# PSOCIAL YCHOLOGY

## ROBERT S. FELDMAN
*University of Massachusetts at Amherst*

PRENTICE HALL, Englewood Cliffs, New Jersey 07632

**Library of Congress Cataloging-in-Publication Data**

Feldman, Robert S. (Robert Stephen), 1947–
   Social psychology / Robert S. Feldman.
     p. cm.
   Includes bibliographical references and index.
   ISBN 0-13-830514-5
   1. Social psychology     I. Title
HM251.F373     1995           94-17697
302—dc20                    CIP

Executive editor: Peter Janzow
Editor: Heidi Freund
Editorial assistant: Jennifer Fader
Development editor: Barbara Muller
Project Managers: Hilda Tauber/Andrew Roney
Copyeditor: Virginia Rubens
Interior and cover design: Thomas Nery
Design director: Paula Martin
Manufacturing buyer: Tricia Kenny
Director, Image Resource Center: Lorinda Morris-Nantz
Photo research: Rhoda Sidney; Joelle Burrows
Cover Art: Paul Klee; *Red Vest (Rote Weste)*, 1938.
   Colored paste on burlap, 25 1/2 x 17 in. (65 x 43 cm).
   Kunstsammlung Nordrhein-Westfalen, Düsseldorf

Photo credits appear on pp. 551–552, which constitute a
continuation of the copyright page.

©1995 by Prentice Hall, Inc.
A Simon & Schuster Company
Englewood Cliffs, New Jersey 07632

Printed in the United States of America
10 9 8 7 6 5 4 3 2 1

ISBN 0-13-830514-5

Prentice-Hall International (UK) Limited, *London*
Prentice-Hall of Australia Pty. Limited, *Sydney*
Prentice-Hall Canada Inc., *Toronto*
Prentice-Hall Hispanoamericana, S.A., *Mexico*
Prentice-Hall of India Private Limited, *New Delhi*
Prentice-Hall of Japan, Inc., *Tokyo*
Simon & Schuster Asia Pte. Ltd., *Singapore*
Editora Prentice-Hall do Brasil, Ltda., *Rio de Janeiro*

*To my family*

# ABOUT THE AUTHOR

Robert S. Feldman is Professor of Psychology at the University of Massachusetts, where he is head of the Personality and Social Psychology Division. A graduate of Wesleyan University with High Honors, he earned a Masters and Ph.D. at the University of Wisconsin, Madison.

Author of more than 100 books, chapters, articles, and presentations, his most recent texts include the edited volume *Applications of Nonverbal Behavioral Theory and Research* (Erlbaum) and, with Bernard Rimé, *Fundamentals of Nonverbal Behavior* (Cambridge University Press). He is a recipient of grants from the National Institute of Mental Health and the National Institute of the Disabilities and Rehabilitation Research, which support his research on nonverbal behavior. He is also a former Fulbright lecturer and research scholar.

During the course of his two decades as a college teacher, he has taught social psychology at the University of Massachusetts as well as at Mount Holyoke College, Wesleyan University, and Virginia Commonwealth University. He lives with his wife and three children in Amherst, Massachusetts, overlooking the Holyoke mountain range.

# BRIEF CONTENTS

# CONTENTS

■  **PART II**      SOCIAL COGNITION: PERCEIVING
THE SOCIAL WORLD

■ **PART III**      **THE SELF**

■ PART V        HELPING AND HURTING OTHERS

■ PART VI           FORMULATING PERSPECTIVES ON THE WORLD

■  PART VII    SOCIAL INFLUENCE

# PREFACE

A glance at any daily newspaper illustrates the extremes of human social behavior. We see violence, heroics, war, political scandal, terrorism, bravery, and a multitude of other manifestations of the extraordinary range of social conduct. At the same time, our own personal lives, involving friends, family, neighbors, lovers, acquaintances, and even chance encounters with total strangers, reflect the stuff of social behavior.

Each of our experiences with our social environment raises a host of questions. What are the sources and consequences of kindness and cruelty? Why and how are people susceptible to the influence of others? How do we develop and maintain our relationships with other individuals? How do people come to grips with the meaning of their social environment? How does the culture in which we live influence our behavior?

The discipline of social psychology seeks to answer such questions. Embracing a vast range of human behavior, the field seeks to address the fundamental issues that underlie our social world. It is a discipline that holds the promise of providing real improvements in the human condition.

The central challenge in writing an introduction to a social psychology textbook is to capture the essence of a dynamic, ever-changing discipline. Social psychology must be presented in a way that fosters readers' intrinsic interest in social psychological phenomena while maintaining scientific integrity and accuracy.

## The Goals and Design of This Book

In order to meet this challenge, *Social Psychology* was written with three major goals in mind. First and foremost, the book provides a broad, balanced overview of the field of social psychology. It is designed to introduce readers to the theories, research, and applications that constitute the discipline, examining both the traditional areas of the field as well as more recent innovations.

The book pays particular attention to the applications developed by social psychologists. While not slighting theoretical material, the text also emphasizes what social psychologists know and how this knowledge may be applied to real-world problems. In fact, the very structure of the book is designed to make the applied material as prominent as the theoretical material.

Specifically, following an introductory chapter, chapters are organized into pairs that address seven key questions. The first chapter of each pair emphasizes theoretical approaches to answering the key question; the second chapter of each pair is oriented toward topics of a more applied nature that address the same question. Although neither theory nor applications are rigidly isolated in particular chapters, this unique structure emphasizes the scope and diversity of the field, and it illustrates how social psychologists use theory, research, and applications to help solve significant social problems. The structure is supported by introductions to each pair of chapters, as well as chapter epilogues that pave the way toward the next chapter.

*The Second Goal*   The second major goal of the text is to tie social psychology explicitly to students' lives. The findings of social psychologists have a significant degree of relevance to students, and this text is meant to illustrate how these findings can be applied in a meaningful, practical sense. For instance, applications are presented within a contemporaneous framework. The book includes current news items, timely world events, and contemporary uses of social psychology that are designed to draw readers into the field. Numerous descriptive scenarios and vignettes reflect everyday situations in students' lives, explaining how they relate to social psychology.

For example, each chapter begins with an opening prologue that provides a real-life situation relating to the chapter subject area. All chapters also have an "Informed Consumer of Social Psychology" section, which explicitly suggests ways to apply social psychological findings to students' experience. Each chapter also includes a feature called "Social Psychology at Work" that discusses ways social psychology research is being used to answer problems of an applied nature.

*The Third Goal*   Finally, the third goal of the text is to make the field of social psychology engaging, accessible, and interesting to students. The book is user-friendly and written in a direct, conversational voice, meant to replicate as much as possible a dialogue between author and student. To that end, it includes a variety of pedagogical features. Each chapter contains a "Looking Ahead" overview that sets the stage for the chapter, a running glossary, a numbered summary, a list of key terms and concepts, and an annotated reading list for students.

In addition, each chapter has three "Review and Rethink" sections. The Review and Rethink sections provide an enumeration of the key concepts and questions that promote and test critical thinking. The book also contains numerous full-color illustrations to accompany the written material and promote learning.

*What this text is not meant to do.* It is important to note that the book is not meant to be an applied psychology text, nor is it designed to be a theories-oriented text. Instead, it seeks to blend and integrate theory, research, and applications. Furthermore, rather than concentrating on a few isolated areas and presenting them in great depth, the emphasis is on illustrating the breadth of the field of social psychology. Concentrating on the scope of the field permits the examination of a variety of evolving and nontraditional areas of social psychology. Finally, the text is not meant to provide a detailed historical record of the development of social psychology. Instead, it seeks to illustrate the field of social psychology as it now stands and is evolving. While covering the classic studies, the decided emphasis is on the field in its current state.

In sum, this text seeks to provide a broad-based overview of the field of social psychology, emphasizing its theories, research, and applications. It is meant to show the relevance of social psychology to students' lives while acquainting them with the scientific basis of the discipline. It is designed to be a user-friendly text, one that captures the excitement—and promise—of a growing, developing scientific field.

*Specific Features*

• **Part-opening descriptions.** Part-openers pose a question that orients and guides students to the major issue addressed in the pair of chapters that follow.

# HOW DOES OUR MEMBERSHIP IN SOCIETY AND CULTURE AFFECT OUR SOCIAL LIVES?

In this final part of the book, we consider how our membership in groups, organizations, and society influences our lives. This pair of chapters links the everyday groups to which we belong to the larger institutions of society, moving from our understanding of how people in groups

- **Chapter-opening prologues.** Each chapter begins with a short vignette describing an individual or situation that is representative of basic social psychological phenomena— for instance, the David Koresh cult tragedy (Chapter 2 on social cognition); the pop singer Madonna (Chapter 4 on the self); and genocide in Bosnia (Chapter 12 on conformity, compliance, and obedience).

## PROLOGUE: HIDDEN VIOLENCE

Were it not for the person accused of killing her, the murder of Nicole Brown Simpson would probably have gone unnoticed by the public at large. She merely would have been one of the almost 5,000 women who are murdered each year in the United States, about one-third at the hands of their boyfriends or husbands.

However, because football and movie star O.J. Simpson was accused of her murder, her death became the focus of world-wide attention. The case received enormous publicity, and the picture of domestic violence that apparently was a part of the Simpsons' life was not a pretty one. Nicole Simpson had called the police eight times, alleging that she had been beaten. Simpson pleaded "no contest" to striking and threatening to kill his wife in 1989, accepting a fine of $700 and performing community service. On one occasion when his wife had called the police, O.J. Simpson urged that they

- **Social Psychology at Work.** Each chapter includes this feature that describes current social psychological research or research issues, applied to everyday problems. Among these features are discussions of a controversial poll conducted by a U.S. presidential candidate, the most effective emotional context of advertisements, and on-the-job influence tactics.

## SOCIAL PSYCHOLOGY AT WORK

### AND THE QUESTION IS: HOW FAIR IS THIS SURVEY?

Examine the following question, and consider how you think most people would respond:

> If our government wants the American people to pay more taxes, should it provide leadership by example—all sacrifice begins at the top—by cutting Congress's and the President's salaries by 10 percent and reducing their retirement plans to bring them in line with those of the American people?

reworded, and more balanced, version: "Should laws be passed to prohibit interest groups from contributing to campaigns, or do groups have a right to contribute to the candidates they support?"

As you can see in Figure 1-9, the two versions of the question produced very different responses. Although most people agreed with Perot's version, endorsing the need to

- **Informed Consumer of Social Psychology.** This feature in every chapter gives information on specific uses that can be derived from research conducted by social psychologists. Examples include how to deal with anger, how to reduce the risk of date rape, and how to draw appropriate conclusions from the behavior of others.

## THE INFORMED CONSUMER OF SOCIAL PSYCHOLOGY

### REDUCING PREJUDICE AND DISCRIMINATION

Are prejudice and discrimination destined to color our interactions with others, or are there ways we can reduce them? Social psychologists have devised several means of reducing prejudice and discrimination against minority groups in society. Among the most important:

- *Creating opportunities for contact between members of majority and minority groups.* No strategy for reducing prejudice has received

run high, such as has been the case in some cases of court-ordered desegregation, there can actually be an increase in prejudice (Stephan, 1986; Gerard, 1988).

Does this mean we should give up on attempting to produce more integrated schools and to increase the frequency of contact between people of different races? Not at all. According to the **contact hypothesis**, direct contact

- **Review and Rethink sections.** Three short recaps of the chapter's main points are provided at appropriate places and followed by questions designed to provoke critical thinking.

## ▶ REVIEW & RETHINK

### *Review*

- In reaching decisions, groups move through a series of four stages and employ social decision schemes and social combination rules.
- Although groups typically come to more accurate solutions more quickly than individuals, they are less efficient than individuals working alone.
- Group polarization and groupthink affect the quality of decisions.

### *Rethink*

- What are the steps in group decision making?
- In what type of group is social loafing most likely to occur?

- **End-of-chapter material.**
Each chapter ends with a
summary, a list of key terms
and concepts, relevant supple-
mental readings, and an epi-
logue. This material helps
students to study and retain
the information in the chapter
and also guides their future
study.

---

LOOKING
BACK  ◄ ◄ ◄ ◄ ◄ ◄ ◄ ◄ ◄ ◄ ◄ ◄ ◄ ◄ ◄ ◄ ◄ ◄ ◄ ◄ ◄ ◄ ◄ ◄ ◄ ◄ ◄

**What models explain the basic structure of organizations?**

1. Organizations—groups of people working together to attain common goals—operate
according to several different models. The bureaucratic model represents the attempt to
apply rationality and efficiency to the functioning of organizations. The human relations
model emphasizes the social psychological structure of an organization. Contingency models
focus on how specific features of an organization's environment affect the way it operates.

2. Because none of the previous approaches has proven fully successful, some organizations

---

## EPILOGUE

Our journey through the field of social psychology has
ended with a consideration of groups and organizations.
Beginning in the previous chapter, where we discussed how
aggregates of people join together to form groups, we moved
to the larger arena of organizations. We considered different
models of organizations and the basic processes that underlie
their functioning. Finally, we discussed culture and society,
reflecting on the contributions social psychologists have made
to the quest for peace and world justice.

As we've seen throughout this book, social psychologi-

cal theory and research have made significant contributions to
our understanding of how the social world operates. At the
same time, such work has led to significant applied contributions, producing real improvement in people's lives.

Yet the story of social psychology remains incomplete.
The field is advancing on many fronts, continuing to unfold
and grow. New theories are being developed, research continues, and applications continue to be derived. To quote poet
Robert Browning, "The best is yet to be."

---

*Teaching Supports That
Accompany the Book*

Social Psychology is accompanied by the following set of teaching and learning tools that
constitute a support package of computer, video, and print supplements.

---

*Supplements for Instructors*

- *Instructor's Resource Manual* prepared by Marianne Miserandino. Material from each chapter
of the text has been assembled as a guide for planning class lectures and activities. The manual features chapter overviews, learning objectives, lecture suggestions, demonstration
activities, discussion topics, and audiovisual resources.
- *Test Item File* prepared by Chris Leone. A test bank with over 1600 questions, this supplement allows instructors to develop any number and variety of tests covering key terms, concepts, and applications from the textbook. Conceptual, applied, and factual questions are
available in multiple choice, short answer, true/false, and essay forms.
- *"800-Number" Telephone Test Preparation Service.* Instructors can call a special toll-free number
and select up to 200 questions from the Test Item File. The test (with an alternate version,
if requested) and answer key are mailed within 48 hours, ready for duplication.
- *Prentice Hall Test Manager 2.0* (3.5″ IBM, Macintosh Formats). A computerized testing package featuring full control over printing with print preview, mouse support, on-screen VGA
graphics with import capabilities for TIFF and PCX file formats and the ability to export
your files to WordPerfect, Word, and ASCII.
- *Handouts and Transparency Masters* prepared by Alan Swinkels. This is an extensive set of
questionnaires, activities, and visual aids for stimulating classroom discussion.

- *ABC News/Prentice Hall Video Library for Social Psychology.* This customized video library features segments from a variety of award-winning ABC News programs and provides a contemporary look at such topics as cultural diversity, gender, prejudice, and relationships.

---

*Supplements for Students*

- *Readings in Social Psychology,* compiled and edited by Robert S. Feldman and Erik
Coats. Like the text, this reader is also organized in a paired chapter format. Each
of the 15 chapters contains two readings, one classic from a primary source, the
other from a contemporary secondary source. Critical thinking questions, focused
on methodology and ethics, conclude each selection.

- *Student Workbook, Study Guide, and Cases* written by Pamela Regan. A unique feature of this study guide is the real-life cases—five per chapter, for a total of 75. Each case is approximately one page long and describes a typical social interaction—i.e. buying a used car, visiting a doctor—or newsworthy events like last year's World Trade Center bombing. After reading the vignette, students are asked a series of quesitons in which they must analyze what transpired from a social psychological perspective.
- *The New York Times Program. The New York Times* and Prentice Hall are sponsoring a *Themes of the Times* program designed to enhance student access to current information in the classroom.

  Throughout this program, the core subject matter provided in the text is supplemented by a collection of time-sensitive articles from one of the world's most distinguished newspapers, *The New York Times.* These articles demonstrate the vital, ongoing connection between what is learned in the classroom and what is happening in the world around us.

  To enjoy the wealth of information of *The New York Times* daily, a reduced subscription rate is available in deliverable areas. For information, call 1-800-631-1222.

  Prentice Hall and *The New York Times* are proud to co-sponsor *Themes of the Times.* We hope it will make the reading of both textbooks and newspapers a more dynamic, involving process.

## *Acknowledgements*

I am grateful to the following reviewers who provided a wealth of comments, criticism, and encouragement: Christopher Leone, the University of North Florida; Marianne Miserandino, Beaver College; Joan Rollins, Rhode Island College; Sue Cloninger, Russell Sage College; Nicholas Christenfeld, University of California at San Diego; Carl Denti, Dutchess Community College; Lee Jussim, Rutgers University; Galen V. Bodenhausen, Ph.D., Michigan State University; Michael A. McCall, Ph.D., Ithaca College; Dean Keith Simonton, Ph.D., University of California at Davis; Mark R. Leary, Wake Forest University; William F. Ford, D.A., Bucks County Community College; Carolin Showers, Ph.D., University of Wisconsin; Bernardo J. Carducci, Ph.D., Indiana University–Southeast; and Dr. Lauren Perdue, Potsdam State College.

In addition to the reviewers, I am grateful to many others for their help, direct and indirect, recently and in the past. I was introduced to social psychology at Wesleyan University by Karl Scheibe, and his example of teacher–scholar remains an inspiration. My graduate work was done at the University of Wisconsin, where the late Vernon Allen honed my appreciation for the discipline. I could not have asked for a finer education.

My colleagues at the University of Massachusetts provide an atmosphere in which all types of intellectual endeavors are nurtured and supported, and I am grateful to them for making the university a terrific place to work. I have also been continually inspired and challenged by our graduate students, who have been helpful in many ways.

Several individuals deserve particular mention. Heidi Freund, Psychology editor at Prentice Hall, was a wonderful help and sounding board during every stage of this project, and I am very appreciative of all her hard work and enthusiasm. Barbara Muller, my developmental editor on the book, nudged, prompted, and prodded me into producing a manuscript several magnitudes better than would have been possible without her wonderful efforts. She is a first-rate editor.

In addition, I thank Chris Rogers, who started me thinking about doing a book exactly of this sort, and Rhona Robbin, who continues to teach me so much about writing. I also thank Jim Anker and Susan Brennan, who steered me to Prentice Hall.

My production manager, Andrew Roney, turned the business of production into an art. Several other folks at Prentice Hall, including designer Thomas Nery and photo researcher Rhoda Sidney, provided an aesthetic expertise that gives this book such an elegant look. Lauren Ward, marketing manager, has brought a creative and enthusiastic touch to the project, and I am grateful for her good ideas. My thanks also go to Pete Janzow and Phil Miller, who, always hovering in the background, unceasingly pushed for excellence.

Finally, I am very grateful to John Graiff, who was involved at every critical juncture in the writing and production of the book. I also thank Erik Coats, who likewise helped a great deal and was always eager to provide (often unsolicited) criticism and suggestions. They both did a terrific job, and I, as well as readers of this book, are in their debt.

Ultimately, I thank my family, to whom I owe most everything.

*Robert S. Feldman*
*University of Massachusetts, Amherst*

# SOCIAL PSYCHOLOGY

### PART I

# WHAT ARE THE ROOTS OF SOCIAL PSYCHOLOGY?

We begin our journey into the field of social psychology by examining its foundations. We discuss the discipline's intellectual roots, considering the historical forces that led to the development of social psychology and speculating on impending advances. We also focus on the research methods used by social psychologists, examining how theory and research work hand in hand to provide us with explanations of the social behavior we find in the world around us. Chapter 1 introduces the principles on which the field is built. ■

# AN INTRODUCTION TO SOCIAL PSYCHOLOGY

# PROLOGUE: A VERY PUBLIC BEATING

No one who has seen the videotape will forget the images: Rodney King, an African-American male, lying on the ground, suffering repeated blows from a group of white police officers. One officer hits him on the head and shoulders with a nightstick, wielding it like a baseball bat. Another also swings his nightstick at King, adding his blows to those of the others, while a third officer joins in with occasional kicks.

Rodney King's beating ultimately led to extensive rioting in Los Angeles when the police who conducted the beating were found innocent. Months later, the devastation from the rioting remained.

The wire from a battery-operated electric stun gun, fired at King earlier, is wrapped around part of his body.

After beating him for almost two minutes, the police officers tie King's hands behind his back and drag him to the side of the street. Bleeding, he is left unattended until an ambulance arrives about five minutes later. At the hospital, physicians find that King has a ruptured eye socket, a broken leg, a shattered cheekbone, and several other fractures.

Yet the injuries that King suffered were only part of the outcome of the beating. When the officers who had battered King were tried for using excessive force, they were found innocent. Following this verdict, rioting broke out that left dozens of people dead and billions of dollars in damage. The crisis strained race relations beyond the breaking point, and fear and suspicion among people of different races remained high in the wake of the rioting. Later the officers were tried for depriving King of his civil rights and were found guilty, but this verdict did not erase the bitter memories of the initial incident.

## LOOKING AHEAD ▶▶▶▶▶▶▶▶▶▶▶▶▶▶▶▶▶▶▶▶▶▶▶▶▶▶

Although Rodney King's beating and the rioting it eventually led to can be viewed merely in terms of physical injury, loss of life, and the destruction of property, the incident also had significant social psychological overtones. For instance, social psychologists might view the incident in these terms:

- A social psychologist who specializes in understanding how people make judgments of others might consider how prejudice and stereotypes shaped the police officers' perceptions of King.
- Social psychologists who focus on the self might examine how the police officers' views of themselves changed as a result of their involvement in the beating.
- Social psychologists who specialize in understanding relationships might consider how the officers' ties with friends in the community changed as a result of the beating.
- Social psychologists who study helping and socially responsible behavior might ask why the many bystanders, who viewed the beating, did nothing to intervene.
- Finally, social psychologists who study the legal system would be interested in the trial of the police officers, investigating the nature of the jury's deliberations and whether the jurors were biased in some manner.

Although each of these approaches considers a different aspect of the King beating and its aftermath, they all derive from the same discipline: social psychology. As we will see, the scope of social psychology is wide and in some ways as varied as the range of human behavior we find in different social situations.

In this chapter, we orient ourselves to the field of social psychology. After defining the field, we consider the general topics it covers and the boundaries of the discipline. We also discuss demographics and the history of the field, examining how social psychology has evolved over the last hundred years and speculating on the future of the discipline.

Next, we turn to the research techniques used in social psychology. We explore how social psychologists construct and refine specific research questions, and we discuss the various ways that research can be carried out. Finally, we consider some threats to the accuracy and validity of research findings—threats that make research on social psychological topics particularly challenging.

In sum, you'll find the answers to these questions after reading this chapter:

- What is the scope of social psychology?
- What were the major milestones and trends in the development of the field, and what is the future likely to hold?
- How do experimental and correlational research differ, and what are the major types of studies carried out by social psychologists?
- What are the major threats to the validity of research findings?

# ORIENTATION TO SOCIAL PSYCHOLOGY

In some ways, all of us are novice social psychologists. For instance, if you've ever wondered why you've been persuaded to buy a jacket that cost more than you intended to spend, you've asked the same question that a social psychologist would ask. If you've watched in amusement as a friend unsuccessfully tried to strike up a romantic liaison at a party, you've made the same kind of observation that a social psychologist might make. And if you were part of a group project in a class and tried to figure out why some of the students did more work than others, you were raising the same sort of query that a social psychologist would raise.

**social psychology**
the scientific study of how people's thoughts, feelings, and actions are affected by others.

**Social psychology** is the scientific study of how people's thoughts, feelings, and actions are affected by others. Members of the discipline seek to investigate and understand the nature and causes of people's behavior in social situations.

In some ways, the definition of social psychology is disarmingly simple. However, in a field that covers as much territory as social psychology, it is necessary to probe behind the definition. In fact, it is useful to consider separately the implications of each of the parts of the definition.

- Social psychology is a *scientific* discipline. Social psychologists do not rely on abstract, untested theories. Instead, as we'll see in the latter part of this chapter, they use precise, methodical, and systematic means of investigation in order to understand phenomena. This does not mean that social psychologists do not develop theories. They do. However, they don't conclude with a theory, but rather use scientific procedures to test its adequacy.

- Social psychology focuses on *people*. Although some research focuses on the social lives of non-humans, by far the vast majority of research conducted by social psychologists studies humans. Social psychologists seek to identify the broad, universal principles that underlie all social behavior, but they do not ignore the consequences of membership in particular cultures and ethnic groups. In fact, a significant part of the field considers how people who are members of different ethnic, racial, and other demographic groups interact.

• Social psychology considers people's *thoughts*. Much of contemporary social psychology is devoted to a decidedly cognitive approach that scrutinizes the thinking processes of individuals in order to understand social behavior. Social psychologists largely reject the view, propounded by some behavioral psychologists, that we should concentrate solely on observable behavior. Instead, they suggest that thinking processes, although not directly accessible to investigators, can be inferred from people's reports of their own experiences.

• The *feelings* that people experience are a central part of social psychology. Our likes and dislikes and emotions are investigated by social psychologists, who use a variety of means to measure our feelings about social stimuli. In fact, some social psychologists study physiological reactions, such as heart and respiration rates, as a means of assessing how people feel in a given situation.

• Finally, social psychologists study people's *actions*. By examining behavior—ranging from whom we choose as romantic partners to what brand of toothpaste we purchase—social psychologists come to understand how the social world in which we live affects our behavior.

Given the broad definition of the discipline of social psychology, it is clear that the field covers a wide swath of territory. As a consequence, many diverse areas of study fit comfortably within the discipline. Some social psychologists focus on social influences on the individual, some on the social interaction between two or more individuals, and still others on group processes.

For example, many social psychologists concentrate on the consequences of social influences on individuals and the way they understand the world (see Figure 1-1). Even when we are alone, the way we think and behave is affected by others. And the influence of others on our behavior is even more profound when they are physically present. Accordingly, social psychologists interested in the individual person study such basic processes as perception, learning, and the ways information is acquired and processed. More specifically, social psychologists concerned with individual processes might examine how we make judgments about other people, how people learn attitudes, and how jurors determine whether a defendant is guilty or innocent.

Social interaction between and among people represents a second principal focus of social psychologists. Those who take this approach are interested in the unique characteristics of social behavior when two or more people are talking, working, bargaining, planning, or engaging in any of the myriad activities that people do together. For exam-

| FIGURE 1-1   Major Approaches in Social Psychology: Avenues to Understanding | |
| --- | --- |
| **CATEGORY** | **SAMPLE TOPICS** |
| Influence of social factors on the individual | Judging others |
| | Stereotypes |
| | Self-presentation |
| | Health |
| Social interaction between and among people | Liking and loving |
| | Interpersonal relationships |
| | Aggression and helping |
| | Attitudes and persuasion |
| Group processes | Conformity |
| | Jury behavior |
| | Politics |
| | Organizations |
| | Culture |

The field of social psychology examines the behavior of people when they are in groups, with another person, and even when they are alone.

ple, these social psychologists investigate how one person can influence another, why we begin to like someone and fall in love, and why people are aggressive or helpful to others.

Group processes is the third primary focus of social psychologists. Those taking this approach study the properties of groups, such as roles, status, group pressure, and communication patterns in groups. On a broader stage, social psychologists study organizations, societal institutions such as the political and legal systems, and culture. Questions about how to maintain our independence in group situations, how to promote the effective functioning of organizations, and how culture influences our views of the world illustrate the range of the group processes focus.

## The Boundaries of Social Psychology: Demarcating the Field

Our discussion of the wide sweep of social psychology may leave you wondering if there is anything the field excludes. In fact, the field does have boundaries, although, as we'll discuss later, they are not rigid.

As you can see in Figure 1-2, the discipline of social psychology is part of the broader field of psychology, which itself is situated in the general realm of social sciences. Although members of related disciplines may address issues that are similar to those of social psychologists, they adopt special—and different—perspectives according to their particular discipline.

Within the field of psychology, social psychology's closest companion is the area of personality psychology. Personality psychology focuses on the identification of the individual characteristics or traits that differentiate one person from others and the processes that explain the consistencies of an individual's behavior. Like social psychologists, personality psychologists focus on the individual. However, personality psychologists look at individuals primarily in terms of what makes them different from one another, whereas social psychologists seek to determine the similarities that join us as individuals and explain our behavior in general. A personality psychologist would ask, for example, why some people are more prejudiced than others. A social psychologist would consider how prejudice arises in general and whether there are ways to diminish its damaging consequences.

Outside of the field of psychology, social psychology's nearest cousins are sociology and anthropology, two disciplines that have related but distinct vantage points. Sociology is the science of society and social institutions. It focuses on how members of groups

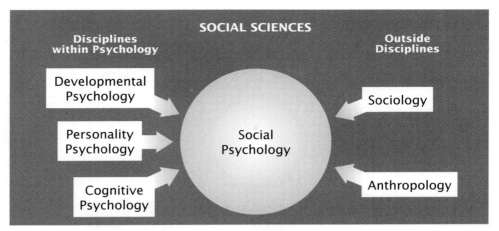

**FIGURE 1-2    Situating Social Psychology** Social psychology is allied with several other disciplines outside the field, as well as being related to several subareas within psychology.

are subject to culturally universal influences that determine how the group as a whole performs. When sociologists consider group behavior they are apt to concentrate on the behavior of the group as a single entity. In contrast, when social psychologists look at a group, their focus will be centered on the individual members of the group.

Let us suppose we are interested in how the racial makeup of a school affects the school's educational effectiveness. A sociologist would be most apt to compare the overall success of school graduates in different types of schools. In contrast, a social psychologist might approach the issue by looking at individual students, perhaps probing how socioeconomic background might affect particular students' performance.

Anthropology, the study of the consequences of culture on human behavior, is another discipline closely related to social psychology. Anthropology takes a broad approach to social phenomena, concentrating on the universals in a given culture and placing only minor emphasis on the individual. For instance, anthropologists might examine how family structure is related to economic productivity in different cultures. In contrast, social psychologists, taking their more individualistic approach, might investigate whether certain forms of child-rearing practices lead to higher levels of motivation to achieve in individual children.

Differing areas of interest are not the only factors that distinguish social psychology from other disciplines: The methods used by social psychologists to investigate problems are also distinctive. Sociologists and anthropologists are most likely to examine existing situations, assessing them as they naturally occur. For example, a sociologist interested in relationships might examine marriage and divorce statistics, attempting to derive an understanding of the phenomenon by looking at statistical trends.

In contrast, social psychologists rely most heavily on experimental methods in which they actively manipulate a variable, thereby permitting them to examine the consequences of the manipulation. To study relationships, then, a social psychologist might set up an experiment to see under what conditions people are attracted to one another.

*The Demographics of Social Psychology: The Changing Face of the Discipline*

Who are social psychologists? Of the approximately 2,500 members of the American Psychological Association who identify themselves as social psychologists, most are male, and most are white. Like other areas of psychology (as well as other scientific fields), social psychology has been traditionally dominated by white men.

However, the profile of the discipline is changing due to the number of women entering the field. Each year more women are receiving graduate degrees in social psychology, significantly expanding the proportion of women making up the field. In fact, recent figures show that more women than men are enrolled in graduate social psychol-

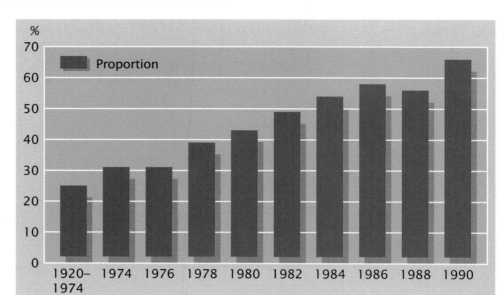

**FIGURE 1-3    Proportion of Ph.D.s in Social Psychology Awarded to Women** Although the proportion of women who received Ph.D.s in social psychology was small until the 1980s, in the past two decades the proportion has increased dramatically. In fact, since 1984, more women than men have received doctorates in the field.    *(Source:* APA, 1993.*)*

ogy programs, and since 1984 more women than men received doctoral degrees in social psychology (see Figure 1–3). These figures suggest that eventually women will constitute the majority of social psychology practitioners. Furthermore, despite the fact that it is only recently that significant numbers of women have entered the field, women have made important contributions to the field. For example, eight of the 50 most frequently cited authors in social psychology texts are women (Gordon & Vicari, 1992a; 1992b).

Racial minorities are also finding increasing representation in the field, although progress has been far slower than the advances in representation made by women. For example, just 6 percent of all social psychologists who identify their racial background on surveys are members of minority groups. However, minority representation is likely to increase, since 12 percent of the recent graduates of social psychology doctoral programs were ethnic minorities. Of the total number of doctorates awarded in the field, 3 percent went to Hispanics, 3 percent to Asians, and 6 percent to African-Americans (APA, 1993).

The lack of minority representation in social psychology represents a serious problem, for several reasons. The discipline of social psychology may be impaired by a lack of minority perspectives, with important questions being overlooked or going unasked. In addition, minority social psychologists act as role models for younger minority students. Consequently, unless the numbers of current minority social psychologists are enlarged, the field will be hampered by a lack of minority representation.

Regardless of their gender and race, social psychologists tend to have educational backgrounds that are fairly uniform. Almost all social psychologists have masters and Ph.D. degrees in psychology, although some individuals who identify with the discipline have degrees in sociology. The Ph.D. is a research degree, meaning that all social psychologists are trained in research methods in order to conduct research. It typically takes four to five years to receive the Ph.D., and the study includes carrying out original research in the form of a dissertation.

Compared with other kinds of psychologists, social psychologists are a prolific lot. Despite the fact that less than 3 percent of all psychologists belonging to the American Psychological Association identify themselves as social psychologists, more than 10 percent of the articles indexed in the leading register of psychological publications are on topics pertaining to social processes, social issues, and experimental social psychology (PsychINFO, 1991).

Pinpointing the birth of a discipline that covers as much territory as social psychology is largely impossible—and, in some ways, not terribly productive. The most historically-minded might point to Plato and Aristotle, who in fact wrote extensively about social behavior (Allport, 1985). Yet to point to any single person as the founding parent of social psychology is rather an exercise in futility. Scientific disciplines develop slowly, coming to life typically not in a sudden revolutionary intellectual leap forward but as a consequence of evolutionary changes in approaches, perspectives, and interests.

**THE FIELD IN ITS INFANCY.**    Two dates stand out if we are to seek the birth of the field: 1897 and 1908. In 1897, Norman Triplett carried out what has come to be considered the first experiment in social psychology. Triplett, as we shall discuss again in Chapter 14, was interested in the effects of competition on performance, and he conducted an experiment to compare the performance of participants who were alone with those who were in groups (Triplett, 1897).

Although the vantage point of some 100 years affords the luxury of criticizing various aspects of Triplett's methods, his study remains a notable moment in the birth of the field, as the first experiment in which social psychological variables were studied. Triplett was also asking a question that has endured: Even today, contemporary social psychologists are researching the effects of others' presence on behavior.

Another way of establishing the beginning of the field of social psychology is to consider the publication of textbooks on the discipline. This happened in the first decade of the twentieth century, when two books with "social psychology" in their titles were published. One was written by the American Edward Ross (1908), and the other by the English psychologist William McDougall (1908).

The publication of these textbooks was unmistakable testimony that a new discipline had emerged, one with a distinctive perspective and orientation. For instance, McDougall endorsed the view that social behavior was largely produced by instinctual factors. Today such a perspective is rejected by almost all social psychologists, but it held sway for several years in the early development of the field and was seen as evidence that social behavior could be studied in a systematic, methodical manner.

Still, it was not until the 1920s that social psychology could be said to have outgrown its infancy. In 1924 a third book with "social psychology" central to its title was published, this one written by Floyd Allport. The approach and emphasis of Allport's book in some ways is remarkably similar to that taken by contemporary social psychologists. For instance, Allport considered such topics as the comprehension of emotions via facial expressions and the consequences of an audience on performance—two areas that are widely researched even today.

**PSYCHOLOGY'S ADOLESCENCE.**    Allport's text gave impetus to the growing field of social psychology, and the field entered an adolescence marked by rapid spurts forward. For example, in the 1930s, Muzafer Sherif began a series of pioneering studies on social norms, the shared rules that influence our behavior (Sherif, 1935, 1936). In systematically studying these norms, Sherif laid the groundwork for subsequent research on conformity and other forms of social influence.

During the same period, one of social psychology's towering figures emerged: Kurt Lewin. Lewin, a German social psychologist who emigrated to the United States when the Nazis came to power, developed a theory meant to explain how the interaction between people's environment and their personal characteristics combined to produce social behavior (Lewin, 1931, 1935, 1936). Lewin's contribution went well beyond the theoretical; his research vividly illustrated how theoretical concepts could shed light on solutions to the most practical, everyday problems. It also illustrates how the impetus for research may come from the basic values that social psychologists hold.

Lewin—who was deeply affected by the ravages of World War II—attempted to contribute to the war effort in several ways. For example, he studied ways of convincing people to make dietary changes, persuading them to eat less-preferred, but more readily available, foods during the war (Lewin, 1943). Similarly, he examined different styles of leadership, attempting to demonstrate the benefits of democratic government over more authoritarian and laissez-faire doctrines (Lewin, Lippitt, & White, 1939). Lewin's work provided the foundation for contemporary research on attitude change, persuasion, and political psychology (discussed in Chapters 11 and 13).

**THE FIELD ENTERS ADULTHOOD.**    Following the end of World War II, social psychology embarked on a golden period in which unabashed confidence reigned. Social psychologists believed that the solutions to significant social problems were within their grasp. The government agreed, generously funding social psychological research. Much of the research focused on groups and group behavior, examining group productivity, interactions among members of groups, and the influence of groups on attitudes. In social psychology, the 1950s, in fact, could be considered the decade of the group.

The emphasis on groups did not last, however. In the late 1950s, Leon Festinger published a book that was to influence a generation of social psychologists: *A Theory of Cognitive Dissonance* (Festinger, 1957). As we discuss in Chapter 10, Festinger argued that when people hold opposing attitudes they experience unpleasant feelings, which they are motivated to reduce. This simple principle led to some surprising findings. For instance, social psychologists learned that people sometimes grow to like the things that cause them to suffer most (Aronson & Mills, 1959), and that receiving a small reward for saying things we don't believe is more effective in producing attitude change than receiving a large reward for doing the same thing (Festinger & Carlsmith, 1959).

The theory of cognitive dissonance led not only to a large number of studies designed to test the theory, but also to other research that focused more on people's personal thoughts, or cognitions, and less on the social processes between individuals. In addition, the norm for social psychological experiments became studies that included elaborate deceptions, motivated by social psychologists' desire to engage experimental participants in involving, dramatic situations. Furthermore, experimental results that were counterintuitive, yielding findings that common sense would be unable to predict, became prized within the field.

**CRISIS.**    The 1960s and 1970s brought a rapid expansion of the field, and the number of social psychologists and the range of topics they studied increased substantially. At this same heady time, though, the field entered a period of crisis. Social psychologists began to express self-doubt about the efficacy and utility of their science. These doubts took several forms.

Some social psychologists complained that the field involved merely the study of social practices at a given moment and that social psychology was unable to identify universal, fundamental social principles that spanned multiple historical and cultural eras (Gergen, 1967, 1973). Other social psychologists argued that the dominant form of data collection in the field—the laboratory experiment—was severely limited. As we'll discuss later in this chapter, critics suggested that laboratory experiments, especially those that use college students as participants, were not representative of the world outside the laboratory. In addition, the extensive use of experiments that deceived subjects regarding their true purpose raised concerns regarding the ethics and validity of a science that routinely utilized trickery in its experiments (Kelman, 1967, 1968; Stricker, Messick & Jackson, 1968; Forward, Canter, & Krisch, 1976).

Although the crisis in social psychology was real, it did not diminish the output of theory or research. In fact, the 1970s saw the emergence of several major areas of research, which have had lasting influence. For instance, social psychologists began to focus on attribution, the processes by which we determine the reasons behind behavior (Jones & Harris, 1967). Furthermore, gender became an established area of study, as social psychologists grappled with the factors that lead to differences in the behavior of men and women (Maccoby & Jacklin, 1974).

Ironically, the crisis in social psychology, which proved to be only temporary, in the end strengthened the discipline. Social psychologists focused increasing attention on historical and cultural factors, taking them into account in the development of theory and the choice of experimental procedures. Moreover, ethical concerns led to the development of new alternatives to the traditional laboratory experiment, especially in terms of the use of experiments that deceived subjects as to their true purpose. We will discuss these alternatives later in the chapter.

**CURRENT DEVELOPMENTS.**    Today, the field of social psychology is a mature, multifaceted discipline. As we've already seen, the scope of the field is broad. Social psychologists' interests range from the most individualistic aspects of social life to sweeping questions about society and culture.

Two major trends mark contemporary social psychology. One is an increased emphasis on how cognitive factors—our thoughts, beliefs, attitudes, and general understanding of the world—influence social behavior. In an approach that has been mimicked by other disciplines in the broader field of psychology, many social psychologists have embraced the belief that cognitions are a primary aspect of social behavior. Consequently, social psychologists who specialize in cognitive factors have argued, quite convincingly, that our understanding of social behavior is not complete without knowledge of how people understand the world around them. For instance, cognitive approaches lead to such questions as how people act as naive scientists, seeking to uncover the causes of our own and other people's behavior; what errors and biases distort our perceptions of others; and how our goals and motivation affect the choices we make in terms of strategies for understanding the world (Higgins & Sorrentino, 1990; Fiske & Taylor, 1991).

A second major trend in the field is the increasing application of the findings of social psychologists in settings outside the laboratory. Of course, social psychology has always had an interest in applying its findings, as illustrated by Kurt Lewin's early work

Social psychologists increasingly are applying their knowledge outside the laboratory, as in political campaigns and business organizations.

on changing dietary preferences during World War II. However, the most recent decades have seen the emergence of several subdisciplines within social psychology that are centered on particular social issues.

For instance, the social psychology of personal health (which we discuss in Chapter 5), of law (Chapter 13), and of industrial and business settings (Chapter 15) have developed as major topical areas in the field. Social psychologists focusing on these areas might ask questions such as, "How do the interpersonal skills of physicians affect patient recovery rates?"; "How do juries reach decisions?"; and "How do pay scales affect worker performance?" In each case, social psychology theory and research have been applied in an effort to solve vexing social problems.

## The Future of Social Psychology

Although even the most scientific of crystal balls is partially clouded, it is possible with a certain degree of confidence to make some predictions about where the field of social psychology is headed. Two forecasts can be made with some certainty: (1) There will be an increasing emphasis on multiculturalism in social psychology; (2) The traditional boundaries that have demarcated the field of social psychology from other areas are likely to become increasingly indistinct.

**DEVELOPING A CULTURALLY DIVERSE DISCIPLINE.** An examination of simple demographic patterns in the United States is sufficient to point to the need for greater understanding of the role of culture in people's social worlds. For example, the proportion of Hispanics is expected to more than double in the next 50 years (U.S. Bureau of Census, 1993). As the minority population continues to grow at a rapid pace, social psychologists have begun to recognize the need for taking cultural factors into account (Klineberg, 1990).

How does a concern with culture correspond to the explicit desire of social psychologists to identify universal principles of social behavior? The answer is that general principles can be identified only if social psychology takes into account the people's cultural and subcultural backgrounds. For instance, social psychologists will never know just how universal their findings relating to social behavior are unless they examine them using research participants who represent a spectrum of backgrounds. Furthermore, because the very questions that social psychologists ask are a consequence of a particular cultural context, it is necessary to take cultural factors into account.

In fact, social psychology is already taking issues of cultural diversity into account. For example, as we discuss in Chapter 7, researchers examining close relationships have attempted to identify the factors that affect the choice of a marriage partner. By addressing the question cross-culturally, they have been able to identify some universal principles that guide the kinds of choices that are made—principles that never would have been identified unless research was conducted in several very different types of cultures (Buss et al., 1990).

Similarly, researchers looking at the development of relationships have traditionally focused on heterosexual alliances and have largely ignored homosexual relationships. Today, however, social psychologists have come to recognize that a full understanding of liking and loving (as well as other social psychological phenomena) must consider nontraditional populations, such as gays and lesbians. Consequently, some research has sought to identify the factors that lead to the development, maintenance, and deterioration of gay relationships to determine similarities and differences from heterosexual relationships (Herek et al., 1991; Kurdek, 1991).

Another factor that has led to burgeoning interest in multiculturalism within the discipline of social psychology is the increasing influence of social psychologists who live and work outside the United States. Although the bulk of social psychological research and theory-building is done in the U.S., social psychologists are active in every part of the globe. Social psychologists in Japan, Hong Kong, Australia, and other parts of the world interact intellectually through publication in each others' journals and through presentation of research at social psychology conventions held throughout the world.

For instance, the *European Journal of Social Psychology* publishes influential research that vies in importance with work published in the major U.S. journal, the *Journal of Personality and Social Psychology*. In addition, joint meetings are often held between U.S. social psychology organizations and those representing social psychologists in other countries. It is clear this intellectual cross-pollination of ideas will promote substantial advances in the discipline (Hewstone et al., 1988).

**A BLURRING OF BOUNDARIES.**   Our second prediction about the future of social psychology is that the traditional boundaries between different disciplines are likely to become increasingly indistinct. For example, the point at which the field of social psychology leaves off and other disciplines begin is likely to become progressively ambiguous (Krahe, 1992). Social psychological findings have been used with increasing frequency outside the traditional boundaries of the field. Hence, educators interested in cooperative learning draw on the social psychological literature on groups; business executives consider the work of social psychologists in designing their advertising campaigns; politicians look to social psychological findings to get votes; and salespersons use persuasive techniques designed by social psychologists (Baron & Greenberg, 1990; Feldman, 1990; Perloff, 1993). As we will see throughout this book, the work of social psychologists has had significant implications for a variety of areas.

Moreover, the relationship between social psychology and other disciplines is not a one-way street. Social psychologists have embraced, and profited from, work going on in other disciplines—a tendency that will likely grow. For example, social psychology has benefited from findings in allied disciplines such as clinical psychology, industrial–organizational psychology, sociology, and anthropology (Jahoda, 1986; Fiske, 1991). In fact, the overlap between certain other disciplines and social psychology is likely to spawn subdisciplines. One sign of this overlap is the founding of the *Journal of Social and Clinical Psychology*, which reports work on such topics as how victims of trauma cope with their adversity (Janoff-Bulman, 1992).

As the lines between disciplines are growing increasingly blurred, traditional distinctions between various types of research are likely to continue to grow less distinct. In particular, social psychologists have traditionally distinguished between purely **theoretical research**—research designed specifically to test some explanation of social behavior— and **applied research**—research meant to provide practical solutions to immediate problems.

As the field of social psychology develops further, the distinction between theoretical and applied research may well diminish. Even the most practical research has relevance to theory-building efforts, since results of applied studies are invariably used not only for their immediate applications to the problem at hand but also for their implications for theory. Furthermore, work in applied areas can illuminate where gaps exist in theoretical formulations (Hedrick, Bickman, & Rog, 1993).

At the same time, theory can lead to solutions to applied problems—solutions that might otherwise be overlooked. Theories are able to suggest new approaches and strategies for dealing with the problems facing society. In fact, the process is parallel to what occurs in other sciences—as when, for example, theories about the structure of DNA molecules ultimately lead to approaches to fighting specific diseases.

In sum, social psychologists are increasingly recognizing that theoretical and applied research have similar underlying goals. Whether their aims are explicit or implicit, social psychologists have a fundamental commitment to building knowledge, a concern regarding the quality of life, and an interest in how the findings of social psychology are ultimately utilized and employed (Smith, 1990). While the paths to these

**theoretical research**
research designed specifically to test some explanation of social behavior.

**applied research**
research meant to provide practical solutions to immediate problems.

goals may differ, depending on the orientation of a particular social psychologist, the interaction between theory and applied research in the quest for improving the human condition has become increasingly accepted (Snyder, 1993).

In its continuing emphasis on finding solutions to social problems, the discipline is echoing earlier calls for melding theoretical and applied research. As Kurt Lewin wrote more than fifty years ago:

> Many psychologists working today in an applied field are keenly aware of the need for close cooperation between theoretical and applied psychology. This can be accomplished in psychology . . . if the theorist does not look toward applied problems with high-brow aversion or with a fear of social problems, and if the applied psychologist realizes that there is nothing so practical as a good theory (Lewin, 1951, p. 169).

Lewin's dictum that there is "nothing so practical as a good theory" captures a central characteristic of the field of social psychology—the interactive relationship that exists between theories and applications. In fact, that relationship is symbolized by the very structure of this book, in which chapters that are more theoretical in nature are paired with chapters covering more applied topics. (For instance, Chapter 2, covering the processes that underlie how we develop an understanding of others, is paired with Chapter 3, which discusses prejudice, stereotypes, and discrimination.) Still, as we will see, even the most theoretically oriented chapters contain material of an applied nature; and the more applied chapters carry their share of theoretical material. There is truly an interchange of theory and applications within the field.

In considering the kinds of questions social psychologists ask, we have been introduced to the basic subject matter of the discipline—but our introduction to the discipline is incomplete. Social psychologists don't just raise questions; they answer them. Before beginning our journey through the field of social psychology, then, we need to consider how social psychologists find answers to the questions they ask. In the next section, we discuss the paths followed by social psychologists in the conduct of research.

## ▶ REVIEW & RETHINK

### Review

- Social psychology is the scientific study of how people's thoughts, feelings, and actions are affected by others.
- Although the roots of the discipline can be traced to Plato and Aristotle, the field has been a scientific discipline for less than 100 years.
- Major recent trends include an increased emphasis on cognitive factors and the application of knowledge outside the laboratory.
- In the future, it is likely that there will be increasing emphasis on multiculturalism in social psychology and that the traditional boundaries that have demarcated the field of social psychology from other areas are likely to become increasingly blurred.

### Rethink

- Many of the concerns of contemporary social psychologists were also the concerns of philosophers more than 2,000 years ago. If the topics of interest were the same for both of these groups, why aren't these ancient thinkers considered "psychologists"? What distinguishes contemporary social psychology from early philosophy?
- Most social psychologists believe that their research will yield knowledge that could be used to improve the lives of others and the world in which they live. What dangers exist for a discipline with such aspirations?
- Using the definition of social psychology provided in this chapter, discuss the field's movement into such areas as health, business, and law.

# RESEARCH IN SOCIAL PSYCHOLOGY

*As Rodney King lay on the pavement, he received repeated blows from police billy clubs. Dozens of spectators witnessed the beating, yet not one person—police or civilian—intervened in a meaningful way. As shown in the videotape, the beating continued as some onlookers chatted with one another.*

Why didn't anyone come to King's rescue? Although the civilians observing the scene might have felt constrained because the police were possibly involved in official, legitimate law enforcement activities, this does not explain why other police officers were unmoved by King's increasingly desperate situation. Although one officer did raise his arm in front of another police officer who was wielding a club, the move was ineffectual and the officer continued to bludgeon King. Some of the other officers present later admitted they thought the violence was unwarranted, but they felt unable to act.

Perhaps the most obvious explanation for the lack of police intervention was the presence of a higher-ranking police officer on the scene. After all, if he didn't stop the beating, why should a lower-ranking officer take responsibility? However, a more subtle social psychological process can also account for the lack of police intervention. According to this explanation, it was the very fact that a large number of police officers were on the scene that was responsible for the lack of intervention. In fact, this explanation suggests that had fewer police officers been present, it would have been more likely that someone would have intervened.

Although this argument may strike you as counterintuitive, it is consistent with decades of social psychological research. This work has produced a general principle: The fewer the number of bystanders present in an emergency situation, the more likely it is that a given individual will intervene. The way social psychologists reached this surprising conclusion illustrates the paths they take in doing research.

## *Theories and Hypotheses: Framing the Question*

Questions lie at the heart of all research. Why do we conform to group pressure? How do we encourage people to help one another? How does the appearance of a defendant affect a jury's deliberations?

**DEVELOPING THEORIES.** Typically, social psychologists' questions come from **theories**—broad explanations and predictions of phenomena of interest. All of us develop theories of social behavior (Sternberg, 1985). For instance, we may assume that people follow certain standards of dress and behavior because they wish to be popular. Whenever we develop such an explanation, we are actually building our own theories.

**theories**
broad explanations and predictions of phenomena of interest.

However, our personal theories usually rest on unverified observations, developed in an unsystematic manner—hardly the stuff from which a science is developed. In contrast, the theories of social psychologists are more formal, based on a systematic and orderly integration of prior social psychological findings and theorizing. Such theories summarize and organize prior observations, and permit social psychologists to move beyond observations and make deductions that are not readily apparent from the individual pieces of data that already exist. Consequently, theories provide a guide to the future collection of observations and suggest the direction in which research should move.

Suppose, for example, you were interested in developing an explanation for why bystanders are reluctant to intervene in emergency situations—an issue that social psychologists Bibb Latané and John Darley tackled some 30 years ago. The impetus for

"SHOULDN'T YOU BE OUT OBSERVING THE HUMAN COMEDY?"

*© 1994 Charles Barsotti and The Cartoon Bank, Inc.*

Latané and Darley's theorizing was the 1964 murder of Catherine Genovese in New York. During her 30-minute ordeal, Genovese was repeatedly pursued and stabbed, while she screamed for help. Although approximately 40 people heard her cries, not one person intervened.

In their quest to explain why no one helped Genovese, Latané and Darley developed the theory of diffusion of responsibility (Latané & Darley, 1970). Their theory suggested that the greater the number of bystanders or witnesses to an event that requires help, the more the responsibility for helping is perceived to be shared by the bystanders. Because of this sense of shared responsibility, then, the more people present in an emergency situation, the less personally responsible each person feels, and the less likely that any single person will provide help (Darley & Latané, 1968).

**FORMULATING HYPOTHESES.**    Although Latané and Darley's theory makes sense, its development marked merely the first step in a series of stages. The next challenge they faced was to formulate a hypothesis. A **hypothesis** is a prediction stated in a way that permits it to be tested.

**hypothesis**
a prediction stated in a way that permits it to be tested.

Hypotheses must be drawn from theories. Theories provide a background and basis for producing reasonable hypotheses, which can fit together with other known explanations of social phenomena. In this way, we can build a body of information from which to determine the validity of the explanation.

Of course, social psychologists develop hypotheses from sources other than theories. They may have hunches and intuitions like anyone else, but without a valid theoretical underpinning, a hypothesis will do little to explain human social behavior in a larger sense, and consequently will not advance our understanding of social behavior terribly far.

Based on their general diffusion of responsibility theory, Latané and Darley derived a straightforward hypothesis: The more people who witness an emergency, the less likely it is that a bystander will provide help (Latané & Darley, 1968). It is important to note that this is just one of several hypotheses that could be derived from their theory.

**CHOOSING A RESEARCH STRATEGY.**    After a hypothesis is settled upon, researchers must devise a strategy to test its validity. There are two major classes of research to choose from—experimental research and correlational research. **Experimental research** is

**experimental research**
research designed to discover causal relationships between various factors, in which the researcher deliberately introduces a change in a situation in order to observe the effect that change has upon the situation.

**correlational research**
research that seeks to identify whether an association or relationship between two factors exists—regardless of whether one factor produces changes in the other.

designed to discover causal relationships between various factors. In experimental research, the researcher deliberately introduces a change in a situation in order to observe the effect that change has upon the situation. For instance, experimental research has the potential to identify whether the presence of more people in an emergency situation *causes* less helping.

In contrast, **correlational research** seeks to identify whether an association or relationship between two factors exists. Correlational research cannot be used to determine whether one factor *causes* changes in the other. For example, correlational research could tell us whether the presence of more people in an emergency is *related to* or *associated with* less helping—but not whether their presence causes less helping.

Because experimental research can identify cause–effect relationships, it represents the first-choice strategy of most social psychologists. However, correlational research also provides invaluable information, particularly in situations in which it is impossible to carry out experiments because of ethical or logistical constraints. And, as we'll see, both types of research offer significant benefits—and some pitfalls, as well. (Figure 1-4 outlines the two classes of research.)

## Experimental Research: Establishing Cause–Effect Relationships

**experiment**
procedure to test a hypothesis.

**treatment**
the procedure in an experiment provided by an investigator.

**treatment group**
the group that receives the treatment in an experiment.

**control group**
the no-treatment or alternative-treatment group in an experiment.

**conditions**
the differing treatments that are given to the different groups in an experiment.

In order to run an **experiment** to test a hypothesis, a researcher must first devise at least two different experiences, or treatments. A **treatment** is the procedure provided by an investigator. One group of participants receives one of the treatments, while other groups of participants receive either no treatment or alternative treatments. The group receiving the treatment is known as the **treatment group**, while the no-treatment or alternative-treatment group is called the **control group**. The differing treatments that are given to the two groups are called the experimental **conditions**. (A medical analogy is helpful here: in an experiment to test the effectiveness of a drug in *treating* a disease, one group of subjects would receive the drug—that is, would be part of the *treatment* group. In contrast, another group of subjects would not receive the drug treatment; they would be part of the no-treatment *control* group. In this example, there are two conditions: the treatment condition and control condition.)

The central feature of an experiment, then, is the comparison of the effects of different treatments on different groups of participants. The use of both treatment and control groups permits researchers to rule out the possibility that something other than the experimental manipulation produced the results found in the experiment. For example, if no control group was used, experimenters couldn't be certain whether or not some other variable—such as the temperature of the room, the time of day the study was being conducted, or even the mere passage of time—produced the changes observed. By

| | **EXPERIMENTAL RESEARCH** | **CORRELATIONAL RESEARCH** |
|---|---|---|
| *Process* | Researcher manipulates a situation in order to observe the outcome of the manipulation | Researcher examines previously existing situations |
| *Desired outcome* | Information regarding how one factor causes changes in another | Identification of associations between factors |
| *Types* | Field experiments Laboratory experiments | Naturalistic observation Archival research Survey research Evaluation research |

FIGURE 1-4    Research Strategies

employing a control group, experimenters can isolate the true cause of their results, thereby permitting inferences about cause–effect to be drawn.

Before experimenters can actually develop an experiment, a decision must be made regarding operationalization of the hypothesis. **Operationalization** is the process of translating a hypothesis into specific testable procedures that can be measured and observed. For instance, if we were interested in how the number of bystanders affects helping in an emergency situation, we could operationalize "number of people" as two, three, ten, *or* any other number; "helping" as the number of minutes that pass before subjects call the police *or* directly intervene *or* avert their eyes *or* do something else; and the "emergency situation" as one in which someone breaks a leg *or* has a seizure *or* some other type of emergency.

There are many ways of operationalizing a hypothesis. Logic and ethical constraints dictate what will be chosen by an experimenter. Obviously, however, the way a hypothesis is operationalized is crucial in determining the kinds of conclusions that may be drawn from a study.

In choosing the operationalization to be used in an experiment, researchers are guided by their formulation of the independent variable and dependent variables. The **independent variable** is the variable that is manipulated in the experiment by the researchers. In contrast, the **dependent variable** is the variable that is measured in an experiment and is expected to change as a result of the experimental manipulation. (A straightforward way of remembering: a hypothesis predicts how a dependent variable *depends* on the manipulation of the independent variable.)

For instance, let's return to the hypothesis developed by Latané and Darley: The more people who witness an emergency, the less likely it is that help will be provided. In order to test this hypothesis, Latané and Darley decided to manipulate the number of people present during an emergency situation and determine how the number of people present affected their level of helping (Darley & Latané, 1968). Consequently, the independent variable was the number of people present, and the dependent variable was the level of helping displayed by participants in the study.

Once they had identified the independent and dependent variables, Latané and Darley had to determine what operationalization they should use. They could have chosen any one of several paths. For instance, they could have decided to operationalize the "number of people present" (their independent variable) as groups of one, two, three, or even six individuals exposed to an emergency situation.

They could have operationalized the emergency situation itself by placing participants in an increasingly smoky room, by having them hear a woman fall and apparently break an ankle, or by having them listen to someone having an epileptic seizure in an adjoining room. Finally, they could have determined that the measure of helping—the dependent variable—should be how quickly a participant responded to the emergency, or simply whether the participant responded at all. (In fact, Latané and Darley [1970] used each of these operationalizations in a series of several experiments designed to test the hypothesis.)

**CHOOSING A RESEARCH SETTING.**    In determining the operationalizations to employ in their research, Latané and Darley also had to choose a setting for the study. Their choices centered on two basic alternatives: the laboratory or the field. A **laboratory study** is a research investigation conducted in a controlled setting explicitly designed to hold events constant. A laboratory may be a room or building designed for research, such as in a university's psychology department. In contrast, a **field study** is a research investigation carried out in a naturally occurring setting. Research that is conducted on a street corner, on a bus, or in a classroom are examples of field studies.

Both laboratory and field studies carry advantages and drawbacks. In laboratory studies, the environment can be controlled to the smallest detail, permitting an investigator to create a world that involves and engages participants. In contrast to field studies,

---

**operationalization**
the process of translating a hypothesis into specific testable procedures that can be measured and observed.

**independent variable**
the variable that is manipulated in the experiment by the researchers.

**dependent variable**
the variable that is measured in an experiment and is expected to change as a result of the experimental manipulation.

**laboratory study**
a research investigation conducted in a controlled setting explicitly designed to hold events constant.

**field study**
a research investigation carried out in a naturally occurring setting.

the laboratory setting protects the study from unexpected and inadvertent intrusions, which may often occur in field settings.

On the other hand, laboratory studies may appear artificial and contrived in comparison to field studies. Participants in laboratory research certainly are aware that they are in a study, and their behavior (as we discuss more completely later in the chapter) can reflect this recognition. If this occurs, there may be a problem with **generalization**—the application of the results of a study to other settings and subject populations beyond those immediately employed in the experiment.

**generalization**
the application of the results of a study to other settings and subject populations beyond those immediately employed in the experiment.

Although the laboratory study presents potential problems of generalization, it remains the dominant research technique utilized by social psychologists. The reason is that the drawbacks of laboratory research can, to a large extent, be overcome through the use of a well-designed study. In laboratory research, it is not necessary, or even appropriate, to re-create a situation exactly as it appears outside the laboratory in order to understand a naturally occurring phenomenon. For example, if we're interested in re-creating an emergency situation in the laboratory, we don't need to include every component of an actual emergency in the real world, such as a dirty street, cars parked along the road, a mother pushing a baby carriage who happens to be passing by, and so forth.

Instead, a laboratory study attempts to isolate the component parts of a phenomenon in order to capture its essence. Furthermore, because events in a well-designed laboratory study can be controlled in a way that typically is impossible in the field, more accurate inferences about cause–effect relationships often can be made.

On the other hand, we shouldn't be fooled into thinking that either laboratory or field research is inherently better than the other. Instead, the choice depends on the nature of the question being asked by the investigators and the type of operationalization of independent and dependent variables that the investigator chooses to study. Both the laboratory and the field can provide answers to the kinds of questions social psychologists ask.

**RANDOM ASSIGNMENT OF SUBJECTS TO CONDITION.** The final key to the successful design of an experiment involves the assignment of **subjects**, as participants are known, to treatment and control groups. In **random assignment**, subjects are assigned to an experimental group or "condition" on the basis of chance and chance alone. The statistical laws of probability ensure that particular subject characteristics—such as intelligence, motivation levels, sex, height—will be represented in approximately equal numbers in each condition, as long as subjects are assigned on a completely random basis. Random assignment is a simple yet elegant procedure that safeguards researchers' ability to make appropriate interpretations of experimental results.

**subjects**
participants in an experiment.

**random assignment**
in an experiment, the method of assigning subjects to particular groups on the basis of chance.

The virtue of random assignment becomes apparent when we consider alternatives. Suppose, for example, we assigned the first 20 volunteers for a study to the treatment condition, and the second 20 volunteers to a control condition. It is possible that those who volunteer earliest might have different personality characteristics than those who volunteer later. Perhaps, for example, the early volunteers are more motivated, greater risk-takers, or smarter than the late-volunteering subjects. If the experimental results subsequently show a difference between those subjects in the treatment condition and those in the control condition, we would then be unable to attribute the difference to the experimental manipulation alone—it is possible that differences in subject characteristics produced the results.

In contrast, random assignment would assign subjects to conditions entirely on the basis of chance. If there were two conditions, each subject would have a 50–50 chance of being in either condition. Consequently, every highly intelligent subject would have a 50–50 chance of being assigned to a particular condition; every risk-taker would have a 50–50 chance of being assigned to a condition; and so forth for every subject characteristic. The outcome of such a procedure is that there will be roughly the same number of highly intelligent subjects, risk-taking subjects, and so on, in each condition.

**confounding**
situation in an experiment in which factors other than the independent variable are allowed to vary.

Through random assignment to conditions, then, it is possible to avoid confounding results. **Confounding** refers to instances in which factors other than the independent variable are allowed to vary. If this occurs, a researcher cannot determine whether changes in the dependent variable are due to the manipulation of the independent variable or to the other, confounding factors.

For instance, if in one condition of an experiment, all the subjects were highly intelligent, and in the other condition all the subjects were not terribly smart, we would say that confounding has occurred. We would not be able to separate the effects of subject intelligence from the effects due to the experimental manipulations. Consequently, random assignment helps ensure that any potential confounding factors are distributed equally across the various experimental conditions, allowing researchers to interpret results with more certainty.

**control**
the degree to which an experimenter is able to limit and restrict events within the experiment to those that are intended.

The use of random assignment is one more way in which experimenters seek to maintain control in experiments. **Control** is the degree to which an experimenter is able to limit and restrict events within the experiment to those that are intended. The greater the control over an experimental situation, the greater the confidence an experimenter can have that the results of a study reflect just the experimental manipulations and not any extraneous factors. In contrast, the less control that exists within an experiment, the higher the probability that the experimental results are confounded by unintended factors.

**THE ESSENTIALS OF AN EXPERIMENT.**    We've now considered the key elements of experimental research. To review, experiments are composed of the following:

- *A hypothesis*, a prediction stated in a way that permits it to be tested.
- *An independent variable*, the variable that is manipulated in the experiment by the researcher.
- *A dependent variable*, the variable that is measured in an experiment and is expected to change as a result of the experimental manipulation.
- *An experimental procedure* in which subjects are randomly assigned to different experimental groups or conditions of the independent variable.

Only when every one of these elements is present can researchers be assured that they have created a true experiment, one that will allow them to determine cause–effect relationships.

**EXPERIMENTAL RESEARCH IN ACTION.**    Let's return to Latané and Darley's hypothesis for a moment and consider how it was tested in an actual experiment. In a classic study, Bibb Latané and colleague Judith Rodin (1968) invited subjects to participate in a survey of game and puzzle preferences. This was not the true purpose of the study, but the experimenters surmised that they had to disguise the actual purpose in order to get a true assessment of subjects' behavior in emergency situations. (How could they announce an emergency in advance?)

Upon arrival, an attractive woman led the subjects to the testing room, and gave them a series of questionnaires to complete. The woman then moved to a different part of the room, separated by a room-dividing curtain. A few minutes later, while subjects were filling out the questionnaire, they heard a loud crash and scream that made it sound as though the chair had collapsed and the woman had crashed to the ground. The subjects heard a woman moan, "Oh, my God, my foot . . . I . . . I . . . can't move . . . it. Oh . . . my ankle . . . I . . . can't get this . . . thing . . . off me." She cried and moaned for about a minute longer, but the cries eventually faded away. Eventually, she mumbled something about going outside and was heard knocking over a chair and closing the door behind her. (In actuality, the "emergency" was a tape recording, repeated in every experimental session.) The "emergency" took just over two minutes.

The primary independent variable of the study was whether subjects were (1) alone or (2) with another subject while they filled out the questionnaires. Subjects were assigned randomly to one of these two conditions (see Figure 1-5).

The major dependent variable was whether subjects offered aid to the supposed victim. We might expect a fairly high level of helping, since the costs of offering assistance were so low—getting up from a table and entering another part of the room. In fact, a clear majority—70 percent of the subjects—did help, but only when they were in the condition in which they were alone. When subjects were in the condition in which they were working in the same room with another subject, only 40 percent of them helped—a substantial difference.

The findings are surprising only to those who are unaware of Latané and Darley's original hypothesis. Recall that they predicted, based on the concept of diffusion of responsibility, that the more people who witness an emergency, the less likely it is that help will be provided. And this situation is exactly what occurred: Less help was offered in the condition when two people were present than in the condition when one was present.

One last step remained for the researchers: In order to make sure that the difference in helping between the two conditions was a real one, they had to conduct several

**FIGURE 1-5    The Ingredients of an Experiment** Latané and Darley's hypothesis of diffusion of responsibility is tested in this experiment. Beginning with a hypothesis, the researcher identified subjects and then randomly assigned them to one or two conditions: **(1)** working alone, or **(2)** working with others. Consequently, the independent variable was the presence or absence of others. The dependent variable—what was measured in the experiment—was how long it took subjects to help in the emergency. The final step was to analyze results statistically by comparing differences between conditions.

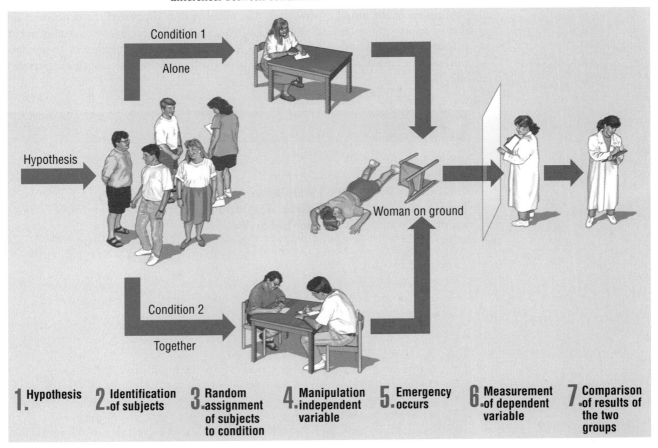

1. Hypothesis  2. Identification of subjects  3. Random assignment of subjects to condition  4. Manipulation independent variable  5. Emergency occurs  6. Measurement of dependent variable  7. Comparison of results of the two groups

statistical tests. These tests established that the difference was large enough to warrant the conclusion that it was statistically meaningful and not merely the outcome of chance. In the parlance of research methods, Latané and Rodin could state that the differences found in the experiment were large enough to reach statistical significance. **Statistical significance** represents an outcome that would be expected to occur by chance less than five times out of 100. In other words, a significant difference is one in which there is a 95 percent or better probability that the difference an experimenter finds is due to real differences between two groups rather than to chance.

**statistical significance**
represents an outcome that would be expected to occur by chance less than five times out of 100.

Latané and Rodin's experiment had all the ingredients of a true experiment. As shown in Figure 1-5, they started with a hypothesis. Their independent variable was whether subjects were alone or together with another person, and their dependent variable was whether subjects helped or not. They randomly assigned subjects to one of the two experimental conditions.

Although the results of this study confirmed the hypothesis, one study cannot unequivocally confirm a theory. Before accepting experimental results, social psychologists demand **replication**, in which experiments are repeated in order to verify the original results. Sometimes replications are exactly the same as an original experiment in order to corroborate the initial results, but more frequently they represent conceptual replications. In a conceptual replication, most features of the original experiment are kept intact, but some components are modified in order to build upon and extend the original results.

**replication**
the process of verifying the original results of an experiment by reproducing the procedure.

Latané and Darley carried out several different conceptual replications to establish the diffusion of responsibility principle (Darley & Latané, 1968). They were joined by other researchers interested in the same issues (Bickman, 1971). By using a variety of approaches and techniques, different social psychologists were able to establish the viability of the theory. In fact, some 50 studies were carried out in the decade following the publication of the initial experiments, and together they supported the concept of diffusion of responsibility (Latané and Nida, 1981). In sum, we can say with confidence that, at least in emergency situations, more is less: The greater the number of bystanders or witnesses to an event that requires help, the less likely it is that any single person will offer help.

# ▶ REVIEW & RETHINK

## Review

- The two major classes of research are experimental research, which can establish cause–effect relationships, and correlational research, which identifies whether an association or relationship exists between two factors.
- Theories are broad explanations and predictions of phenomena of interest, while a hypothesis is a prediction, derived from a theory, stated in a way that permits it to be tested.
- The essentials of an experiment include a hypothesis, independent and dependent variables, and a procedure in which subjects are randomly assigned to experimental groups or conditions.

## Rethink

- Why is it important for social psychologists to derive hypotheses that they use to test theories? Is it possible to form theories from hypotheses?
- What is the function of control groups in psychological experiments? Imagine a study in which college students took a math test before and after a training program designed to improve math skills. Would a control group be necessary in this study? Why or why not?

• Why is it important to assign subjects into conditions in a random fashion? What confounding factors can be controlled by using random assignment? Can you think of confounding factors that would not be controlled by using random assignment?

*Correlational Research: Establishing Associations Between Variables*

No matter how ingenious a researcher, there is no way to study subjects' reactions to the stress of a natural disaster by manipulating their exposure to an earthquake. Similarly, researchers cannot experimentally manipulate the sex of subjects in order to study whether male and female students are treated differently by their employers. Nor can we cut off a hand of subjects in one treatment condition in order to study subjects' reactions to being physically challenged. In each of these cases, practical, ethical, and moral constraints preclude the manipulation of variables that are necessary to conduct a true experiment.

However, there is an alternative class of research: correlational research. As we discussed earlier, correlational research examines the relationship between two (or more) variables to determine whether they are associated or "correlated." Correlational research basically has three possible outcomes:

• When values of one variable are high, values of the second are also high; and when values of the first variable are low, the values of the second are also low. This situation produces a *positive correlation*. For example, if we assumed that *more* people present in an emergency situation would result in *more* helping (a prediction contrary to that of Latané and Darley), we would expect to find a positive correlation between number of people and helping (see Figure 1-6).

• When values of one variable are high, values of the second are low; and when values of the first variable are low, the values of the second are high. This produces a *negative correlation*. For instance, if Latané and Darley's hypothesis is correct in predicting that as *more* people are present, *less* helping will occur, we would expect to find a negative correlation.

• Finally, no relationship may exist between the two variables. This yields a finding of "no correlation." If, for example, the number of bystanders present was unrelated to helping, no correlation would be present.

**FIGURE 1-6    Types of Correlations** These graphs indicate three types of possible relationships between variables. In **a**, we find a positive correlation between the amount of helping and the number of people present (as values of one variable rise, so do the values of the other variable). In **b**, as the number of people increases, the amount of helping declines (as values of one variable fall, values of the other variable rise). Finally, in **c**, we see no relationship between the two variables; they are uncorrelated.

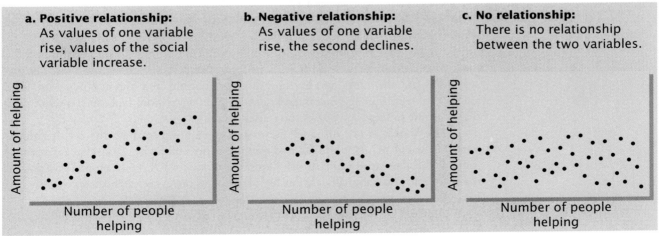

*© 1993 OHMAN. Reprinted with permission of Tribune Media Services.*

**FIGURE 1-7    Correlation Is Not the Same as Causation.**
Researchers who discovered that heart disease was correlated with a certain pattern of balding didn't mean to imply that balding was the cause of heart disease.

The strength of a correlation is represented by a mathematical score ranging from +1.00 to −1.00. The closer a correlation comes to positive or negative 1.00, the stronger the relationship between the two variables. Hence, a strong positive correlation would be close to +1.00, and a strong negative correlation would be close to −1.00. Conversely, weak or no relationships result in a correlation that will hover around .00.

The most critical point about correlations is that no matter how strongly two variables are correlated with one another, the correlation does not imply that the two variables are linked causally. Such a finding means only that they are associated with one another. Although it may mean that one variable causes the changes in the other, it is equally plausible that it does not. It is even possible that some third, unmeasured—and previously unconsidered—variable is causing both variables to increase or decrease simultaneously.

Let's take a concrete example. Suppose you were a social psychologist who hypothesized that the long-term consequences of exposure to violence on television produced aggression in children. Because it is not possible to control everything children watch on television during their entire childhood, experimental research on the long-term effects of viewing is simply not practical. Consequently, you would be compelled to use correlational research.

Stated in correlational terms, your hypothesis would be that there is a positive correlation between the amount of aggressive television programs children view and the aggressive behavior they display. Now suppose you conduct an experiment and find that the results support your hypothesis: Children who are exposed to the most televised aggression are the most apt to show high aggression, and those exposed to lower amounts of television aggression tend to show lower aggression. Does such a result mean that exposure to television aggression causes children's aggression?

The answer is no. Although it would be tempting to draw the conclusion just stated, it would be inappropriate and quite possibly inaccurate. Consider, for instance, some of the alternative explanations illustrated in Figure 1-8. For example, it is possible that children who habitually exhibit high aggression prefer to watch shows that are high in aggressive content because of their own aggressive tendencies.

Similarly, it is just as plausible that some third factor produces both viewer aggression and observation of highly aggressive television shows. For example, neglectful par-

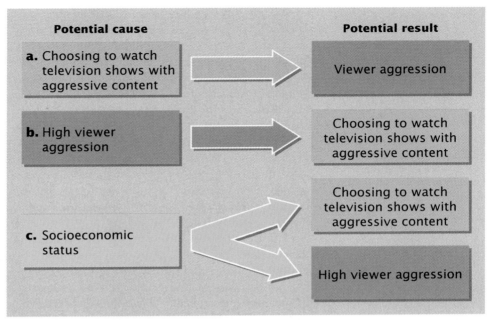

**FIGURE 1-8    The Causal Possibilities: The Relationship between Exposure to Television Violence and Aggressive Behavior** At least three possible causal paths underlie a positive correlation between televised violence and aggression: **a.** watching shows with aggressive content leads to viewer aggression; **b.** people who act aggressively choose to watch shows containing violence; and **c.** a third factor—socioeconomic status—leads to both watching aggression on television and acting aggressive.

ents may tolerate high levels of television viewing and high levels of aggression in their children. Their lack of discipline may produce unrestrained, uncontrollable children who do whatever they desire, including watching large amounts of television and behaving aggressively. No causal links may exist, then, between televised aggression and aggressive behavior.

Despite their inability to draw causal connections from correlational research, social psychologists regularly carry out research of this nature because it enables them to study areas that could not be examined in a laboratory. Conclusions from such research have illuminated important issues and have led to significant advances in the field. In fact, social psychologists have developed an inventory of several correlational procedures that illustrate a range of possibilities of collecting data. (See Figure 1-4.) We'll discuss some of the major ones: naturalistic observation, archival research, survey research, and evaluation research.

**NATURALISTIC OBSERVATION.** Every day of our lives, we engage in naturalistic observation. As we walk down college corridors, stand on street corners, or grab breakfast at a restaurant, most of us are taking mental note of what people around us are doing.

Social psychologists make the same kinds of observations, although in a considerably more systematic manner. In **naturalistic observation**, investigators simply observe some naturally occurring behavior without intervening or making changes in the situation. For instance, a social psychologist interested in the size of naturally occurring groups may examine various locations (parks, streets, restaurants) to determine how many people are usually found together. The critical point is that researchers using naturalistic observation do not intervene and modify the situation, as they might if they were carrying out an experiment. Instead, they seek to record what they find in as careful and unbiased a manner as possible.

There are actually two sorts of naturalistic observation: nonparticipant and participant observation. In **nonparticipant observation**, the researcher records people's behav-

**naturalistic observation**
a process in which investigators observe some naturally occurring behavior but do not intervene in the situation.

**nonparticipant observation**
the type of naturalistic observation in which the researcher records people's behavior in a given setting but does not actually enter into it.

ior in a given setting but does not actually enter into it. For example, an experimenter interested in understanding how often people obeyed traffic regulations could secretly record the number of times people passed through a stop sign without fully stopping. Similarly, nonparticipant observation can take the form of indirect, unobtrusive measures. For instance, one ingenious study using nonparticipant observation examined the rate of replacement of tiles in front of different exhibits in a children's museum to determine which was the most popular (Webb et al., 1966). (For the record, hatching chicks were the favorite!)

**participant observation**
the type of naturalistic observation in which the researcher actually engages in the activities of the people being observed.

In contrast, **participant observation** occurs when an observer actually engages in the activities of the people being observed. In one classic study, for example, an investigator interested in the behavior of friendship patterns among neighborhood residents actually moved into the community and participated in various leisure-time activities. In this way, the researcher was able to learn, first-hand, the relationships among people living in the area (Whyte, 1981).

Both nonparticipant and participant observation have assets and drawbacks. Participant observers are able to get close to the people being studied and may be in a better position to understand fully what is actually occurring in a field setting. On the other hand, a participant observer runs the risk of inadvertently influencing the activities of the people being studied. If that occurs, the observed behavior may not reflect what subjects would have done had the observer not been participating in their activities.

**reactivity**
behavior that occurs as a result of subjects' awareness that they are being studied.

If subjects are aware that they are being observed, another problem may occur: subject reactivity. **Reactivity** is behavior that occurs as a result of subjects' awareness that they are being studied. Although reactivity typically declines over time, as subjects become acclimated to being studied, it can be a serious problem in short-term observational studies.

ARCHIVAL RESEARCH.     Suppose a friend asserted that the phases of the moon affected people's behavior, making them act "crazy." What might you do to verify or refute the accuracy of your friend's claim?

**archival research**
research in which an investigator analyzes existing records or documents in an effort to confirm a hypothesis.

One approach would be to employ archival research. In **archival research**, researchers analyze existing records or documents in an attempt to confirm a hypothesis. For example, in this case you might consult the *Farmer's Almanac* for a five-year period to document when changes in the moon's phases occurred. By examining records of admissions to mental hospitals and correlating them with the moon's phases, you might be able to confirm—or deny—such a hypothesis.

Archival research has the advantage of being completely nonreactive: Subjects do not know they are being observed, and their behavior will be uninfluenced by the observation. Even more important, researchers can test hypotheses that span vast periods of time, history, and culture. Consequently, archival research can confirm the validity of principles developed in the present from data that has been collected in the past.

However, there are disadvantages to archival research. Sometimes the data needed to confirm a hypothesis simply do not exist or are unavailable or incomplete. Even when such data can be collected, the sheer mass may be so great that it is hard to tell what is and is not important. Finally, the researcher is at the mercy of the original collectors of the material. If they have done a poor job, the results of archival research will be inclusive at best, and misleading at worst (Jones, 1985; Stewart & Kamins, 1993).

SURVEY RESEARCH.     Are you a Democrat, a Republican, an independent, or none of the above? Should women have the right to obtain an abortion? Do you believe that homosexuality should be grounds for discharge from the military?

**survey research**
research in which an investigator chooses people to represent some larger population and asks them a series of questions about their behavior, thoughts, or attitudes.

Questions like these are typical of those asked in surveys, one of the most direct techniques for determining how people think and feel about a topic. In **survey research**, people chosen to represent some larger population answer a series of questions about

The care with which surveys are carried out varies considerably. For instance, telephone surveys cannot include people who do not have a phone in their sample, thereby omitting individuals who are particularly disadvantaged. The U.S. Census, in contrast, attempts to contact every household in the United States.

their behavior, thoughts, or attitudes. If the sample of people surveyed has been scientifically selected, researchers are able to draw quite accurate inferences from the larger population. For example, the outcome of presidential elections usually can be predicted within one or two percentage points if a sample of just a few thousand voters is surveyed—provided the sample is painstakingly identified (Fowler, 1993).

Although survey research is a proven technique for learning about people's behaviors and attitudes, the data obtained cannot always be taken at face value. For one thing, people do not always respond accurately. They may not precisely remember their own past behavior; they may not wish to reveal information about themselves; or they may not even know how they feel and may answer without giving the issue full consideration. Because people may try to present themselves favorably, their answers may not be fully honest. Consequently, one major drawback of survey research is that the researcher is not able to directly observe behaviors in question but instead must rely on the accuracy of those who are surveyed.

## SOCIAL PSYCHOLOGY AT WORK

# AND THE QUESTION IS: HOW FAIR IS THIS SURVEY?

Examine the following question, and consider how you think most people would respond:

> If our government wants the American people to pay more taxes, should it provide leadership by example—all sacrifice begins at the top—by cutting Congress's and the President's salaries by 10 percent and reducing their retirement plans to bring them in line with those of the American people?

Regardless of how one personally feels about the issues involved, it is clear that the question is hardly worded in a neutral manner. In fact, the item seems purposely designed to elicit agreement on the part of most people who are asked to respond.

The question is one of a series of 17 included in a survey designed by politician H. Ross Perot (see Figure 1-10). Perot paid for the survey to be inserted into *TV Guide*, supposedly to learn about readers' political attitudes. However, the wording of the questions made any results highly suspect, and professional survey researchers criticized what they saw as the bias of the survey (Kolbert, 1993; Wilber, 1993).

In order to prove the point, the television network CNN conducted its own survey, which compared questions from Perot's survey with more neutral ones. For example, on the issue of interest groups, the CNN survey asked one half of the sample Perot's query, "Should laws be passed to eliminate all possibilities of special interests giving huge sums of money to candidates?" The other half of the sample was asked a reworded, and more balanced, version: "Should laws be passed to prohibit interest groups from contributing to campaigns, or do groups have a right to contribute to the candidates they support?"

As you can see in Figure 1-9, the two versions of the question produced very different responses. Although most people agreed with Perot's version, endorsing the need to restrict interest groups, only a minority were in favor of restrictions when the wording was put in more neutral terms.

Clearly, the way in which a question is worded affects the responses dramatically. But the wording of the questions was not the only potential source of bias in the poll. For instance, readers of *TV Guide* do not necessarily embody a representative sample of U.S. voters. Moreover, two other factors undermined the objectivity of the survey: The survey included a place for respondents to provide their names and addresses, and it included a request for a monetary contribution to a political organization. A lack of anonymity may have made respondents less than forthright in their responses, and the call for donations may have limited responses from people of limited economic means.

In sum, it is clear that the conclusions that can be drawn from a survey are only as good as the objectivity of the questions that are asked and the representativeness of the sample. If either is in doubt, it is impossible to interpret accurately the meaning of any survey's results.

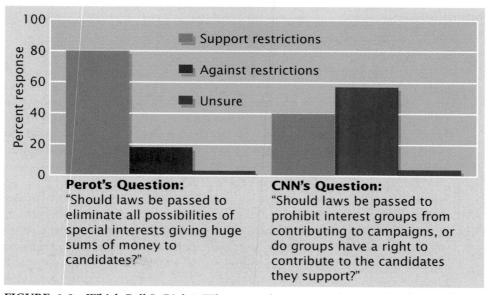

**FIGURE 1-9  Which Poll Is Right?** When researchers compared the results of two polls, one using Ross Perot's wording and the other worded in a more neutral fashion by CNN, the responses were quite different. *(Source:* Kolbert, 1993.)

**Ross Perot Presents**
**THE FIRST NATIONAL REFERENDUM - GOVERNMENT REFORM**
**Sponsored By United We Stand America** ₛₘ
**SUNDAY, MARCH 21**
**NBC TV & RADIO  8:00pm EST (7:00pm CST/8:00pm PST)**

Your response allows the people of America to speak to Congress and the White House on these vital issues. Complete your ballot and mail it in to be tabulated.

**United We Stand America** ₛₘ
**NATIONAL REFERENDUM-GOVERNMENT REFORM**

(Please darken box completely)
YES NO

1. Do you believe that for every dollar of tax increase there should be $2.00 in spending cuts with the savings earmarked for deficit and debt reduction?.............................. ☐ ☐

2. Should the President present an overall plan including spending cuts, spending increases, and tax increases and present the net result of the overall plan, so that the people can know the net result before paying more taxes?.............................. ☐ ☐

3. Should the President issue a quarterly, audited financial report to the people so we can know whether or not the results of the debt reduction plan are being achieved as scheduled?.............................. ☐ ☐

4. Do you want a Constitutional Balanced Budget Amendment, with emergency funding limited exclusively to National Defense?.............................. ☐ ☐

5. Should the President have the Line Item Veto to eliminate waste?.............................. ☐ ☐

6. If our government wants the American people to pay more taxes, should it provide leadership by example - all sacrifice begins at the top - by cutting Congress' and the President's salaries by ten percent and reducing their retirement plans to bring them in line with those of the American people?.............................. ☐ ☐

7. Should Congress agree to term limits that would automatically take effect if the specific debt reduction time table is not achieved?.............................. ☐ ☐

8. Should Congress and officials in the White House set the example for sacrifice by eliminating all perks and special privileges currently paid by taxpayers?.............................. ☐ ☐

9. Do you feel past international trade agreements have caused loss of jobs in this country?.............................. ☐ ☐

10. Should we eliminate foreign lobbyists completely - no loopholes - and make it a criminal offense?.............................. ☐ ☐

11. Should we dramatically reduce the role of domestic lobbyists to provide only information - not money directly or indirectly?.............................. ☐ ☐

12. Should we eliminate political action committees and soft money contributions to campaigns?.............................. ☐ ☐

13. Should laws be passed to eliminate all possibilities of special interests giving huge sums of money to candidates?.............................. ☐ ☐

14. Do you believe that Congress should not exclude itself from legislation it passes for us, and should correct this discrepancy immediately?.............................. ☐ ☐

15. Should major new programs such as health care reform be first presented to the American people in detail, and then tested in pilot programs to prove their cost effectiveness before they are implemented nationwide?.............................. ☐ ☐

16. Should the electoral college be replaced with a popular vote for the Presidential election?.. ☐ ☐

17. Was this TV forum worthwhile?  Do you wish to continue participating as a voting member of United We Stand America?.............................. ☐ ☐

PRINT IN UPPER CASE ONLY

FIRST NAME          M.I.   LAST NAME

STREET/RURAL ROUTE                                        APT#

CITY                                              STATE    ZIP

A/C      PHONE                          US CONGRESSIONAL DIST. (If known)

*Please see reverse side for United We Stand America Membership Information. (detach card here)*

**FIGURE 1-10    A Biased Survey?**  The wording of the questions in this poll makes any findings highly suspect, according to professional pollsters.

Another potential problem with surveys concerns the way the questions are worded. As discussed in the accompanying *Social Psychology at Work* feature, unless questions are posed in a neutral, impartial manner, people's responses will be biased.

**EVALUATION RESEARCH.**    In recent years, the U.S. government has invested millions of dollars to encourage the public to follow safer sex practices in order to prevent the spread of AIDS. How successful have these efforts been?

**evaluation research**
a technique designed to determine the effects of a research program—specifically, whether it is meeting its goals—and to contribute information to help improve the program in the future.

In order to answer this question, social psychologists would turn to evaluation research. **Evaluation research** is a technique designed to determine whether a program is meeting its goals and to contribute information to help improve the program in the future. The program in question might be a small, local one ("Is the college's new program to reduce freshman student dropouts effective?") or a large-scale assessment of the effectiveness of a national program ("Is Head Start successful in increasing student scholastic achievement?").

The outcome of evaluation research is often controversial and can be related to politics. Consider, for instance, the Head Start program. Although the program has been in place for several decades, there is still no definitive evidence concerning its success in improving student performance. In fact, the evidence is quite contradictory, with some studies showing positive gains for the program and others yielding little or even contrary evidence for the effectiveness of the program. Because such a mixture of results can produce alternative interpretations, it is not surprising that political considerations have played a role in the evaluation of the program (DeParle, 1993).

As a consequence of the ambiguous nature of such studies, social psychologists may be the targets of political pressure, particularly by program advocates and administrators who feel threatened by a negative evaluation. Although such real-world pressures can make the program evaluator's job a difficult one, program evaluation is an activity in which social psychologists are increasingly involved (Kushler, 1989; Archer, Pettigrew, & Aronson, 1992; Mohr, 1992).

*Threats to Research Validity: On the Social Psychology of Doing Research*

So far, we've been discussing research as if subjects were fairly passive responders to stimuli, reacting to events in experiments with little awareness or concern that they are, in fact, participating in an experiment. However, those of us who have been subjects in a study know that nothing could be further from the truth. Subjects constantly wonder about questions such as these: What is happening? What does this mean? Why am I being told this? What is the experimenter trying to prove? In their attempts to answer questions such as these, subjects may pose some serious threats to the validity of any findings the experiment produces.

**DEMAND CHARACTERISTICS.**    If a stranger came up to you on the street and asked you to answer 20 pages of math problems, you would probably refuse. But if an experimenter asked you to do the same thing in the course of an experiment, you would probably be considerably more agreeable to the request. The reason? You would likely assume that the task had some meaning, particularly in light of the presumed expertise and authority of the experimenter.

Subjects who participate in an experiment make interpretations about what the experimenter is looking for. Moreover—and even worse in terms of the validity of the results—they may act upon their interpretations. They may try to "help" experimenters by conforming to their guess of the hypothesis; or, if so inclined, they may try to disprove the hypothesis. In either case, their behavior in experiments is not necessarily a valid representation of real-life behavior; rather, it is an indication of how subjects feel they ought to behave.

**demand characteristics**
the cues that subjects use in an experiment to provide information regarding what is expected or regarding appropriate behavior.

**Demand characteristics** refer to the cues that subjects receive in an experiment that provide information regarding what is expected or appropriate behavior (Aronson et al., 1990). These may include the location of the experimental laboratory, the demeanor of the experimenter, or the kind of equipment involved in the study. Any of these factors might be sufficient to lead subjects to develop their own notion about what kind of behavior the experimenter is looking for.

**deception**
research methods that disguise or mislead subjects regarding the actual purpose of a study.

The most common way to prevent demand characteristics from biasing the results of an experiment is through the use of deception. When social psychologists use the term **deception**, they mean research methods that disguise or mislead subjects regarding the actual purpose of a study. If subjects then attempt to change their behavior in order to support (or refute) this fake hypothesis, such behavior is presumably unlikely to affect responses relevant to the true question of interest.

In many cases, social psychologists employ elaborate deceptive scenarios in experiments in order to disguise the true purpose of the experiment. They not only conceal the hypothesis, they also use **confederates**—employees or colleagues of the experimenter who pose as subjects, in order to produce a scene that has a certain impact on subjects, engaging and involving them in order to create the needed conditions (Suls & Rosnow, 1988; Aronson et al., 1990).

**confederates**
employees or colleagues of the experimenter who pose as subjects in an experiment and who may be used to produce a scene that has impact on subjects, engaging and involving them.

The frequent use of deception in social psychological experiments raises concerns of both a methodological and an ethical nature. For instance, some critics argue that the use of deception will ultimately lead to a scarcity of untainted, "naive" subjects (subjects who are taken in by the experimental deception). They suggest that the problem will grow as social psychologists' routine use of deception becomes increasingly well-known by the general population and particularly among college students, who, as we will mention later, serve as the discipline's most frequent subjects (Kelman, 1967; Greenberg & Folger, 1988).

However, at least some research on the use of deception in experiments suggests otherwise. For example, survey data collected over the last two decades shows little change in college students' attitudes toward research. Subjects have apparently not become more suspicious or distrustful of psychologists (Sharpe, Adair, & Roese, 1992).

Other critics of social psychology's use of deception raise ethical concerns. They suggest that there is something inherently contradictory about a discipline that calls itself a science—which implies an open and public quest for knowledge—and yet uses deception as a major research tool. Furthermore, the use of deception raises several related ethical dilemmas, including such issues as whether people should be studied without their knowledge, whether the true purpose of experiments should be revealed to subjects, whether research procedures place people under stress, whether subjects should be actively deceived, and whether research should induce subjects to engage in behaviors that they otherwise would be unlikely to carry out (Cook, 1976; Greenberg & Folger, 1988; Aronson et al., 1990; Mann, 1994; Rosenthal, 1994).

In order to deal with such ethical issues, social psychologists adhere to a strict set of ethical guidelines that protects the rights of subjects (American Psychological Association, 1990). These ethical principles require that subjects be told enough about the experiment to give their **informed consent**—that is, that they agree to proceed as subjects after the possible risks and benefits have been fully disclosed and explained. The only time informed consent is not required is when the risks to subjects are minimal, as when a study using naturalistic observation is conducted in a public setting such as a street corner or shopping mall.

**informed consent**
agreement between the researchers and the subjects in an experiment in which the researchers fully disclose and explain to the subjects the possible risks and benefits of the experiment.

Furthermore, the ethical principles state that deception should be used only if no other techniques are available; that subjects should not be harmed or placed in discomfort; that a full debriefing be done following the study; and that the benefits of participation should outweigh the risks for people who act as subjects. Institutions in which research is conducted must have review boards, composed of professionals not involved in the research, who evaluate every experiment before it is run to ensure that the methods employed strictly follow ethical guidelines (Gurman, 1994).

**EXPERIMENTER EXPECTATIONS.**    In most studies, the experimenter plays a central role in the proceedings. Consequently, it seems reasonable that the experimenter's behavior, personal qualities, and expectations can have an effect upon subjects' behavior.

If experimenters treated all subjects the same way, there would not be a problem, since the experimenter's effects would be roughly the same on all subjects. However, experimenter behavior and characteristics that affect some subjects in one way and others in a different way create a problem. If, for instance, an experimenter treated attractive

**experimenter expectations**
a situation that may arise in an experiment in which the experimenter unintentionally communicates cues to subjects about the way they are expected to behave in a given experimental condition.

subjects differently from unattractive subjects, the outcome of the experiment clearly could be affected (Blanck, 1993).

The most threatening form of experimenter effects is due to **experimenter expectations**, in which an experimenter unintentionally communicates cues to subjects about the way they are expected to behave in a given experimental condition (Rosenthal, 1976; Harris, 1991). For example, an experimenter who hypothesizes that subjects will act aggressively in one condition and passively in another may relate to subjects in a way that evokes aggression from them in the first condition and passivity from them in the second. Experimenters may not be aware of their behavior, but the expectations may be communicated inadvertently from the kinds of things the experimenter says and does.

Although experimenter expectations can never be completely eliminated, there are several techniques that can reduce their likelihood. For instance, if the people who carry out the experiment are unaware of the experimental hypotheses that are being tested, they obviously will be unable to let their expectations be communicated to subjects. In addition, experimenters may employ substitutes, such as providing subjects with tape-recorded instructions. The difficulty with this solution, however, is that it raises problems of its own, as it may produce an experiment that is uninvolving and sterile.

**CHOOSING RESEARCH PARTICIPANTS: The subject of subjects.**    If a goal of social psychology is to discover principles that apply to people in general, it would seem logical to use research participants who somehow represent "people in general."

Obviously, even the most ingenious experimenter will be unable to find subjects who are fully representative of everyone. In fact, the field of social psychology has been criticized for its reliance on college students as subjects. As with other fields within psychology, critics have noted that the discipline is developing a science of "the behavior of the college sophomore" (Rubenstein, 1982).

If college students were representative of the population at large, their frequent use would not be problematic. However, college students tend to be younger, have a higher socioeconomic status, and be better educated than the rest of the population of the United States. They may also differ on important social psychological dimensions. For instance, their attitudes may be less established than in older adults, and consequently they may be more susceptible to social influence (Sears, 1986).

The subjects of social psychological experiments also tend to be disproportionately white. Remarkably, the percentage of research studies on African-Americans has declined from the early 1970s to the late 1980s, even as awareness and sensitivity about minority inclusion have risen. Although the decline may be traced to several causes, such as fears associated with conducting socially sensitive research or changes in topical areas, the lack of research involving African-Americans is troubling. As one consequence, government agencies that fund research now ask researchers to indicate how they intend to include underrepresented populations when they submit research proposals (Graham, 1992; NIH, 1993).

# THE INFORMED CONSUMER OF SOCIAL PSYCHOLOGY

## THINKING CRITICALLY ABOUT SOCIAL PSYCHOLOGY

"The Ten Best Ways to Build a Relationship!"

"How to Read Another Person Like a Book"

"Rescuing Your Child from a Cult"

We encounter information relevant to social psychology not only in textbooks but in the daily newspaper, on the 6 o'clock news, or in a shopping mall bookstore. We are constantly confronted—even bombarded—with apparent wisdom relating to people's social lives, such as the titles cited above.

We face a formidable challenge when we attempt to sort through this information and separate appropriate claims from inappropriate ones. Several principles, derived from the strategies used by social psychologists in their exploration of the underpinnings of social behavior, can aid in evaluating such material (Coats, Feldman, & Schwartzberg, 1994):

- *Identify and challenge assumptions.* Every statement has multiple underlying assumptions. For instance, when someone claims that allowing homosexuals in the military will reduce unit cohesion, they may be making any one of several underlying assumptions: (1) all homosexuals behave in similar ways; (2) unit cohesion is critical to the military's effectiveness; (3) unit cohesion is affected by the sexual orientation of those in the unit; (4) homosexuals are not already serving in the military. Regardless of whether one agrees or disagrees with such underlying assumptions, the point is that these assumptions must be considered before the original statement can be rejected or accepted.

- *Consider factual accuracy and logical consistency.* In critically evaluating the claims that people make, it is important to consider the validity of the evidence on which a claim is staked. Claims need to be substantiated, and the source of the information needs to be verified. The very fact that something is printed in a magazine or newspaper—or even in a textbook!—does not guarantee that it is correct; writers are human, and they make human errors. Furthermore, it is important to consider the logic behind an argument's conclusions. For instance, hearing that "no other toothpaste is recommended more than Toothwasher" doesn't mean that Toothwasher is the toothpaste most often recommended—just that nothing else is recommended more. In fact, such a statement suggests that other toothpastes may be just as good as Toothwasher.

- *Consider context.* An assertion may be valid in some contexts, but not in others. In fact, very few claims are universally applicable. Consider, for instance, the old proverb "Two heads are better than one." If we interpret this to mean that two people working on a problem are more likely to arrive at an accurate solution than one person, then social psychological research is supportive, as we'll see in Chapter 14. But if we consider the proverb in the context of whether two people working on a problem are more efficient than one person, the answer is just the opposite. According to the same body of research, groups are less efficient than individuals working alone.

Identifying accurate information derived from social psychology represents a formidable challenge to consumers.

Context is also crucial in terms of cultural factors. Although we tend to be embedded in our own culture, it is important to keep in mind that people from different cultures may respond in diverse ways. Just as social psychologists struggle with the challenge of determining the degree to which principles are universal, all of us need to keep in mind the potential limitations of broad claims.

- *Imagine and explore alternatives.* Evaluating the claims of others consists of more than just poking holes in their arguments. It is also useful to generate new ideas and alternative explanations. For instance, one approach is to assume that an assertion is wrong, and to think of arguments for its opposite. If we can develop plausible alternative explanations, the shortcomings of the original claims may become apparent.

By adhering to these guidelines, you can become more astute in your evaluations of the claims that you encounter in the popular press, as well as those espoused by friends, teachers, and other acquaintances. Furthermore, the same criteria can be used to appraise the theories and research carried out by social psychologists. By applying a critical eye to the assertions you encounter, you'll be better able to appreciate the very real advances in our understanding of behavior that social psychologists have accomplished.

▶ # REVIEW & RETHINK

## Review

- Correlational research examines the relationship between two (or more) variables to determine whether they are associated.
- The major types of correlational research are naturalistic observation, archival research, survey research, and evaluation research.
- Threats to the validity of experiments include demand characteristics, experimenter expectations, and the characteristics of the subjects used in the study.

## Rethink

- What benefits are provided by an experimental design in which the experimenter is "blind" to the hypotheses being tested? Are there any costs involved in keeping experimenters blind?
- What type of correlation would you expect to find between height and weight? How might this correlation affect the results of a study that demonstrates a positive association between height and a tolerance for alcohol?
- Consider these four types of research studies: (1) an experiment conducted in the field, (2) an experimental study conducted in a laboratory, (3) a correlational study using naturalistic observation, and (4) a correlational study using archival research methods. Which would you use to answer the following questions:
  (a) Are elementary school teachers more nonverbally supportive of their younger pupils?
  (b) Does nonverbal support from their classroom teacher help children learn more effectively?
  (c) Does the presence of a full moon produce a change in normal behavior?
  (d) Will rewarding someone for doing something that they always enjoyed reduce their inherent pleasure in performing the task?
  (e) Will watching one hour of violent television programming increase aggressive behavior?
- What benefits does correlational research have over experimental research methods? Are experimental designs always preferable when feasible?

# LOOKING BACK ◀ ◀ ◀ ◀ ◀ ◀ ◀ ◀ ◀ ◀ ◀ ◀ ◀ ◀ ◀ ◀ ◀ ◀ ◀ ◀ ◀ ◀ ◀ ◀ ◀ ◀ ◀

### What is the scope of social psychology?

1. Social psychology is the scientific study of how people's thoughts, feelings, and actions are affected by others. Social psychologists focus on the consequences of social influences on individuals and the way they understand the world; on social interaction between and among people; and on group processes.

2. Within the broader field of psychology, social psychology's closest companion is the subdiscipline of personality psychology. Outside psychology, sociology and anthropology are closely related to social psychology.

3. Although the field of social psychology is made up primarily of white males, demographic trends are changing, as increasing numbers of women get degrees in the area. However, the record on minority representation is less positive: Only 3 percent of social psychologists are Hispanic and 6 percent African-American.

### What were the major milestones and trends in the development of the field, and what is the future likely to hold?

4. Although the roots of social psychology were foreshadowed by Plato and Aristotle, the scientific discipline of social psychology can be traced to 1897, when the first social psychological experiment was conducted, and to 1908, when two social psychology texts were published. However, it was not until the 1920s that social psychology became an established, independent discipline. The 1930s saw the emergence of such pioneers as Muzafer Sherif, who studied social norms, and Kurt Lewin, who made both theoretical and applied contributions.

5. Following World War II, social psychology flourished. Group behavior was a central topic at that time, a trend that continued well into the 1950s. By the 1960s, however, another shift occurred, and the emphasis changed to within-individual social processes, compared with the earlier emphasis on between-individual processes. Attribution theory, which focuses on the processes by which people determine the reasons behind behavior, and gender studies became established and influential areas of research.

6. Despite a rapid expansion, some social psychologists argued that the field was in crisis because it was unable to identify universal, fundamental principles that spanned historical and cultural eras. Ultimately, concerns about the crisis in the field led to a strengthening of the discipline.

7. Over the last decade, the field has focused on the role of cognitive factors in social behavior. Applications of social psychological theory and research have also grown. Although it is difficult to forecast the future, two trends are likely: There will be an increasing emphasis on multiculturalism in social psychology; and the traditional boundaries that have demarcated the field of social psychology from other areas are likely to become increasingly indistinct.

### How do experimental and correlational research differ, and what are the major types of studies carried out by social psychologists?

8. Research, which may be experimental or correlational, begins with a question derived from theories—broad explanations and predictions about phenomena of interest. These questions are put in the form of a hypothesis—a prediction stated in a way that permits it to be tested. Experimental research is designed to discover causal relationships between various factors. In contrast, correlational research seeks to identify whether an association or relationship between two factors exists—regardless of whether one factor produces changes in the other.

9. Experimental research includes at least two conditions: a treatment group and a control group. In an experiment, the independent variable is the variable that is manipulated, while the dependent variable is the variable that is measured and expected to change as a result of the manipulation of the independent variable. Operationalization is the process of translating a hypothesis into specific testable procedures that can be measured and observed.

10. Research takes place either in the laboratory—a controlled setting explicitly designed to hold events constant—or in the field, a naturally occurring setting. Whatever the location of the study, subjects in true experiments must be assigned to a condition by means of random assignment, in which subjects are assigned to particular groups on the basis of chance. Random assignment avoids confounding, in which factors other than the independent variable are allowed to vary.

**11.** Although correlational research cannot determine causality, it includes several significant types of research. Among the most frequently used are naturalistic observation (including participant and nonparticipant observation), archival research, survey research, and evaluation research.

### What are the major threats to the validity of research findings?

**12.** Several situations threaten the validity of research findings. They include demand characteristics, experimenter expectations, and the use of inappropriate subjects.

**13.** Among the strategies for evaluating material relevant to social psychology are identifying and challenging assumptions, considering factual accuracy and logical consistency, considering context, and imagining and exploring alternatives.

# KEY TERMS AND CONCEPTS

*social psychology (p. 6)*

*theoretical research (p. 15)*

*applied research (p. 15)*

*theories (p. 17)*

*hypothesis (p. 18)*

*experimental research (p. 19)*

*correlational research (p. 19)*

*experiment (p. 19)*

*treatment (p. 19)*

*treatment group (p. 19)*

*control group (p. 19)*

*conditions (p. 19)*

*operationalization (p. 20)*

*independent variable (p. 20)*

*dependent variable (p. 20)*

*laboratory study (p. 20)*

*field study (p. 20)*

*generalization (p. 21)*

*subjects (p. 21)*

*random assignment (p. 21)*

*confounding (p. 22)*

*control (p. 22)*

*statistical significance (p. 24)*

*replication (p. 24)*

*naturalistic observation (p. 27)*

*nonparticipant observation (p. 27)*

*participant observation (p. 28)*

*reactivity (p. 28)*

*archival research (p. 28)*

*survey research (p. 28)*

*evaluation research (p. 32)*

*demand characteristics (p. 32)*

*deception (p. 32)*

*confederates (p. 33)*

*informed consent (p. 33)*

*experimenter expectations (p. 34)*

# FOR FURTHER RESEARCH AND STUDY

Lindsey, G., & Aronson, E. (1985). *Handbook of social psychology* (3rd ed.). New York: Random House.

A comprehensive overview of the field of social psychology in two volumes. Although it may be tough going for the novice, it covers the span of the discipline.

Dane, F. C. (1988). *The common and uncommon sense of social behavior.* Belmont, CA: Brooks/Cole.

Hunt, M. (1985). *Profiles of social research: The scientific study of human interactions.* New York: Russell Sage.

Two riveting views of how social psychologists come to ask, and answer, questions regarding social behavior.

Aronson, E., Ellsworth, P. C., Carlsmith, J. M., & Gonzales, M. H. (1990). *Methods of research in social psychology* (2nd ed.). New York: McGraw-Hill.

An easy-to-read, engaging, and comprehensive look at methods for doing research. It covers both experimental and correlational research, with an emphasis on laboratory experiments.

*Journal of Personality and Social Psychology; Personality and Social Psychology Bulletin; European Journal of Social Psychology.*

For up-to-the-minute theory and research in social psychology, these journals are the best. Although the articles are highly technical, they give a sense of what the primary sources in social psychology are like.

# EPILOGUE

As our introduction to the discipline has indicated, the scope of the field of social psychology is broad. We've traced it from its early beginnings to its present status, and discussed the research procedures that social psychologists use to answer the questions they ask.

We're now ready to consider the substance of the discipline in the remainder of the book. We'll trace a route that starts with the individual in a social context and moves on to larger social units in society, including groups, organizations, and ultimately culture. As we continue our exploration of the field and its findings, you'll encounter a discipline that has genuine utility and relevance to your life. The issues that social psychologists investigate, whether in the laboratory or in the field, from a theoretical or an applied perspective, have the potential for improving all of our lives.

# HOW DO PEOPLE MAKE SENSE OF THEIR SOCIAL ENVIRONMENT?

Our journey into the world of social psychology continues as we contemplate the question of how people make sense of their social environment. We consider how people come to understand the causes and meaning of others' behavior, and how such understanding affects their social interactions. We also see the circumstances under which people are most accurate and when they are most prone to error in the conclusions they draw about others' behavior.

In Chapter 2, we consider how people form impressions of other individuals and how they explain the causes of their behavior. In Chapter 3, we discuss how our understanding and treatment of others is colored by their membership in racial, gender, and other types of social groups as we examine stereotyping and prejudice. We end by considering how to reduce the prejudice and discrimination that victimizes us all. ■

# CHAPTER TWO

# SOCIAL COGNITION
## PERCEIVING AND UNDERSTANDING INDIVIDUALS

# PROLOGUE: MESSIAH OR MADMAN?

To law enforcement officials at the FBI, David Koresh was a criminal, having illegally amassed a storehouse of weapons. Leader of the Branch Davidians, a cult on the fringes of organized religion, Koresh was seen as a strange but charismatic eccentric who enticed innocent people to join him in his bizarre view of religion and the world. To the FBI, his illegal

The fire at the Branch Davidian compound in Waco, Texas, resulted in the deaths of dozens of David Koresh's followers.

purchase of so many weapons was proof that he was fraudulent, corrupt, and disturbed—a madman with no regard for others.

David Koresh had a different view. To him, amassing a stockpile of weapons was just a reaction to the situation in which he found himself. In his view of the world, articulated soon before he died, he was an innocent prophet, a messiah who was simply protecting his flock from an increasingly hostile world. His acquisition of weapons was a sensible, prudent response to the actions of others who were evil.

We'll never know which of the two views was more accurate. Indeed, when Koresh and dozens of his followers died in a fiery blaze following an FBI siege, both opinions seemed to hold some validity. Koresh's view that the world was a hostile place, stacked against him, certainly seemed valid. But law enforcement officers, too, had support for their views: Who but a madman would allow men, women, and children to die in such a cataclysmic manner?

## LOOKING AHEAD ▷▷▷▷▷▷▷▷▷▷▷▷▷▷▷▷▷▷▷▷▷▷▷▷▷▷

The difference between these two views of the reasons for Koresh's behavior illustrates a problem that all of us face continually: attributing the causes of behavior. How do we determine what motivates behavior, what a given act represents, what characteristics people have, and how to form an overall impression from individual traits? In short, how do we make the leap from what we see of people's appearance and behavior to what lies beneath the surface?

In this chapter, we begin to investigate how social psychologists have answered these questions by examining social cognition, the processes people employ to understand others and themselves. We start by considering how people perceive others, how they form impressions of others based on the particular combination of traits they encounter. Next, we examine how people draw conclusions regarding the causes of others' behavior. We'll consider how observers try to analyze how much of another's behavior is caused by personality traits and how much is due to characteristics of the situation.

Finally, we examine how people organize and store in memory information about others, and how this process affects their views of others. We'll also consider some biases that cloud our ability to view others accurately and some ways to view others with greater clarity.

In short, after reading this chapter, you'll be able to answer these questions:

- How do we combine people's individual personality traits into an overall impression?
- How do we make judgments about the causes of others' behavior from their actions?
- What kinds of systematic errors are we vulnerable to when we consider others' behavior?
- How do we organize and remember information about social stimuli, and how does this process affect our social judgment?

# SOCIAL COGNITION: AN ORIENTATION

To his friends and neighbors, Ted Bundy seemed personable and humane. Yet there was another side to him: Ted Bundy brutalized and murdered dozens of women. When he was brought to trial, he was suspected of killing more than 100 people. But even after he was convicted and executed, many of his acquaintances still could not believe he was capable of such crimes. How could these people have misjudged Bundy so fundamentally?

Clearly, we are not always accurate in discerning what others are like, in explaining their actions, and in predicting their future behavior. On the other hand, at times we seem to be remarkably talented in understanding others and judging and predicting their behavior. Like a social psychological Sherlock Holmes, we can look at just a small snippet of people's behavior and construct elaborate, and sometimes quite accurate, profiles about their underlying characteristics, and we can often make precise predictions about their future behavior.

**social cognition**
the study of how people understand and make sense of others and of themselves.

**Social cognition** is the study of how people understand and make sense of others and of themselves. Research on social cognition covers a wide territory, encompassing many of the central areas of social psychology. For instance, social cognitive approaches can be found in such diverse topics as the study of attitudes (Chapter 10; Chaiken, 1980; Petty & Cacioppo, 1986; McCann, Higgins, & Fondacaro, 1991), groups (Chapter 14; Stangor, Sullivan, & Ford, 1991; Mackie, Worth, & Allison, 1990), and prejudice and stereotyping (Chapter 3; Fiske, 1992a, 1992b; Devine & Sherman, 1992). The central theme of this research work is the search for an understanding of how people mentally represent and think about others, as well as an exploration of the mental strategies people use to make sense of their social worlds.

In their study of social cognition, social psychologists have followed three major avenues (summarized in Figure 2-1). The first approach, which was the historical forerunner for a good deal of current work in social cognition, focuses on the perception of others, or person perception. **Person perception approaches** consider the way we assess and combine the traits of another to form an overall impression. These approaches are based on the view that we are thoughtful and fairly rational perceivers of others, who notice the traits of others and pull them together in a consistent framework (Heider, 1958; Kelley, 1950).

**person perception approaches**
approaches to social cognition that consider the way an individual's traits are assessed and combined to form an overall impression.

More recent work in social cognition has taken a somewhat different tack, focusing less on how we form impressions of others' personal traits and more on the *causes* of others' behavior. **Attribution approaches** seek to identify how we understand the causes of behavior—our own and others' (Jones & Davis, 1965; Kelley, 1967). According to attribution theorists, we act as "naive scientists," rationally weighing and combining different sources of information. By deliberating about the relative influence of people's actions and the situation in which they are behaving, we make systematic judgments about the reasons behind the behavior (Zelen, 1991).

**attribution approaches**
approaches to social cognition that seek to identify how people understand the causes of others' and their own behavior.

The third and final approach to social cognition focuses on how we interpret the meaning of others' behavior and traits. **Schema approaches** consider how we organize

**schema approaches**
approaches to social cognition that consider how information is organized and stored in memory and how this information is used as a guideline to understand behavior.

Social cognition is the study of how we understand and make sense of others and ourselves. We quickly draw conclusions about people, even on first encounter.

**FIGURE 2-1    Major Approaches to Social Cognition**

| APPROACH | MAJOR QUESTION ADDRESSED BY PERCEIVER | MAJOR GUIDING PRINCIPLE USED BY PERCEIVER |
|---|---|---|
| Person perception approaches | How are traits combined to form an overall impression? | Rational combining of trait information |
| Attribution approaches | What are the causes of behavior? | Naive scientist model |
| Schema approaches | How is the meaning of behavior and traits interpreted? | Cognitive miser model |

information and store it in memory, and how we use this information to understand behavior.

Schema approaches hold a view of information processing different from that of attribution approaches. Instead of seeing us as the "naive scientists" of the attribution approach, schema approaches view us as Scrooge-like cognitive misers. This **cognitive miser model** suggests that because of limited information-processing capabilities, we expend no more than the minimum effort necessary to solve a social problem or answer a social question. In order to save ourselves from the task of constantly gauging our impressions of others, then, we do what we can to minimize the expenditure of cognitive effort. In sum, rather than acting as diligent and industrious naive scientists, cognitive misers seek efficiency in the way they make judgments of others (Fiske & Taylor, 1991; Taylor, 1981).

As we'll see throughout this chapter, each of the three approaches to social cognition—the person perception, attribution, and schema approaches—has yielded significant information about the way we come to understand others, as well as ourselves. It is important to keep in mind that these approaches, which we'll discuss in turn, supplement one another and are not necessarily contradictory. Focusing on different kinds of information and different questions that we ask about the nature of human behavior,

**cognitive miser model**
model associated with the schema approaches to social cognition that suggests that because of people's limited information-processing capabilities, they expend no more than the minimum effort necessary to solve a social problem or answer a social question.

these approaches provide us with a palette we can use to paint a full portrait of the people we encounter in our social world.

# PERSON PERCEPTION: FORMING IMPRESSIONS OF OTHERS

Warm. Industrious. Critical. Practical. Determined.

If you were told that someone embodied this list of traits, you probably would quickly form an impression that was fairly positive. However, suppose the list contained these traits:

Cold. Industrious. Critical. Practical. Determined.

Although only one trait is different (the substitution of "cold" for "warm"), the assessment you would make would probably be quite different and would likely be considerably more negative. The reasons for this difference in overall impression are reflected in work on person perception, which considers the way people assess and integrate others' traits and characteristics to form an overall impression.

*First Impressions: Using People's Outward Appearance to Draw Inferences*

Do blondes have more fun? Are fat people jolly? Do people who wear glasses study more? Most people seem to think so.

Although we're taught that appearances can be deceiving, we often act as if we've never heard such warnings. Study after study has shown that people use clues such as clothing, eyeglasses, and jewelry to form judgments about what others are like (Alley, 1988; Bull & Rumsey, 1988; Berry, 1990; Workman & Johnson, 1991; Marino et al., 1991). Although such judgments are made every day, there is often no evidence to support them.

Physical attractiveness also represents a powerful contributor to people's judgments of others. As we'll discuss more in Chapter 6, physical attractiveness plays a significant

Because physical attractiveness plays an important role in determining how others are perceived, many people invest considerable energy in keeping themselves in good shape.

role in determining how much people are liked (see, for example, Hatfield & Sprecher, 1986; Feingold, 1992). Even the configuration of a person's face affects the judgments that others make. For example, facial characteristics typical of baby-faced individuals—relatively large eyes and small noses—are viewed as signs of powerlessness, submissiveness, and social incompetence (Zebrowitz, 1990; Zebrowitz, Olson, & Hoffman, 1993).

Clearly, however, we do not base our judgments of others solely on physical appearance. We also use people's nonverbal behavior as an indication of their inner feelings. A large body of research suggests people can accurately identify at least the basic emotions of happiness, surprise, sadness, anger, disgust, and fear from facial expressions (Feldman & Rimé, 1991). Furthermore, these emotions are displayed universally across cultures, and they are identified with high degrees of accuracy by observers who live in very different cultures (Ekman & O'Sullivan, 1991) (see Figure 2-2).

We use other kinds of nonverbal behavior as an additional source of information about an individual. For example, body language, and in particular the gestures that accompany speech, provide data used in the development of inferences about others (Rimé & Shiaratura, 1991; Ricci Bitti & Poggi, 1991).

Unlike the basic facial expressions, which are interpreted by observers in fairly similar ways across cultures, gestures have quite different meanings from one culture to another. For example, in North America people interpret the "A-OK" gesture (see Figure 2-3) as very positive, meaning "everything's great." On the other hand, in many other cultures, the gesture represents the female sexual anatomy. In Greece, for instance, if a male uses the sign when interacting with a female, it is viewed as a sexual proposition. If a male gestures in the same way during a conversation with another male, it is considered an insult to the recipient's masculinity. Clearly, the meaning of gestures differs significantly across cultures (Morris et al., 1979; Ricci Bitti & Poggi, 1991).

*Cognitive Math: 1 + 1 Doesn't Always Equal 2*

Although such features as appearance and nonverbal behavior provide clues regarding the personality and character of others, the bits of information are like pieces of an incomplete puzzle, randomly strewn about on a table top. How do people take these individual pieces and combine them into a full, complete picture? How, in other words, do we form an overall impression of others based on the bits and pieces of cognitive data that we are able to collect?

This question has been asked throughout the history of social psychology, and it has received many different answers. One of the first responses came almost 50 years ago, when social psychologist Solomon Asch argued that certain personal attributes, which he termed central traits, played an unusually influential role in determining a general impression (Asch, 1946; Watkins & Peynircioglu, 1984; Asch & Zukier, 1984). **Central traits** are characteristics that serve to organize an impression of another person and provide a framework for interpreting information that is subsequently received.

**central traits**
characteristics that serve to organize an impression of another person and provide a framework for interpreting information that is subsequently received.

Asch's proposition received support in a classic study by social psychologist Harold Kelley (1950) that examined students' impressions of a professor. In the experiment, students were given one of two descriptions of a lecturer whom they had never met. Then they took part in a discussion led by the lecturer. One group of students was told that the lecturer had the five traits listed earlier—that he was "a rather warm person, industrious, critical, practical, and determined." In contrast, the second group of students was told that the same lecturer was "a rather cold person, industrious, critical, practical, and determined."

As you might guess, the replacement of the word "cold" for "warm" in the second description made a dramatic change in the way the lecturer was perceived in the two conditions. Although the lecturer's behavior did not vary between the two groups, students who were told that the lecturer was cold rated him far less positively after the discussion than those who were told he was warm.

Asch's interpretation of these findings, which were replicated in a more recent experiment (Widmeyer & Loy, 1988), was that the presence of a central trait altered the

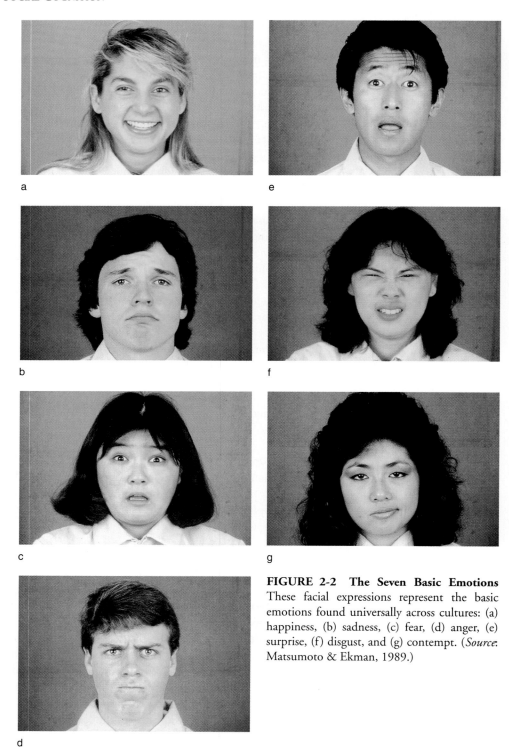

**FIGURE 2-2  The Seven Basic Emotions** These facial expressions represent the basic emotions found universally across cultures: (a) happiness, (b) sadness, (c) fear, (d) anger, (e) surprise, (f) disgust, and (g) contempt. (*Source:* Matsumoto & Ekman, 1989.)

**cognitive algebra approach** an explanation for impression formation that suggests that perceivers consider each individual trait, evaluate each trait individually in isolation from the others, and then combine the evaluations into an overall judgment.

meaning of additional descriptive traits. For instance, in the context of the description of an individual, the word "determined" takes on a very different meaning depending on whether it is preceded by the central trait of "warm" or "cold."

The notion of central traits was not to go unchallenged as the field of social psychology developed. The most immediate disagreement resulted from what has been called the cognitive algebra approach. According to the **cognitive algebra approach,** perceivers consider each individual trait; evaluate each trait individually, in isolation

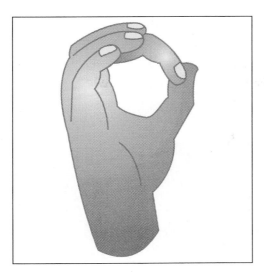

**FIGURE 2-3  What Does This Mean?** Your understanding of the meaning of this gesture depends on your cultural origin. In North America, people interpret it as meaning "everything's great." In contrast, in Greece, the gesture represents the female sexual anatomy.

from the others; and then combine the evaluations into an overall judgment (Anderson, 1965, 1981). In this procedure, the meaning of the individual traits is relatively fixed and does not change according to what other traits are present.

For instance, suppose we encounter a person who appears adventurous and bold, but unintelligent. If we assign values to each trait, we simply combine those values to form an overall judgment. The positive traits of "adventurous" and "bold" add to the final impression; the negative trait of "unintelligent" subtracts from it. However, the value of each trait doesn't change as a result of the presence (or absence) of others.

The relative merits of the cognitive algebra and central trait views were hotly debated by social psychologists, and the two approaches became increasingly refined. For instance, cognitive algebra theorists found that our impressions of others are more accurate when we consider the importance of each piece of information (Kaplan, 1975). Furthermore, negative information is usually weighted more heavily than positive information. Consequently, a supposedly "balanced" letter of recommendation that contains equal amounts of positive and negative information about a graduate school applicant is likely to result in an overall negative interpretation of the applicant (Skowronski & Carlston, 1989; Klein, 1991; Taylor, 1991; Vonk, 1993).

However, neither the cognitive algebra nor the central trait view emerged as predominant, as it became increasingly clear that neither approach provided a complete account of impression formation (Ostrom, 1977). Still, the approaches led to a considerable amount of research. For instance, as we see next, they helped explain the puzzling phenomenon that the order in which we receive information about a person influences the nature of our ultimate overall impression.

*Order Effects in Person Perception: The First Shall Be Last?*

Does it matter whether we initially learn that another person is "intelligent, industrious, impulsive, critical, stubborn, and envious," or learn the same information but in the reverse order?

Although logically it shouldn't matter, the reality is different. According to an early study by Asch, people who hear the list with the more positive attributes first form a more positive impression than those who hear it in the reverse order (Asch, 1946). This finding is consistent with subsequent research, which has shown that there is a strong and pervasive primacy effect in the influence of information (Titus, 1991; McKelvie, 1990). A **primacy effect** occurs when early information has a stronger impact than later information.

**primacy effect**
the effect on perception when information received early has a stronger impact than information received later.

First impressions do matter, according to research on order effects in person perception.

Primacy effects are found not only in the realm of traits, but even when a single dimension of behavior varies over time. For instance, consider school performance. Which ultimately leaves a better impression: doing better initially in class and then declining, or starting off poorly and improving?

Experimental results are clear in illustrating a primacy effect, in which the earliest information plays the dominant role in determining the ultimate evaluation. For example, in one study, early performance on a 30-item test was considered by subjects to be more indicative of a person's true ability than performance later on the same test—even if the person showed substantial improvement or declines in performance (Jones & Goethals, 1972).

**recency effect**
the effect on perception when information received later has a stronger impact than information received earlier.

On the other hand, **recency effects**, in which later information is given more weight than earlier information, occasionally occur. For example, people who are strongly motivated to pay attention to incoming information are likely to weight later information more heavily. Similarly, if the time span between the receipt of initial and later information is great enough, primacy effects are reduced and recency effects occur (Stewart, 1965; Kruglanski & Freund, 1983).

Why are we susceptible to primacy and recency effects? One answer is that we often pay less attention to information as time goes on. Consequently, as the amount of information we have available increases, we focus on the new information less closely, even if it contradicts earlier information (Belmore, 1987). In addition, primacy effects are congruent with Asch's speculation that information received earlier influences our perception of the meaning of additional information. For example, when we first learn that a person is envious, hearing later that she is intelligent takes on a less positive meaning than if we had initially learned that bit of information (Asch & Zukier, 1984).

The existence of both primacy and recency effects suggests that the cognitive algebra approach does not provide a full account of social cognition. Furthermore, neither the central trait nor the cognitive algebra approach fully considers how people uncover the causes of others' behavior, nor how they categorize and organize traits in their own minds. These shortcomings led to the development of two additional approaches to social cognition: the attributional approach (which we discuss next) and the schema approach.

► REVIEW & RETHINK

*Review*

- Social cognition is the study of how people understand and make sense of others and themselves.
- The three major approaches to social cognition are the person perception, attribution, and schema approaches.
- Person perception approaches consider the way an individual's traits are assessed and combined to form an overall impression. Both central trait and cognitive algebra approaches have been employed to understand how information is integrated when people form impressions of others.
- Primacy and recency effects influence person perception.

*Rethink*

- What are the broad similarities and differences between the three major approaches to social cognition? Could they all, in part, be accurate?
- What are the two major explanations for the primacy effect phenomenon? Can the logic of these explanations be reconciled with the existence of recency effects?
- What are central traits, and how do they differ from "primacy effects"?
- What basic difference separates cognitive algebra theorists from central trait theorists? What would each have to say about the importance of first impressions and the potential for changing them?

# ATTRIBUTION: EXPLAINING THE CAUSES OF BEHAVIOR

*Over the course of the semester, Kate has come to have great respect for her history professor, Professor Kirk. Even though she isn't doing all that well in class, she likes his effusive, outgoing lecture style and the way he keeps ancient history entertaining and provocative. Near the end of the term, she sees Professor Kirk in the campus center coffee bar, and she decides to tell him how much she likes the class. Expecting a cordial response, she is startled by his cool and indifferent reaction. She leaves feeling confused and a little foolish, and wondering why he reacted in the manner he did.*

Kate's attempt to understand the professor's reaction illustrates several central issues in attribution, the process in which people attempt to identify the causes of others' (as well as their own) behavior. In this case, Professor Kirk's behavior can be explained by considering the central attributional dilemma he faces: whether to attribute Kate's compliment to situational or dispositional causes.

*Situation or Disposition? A Central Attributional Dilemma*

**situational causes**
reasons for behavior that rest on the demands or constraints of a given social setting.

In seeking to explain another person's behavior, people have two general categories of causes: situation and disposition. **Situational causes** are reasons for behavior that rest on the demands or constraints of a given social setting. Most situations call for certain kinds of behavior. For instance, people in a lecture class basically sit, take notes, and ask or answer questions. They don't stand up in the middle of the class and practice yodeling. Likewise, if the setting is a baseball game, it's a miserably hot day, and the home team is behind by six runs, the manager's temper tantrum when a runner is called out is proba-

Every situation calls for certain types of expected behavior. For instance, boisterous and frenzied behavior may be the norm at a rock concert; quiet, sedate behavior would be the exception.

bly due to the situation and not to the manager's bad temper. Certain circumstances, then, produce particular kinds of behavior.

In contrast, behavior may also be caused by dispositional causes. **Dispositional causes** are reasons for behavior that rest on the personality traits and characteristics of the individual carrying out the behavior. Some people are habitually friendly, or hostile, or energetic, regardless of the particular situation in which they find themselves. Consequently, when they act friendly, hostile, or energetic, respectively, the cause of their behavior is most likely their disposition.

In the case of Professor Kirk, for instance, Kate's compliment placed him in a quandary in terms of interpreting her behavior. Is Kate's compliment due to her disposition ("She really seems nice and friendly and sincere, and she must really like the course")? Or is her compliment due to situational constraints ("She must be saying that in order to raise her grade; students always tell me they like my class—just before the end of the term")?

In this case, two things argue against a dispositional attribution. First, Professor Kirk doesn't know Kate, and therefore he has no information about how friendly she is. Second, and even more important, situational constraints against saying anything except what Kate did say are extremely strong (would you go up to a professor and tell him how much you hated his class?). Consequently, given that he doesn't know Kate and can't easily attribute her behavior to dispositional causes, Professor Kirk is most likely to attribute her remarks to situational (and less flattering) motives.

But what of Kate? Like Professor Kirk, she is faced with the attributional puzzle of determining the causes of another's behavior—in this case, the behavior of Professor Kirk. If she looks to dispositional causes, she's faced with an inconsistency, because Kirk seems warm and outgoing in class but cold in person. A more likely conclusion, then, is that his cool behavior toward Kate is due not to dispositional factors but to situational causes. Kate sadly concludes that Professor Kirk is reacting to her specifically (a situational stimulus) and that he really doesn't like her very much.

Such reasoning illustrates a general principle about attributions: Behavior will be attributed to a situational cause when external reasons are more likely or plausible. Con-

**dispositional causes**
reasons for behavior that rest on the personality traits and characteristics of the individual.

The same behavior can have very different meanings, depending on the situation. For instance, the tears of a beauty contest winner indicate an emotional response that is quite different from those of the man whose farm was destroyed by a tornado.

versely, behavior will be attributed to dispositional factors when external causes are unlikely (Hilton et al., 1990). This point was demonstrated in an experiment in which participants were asked to rate the personality of a job applicant. To some subjects the applicant presented himself as having the characteristics that were a prerequisite for the job; to other subjects he presented himself as not having those characteristics (Jones, Gergen, & Davis, 1961).

When the applicant indicated that he had traits that were necessary for the job, subjects were not terribly confident about their ratings of the candidate—they thought he might be trying to make a certain impression in order to get the job. But when the candidate indicated that he had traits that were contrary to ones related to the job requirements, subjects were considerably more confident about their ratings.

We can see the operation of this principle in politics. When a Democratic senator follows a Democratic president's wishes and votes in favor of a bill, the most likely attribution is a situational one: the senator is voting because of pressures to remain loyal to the president. But if the senator votes against the president's position, we are much more likely to make a dispositional attribution, because the senator is acting contrary to the external pressures of the situation.

Attribution approaches assume that people make their attributions on the basis of mini-experiments that they carry out in their minds. Implicitly using the principles behind experimentation that we discussed in Chapter 1, people seek to identify the "why?" behind the behavior of others. However, because the process is not immune to biases and error, social psychologists speak of "naive scientists" going about the task of forming attributions (Harvey, 1989; White, 1992). Like scientists, people attempt to make systematic use of the social data at hand; like naive scientists, though, they are not always exact in the way they interpret information (Trope & Higgins, 1993).

As we discuss next, two major theories of attribution seek to explain the systematic processes people use in forming attributions: Jones and Davis's theory of correspondent inferences, which considers how we infer intentions, traits, and dispositions; and Kelley's model of causal attribution, which focuses on how we consolidate different sorts of information to make attributions.

### JONES AND DAVIS'S CORRESPONDENT INFERENCE THEORY: FROM ACTS TO DISPOSITIONS.
Consider the following situation:

> *Dan is alone in his dorm room, working on a term paper. There is a knock at the door, but Dan ignores it. The knock becomes louder and a voice outside the door says, "C'mon, Dan. I know you're in there. I just want to talk to you for a minute about catching a quick movie." Dan answers the door, talks to the visitor for half an hour, and finally decides to go to the movie.*

As an observer of this scene, what kind of judgment would you make about the motives behind Dan's behavior? Social psychologists Edward Jones and Keith Davis (1965; Jones, 1979, 1990) developed a theory of attribution that helps us understand how an observer would answer this question. Further, the theory covers the more general case of how we use a person's behavior to make inferences about that individual's enduring personality traits and motivations.

The Jones and Davis theory examines **correspondent inferences**—observers' notions of how closely an overt behavior or action represents a specific underlying intention, trait, or disposition. The more a behavior appears to reflect the underlying disposition, the greater is the correspondence between these two factors (Jones, 1990).

According to Jones and Davis, we learn most from behaviors of others that lead to unique or *noncommon effects*. The theory assumes that any behavior leads to a particular set of consequences. However, the behaviors that are most helpful in forming correspondent inferences are those that result in consequences that other, alternative behaviors would not have produced.

For example, if we knew that Dan could work on his term paper equally well whether he was alone or chatting with a visitor, we would know little about his motivation for completing the paper because there are no noncommon effects. However, one fact is clear: if he chats with the visitor, he is unable to continue writing; but if he does not answer the door, he can continue to write. We can say, then, that the two alternative behaviors (chatting versus not answering the door) have noncommon effects. The choice of behavior to talk to the visitor, then, is informative, suggesting that Dan's motivation to write his term paper is not particularly high.

One additional factor that colors our attributions is the *social desirability* of a behavior—the degree to which society encourages and values a behavior. The greater the social desirability of a behavior, the more difficult it is to draw a correspondent inference between the act and disposition. For example, because the visitor knew that Dan was in his room, it would have been an outright insult for Dan to refuse to open the door. Because Dan's behavior—answering a knock at his door—has an element of social desirability, it is relatively uninformative about what it represents. On the other hand, if Dan had refused to answer the door, even in the face of repeated requests, his behavior would clearly be low in social desirability. As a result, it would tell more about Dan's motivations and disposition, suggesting that Dan was strongly committed to completing his term paper.

Another basis for making attributions relates to the degree of *choice* an individual is seen to have in carrying out a behavior. For instance, if you are assigned by a teacher to argue in favor of capital punishment in a debate, it is unlikely that your classmates would assume that you necessarily believed in what you were saying. On the other hand, had you chosen, on your own, to argue that side of the issue, then it is a fair assumption that you believed what you were arguing. Similarly, if Dan chooses to invite a visitor into his room, his behavior is more informative than if the visitor barges in without an invitation to come in.

Jones and Davis's theory of correspondent inferences considers how observers take a small part of a person's behavior and use it to determine how representative that sample is of the person's underlying traits and other characteristics. But that is only one aspect of

**correspondent inferences**
observers' notions of how closely an overt behavior or action represents a specific underlying intention, trait, or disposition.

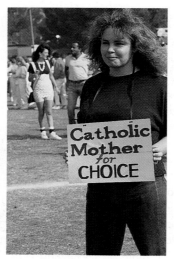

For a Catholic mother, taking a pro-choice position on abortion may well be lower in social desirability than taking an anti-abortion stance. Because it is low in social desirability, though, her behavior allows observers to be more confident in drawing correspondent inferences between the behavior and the underlying disposition.

the attribution process. Another approach to attribution, which we discuss next, considers whether a behavior is primarily caused by situational forces or personal factors.

**KELLEY'S MODEL OF CAUSAL ATTRIBUTION: SEARCHING FOR CONSENSUS, CONSISTENCY, AND DISTINCTIVENESS.**    Consider the following situation: You're at a party. You suddenly see your classmate Jenna get angry with another classmate, Josh, and begin to yell at him. What psychological processes operate as you figure out why Jenna yelled at Josh?

Several possibilities come to mind. For instance, Jenna's behavior might be caused by something abut Jenna herself (whom social psychologists would refer to as the "actor" in this context). Perhaps she has a bad temper and is easily angered. That's one possibility: Jenna is yelling at Josh because she has a quick temper. On the other hand, the fight might be caused by something about Josh (the target of the behavior), who may be the kind of person who often angers others by his blunt remarks. That's another possibility: Jenna is yelling at Josh because he said something inflammatory. Still another possibility is that the fight might be caused by the specific situation—something that happened at the party. Perhaps Jenna had consumed a great deal of alcohol and therefore was particularly volatile as a result of being drunk. Consequently, Jenna is yelling because she both drank too much and lost control during a minor disagreement.

In attempting to choose among these potential causes, social psychologist Harold Kelley suggests that people consider three different kinds of information (Kelley, 1972; Kelley & Michela, 1980). First, people use consensus information. **Consensus information** is data regarding the degree to which other people react similarly in the same situation. For example, if others frequently get angry with Josh at parties, there would be high consensus; if it was rare that others got angry with him at parties, there would be low consensus. If there was high consensus regarding Josh's display of anger at parties, an observer would be inclined to attribute the cause of the fight to Josh.

In addition to consensus information, observers use a second category of data, called consistency information. **Consistency information** is knowledge regarding the degree to which people react in the same way in different situations. If Jenna's behavior is highly consistent (she often gets angry at Josh and frequently fights with him) there is high consistency. If she occasionally gets angry with Josh at parties, but not always, her behavior is of low consistency. Information that is low in consistency is not very informative.

Finally, the third category of data available to an observer is distinctiveness information. **Distinctiveness information** refers to the extent to which the same behavior occurs in relation to other people or stimuli. For example, if Jenna gets angry only with Josh, and doesn't get angry with anyone else, getting angry is high in distinctiveness. But if she frequently gets angry at her dates and reacts by fighting with them, the behavior of getting angry is low in distinctiveness.

Taking into account information about consensus, consistency, and distinctiveness allows people to attribute a certain behavior either to dispositional factors (something about the person) or to situational factors (something about the target person or the particular circumstances). More precisely, when consensus and distinctiveness are low and consistency is high, people tend to make dispositional attributions (see Figure 2-4). On the other hand, when consensus, consistency, and distinctiveness are all high, people tend to make attributions to external, situational factors (Reynolds & West, 1989; Iacobucci & McGill, 1990).

More concretely, if others don't get angry with Josh (low consensus); Jenna often gets angry with Josh (high consistency); and Jenna gets angry with most of her dates (low distinctiveness), an observer would be most likely to conclude that it is something about Jenna that led to her anger. On the other hand, if people in general and specifically Jenna frequently get angry with Josh (high consensus and high consistency), and Jenna gets angry only with Josh but not other dates (high distinctiveness), then the source of Jenna's anger will be most likely attributed to Josh.

---

**consensus information**
data regarding the degree to which other people react similarly in the same situation.

**consistency information**
knowledge regarding the degree to which people react in the same way in different situations.

**distinctiveness information**
knowledge regarding the extent to which the same behavior occurs in relation to other people or stimuli.

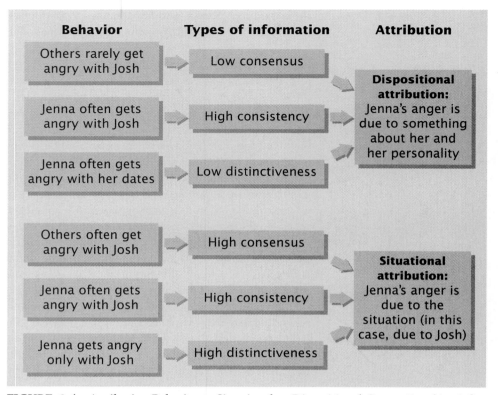

**FIGURE 2-4    Attributing Behavior to Situational or Dispositional Causes** By taking information about consensus, consistency, and distinctiveness into account, people attribute behavior either to dispositional factors (something about the person) or to situational factors (something about the target person or the particular circumstances). Specifically, when consensus and distinctiveness are low and consistency is high, people make dispositional attributions. In contrast, when consensus, consistency, and distinctiveness are all high, people make attributions to external, situational factors.

Kelley's attribution model has been well supported by subsequent research. In the typical study, subjects are provided with differing kinds of information, and the kinds of attributions that they make are traced (McArthur, 1972; Harvey & Weary, 1984; Forsterling, 1989; Cheng & Novick, 1990). Furthermore, even when some of the three sources of information are absent, people still make causal inferences similar to the ones predicted by the model. For instance, simply knowing that a behavior is of low distinctiveness can lead observers to attribute its cause to internal (dispositional) factors. Furthermore, learning that there is high consensus associated with a particular behavior is sufficient to lead an observer to attribute the cause to external (situational) factors, even without any other information (Orvis, Cunningham, & Kelley, 1975).

However, Kelley's model is not infallible (Cheng & Novick, 1990). Although the theory works well when people have concrete, explicit information regarding consensus, distinctiveness, and consistency, it does not work quite so well when people must seek, find, or recognize the information on their own. For example, reading about the high reliability of Toyota automobiles in a consumer testing magazine theoretically should provide a powerful, objective source of consensus information. However, such information may have less impact on a person's attributions than the complaints of a next-door neighbor about the unreliability of her particular Toyota (Nisbett & Ross, 1980; Davidson & Hirtle, 1990; Heller, Saltzstein, & Caspe, 1992).

In sum, although the general principles of Kelley's theory appear to be valid, it provides the most accurate description of how people make attributions when they have clear and unambiguous information on which to base the attributions. It also is most accurate when people encounter unexpected events, which they are unable to explain in terms of what they already know about the person or situation (Nisbett & Ross, 1980; Bohner et al., 1988).

*Biases in Attribution: The Fallibility of the Naive Scientist*

Let's face it: We don't always have the ability, motivation, or simply the time to sort through behavior and come up with an accurate accounting of the motives behind behavior. Consequently, people are not always as rational in making attributions as the various attributional theories might suggest. The naive scientist within us sometimes falls prey to a variety of biases and errors. We turn now to some of the most frequent pitfalls.

THE FUNDAMENTAL ATTRIBUTION ERROR: WHAT YOU SEE IS NOT (NECESSARILY) WHAT YOU GET.   As we discussed at the beginning of the chapter, at the same time that law enforcement officers concluded that David Koresh's behavior was produced by psychological delusions and character flaws, Koresh claimed that he was simply reacting to the circumstances in which he found himself.

Although the particulars of Koresh's situation were more extreme than most everyday occurrences, they are typical of social psychological processes that are hardly unique. In fact, the assumption that other people's behavior represents some inner trait underlies one of the most common and powerful attributional biases: the fundamental attribution error. The **fundamental attribution error** is the tendency to overattribute others' behavior to dispositional causes, and the corresponding failure to recognize the importance of situational causes (Ross, 1977; Ross & Nisbett, 1991).

**fundamental attribution error**
the tendency to overattribute others' behavior to dispositional causes, and the failure to recognize the importance of situational causes.

The fundamental attribution error is pervasive. For instance, letters to advice columns such as "Ann Landers" or "Dear Abby" provide a good illustration of the phenomenon. When social psychologists Thomas Schoeneman and Daniel Rubanowitz analyzed the letters (1985; Fischer, Schoeneman, & Rubanowitz, 1987), they found that writers tended to attribute the cause of their circumstances to the situation when describing their problems ("I'm always late to work because the bus doesn't run on time," or "We're having marital problems because my wife won't sleep with me any more"). On the other hand, observers reading the letters were more apt to see the problem in terms of the characteristics of the person writing the letter ("She's too lazy to take an earlier bus" or "He should take a bath more often").

Why should the tendency to view others' personality characteristics as the cause of their behavior be so strong? One reason is merely perceptual. When we view the behavior of other people, the information that is most conspicuous is that which comes from the individual. Typically, the environment is static and unchanging, while the person moves about and reacts—making the person the focus of attention. Because to an observer the environment appears less obvious, observers are more likely to use a dispositional explanation (McArthur, 1981).

Another reason for the fundamental attribution error rests on the presumed basic process observers follow when they make an attribution. Specifically, social psychologist Daniel Gilbert has speculated that the attribution process actually consists of two sequential stages (Gilbert, 1989; Gilbert, Krull, & Pelham, 1988; Gilbert et al., 1992). Gilbert argues that the first step people take is to make a fast, automatic dispositional attribution, inferring that personal characteristics explain the behavior. However, once they make this quick initial determination, people then correct or adjust it by taking into account situational constraints that may have produced the behavior. This followup correction is more thoughtful and occurs at a relatively slower, more leisurely pace.

Because the situational correction is sluggish, the process is relatively easy to disrupt. For example, if people are distracted by some outside diversion or do not pay close attention, they are apt to make do with their initial—dispositional—judgment. Hence, people are likely to overemphasize dispositional judgments not because they carefully weigh the possible situational or dispositional causes of a person's behavior and then attribute the behavior to dispositional factors. Instead, they often stop at the first stage of

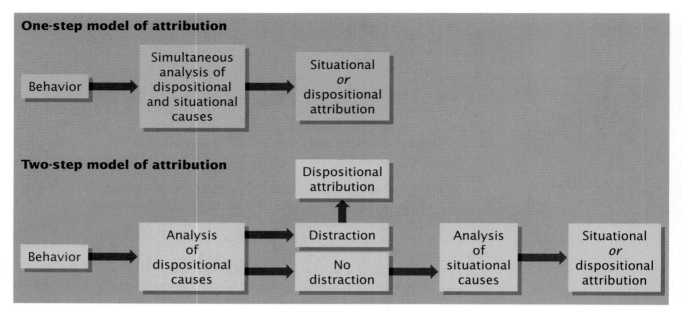

**FIGURE 2-5   Two Attributional Models** According to the one-step model of attribution, people simultaneously analyze whether a behavior is due to dispositional or situational causes. In contrast, the two-step model suggests they first analyze dispositional causes, and then consider situational possibilities.

the attributional process, considering only their initial dispositional judgment and not sufficiently correcting it with additional data that may be available (Gilbert & Osborn, 1989). (See Figure 2-5.)

To test this reasoning, Gilbert devised an experiment in which subjects were led to be "cognitively busy" in some conditions (Gilbert, Pelham, & Krull, 1988). In the study, all subjects watched a silent videotape of a woman who appeared to be extremely anxious, biting her nails, twirling her hair, tapping her fingers, and shifting in her chair. However, some subjects were told that the woman was discussing such anxiety-provoking subjects as her sexual fantasies, while other subjects were told that she had been taped while discussing bland topics, such as world travel. Subjects were then asked to characterize how anxious the woman typically was. In other words, they had to indicate how dispositionally anxious she was.

Clearly, a typical person might reasonably appear nervous while discussing topics designed to be anxiety producing. Hence, although observers might first make a dispositional attribution (she is a nervous person), they should subsequently correct it with a situational attribution (she acts nervous because of the anxiety-producing topics she is discussing). On the other hand, observers who are distracted might never get to the second stage, and they would likely stick with their uncorrected dispositional attribution.

In the experiment, half of the subjects were distracted as they watched the woman on the tape by being asked to memorize the list of topics the woman was supposedly discussing. The remaining subjects watched the tape without such distraction. The prediction, then, was that those who were cognitively busy would be prone to make dispositional attributions, regardless of topic, while those who were undistracted would make attributions that were less dispositional when supposedly anxiety-producing topics were discussed.

As you can see in Figure 2-6, the predictions received clear support. Cognitively busy subjects were unaffected by the nature of the topics. In contrast, those subjects who were not distracted took the topic into account, making attributions that were more dispositional when the woman acted nervous while discussing the bland topics.

In sum, the two-stage account of attribution seems accurate: we first make dispositional characterizations, and then, if we're not otherwise cognitively busy, we take situa-

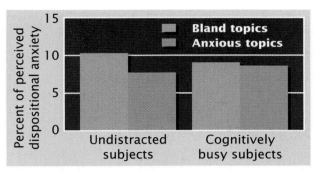

**FIGURE 2-6   Cognitively Busy and Undistracted Subjects' Attributions** Undistracted subjects made stronger dispositional attributions when the woman on the tape was thought to be discussing bland topics than when she was supposedly discussing "anxious" topics. In contrast, subjects who were cognitively busy never corrected their initial dispositional attribution, regardless of the nature of the topic. *(Source:* Adapted from Gilbert, Pelham, & Krull, 1988, p. 735.*)*

tional information into account. As Gilbert has observed, "Perceivers do not ponder, 'Did Arthur take the money because he is dishonest [dispositional causation], or because his friends pressured him to do so [situational causation]?' Rather, perceivers of such behavior first draw a dispositional inference ('Arthur is dishonest') and then correct this inference with information about the situational constraints on the actor ('But given that his friends pressured him to take the money, I guess he isn't *really* dishonest')" (Gilbert, 1989, p. 193).

**CULTURAL INFLUENCES ON ATTRIBUTION.**    Despite its pervasiveness, the fundamental attribution error does not always operate. In fact, in some cases, people overestimate the role of situational causes. For example, when people are made aware of situational constraints operating in a setting, they are more likely to attribute the cause to situational factors (Quattrone, 1982).

Furthermore, research conducted in non-Western cultures calls into question just how fundamental to the human species is the fundamental attribution bias. For example, social psychologist Joan Miller (1984) asked subjects of different ages in the United States and India to make attributions regarding a series of positive and negative events.

When school-age children made attributions, there was little difference between the members of the two cultures, and neither culture was more apt to choose dispositional over situational attributions. However, as the subjects aged, the differences between members of the two cultures became more pronounced. In fact, when adult subjects were examined, only subjects from the United States showed the fundamental attribution bias; they were much more likely to make dispositional attributions than Hindu Indian subjects. In sharp contrast, with increasing age, the Hindu Indians showed more reliance on situational explanations than the American subjects (see Figure 2-7).

These results, and subsequent research, suggest that Hindu Indians emphasize social responsibility and societal obligations in a fundamentally different manner from people in Western cultures. Similarly, other facets of culture, such as language, may promote the use of situational, over dispositional, attributions. For instance, people who use English might say, "I am late," suggesting a dispositional cause ("I tend to be a tardy person"); in contrast, when users of the Spanish language report the same occurrence, their language expresses it as follows: "The clock caused me to be late," suggesting a situational cause for their tardiness (Zebrowitz-McArthur, 1988). Finally, attributional differences in cultures may help account for differences in academic achievement, as we discuss in the following Social Psychology at Work feature.

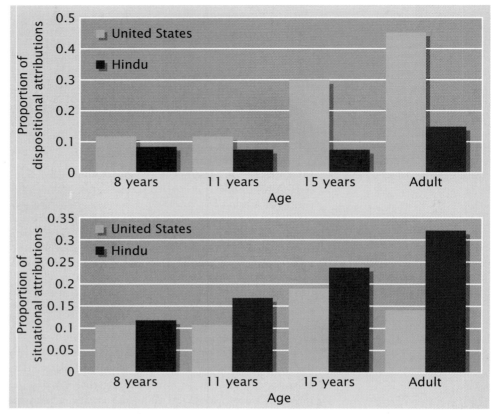

**Figure 2-7  Is the Fundamental Attribution Bias Universal?** As United States subjects grew older, they were much more likely to attribute the causes of behavior to dispositional causes (illustrating the fundamental attribution bias), whereas Hindus' attributions to dispositional causes remained fairly stable (top). In contrast, with increasing age, the Hindu Indians showed more reliance on situational explanations than the American subjects (bottom). Such results call into question the universality of the fundamental attribution bias.    *(Source:* Based on Miller, 1984.*)*

## SOCIAL PSYCHOLOGY AT WORK

## ATTRIBUTIONS AND ASIAN ACADEMIC EXCELLENCE

The evidence could not be more compelling: By the time they have reached the upper grades of public school, the average student in Japan is doing better in school than the average U.S. student. The situation doesn't start this way: In first grade there is relatively little difference in mathematics performance between Japanese and American students. By fifth grade, however, Asian students consistently outperform American students on standardized tests of math achievement. Results on reading tests are similar: While Americans actually outperform Japanese in reading scores in the first grade, by fifth grade the Japanese children have caught up with the Americans (Stevenson & Lee, 1990). Why do Japanese students end up outperforming those in the United States?

While several reasons for the difference have been suggested—ranging from the Japanese students' spending many more days in school to greater cultural pressure to excel scholastically—one of the most compelling explanations rests on differences in the kind of attributions made about the causes of academic performance. According to work by educational psychologist Harold Stevenson and colleagues, people in Western and Asian societies hold very different attributions about the underlying causes of academic performance. Specifically, Westerners are more likely to point to stable, internal causes for a student's performance (such as a student's native level of intelligence), while Asians are more apt to see temporary, situational factors (such as a lack of effort) as responsible for the performance.

The Asian view is derived in part from Confucian writings about the importance of effort in achievement. Furthermore, as we will discuss in Chapter 15, Asian society

**Figure 2-8 Mothers' Beliefs in Equal Ability** Compared with mothers in the United States, mothers in Taiwan and Japan were more likely to feel that all children have the same degree of underlying, innate ability. Subjects responded using a 7-point scale, where 1 = strongly disagree and 7 = strongly agree.
*(Source:* Stevenson & Lee, 1990.*)*

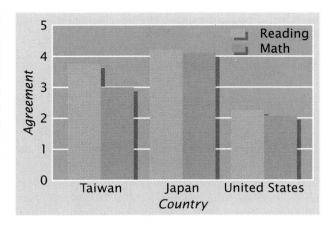

minimizes individual differences in achievement across all domains and accentuates the role of hard work and perseverance. In contrast, Americans are more likely to emphasize the importance of innate ability in making causal attributions for a person's performance. If a student does not do well, Western culture may assume he or she lacks the intellectual abilities necessary for good performance, whereas Asian culture may assume he or she is not working hard enough.

The Western stress on innate ability is manifested in several ways. For example, when mothers in Japan, Taiwan, and the United States were asked to indicate the degree to which they felt that everybody in their children's class had similar abilities, striking differences between countries emerged. The mothers in the two Asian countries agreed that students in their children's class all had about the same amount of reading and math ability. In contrast, mothers in the United States disagreed, believing that there were significant differences in innate ability (see Figure 2-8).

Obviously, such differences in attributions regarding the cause of academic performance influence people's reactions to poor performance. For Japanese and Taiwanese students, poor performance is seen as a temporary state, one that hard work will remedy. For U.S. students, however, poor performance is an indication of lack of ability, which may lead to discouragement and withdrawal from academic endeavors, rather than diligence and perseverance to overcome their difficulty.

We don't know for sure how much the differences in attributional patterns between Asians and Westerners account for the overall differences in achievement between students in the two cultures. What is clear is that attributing performance to causes that can be modified, such as hard work, is far more utilitarian than assuming that performance is caused by fixed, unchangeable factors. These findings also suggest a strategy for improving school performance: As we'll discuss in Chapter 4, it may be possible to change people's attributions to help minimize the academic gap between Western and Asian students (Stevenson, 1992; Stevenson & Stigler, 1992).

Clearly, then, the social lens through which people view the world influences their susceptibility to the fundamental attribution error. In sum, although the fundamental attribution error is a common source of bias in Western society, its universality is open to question (Miller, Bersoff, & Harwood, 1990; Miller & Bersoff, 1992).

**THE PERSON POSITIVITY BIAS: LOOKING FOR THE BRIGHT SIDE OF OTHERS.**    Like Pollyana, the heroine of Eleanor Porter's 1913 novel who could see no evil in the world, many of us have a blind optimism about others. This tendency to see the world in positive terms reflects the person positivity bias. The **person positivity bias**, or "Pollyanna effect," is the tendency to rate others in a generally positive manner (Sears, 1982; Miller & Felicio, 1990; Granberg & Holmberg, 1990).

The person positivity bias operates in several domains. For example, when subjects are asked during an experiment to rate people they have just met, they tend to judge them positively. Similarly, people's evaluations of important historical and public figures—such as presidents—tends to be generally positive.

On the other hand, there are exceptions to the person positivity bias. People may tend to rate positively their own representative to the U.S. Congress, while holding negative attitudes towards Congress as an entity. Although humorist Will Rogers may never

**person positivity bias**
the tendency to rate others in a generally positive manner, also known as the "Pollyanna effect."

have met a person he didn't like (to paraphrase his famous quote), not all of us would feel the same.

### MOTIVATIONAL BIASES: WANTING TO LOOK GOOD AT THE COST OF ACCURACY.

Have you ever had the opportunity to teach or tutor someone? If your student later did well on a test, how did you explain the success? If you're like most people, you probably gave yourself a bit of credit. But suppose the student did poorly. Were you equally ready to claim responsibility for your student's failure?

**motivational bias**
sources of error that stem from a need to present oneself well, either to impress others or to maintain one's own sense of self-esteem.

Probably not. The reason stems from several biases that fall into the collective category of motivational biases. **Motivational biases** are sources of error that stem from a need to present oneself well, either to impress others or to maintain one's own self-esteem. Unlike the more cognitively oriented attributional biases that we've considered up to now, motivational biases don't originate from failures or inadequacies in examining and drawing conclusions from information that is presented to us. Instead, they result from the desire to achieve some goal, such as making oneself look good.

The operation of motivational biases in attribution was demonstrated in a classic study in which experienced teachers taught a lesson to pupils, whose performance—both in terms of its level and its progression—was manipulated by the experimenters (Beckman, 1970). When pupils' performance improved, the instructors tended to attribute the improvement to their abilities as teachers. But when the pupils' performance declined, the instructors attributed the failure to the students.

On the other hand, a group of uninvolved observers, who had no responsibility for the students' performance, attributed good performance to the students and bad performance to the teachers—the exact opposite pattern from instructors' attributions. Clearly, the kind of involvement a person has in a situation has a powerful effect on that person's causal attributions.

**self-serving bias**
the tendency to attribute personal success to internal factors (such as skill, ability, or effort), while attributing failure to external factors (such as bad luck).

In fact, a general attributional bias, known as the self-serving bias, sometimes occurs when people feel they may be responsible for others' behavior. The **self-serving bias** is a general tendency to attribute success to internal factors—such as skill, ability, or effort—while attributing failure to external factors, such as chance or a particular situa-

Coaches who attribute their team's success to their own skill, ability, or effort in coaching (internal factors), and attribute their team's failures to their poor players (external factors), are reflecting the self-serving bias.

Belief in a just world can lead a gambler to feel that she deserves to win, if she has suffered in other areas of her life.

tion. For instance, coaches may feel their team's successes are due to their coaching, while a poor record is due to the poor performance of their players. Movie directors may assume that good reviews are brought about by their accomplished directing, but poor reviews are due to the lousy script. Authors may surmise that the success of a book is due to their writing skill, but that failure is caused by poor editing and marketing (Schlenker, Weigold, & Hallam, 1990; Schlenker & Weigold, 1992).

In some cases, motivational biases take a particularly cruel twist, when observers, in order to maintain their view of the world, hold victims of disaster responsible for their own misfortune. This misattribution may stem from the fact that most of us hold a **belief in a just world**—the notion that people get out of life what they deserve. Such a belief can easily lead to the converse belief, that people tend to deserve what happens to them (Lerner, 1980).

Although the just world belief results in positive evaluations of others who have good things happen to them, since the judgment is generally that people deserve their good fortune, it can produce unwarranted negative impressions when disaster strikes. For instance, crime victims may be perceived as having done something to invite the crime, such as leaving their doors and windows unlocked (Saunders & Size, 1986; Dye & Roth, 1990; Best, Dansky, & Kilpatrick, 1992). Victims of kidnapping, rape, and assault are often asked what they did to bring on the misfortune (McCaul et al., 1990). People with AIDS may be thought to have brought it on themselves through their own moral failings (Cadwell, 1991; Berrenberg, Rosnik, & Kravcisin, 1991; Anderson, 1992); wives who are battered may be considered to have acted in a way that provoked their beatings (Saunders & Size, 1986; Kristiansen & Giulietti, 1990); and victims of assault may be assumed to have tempted the perpetrators by carelessly wandering into unsafe areas (Symonds, 1975; Hunter & Ross, 1991).

Such blame-the-victim attributions reflect **defensive attributions**—attributions that enable observers to deal with perceived inequities in others' lives and to maintain the belief that the world is just. Presumably, blaming the victim permits observers to distance themselves from the misfortune of others. It is highly threatening to admit that negative events might happen just on the basis of chance; in order to protect themselves against this reality, people tend to view negative outcomes as being deserved. By making such attributions, people are able to preserve their belief that they themselves are less likely to suffer adversity (see, for example, Thornton et al., 1986; Thornton, 1992).

Of course, people are likely to make defensive attributions only to the extent that they feel threatened by the misfortune of others. In particular, people who live in cultures with high levels of fatalism—the acceptance of events as inevitable—may be less susceptible to just world beliefs than those in less fatalistic societies. Hence, one might expect that Asian cultures, which are particularly fatalistic, would be less susceptible to defensive attributions (Yang & Ho, 1988).

**belief in a just world**
the notion that people tend to deserve what happens to them.

**defensive attributions**
attributions that help observers deal with perceived inequities in others' lives in order to maintain the belief that the world is just.

## ▶ REVIEW & RETHINK

### Review

- The two major causes to which we attribute people's behavior are situational causes and dispositional causes.
- The Jones and Davis attribution theory focuses on correspondent inferences—observers' notions of how closely an overt behavior or action represents a specific underlying intention, trait, or disposition.
- Kelley's model of causal attribution considers causes of behavior in terms of consensus, consistency, and distinctiveness information.
- Among the biases in attribution are the fundamental attribution error, the person positivity bias, and motivational biases.

### Rethink

- According to Kelley's attribution theory, what three questions do observers ask themselves when they are trying to make sense of another's behavior?
- How does the Jones and Davis attribution theory differ from Kelley's model?
- Identify the attributional bias in each of the following sentences.

   a. In general, people hate Congress but love their congressional representative.

   b. Alex Trebeck (the host of the TV game show *Jeopardy*) is one of the smartest people I have ever known.

   c. I know that the lottery is a long shot, but I can't help but think that I'll win because I need the money so badly.

   d. I did all I could to study for that exam, but fate was against me. The instructor managed to ask only questions I was unsure about.

- What explains the fundamental attribution error?

## SCHEMAS: ORGANIZING IMPRESSIONS

Consider what it would be like if each time you encountered an individual, it was necessary to make a novel, unique judgment about that person. And think how difficult and time-consuming it would be if each time you encountered that person in the future, you had to revise your impression to incorporate information about his or her particular behavior on that occasion.

**schemas**
organized bodies of information stored in memory.

The primary way we simplify and organize impressions of others is through schemas. **Schemas** are organized bodies of information stored in memory. The information in a schema provides us with a representation of the way the social world operates, and it enables us to categorize and interpret new information related to the schema (Rumelhart, 1984; Fiske & Taylor, 1991).

We all hold schemas relating to everyday objects in our environment. Most of us, for instance, hold a schema for automobiles. We have an idea of what they look like, how they are used, what they can do for us, and how to differentiate them from other vehicles such as trucks or wagons or bicycles. More importantly, from a social psychological point of view, we hold schemas for particular people (our mother, girlfriend, boyfriend, brother, or sister) and for classes of people playing a particular role (mail carriers, teachers, or librarians). Each of these schemas provides a way of organizing behavior into meaningful wholes.

**prototypes**
schemas that organize a group of traits into meaningful personality types or categories.

The personality types that we derive when perceiving others are organized into schemas known as prototypes. **Prototypes** are schemas that organize a group of traits

What is your schema of a car salesperson?

into meaningful personality types or categories. Prototypes represent the typical or average example of a category. We can think of a prototype, then, as a schema of a particular personality type.

For example, consider the prototype of "committed person," an individual who is concerned, involved, and dedicated to a particular cause (Cantor & Mischel, 1979). As you can see in Figure 2-9, this prototype can be divided into different levels of a hierarchy that relate to different levels of specificity. For instance, at the most specific level, called the subordinate level, the prototype consists of different types of committed individuals, such as monks, nuns, and activists for a particular cause. The middle level is represented by general classes of people: the religious devotee or the social activist. Finally, the subordinate and middle levels of specificity are subsumed under the broader superordinate level, which encompasses as a whole the prototype of a committed person.

Just as we have mental prototypes to represent particular types or classes of people, we have scripts to mentally represent particular situations. A **script** is the organized knowledge people hold regarding a particular situation and the way events in that situation unfold (Abelson, 1981). For instance, most of us have a script for "classroom behavior." It includes walking into a class, finding a seat, taking out pen and paper to take notes, and listening as the professor lectures. Like the script of a play, the script for a social scenario describes a sequence of actions (sitting down, taking out a pen), props (pen and notebook), roles (student, professor), and sequence rules (sitting down before taking notes).

The components of scripts are mentally organized into hierarchies, similar to the way that prototypes are arranged in hierarchies. For instance, exam-taking behavior and review session behavior are subordinate to general classroom behavior. In turn, classroom behavior may be subordinate to college behavior in general (Price & Goodman, 1990).

**script**
the organized knowledge people hold regarding a particular situation and the way events in that situation unfold.

**FIGURE 2-9 Prototype of the "Committed Person"** The prototype of the "committed person" can be divided into different levels of a hierarchy, ranging from the more general to the more specific. *(Source:* Cantor & Mischel, 1979.*)*

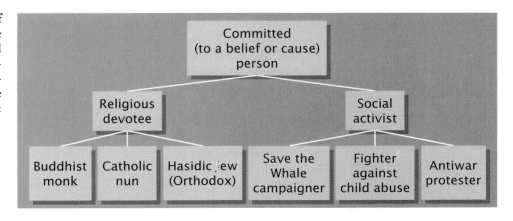

*The Value of Schemas: Furnishing a Social Framework for Old and New Information*

Schemas, prototypes, and scripts are important to our social lives for several reasons. For one thing, they influence the way we understand and interpret information about the social world. Further, they help determine how we remember material to which we have been exposed previously. Finally, they influence the inferences we draw regarding incomplete information.

**THE UTILITY OF SCHEMAS: RECALLING AND INTERPRETING THE WORLD.**    To illustrate the utility of schemas in organizing our understanding of social events, social psychologists Susan Fiske and Shelley Taylor (1991) provide an example based on an ancient Native American folktale. In the folktale, the hero participates in a battle and is shot by an arrow, but he feels no pain because he is in the company of ghosts. When he returns to his home and recounts the story, something black emerges from his mouth, and he dies the next morning.

For those of us unschooled in the Native American culture, the story makes little sense, and so we omit, add, change, or interpret aspects of it to fit in with our schemas. However, for someone familiar with the culture, the story is easily understood. For example, the hero doesn't feel pain because he has ghosts as companions, and the "black thing" coming from his mouth was his departing soul. The point is that previous experience, and more broadly our culture, provide us with schemas that allow us to understand and interpret the meaning of the social world around us. When we do not have such a schema, our comprehension is reduced.

One central way that schemas aid people's comprehension of others' and their own behavior is through their influence on memory. Schemas affect memory both in terms of what information is initially stored and how well it can later be recalled (Cowan, 1992).

What we remember about others reflects the schemas that are seen as relevant in a social setting. In particular, we tend to recall material that is relevant and consistent with a schema and forget information that is irrelevant and inconsistent (Laszlo, 1986; Hansen, 1989). For instance, we tend to remember those pieces of information that fit with our notion of the way people representing certain schemas behave, and at the same time ignore or forget data that does not seem to fit (VanManen & Pietromonaco, 1993).

In an experiment illustrating this point, subjects watched a videotape of a woman celebrating her birthday with her husband (Cohen, 1981). In one condition, the subjects were told that she was a librarian, while in another they were told that she was a waitress. If the subjects thought she was a librarian, they later recalled her as wearing glasses and enjoying classical music. On the other hand, subjects who thought she was a waitress reported that she drank beer and owned a television. Obviously, what was remembered was based on which particular schema was aroused by the occupational information.

Furthermore, our memories do not just consist of dry, factual information about people; they also harbor emotional content. For example, a woman who has been raped may recall and reexperience the terror she suffered when she finds herself in a location or under circumstances that remind her of where and when she was raped. It is not surprising, then, that when people encounter a person or situation relevant to a schema, the emotion attached to the schema may be triggered. For instance, if we confront a member of the clergy, our "clergy" schema may be aroused, and we may experience whatever emotions are attached to that schema. Similarly, if we meet a woman who reminds us of our mother, the emotions associated with our relationship to our mother may be aroused (Fiske & Pavelchak, 1986; Fiske & Neuberg, 1990).

Furthermore, obvious physical characteristics, such as age, sex, and race, are used to place others into relevant schemas at the very first moments of perception. This initial influence of schemas occurs with great speed and seemingly automatically, without the involvement of critical thinking (Gilbert & Hixon, 1991).

Because they are so readily discerned, overt physical characteristics may be represented in primary, universal schemas. Such schemas may be so powerful that they decrease awareness of other, potentially more pertinent, social information relating to the person's specific characteristics (Brewer, 1988; Brewer & Lui, 1989). For example, once someone is categorized as an "old woman," the schema relevant to such a category may overwhelm other types of information. (What comes to mind when you think of the category?) As we will see in Chapter 3 when we discuss prejudice and stereotyping, schemas may be so powerful that they prevent people from noting and remembering potentially more relevant information. When this happens, people may be viewed from the perspective of their connection to a schema, rather than in terms of more personal, individualistic information.

**PRIMING: PLANTING IDEAS IN PEOPLE'S MINDS.**   So far, we have been discussing schemas in terms of how they affect our recall and interpretation of people and events. However, schemas play another role: they prepare us for the future receipt of information through the phenomenon of priming.

**priming**
the process by which recent exposure to stimuli such as people, ideas, or even mere words influences the interpretation of new information.

**Priming** is the process by which recent exposure to stimuli such as people, ideas, or even mere words influences the interpretation of new information. Priming readies people to respond in a particular manner when relevant information is brought to mind (Bower, 1986; Tulving & Schacter, 1990).

Suppose, for instance, that you watch *Cujo,* the horror movie about a vicious, evil dog who tries to murder its owner. If you encounter a dog soon after viewing the film, it would not be too surprising if even the most innocent behavior of the real dog seemed menacing to you. Similarly, a physician who attends a lecture on the prevalence of child sexual abuse may be primed to identify cases of abuse in the next patient she treats.

Priming has been demonstrated in a variety of circumstances and contexts (e.g., Bargh, 1989; Philippot et al., 1991). Some of the earliest research focused on how merely exposing people to a list of words predisposed them to judge another person in a way that was congruent with the words on the list. For instance, in one of the original priming experiments, subjects heard one of two lists of words during what they thought was a memory experiment (Higgins, Rholes, & Jones, 1977). In one condition, the words had positive connotations, such as brave, independent, and adventurous; in the other, they were not-so-positive, such as reckless, foolish, and careless. Later, in what these same subjects thought was another study, subjects were asked to make judgments about a man who engaged in such activities as navigating a sailboat across the Atlantic and participating in a car demolition derby.

The findings were clear. Subjects with previous exposure to the more positive words rated the man more favorably than those with previous exposure to the negative words. In sum, the initial words seem to have activated the equivalent of either "adventurous" or "foolhardy" schemas, and these schemas created either a positive or negative mindset in the subjects.

Priming effects occur even when people are not consciously aware that they have been exposed to relevant prior information. For example, in some experiments, stimulus words are presented so quickly that subjects report having no conscious awareness of being exposed to them. Even under such conditions, the nature of the words affects later judgments and evaluations. Obviously, exposure to the words—even though it occurs without conscious knowledge—acts as a prime (Bargh & Pietromonaco, 1982; Niedenthal & Cantor, 1986; Bargh, 1989).

It is important to keep in mind that priming does more than just affect people's judgments of others. It also can have important consequences in the way we treat them. For instance, in one experiment participants were primed through exposure to categories of people who, at the time, were viewed as hostile and competitive (such as rock star Alice Cooper and Indiana basketball coach Bobby Knight). After such exposure, subjects were placed in a situation in which they interacted with a partner. The primes had their expected effect: Subjects who had been primed acted toward their partners in a more hostile, competitive way than subjects who were not primed (Herr, 1986). Obviously, priming can be a potent phenomenon.

*The Biases of Schemas: The Fallibilities of the Cognitive Miser*

Although schemas play a central role in the way we organize our social world, they have their drawbacks. Earlier in the chapter we mentioned how people may act like "cognitive misers" due to restrictions in their information-processing capabilities. As cognitive misers, they take shortcuts in the way they consider information and may unwittingly value efficiency over accuracy in the way they come to judgments.

Consider, for instance, an experiment in which subjects were exposed to a conversation between two business executives (Holtgraves, Srull, & Socall, 1989). In some conditions they were led to believe that Robert was the boss of a company, and that Michael was his subordinate. In other conditions, though, Robert and Michael were presented as equals with similar status. Two days later, subjects were asked to remember what Robert had said in the conversation.

As Figure 2-10 shows, the nature of the recollections depended on how the two people had been described earlier. When Robert was presented as the boss, he was recalled as acting in a considerably more assertive manner than when he was initially presented as having an equal status with Michael. Subjects' schema of "boss," which presumably had been activated in the first condition, biased their recollections of how Robert had behaved.

Clearly, the use of schemas may lead people to view the social world in an inaccurate and biased manner. Several other factors related to schema can also lead to errors in our perception of others.

**THE REPRESENTATIVENESS HEURISTIC: CONSIDERING MENTAL MATCHES.** Suppose you meet a student named Nick at a party. Nick seems highly intelligent, neat, orderly, but a bit dull. Although he has a strong sense of morality, he seems to be self-centered, lacking feelings and sympathy for others. Assume you find out that he is a writer (although someone mentions his writing is fairly dull), and that he occasionally makes corny puns and has flashes of a science-fiction imagination. When you talk about Nick to a friend

**FIGURE 2-10  Recall Is Consistent with One's Schema** Subjects' recollection of the nature of an earlier conversation depended on whether they thought one of the conversants was a boss or a person of equal status.
*(Source: Adapted from Holtgraves, Srull, & Socall, 1989, p. 155, Table 3.)*

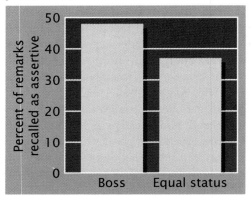

the next day, you pause when the friend asks what Nick's major is. For some reason, you never found out. But you're willing to take a guess, since most of the people at the party were either humanities majors or computer science majors. You guess and say that he seems like the kind of guy who is involved in computer science.

How do you come to such a conclusion? The most likely process involves mentally comparing Nick with your perception of what humanities majors and computer science majors are like. Because he fits fairly well with your schema of a computer science enthusiast, you come up with the theory that he is most likely a computer science major.

If this scenario sounds plausible to you, it is because of the representativeness heuristic. The **representativeness heuristic** is a rule we apply when we judge people by the degree to which they represent a certain category. Although the representativeness heuristic can often be helpful in guiding our judgments of others, it can also lead us astray. In particular, it can lead us to ignore other information that might inform our judgments.

For instance, suppose you learned that 80 percent of the people at the party were humanities majors and 20 percent were computer science majors. Would such additional information change your guess of Nick's major?

If you are like most people, the answer is No. When confronted with such a situation—similar to one used in a classic experiment carried out by social psychologists Daniel Kahneman and Amos Tversky (1973)—most individuals stick with their original judgment. Unfortunately, such judgments are not necessarily correct. If one were to accurately follow the laws of logic and probability, the answer should be revised. After all, given that it is considerably more likely that any single individual at the party is a humanities major, the most logical decision would be that Nick is a humanities major.

**BASE-RATE FALLACY: IGNORING THE DATA.**    The reason that most people make the wrong choice is that they ignore base-rate information. **Base-rate information** is data regarding the frequency with which some event occurs in the general population. Although the use of base-rate information should increase judgmental accuracy, people often ignore it. For instance, people disregard base-rate data as a result of a bias known as the base-rate fallacy. The **base-rate fallacy** is the tendency to underemphasize base-rate data because of the influence of more prominent, although ultimately less meaningful, information (Bar-Hillel, 1980; Taylor & Thompson, 1982).

An illustration of the base-rate fallacy is provided by an experiment in which participants read a vivid, lively description of a Puerto Rican woman who lived on welfare for many years (Hamill, Wilson, & Nisbett, 1980). According to the description, she led a comfortable, contented life with her many children. In one condition, participants were provided with base-rate information that people on welfare tend to stay on welfare for long periods of time—information that was congruent with the scenario. In the other condition, subjects received base-rate information that was contradictory to the scenario. This information (which was factual, by the way) suggested that most welfare recipients were on welfare for only a relatively short time.

When subjects were asked to evaluate the scenario, the base-rate information made little impact on participants' views of welfare in this experiment. Even when subjects received base-rate information that contradicted the scenario, participants focused on the more colorful and involving scenario, ignoring the base-rate data. Plainly, the base-rate fallacy is a powerful bias.

On the other hand, even if it is taken into account, base-rate information ultimately can result in erroneous conclusions if the information is inaccurate. For instance, popular television programs portray a level of violence that far exceeds what is found in the real world. However, heavy television viewers, who use what they see on television as base-rate information, tend to substantially overestimate the amount of real violence. In turn, this leads heavy viewers to be more fearful and anxious about violence than is warranted by the facts (Liebert & Sprafkin, 1988).

---

**representativeness heuristic**
a rule in which people are judged by the degree to which they represent a certain category.

**base-rate information**
data regarding the frequency with which some event occurs in the general population.

**base-rate fallacy**
the tendency to underemphasize base-rate data because of the influence of more prominent, although ultimately less meaningful, information.

**AVAILABILITY HEURISTIC: USING WHAT POPS INTO YOUR HEAD.**     Quick. Which do you think are more prevalent in the English language, words beginning with the letter "r," or words that have "r" as the third letter?

Most people guess that words beginning with "r" are most common. But they're wrong. The letter "r" occurs considerably more often as the third letter of English words than as the first. The reason most people make this mistake is a phenomenon known as the availability heuristic.

The **availability heuristic** is a rule we apply in judging the likelihood of an event by considering the ease with which it can be recalled from memory. Thus, because words that start with "r" are relatively easy to remember, we assume that they are more prevalent. Similarly, many more people are fearful every time they take an airplane flight than when they go for a car ride—despite statistics showing that airplanes are much safer than autos. One reason is that airplane crashes are much more publicized than auto crashes and therefore much more easily retrievable from memory. The availability heuristic, then, leads people to assume that they are more likely to crash in a plane than in a car (Slovic, Fischhoff, & Lichtenstein, 1976; Schwarz et al., 1991).

The availability heuristic can easily skew our perception of what others believe. For instance, college students attending a college where liberal viewpoints predominate may assume that since most of their acquaintances share their liberal opinions on abortion, the general population shares such views. However, once they leave campus and interact with a broader cross-section of the population, these students may be surprised to learn the degree of variability in viewpoints.

Indeed, the tendency to believe that others share our views, spawned from the availability heuristic, is so powerful that it can produce another bias: the false consensus effect. The **false consensus effect** is the tendency to overestimate the degree of agreement with our own opinions, beliefs, and attributes (Ross, Greene, & House, 1977; Marks & Miller, 1987; Ross & Nisbett, 1991).

For instance, if we think that strict environmental laws should be passed, we assume that other people believe the same thing. By the same token, if we believe in the death penalty, we think that others hold the same views. If we smoke, we think that many others smoke. Across a variety of issues, people consistently exaggerate the number of individuals who agree with their position (Granberg, 1987; Marks & Miller, 1987).

**availability heuristic**
a rule for judging the likelihood of an event by considering the ease with which it can be recalled from memory.

**false consensus effect**
the tendency to overestimate the degree of agreement with our own opinions, beliefs, and attributes.

Because airplane crashes receive more publicity than auto crashes, the availability heuristic leads people to recall plane crashes more readily. This leads them to the erroneous conclusion that airplanes are less safe than autos.

Why does this occur? One reason may be that people want to believe that others agree with them, because this belief provides evidence that their own behavior or choices are reasonable (Marks & Miller, 1987). But there are additional reasons for the effect. For instance, we often remember examples of people who agree with us more than examples of those who disagree. Because such instances of agreement are easier to recall, we are misled into thinking that more people hold our position than is actually the case.

Finally, as we will discuss further in Chapter 6, we choose our friends on the basis of similarity of attitudes, beliefs, and values. As a result, we're exposed more often to instances of agreement with our positions than with instances of disagreement (Wetzel & Walton, 1985). Consequently, we overestimate the degree of agreement with our particular position—leading to the false consensus effect.

### The Motivated Tactician: The Rise and Fall of the Cognitive Miser

**motivated tactician model**
an approach to social cognition that suggests that the way people view the world depends on their goals, motivations, and needs.

So far, our discussion of the schema approach to social cognition has taken the cognitive miser model at face value. From this perspective, people are relatively limited in their abilities to process complex information. In order to maximize their success in judging social situations accurately, they hoard their resources, seeking the most efficient solution to questions of why people behave the way they do.

The most recent work in social cognition takes a somewhat different approach, however. In the **motivated tactician model**, the way people view the world depends on their goals, motivations, and needs (Fiske, 1992). If accuracy in understanding others is the predominant goal, the motivated tactician may sacrifice speed in order to come up with an accurate understanding of a social situation—an understanding that enhances the possibility of smooth or effective social interaction. On the other hand, if accuracy is relatively unimportant, the goal of making a rapid decision may prevail, and accuracy may decline (Fiske & Neuberg, 1990; Hilton & Darley, 1991; Snyder, 1992).

But why, you may be wondering, would there ever be a case in which accuracy is inconsequential? The answer is that in some ways absolute accuracy isn't necessary for smooth social functioning. In a number of situations we construct our own social realities, and then act upon those realities. In fact, as we see next, sometimes the perception of reality that we construct takes on a life of its own, as our expectations about the world are transmitted to others and affect their behavior.

### The Self-Fulfilling Prophecy: Turning Cognition into Reality

Suppose you were a teacher who received the following information at the start of the school year:

*All children show hills, plateaus, and valleys in their scholastic progress. A study being conducted at Harvard with the support of the National Science Foundation is interested in those children who show an unusual forward spurt of academic progress. . . .*

*As part of our study we are further validating a test that predicts the likelihood that a child will show an inflection point or "spurt" within the near future. This test, which will be administered in your school, will allow us to predict which youngsters are most likely to show an academic spurt. . . . The development of the test for predicting inflections or "spurts" is not yet such that every one of the top 10 percent will show the spurt or "blooming" effect. But the top 20 percent of the children will show a more significant inflection or spurt in their learning within the next year or less than will the remaining 80 percent of the children (Rosenthal & Jacobson, 1968, p. 66).*

How would you react to such information? Would you treat your students differently, according to the kind of the information you receive about them?

Teachers may favor students for whom they hold more positive expectations of future academic performance, leading to a self-fulfilling prophecy.

**self-fulfilling prophecy**
the tendency for people to act in a way that is congruent with their expectation, belief, or cognition about an event or behavior, thereby increasing the likelihood that the event or behavior will occur.

Although most of us would want to think that we would treat people in an unbiased, equitable manner, the information that we have discussed throughout this chapter so far might lead you to suspect that this might not be the case. As active social perceivers, it seems reasonable that we would use the information to help in the formation of impressions of our students, and we would potentially treat students differently on the basis of our newly formed impressions. This inclination to act as if our expectations were true is reflected in the self-fulfilling prophecy.

A **self-fulfilling prophecy** is the tendency for people to act in a way that is congruent with their expectation, belief, or cognition about an event or behavior, thereby increasing the likelihood that the event or behavior will occur (Snyder, 1984). Self-fulfilling prophecies operate in a variety of contexts. For instance, patients who, on the advice of a physician, take biologically ineffective medication (a placebo) may feel better simply because they expect to feel better. Similarly, the experimenter expectancy effect that we discussed in Chapter 1—in which experimenters' hypotheses lead to behavior that ultimately brings about the expected behavior on the part of subjects—is an example of the self-fulfilling prophecy.

Might teacher expectations produce academic performance consistent with the expectation? To answer that question, social psychologists Robert Rosenthal and Lenore Jacobson (1968) told each teacher in a school that five students who would be in his or her class during the upcoming school year supposedly were likely to "bloom" according to test results. In reality, each of the students was chosen at random from the class list. Despite the fact that the information was bogus, a year later, when all children in the school took a battery of tests, many of the students designated as "bloomers" had gained significantly more than students about whom teachers had received no information.

How did the teachers confirm their expectations? According to subsequent research, teachers who expect a student to perform well begin to behave in a way that elicits the expected behavior. They seem to create a more positive social climate, furnish more precise feedback, and allow more performance opportunities for students expected to do well than for those for whom they hold lower expectations. In turn, students flourish in such an environment and, as can be seen in Figure 2-11, actually begin to behave congruently with the expectation (Harris, 1991; Rosenthal, 1991).

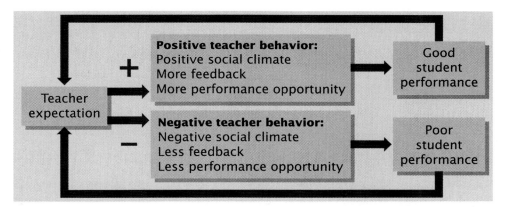

**FIGURE 2-11    Teacher Expectations Can Affect Student Performance** Holding a positive or negative expectation about a student can actually bring about student behavior congruent with the expectation.

By the way, it is not just teachers who communicate their expectations to students. The process works in reverse as well: Students' expectations about their teachers' abilities can be communicated to the teacher and can affect the teacher's behavior. For instance, when students in an experiment were led to believe that their teacher was particularly good or bad, they behaved in ways that actually elicited the expected behavior on the part of the teacher. Teachers whose students expected them to do a good job actually did a better job; those whose students expected them to do poorly did worse. In sum, our teachers' behavior may be at least partially a consequence of the way we treat them (Feldman & Theiss, 1982; Jamieson et al., 1987).

If the self-fulfilling prophecy operates in academic realms, we should not be surprised that it plays a significant role in other domains, such as in our perception of others' personality and behavior. For instance, when we form expectations about what other people are like, these expectations then influence the kind of interaction we subsequently have with them.

A classic experiment illustrates the power of expectations in defining the kinds of interactions we have with others (Snyder & Swann, 1978). In the experiment, subjects were led to believe that a student they were about to interview was either introverted or extroverted. They were then given a list of questions to ask the student during the interview. As expected, subjects chose a disproportionate number of questions that elicited information that was congruent with the specific expectation that they had been given. When they thought a subject was extroverted, they chose to ask such things as "What would you do if you wanted to liven things up at a party?"; when their expectation was that the subject was introverted, they asked questions such as "What factors make it really hard for you to open up to people?" Clearly, they appeared to seek confirmation for the validity of their prior impression.

More striking were the results that the choice of questions brought about. According to impartial judges, who heard tapes of the interviews, students who were asked more questions about their supposed extroversion came across as more extroverted, while those who were asked questions about their ostensible introversion appeared more introverted.

The results of this study and of subsequent research are clear in demonstrating the power of our expectations in bringing about behavior that confirms our expectations (Eden, 1990; Jenner, 1990; Harris et al., 1992). They also accentuate the importance of developing accurate impressions and attributions in the first place. If our expectations about others not only affect our behavior but also provoke others to act in a way that is congruent with those expectancies, we certainly need to be cautious in the kinds of conclusions we draw about others (Snyder, Campbell, & Preston, 1982; Slowiaczek et al., 1989; Snyder, 1992). We next consider several ways in which we can increase the accuracy of our impressions.

---

# THE INFORMED CONSUMER OF SOCIAL PSYCHOLOGY

## DRAWING THE RIGHT CONCLUSIONS FROM OTHERS' BEHAVIOR

Social psychologist Susan Fiske argues that people are "good-enough perceivers" (Fiske, 1992). What she means is that people are generally sufficiently accurate in their perceptions of others to ensure their reasonably successful navigation through the social seas. But is it possible for people to change from just "good-enough" to "excellent"? Social psychologists have discovered several means of increasing the validity of one's interpretations of others and their behavior (Funder, 1987; Darley et al., 1988; Neuberg, 1989; Colvin & Funder, 1991; Kunda, 1991; Sanitioso & Kunda, 1991). Among them:

- *Make accuracy a goal.* Simply keeping in mind the objective of discovering people's true characteristics will help you to be more accurate in your impressions and will decrease the impulsiveness with which you make some judgments.

- *Keep in mind the biases that distort attributions.* For instance, your awareness that we tend to overemphasize the dispositional determinants behind behavior that we observe—the fundamental attribution error—should lead you to ask yourself what situational constraints may be at work as you observe another person's behavior.

- *Be alert for incongruent and negative information.* Even after you've made up your mind about someone's motivations in a given situation, stay alert for new data that may lead to a mid-course correction.

- *Don't rush to judgment.* Although people are sometimes quite accurate in inferences based on brief slices of behavior (Ambady & Rosenthal, 1992, 1993), the more information you can garner about people, across very different kinds of situations, the more accurate your judgments will be.

- *If all else fails, keep in mind that bias does not equal error.* Just because judgments may deviate from formal rules of logic does not mean they are wrong. For example, sometimes dispositional factors do adequately explain the causes of people's behavior, and in such cases the fundamental attribution error will only act to increase the accuracy of judgments.

---

# ► REVIEW & RETHINK

## Review

- Schemas are organized bodies of information stored in memory.
- Priming is the process by which recent exposure to stimuli such as people, ideas, or even words influences the interpretation of new information.
- Among the biases related to the use of schemas are the representativeness heuristic, the base-rate fallacy, the availability heuristic, and the false consensus effect.
- Acting on our expectations can lead to the operation of self-fulfilling prophecies.

## Rethink

- What is a prototype and how are prototypes related to schemas?
- In what ways do scripts differ from schemas? Describe a possible script and a possible schema for how to behave when meeting new people.
- What is the availability heuristic, and can this heuristic help explain the priming effect?
- What is the false consensus effect, and how is it related to the person positivity bias discussed earlier in the chapter?
- What is the sequence of events involved in the self-fulfilling prophecy? Give an example.

# LOOKING BACK

◄ ◄ ◄ ◄ ◄ ◄ ◄ ◄ ◄ ◄ ◄ ◄ ◄ ◄ ◄ ◄ ◄ ◄ ◄ ◄ ◄ ◄ ◄ ◄ ◄

### How do we combine people's individual personality traits into an overall impression?

1. Social cognition is the study of how people understand and make sense of others and themselves. Three main approaches characterize this area of social psychology. Person perceptions consider how an individual assesses and combines the traits of another to form an overall impression. Attribution approaches seek to identify how people understand the causes of others', and their own, behavior; according to attribution theorists, people act as "naive scientists," rationally weighing and combining different sources of information. Schema approaches consider how people organize and store information in memory, and how they use this information as a framework to understand others' and their own behavior.

2. Although sometimes our impressions are based on outward, surface features, we often combine various traits to form an overall impression. The central traits theory suggests that certain characteristics serve to organize an impression and provide a framework for interpreting subsequent information; hence these central traits have the major influence on a person's final judgment of another. In contrast, the cognitive algebra approach suggests that perceivers consider each individual trait, evaluate each trait individually, and then combine the evaluations into an overall judgment. No approach has been fully successful in explaining the judgment process, in part because of such phenomena as primacy and recency effects.

### How do we make judgments about the causes of others' behavior?

3. Attribution studies consider how people understand the causes of others', and their own, behavior. In considering that people act like "naive scientists," attribution theories seek to explain how people look for situational and dispositional causes behind behavior.

4. Jones and Davis's correspondent inference theory of attribution focuses on correspondent inferences—observers' notions of how closely an overt behavior or action represents a specific underlying intention, trait, or disposition. To make that judgment, observers focus on the unique or noncommon effects of behaviors.

5. Kelley's model of causal attribution focuses on the role of three different kinds of information: Consensus information concerns the degree to which other people react similarly in the same situation. Consistency information concerns the degree to which people react in the same way in different situations. Distinctiveness information concerns the extent to which the same behavior occurs in relation to other people or stimuli. When behavior exhibits low consensus and distinctiveness and high consistency, people tend to make dispositional attributions; when behavior exhibits high consensus, consistency, and distinctiveness, people tend to attribute the behavior to external, situational factors.

### What kinds of systematic errors are we vulnerable to when we consider others' behavior?

6. The fundamental attribution error, which is pervasive and powerful, is the tendency to overattribute others' behavior to dispositional causes and to underemphasize the role of situational causes. Other biases include the person positivity bias or Pollyanna effect, and the motivational biases, which are due to a desire to present oneself well. One of the motivational biases is the self-serving bias, which is a general tendency to attribute success to internal factors (skill, ability, or effort) and failure to external factors (chance or something about the situation). Another motivational bias is the belief in a just world—the notion that people get out of life what they deserve and that people deserve what happens to them.

### How do we organize and remember information about social stimuli, and how does this process affect our social judgment?

7. Schemas are organized bodies of information stored in memory. They provide a representation of the way the social world operates, and they enable us to categorize and interpret

new information related to the schema. Two major types of schemas are prototypes (for personality information) and scripts (for information regarding particular situations).

8. Priming is the process by which recent exposure to stimuli—such as people, ideas, or even mere words—influences the interpretation of new information. Priming prepares people to respond in a particular manner when relevant information is brought to mind.

9. The use of schemas may lead to mistakes in social judgment. There are four major sources of such errors. The representativeness heuristic occurs when people are judged by the degree to which they represent a certain category. The base-rate fallacy is the tendency to underemphasize base-rate data because of the influence of more prominent, although ultimately less meaningful, information. The availability heuristic occurs when likelihood of an event is judged by considering the ease with which it can be recalled from memory. And the false consensus effect is the tendency to overestimate the degree of agreement with our own opinions, beliefs, and attributes.

10. A self-fulfilling prophecy is the tendency for people to act in a way that is congruent with their expectation, belief, or cognition about an event or behavior, thereby increasing the likelihood that the event or behavior will occur. Self-fulfilling prophecies lead people to act in a way that makes their social judgments become reality.

11. In order to avoid making errors in social judgment, there are several strategies to follow. These include making accuracy an explicit goal, being aware of potential biases, being alert for incongruent and negative information, avoiding rushed judgments, and recalling that bias does not always lead to error.

# KEY TERMS AND CONCEPTS

*social cognition (p. 44)*

*person perception approaches (p. 44)*

*attribution approaches (p. 44)*

*schema approaches (p. 44)*

*cognitive miser model (p. 45)*

*central traits (p. 47)*

*cognition algebra approach (p. 48)*

*primacy effect (p. 49)*

*recency effect (p. 50)*

*situational causes (p. 51)*

*dispositional causes (p. 52)*

*correspondent inferences (p. 54)*

*consensus information (p. 55)*

*consistency information (p.55)*

*distinctiveness information (p. 55)*

*fundamental attribution error (p. 57)*

*person positivity bias (p. 61)*

*motivational bias (p. 62)*

*self-serving bias (p. 62)*

*belief in a just world (p. 63)*

*defensive attributions (p. 63)*

*schemas (p. 64)*

*prototypes (p. 64)*

*script (p. 65)*

*priming (p. 67)*

*representativeness heuristic (p. 69)*

*base-rate information (p. 69)*

*base-rate fallacy (p. 69)*

*availability heuristic (p. 70)*

*false consensus effect (p. 70)*

*motivated tactician model (p. 71)*

*self-fulfilling prophecy (p. 72)*

# FOR FURTHER RESEARCH AND STUDY

Fiske, S. T. & Taylor, S. E. (1991). *Social cognition* (2nd ed.). New York: McGraw-Hill.

A definitive, comprehensive introduction to social cognition, detailing how people come to judgments about others and the reasons for their behavior.

Plous, S. (1993). *The psychology of judgment and decision making.* New York: McGraw-Hill.

A lively look at how we make judgments, including an examination of the kinds of biases that influence our decisions about what others are like.

Jones, E. E. (1990). *Interpersonal perception.* New York: Freeman.

This treatment of social perception by one of the major leaders in the field focuses on how people come to understand the particular behaviors of others and themselves.

Gilovich, T. (1991). *How we know what isn't so: The fallibility of human reason in everyday life.* New York: Free Press.

A close-up view of how the errors we make in social reasoning can have major consequences.

# EPILOGUE

In our discussion of both our abilities and our imperfections as social observers, we've focused on how a single observer makes judgments about a single person. But many of our social judgments encompass multiple individuals, people whose membership in certain groups is used to make inferences. Hence, up to now we've largely ignored factors such as sex, race, ethnicity, and other characteristics that are among the most potent determinants of how people react to others.

In the next chapter, we focus on how we perceive and understand groups. We look at how the work done by social psychologists addresses some of the most critical—and intractable—societal problems, including race relations, sex discrimination, and stereotyping and prejudice in general. We'll see how the specific principles of social judgment that we've been discussing can be applied beyond the individual level to the broader societal sphere. In addition, we'll consider how some of the same research that has led to our understanding of the basic processes of social perception also points us toward solutions and remedies for some of the difficult problems our world faces.

### CHAPTER THREE

# PREJUDICE, DISCRIMINATION, AND STEREOTYPES

## PERCEIVING AND UNDERSTANDING GROUPS

There had been a keg in the kitchen and necking on the couch, maybe a joint or two smoked outside, more than 30 teenagers talking and drinking and flirting on a hot August night in the South Florida city of Coral Springs, which calls itself "America's Best Hometown." About 11 P.M., Luyen Phan Nguyen, an easygoing 19-year-old Vietnamese-American, walked into the party. As a child, he had survived danger on the ocean and a deserted island in Malaysia, and as a teenager he'd hurt his knee trying to play the American game of football. Nguyen was going to be a doctor like his father, who had brought his family to the USA so his children could grow up free and safe.

Luyen's life ended that night while other American kids called him "chink" and "Viet Cong." As they beat Luyen in a grassy courtyard, between the palm trees and the swimming pool with aqua trim, one of the young partygoers was heard to scream, inexplicably, "I should have killed you in 'Nam, you f---ing gook!" Twenty or so partying teenagers watched it all. (Lovely, 1993, p. 4)

Luyen Phan Nguyen

# LOOKING AHEAD

▶ ▶ ▶ ▶ ▶ ▶ ▶ ▶ ▶ ▶ ▶ ▶ ▶ ▶ ▶ ▶ ▶ ▶ ▶ ▶ ▶ ▶ ▶ ▶ ▶ ▶ ▶ ▶ ▶ ▶

The senseless hatred that led to Luyen's death is mirrored in scores of other crimes perpetrated against people because of their race, religion, sexual orientation, or ethnicity. In fact, a study by the National Institute Against Prejudice and Violence found that 7 percent of all adults had been the targets of verbal abuse or violence during the previous year due to their membership in a particular group (Levin & McDevitt, 1993).

Furthermore, ill treatment due to group membership is not just manifested in extreme and violent acts. Prejudice, discrimination, and stereotyping occur in everyday situations: when a woman is passed over for a promotion because of her gender; when an African-American receives poor service in a store because of his race; and when a physician uses condescending baby-talk with an elderly patient.

In this chapter, we consider the roots of prejudice and discrimination. We begin by differentiating three fundamental concepts used to explain why people demonstrate bias and bigotry toward others: prejudice, discrimination, and stereotypes. We discuss the psychological definition of a minority group, and we learn how a numerical advantage is not necessarily a defining characteristic. We also examine what lies behind prejudice and discrimination, how any group that is different from our own may be subject to prejudice and discrimination, and why group membership may be a source of self-esteem.

Finally, we focus on the two most frequent manifestations of bias: prejudice based on gender and on race. We consider how these prejudices affect the way people view others and the damaging consequences of discrimination. We end on a positive note, discussing ways to reduce prejudice and discrimination.

In sum, after reading this chapter, you'll be able to answer these questions:

- What differentiates prejudice, discrimination, and stereotyping?
- How is prejudice learned and maintained?
- How do stereotypes provide the cognitive foundations for prejudice and discrimination?
- How prevalent is racism, and is it inevitable?
- Why does sexism occur, and what are the roots of gender stereotyping?
- What are some ways social psychologists have devised to reduce prejudice and discrimination?

# THE BASIC PRINCIPLES OF HATRED

*Cambodian, Vietnamese, and Laotian refugees, resettled in the United States, are facing a rash of physical assaults, including beatings, rock throwing, vandalism, arson, intimidation, and racial slurs. According to one state attorney general, "Often, these individuals cannot even walk along the public street without being physically attacked and threatened because of their race or national origin." (U.S. Commission on Civil Rights, 1990, p. 2)*

*A female Jewish student was shot five times with a BB gun on a large state college campus. As the attacker fired, he shouted "Heil Hitler" and other anti-Semitic epithets. An underground campus newspaper hailed the assailant as a hero and suggested that next time he use a flamethrower on the victim.*

*Five white cadets at a military academy, wearing masks and white sheets, entered the room of an African-American cadet. While shouting obscenities, they threw a burned paper cross onto the floor.*

These incidents, recorded by the U.S. Commission on Civil Rights (1990), illustrate that ethnic and racial hate is alive and well in U.S. society today. But it is not only in such obvious physical and verbal attacks that we find hostility and rancor. When people presume that someone is likely to behave in a certain way because she is a woman, or an African-American, or gay or lesbian, such assumptions spring from the same foundations as more visible and overt forms of prejudice and discrimination.

Seeking to understand such acts and assumptions, social psychologists first have sought to delineate and clarify the basic concepts of prejudice, stereotypes, and discrimination.

*The Basic Concepts: Distinguishing Prejudice, Stereotypes, and Discrimination*

**prejudice**
the negative (or positive) evaluations or judgments of members of a group that are based primarily on membership in the group and not necessarily on the particular characteristics of individual members.

**Prejudice** refers to the negative (or positive) evaluations or judgments of members of a group that are based primarily on membership in the group, and not necessarily on the particular characteristics of individual members. For example, gender prejudice occurs when a person is evaluated on the basis of being a male or female and not because of his or her own specific characteristics or abilities.

Although prejudice is generally thought of as a negative evaluation of group members, it can also be positive: As we'll see, at the same time people dislike members of other groups, they may also positively evaluate members of their own group. In both cases, the assessment is unrelated to qualities of particular individuals; rather, it is due to the specific group to which individuals belong.

The cognitive framework that maintains prejudice is a stereotype. A **stereotype** is a set of beliefs and expectations about members of a group that is held simply on the basis of their membership in the group. Stereotypes are oversimplifications that we employ in

**stereotypes**
a set of beliefs and expectations about members of a group that are held simply on the basis of their membership in the group.

an effort to make sense of the complex social environment in which we live (Andersen & Klatzky, 1987).

Stereotypes can be thought of as particular kinds of schemas—those cognitive bodies of information we discussed in the previous chapter. Schemas relating to stereotypes organize and simplify information and provide a framework for prejudiced individuals to view others' behavior (Macrae, Milne, & Bodenhausen, 1994). Such schemas distort a person's perception so that others are viewed through the lens of prejudice.

The existence of stereotypes, like that of all schemas, means that information consistent with the schema is more conspicuous to the prejudiced person and is remembered more easily than other information. As a result, information inconsistent with the stereotype is ignored and readily forgotten. In addition, stereotypes determine how information is interpreted, so that even when people are exposed to data contrary to their stereotype, they may interpret the information in a way that supports their prejudice (Wyer, 1988; Fiske & Neuberg, 1990; Hamilton, Sherman, & Ruvolo, 1990; Biernat, Manis, & Nelson, 1991).

**discrimination**
the behavioral manifestation of stereotypes and prejudice.

Ultimately, stereotypes may increase the chances of discrimination occurring. **Discrimination**, the behavioral manifestation of stereotypes and prejudice, refers to negative (or sometimes positive) actions toward members of a particular group due to their membership in a particular group. Although prejudice and discrimination often go hand in hand, one may be present without the other. A person who harbors prejudice may not necessarily engage in overt discrimination, because the target of his or her prejudice may not be present. For example, someone may dislike Turks without ever having had an opportunity to interact with them. Furthermore, laws against discrimination, as well as strong social norms or standards, may prevent overt discrimination, although it still may occur in more subtle ways. Hence, the presence of prejudice does not always lead directly to discrimination.

On the other hand, the presence of discrimination is a fairly good indication that prejudice also exists. But not always. For instance, the white president of a company may impede the hiring of a Korean-American executive for a post because she thinks that person would have difficulty dealing with the business's prejudiced customers. In this case, then, there would be discrimination without prejudice.

## Minority Groups: Not Just a Matter of Numbers

Towards whom are prejudice, stereotyping, and discrimination directed? In most cases, it is towards members of minority groups. Of the concepts we've discussed, the term minority group seems to be the easiest to conceptualize. However, minority groups are not just groups that are numerically smaller than majority groups.

For instance, in some parts of the southern United States, African-Americans far outnumber whites; in South Africa, whites make up only a small percentage of the population; and in the U.S. there are slightly more females than males. But in each of these three examples, we can make a good argument that those in the numerical minority should actually be considered the majority, since the numerically smaller group historically has had considerably more power, control, and influence than the numerical majority. From a social psychological point of view, then, a **minority group** is a group in which the members have significantly less power, control, and influence over their own lives than do members of a dominant group (Simpson & Yinger, 1985; Schaefer & Lamm, 1992).

**minority group**
a group in which the members have significantly less power, control, and influence over their own lives than do members of a dominant group.

Social psychologists consider minority groups in terms of psychological, as opposed to strictly numerical, characteristics. Specifically, minorities make up subordinate parts of a society, have physical or cultural characteristics that are held in relatively low esteem by dominant groups, and are aware of their minority status. Furthermore, minority membership is passed on through norms that encourage affiliation and marriage with other minority group members. In some ways, then, being a minority or majority group member is something of a state of mind, regardless of what the absolute numbers imply.

Although blacks are a numerical majority in South Africa, it is only recently that they have gained a significant degree of political power. Until Nelson Mandela became head of the government, blacks were psychologically a minority group.

# THE ROOTS OF PREJUDICE

Female. African-American. Muslim. Gay.

What images come to mind when you read or hear each of these words? For most people, encountering a description of a person that includes such a label is enough to summon up a rich network of impressions, memories, and probably even predictions of how a person who embodies such a label will behave in a given situation. The presence of such connections suggests that we are all susceptible to prejudice.

But where does prejudice originate? Social psychologists have considered several answers, ranging from early learning to basic cognitive processing (Duckitt, 1992).

## Social Learning Explanations: The School of Stereotyping

**social learning view**
the theory that people develop prejudice and stereotypes about members of various groups in the same way they learn other attitudes, beliefs, and values.

People are not born feeling prejudice and showing discrimination to members of different religions, ethnic groups, or races. It is something that is taught to us, in much the same way that we learn that $2 + 2 = 4$.

The **social learning view** suggests that people develop prejudice and stereotypes about members of various groups in the same way they learn other attitudes, beliefs, and values (as we'll discuss further in Chapter 10). For instance, one important source of information for children regarding stereotypes and prejudice is the behavior and teaching of parents, other adults, and peers (Kryzanowski & Stewin, 1985; Zinberg, 1976). Through direct reinforcement and observing the reinforcement of others, people learn about members of other groups. And such learning begins at an early age: By the age of three or four, children are able to distinguish between African-Americans and whites, and even at that age they can possess preferential feelings for members of their own group over others (Katz, 1976).

But children are not the only ones who learn stereotypes and prejudice from others. Although there have been significant improvements in the past decade, television and other media often portray minority group members in shallow, stereotyped ways. For instance, *Hangin' With Mr. Cooper,* a network television program, portrayed African-

American Mark Cooper as a bug-eyed substitute teacher, repeatedly expressing surprise with prolonged shouts of "damn." Another program, *Out All Night,* featured a lecherous African-American who preens before an attractive woman and pronounces, "Right now I'm delivering pizza. And in my personal life as well as in my work, I deliver hot and on top!" (Hammer, 1992).

Such portrayals of African-Americans perpetuate some of society's most distasteful and undesirable stereotypes. In fact, an observer of television might conclude that most African-American males are lechers, shiftless buffoons, or speak primarily in jive. Other groups are stereotyped in the media in equally derogatory ways: Godfather-like Italian mobsters, greedy Jewish businessmen, inscrutable Asians, and airheaded blonde women are frequent characters in television and film (Jussim, Milburn, & Nelson, 1991; Hyler, Gabbard, & Schneider, 1991).

Repeatedly observing such characters takes a toll. For people whose exposure to minority group members is limited to what they see in the media, such portrayals cultivate and maintain unfavorable views of minority groups (Hammer, 1992a; Evans, 1993).

On the other hand, the situation is not entirely bleak. The different media have shown increased sensitivity to the way in which minority group members are portrayed. The number of positive portrayals of minorities shown on television, in particular, has increased dramatically. For instance, such television programs as *L.A. Law, I'll Fly Away,* and *The Cosby Show* have had strong, responsible, and successful African-American men and women as major characters. If we expect that negative media portrayals perpetuate stereotypes and, ultimately, prejudice—as social learning theory suggests—it also stands to reason that positive media portrayals should lead to a reduction in stereotyping and prejudice (Evuleocha & Ugbah, 1989).

Children learn the prejudices of their parents through social learning processes. These young children were not born discriminating against gays and lesbians, but were taught their prejudice.

## Realistic Conflict: The Clash of Competition

**realistic conflict theory** the notion that prejudice is the outcome of a direct competition over valued, but limited, resources.

Put into a small cage two rodents who are unfamiliar with one another, and they are likely to fight over the limited amount of space available. Does prejudice begin in the same way, when two groups compete over scarce resources?

According to realistic conflict theory, the answer is yes. **Realistic conflict theory** argues that prejudice is the outcome of direct competition over valued, but limited, resources (Hilton, Potvin & Sachdev, 1989; Brown & Williams, 1984). In this view, the things we value most in life—a good job, a safe and comfortable environment, and a high standard of living—are limited, and people must compete with others to obtain what they consider their fair share. If they perceive that members of minority groups prevent their attaining those higher standards, they will view those minorities in an increasingly hostile manner. Consequently, prejudice develops, fueled by the competition for the desired resources (White, 1977; Simpson & Yinger, 1985) (see Figure 3-1).

For example, consider a noisy, crowded city—an environment that is dirty, unsafe, and impersonal. If residents who are members of majority groups blame the difficulties of urban life on the presence of a particular minority, they may act in a hostile and antagonistic manner toward the minority group members. Similarly, in times of high unemployment in which there is competition for a handful of jobs, prejudice may be directed toward members of minority groups if they are seen to be taking jobs away from majority group members.

In extreme cases, the conflict between members of different groups turns to violence. For instance, an examination of lynchings of African-Americans in the American South more than 50 years ago shows a clear—and strong—negative relationship with several indicators of economic well-being: The worse the economy, the greater the number of lynchings (Hovland & Sears, 1940; Hepworth & West, 1988).

**COMPETITION AT ROBBER'S CAVE.** Experimental evidence, as well, supports the argument that competition leads to stereotyping, prejudice, and ultimately conflict. For example, social psychologist Muzafer Sherif (1966) conducted a classic field study held at a boys' summer camp called Robber's Cave. Two groups of middle-class 11- and 12-

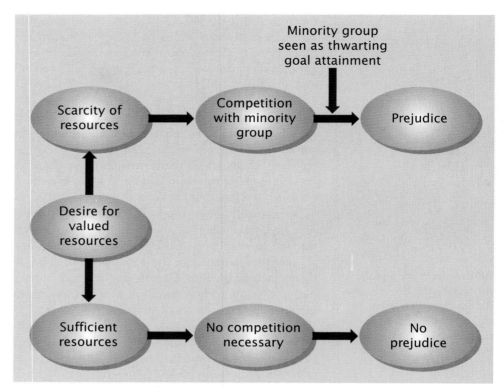

**Figure 3-1    Realistic Conflict Theory** According to realistic conflict theory, prejudice is the outcome of direct competition over limited resources. If there are insufficient resources, prejudice will occur, but if the resources are adequate, prejudice will be avoided.

year-olds—who did not know they were in an experiment—were settled on opposite sides of the camp. Initially, each group was unaware of the other's existence. Then, after the two groups had been established, the researchers devised a tournament of games in which the two groups competed for a series of attractive prizes that only one group could win. According to realistic conflict theory, the conditions were clearly ripe for stereotyping and prejudice to develop: There was competition between the two groups over scarce resources.

The results were more than the researchers bargained for. Not only did the groups compete vigorously during the games, but the competition soon went well beyond the tournament. The groups picked fights, raided each other's campsites, and generally behaved in a belligerent and combative manner. According to the researchers, an outside observer would characterize the children as "wicked, disturbed, and vicious bunches of youngsters" (Sherif, 1966, p. 58). In just two short weeks, the groups developed a deep-seated malice toward each other.

Although it was easy to foster antagonism between the two groups, taming it proved to be considerably more difficult, and the researchers' first efforts were inadequate. For instance, members of the two groups were brought together to share pleasant experiences, such as watching a movie. However, as soon as the lights were dimmed, fights broke out. Moral exhortations also proved useless. Even the introduction of a third group, which was supposed to act as a kind of common enemy, was ineffective in reducing hostility.

**superordinate goals**
goals simultaneously shared by members of conflicting groups.

Fortunately, though, one procedure did work: the introduction of **superordinate goals**—goals which are simultaneously shared by members of conflicting groups and which can only be achieved through the members of different groups jointly contributing resources or working together. Reasoning that it was common goals that led to the formation of the groups initially, the researchers surmised that the introduction of goals that were

As the economy worsened in the 1920s and 1930s, the number of lynchings of African-Americans increased in the South. Such findings support realistic conflict theory, which suggests that prejudice is the outcome of direct competition over limited resources.

common to both groups—superordinate goals—might be effective in uniting the two groups.

They were right. The researchers arranged for a series of apparent emergencies. For instance, the water supply broke down, and the boys were forced to work jointly if they wanted water to drink. After a number of such events, group hostility was reduced, friendships developed across group lines, and the superordinate goals became effective in unifying the previously hostile groups.

Subsequent work has suggested that it was probably not only the jointly held goals that reduced the group hostility. An additional process may have been at work: a cognitive recategorization in which members of the two separate groups came to see each other as members of a single group (Gaertner et al., 1989).

**RELATIVE DEPRIVATION.**    Does the study at the Robber's Cave provide us with a microcosm of society? Do stereotypes and prejudice develop merely as a result of competition between groups sparring over scarce resources?

Although the results of the study clearly support realistic conflict theory, they do not represent the total picture. Some research suggests that competition cannot by itself lead to stereotyping and prejudice. For instance, whites who reluctantly comply with local school busing plans to promote the desegregation of their local schools often show no more prejudice toward African-Americans than do those who are not personally involved (Sears & Kinder, 1985; Sears & Funk, 1991). Such findings suggest that prejudice involving competition is not just a result of the absolute level of resources that people feel they lack. Instead, it is the relative deprivation they experience that is crucial.

**relative deprivation**
the sense that one lacks a desired resource in comparison with another group, which is perceived to have more.

**Relative deprivation** is the sense that one lacks a desired resource in comparison with another group, which is perceived to have more. Relative deprivation may arise as people view the world around them, particularly as it is mirrored on television and film. For instance, in the 1960s, minority group members saw that the economy was prospering for most people—except for members of minority groups, who lagged well behind the majority. The perception that for them the "American Dream" was going unfulfilled

led to violence and rioting against the white majority in some urban areas of the United States (Sears & McConahay, 1981).

Similarly, majority group members may blame members of minority groups for their feelings that they are faring poorly, resulting in prejudice against minority group members. What is important here is not so much that people see their absolute level of economic well-being threatened or injured by minority group members, but how their economic success compares to those of other groups (Danziger & Wheeler, 1975; Brown et al., 1986; Olson, Herman, & Zanna, 1986).

However, neither realistic conflict theory nor relative deprivation approaches to stereotyping and prejudice provide the full story. In most cases, minority group members represent no credible threat; often, members of minorities are hardly in a position to threaten the well-being of majority group members. In fact, in the struggle for scarce resources, minority group members are most often at a distinct disadvantage. Stereotyping and prejudice, then, are produced by factors beyond realistic conflict. One likely candidate: the role that people's membership in racial, religious, ethnic, and gender groups plays in people's identity.

## Social Identity Theory: The Self-Esteem of Group Membership

**social identity theory**
the notion that people use group membership as a source of pride and self-worth.

Think about your ethnic or religious identity for a moment. Are you proud of it? Does it make you feel good to be part of the group? Would you feel threatened if your group were criticized or attacked?

According to social psychologists Henri Tajfel (1982) and John Turner (1987), the groups to which we belong play a crucial role in maintaining our personal self-esteem. Their **social identity theory** suggests that we use group membership as a source of pride and self-worth. However, in order to feel such pride, we must assume that our group is, in fact, superior to others. As a result, our quest for a positive social identity leads us to inflate the positive aspects of the group to which we belong and belittle groups to which we do not belong (Tajfel & Turner, 1986; Tajfel, 1974; Turner et al., 1992).

Certainly, there is ample evidence that members of various cultural groups tend to see their own groups in more positive terms than others. For instance, one cross-cultural investigation of 17 different societies found that, universally, people rated the group to which they belonged as more peace-loving, virtuous, and obedient than other groups (LeVine & Campbell, 1972). Even in cases in which objective behavior displayed by different groups is similar, people interpret the behavior quite differently (Campbell, 1967).

One goal of this gay rights demonstration was to instill a sense of group pride.

Hence, groups to which we belong are described as generous, but the same behavior, when practiced by a minority group, is viewed as wasteful and extravagant. Members of our own group are seen as devoted; members of other groups are cliquish.

Of course, not all groups allow us to obtain the same sense of self-worth. It is important for groups to be small enough so that people can feel somewhat unique and special. In fact, minority group membership sometimes produces stronger feelings of social identity than majority group membership (Brewer, 1991). Minority group leaders of the past who used slogans such as "Black is Beautiful" and "Gay Pride" reflected awareness of the importance of instilling group pride.

If people's self-esteem is tied to their group identity, does that mean that assaults on self-esteem will lead to more positive appraisal of their own group and increased belittlement of other groups? The answer seems to be yes. For instance, one experiment tested this theory using a group of English-speaking Canadian subjects (Meindl & Lerner, 1985). In a ruse designed to make subjects experience a temporary loss of self-esteem, some subjects were led to drop a batch of computer cards that they were told was quite important. The rest of the subjects were not subjected to this self-esteem loss.

A short time later, another experimental manipulation made subjects contemplate their identity as English-speaking Canadians. Finally, subjects were asked to rate French-speaking Canadians (a group to which they did not belong) on a variety of traits.

Compared with those who had not endured the temporary self-esteem loss that came from dropping the cards, the subjects who dropped the cards and felt awkward made more extreme and biased ratings of the French-speaking group members. On the other hand, subjects who were not reminded of their identity as English-speaking Canadians did not judge the French-speaking group members in a more biased manner, regardless of whether their self-esteem had been lowered or not (see Figure 3-2).

In short, according to social identity theory, membership in a group provides people with a sense of personal identity and self-esteem (Crocker & Luhtanen, 1990). When a group is successful, self-esteem can rise; and, conversely, when self-esteem is threatened, people feel enhanced attraction to their own group and are more prone to disparage members of other groups.

**FIGURE 3-2   The Self-esteem That Comes from Group Membership** Subjects whose group membership had been made salient and whose self-esteem had been lowered showed more extreme and biased ratings of members of the group to which they did not belong. On the other hand, subjects who were not reminded of their group identity did not judge outgroup members in a more biased manner, regardless of whether their self-esteem had been lowered. *(Source:* Meindl & Lerner, 1985, Table 1.*)*

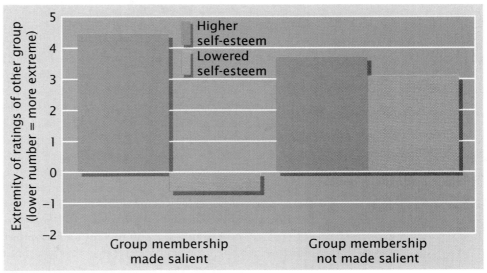

▶ **REVIEW & RETHINK**

### Review

- Stereotypes, discrimination, and minority groups are primary concepts in the study of prejudice.
- Among the explanations for prejudice are social learning approaches and realistic conflict theory.
- Social identity theory suggests that people derive a sense of pride from group membership, leading to exaggeration of their group's positive aspects and other groups' negative aspects.

### Rethink

- What is prejudice and how does it differ from stereotypes and discrimination?
- How do social psychologists define a minority group? In what way is being a minority group member a state of mind?
- According to the realistic conflict theory, how does prejudice arise? Can this theory explain the conditions that pervaded the American South at the turn of this century?
- According to social identity theory, how would a person feel about herself or himself after being given a chance to discriminate against a group to which they do not belong? After a basketball game, would the winning or losing team be more likely to exhibit discriminatory behavior?

*The Cognitive Foundations of Prejudice: Viewing the World Through Stereotypes*

We all have a natural tendency to categorize, to sort objects into groupings. If you are asked what kinds of dishes you have in your kitchen cupboard, for instance, you are unlikely to reply with a list of each individual plate ("Let's see, plate number one is blue and has a chip; number two is also blue and . . ."). Instead, you'll probably respond that you have eight dinner plates, eight salad plates, five bowls, and so forth.

In the same way, we use social categorization to sort out the world of people around us. In particular, we are influenced by such visually conspicuous physical features as race, sex, and age to categorize and form schemas about members of different groups. Even when we have just met someone for the first time, social categorization processes thus provide us with a rich—although not necessarily accurate—set of expectations about what this new acquaintance is like (McCann et al., 1985; Brewer, 1988; Brewer & Lui, 1989).

Cognitive approaches to prejudice suggest that such social categorization processes lie at the heart of prejudice. Social categorization leads to the development of stereotypes—beliefs and expectations about members of a group that are held solely on the basis of their membership in the group. Certainly, social categorization plays an important role in how we view others. For example, once people have been cognitively sorted into a social category, they seem more like other members of that category than is actually the case (Wilder, 1986). Also, people who assert that members of a particular group "all act the same" or "all look alike" may be doing so because they believe there is less variability among members of a group than is actually the case. As a result, people minimize the differences among people who belong to the same classification and—at the same time—overestimate the degree of difference between people who fall into different social categories (Wilder, 1981; Capozza & Nanni, 1986).

One fundamental way in which people are categorized is on the basis of ingroup and outgroup membership. An **ingroup** is a group to which a person feels he or she belongs; an **outgroup** is a group to which a person feels he or she does not belong. For instance, a white male may perceive that he is a part of the ingroup of white males; non-

**ingroup**
a group to which a person feels he or she belongs.

**outgroup**
a group to which a person feels he or she does not belong.

white, non-males would be thought of as outgroup members. The categorization of people into ingroups and outgroups results in several biases.

**INGROUP–OUTGROUP BIAS: THE US-VERSUS-THEM MENTALITY.**    Suppose you were part of a group of ten people that was randomly divided into two groups. How would you react toward the members of your own team, and would you favor them over the members of the other team?

A good deal of research suggests that just on the basis of a random assignment to two teams, most people would come to value their own team and discriminate in favor of them. The reason: the ingroup–outgroup bias. The **ingroup–outgroup bias** is the tendency to hold less favorable views about groups to which we do not belong, while holding more favorable opinions about groups to which we do belong (Wilder, 1986, 1990; Perdue et al., 1990).

In an experimental procedure that is typical for eliciting ingroup–outgroup biases, subjects are divided into two groups, supposedly on the basis of their preferences for one of two artists. In reality, they are randomly assigned to one of the two groups, producing an ingroup to which the person belongs and an outgroup. Later in the experiment, subjects are asked to distribute a sum of money to a member of their own group and to a member of the outgroup, using one of several distribution rules. One method is to follow an equality rule, in which each person receives a similar amount. A second approach that subjects can follow is to maximize the outcome so that the total amount distributed is highest without regard to group membership. Finally, a third potential strategy is to show bias in favor of the ingroup.

Results of studies using this basic procedure identify a consistent pattern: Not only do subjects tend to reward members of their own group at the expense of members of other groups, but they do so in a way that magnifies the differences in reward between the two groups (see, for example, Tajfel, 1982; Wilder, 1990).

What is particularly striking about results such as these is that the ingroups and outgroups are so minimally differentiated from one another. There is no direct, face-to-face interaction between subjects, either within their own group or with members of the other group. The subjects are anonymous, and the categorization is based on a criterion that is unrelated to subjects' earlier behavior. In sum, membership in the groups is determined in a totally arbitrary manner. Given the discriminatory behavior toward outgroups that occurs in situations such as these, it is hardly surprising that the bias against the outgroup would be even stronger when the outgroups have very obvious and salient differences from ingroups.

The ingroup–outgroup bias is consistent with the self-serving bias that we discussed in Chapter 2. People see the success of their group as a manifestation of their own group's abilities, while they see their group's failures as brought about by circumstance. On the other hand, people attribute outgroup success to luck or extraordinary, atypical hard work, while they believe outgroup failure illustrates ineptness (Brewer & Kramer, 1985; Hamilton & Trolier, 1986).

The bias against outgroup members and the favoring of ingroup members may have its roots in basic perceptual phenomena (Turner, 1987). For instance, people pay more attention to stimuli that are unusual, novel, or distinct than to those that are typical, familiar, and nondistinctive. Indeed, categorization leads to a perceptual distortion in which objects in the same category (the ingroup) appear more similar to one another and more other different from objects in other categories (outgroups) than if they had not been categorized (Wilder, 1986; Turner, 1987; Herringer & Garza, 1987).

As a consequence, minority group characteristics (such as race, facial configuration, and dialect or accent) that differentiate the members from majority group members may be particularly salient. And majority group members will use these perceived differences in appearance to infer that other differentiations exist. Ultimately—to people in both the majority and the minority—outgroup members are viewed more negatively and

**ingroup–outgroup bias**
the tendency to hold less favorable views about groups to which we do not belong, while holding more favorable opinions about groups to which we do belong.

ingroup members are seen in a more positive light. The bottom line: Stereotypes about outgroup members may develop through the way in which we categorize different people as we seek to understand and simplify our own social environment.

**OUTGROUP HOMOGENEITY BIAS.**   Sorting people into categories produces several other biases in social perception that lead to stereotyping. For instance, the **outgroup homogeneity bias** is the perception that there is less variability among the members of outgroups than within one's own ingroup. We assume that members of other groups are similar to one another, while we are keenly aware of the differences among members of our own group (Linville & Jones, 1980; Linville, 1982; Linville, Fischer, & Salovey, 1989; Mullen & Hu, 1989).

Why do people assume that the outgroup is so homogeneous? One reason is that they have less complex conceptualizations of outgroup members. Whites asked to describe African-Americans tend to use fewer descriptive dimensions, just as young people have more general and incomplete views of older people. In contrast, people tend to have considerably more strongly differentiated views of members of their own group. If you are Hispanic, all Hispanics don't seem similar; if you're white, all whites don't appear to act alike (Linville, 1982; Judd, Ryan, & Park, 1991; Ostrom et al., 1993).

Another reason for the outgroup homogeneity bias is a lack of contact with outgroup members. If people rarely interact with members of outgroups, they are unlikely to view them as individuals with differing opinions, beliefs, values, and traits. Even when they do interact, the circumstances may be limited, thereby preventing the development of more complex, heterogeneous views of outgroup members (Quattrone, 1986; Judd & Park, 1988).

**ILLUSORY CORRELATION: THE FICTITIOUS MISSING LINK.**   In our search for order in the world, we sometimes mistakenly perceive that a relationship exists between two variables—even when, in reality, there may be little or no relationship at all. **Illusory correlation** occurs when a perceiver overestimates the strength of a relationship between two variables. Illusory correlation is at work when two factors that are only minimally related to one another are perceived as being closely related.

For those not in the military, the outgroup homogeneity bias leads to assumptions that there is relatively little variability among members of that particular outgroup. However, a closer look at the photo illustrates that even superficially a significant degree of variation exists.

**outgroup homogeneity bias**
the perception that there is less variability among the members of outgroups than within one's own ingroup.

**illusory correlation**
the overestimation by a perceiver of the strength of a relationship between two variables.

Illusory correlation helps explain why stereotypes develop and survive, even in the face of little supportive evidence (Mullen & Johnson, 1990; Meehan & Janik, 1990; Hamilton & Rose, 1980). Illusory correlation operates, for example, when people overestimate how often members of minority groups engage in relatively unusual, rare behaviors. Social psychologist David Hamilton (1979; Hamilton & Gifford, 1976) observes that members of a majority group have relatively few interactions with members of minority groups; that negative, undesirable behaviors are fairly infrequent; and that most of our interactions with others are positive, pleasant ones. Furthermore, largely because of their rarity, both interaction with minority group members and negative behavior are highly distinctive when they do occur. Thus, the ingredients for illusory correlation are present: two rare, distinctive variables that are actually only occasionally associated with one another produce the perception that they are actually strongly related to one another.

How likely is such a scenario? Quite plausible, actually. For instance, newspapers may report the racial identity of minority group members who commit crimes, but fail to state the racial identity of majority group members who commit the same type of offense. In the minds of the public, then, crimes (relatively unusual, rare events) get linked with minority group members. The ultimate result is that the illusory correlation bias results in the development or reinforcement of a stereotype about minority group members.

**THE ULTIMATE ATTRIBUTION ERROR: HEADS I WIN, TAILS YOU LOSE.**    In extreme cases, stereotypes lead people to make inaccurate attributions regarding the causes of both minority and majority group members' behavior. More specifically, social psychologist Thomas Pettigrew (1979; Jemmott, Pettigrew, & Johnson, 1983) suggests that people holding stereotypes are prone to the ultimate attribution error, which is an extension of the fundamental attribution error that we discussed in Chapter 2. You will recall that the fundamental attribution error refers to the tendency of observers to overattribute behavior of others to stable traits and dispositions and the corresponding failure to recognize the importance of situational factors. The **ultimate attribution error** goes several steps further. It suggests that when people holding strong stereotypes view negative behavior on the part of a minority group member, they will attribute it to dispositional characteristics; but when they see a minority group member engaging in positive behavior, they will attribute the behavior to situational factors.

Hence, when a minority group member acts in an undesirable way, the attribution is something on the order of "that's the way those people are" or "they're born like that." But the view is different when a minority group member is seen engaging in desirable behavior. In order to be consistent with their negative stereotype, people go through some cognitive acrobatics to find an attribution that fits their view. It's not all that hard, it turns out: There are at least four ways in which a person holding a stereotype can approach the problem (Pettigrew, 1979; Jemmott, Pettigrew, & Johnson, 1983; Rothbart & John, 1985):

**ultimate attribution error** the tendency among people holding strong stereotypes to attribute negative behavior on the part of a minority group member to dispositional characteristics, and correspondingly, to attribute positive behavior on the part of a minority group member to situational factors.

1. *The exceptional case.* First, the positive act can be viewed as an exceptional case, and the person can be differentiated from other members of the minority group ("He's the exception that proves the rule," or "She's so different from most other African-Americans"). In fact, the perceiver might even perceive the positive behavior as deviant in some ways.

2. *Special advantage or luck.* A second way in which a person holding a negative stereotype can explain positive minority group behavior is by deciding that the behavior is due to some kind of special advantage or simply to luck ("She must have gotten into medical school because of affirmative action" or "What a lucky person to get the job").

3. *The situational context.* There is a third way in which a person holding negative stereotypes can explain positive acts on the part of minority group members: The actions are seen as being caused by situational factors outside the control of the individual, rather than by some personality or dispositional factor ("Anyone in that position would have done well"). In other words, the minority person's membership in the minority group is overlooked as a

causal explanation; the particular role or position that the person occupies is assumed to be the explanation for his or her behavior.

4.  *Extraordinary motivation and effort.* Finally, an observer may assume that a successful minority group member has shown disproportionate, unusually high, and perhaps even excessive motivation to succeed and overcome minority membership. In this view, the underlying negative characteristics of the minority group are still present, but exceptional motivation has enabled this particular individual to overcome his or her "true" state. Curiously, though, the success of minority group members allows people holding the stereotype to deny that prejudice and discrimination have negative consequences for the targets of prejudice, since some people do manage to be successful.

These four attributions for desirable minority group member behavior clearly represent a damned-if-you-do, damned-if-you- don't, no-win situation. If minority group members engage in a negative act, their behavior is seen as a confirmation of an underlying flaw of that minority. If the behavior is positive, any one of the four unflattering causes will be used to avoid acknowledging the value of the individual and his or her behavior.

The operation of the ultimate attribution error can be seen in a study by Donald M. Taylor and Vaishna Jaggi (1974). In the experiment, a group of Hindu office clerks in southern India were asked to choose the reasons for the behavior of a person described in a short passage. The passage described a shopkeeper being either generous or cheating a customer; a teacher rewarding or punishing a student; a person helping or ignoring an injured individual; or a householder sheltering or ignoring a person caught in the rain. For each situation, subjects were asked to choose a reason for the behavior that represented either a primarily internal attribution (related to personal, dispositional characteristics) or a primarily external attribution (related to the situation).

The crucial variable in the study was whether the person in the passage was identified as a member of the observer's own ethnic group (which was Hindu) or was described as a member of another group (Muslim) which was often the target of discrimination and negative stereotypes in southern India at that time.

As shown in Figure 3-3, the findings were clear. When the person in the passage was identified as a member of the observer's own group (Hindu), positive behavior was generally attributed to internal causes, while negative behavior tended to be perceived as due only minimally to internal causes. In contrast, when the person was a member of the

**FIGURE 3–3   The Ultimate Attribution Error** When Hindu subjects read about positive behavior on the part of an in-group (Hindu) actor, they made internal attributions, while negative behaviors were not seen as indicative of internal characteristics. In contrast, attributions were made in the opposite direction when the actor was an out-group member. Percentages refer to percentage of subjects making internal attributions.   *(Source:* Adapted from Taylor & Jaggi, 1974, Table 2.)

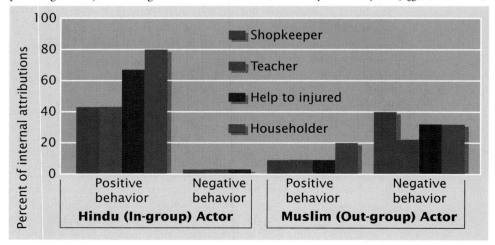

other (Muslim) group, positive behavior was attributed to internal causes much less frequently than was negative behavior.

Such findings unequivocally demonstrate the ultimate attribution error, and they illustrate its treacherous nature. They suggest that no matter how exemplary the behavior of a minority group member is, people holding negative stereotypes may not alter their underlying negative views of the group to which the member belongs (Wilder, 1984). The ultimate attribution error puts the target of prejudice in a clear, no-win situation from which escape is seemingly impossible: Nothing can be done to change an observer's evaluation.

> # REVIEW & RETHINK

## Review

- Cognitive approaches to prejudice suggest that social categorization processes lead to stereotypes.
- One primary categorization is the distinction between ingroups and outgroups.
- Among the cognitive biases relating to prejudice are the ingroup–outgroup bias, the outgroup homogeneity bias, illusory correlation, and the ultimate attribution error.

## Rethink

- What are the characteristics that our culture commonly uses to form ingroups and outgroups? Are these the only characteristics that logically can be used to form such groups?
- What is the outgroup homogeneity bias? Is it possible that such a bias could be used to reduce prejudice?
- What is the ultimate attribution error, and how does it differ from the fundamental attribution error?
- How might illusory correlation affect attitudes toward women in contemporary culture?

# RACISM AND SEXISM: THE CONSEQUENCES OF PREJUDICE

*When Philip McAdoo, a 22-year-old senior at the University of North Carolina, stopped one day to see a friend who worked on his college campus, a receptionist asked if he would autograph a basketball for her son. Because he was African-American and tall, "she just assumed that I was on the basketball team," recounted McAdoo.*

*Jasme Kelly, an African-American sophomore at the same college, had a similar story to tell. When she went to see a friend at a fraternity house, the student who answered the door asked if she was there to apply for the job of cook.*

*White students, too, find racial relations difficult and in some ways forbidding. For instance, Jenny Johnson, a white 20-year-old junior, finds even the most basic conversation with African-American classmates difficult. She describes a conversation in which African-American friends "jump at my throat because I used the word 'black' instead of African-American. There is just such a huge barrier that it's really hard . . . to have a normal discussion" (Sanoff & Minerbrook, 1993, p. 58).*

Even at colleges with significant minority populations, members of minority groups often face racism on a daily basis.

The consequences of prejudice can be seen not only in the blaring headlines of conspicuous, flagrant racial incidents. They are also the stuff of daily life for members of groups that are the victims of prejudice and discrimination. And majority group members, too, are affected by a world afflicted with prejudice and discrimination.

We turn now to a discussion of two of the major manifestations of prejudice: racism and sexism. **Racism** is prejudice directed at people because of their race; **sexism** is prejudice directed at women or men because of their gender. Although, lamentably, there are many other types of "isms" that we could consider, such as ageism (prejudice against the elderly), racial and sexual prejudice represent the problems of prejudice and discrimination that have been most often addressed by social psychologists.

To make matters worse, the problems of racism and sexism are not likely to go away—although the targets of prejudice may ultimately shift in the future as the population distribution undergoes major changes. For instance, current projections of the population makeup of the United States suggest that by the year 2000, non-Hispanic whites will make up less than 82 percent of the population, and by the year 2050, the non-Hispanic white population will decline to less than 53 percent of the total population of the United States (see Figure 3-4).

**racism**
prejudice directed at people because of their race.

**sexism**
prejudice directed at people because of their gender.

## Racism: Shades of Hatred

In his classic novel, *Invisible Man*, Ralph Ellison, an African-American, wrote, "I am an invisible man. I am a man of substance, of flesh and bone, fiber and liquids—and I might even be said to possess a mind. I am invisible, understand, simply because people refuse to see me" (Ellison, 1952, p. 3).

More than 40 years later, there is still an unfortunate truth to Ellison's words. Despite enormous strides in the civil rights arena, including an end to legal segregation

**FIGURE 3-4    U.S. Racial and Ethnic Population Projections** Current projections of the population makeup of the United States suggest that by the year 2000, the proportion of non-Hispanic whites will decline as the proportion of minority group members increases. *(Source:* U.S. Census Bureau, 1993.)

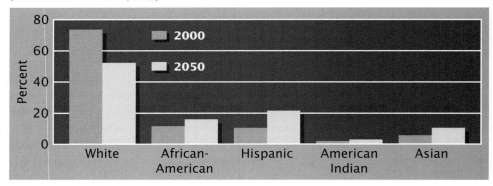

in the United States, African-Americans still fall behind whites on many crucial measures of economic and social success. Only half as many African-Americans as whites have completed college; the African-American unemployment rate is more than double that of whites; and three times as many African-Americans as whites live below the poverty level (Bureau of the Census, 1993).

Curiously, such grim social and economic facts fly in the face of data regarding white society's stated views regarding African-Americans, which, at least on the surface, have become considerably more positive. For example, studies of stereotypes begun in the 1930s and continued through subsequent decades show that many of the more blatant negative views of African-Americans, which people admitted freely in the first half of this century, have been moderated. In general, when directly asked, fewer people feel that African-Americans as a group harbor such negative traits as "laziness" or "ignorance"—stereotypes that were believed and freely admitted as recently as the 1950s (Katz & Braly, 1933; Karlins, Coffman, & Walters, 1969; Dovidio & Gaertner, 1986). Furthermore, whites tend to feel that race relations between whites and African-Americans have been improving—a view not shared by African-Americans, who tend to think just the opposite, as indicated in Figure 3-5 (McQueen, 1991).

**MODERN RACISM.**    But has the white majority, by and large, really become less prejudiced? Some social psychologists suggest that despite the apparent reduction of visible stereotyping of African-Americans and other racial minorities, a new kind of racism has taken its place. According to social psychologists Samuel Gaertner and John Dovidio, overt racism has been replaced by modern racism. **Modern racism** is a subtle form of prejudice in which people appear, on the surface, not to harbor prejudice, but actually do hold racist attitudes. According to this view, if we scratch the apparently nonracist surface of many people, we will find bigotry lurking beneath (Gaertner & Dovidio, 1986; McConahay, 1986; Dovidio & Gaertner, 1991).

Modern racism arises because people often hold several competing beliefs and values. They want to see themselves as part of the mainstream of society and as fair, humanitarian, and egalitarian (Katz & Hass, 1988). At the same time, though, they may still hold somewhat negative views of members of groups other than their own. In most cases, they keep their prejudice under wraps, but when placed in a situation in which they are given social support for racism, they are willing to express, and sometimes to act on, their unfavorable opinions.

For instance, most people avoid publicly endorsing overtly racist statements, because of social pressures against such behavior. But when more subtle measurement

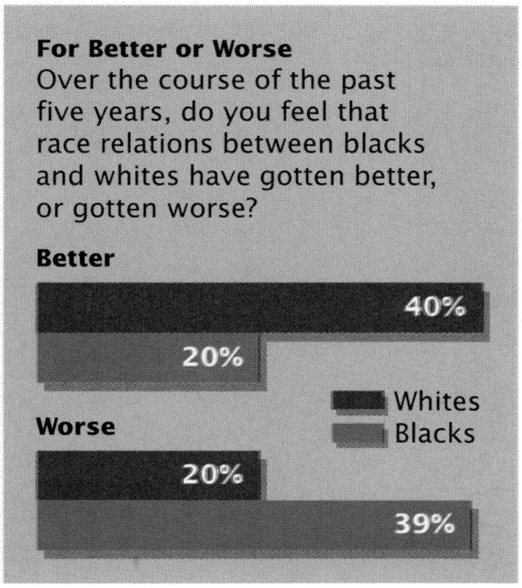

**modern racism**
a subtle form of prejudice in which people appear, on the surface, not to harbor prejudice, but who actually do hold racist attitudes.

**For Better or Worse**
Over the course of the past five years, do you feel that race relations between blacks and whites have gotten better, or gotten worse?

**Better**
40%
20%

■ Whites
■ Blacks

**Worse**
20%
39%

**FIGURE 3-5 Improvements in Race Relations Are in the Eyes of the Beholder**
The views of whites and African-Americans are almost the mirror image of one another. Whites tend to feel that race relations between whites and African-Americans have been improving, while African-Americans tend to think they have become worse.
(*Source:* Wall Street Journal/NBC News Poll, reported in McQueen, 1991)

techniques are used, it becomes clear that many negative stereotypes of African-Americans and members of other racial groups remain in force (Pettigrew, 1989; McConahay, Hardee, & Batts, 1981).

Consider, for example, the results of a large-scale survey of whites, African-Americans, and Hispanics conducted in 300 United States communities in the late 1980s (Smith, 1990). To measure prejudice, the study employed a novel technique that circumvented people's desire not to appear prejudiced. In the survey, participants were asked to indicate whether people in each of several racial groups were closer to one or the other end of a series of seven-point scales. For instance, survey respondents were asked whether members of a racial group were closer to scale end-points marked "hard-working" (at one end of the scale) or "lazy" (at the opposite end of the scale). By comparing the ratings given to the various racial groups, the researchers were able to determine which racial groups were the targets of the greatest stereotyping. As shown in Figure 3-6, compared with their beliefs about whites, survey respondents held quite negative stereotypes about members of each of the three racial groups studied (African-Americans, Asians, and Hispanics). For instance, 77 percent of respondents thought that African-Americans were more likely than whites to "prefer to live off welfare." Overall, African-Americans, Asians, and Hispanics were seen as lazier, more prone to violence, less intelligent, and less patriotic than whites. In sum, when their underlying beliefs are tapped, people express negative stereotypes about members of minority groups—an example of modern racism.

Modern racism may also account for the results of polls that ask about the use of affirmative action programs. In general, a majority of people, both white and African-American, express favorable attitudes toward affirmative action (see Figure 3-7). But when alternate wording is used, the results can be quite different. For instance, when another poll addressed the same issue but expressed "affirmative action" as racial "preferences," the proportion of people in favor dropped substantially (Brennan, 1991).

**IS RACISM INEVITABLE? A LESS PESSIMISTIC VIEW.**    Although the modern racism view suggests that racism is inevitable and that if you scratch the surface of most people, you'll find racists lurking beneath, some social psychologists think this may be an overly pessimistic view. For instance, social psychologist Patricia Devine suggests that we should not assume that just because people sometimes experience prejudiced thoughts, they

**FIGURE 3-6  Prejudice: Alive and Well in the United States** Compared with their beliefs about whites, survey respondents viewed minorities more negatively on each of the characteristics illustrated in the figure. The higher the percentage, the more respondents who felt the characterization (such as "poor," "lazy," and so forth) was more appropriate for a minority group than for whites.    *(Source: Smith, 1990.)*

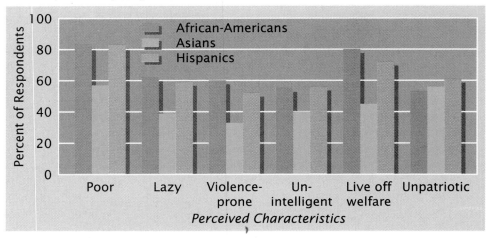

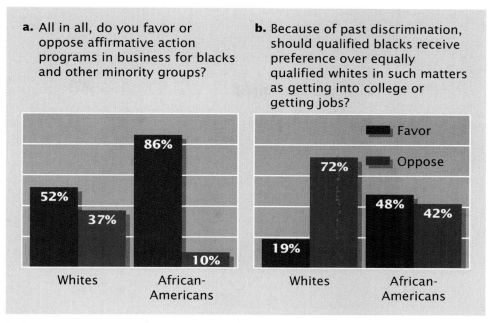

**a.** All in all, do you favor or oppose affirmative action programs in business for blacks and other minority groups?

**b.** Because of past discrimination, should qualified blacks receive preference over equally qualified whites in such matters as getting into college or getting jobs?

**FIGURE 3–7    Does Modern Racism Account for What People Say They Think about Affirmative Action?** A majority of both whites and African-Americans express favorable attitudes toward affirmative action (as seen in a). But when alternate wording is used, the results can be quite different. For instance, when another poll addressed the same issue but expressed "affirmative action" as racial "preference," the proportion of people in favor dropped substantially, (see b). *(Source:* Brennan, 1991.*)*

should automatically be branded as racist. Instead, she suggests that even those who completely reject prejudice may sometimes experience unintentional prejudice-like thoughts or feelings due to prior learning (Devine, 1989; Devine et al., 1991).

In this view, then, racism is something akin to a lingering bad habit that surfaces despite people's best efforts to avoid it. This view is based on a critical distinction between automatic versus controlled information processing (Shiffrin & Schneider, 1977; Shiffrin & Dumais, 1981). Automatic information processing is largely involuntary; it involves the unintentional activation of well-learned responses found in memory. Such processing occurs in spite of voluntary efforts to suppress or circumvent it. In contrast, controlled information processing involves voluntary, intentional processes and relates to decision making and problem solving.

Automatic and controlled processing can operate independently of one another (see Logan & Cowan, 1984; Bargh, 1989a). Consequently, it is possible that in the presence of a member of a minority group, a person may automatically activate racist stereotypes about minority groups, learned through society's stereotypic vision of minorities. Furthermore, given the pervasiveness of racial stereotypes in society, they can be activated automatically by both high- and low-prejudice people. For example, automatic processing may activate thoughts that minorities are often involved in criminal activities—a frequent societal stereotype—regardless of whether a person is or is not prejudiced.

At the same time, though, more controlled processes will likely produce different consequences for high- and low-prejudice individuals. High-prejudice people are likely to have strongly held beliefs that are congruent with the cultural stereotypes, leading them to show biased behavior even when controlled processing subsequently occurs. For instance, because they hold beliefs congruent with the societal stereotype that minorities are often involved in crime, they are likely to show biased behavior even if controlled processing occurs.

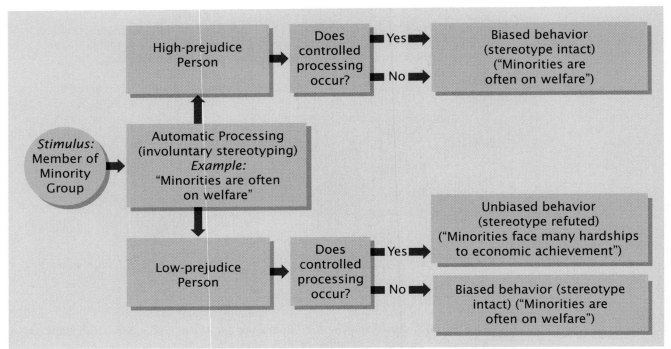

**FIGURE 3-8    Prejudice and Automatic and Controlled Processing** According to Patricia Devine, both high- and low-prejudice people engage in automatic information processing that makes them susceptible to societal stereotypes. However, when low-prejudice persons engage in controlled processing, unbiased behavior is the consequence.    *(Source:* Based on Devine, 1989; Devine et al., 1991.*)*

In contrast, low-prejudice individuals are likely to hold beliefs discrepant from the stereotype. When controlled processing occurs for low-prejudice individuals, then, there will be a conflict between automatic and controlled processing (see Figure 3–8).

How is this discrepancy manifested? When unprejudiced people are permitted the luxury of time and attention to their thoughts, they are apt to use more controlled cognitive processes. Ultimately, the use of controlled processing allows those who are relatively unprejudiced to react with little or no racism to situations involving minority group members. On the other hand, in situations in which controlled, thoughtful processing is obstructed or impeded in low-prejudice individuals, or where such people are not terribly attentive, the underlying automatic process may lead to behavior that shows prejudice—even though they are relatively unprejudiced individuals (Devine, 1989).

It should be clear that this view of prejudice does not see racism as inevitable in our society. Instead, it suggests that when people are more attentive and thoughtful, they can overcome any underlying negative stereotypes they may have learned as part of their membership in a society that makes such vast distinctions among racial groups (Monteith, 1993). It also raises the possibility that even these underlying, automatic processes are subject to change. If society as a whole is able to transmit less racist messages, it seems plausible that the production of negative stereotypes will not be an automatic cognitive reaction.

*Sexism: Prejudice and Gender*    Upon learning of the birth of a child, what's the first question you're likely to ask? For almost everyone, it's "Boy or girl?"

In fact, "It's a boy" or "It's a girl" are almost always the initial words spoken in the delivery room upon the emergence of an infant into the world. And as soon as the gender of the child becomes known, other things quickly ensue: girls are wrapped in pink, boys in blue; the style of clothing differs for boys and girls; and the toys given to boys and girls differ. From the moment of birth, boys and girls are treated quite differently (Malatesta & Lamb, 1987; Fogel, Toda, & Kawai, 1988).

The type of clothing used to dress boys and girls differs significantly, starting from the moment of birth and continuing throughout childhood.

**GENDER ROLES AND STEREOTYPES.**    The difference in the way boys and girls are treated is a result of **gender roles**, the set of expectations, defined by society, that indicate what is appropriate behavior for men and women.

If the gender roles for men and women were similar, they would have only a minimal impact upon men's and women's lives. However, the contrary is true: The expectations are so different that they often lead to bias and stereotyping. Such stereotypes produce sexism, negative attitudes, and behavior toward people based on their sex (Bem, 1984, 1993).

In our society, stereotypes about males and females fall into quite consistent, well-established patterns. For instance, a classic study in the 1970s identified several traditional stereotypes for males and females. In the study, a group of male and female college students were given a list of traits and asked to indicate which were more appropriate for the typical man and which applied more to the typical female (Broverman et al., 1972). As you can see in Figure 3-9, results showed that the traits fell into two clusters, one

**gender roles**
the set of expectations, defined by society, that indicate what is appropriate behavior for men and women.

| FIGURE 3-9    Common Stereotypes About Men and Women | |
| --- | --- |
| **TRAITS PERCEIVED AS CHARACTERISTIC OF MEN** | **TRAITS PERCEIVED AS CHARACTERISTIC OF WOMEN** |
| Aggressive | Talkative |
| Independent | Tactful |
| Unemotional | Gentle |
| Self-confident | Religious |
| Very objective | Aware of feelings of others |
| Likes math and science | Interested in own appearance |
| Ambitious | Neat |
| Active | Quiet |
| Competitive | Strong need for security |
| Logical | Enjoys art and literature |
| Worldly | Easily expresses tender feelings |
| Direct | Does not use harsh language |
| Adventurous | Dependent |

*Source:* Adapted from Broverman et al., 1972.

relating to competence and one relating to warmth and expressiveness. Traits relating to warmth and expressivity were judged most appropriate for females, while competency traits were seen as most appropriate for males. Because Western society traditionally holds competence in higher esteem than warmth and expressivity, such differences in perception favor males over females.

Subsequent research has shown the persistence of gender role stereotyping. Although we might expect that the growth of the women's movement and feminism would have blunted the amount of stereotyping, this in fact has not happened. Differences between what is expected of men and of women remain (Deaux & Lewis, 1984; Werner & LaRussa, 1985; Signorella & Frieze, 1989).

Furthermore, although both men and women are perceived as having various positive traits, this has not meant that men and women are seen as equals. Numerous studies suggest that men are held in higher esteem than women (Eagly & Mladinic, 1989; Williams & Best, 1990). For instance, one 25-nation study found that certain adjective descriptions were similar across cultures: Women were seen as sentimental, submissive, and superstitious, while men were seen as adventurous, forceful, and independent (see Figure 3-10).

In addition, there were differences based on the dominant religion of the country. In predominantly Catholic countries, women were seen more favorably, whereas in Muslim countries women were perceived in a more negative light. In every country studied,

## FIGURE 3-10    Descriptive Adjectives Applied to Men and Women

The Williams and Best (1990) study found that the following descriptive terms were most closely associated with men or with women, respectively, in at least 20 of the 25 countries examined.

### ADJECTIVES ASSOCIATED WITH MALES

| | | | |
|---|---|---|---|
| Active | Daring | Inventive | Rude |
| Adventurous | Determined | Lazy | Self-confident |
| Aggressive | Disorderly | Logical | Serious |
| Ambitious | Dominant | Loud | Severe |
| Arrogant | Egotistical | Masculine | Showing initiative |
| Assertive | Energetic | Opportunistic | Stern |
| Autocratic | Enterprising | Progressive | Stolid |
| Clear-thinking | Forceful | Rational | Strong |
| Coarse | Hardheaded | Realistic | Unemotional |
| Courageous | Hardhearted | Reckless | Wise |
| Cruel | Independent | Robust | |

### ADJECTIVES ASSOCIATED WITH FEMALES

| | |
|---|---|
| Affected | Gentle |
| Affectionate | Mild |
| Attractive | Sensitive |
| Charming | Sentimental |
| Curious | Sexy |
| Dependent | Softhearted |
| Dreamy | Submissive |
| Emotional | Superstitious |
| Fearful | Talkative |
| Feminine | Weak |

*Source:* Adapted from Williams, J. E., and Best, D. L. (1990). Measuring sex stereotypes: A multi-nation study. Newbury Park, CA: Sage.

gender stereotypes emerged early, in most cases before the age of five, and they tended to be fully developed by the time children began adolescence (Williams & Best, 1990).

Gender stereotyping is also mirrored in people's perception of which occupations are most appropriate for men and women. For example, even though women are an increasingly large presence in the work force, they are still perceived as best suited to jobs traditionally filled by women: secretary, teacher, cashier, and librarian. Men, in contrast, are viewed as better suited for such professions as doctor, police officer, and construction worker (Gettys & Cann, 1981; Eccles, 1987; Bridges, 1988). (For more on gender stereotyping in the workplace, see the accompanying Social Psychology at Work feature.)

## SOCIAL PSYCHOLOGY AT WORK

## *HOPKINS V. PRICE WATERHOUSE:* GENDER ROLE STEREOTYPING ON TRIAL

In many ways, she was the ideal worker. An employee at one of the largest accounting firms in the country, Price Waterhouse, she had brought in $25 million worth of new business. She produced more billable hours than anyone else at her level. She was viewed as hard-working, driven, and exacting.

But largely because Ann Hopkins was a "she" and not a "he," she was not promoted to the rank of firm partner. At least that was the determination made by the United States judicial system, which found that "gender-based stereotyping played a role in this decision" (*Hopkins v. Price Waterhouse*, 1990, p. 1).

Executives at Price Waterhouse disagreed that sex discrimination had played a role in their decision to deny her promotion to partner. Instead, they said that she had interpersonal problems, labeling her as "macho," saying she needed a "course at charm school," and claiming that she "overcompensated for being a woman." She had received warnings that her chances for promotion were in jeopardy and that she could benefit if she would "walk more femininely, talk more femininely, dress more femininely, wear make-up, have her hair styled, and wear jewelry" (*Hopkins v. Price Waterhouse*, 1985, p. 1117).

Because she did not fit the female stereotype, Ann Hopkins's employers did not promote her to partner—despite her exemplary job performance.

According to social psychologist Susan Fiske, who testified as an expert witness at one of several sex discrimination trials involving Hopkins and Price Waterhouse, such criticisms reflected blatant sex stereotyping. During Hopkins's first trial, Fiske presented evidence that the conditions at Price Waterhouse were ripe for sex stereotyping.

In her testimony, Fiske noted that stereotyping was most likely to occur when a victim is isolated and in a unique position in an otherwise homogeneous environment. This certainly was true at Price Waterhouse: Only 2 percent of the partners were women, and the number of women in the profession as a whole was low. In addition, the traits stereotypically thought to characterize women in general do not fit with the aggressiveness and competitiveness required of a manager. Stereotyping is also likely when the criteria used for evaluation are ambiguous and when the information about a person is open to multiple interpretations and is limited (Fiske et al., 1991).

Fiske noted that for these and several other reasons, Hopkins was the victim of stereotyping. The courts agreed. In its ruling, the U.S. Supreme Court wrote the following:

> In the specific context of sex stereotyping, an employer who acts on the basis of a belief that a woman cannot be aggressive, or that she must not be, has acted on the basis of gender. . . . We are beyond the day when an employer could evaluate employees by assuming or insisting that they matched the stereotype associated with their group. . . . An employer who objects to aggressiveness in women but whose positions require this trait places women in an intolerable Catch 22: out of a job if they behave aggressively and out of a job if they don't. [The law] lifts women out of this bind. (*Price Waterhouse v. Hopkins*, 1989, pp. 1790-1791)

As Fiske et al. (1991) note, "One could not have asked for a better understanding of the psychology of stereotyping" than that shown by the Supreme Court. It also illustrates another point—that the experimental and theoretical work conducted by social psychologists can have a substantial impact on areas critical to social policy.

**communal professions**
professions based on relationships.

**agentic professions**
professions based on accomplishing tasks.

According to social psychologists Alice Eagly and Valerie Steffen (1984), women are seen as most appropriately filling **communal professions**—that is, professions associated with relationships. In contrast, men are perceived as best suited for **agentic professions**—professions that are associated with getting things accomplished. Traditionally, professions relating to communal concerns are of lower prestige and are lower paying than are agentically oriented professions (Eagly & Steffen, 1984, 1986).

Society's messages are heard by both men and women. For instance, when first-year college students are asked to indicate their likely career choice, women are unlikely to indicate they will enter traditionally male-dominated careers, such as engineering or computer programming. Furthermore, when asked to guess their entering and peak salaries, women expect to be paid less than men (Major & Konar, 1984; Glick, Zion, & Nelson, 1988; Martin, 1989; CIRE, 1990). Such expectations are not unwarranted: On average, women earn 70 cents for every one dollar that men earn, and—as can be seen in Figure 3-11—in some professions the discrepancy is even greater. Women who are minority group members fare even worse: African-American women earn 62 cents for every dollar men make, while Hispanic women earn just 54 cents for every dollar men earn (U.S. Bureau of Labor Statistics, 1993).

**SOURCES OF GENDER STEREOTYPES.**    Those blue and pink baby blankets that male and female babies are wrapped in at birth are just the start of a lifetime of being treated dif-

**FIGURE 3-11   Women's Wages Remain Lower Than Men's** Women's salaries still do not match those of men, even within the same profession. This graph shows women's median wages in a given profession as a proportion of the wages that men receive.    *(Source:* U.S. Bureau of Labor Statistics, 1992.*)*

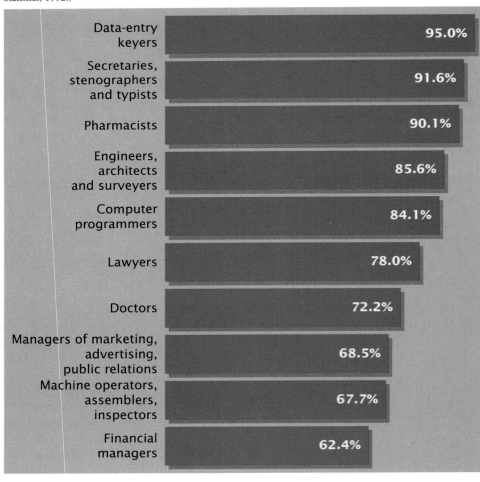

ferently because of one's sex. For instance, middle class mothers speak more to their female children than to their male children, while fathers play more roughly with their infant sons than with their daughters. Even though the extent of behavioral differences in the way parents treat their sons and daughters may not be great, there is little doubt that adults, in general, treat male babies and children differently from female ones (Houston, 1983; Eccles, Jacobs, & Harold, 1990; Lytton & Romney, 1991).

It is not difficult to see how such differences in treatment are translated into differences in differential gender schemas. According to social psychologist Sandra Bem (1987), a **gender schema** is the cognitive framework that organizes information relevant to gender. Gender schemas are particularly powerful, as sex represents one of the most salient and potent social categories that people employ (Stangor et al., 1992).

Bem suggests that gender schemas are learned early in life, and, like the other schemas that we discussed in Chapter 2, they provide a lens through which people view the world. She also suggests that there are individual differences in how widely gender schema are applied. For some people, gender schemas are relatively less developed, and these individuals are more apt to employ non-gender-related schema to social settings. Others, though, use gender schema far more readily (Bem, 1982, 1983, 1993).

One experiment, conducted by Deborrah Frable and Sandra Bem (1985), clearly illustrates differences in how people use gender schema. In the study, subjects were first categorized into people whose gender schemas were well developed and strong and those who had relatively weak, circumscribed gender schemas. Next, all subjects listened to a group discussion.

When later asked to recall who said what in the discussion, the subjects with the strongest gender schemas were apt to confuse people of the opposite sex with one another (see Figure 3-12). On the other hand, subjects with less pronounced gender schemas demonstrated no propensity to mix up people of the opposite sex. Apparently, people with extremely strong gender schemas were categorizing group discussion members on the basis of sex and to the exclusion of other factors that would have permitted them to see the group discussion members as individuals.

How do we reduce the detrimental consequences of evaluating people according to gender schema? According to Sandra Bem, one way is to encourage children to be **androgynous**, a state in which gender roles encompass characteristics thought typical of both sexes. For instance, androgynous males may sometimes be assertive and pushy (typically thought of as male-appropriate traits), but they may also behave with warmth and tenderness (typically seen as female-appropriate traits).

**gender schema**
the cognitive framework that organizes information relevant to gender.

**androgynous**
a state in which gender roles encompass characteristics thought typical of both sexes.

Gender schemas are powerful, sometimes causing teachers to inadvertently pay more attention to boys than to girls in their classroom.

# Doonesbury

BY GARRY TRUDEAU

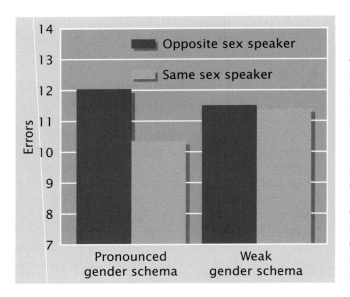

**FIGURE 3-12 Do Members of the Opposite Sex All Look Alike? It Depends on Who's Looking** When subjects with strong gender schemas were asked to recall the gender of people in a discussion, they were more likely to confuse members of the opposite sex than those of their own sex—suggesting that members of the opposite sex "all looked alike" to them. In contrast, those with weak gender schemas were no more likely to confuse members of the opposite sex than those of their own sex. *(Source:* Based on Frable & Bem, 1985.)

**contact hypothesis**
the theory that under the appropriate conditions, direct contact between hostile groups will reduce prejudice.

**jigsaw technique**
a procedure for increasing intergroup interaction in which people are given a small amount of information and then required to teach the material to a set of partners in a group.

Similarly, androgynous females may behave with empathy and tenderness, but also may be competitive, aggressive, and independent. The key point is that androgynous people do not react to individual situations on the basis of traditional expectations about what constitutes masculine or feminine behavior. Instead, they draw upon both sets of characteristics, behaving in a way that is appropriate for a given situation.

The idea of the androgynous man and woman does not mean that men and women should be expected to behave in exactly the same way, nor that the differences between men and women, of which there are many, should be altogether minimized or ignored. Similarly, it does not imply that the use of gender schemas necessarily leads to sexism. What the concept does suggest is that rather than acting in ways that society deems appropriate for men and women, people should behave in a human way, based on freely made choices.

---

# THE INFORMED CONSUMER OF SOCIAL PSYCHOLOGY

# REDUCING PREJUDICE AND DISCRIMINATION

Are prejudice and discrimination destined to color our interactions with others, or are there ways we can reduce them? Social psychologists have devised several means of reducing prejudice and discrimination against minority groups in society. Among the most important:

• *Creating opportunities for contact between members of majority and minority groups.* No strategy for reducing prejudice has received greater attention than the idea that contact between a prejudiced person and the target of prejudice will lead to more favorable attitudes (Allport, 1954; Miller & Brewer, 1984; Stephan, 1985). For instance, one rationale for school desegregation is that contact in schools will lead to a reduction in prejudice.

It turns out, though, that not just any contact will do. For instance, school desegregation has not proven to invariably produce reductions in prejudice. In fact, when emotions

run high, such as has been the case in some cases of court-ordered desegregation, there can actually be an increase in prejudice (Stephan, 1986; Gerard, 1988).

Does this mean we should give up on attempting to produce more integrated schools and to increase the frequency of contact between people of different races? Not at all. According to the **contact hypothesis**, direct contact between hostile groups will reduce prejudice only under certain conditions. Decades of research have identified what such "certain conditions" include. They encompass contact between people who have relatively equal status; who have close, intimate contact; and who cooperate with one another or who are dependent on one another. Hence, a prejudiced white woman who hires a Hispanic maid is unlikely to surrender her prejudices on the basis of such contact. On the other hand, a prejudiced white woman who works with a Hispanic on a committee to improve children's schools is considerably more likely to show reductions in prejudice.

Why can contact be effective? The answer is in the changes that can be accomplished in schemas regarding stereotyped groups. As the degree of contact increases, schemas become more detailed, accurate, and individualized (Gaertner et al., 1990; Desforges et al., 1991).

• *Using the jigsaw technique.* The jigsaw technique is a classroom procedure for increasing intergroup interaction. Based on the way that a jigsaw puzzle is constructed by taking small pieces and placing them together, students who participate in the **jigsaw technique** are given a small amount of information and then required to teach the material to a set of partners in a group. When the information from all the students is put together, it forms a meaningful whole, enabling the group to understand the lesson in its entirety. Several studies have shown that the jigsaw technique not only results in effective learning, but also promotes self-esteem, interpersonal attrac-

tion, and empathy for members of different ethnic and racial groups (Aronson et al., 1978; Aronson & Bridgeman, 1979; Aronson, 1988).

• *Making humanitarian values more conspicuous.* Rather than hoping that contact will bring about changes in stereotypes and schemas indirectly, there is a more direct approach—illustrating how values regarding equality and fair treatment conflict with negative stereotyping. For example, in some experimental studies, people are forced to confront the fact that the positive values they hold regarding equality and freedom are not consistent with their negative perceptions of minority group members (see, for example, Rokeach, 1971). When such inconsistencies are pointed out, prejudice is reduced. Similarly, when people overhear others strongly condemning racism, they are considerably more apt to make strong statements themselves against prejudice. Apparently, situations in which public standards, or norms, against racism are more prominent—such as public condemnations—can reduce its occurrence (Blanchard, Lilly, & Vaughn, 1991; Fiske & Von Hendy, 1992).

---

## ▶ REVIEW & RETHINK

### Review

• Racism is prejudice directed at people because of their race. Although overt indications of racism have declined, modern racism is still strong even if more subtle.

• Sexism—prejudice directed at people because of their gender—arises from strong gender roles.

• Among the means of reducing prejudice and discrimination are increasing contact between majority and minority group members, using the jigsaw technique, and making humanitarian values more salient.

### Rethink

• Does the existence of modern racism suggest that there has been little progress in the reduction of prejudice toward minority group members?

• Does the projected increase in the proportion of minority group members have implications for the amount of prejudice in society?

• Are the ways of reducing prejudice that have been discussed equally applicable to combating racism *and* sexism, or is there something unique about one or the other type of prejudice?

---

# LOOKING BACK

◀ ◀ ◀ ◀ ◀ ◀ ◀ ◀ ◀ ◀ ◀ ◀ ◀ ◀ ◀ ◀ ◀ ◀ ◀ ◀ ◀ ◀ ◀

### *What are the distinctions between prejudice, discrimination, and stereotyping?*

1. Prejudice refers to the negative or positive evaluations or judgments of members of a group that are based primarily on membership in the group. A stereotype is a set of beliefs and expectations about members of a group that is held solely on the basis of their membership in the group. Discrimination is the behavioral manifestation of stereotypes and prejudice.

2. Prejudice is often targeted at minority groups, which are groups in which members have significantly less power, control, and influence over their own lives than do members of a dominant majority.

### *How is prejudice learned and maintained?*

3. Social learning explanations of prejudice suggest that people develop prejudice and stereo-types about members of various groups through direct reinforcement and teaching. In contrast, realistic conflict theory suggests that prejudice is the outcome of direct competition between members of different groups over valued but limited resources. Competition alone, though, does not always produce prejudice; the presence of relative deprivation, the sense that one lacks a desired resource in comparison with another group, may be crucial.

4. Social identity theory states that people use group membership as a source of pride and self-worth, leading them to inflate the positive aspects of their own group and belittle groups to which they do not belong.

### *How do stereotypes provide the cognitive foundations for prejudice and discrimination?*

5. Cognitive approaches to prejudice suggest that social categorization processes lead to stereotypes. One primary categorization is in terms of ingroups (a group to which a person feels he or she belongs) and outgroups (a group of which a person feels that he or she is not a part).

6. Among the biases that lead to stereotyping is the ingroup–outgroup bias—the tendency to hold less favorable views about groups to which we do not belong, while holding more favorable opinions about groups to which we do belong. The outgroup homogeneity bias is the perception that there is less variability among the members of outgroups than within one's own ingroup.

7. Illusory correlation occurs when a perceiver overestimates the strength of a relationship between two variables. The ultimate attribution error suggests that when people holding strong stereotypes view negative behavior on the part of a minority group member, they will attribute it to dispositional characteristics; but when a minority group member is seen engaging in positive behavior, the behavior is attributed to situational factors.

### *How prevalent is racism, and is it inevitable?*

8. Racism is prejudice directed at people because of their race. Although on the surface, overt manifestations of racism have declined, modern racism, in which people hold underlying racist attitudes, still exists.

9. On the other hand, even unprejudiced people may experience unintentional negative thoughts and feelings due to prior learning. These negative reactions are the result of the distinction between automatic versus controlled information processing.

### *Why does sexism occur, and what are the roots of gender stereotyping?*

10. Sexism is prejudice directed at women or men on the basis of their gender. Sexism arises out of strong societal gender roles, the set of expectations that indicate what is appropriate behavior for men and women.

11. As a consequence of gender stereotyping, women are seen as most appropriately filling communal professions (which emphasize relationships), while men are perceived as best filling agentic professions (in which the emphasis is on getting things done). One source of stereotyping is in gender schemas, the cognitive framework that organizes information relevant to gender.

### *What are some ways to reduce prejudice and discrimination devised by social psychologists?*

12. Among the ways to reduce prejudice and discrimination are to create opportunities for contact between members of majority and minority groups, to use the jigsaw technique, and to make humanitarian values more conspicuous.

## KEY TERMS AND CONCEPTS

*prejudice (p. 80)*

*stereotype (p. 81)*

*discrimination (p. 81)*

*minority group (p. 81)*

*social learning view (p. 82)*

*realistic conflict theory (p. 83)*

*superordinate goal (p. 84)*

*relative deprivation (p. 85)*

*social identity theory (p. 86)*

*ingroup (p. 88)*

*outgroup (p. 88)*

*ingroup–outgroup bias (p. 89)*

*outgroup homogeneity bias (p. 90)*

*illusory correlation (p. 90)*

*ultimate attribution error (p. 91)*

*racism (p. 94)*

*sexism (p. 94)*

*modern racism (p. 95)*

*gender roles (p. 99)*

*communal professions (p. 102)*

*agentic professions (p. 102)*

*gender schema (p. 103)*

*androgynous (p. 103)*

*contact hypothesis (p. 104)*

*jigsaw technique (p. 104)*

## FOR FURTHER RESEARCH AND STUDY

Allport, G. W. (1954). *The nature of prejudice.* Reading, MA: Addison-Wesley.

A classic in every respect, this book makes for fascinating reading. Although many of the applications and examples are dated, the book provides a rich source of hypotheses and explanations regarding prejudice.

Dovidio, J. F., & Gaertner, S.L. (Ed.) (1986). *Prejudice, discrimination, and racism.* Orlando, FL: Academic Press.

A group of experts summarizes the field of prejudice, with particular emphasis on the relations between whites and African-Americans.

Taylor, D. M., & Moghaddam, F. M. (1987). *Theories of intergroup relations: International social psychological perspectives.* New York: Praeger.

This volume illustrates the worldwide scope of prejudice and discrimination.

Bem, S. L. (1993). *Lenses of gender.* New Haven, CT: Yale University Press.

Unger, R., & Crawford, M. (1992). *Women and gender: A feminist psychology.* New York: McGraw-Hill.

Two comprehensive examinations of the ways in which gender permeates every aspect of modern society.

## EPILOGUE

In this chapter we've considered how we perceive people on the basis of their membership in particular groups. It is clear that powerful social psychological forces often lead people to make judgments based primarily on the basis of group membership, and that concerns about prejudice, stereotyping, and discrimination remain among the most stubborn and enduring social issues of our time.

Yet the problems are not insurmountable. As we discussed in both this chapter and the previous one, in which we considered how people develop an understanding of other individuals, our social cognitive capabilities provide at least the potential for accurate and discerning judgments of others. Certainly, the theory and research discussed in these two chapters paves the way for a more precise understanding of what others are like and the causes of their behavior. Even more important, the material contributes to efforts to diminish the corrosive consequences of prejudice, stereotyping, and discrimination.

# HOW DOES OUR SENSE OF SELF INFLUENCE OUR SOCIAL BEHAVIOR, PSYCHOLOGICAL WELL-BEING, AND PHYSICAL HEALTH?

We continue our travels through the field of social psychology by looking inward, examining how our sense of self influences our social behavior and our physical and psychological well-being. We explore how people define themselves and how people's view of themselves as individuals influences their interactions with others. We also consider the social psychological factors that influence both psychological well-being and physical health.

In Chapter 4, we focus on the self, considering its components and the way we look at ourselves. We examine the inaccuracies that develop in the way we view ourselves, and we look at the ways we endeavor to present ourselves to others. In Chapter 5, we build on our understanding of the self to consider the subject of mental and physical well-being, examining how our view of ourselves and the world affects our psychological and physical health. ■

# CHAPTER FOUR

# THE SELF

## PERCEIVING AND UNDERSTANDING OURSELVES

# PROLOGUE: WOMAN OF MANY FACES

When Madonna looks in the mirror, who does she see?

Is the image she sees that of the naked hitchhiker portrayed in her best-selling book of photos, *Sex*? Is it the schoolgirl of her past, with her strict Catholic upbringing? Is it the

The singer Madonna has adopted, and discarded, a variety of public identities over the course of her career. Is there a "real" Madonna?

feminist about whom scholarly tomes are written? Is it the punk rocker, the lesbian lover, or the person said to have been involved with Warren Beatty?

When she is gazing at the mirror, does she see the movie star, or the singer, or the woman who wore a gold capped tooth engraved with the letter "D" (the initial of an associate who appeared in *Sex* with her)? Does she see a publicity hound, or the person who complains to an interviewer, "Sometimes, I just want to go to a movie and not have someone pull on my shirt, you know what I mean? I mean, I can't go grocery shopping . . ." (Leland, 1992, p. 103).

The answer, most likely, is "none of the above." The woman who has relentlessly invented, adopted, and discarded a series of public identities over the past few years undoubtedly has a view of herself that is very different from the images that she projects to the rest of the world. Madonna is a master of self-presentation, and her outer behavior is most likely not a reflection of her private, inner self. We see what she wants us to see.

## LOOKING AHEAD ▶▶▶▶▶▶▶▶▶▶▶▶▶▶▶▶▶▶▶▶▶▶▶▶▶▶▶

Although Madonna's pursuit and abandonment of public identities is extreme, her behavior spotlights a fundamental question that all of us ask: Who am I?

In the last decade, social psychologists have come to see the study of the self as central to the field. It has become increasingly clear that the way people view their own inner selves has important implications for how they interact with others, making the self an important social topic.

We begin this chapter with a discussion of the nature of the self, considering its structure and how people perceive the components of the self. We also examine how people use others to understand their own abilities, emotions, and attitudes.

We then turn to the ways in which people evaluate themselves, considering issues related to the emotional response associated with the self. We also look at the systematic biases that affect the way we view the self.

Finally, the chapter considers how people present themselves to others. We discuss how people monitor their behavior in order to effectively manage the impressions they give. We consider both verbal and nonverbal strategies for self-presentation, and we end by discussing effective strategies for impression management.

In sum, after reading this chapter, you'll be able to answer these questions:

- How do people use others' (and their own) behavior to assess their abilities, emotions, and attitudes?

- How do self-esteem and self-awareness affect people's interactions with others?
- What biases exist in the way people view themselves?
- What self-presentation strategies do people employ, and which are most effective?

# DEFINING THE SELF

If you've ever had dogs or cats as pets, perhaps you've seen them the first time they catch a glimpse of themselves in a mirror. Although they may appear to be interested or startled by the image they behold, their reaction is not due to their understanding that they are encountering an image of themselves. Far from it: Except for certain apes, animals other than humans do not recognize likenesses of themselves, and they do not appear to have a sense of themselves as individuals (Gallup, 1977).

People, however, begin to develop a sense of themselves at an early age. Even infants as young as 12 months appear to recognize themselves: They are startled when they see in a mirror that a spot of red rouge has been dabbed on their noses, as researchers have done in studies of self-awareness (Lewis & Brooks-Gunn, 1979; Lipka & Brinthaupt, 1992).

The knowledge that we exist as individuals, separate from everyone else, emerges by the age of 18 months. Before then, according to child development experts, children feel totally merged with their caretakers, unable to distinguish themselves from these caretakers and other people (Mahler, Pine, & Bergman, 1975). As they get older, though, children soon develop a sense of themselves as separate individuals, ultimately developing a self-concept.

## Forming a Self-Concept: Who Am I?

**self-concept**
a person's sense of identity, the set of beliefs about what he or she is like as an individual.

**Self-concept** is a person's sense of identity, the set of beliefs about what he or she is like as an individual (Breakwell, 1992; Hattie, 1992). When we think of ourselves as sociable, energetic, outgoing, a little chubby, and temperamental, we're describing aspects of our self-concept. (Before continuing, consider the ingredients of your own self-concept; most people have well-defined, explicit, and fairly precise knowledge about what they are like.)

**SELF-SCHEMA: ORGANIZING A SELF-CONCEPT.** While a person's self-concept is made up of a variety of attributes, the "glue" that holds these impressions together is known as a self-schema. A concept derived from the work on social cognition that we discussed in Chapter 2, a **self-schema** is the organized body of information that relates to a person's self. According to social psychologist Hazel Markus, self-schemas, like other schemas, are based on prior experience, and they guide both people's understanding of what is currently happening and their expectations about what to anticipate in the future (Markus, 1977; Pace, 1988).

**self-schema**
the organized body of information that relates to a person's self.

Unlike the broader notion of self-concept, which includes the entire sum of a person's impressions about himself or herself, self-schemas are more specific and relate to particular personality dimensions (see Figure 4-1). For example, some people may be particularly concerned with the domain of independence, and have a particularly well-developed sense of their independence (or lack of it). They would be said to have a self-schema relating to independence. To others, the domain of independence might be of little concern. These individuals would be seen as lacking a self-schema for independence (Markus, 1977; Markus & Nurius, 1986; Fiske & Taylor, 1991).

Self-schemas serve several functions. They help people sift and filter information relevant to the self-schema, making them more aware of and quick to respond to information that is consistent with the schema (Markus & Sentis, 1982). Moreover, self-

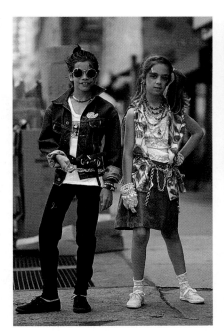

As people grow older, they develop a sense of who they are—their self-concept.

schemas help people remember information related to the schema. For instance, people who hold an independence self-schema are more likely to notice other people's behavior that is indicative of independence. In addition, they will be more likely to recall times when they have acted independently in the past as opposed to someone who does not hold such a self-schema (Pietromonoco & Markus, 1985).

Self-schemas also affect the way people perceive and integrate information into meaningful units. Just as a computer programming expert can scan a multipage printout of computer codes and perceive its broad, underlying patterns, people who hold self-schemas in a given domain consider social information in broader groupings, or "chunks," of information than those who don't hold such self-schemas.

To illustrate this phenomenon, Hazel Markus and colleagues conducted a study with men who either had or lacked a well-defined self-schema related to masculinity (Markus, Smith, & Moreland, 1985). In the experiment, the subjects were shown two films. In one film, they viewed men who were involved in stereotypically masculine activities such as weight-lifting or watching a baseball game. In the other film, the activities portrayed were irrelevant to masculine stereotypes, such as playing a record or eating an apple. While the men were watching each film, they were asked to signal when they thought a "meaningful" grouping, or "chunk," of behavior had occurred.

The results were clear. When the film was relevant to the masculinity stereotypes, the men with masculinity self-schemas perceived the film as having larger groupings, or chunks, than those who did not hold a masculinity self-schema (see Figure 4-2). In contrast, when the film had nothing to do with masculinity-relevant information, the size of the chunks did not vary between those who did or did not have the masculinity self-schema. The data supported the notion that the men with masculinity self-schemas functioned like "masculinity experts" and viewed masculinity-relevant information as a specialist would—in broad, meaning-filled units.

**POSSIBLE SELVES AND IDENTITY.**    In addition to helping guide our current behavior, self-schemas aid in our consideration of what we might become in the future. A portion of the self is comprised of **possible selves**—those aspects of self that relate to the future. Possible selves reflect our aspirations, our concerns, and our view of what is likely to happen to us. For instance, a law student may hold several possible selves about her future, seeing herself as a corporate lawyer, a prosecuting attorney, or a Supreme Court justice.

**possible selves**
the aspects of the self that relate to the future.

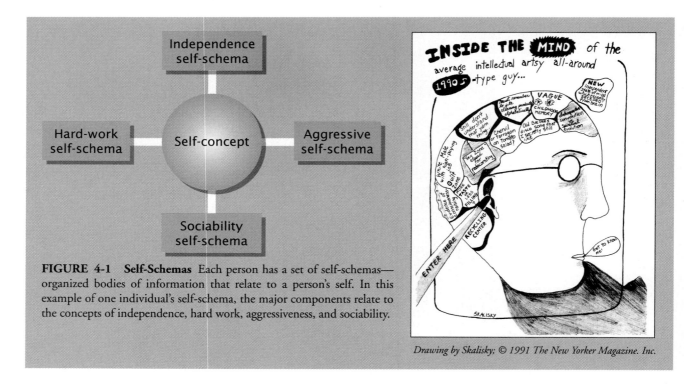

**FIGURE 4-1  Self-Schemas** Each person has a set of self-schemas—organized bodies of information that relate to a person's self. In this example of one individual's self-schema, the major components relate to the concepts of independence, hard work, aggressiveness, and sociability.

*Drawing by Skalisky; © 1991 The New Yorker Magazine. Inc.*

**identity**
the combination of roles and group categories to which a person belongs, along with the set of personal meanings and experiences related to the roles and categories.

Advertisements for diet programs may suggest that a person who is overweight harbors a "possible self" who is slender.

Obviously, such alternatives represent only possibilities, but they help influence a person's current behavior and the choices that person makes. In fact, people make use of possible selves to consider their future throughout life, even extending into old age (Markus & Nurius, 1986; Ryff, 1991; Ruvolo & Markus, 1992).

In addition to considering the self in terms of self-concept and self-schemas, some social psychologists have focused on the notion of identity. **Identity** reflects the roles and group categories to which a person belongs, along with the set of personal meanings and experiences related to those roles and categories. In other words, identity is a combination of social identity (roles or group membership categories to which a person belongs) and personal identity (traits and behaviors that people find descriptive of themselves and that are linked to social identity categories) (Tajfel, 1974, 1979; Widdicombe, 1988; Dollinger & Clancy, 1993).

According to social psychologist Kay Deaux (1993), each of us "packages" our own identity, both in terms of the categories that are important to us and the meaning that we attach to the categories. For example, when a group of Hispanic first-year college students were asked to list their identities and the characteristics associated with each identity, they came up with very different representations of the same identity. As you can see in Figure 4-3, a comparison of two of the subjects' reports reveals a very different pattern of responses (Ethier & Deaux, 1990).

Furthermore, people arrange their identities in hierarchies, clustering together similar identities and attributes relating to particular identities. As we can see in Figure 4-4, the one individual's identities of wife and mother, which share similar attributes, are viewed in terms of being accepting, reliable, and understanding. The related identity of friend is characterized by the attributes of happy, peaceful, and appreciative (Deaux, 1992).

It is important to keep in mind that the view of identity depicted in Figure 4-4 is a unique one, produced from the responses of a single subject. Other individuals would characterize their identities in their own, special manner. But where do such hierarchies come from? More broadly, how do we develop a sense of ourselves as singular unique individuals?

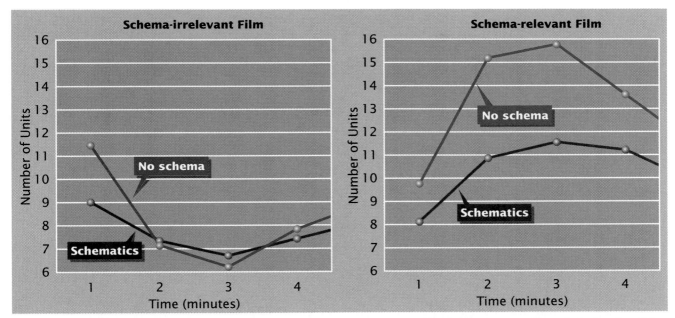

**FIGURE 4-2    Self-schemas and Perception of Information**  Regardless of whether they did or did not hold a masculinity self-concept, subjects who watched a film showing people involved in activities unrelated to a masculinity self-schema perceived the same number of units or chunks of information (as illustrated in the first graph). In contrast, when the film was relevant to the masculinity self-schema, people who held the masculinity self-schema employed different-sized chunks from those who did not have the masculinity self-concept (as illustrated in the second graph). *(Source:* Markus, Smith, & Moreland, 1985.)

Ironically, our view of ourselves is built largely on experience with other people. From the earliest beginnings of both psychology and sociology, theorists have argued that without the presence of others, we would be unable to develop a sense of who or what we are.

**FIGURE 4-3    Self-Identities of Two Hispanic Students**

As these descriptions indicate, when two Hispanic students were asked to describe their identities as "Hispanic" and "student," their representations were quite different.

|  | CHARACTERISTICS | |
| --- | --- | --- |
| IDENTITY | SUBJECT 1 | SUBJECT 2 |
| Hispanic | Confused | Proud |
|  | Proud | Loyal |
|  | On guard | Happy |
|  | Representative | Part of a big family |
|  | Questioning | Lucky |
|  | Aware | Cared for |
|  | Token | Stand out in good and bad ways |
|  | Excluded | Social |
|  |  | Religious |
| Student | Conscientious | Hard |
|  | Flexible | Big change |
|  | Self-sacrificing | Pressure |
|  | Curious | Freedom |
|  | Assertive | Responsibilities |
|  | Demanding | New environment |

*Source:* Ethier & Deaux, 1990.

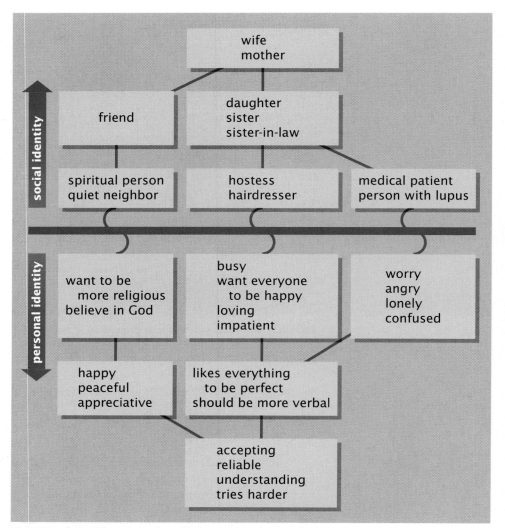

**FIGURE 4-4    The Hierarchy of Identity** People classify their identities into hierarchies. The levels of identity at the top relate to the social aspects of identity, while those in the bottom half of the figure are aspects of identity pertaining to personal characteristics.    (*Source:* Based on Deaux, 1992.)

For instance, William James, one of the founders of the discipline of psychology, suggested that our personal identity could not exist without feedback and judgments from others (James, 1890). Sociologist Charles Horton Cooley (1902) referred to the "looking-glass self" as a means of explaining how we use others as mirrors to perceive ourselves. He suggested that other people provide us with the data that we use to formulate the core of our self-concept.

More recent work has supported these speculations (Gecas & Schwalbe, 1983; Burkitt, 1992). For instance, as we see next, people use others to hone their views of their own skills and capabilities. Indeed, even when we consider the realm of emotions and feelings, people seem to rely on others to define what they are experiencing at a given moment.

*Social Comparison: Using Others to Clarify Where We Stand*

Ed Koch, a former mayor of New York City, became famous for the question he asked his constituents as he traveled around the city: "How am I doing?" In fact, this same question may be one that all of us ask ourselves in order to determine how we compare to others.

Class reunions offer an opportunity for social comparison with a similar comparison group.

**THE NEED FOR SOCIAL COMPARISON.**    According to a theory developed by social psychologist Leon Festinger (1954), people have a need to evaluate their own behavior, abilities, expertise, and opinions—leading to a desire for **social comparison.** In many cases, the answers come easily; objective, physical evidence provides the answer. For instance, if a student thinks her route from home to campus is shorter than the route a friend takes, she can objectively determine whether her opinion is correct by using her car odometer and measuring the mileage of the two routes.

But suppose she wants to know how good a tennis player she is. Here, objective means are lacking. According to Festinger, in this case she will turn to social reality to satisfy her needs for evaluating her ability. **Social reality** refers to understanding that is derived from how other people act, think, feel, and view the world.

For instance, the college student who wishes to determine how well she plays tennis will compare her abilities with those of other tennis players. But who is the most useful comparison person? Unless the student is a top-ranked pro, she already knows she doesn't play as well as Steffi Graff or Monica Seles, but she also knows that she plays better than someone who has just taken up the game. Consequently, the most likely candidates are people who are fairly similar to her own level of experience, who provide the closest comparisons.

This example illustrates a general rule: People determine their ability by comparing themselves to others who are similar to themselves along relevant dimensions. Consequently, when we cannot objectively evaluate our ability, we look for answers to others who are similar (Goethals & Darley, 1977; Wood, 1989; Suls & Wills, 1991).

On the other hand, we don't always use similar others as guides to our abilities. If we are motivated to make ourselves look good, we may employ **downward social comparison**, in which we compare ourselves with others who are inferior or worse off than we are. By comparing ourselves with those less fortunate than ourselves, we obviously can make ourselves look better in comparison (Wills, 1981). In most cases, though, the people we are most apt to use for purposes of comparison are those who are similar to ourselves.

Perhaps it is not surprising that we use others to develop a self-schema regarding our abilities. But some social psychologists have taken this notion a step beyond the domain of abilities. If we use information from others to determine something as stable as our own abilities, they asked, might not information from others also be used to determine what we are emotionally experiencing at any given moment?

**THE TWO-FACTOR THEORY OF EMOTIONS: DETERMINING HOW WE FEEL.**    According to social psychologists Stanley Schachter and Jerome Singer, the answer is an emphatic yes (Schachter & Singer, 1962). In what has become a classic experiment, the two researchers demonstrated that how people label their emotional experiences may depend in large measure on the information provided by others and on the situation in which they find themselves.

---

**social comparison**
the need to evaluate one's own behavior, abilities, expertise, and opinions by comparing them to those of others.

**social reality**
a person's understanding that is derived from how other people act, think, feel, and view the world.

**downward social comparison**
a situation in which one compares oneself with others who are inferior or worse off.

In the study, subjects were told that they would be given injections of a "vitamin" called Suproxin. In reality, they were given epinephrine, a drug that causes increases in physiological arousal such as increased heart rate and flushing of the face, responses that occur during natural emotional experiences. One group of subjects was informed of the drug's effects, while another was not.

Subjects were then asked to complete a series of questionnaires. In both groups a confederate acted either very joyful and exhilarated—lobbing papers into a wastebasket and throwing paper airplanes—or quite angry. Subjects then were asked to describe their own emotional states. Those who had been informed of the effects of the epinephrine were generally unaffected by the confederate's behavior; they attributed their physiological arousal to the drug, and thus were not faced with the need to find an explanation for their arousal.

On the other hand, subjects who were uninformed of the drug's effect upon them were affected by the confederate's behavior: When the confederate acted euphoric, they reported feeling happy, but when he acted angry, they reported feeling angry. Basically, subjects who experienced unexplained physiological arousal functioned as problem solvers. In attempting to explain their arousal, they turned to the environment and used external cues, in the form of others' behavior, to label their own emotional state.

**two-factor theory of emotion**
the notion that emotions are a joint result of nonspecific physiological arousal and the interpretation of the arousal.

In sum, the Schachter and Singer experiment pointed to a **two-factor theory of emotion**, in which emotions are a joint result of (1) nonspecific physiological arousal and (2) the interpretation of the arousal. Unfortunately, the validity of the theory remains far from certain. The methods and theoretical arguments of the original experiment have been criticized, and attempts to replicate the findings have not been consistently successful (see, for example, Marshall & Zimbardo, 1979; Reisenzein, 1983; Chwalisz, Diener, & Gallagher, 1988). Still, one basic premise of the original study has remained supported: When people are unsure about how they feel, they may infer their emotional state by observing the behavior of others and the nature of the situation in which they find themselves (e.g., Sinclair et al., 1994).

## Defining Ourselves Through Our Behavior

The two-factor theory of emotions suggests that we can use a combination of internal arousal and situational cues to make inferences about the nature of our emotional state. What other sources of information might we employ to better understand our inner self?

One likely candidate is our own behavior. According to social psychologist Daryl Bem, people sometimes make attributions regarding the causes of their own behavior in a manner equivalent to the kinds of attributions they make regarding the causes of others' behavior (Bem & McConnell, 1970; Bem, 1972).

**self-perception theory**
the notion that people become aware of their own attitudes, dispositions, emotions, and other internal states in the same way that they learn about those of other people.

**SELF-PERCEPTION THEORY.**    Building on the work on social cognition that we discussed in Chapter 2, Bem's **self-perception theory** suggests that people come to be aware of their own attitudes, dispositions, emotions, and other internal states in the same way that they learn about those of other people—through observation of behavior. To the extent that situational cues or past experience are irrelevant, weak, or ambiguous, the theory suggests that people use the basic principles of attribution theory to identify the causes of the behavior they have observed in themselves. Moreover, they use the same principles to assess their own inner states that they employ when they consider the inner states of others.

A few examples help clarify Bem's theory. If you saw someone patiently helping an elderly woman cross a busy street, it would be reasonable to infer that the helper is altruistic or perhaps favorably disposed toward the elderly. But suppose that person is you, and at an intersection you find yourself helping the individual cross the road. When you look back to analyze your own behavior, Bem's theory suggests that you would make the same kind of attributions about your own behavior that you did about the other's behavior—i.e., that you have an altruistic streak and hold positive attitudes toward the elderly. (We'll discuss the role of self-perception in the domain of attitudes in Chapter 10.)

Consider another example: As part of an experiment, you are looking at a group of attractive nudes, all of which are sexually appealing. When you see some of them, though, your heart rate (which is being monitored and amplified through a speaker) speeds up or slows down, while with others it stays the same. You're then asked which one you liked best.

If you're like the real subjects in this study, which was actually carried out, you'll probably choose the one for which your heart rate changed rather than the ones for which it remained stable (Valins, 1966). What is particularly intriguing about these results is that in the experiment, the heart-rate changes that the subjects heard were false: The experimenter used bogus tape recordings of accelerating, decelerating, and steady heartbeats to lead subjects to believe there had been actual variations in their own heartbeats.

In sum, Bem's theory of self-perception indicates that people will apply the same principles of attribution to their own behavior that they use with others. Through this process, they are able to understand and infer their attitudes and make attributions regarding why they have engaged in certain behavior.

**OVERJUSTIFICATION: TURNING PLAY INTO WORK.**   Consider this situation: Bob's son, Jonathan, is 8 years old and loves to use machinery of any kind. Each week he begs Bob to be permitted to use the power lawn mower. Despite some qualms about safety, Bob usually agrees, because Jonathan does an excellent job. In fact, he does such a good job that Bob is considering paying Jonathan so that he'll continue to mow the lawn enthusiastically. Should Bob pay him?

In the light of self-perception theory, the answer is clearly no. Here's why: According to a derivative of self-perception theory, rewarding Jonathan will make him lose his intrinsic motivation—motivation that causes people to participate in an activity for their own enjoyment, not for the reward it will get them. Instead, his effort will be produced by extrinsic motivation—motivation that causes people to participate in an activity for a tangible reward.

The phenomenon in which intrinsic motivation is replaced with extrinsic motivation is known as overjustification. **Overjustification** occurs when incentives are used to bring about behavior that would have been done voluntarily, without any incentive (Lepper, Greene, & Nisbett, 1973; Condry, 1977; Lepper, 1983; Deci & Ryan, 1985).

**overjustification**
a situation in which incentives are used to bring about behavior that would have been done voluntarily, without any incentive.

When people are rewarded for something they have done, two explanations for their behavior are possible—their own interest in the task (intrinsic motivation), and the external reward (extrinsic motivation). If the reinforcement is clear and unambiguous, the reinforcement provides the most reasonable cause of the behavior. But if no external reinforcement is present, the person's own interests, dispositions, or motivations provide the most reasonable explanation of the behavior.

In terms of the earlier example of Bob and Jonathan, providing Jonathan with a financial reward for mowing the lawn provides him with clear, external reinforcement. As a result, Jonathan may begin to view his own behavior in terms of the external reward—rather than in terms of his internal motivation. The result: He'll be less apt to view mowing as an enjoyable, intrinsically motivated behavior. Clearly, for Bob to pay Jonathan would be a strategic error.

Overjustification effects have been demonstrated in many contexts. For example, in one experiment a group of nursery school children were promised a reward for drawing with magic markers—a pastime for which they had previously shown great enthusiasm (Lepper & Greene, 1978). However, once the reward was promised, their enthusiasm for the task dropped and they showed considerably less zeal for drawing. Apparently, the promise of a reward undermined their intrinsic motivation for the task.

This phenomenon occurs with adults as well: People rewarded for tasks they already like not only begin to enjoy the task less, but the quality and creativity of their work also declines (see, for example, Amabile, 1983; Amabile, Hennessey & Grossman, 1986; Seta & Seta, 1987). Through overjustification, then, play can clearly be turned into work.

ACTION IDENTIFICATION: LEVELS OF DOING.    What are you doing at this moment?

The most obvious answer is "reading a book." But consider some alternative responses you might have made: "looking at a string of letters on a page" or "learning social psychology" or "desperately trying to finish a chapter before a test" or "becoming a better human being." Each is equally valid, but they vary in terms of the level of abstraction with which they seek to respond to the question.

**action identification theory**
the theory that people's interpretation of their own behavior varies in terms of whether the behavior is seen at a high or low level.

According to action identification theory, proposed by Robin Vallacher and Daniel Wegner (1985, 1987), the kind of answer that you do give has important implications. **Action identification theory** suggests that people's interpretation of their own behavior varies in terms of whether the behavior is seen at a high or low level. High-level interpretation looks at the broad scenario, taking an abstract approach. In contrast, low-level interpretation looks at the minutiae of people's behavior, breaking behavior down into its parts.

Action identification theory suggests that the level at which people typically view their current actions has implications for future behavior. For example, identification of actions at higher levels leads to greater stability in future behavior. Consequently, people who tend to view their actions at higher levels find it more difficult to modify subsequent behavior.

More specifically, action identification done at high levels may make it harder to change maladaptive behaviors. For instance, alcoholics who identify their drinking behavior at high levels ("drinking helps me to relax in social situations") may find it more difficult to break the drinking habit than those who identify their drinking behavior in terms of its lower-level components ("beer quenches my thirst"). In sum, the level at which we perceive our own actions affects the stability of behavior and its susceptibility to change (Wegner, Vallacher, & Dizadji, 1989).

*The Self in a Cultural Context: Squeaky Wheel or Pounded Nail?*

In Western cultures, the "squeaky wheel gets the grease." In Asian cultures, "the nail that stands out gets pounded down."

These two maxims represent quite different views of the world. The Western saying suggests that to get the attention one deserves, it is best to be special and different and to make one's concerns known to others. The Asian perspective is quite different, suggesting that one ought to try to blend in with others in society and refrain from making waves or being noticed.

The two maxims, and the reasoning that lies behind them, illustrate profound cultural differences in how people view the self. According to Hazel Markus and Shonobu Kitayama (1991), people in Asian society have an interdependent view of themselves. They see themselves as part of a larger social network in which they work with others to maintain social harmony. Individuals in interdependent societies strive to behave in accordance with how others think, feel, and behave.

People living in many Western countries, in contrast, have an independent perspective on the self. They tend to see themselves as self-contained and autonomous, competing with others to better their own lot in life. Individuals in independent societies strive to behave in a way that expresses their own uniqueness. They consider their behavior to be brought about by their own special configuration of personal characteristics (see Figure 4-5).

The difference between Asian and Western views of self have several consequences. For instance, Markus and Kitayama reported that students in India see themselves as

People in Asian societies have a more interdependent view of themselves than those in Western countries. They see themselves as part of a larger social network in which they strive to maintain social harmony.

more similar to one another than do American college students. While American students emphasized qualities they felt differentiated themselves from others, Indian students emphasized qualities they shared with others.

Furthermore, Westerners are more apt to experience emotions that are related to their view of themselves as independent, unconnected individuals—emotions such as jealousy and anger. In contrast, people living in Japan are more likely to experience "other-focused" emotions, in which the emotion is related to cooperation with others. Specifically, the Japanese language describes emotions that are not even present in the English vocabulary, such as feeling "oime," which refers to being indebted to another.

Finally, people living in independent cultures see achievement in terms of personal gains, viewing themselves as better or worse off than others. They compare their salaries

**FIGURE 4-5    Representations of the Self in Two Cultures** In a typically American view of the self, people see themselves as independent, self-contained, and autonomous. In an Asian view of the self, people see themselves as interdependent, related to a large social network with others. (*Source:* Markus & Kitayama, 1991.)

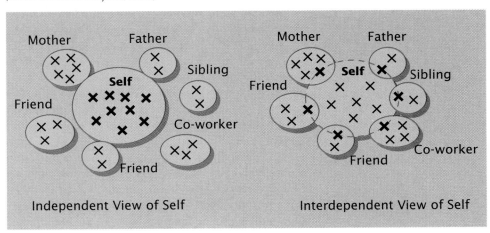

and their grades with their peers, and they receive individual awards for good performance. The self-concept of people in independent cultures, then, is based on personal, individual successes and failures.

The perspective of those in interdependent cultures is different. In these cultures, people are rewarded on the basis of their contribution to group achievement. For example, an employee's contribution to a company might be evaluated in terms of how well the employee contributes to the company's overall success. If the company does well, all workers receive the benefits; if the company does not do well, everyone suffers. It is as if students in a class received grades based not just on their own performance but on how their classmates, as a whole, fared on the final exam.

► # REVIEW & RETHINK

## Review

- Self-concept is a person's sense of identity, the set of beliefs about what he or she is like as an individual.
- Self-schemas organize information relating to a person's self. In addition to descriptive self-schemas, people have possible selves relating to the future, and they also have identity.
- People use social comparison to clarify their abilities and, according to one theory, use others to interpret their emotions.
- Self-perception theory explains how people come to understand their own internal states by acting as observers of their own behavior.

## Rethink

- What is a self-schema? Describe its relationship with self-concepts.
- What are possible selves? How can possible selves help us attain future goals?
- What two types of identity do people have? Which of these is more important for most Americans, and which is more important for most Asians?
- Without comparing yourself to anyone else, try to answer the questions, "How good a tennis player am I?" and "How outgoing am I?"
- Compare self-perception theory with the two-factor theory of emotion. How does each theory explain how people know they are experiencing an emotion? How do the theories explain how people know which emotion they are experiencing?

## EVALUATING AND PROTECTING THE SELF

If you're like most people, you see yourself not just as a student, but as a good, bad, or indifferent student. You don't consider yourself simply as having a face and body, but as having an attractive or an unattractive one. You probably don't think of your personality as composed of just a neutral set of characteristics, but as being made up of traits that you like or you dislike.

When it comes to the self, we are not neutral, unbiased observers. Instead, we evaluate the self, considering it in terms of positive and negative dimensions. Moreover, we try to protect our view of self, reacting to threats by attempting to change the situation or the way in which we view it. As we will see, these self-protective efforts sometimes color our behavior and the way we view the world.

*"I like to think of myself as a nice guy. Naturally, sometimes you have to step on a few faces."*

## Self-Esteem: Rating the Self

**self-esteem**
the affective component of self, a person's general and specific positive and negative self-evaluations.

**Self-esteem** is the affective component of self—a person's general and specific positive and negative self-evaluations. In contrast to self-concept, which reflects our beliefs and cognitions regarding the self, self-esteem is more emotionally oriented (Baumeister, 1993).

Just as the self is composed of multiple self-schemas, self-esteem is not one-dimensional. Instead, we may view particular parts of the self in more or less positive ways. For instance, a person may hold his academic self-schema in high regard, but consider his weight and body type self-schema negatively (Marsh, 1986; Pelham & Swann, 1989; Moretti & Higgins, 1990).

Furthermore, self-esteem varies over time: Depending on the situation, sometimes we feel quite good about ourselves, and other times we may feel negatively (Kernis et al., 1993). For instance, transitions between different schools often result in lower self-esteem. Hence, students who leave elementary school and enter junior high school often show a drop in self-esteem, which then gradually rises (Eccles et al., 1989).

Although everyone occasionally goes through times of low self-esteem, such as after an undeniable failure, some people are chronically low in self-esteem. In such cases, the consequences can be profound, including physical illness, psychological disturbance, or—as we'll discuss in the next chapter—a general inability to cope with stress (Baumeister, 1993).

One reason that low self-esteem is so damaging is that it becomes part of a cycle of failure that is difficult to break. For example, consider students with low self-esteem who are facing an upcoming test. As a result of their low self-esteem they expect to do poorly. In turn, this expectation produces high anxiety and may lead them to reduce the amount of effort they apply to studying. After all, why should people who expect to do badly bother to work too hard? Ultimately, of course, the high anxiety and lack of effort produce just what was expected—failure on the test. Unfortunately, the failure simply reinforces the low self-esteem, and the cycle continues (see Figure 4-6).

The cycle of failure brought about by low self-esteem is not unalterable, however. Social psychologist Albert Bandura suggests that such self-defeating behavior can be overcome by increasing a person's sense of self-efficacy. **Self-efficacy** refers to learned

**self-efficacy**
an individual's learned expectations that he or she is capable of carrying out a behavior or producing a desired outcome.

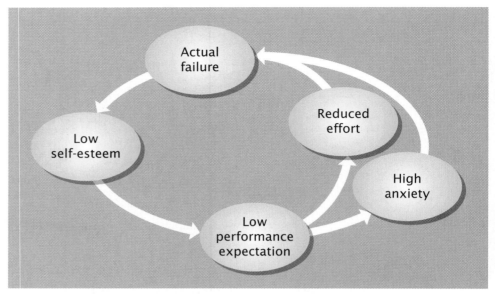

**FIGURE 4-6    The Cycle of Low Self-Esteem** People with low self-esteem who expect to do poorly on a test will probably experience high anxiety and not work as hard. As a result, they actually fail, which in turn confirms their negative view of themselves.

Would being President Bill Clinton's younger brother hurt your self-esteem? Only if you had political aspirations of your own, according to self-evaluation maintenance theory. If you had different, non-political goals, then President Clinton's achievements would more likely be a source of pride.

expectations that one is capable of carrying out a behavior or producing a desired outcome in a particular situation (Bandura, 1982, 1986, 1988, 1993; Schunk, 1991).

When people expect to be successful, they tend to exert greater effort and show greater persistence when faced with a challenging task—thereby increasing the likelihood of success. This is particularly true in academic realms. People high in self-efficacy regarding their scholastic ability are successful—a finding that holds true both for students and college professors (Bandura & Schunk, 1981; Scheier & Carver, 1992; Taylor et al., 1984).

How do we develop a sense of self-efficacy? There are several sources. For one thing, observing our prior successes and failures at a task leads to self-efficacy. If people try rollerblading and have little success, they will be less apt to attempt it again. On the other hand, if their initial attempts have been reasonably promising, they'll be considerably more likely to try it again in the future.

Self-efficacy also comes from observation of others' success, as well as through direct reinforcement and urging from others. Finally, our sense of self-efficacy can emerge when we are in a relatively relaxed physiological state, which actually enhances the possibility that we will succeed (Bandura, 1988).

*Self-Evaluation Maintenance: When Others' Success Hurts*

**self-evaluation maintenance theory** a theory that predicts that people will react to the accomplishments of important people in their lives by showing either jealousy or pride.

Did you ever wonder what it would be like to be the brother or sister of a U.S. president? Despite allowing you the opportunity to hang out in the White House, it might not be something all that desirable for your self-esteem—at least according to self-evaluation maintenance theory.

In the view of social psychologist Abraham Tessor, **self-evaluation maintenance theory** predicts that people will react to the accomplishments of important people in their lives by showing either jealousy or pride (Tessor, 1988). What determines which of the two reactions will occur?

The critical factor is the relevance of the other person's success to one's self. For instance, someone who has political aspirations of his or her own or who wants to be in the limelight might experience jealousy when a sibling becomes president or experiences other political success. On the other hand, if the success is not central to one's view of oneself and poses no threat, then the sibling's success will be a source of pride and positive emotions.

### Self-Awareness: Focusing on the Me in One's Life

**self-awareness**
a state in which attention is focused on the self.

**private self-consciousness**
an individual's awareness of inner thoughts, feelings, and self-evaluations.

**public self-consciousness**
an individual's awareness of his or her outward behavior and appearances that are visible to others.

Seeing ourselves in a mirror leads to self-awareness, in which attention is focused on one's self.

For most of us, it is hard to resist taking a peek at ourselves as we pass by a mirror or a reflecting store window. And it's equally hard, once we've seen that image, not to engage in a bit of self-reflection.

At least that's the suggestion made by research on self-awareness. **Self-awareness** is a state in which attention is focused on the self. According to social psychologist Robert Wicklund and colleagues, certain situations, such as seeing oneself in a mirror, having one's picture taken, or giving a talk in front of an audience, bring about a state in which people become more conscious of themselves (Duval & Wicklund, 1972; Wicklund, 1975; Wicklund & Frey, 1980; Hass & Eisenstadt, 1990; Duval, Duval, & Mulilis, 1992).

Wicklund argued that being in a state of self-awareness leads to a particular consequence: People begin to focus on how their actual self compares to ideal standards they hold for themselves. Typically, the result is an unpleasant affective state, as people find their actual selves less than ideal, leading to temporary loss of self-esteem.

Once people become aware of the discrepancies between their actual and ideal selves, there are two main ways of resolving the situation. One is simply to flee: They may move away from a mirror, or refuse to have their picture taken. A second strategy is to attempt to decrease the discrepancy between their actual and ideal selves. To that end, people who are highly self-aware tend to behave in accordance with their ideal self. Research on self-awareness has shown that people placed in a self-aware state tend to be more helpful to others, to work harder, and to be more honest than those who are not self-aware (Gibbons & Wicklund, 1982; Gibbons & Wright, 1983; Gibbons, 1990).

Clearly, self-awareness may lead to positive outcomes. But what if people choose to escape the situation? Although in many instances self-awareness can be readily avoided, in some cases it is inescapable. (Consider a professor, who must repeatedly appear in public to give lectures, or a trial lawyer who must argue cases in court.) In such situations, the aversive consequences of self-awareness may become so unpleasant that people will engage in self-injurious behavior, including drunkenness, masochism, and even—in the most extreme cases—suicide (Baumeister, 1988, 1990, 1991).

Are there different forms of self-awareness? According to social psychologist Allan Fenigstein and colleagues, self-awareness can be broken down into two categories—private self-consciousness and public self-consciousness. **Private self-consciousness** refers to awareness of inner thoughts, feelings, and self-evaluations. **Public self-consciousness** consists of a focus on one's outward behavior and appearances that are visible to others.

People tend to vary in the nature of self-consciousness that they are most apt to experience. Some people are chronically high in private self-consciousness; they are most concerned with how they measure up to their own personal standards. In contrast, other people are chronically high in public self-consciousness; they are more concerned with behaving in accordance with societal norms. Researchers have devised a personality scale to distinguish the two types of people; some of the items on the scale are shown in Figure 4-7.

Being high in public self-consciousness has several consequences. Because they are particularly attuned to the impression that their behavior makes on others, people high in public self-consciousness are more easily persuaded by others' arguments, and they are more likely to see themselves as the focus of others' attention. In contrast, people higher in private self-consciousness are more resistant to persuasion and less easily influenced by pressure from others (Carver & Scheier, 1985; Hutton & Baumeister, 1992).

| FIGURE 4-7 Sample Items from the Self-Consciousness Scale |
| --- |

*Items Relating to Public Self-Consciousness*

   I'm concerned about what other people think of me.

   I'm concerned about the way I present myself.

   I usually worry about making a good impression.

   One of the last things I do before leaving my house is look in the mirror.

*Items Relating to Private Self-Consciousness*

   I'm always trying to figure myself out.

   I'm alert to changes in my mood.

   I'm aware of the way my mind works when I work on a problem.

   I'm constantly examining my motives.

*Source:* Fenigstein et al., 1975.

## Misperceptions of the Self: To Thine Own Self Be False

Most of the evidence about the self that we've discussed so far suggests that people are pretty good perceivers of themselves and their own behavior. In fact, one could draw the conclusion that people seem to look at themselves in the same dispassionate manner in which they would look at a stranger, and to apply the principles of social cognition we first discussed in Chapter 2.

As you might suspect, however, this conclusion is not completely true. People seek to protect themselves from damaging, hurtful information, interpreting it in a way that maintains their positive view of themselves. Furthermore, even when self-protection is of little concern, individuals may view and interpret what is happening to them in ways that are very different from how others see the identical situation. Two of the biases that occur regularly when we analyze our own behavior are the actor–observer bias and self-handicapping.

**THE ACTOR–OBSERVER BIAS: YOU SAY I'M AN ANGRY PERSON, I SAY YOU MAKE ME ANGRY.** Suppose you've waited in a long line at a bank, becoming increasingly annoyed. When you finally reach the teller, your anger spills out, and you act hostile and resentful. The teller thinks, "What a mean person." Would you agree?

Most likely not. To you, your behavior is simply a reaction to the situation, and it has little to do with your own personality. You were just in a bad mood after waiting so long.

Your reliance on situational factors to explain your behavior, and the teller's reliance on dispositional factors to explain behavior, is an example of the actor–observer bias (Jones & Nisbett, 1972). The **actor–observer bias** is the tendency for people to attribute their own behavior to situational requirements, while people observing that behavior tend to attribute it to the actor's stable dispositions.

**actor–observer bias**
the tendency for people to attribute their own behavior to situational requirements, while people observing that same behavior tend to attribute it to the person's stable dispositions.

Why is it that people looking for explanations of their own behavior focus on the situation, while observers focus on the qualities of the actor? One reason is perceptual (Storms, 1973; Taylor & Fiske, 1978). When involved in social interaction, people are looking, listening, and responding to what is happening in the environment around them. Thus, their focus is on the external world. In contrast, observers are more apt to focus on the actor's behavior—because it is so striking and vivid—than on the relatively inanimate, lifeless situational factors. In part, then, the bias is due to a difference in focus or perspective.

There's another reason, though, for the actor–observer bias: Actors have more information than observers. They know where they were yesterday, last night, and this morning, and in each situation they behaved differently. In contrast, an observer knows much less. Because actors have seen themselves behave very differently in various situations, they are more likely to look to the situation for an explanation than would an observer.

If you are caught in a traffic jam and honk your horn, you would probably attribute your behavior to your desire to avoid being late to an important appointment—a situational cause. Other drivers, however, would probably view your behavior as an indication that you are impatient and rude—a dispositional cause. The discrepancy in attributions is an example of the actor–observer bias.

In sum, the actor–observer bias occurs due to perceptual factors and to differences in information. It is likely that both contribute to this powerful and pervasive phenomenon. On the other hand, this bias does have its limits. For instance, as we first discussed in Chapter 2, people sometimes fall prey to the **self-serving bias**—the tendency to attribute personal success to internal factors (such as skill, ability, or effort), while attributing failure to external factors, such as bad luck or something about the situation. In short, any time we're motivated to protect our self-concept, the actor–observer bias will be overridden (Gioia & Sims, 1985; Green et al., 1985; Osberg & Schrauger, 1986). In fact, in some cases the desire to protect our self-concept is so great that it goes beyond coloring our perceptions and actually affects our performance—and not always in a positive way, as we see next.

**self-serving bias**
the tendency to attribute personal success to internal factors (such as skill, ability, or effort), while attributing failure to external factors (such as bad luck).

**SELF-HANDICAPPING: ERECTING HURDLES FOR OURSELVES.**    From time to time, most of us experience anxiety and insecurity about the extent of our own abilities. Are we smart enough to succeed in school? Will we do well enough on the job? Will we make the grade?

Unfortunately, the strategy that some people use to deal with this problem actually interferes with their own performance. According to social psychologists Stephen Berglas and Edward Jones, who first described the phenomenon, **self-handicapping** is a tactic in which people set up circumstances that allow them to avoid attributing poor performance to low ability and instead to attribute failure to less-threatening causes (Berglas & Jones, 1978; Jones & Berglas, 1978; Higgins, Snyder, & Berglas, 1990).

**self-handicapping**
a tactic in which people set up circumstances that allow them to avoid attributing poor performance to low ability and instead allow them to attribute it to less-threatening causes.

Consider, for example, a student who goes to a bar the night before a test, and the next day says, "I don't think I'm going to do very well on today's test: I was up late drinking and didn't get a chance to study." If, in fact, the student ends up not doing well on the test, he has an obvious excuse—being drunk. Because being drunk is a temporary, external factor which doesn't relate to a lack of academic competence, it is presumably less threatening to self-esteem than if the student were forced to attribute his failure to a lack of ability (Arkin & Baumgardner, 1985; Duval & Duval, 1987).

Several types of behavior can be used to shift attributional attention away from personal abilities. For example, research has shown a rich variety of self-handicapping strategies—feeling anxiety, being in a bad mood, acting shy, becoming depressed, creating distracting work conditions, and procrastinating (Baumgardner, Lake, & Arkin, 1985; Schouten & Handelsman, 1987; Shepperd & Arkin, 1989; Baumgardner, 1991).

In a broader sense, self-handicapping strategies fall along two dimensions—internal versus external, and acquired versus claimed (Arkin & Baumgardner, 1985). The internal–external dimension relates to whether the excuse pertains to oneself (internal) or to the situation (external). The acquired–claimed dimension relates to whether the handicapping behavior is actually performed (acquired) or is merely claimed, but not necessarily true (claimed).

These two dimensions, when considered jointly, delineate four types of self-handicaps (Leary & Shepperd, 1986). As shown in Figure 4-8, self-handicaps may be internal acquired (such as drug use), internal claimed (as when a person asserts that she is always highly anxious when taking a test), external acquired (choosing overly difficult goals), or external claimed (as when one claims that a test is too hard) (Arkin & Baumgardner, 1985; Leary & Shepperd, 1986; Hirt, Deppe, & Gordon, 1991).

In some instances, self-handicapping may become habitual, as in the case of a person who consistently drinks too much and whose performance in many areas of life suffers. Alcohol provides a ready excuse for explaining failures that might otherwise be attributed to internal factors.

Interestingly, there may be gender differences in self-handicapping, with males being more likely to self-handicap than females (Harris & Snyder, 1986; Shepperd & Arkin, 1989b). Men and women may also differ in the way they self-handicap. Men tend to use more alcohol and drugs, whereas women are more likely to claim stress or physical illness (Hirt, Deppe, & Gordon, 1991).

Individuals who are high in public self-consciousness are more apt to use self-handicapping than people high in private self-consciousness. For example, one study found that when a task was presented as an important one, participants who scored high in public self-consciousness showed a heightened tendency to self-handicap. On the other hand, when the experimenter suggested that the task was not all that important, subjects showed little difference according to whether they were high or low in public self-consciousness (Sheppard & Arkin, 1989).

Why do people self-handicap? The most obvious reason is for self-esteem protection. People who adopt a self-handicapping strategy are rendered blameless for their fail-

**Figure 4-8 Self-handicapping Strategies** Self-handicapping strategies vary along two dimensions: whether they are internal–external or acquired–claimed. The internal–external dimension relates to whether the excuse pertains to oneself (internal) or to the situation (external). The acquired–claimed dimension relates to whether the handicapping behavior is actually performed (acquired) or is merely claimed, but not necessarily true (claimed). (*Source:* Based on Arkin & Baumgardner, 1985.)

|  | **Internal–External Dimension** | |
|---|---|---|
| **Acquired–Claimed Dimension** | Excuse pertains to oneself | Excuse pertains to the situation |
| Excuse is taken on | Using drugs | Choosing overly difficult goals |
| Excuses stated but not necessarily true | Asserting high test anxiety | Asserting test is too difficult |

ure, at least in their own eyes, and this allows them to maintain a positive view of themselves (Jones & Berglas, 1978).

However, self-handicapping also helps protect one's public image. Hence, by self-handicapping, people provide not only to themselves but also to observers a reasonable excuse for failure (Kolditz & Arkin, 1982; Snyder & Higgins, 1988; Luginbuhl & Palmer, 1991). As we discuss in the accompanying Social Psychology at Work feature, self-handicapping may have its benefits.

---

## SOCIAL PSYCHOLOGY AT WORK

## EXCUSES, EXCUSES: WHEN SELF-HANDICAPPING HELPS

"The dog ate my homework." "The water pipe broke in the dorm, and I had to evacuate." "My grandmother died."

Conventional wisdom suggests that we shouldn't make excuses for our behavior and that we should own up to our failures and accept the consequences. Recent research, however, suggests otherwise.

According to social psychologists C. R. Snyder and Raymond Higgins of the University of Kansas, excuses are not all bad (Snyder & Higgins, 1988; Higgins & Snyder, 1989). In fact, people who make excuses may have higher self-esteem, do better on tests of performance, and even have better physical health than those who avoid or refuse to make excuses for their own performance.

Snyder and Higgins consider excuse-making as a process in which people shift attributions for negative events away from causes that are relatively central to their sense of self and toward causes that are less pivotal. By focusing on less-important causes, people are able to improve their image of themselves and their sense of control.

More specifically, Snyder and Higgins argue that successful excuses begin when some negative outcome threatens people's positive views of themselves and their sense of control (see Figure 4-9). Next, excuse-makers develop external attributions for their behavior, making potential threats to self-esteem less potent. In turn, this process leads to a reduction in self-focus and an increase in focus on the situation. Ultimately, this outward focus benefits self-esteem, emotion, health, and even future performance. Moreover, it can aid in the maintenance of people's self-image and sense of control over events in the world. *Continued on next page*

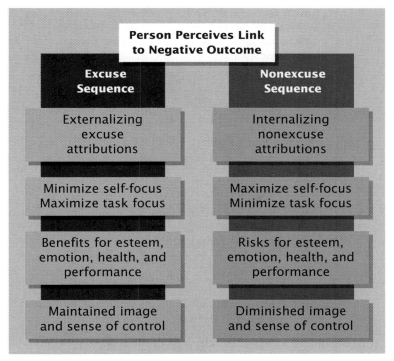

**FIGURE 4-9  Making Excuses** Depending on how one attributes a negative outcome, excuses can be beneficial. (*Source:* Adapted from Snyder & Higgins, 1988, p. 30.)

In contrast, when people don't make excuses in the face of some negative outcome, their attributions for the cause of the unpleasant event can turn inward. In this case, they maximize their self-focus and concentrate on internal attributions. In turn, non-excuse-makers may suffer from a loss of self-esteem, and as a consequence, they may experience negative emotions, poorer health, and impaired future performance. Eventually, such outcomes can lead to a deflated self-image and a loss of the sense of control.

Clearly, excuses can be helpful. But not all kinds of excuses are equally effective. The most effective excuses emphasize how the circumstance being excused was not intentional, and could not be foreseen or controlled. In addition, excuses that are somewhat ambiguous work better than excuses that appear to others to be obvious attempts to justify unpleasant occurrences (Higgins & Snyder, 1989; Higgins, Snyder, & Berglas, 1990).

Effective excuse-makers also try to use excuses that prevent others from labeling their behavior as chronic and habitual. For instance, consider the student who excuses his lack of academic success on tests by explaining that he was out celebrating the night before and had too much to drink. If he continually uses the same excuse, he runs the risk of being labeled an alcoholic—not a particularly successful strategy.

In sum, the right kind of excuses can be a boon to one's self-image. Consequently, if someone complains that you're just making excuses, don't take their criticism too hard: You may be doing yourself a favor.

## ► REVIEW & RETHINK

### Review

- Self-esteem, the affective component of self, is multidimensional and may change over time.
- Self-awareness leads to a focus on how the actual self compares to ideal standards; the discrepancy may result in an unpleasant affective state. In addition, people may be in a state of private self-consciousness or public self-consciousness.
- The actor–observer bias and self-handicapping are two forms of bias in self-perception.

### Rethink

- How do the concepts of self-esteem and self-concept differ? Which is more variable over time and across situations?
- What is private self-awareness and how does it differ from public self-awareness? Which is more likely to be brought on by (1) seeing oneself in a mirror, or (2) having to give a speech in front of a large group?
- How would a person explain his or her own behavior in the following two situations: (1) hiding under the bed covers during an evening thunderstorm; (2) doing well on an exam. How might an impartial observer explain these behaviors?
- Briefly describe four types of self-handicapping and describe a situation in which each would be most effective.

## PRESENTING THE SELF TO THE WORLD

When the late entertainer Sammy Davis, Jr., said, "As soon as I go out of the front door of my house in the morning, I'm on, . . . I'm on," he was merely reflecting what William Shakespeare had written, somewhat more elegantly, three centuries earlier. In Shakespeare's comedy *As You Like It,* the character of Jaques suggests that "All the world's a stage, and all the men and women merely players."

Most social psychologists would be tempted to agree. People don't just passively react to social stimuli. Instead, they attempt to regulate and control the information they

**self-presentation**
the process by which people attempt to create specific, generally positive impressions regarding themselves—also known as impression management.

present to others. Although they may not be fully aware of it, people have agendas that they wish to accomplish during social interactions, and they engage in self-presentation. **Self-presentation**, or impression management, is the process by which people attempt to create specific, generally positive impressions regarding themselves (Schlenker, 1980; Schlenker & Weigold, 1992). One way to do this is through self-monitoring.

## Self-Monitoring: Keeping Tabs on One's Behavior

**self-monitoring**
a regulating of one's behavior to meet the demands of a situation or the expectations of others.

Most of us have acquaintances who appear at ease in almost any social situation, easily fitting in with others. And most of us also know people who seem oblivious to social norms, who act as if driven by an inner compass that does not vary from one situation to another.

The differences between the two types of people reflect differences in self-monitoring (Snyder, 1974, 1979, 1987). **Self-monitoring** describes the regulation of one's behavior to meet the demands of a situation or the expectations of others. Although self-monitoring is related to public self-consciousness, self-monitoring involves more extensive behavioral adjustments to the perceived expectations of others. Self-monitoring focuses on how one presents oneself, whereas self-consciousness emphasizes the object of one's attention.

People who are chronically high in self-monitoring lead very different lives from those who are characteristically lower in the trait. As indicated in the sample items from the scale that measures self-monitoring, presented in Figure 4-10, high self-monitors are social chameleons, changing their colors according to the requirements of the situation (Snyder, 1974; Snyder & Gangestad, 1986). They are attentive to how others expect them to behave, concerned about the appropriateness of their behavior, and adept at changing their behavior to match their understanding of the social situation.

In contrast, low self-monitors are relatively insensitive to the social demands of a given situation. As a consequence, their behavior is more consistent across situations (Ajzen, Timko, & White, 1982; Shaffer, Smith, & Tomarelli, 1982; Prislin, Akrap, & Sprah, 1987; Lippa & Donaldson, 1990). In addition, low self-monitors seem to have a clearer sense of themselves. They see themselves as having a "principled self," based on their own philosophy of behavior, as opposed to the "pragmatic self" of the high self-monitor (Snyder, 1987).

A good deal of research has illustrated stark differences between high and low self-monitors in a variety of domains. For example, high self-monitors seek out information about other people, and they remember that information better (Snyder, 1987). They make more accurate courtroom eyewitnesses than low self-monitors. Given that high self-monitors are so keenly aware of the happenings in their social environment, they pay more attention to what is happening—even in the midst of a crime (Hosch & Platz,

---

**FIGURE 4-10    Sample Items from the Self-Monitoring Scale**

*Items Relating to High Self-Monitoring*

I would probably make a good actor.

I may deceive people by being friendly when I really dislike them.

I can make impromptu speeches even on topics about which I have almost no information.

In different situations and with different people, I often act like very different persons.

*Items Relating to Low Self-Monitoring*

I find it hard to imitate the behavior of other people.

In a group of people, I am rarely the center of attention.

I can only argue for ideas which I already believe.

I feel a bit awkward in company and do not show up quite as well as I should.

*Source:* Snyder, M., & Gangestad, S. (1986).

1984). On the other hand, high self-monitors do not make perfect witnesses; they are likely to be tripped up by leading questions (Lassiter, Stone, & Weigold, 1988).

High and low self-monitors also differ in the nature of their personal relationships. High self-monitors remember more about others, and they appear more friendly and less anxious to observers (Berscheid et al., 1976; Lippa, 1976). Furthermore, the kinds of relationships they have with others is qualitatively different from those of low self-monitors. High self-monitors are more likely to choose their friends on the basis of the particular activity in which they are interested and less on the friend's personal qualities, such as attitude similarity. Thus, if high self-monitors want to play tennis, they'll choose a partner on the basis of tennis ability; low self-monitors, in contrast, will be more apt to choose on the basis of friendship (Snyder, Gangestad, & Simpson, 1983). Dating behavior shows a similar pattern: Low self-monitors choose dates more or less independently of the specific activity, while high self-monitors are more influenced by the nature of the particular activity (Snyder & Simpson, 1984).

In sum, high self-monitors place a premium on responding effectively to the demands of a social situation. They make shrewd and accurate assessments of what behaviors are best suited to a given social situation, and they attempt to carry out those behaviors. Does this mean that it is better to be a "pragmatic" high self-monitor than a "principled" low self-monitor?

The answer depends on one's values. On the one hand, an observer might label the behavior of high self-monitors as superficial, transitory, equivocating, and seeming to lack underlying integrity. (Think of politicians who make promises based on whatever they think their particular audience wishes to hear.) On the other hand, the behavior of a low self-monitor might be viewed as rigid, insensitive, and thoughtless. A skeptic might view low self-monitors as people who are socially incompetent, are unheeding of others, or simply don't care about the social niceties that keep the engine of social relations running smoothly.

The truth, no doubt, lies somewhere in between. Both low and high self-monitors can lead effective social lives. Both low and high self-monitoring strategies permit people to present themselves in ways that balance their desire to expedite social interactions and maintain their own sense of themselves. Furthermore, it appears that the tendency to self-monitor decreases with age. For example, one study that looked at a sample of people ranging in age from adolescence to old age found that self-monitoring scores decline with age (Reifman, Klein, & Murphy, 1989). Apparently, as people become older, they may feel more comfortable in "letting it all hang out."

---

## Self-Presentation: Selling Ourselves to Others

If "all the world's a stage," as Shakespeare wrote, a good deal of time is spent in the consideration of playing roles and developing scripts. No one wants to look foolish, or ignorant, or inept; people want to be seen in the best possible light. To this end, people try to present themselves in positive ways.

Why do we care what others think about us? According to social psychologist Roy Baumeister, two main motives fuel self-presentation goals (Baumeister & Hutton, 1987). The first is audience pleasing. **Audience pleasing** is behavior designed to make an audience feel good. As a rule, people want others to experience a positive reaction to them, either because they generally want to please others or because they want to manipulate others' behavior in particular ways. People may also want to prevent others from holding them responsible for undesirable consequences of their behavior (Baumeister, 1982; Schlenker, 1982; Baumeister, Hutton, & Tice, 1989).

**audience pleasing**
behavior designed to make an audience feel good.

Another reason that people are motivated to make good impressions has to do with self-construction. **Self-construction** is self-presentation meant to corroborate our own view of ourselves. We try to make our behavior match our "ideal self," supporting a positive view of ourselves. Moreover, we self-present in order to "audition" different selves, with the goal of choosing identities that might eventually be incorporated into

**self-construction**
self-presentation meant to corroborate an individual's own view of self.

## FIGURE 4-11   Self-presentational Strategies

The major strategies used in self-presentation, classified according to the attributions we seek others to make.

| | ATTRIBUTIONS SOUGHT | NEGATIVE ATTRIBUTIONS RISKED | EMOTION TO BE AROUSED | PROTOTYPICAL ACTIONS |
|---|---|---|---|---|
| 1. Ingratiation | Likable | Sycophant Conformist Obsequious | Affection | Self-characterization Opinion conformity Other enhancement Favors |
| 2. Self-promotion | Competent (effective, "a winner") | Fraudulent Conceited Defensive | Respect (awe, deference) | Performance claims Performance accounts Performances |
| 3. Intimidation | Dangerous (ruthless, volatile) | Blusterer Wishy-washy Ineffectual | Fear | Threats (Incipient) anger (Incipient) breakdown |
| 4. Exemplification | Worthy (suffers, dedicated) | Hypocrite Sanctimonious Exploitative | Guilt (shame, emulation) | Self-denial Helping Militancy for a cause |
| 5. Supplication | Helpless (handicapped, unfortunate) | Stigmatized Lazy Demanding | Nurturance (obligation) | Self-deprecation Entreaties for help |

*Source:* Adapted from Jones, 1990, p. 198.

our central identity. A relatively introverted person might, for instance, try to act particularly outgoing at a social occasion in order to see how others react. In sum, other people are not the only audience of our self-presentations; sometimes we are seeking to see the impact of our behavior for ourselves.

In addition to the audience pleasing and self-construction motives for self-presentation, social psychologist Edward Jones suggests that an additional motive lies behind self-presentational goals—the attainment of power during social interaction (Jones & Pittman, 1982; Jones, 1990). Jones argues that people attempt to maintain and augment their social power through self-presentation, in order to better attain their own social goals. To Jones, self-presentation involves several strategies, including ingratiation, self-promotion, intimidation, exemplification, and supplication. These are summarized in Figure 4-11.

**INGRATIATION: THE ART OF SELF-PRESENTATION.**   According to Jones (Jones, 1990), one of the keys to effective self-presentation is ingratiation. **Ingratiation** is a deliberate effort to make a favorable impression, often through flattery. Through the use of various ingratiation strategies, people seek to make themselves more likable. For instance, people can ingratiate themselves by agreeing with others' opinions. Other ingratiation approaches include doing favors for others, and praising another person's achievements, conduct, or personality.

**ingratiation**
a deliberate effort to make a favorable impression, often through flattery.

Ingratiation does not always proceed along a smooth path. The dilemma that ingratiators face is that if not done with subtlety and finesse, ingratiation can backfire as the recipient of ingratiation realizes the true motivations of the ingratiation. In fact, there is something of a Catch-22 in ingratiation: The less power a person has in a particular situation, the more apt that person is to try to use ingratiation tactics. At the same time, however, ingratiation from a person with lower power is more likely to be seen for what it is and consequently is generally less effective. For example, when a store employee effusively praises her boss, the boss may suspect that the flattery is an attempt to get a raise.

When presidential candidate Michael Dukakis donned army garb, he was attempting to present himself as a supporter of the military. Unfortunately, Dukakis's self-presentation efforts did not have the intended results, as many voters reacted negatively when seeing this photo.

Sometimes, though, ingratiators have little to worry about, because both ingratiators and the targets of their ingratiation may engage in a kind of conspiracy. Both ingratiators and targets are motivated not to expose ingratiation—ingratiators because they don't want to see themselves as manipulative, and targets because they actually want to believe the flattery they are receiving. This mutual self-deception promotes positive feelings for both parties in the interaction.

**SELF-PROMOTION: CREATING THE IMPRESSION OF COMPETENCE.**    While people using ingratiation focus their efforts on making themselves seem more likable, **self-promotion** techniques are designed to make a person seem more competent. Job interviews represent an instance where self-preservation concerns will be more focused on cultivating an air of competence than likability. In such a case, a person may use self-promotion techniques.

Self-promotion can be carried out in several ways. For example, people may flaunt or boast about their prior successes, and minimize previous failures. They also may admit a minor weakness, secondary to the ability that is of primary concern (Baumeister & Jones, 1978). By admitting a weakness, self-promoters hope to show that although they have both strong and weak points, in general they are confident about their overall ability. In addition, admitting a weakness helps disguise the fact that they are self-promoting.

Of course, the use of self-promotion, like ingratiation, carries several risks. For instance, self-promoters gamble that they will not be seen as conceited or defensive. Furthermore, if it is discovered that their underlying ability is actually less than it was made out to be, they may appear fraudulent. Still, self-promotion remains one of the primary self-presentational strategies (Giacalone & Rosenfeld, 1986; Gardner, 1992).

**INTIMIDATION AND EXEMPLIFICATION.**    Some self-presentation strategies are more blatant. **Intimidation** occurs when people communicate an ability and inclination to provide negative outcomes to others. For instance, a high-level employee who implies that a low-level worker will be dismissed if the low-level worker doesn't provide a particular favor is using intimidation.

Although such a technique certainly lacks refinement and subtlety, it may be useful in bringing about desired outcomes. However, people using intimidation may, in the process, end up being disliked. Consequently, intimidation is often reserved for social situations in which relationships are involuntary, such as disagreeable and tough college professors using intimidation to motivate their students.

**self-promotion**
an individual's efforts or techniques designed to make him or her appear more competent.

**intimidation**
the process of communicating an ability and inclination to provide negative outcomes to others.

A job interview is a setting in which people strive to use self-promotion techniques, in which applicants seek to make themselves appear competent.

**exemplification**
a technique in which people attempt to create an impression of moral superiority and integrity.

In some ways, the self-presentational tactic that is the polar opposite of intimidation is **exemplification**, a technique in which people attempt to create the impression of moral superiority and integrity. Rather than seeking to control a situation through fear, as with intimidation, people using this tactic try to present themselves in such a virtuous light that they control the situation. The danger with exemplification is that people using this tactic may be seen as hypocritical or sanctimonious, as when rich people brag about the amount of money they give to the needy.

**SUPPLICATION: POWER THROUGH NEEDINESS.** A final means of self-presentation is **supplication**, which consists of creating the impression that one is needy, weak, and dependent. For instance, panhandlers may justify their request for some change by saying that they are hungry or homeless; students may beg a professor for a higher grade in a class, pleading that they are on academic probation and will be thrown out of school if they don't get a certain grade. By creating an aura of neediness, supplication attempts to make others feel responsible for our needs. Consequently, others may decide to help. Supplication is usually the self-presentation technique of last resort, used by people with little power.

**supplication**
the process of creating the impression that one is needy, weak, and dependent.

*The Language of Self-Presentation: Maintaining Social Control Through Words and Actions*

Perhaps you've been surprised, and even slightly annoyed, by a telephone salesperson who calls you at home and uses your first name as if you were long-time friends. Or perhaps you've overheard a conversation between a young physician and an elderly patient in which the physician uses the patient's first name, while the patient addresses the physician with her formal title of "Doctor."

**THE SPOKEN WORD AND SELF-PRESENTATION.** As these two examples illustrate, the kind of spoken language that people employ has important self-presentational consequences (Levinson, 1980; Clark, 1985). For instance, the choice of language helps maintain and direct the nature of the social relationship between two speakers. Difference in status between two speakers is often represented in the way the two people address one another. People use first names when addressing close friends, and they use formal titles (Doctor, Congressman, Ms.) and last names when addressing someone of higher status.

Within a status level, there is a fairly strong tendency to reciprocate the level of formality in address.

When two people at different status levels have been addressing each other at different levels of intimacy, such as Mr. Coats (the boss) who addresses his employee as "Erik," the form of address may eventually change as the level of intimacy evolves. However, such changes usually occur only at the behest of the higher-status person. For instance, it is likely that Mr. Coats would need to ask Erik to address him more informally before Erik would do so.

According to social psychologist Roger Brown and colleagues, choices of address are based upon the power semantic and the solidarity semantic (Brown & Gilman, 1960). The **power semantic** is the power or status level that a conversant holds, while the **solidarity semantic** refers to the degree of shared social experience between two people. The power semantic suggests that people of greater power or status ought to be addressed with great formality, while the solidarity semantic operates to allow greater familiarly between people—for example, between close neighbors, friends, or classmates.

In many languages other than English, the existence of distinct forms of "you" allows power and solidarity semantics to be reflected in the form a speaker chooses—whether formal or informal. In French, a speaker must choose between *tu* (familiar) and *vous* (formal); in German, the choice is between *du* (familiar) and *Sie* (formal). Each culture has its own set of rules. For example, the French use *tu* for intimate friends, family, and children, and *vous* for nonfamilial adults. And children use *vous* for all adults except their closest family members.

A number of shifts have occurred in the use of the formal and informal "you" that seem to be reflective of historical and cultural changes in society. In societies in which there has been movement toward greater egalitarianism, the trend has been toward less distinction between use of the formal and informal "you." In modern France, more people are addressed by the informal *tu* than ever before. And at one time, English speakers had a choice between "you" and "thou," a distinction which of course has long since disappeared from everyday conversation.

In addition to conveying the nature of intimacy between conversants, the language one employs also helps create impressions regarding one's political leanings. Thus, people who consistently address women as "Ms.," rather than using "Miss" or "Mrs.," may be making a political statement regarding their views of feminism (Tannen, 1991).

**NONVERBAL BEHAVIOR AND SELF-PRESENTATION: MAKING USE OF DISPLAY RULES.** When people receive a gift that turns out to be terribly disappointing, they rarely frown, pout, or otherwise outwardly display signs of unhappiness. Instead, people in this situation are likely to smile and proclaim how pleased they are to have received, for instance, a package of socks and underwear. What prevents these people from revealing how they are actually feeling are social norms that define appropriate behavior. Social norms are learned early on in life and tell us, among other things, that gift givers should be thanked and made to feel that their gifts are appreciated. Such norms influence not only verbal behavior, but nonverbal behavior as well.

The guidelines that govern what society sees as appropriate nonverbal behavior are known as display rules (Ekman, Friesen, & Ellsworth, 1972; Ekman & O'Sullivan, 1991). **Display rules** are the implicit rules that define what type of nonverbal behavior is appropriate for a given situation or interpersonal relationship, and what type is not. These display rules are mastered during childhood as children's cognitive abilities and control of their facial muscles increase (Feldman, 1982, 1991; Halberstadt, 1991).

There are at least four strategies through which display rules can modify the expression of emotion: intensifying, deintensifying, neutralizing, and masking an emotion (Ekman, Friesen, & Ellsworth, 1972). Using intensification, one exaggerates an expression, such as a smile, to communicate a greater degree of feeling than is actually being experienced. In deintensification, the opposite occurs—the communication of a

**power semantic**
the power or status level that an individual has in relation to another.

**solidarity semantic**
the degree of shared social experience between two people.

**display rules**
the implicit rules that define what type of nonverbal behavior is appropriate for a given situation or interpersonal relationship, and what type is not.

Gabriela Sabatini, on the left, and opponent Mary-Joe Fernandez, following their match in the Australian Open. Display rules prevent us from easily determining from their facial expressions who was the winner and who the loser. (In case you are wondering, Sabatini is congratulating Fernandez on her win.)

felt emotion is minimized. When, for example, we have bested someone in a business negotiation, we may try not to show how happy we are; rather, we try to minimize our true delight.

When people neutralize an expression, they attempt to withhold any indication of how they actually feel. The term "poker face" characterizes situations in which someone attempts to show no emotion of any sort. This is accomplished by neutralizing the non-verbal expressions representative of emotions that are actually being experienced.

The most extreme form of modification of nonverbal behavior occurs when someone masks one expression with another. For instance, you might mask your glee at the funeral of an old and hated rival with appropriate expressions of grief, or you might smile and congratulate the winner of a race for which you had trained extensively. In both examples, the expression that is being displayed is just the opposite of the feeling being experienced.

How successful are people at self-presentation that occurs through the modification of facial expressions? Although the research evidence is not entirely consistent, in many cases people are able to manage and disguise their nonverbal behavior successfully (Miller & Burgoon, 1982; DePaulo, 1991; Miller & Stiff, 1992). However, no matter how much effort they employ, there are always visible differences between true and feigned emotional displays.

For instance, psychologist Paul Ekman and colleagues have found differences between true smiles of enjoyment and those that are produced to conceal negative emotions (Ekman, Friesen, & O'Sullivan, 1988). True smiles, known as "Duchenne smiles," involve a unique pattern of facial muscles that does not appear in false ones (see Figure 4-12, which illustrates the subtle difference between feigned and Duchenne smiles).

Given that display rules are socialized during childhood, it should not be surprising that the use of display rules varies greatly across cultures. For instance, in Asian cultures it is generally considered inappropriate to display emotions, while in Mediterranean and Latin cultures volatile nonverbal displays are expected in social interactions.

In addition to general differences in nonverbal expressiveness, research has found that cultures sometimes differ with regard to the display of a particular emotion. For example, one study found that the Japanese, who place a strong emphasis on group harmony and cohesion within their own ingroup, felt that nonverbal displays of anger and disgust were more appropriately shown to outgroup members than to ingroup members.

a

b

c

**FIGURE 4-12** Which is the true smile? The smile in (a) is a Duchenne (true) smile, while those in (b) and (c) are all false, masking smiles    *Source:* Ekman, Friesen, & O'Sullivan

In comparison, people in the United States, a more individualistic culture, felt that displays of anger, disgust, and sadness were more permissible toward members of ingroups than toward outgroups (Matsumoto, 1990; Lee et al., 1992).

---

# THE INFORMED CONSUMER OF SOCIAL PSYCHOLOGY

## MAKING A GOOD IMPRESSION

Regardless of whether we are high or low self-monitors, all of us are concerned to some degree with presenting ourselves well—as much of the material in this chapter has illustrated. As it turns out, research conducted by social psychologists suggests several effective strategies for making a positive impression. In addition to the specific self-presentation techniques we have already discussed (such as ingratiation, self-promotion, intimidation, exemplification, and supplication), several broad principles underlie successful self-presentation (Kleinke, 1986; Snyder, 1977; Schlenker, 1980; Fiske & Taylor, 1991):

- *Conform to the social norms of a given situation.* Every social situation has particular norms concerning appropriate behavior. At a dance, it is permissible to dance with a friend's date,

but asking for too many dances from that person might be frowned upon. When we attend funerals, society suggests that we should wear dark colors and say only nice things about the recently departed, no matter how much we disliked that person. Keeping situational norms in mind is central to creating a good impression (Sagatun & Knudsen, 1982).

- *Use behavioral matching.* Another way to produce a good impression is to try to match the behavior of others. Research indicates that people in successful interactions coordinate and synchronize their interpersonal interactions, both on a verbal and nonverbal level (Bernieri & Rosenthal, 1991).

- *Use verbal immediacy in your conversations.* "Immediacy" refers to the directness and intensity of a verbal communication. For example, saying "I'd like to go with you to the lecture" is more immediate than saying "I guess I'll go to the lecture." Qualifications such as "maybe," "I suppose," "kind of," and "I think" make communications less immediate, and they are seen by others as being less personal. Consequently, more immediate communications make a more positive impression.

- *Keep verbal and nonverbal behavior congruent with one another.* To be perceived as genuine and trustworthy, it is important that verbal and nonverbal messages match. If you're trying to convey that you are pleased, make sure that your nonverbal behavior matches what you are saying. Otherwise, you may come across as counterfeit and deceptive (Feldman, 1992).

- *Don't overstate your accomplishments—but don't understate them, either.* Honesty *is* the best policy when it comes to discussing your positive assets. If you exaggerate your accomplishments, you'll be seen as a braggart. If you minimize your assets, you're not putting your best foot forward and you may be seen as lacking confidence. Presenting yourself effectively, then, is in part a matter of presenting yourself honestly.

## ► REVIEW & RETHINK

### Review

- People differ widely in their levels of self-monitoring, which consists of the regulation of their behavior to meet the demands of a situation or the expectations of others.
- Self-presentation, the result of audience pleasing and self-construction motivations, occurs through both verbal and nonverbal behavior.
- Several strategies underlie self-presentation, including ingratiation, self-promotion, intimidation, exemplification, and supplication.

### Rethink

- Discuss three possible reasons why people actively use self-presentation techniques.
- High and low self-monitors will often choose different self-promotional techniques. Discuss the types of self-promotion, focusing on which group would be likely to prefer each.
- Using the notions of power semantic and solidarity semantic, explain how an employee might begin referring to his supervisor by his first name instead of "Mr."
- Explain how different norms regarding nonverbal display might have contributed to the stereotype in the United States of "inscrutable Asians." What corresponding stereotypes might Asians hold about Americans?

## LOOKING BACK  ◄ ◄ ◄ ◄ ◄ ◄ ◄ ◄ ◄ ◄ ◄ ◄ ◄ ◄ ◄ ◄ ◄ ◄ ◄ ◄ ◄ ◄ ◄ ◄

### *What are the components of the self?*

1. Self-concept is a person's sense of identity, the set of beliefs about what he or she is like as an individual. Cognitions about identity comprise self-schema—an organized body of information that relates to a person's self, pertaining to specific domains, such as dependence or femininity.

2. In addition to self-schemas, part of the self is comprised of possible selves, those aspects of self that relate to the future. In addition, the concept of identity reflects roles and group categories to which a person belongs, along with the set of personal meanings and experiences related to the roles and categories.

### *How do people use others' (and their own) behavior to assess their abilities, emotions, and attitudes?*

3. Because people have a need to evaluate their opinions and abilities—a need for social comparison—they determine their ability by comparing themselves to others who are similar to themselves along relevant dimensions. In addition, the two-factor theory of emotions suggests that when people are unsure about how they feel, they may infer eir emotional state

by observing the behavior of others and the nature of the situation in which they find themselves.

4.  Self-perception theory suggests that, to the extent that situational cues or past experience are irrelevant, weak, or ambiguous, people become aware of their own dispositions, emotions, attitudes, and other internal states through observation of their own behavior. One derivative of the theory is the concept of overjustification, which may occur when incentives replace intrinsic motivation.

5.  Action identification theory suggests that people's interpretation of their own behavior varies in terms of whether the behavior is seen at a high (abstract) or low (more concrete) level. It asserts that the level at which people typically view their current actions affects the stability of behavior and has implications for future behavior change.

6.  One cultural difference in the view of self is found between Western and Asian cultures. Asian societies have a more interdependent view of their selves, while people living in Western countries have a more independent perspective.

### How can self-esteem and self-awareness color our interactions with others?

7.  Self-esteem is the affective component of self, consisting of a person's general and specific positive and negative self-evaluations. Low self-esteem may lead to a cycle of failure, although it may be overcome by increasing a person's sense of self-efficacy—learned expectations that one is capable of carrying out a behavior or producing a desired outcome in a particular situation.

8.  Self-awareness is a state in which people focus attention on the self. By increasing self-awareness, people begin to focus on how their actual self compares to the ideal standards they hold for themselves, typically resulting in an unpleasant affective state.

9.  The two types of self-awareness are private self-consciousness and public self-consciousness. People vary in the type of self-consciousness that they typically experience.

### What biases exist in the way people view themselves?

10.  The actor–observer bias is the tendency for actors (the individuals involved in a situation) to attribute their behavior to situational requirements, while observers tend to attribute the same behavior to stable dispositions. Perceptual, informational, and social comparison explanations have been suggested to explain the phenomenon.

11.  Self-handicapping is a tactic in which people set up circumstances that allow them to avoid attributing poor performance to low ability and instead can attribute failure to less-threatening causes. Self-handicapping strategies fall along two dimensions—internal versus external, and acquired versus claimed. Not all self-handicapping is strategically wrong; the use of excuses, for instance, can have positive benefits for self-esteem and achievement.

### What self-presentation strategies do people employ, and which are most effective?

12.  Self-presentation, or impression management, is the process by which people attempt to create specific, generally positive impressions regarding themselves. People differ in their typical level of self-monitoring, which consists of regulating one's behavior to meet the demands of a situation or the expectations of others.

13.  Two main motives lie behind self-monitoring efforts—audience pleasing (focused on pleasing others) and self-construction (meant to confirm our own view of ourselves).

14.  Among the self-presentational strategies that people employ are ingratiation, self-promotion, intimidation, exemplification, and supplication. Self-presentation also occurs through the use of particular kinds of language and through efforts to control nonverbal behavior through display rules.

15.  Among the ways that people can make an optimum impression on others are to conform to the social norms of a given situation, to use behavioral matching, to use verbal immediacy in conversation, to keep verbal and nonverbal behavior congruent with one another, and to be accurate in stating one's accomplishments.

# KEY TERMS AND CONCEPTS

*self-concept (p. 112)*

*self-schema (p. 112)*

*possible selves (p. 113)*

*identity (p. 114)*

*social comparison (p. 117)*

*social reality (p. 117)*

*downward social comparison (p. 117)*

*two-factor theory of emotion (p. 118)*

*self-perception theory (p. 118)*

*overjustification (p. 119)*

*action identification theory (p. 120)*

*self-esteem (p. 123)*

*self-efficacy (p. 123)*

*self-evaluation maintenance theory (p. 124)*

*self-awareness (p. 125)*

*private self-consciousness (p. 125)*

*public self-consciousness (p. 125)*

*actor–observer bias (p. 126)*

*self-serving bias (p. 127)*

*self-handicapping (p. 127)*

*self-presentation (p. 131)*

*self-monitoring (p. 131)*

*audience pleasing (p. 132)*

*self-construction (p. 132)*

*ingratiation (p. 133)*

*self-promotion (p. 134)*

*intimidation (p. 134)*

*exemplification (p. 135)*

*supplication (p. 135)*

*power semantic (p. 136)*

*solidarity semantic (p. 136)*

*display rules (p. 136)*

# FOR FURTHER RESEARCH AND STUDY

Jones, E. E. (1990). *Interpersonal perception.* New York: Freeman.

This book is a well-written, straightforward introduction to the ways in which people look at others and themselves. In particular, it provides a useful discussion of the pros and cons of various self-presentational strategies.

Kleinke, C. L. (1986). *Meeting and understanding people.* New York: Freeman.

This practical book summarizes research findings on impression management and presents workable suggestions for presenting oneself in a way that promotes getting along with others.

Snyder, D. R., Higgins, R. L., & Stucky, R. J. (1983). *Excuses: Masquerades in search of grace.* New York: Wiley-Interscience.

A comprehensive look at excuses—those that work and those that don't.

Tannen, D. (1991). *You just don't understand.* New York: Ballantine.

A lively discussion on how the language that men and women use affects the ways in which they are perceived by others.

# EPILOGUE

In our consideration of the self, we've focused on how people view and evaluate themselves, and on their strategies for presenting themselves effectively to the world. To put it another way, we've examined the self in terms of its cognitive, affective, and behavioral components. As we'll see in Chapters 10 and 11, such a three-part consideration of self mirrors the view, held by many theorists, that attitudes are composed of cognitive, affective, and behavioral components.

What we haven't yet discussed, though, is how our sense of self relates to our general well-being, both on a psychological and physical level. In the next chapter we turn to this issue, considering how social psychological factors underlie both our physical and mental health.

To round out our consideration of the self, then, we consider such topics as how our sense of well-being is affected by the kinds of illusions we hold about ourselves and the world, how we cope with stress, and how major health problems have social psychological components. In our discussion of these topics, we'll discover how the understanding of the self that we arrived at in this chapter leads to concrete suggestions regarding how to better people's physical and mental resiliency and coping capabilities.

# CHAPTER FIVE

# WELL-BEING AND HEALTH PSYCHOLOGY

## CARING FOR THE SELF

# PROLOGUE: SPREADING THE ABC'S OF HIV

The din inside the downtown Seattle video arcade is overpowering—guns blasting away, bells ringing wildly. None of the 50 or so teens inside notices the tall kid with a Falcons cap who walks in. He steps up to two boys engrossed in a shooting game. "Hey, brothers, you using condoms?" he asks. They

AIDS represents one of the major health problems of the twentieth century. By the year 2000, it is estimated that one million people in the United States alone will be infected.

nod, barely looking his way. "Need some?" he says, shoving a handful toward them. The boys grab the condoms and stuff them into their pockets. The intruder isn't finished with them. "Know much about AIDS and HIV?" he continues, with the patter of a door-to-door salesman. "Yeah," they answer, in unison. "Then you know you can get it from unprotected sex and from sharing needles?" They nod. He quickly hands them a brochure: "This will answer any other questions you have."

The kid in the Falcons cap is Kevin Turner; and at 19, he is already an experienced warrior on the front lines of the battle against AIDS. He carries his weapon of choice—condoms—in a black leather bag strapped around his chest. Turner works for POCAAN (People of Color Against AIDS Network). Officially, he's a peer educator; unofficially, he's "Mr. Condom," on call 24 hours a day. He gives out hundreds of condoms every week and has been known to burst into conversations when he hears someone talking about sex. "You're going to use condoms, aren't you?" he'll ask. "Here, have a few." (Kantrowitz, 1992, p. 45)

## LOOKING AHEAD

▶ ▶ ▶ ▶ ▶ ▶ ▶ ▶ ▶ ▶ ▶ ▶ ▶ ▶ ▶ ▶ ▶ ▶ ▶ ▶ ▶ ▶ ▶ ▶ ▶ ▶ ▶ ▶

Despite the fact that AIDS is a life-and-death matter and Kevin Turner is working to prevent its spread, his is not an easy job. To many people, the risk of AIDS—as well as other illnesses—seems remote; and motivating people to engage in behavior that protects their well-being is a complicated endeavor.

In this chapter, we continue our focus on the self by considering social psychological issues relating to well-being and health. Issues relating to a sense of well-being and health have become a central part of the discipline, with many social psychologists concentrating on issues of wellness and the prevention and treatment of medical problems.

We begin our discussion by focusing on psychological well-being and mental health. We'll consider how our view of the self influences our perception of well-being, how a sense of helplessness may lead to depression, and how attributional patterns affect psychological health. We also discuss how certain kinds of mistaken illusions we hold may produce a sense of well-being.

Next, we consider stress and coping. We examine the causes of stress, its short- and long-term consequences, and the strategies that have been developed to deal with stress. We then turn to a discussion of three major health issues: coronary heart disease, cancer, and AIDS. We'll look in particular at how social factors affect the course of the disease.

Finally, we discuss physician–patient interactions. We'll see that the way physicians and other health-care workers communicate with patients has important implications for the success of treatment, and we'll discuss patient compliance to medical recommendations.

In sum, after reading this chapter, you'll be able to answer these questions:

- What are the ingredients of a sense of psychological well-being?
- What are the determinants and consequences of stress, and what are the strategies for coping with it?
- What are the social psychological components of coronary heart disease, cancer, and AIDS?
- How do patients' interactions with their physicians affect their health and their compliance to medical treatment?

# PSYCHOLOGICAL WELL-BEING

How are you?

If you're like most people, the answer you give will depend on a constellation of factors. Before you reply, you'll perhaps think about the bruise on your knee, or the headache you've had since you woke up, or the itching poison ivy on your arm. However, you won't stop there: How you assess your well-being depends on psychological factors as well. Your mood, your emotional state, your level of anxiety—all will enter into your response to the question.

In sum, our overall sense of well-being is influenced as much by our everyday state of mind as it is by physiological factors. Building on theory and research on the self that we discussed in Chapter 4, social psychologists have examined the social psychological components that determine people's sense of well-being.

## Self-Complexity and Well-Being: The Benefits of Multiple Selves

**self-complexity**
the phenomenon of viewing oneself as having many distinct facets.

Although mothers who work and raise their children report high levels of stress, they typically have a sense of greater psychological well-being than women who don't have a job outside the home.

Do you see yourself as primarily a woman or man, a student, or a son or daughter? Or is your view of yourself more multifaceted, made up of a complex mixture of roles and attributes?

Although all of us hold various self-schemas of the sort we spoke about in the previous chapter, some people's view of themselves is more complex than others'. According to social psychologist Patricia Linville (1987), **self-complexity** is the phenomenon of viewing oneself as having many distinct facets.

Self-complexity is important because it seems to function as a barrier against illness and depression. People with higher self-complexity show a greater resistance to depression brought about by stress, and even their rate of physical stress-related illness is lower.

How does self-complexity produce its benefits? The answer lies in the multiple roles that self-complexity encompasses. When a person with high self-complexity has difficulties on the job, for instance, she can turn for psychological compensation to successes she is experiencing in other domains of her life. On the other hand, when a woman with low self-complexity, who defines herself primarily in terms of her career performance, has problems on the job, the story is very different. Because she does not have as many alternate selves to which to turn, the consequences of the problems are more profound.

The findings relating to self-complexity help explain an otherwise puzzling phenomenon: Women who juggle jobs and family obligations often report a higher degree of mastery, pride, and competence than women who stay at home to raise their children (Hoffman, 1989; Crosby, 1991). Although they report high levels of stress and typically do a greater percentage of the housework than their husbands (Googans & Burden, 1987; Biernat & Wortman, 1991), women who both work and help raise children still end up with a sense of greater psychological well-being than women who don't have a job outside the home.

One explanation is that the self-complexity of working mothers increases, providing them with a buffer against stress and stress-related illness. When they experience problems in one domain, women who work and raise a family can turn to the positive aspects of their other roles. Ironically, then, the stress of having more than enough to do may sometimes help as much as it hurts.

*Self-Discrepancy Theory: Matching Real and Ideal*

**self-discrepancy theory**
the argument that the discrepancy between people's self-concept and their self-guides leads to negative emotions and ultimately to lower psychological well-being.

Who we are is not always who we would like to be. Despite our desire to be brilliant, likable, and terrific-looking, the truth is that many of us see ourselves as quite different from our ideal.

According to social psychologist E. Tory Higgins's self-discrepancy theory, people compare their self-view to internalized standards called "self-guides." **Self-discrepancy theory** argues that the discrepancy between people's self-concept and their self-guides leads to negative emotions and ultimately to lower psychological well-being (Higgins, 1989).

What are the "self-guides" to which the theory refers? Self-guides are the standards that people strive to attain. There are actually several types of self-guides. *ideal self* is made up of those hopes and aspirations that either the person or others feel are important. The *ought self* is comprised of what people feel they ought to do—the obligations they place on themselves and on others. In sum, the ideal self is what people want to be, and the ought self is what people feel they should be.

According to the theory, both the degree and kind of discrepancy between actual self and self-guides influence an individual's psychological well-being. For instance, significant discrepancies between actual self and ought self can lead to feelings of guilt, shame, fear, and other emotions related to agitation. Inconsistencies between actual and ideal self may promote disappointment, sadness, dissatisfaction, and other emotions related to dejection. Ultimately, such emotions can result in depression and a reduction in self-esteem. Furthermore, such self-discrepancies can produce a chronic sense of indecision and confusion about one's identity (Van Hook & Higgins, 1988; Moretti & Higgins, 1990).

"I'm only a <u>good</u> dane."

© 1994 Mike Twohy and The Cartoon Bank, Inc.

On the other hand, minor inconsistencies between actual self and self-guides can be helpful in sparking efforts to reduce the discrepancy (Higgins, Strauman, & Klein, 1986). In such cases, incongruities between actual self and self-guides could be expected to promote psychological well-being, while people feel a sense of accomplishment as the gap between their various selves is reduced.

*Self-Disclosure and Well-Being: To Tell the Truth*

**self-disclosure**
a situation in which information about the self is exchanged with others.

How open are you with others?

According to some social psychologists, in certain ways, the more you disclose about yourself, the better. According to this reasoning, **self-disclosure**, in which information about the self is exchanged with others, holds several advantages.

For example, as we'll discuss further in Chapter 7, one important consequence of self-disclosure is that it increases the level of intimacy of social interactions (Jourard, 1971; Derlega & Berg, 1987; Derlega et al., 1993). In turn, this increased level of intimacy may provide social support that can help reduce stress. Self-disclosure also may promote more honest responses from others, who may then be in a position to act as a useful sounding board. In such a situation, others ultimately may provide worthwhile feedback that can reduce stress. (For more on the advantages of self-disclosure, see the accompanying Social Psychology at Work feature on the benefits of confession.)

# SOCIAL PSYCHOLOGY AT WORK

# THE BENEFITS OF CONFESSION

Is confession good for the soul?

According to the research of social psychologist James Pennebaker, confession may be good not only for the soul, but also for the mind and the body. Pennebaker and colleagues have found that giving people the opportunity to air their most personal and disturbing experiences, which they typically have kept hidden, has clear health benefits (Pennebaker, 1990).

In a series of experiments, Pennebaker has explored the results of revealing information that people usually keep to themselves. For example, in one study, groups of healthy undergraduates were asked to write over a four-day period a series of anonymous essays about the most traumatic, emotionally upsetting, and stressful events they had experienced during their lifetime. One group was told only to describe the events factually; a second group was instructed to write about their feelings—but not the facts—about them; and a third group wrote about both the facts *and* their feelings concerning the events. There was also a control group that wrote about insignificant topics for the four-day period (Pennebaker & Beall, 1986).

The nature of subjects' confessions had important, long-lasting consequences. Subjects who wrote about the emotions or about the combined facts and emotions of past traumatic events reported feeling the most upset directly following their participation in the study. However, as the results displayed in Figure 5-1 indicate, the long-term outcomes were more positive. Six months after the study, subjects who had written about the facts *and* their emotions reported feeling

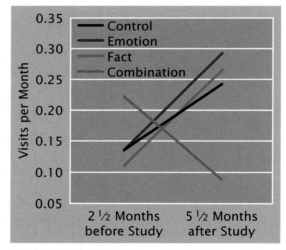

**FIGURE 5-1 The Value of Confession** Subjects who wrote about both the facts and their feelings concerning difficult events showed reduced visits to the student health services five and a half months later.
*(Source: Pennebaker & Beall, 1986.)*

healthier and experiencing fewer illnesses, as well as fewer days of restricted activity due to illness, than subjects in the other groups.

In sum, although initially upsetting to the subjects, the disclosure of traumatic information proved to have lasting benefits. But why should confession be so worthwhile? Pennebaker suggests two reasons. First, the act of inhibiting or restraining traumatic information necessitates effort, both of a physical and a mental nature. This effort results in heightened stress that ultimately produces physical symptoms and stress-related illness. The disclosure of hidden past traumas, even if only during the course of a psychological experiment, provides a temporary respite in the effort required to suppress the information. Ultimately, this results in reduced stress and an enhanced sense of well-being.

There is a second reason why confession is worthwhile: When we discuss past traumatic events, either aloud or in writing, we are forced to translate the occurrence into linguistic terms, thereby confronting the event in a way that may be novel to us. Consequently, the use of language may translate unpleasant events into something more coherent and understandable. Ultimately, this translation makes it possible to cope with stress more easily (Pennebaker, 1990).

---

*Attributional Style and Depression: Learning to Be Depressed*

**learned helplessness**
the belief that no control can be exerted over one's environment.

Have you heard someone say, "No matter how hard I try, I'll never do better in math" or "I could rehearse until doomsday, but I know I'll never learn my lines"?

To psychologist Martin Seligman, such statements would probably represent instances of learned helplessness. **Learned helplessness** is the belief that no control may be exerted over one's environment. When people hold such a belief, they feel they cannot escape from the environment, and they may simply give up—leading, in some cases, to profound feelings of depression (Seligman, 1975).

Seligman first demonstrated learned helplessness in experiments with animals. In one experiment he exposed dogs to a series of moderately painful shocks that were not physically damaging but that could not be avoided. Although at first the dogs anxiously tried to escape the shocks, they ultimately realized that escape was impossible, and they eventually accepted them with seeming resignation. It was their subsequent behavior that proved most puzzling: When the same dogs were later placed in a cage in which they *could* avoid the shocks by jumping over a short barrier, they did not. Instead, they passively accepted the shocks, despite the opportunity to escape them. In contrast, a control group of animals, who had not been exposed earlier to the inescapable shocks, readily jumped over the barrier to avoid the shocks.

The results of the experiment convinced Seligman that the dogs had learned to be helpless. He argued that the animals earlier exposed to the uncontrollable shock had been taught a harsh, although erroneous, lesson—that there was no way to escape from the unpleasant experience, and that the only way to deal with it was passive acceptance.

A series of later experiments convincingly demonstrated that both animals and humans experienced the phenomenon. For instance, college students who were not permitted to escape from a shrill tone in an experiment later made fewer attempts to escape the tone than subjects who had not been exposed earlier to the tone—even when the opportunity to escape was available (Hiroto & Seligman, 1975; Mineka & Hendersen, 1985).

Learned helplessness, the belief that no control can be exerted over one's environment, may prevent battered spouses and children from seeking help.

Learned helplessness has proven to be a durable concept, relevant to both physical health and general psychological well-being. For example, battered children and spouses sometimes do not seek out help even when given the opportunity; they come to passively accept what is happening to them and feel there is no way out. Similarly, learned helplessness provides an explanation for severe depression, in which people come to feel that they are the victims of a hostile world beyond their control. Specifically, clinical psychologist Lynn Abramson and colleagues suggest that depression may be the result of hopelessness, a combination of learned helplessness and an expectation that negative outcomes in one's life are inevitable (Abramson, Metalsky, & Alloy, 1989).

Abramson suggests that depression is related to three major types of attributions: stable versus unstable, internal versus external, and global versus specific. The stable–unstable dimension refers to whether the cause of an event is seen as enduring across time (stable) or as temporary (unstable). The internal–external dimension refers to whether the cause is seen as due to personal characteristics and behavior (internal) or to the situation (external). And the global–specific dimension relates to whether the cause is seen as affecting many different aspects of one's life (global) or is restricted to a particular domain (specific).

**attributional style**

a tendency to make particular kinds of causal attributions across different situations.

Those most prone to depression caused by learned helplessness tend to have a particular **attributional style**—a tendency to make particular kinds of causal attributions across different situations (see Figure 5-2). According to this view, people at risk for depression habitually view positive events in their lives as due to external, unstable, and situation-specific causes. For instance, a person with such an attributional style would attribute getting a good job to external causes ("The employer was desperate to hire"), unstable causes ("It was just luck"), and situation-specific causes ("It probably won't happen again").

At the same time, people prone to depression view negative events as brought about by internal, stable, and global causes. For instance, losing a job would be attributed to internal causes ("I'm no good"), stable causes ("I'll never be any better"), and global causes ("No matter what I do, I fail"). When individuals who characteristically make such attributions for positive and negative events encounter a situation in which they lack control, they are apt to experience depression—as well as several other types of health difficulties (Sweeney, Anderson, & Bailey, 1986; Robins, 1988).

Although learned helplessness provides an explanation for severe depression, it is important to note that it is not the only one. For example, genetic and biological factors may predispose people to the ups and downs of depression and related mental health dis-

**FIGURE 5-2 Attributional Styles Leading to Depression** According to Abramson's theory of depression, people at risk for depression habitually view positive events as due to external, unstable, and specific causes. At the same time, they view negative events as produced by internal, stable, and global causes. Both patterns lead to depression.    (*Source:* Based on Abramson, Metalsky, & Alloy, 1989.)

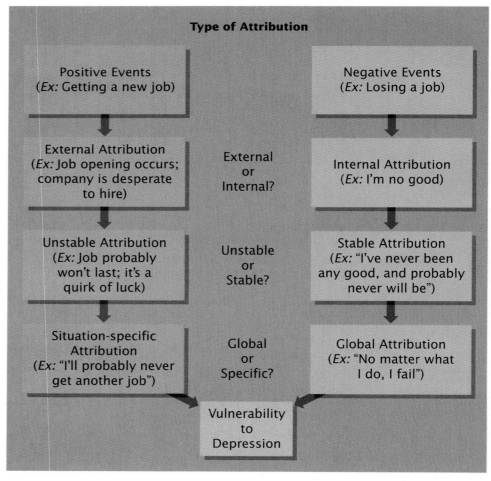

orders (Egeland et al., 1987). In addition, some psychologists argue that depression is the result of maladaptive cognitions. For instance, clinical psychologist Aaron Beck has proposed that depressed people consider themselves as life's losers, blaming themselves whenever anything goes wrong (Beck, Rush, Shaw, & Emery, 1979; Beck, 1991). Because they focus on the negative side of life, they feel incompetent and unable to make constructive changes.

**ATTRIBUTION TRAINING: OVERHAULING FAULTY ATTRIBUTIONS.**    The fact that certain psychological disorders are the result of maladaptive attribution styles suggests a way of restoring psychological well-being—changing people's attributional styles. In fact, social psychologists have developed several forms of **attribution training**, in which inaccurate, harmful attributions are replaced with more accurate and beneficial ones.

**attribution training**
a situation in which inaccurate, harmful attributions are replaced with more accurate and beneficial ones.

In attribution training, social psychologists attempt to alleviate psychological distress and anxiety by replacing internal attributions with external ones. Specifically, the difficulty may be resolved by teaching people to attribute the cause of negative events to some nonthreatening source outside of themselves, and not to their own failings.

Consider, for instance, the plight in which many first-year college students find themselves. If you think back to your own experience, you probably felt some trepidation about your academic performance, how well you compared with your classmates, and whether you were doing as well as you could. If you initially performed poorly, you may have seen this as confirmation of your greatest fears, and perhaps you assumed that you just weren't cut out to make the grade—an attribution based on stable, internal causes.

If you felt this way, you weren't alone: Most first-year college students make similar attributions (Peterson & Barrett, 1987). However, research by social psychologists Timothy Wilson and Patricia Linville (1982, 1985) suggests a way, based on attribution retraining, to break this attributional pattern. They devised a program designed to change first-year students' attributions from stable to unstable causes. Basically, students were exposed to information that led them to attribute their problems to temporary factors that were amenable to change, instead of to permanent, unchangeable causes.

To test their reasoning, the experimenters exposed a group of first-year students at Duke University, who had expressed concern over their first-term performance, to statistical information demonstrating that college students typically improve their grades over the course of their college career. In addition, the subjects watched videotapes of juniors and seniors discussing how their grades had improved since their freshman year.

In comparison to members of a control group, who received no treatment, the students who had experienced the attribution training showed improved grades in the semester following the study, and their dropout rate was significantly lower. As a result, a one-time exposure to information suggesting that first-semester performance was due to unstable rather than stable causes was sufficient to bring about changes in how the students performed.

Other research has shown that it is possible to retrain attributions from internal causes to external ones, resulting in the alleviation of poor performance, psychological distress, and other symptoms. In sum, attribution training, in which inaccurate attributions are replaced with more accurate ones, shows considerable promise (Forsterling, 1985).

**MISATTRIBUTION TRAINING: REPLACING ACCURATE ATTRIBUTIONS WITH INACCURATE ONES.**    In some cases, it is not the inaccuracy of people's attributions that leads to detrimental consequences. In fact, sometimes attributions are all too accurate, producing dysfunctional consequences. In such cases, social psychologists have devised another intervention strategy: misattribution training. In **misattribution training**, people are led to replace their accurate, but harmful, attributions with inaccurate, but more beneficial, attributions.

**misattribution training**
a situation in which people are led to replace their accurate but harmful attributions with inaccurate, but more beneficial attributions.

Consider, for instance, people who have chronic insomnia. For them, going to bed each night is a tension-filled experience: They anticipate having difficulty sleeping, and they lie awake worrying about their problems and experiencing anxiety due to the fact that they are not sleeping. Typically, such insomniacs attribute their inability to sleep to anxiety, to problems in general, or to a host of other personality factors. Such internal attributions make it difficult to go to sleep.

Suppose, however, that insomniacs were told that their inability to get to sleep was due not to anxiety or other internal factors, but to some factor that was essentially beyond their control. It is conceivable that they might fall asleep more quickly than usual, since the usual source of worry—themselves—could not be blamed.

Using this reasoning, Michael Storms and Richard Nisbett (1970) conducted a classic experiment in which they told one group of insomniacs that they would be taking a pill that would relax them and allow them to sleep more easily. In contrast, another group of insomniacs were told that the pill would keep them awake. In reality, the pills given to both groups of subjects were inert sugar pills that had no real physiological effects.

The results of the study supported the prior reasoning. Subjects who were told that they would be able to get to sleep more easily actually took about 15 minutes *longer* to fall asleep than they usually did. In contrast, those who could attribute their initial sleeplessness to the side effects of the pill actually took *less* time to fall asleep than they usually did. Apparently, the fact that these latter subjects could attribute their potential insomnia to an external factor, outside of their own control, provided them with the "excuse" to fall asleep easily.

Later research has supported the benefits of replacing accurate attributions with inaccurate ones (see, for example, Storms & McCaul, 1976; Olson & Ross, 1988). However, misattribution training does not work for all people. For instance, such training seems most effective for relatively introspective and thoughtful individuals (Brockner & Swap, 1983). Still, misattribution training offers a promising route for promoting better health and psychological well-being.

---

*The Benefits of Illusions: Where Wrong Is Right*

Most of us would probably endorse the notion that one of the hallmarks of good mental health is holding a clear, accurate view of both ourselves and the world, and that distorted and inaccurate perceptions are a sign of psychological disorder.

However, not everyone would agree. According to social psychologists Shelley Taylor and Jonathan Brown, looking at things with a clear, honest eye may not be so helpful in terms of mental health (Taylor & Brown, 1988). For instance, victims of depression and people low in self-esteem often see themselves clearly and accurately—warts and all. They make the same sorts of attributions regarding the causes of their misfortunes that neutral, objective observers do, and they are less apt to exaggerate their sense of control over events that are not easily controlled. Holding accurate self-perceptions, then, is not always associated with positive psychological outcomes.

In fact, the peril of having an accurate view of the world and oneself seems so pronounced that Taylor and Brown argue that certain types of inaccuracies regarding oneself and others may actually promote mental health (Taylor & Brown, 1988). Specifically, they suggest that three basic illusions are associated with better psychological functioning: holding unrealistically positive evaluations of self, having an exaggerated sense of control over occurrences in one's life, and being unrealistically optimistic. These positive illusions are related to happiness and contentment, productivity and creativity, and the ability to care about others.

Obviously there are limits to how far people can twist reality, and sometimes it is clearly maladaptive to ignore objective threats and to assume that one can always exert control over any situation. Still, it's clear that some sorts of biased self-perceptions may be beneficial.

## ▶ REVIEW & RETHINK

### Review

- Self-complexity is the phenomenon of viewing oneself as having many discrepant facets, while self-discrepancy theory suggests that the discrepancy between people's self-concept and their self-guides leads to negative emotions and ultimately has psychological costs.
- Learned helplessness has been linked to depression and to particular attributional styles.
- Attribution training and misattribution training both aim to change the type of attributions people make.

### Rethink

- According to Higgins's self-discrepancy theory, what emotions would a person experience who felt that his or her hopes and aspirations were largely going unfulfilled? How would a person's level of self-complexity influence these emotions?
- Some research suggests that thinking about a past negative event may be psychologically harmful, but writing about it may be beneficial. Use Pennebaker's work to explain why this might be true.
- What is the role of cognitive thought processes in the phenomenon of learned helplessness?
- What is the role of accuracy in attribution training? When is attribution training most likely to suceed?

## STRESS AND DISEASE

*It was only 10:34 A.M., and already Jennifer Jackson had put in what seemed like a full day. After getting up at 6:30 A.M., she studied a bit for her American History exam scheduled for the afternoon. She gulped down breakfast as she studied, and then headed off to the campus bookstore, where she worked part-time.*

*Her car was in the shop with some undiagnosed ailment, so she had to take the bus. The bus was late, so Jennifer didn't have time to stop off at the library before work to pick up the reserve book she needed. Making a mental note to try to get the book at lunchtime (although she thought it probably wouldn't be available by then), she sprinted from the bus to the store, arriving a few minutes late. Her supervisor didn't say anything, but she looked irritated as Jennifer explained why she was late. Feeling that she needed to make amends, Jennifer volunteered to sort invoices—a task that she, and everyone else, hated. As she sorted the invoices, she also answered the phone and jumped up to serve a steady stream of customers who were placing special orders. When the phone rang at 10:34 A.M., it was her garage mechanic telling her that the car repair would cost several hundred dollars—a sum she did not have.*

**stress**
the response to events that threaten or challenge a person.

**stressor**
circumstances that produce threats to an individual's well-being.

If you were to monitor Jennifer Jackson's heart rate and blood pressure, you wouldn't be shocked to find that both were higher than normal. You also wouldn't be surprised if she reported feeling stress.

Most of us are well-acquainted with **stress**, the response to events that threaten or challenge a person. Everyday life is filled with **stressors**—circumstances that produce threats to our well-being. And it is not just unpleasant events such as tests or jobs that produce stress; even happy circumstances, such as getting prepared for a week's vacation or winning an election, can produce stress (Sarason, Johnson, & Siegel, 1978; Brown & McGill, 1989).

*Stress and Coping: Reactions to Threat*

**primary appraisal**
the assessment of an event to determine whether its implications are positive, neutral, or negative.

**secondary appraisal**
the assessment of whether one's coping abilities and resources are adequate to overcome the harm, threat, or challenge posed by the potential stressor.

How do circumstances become stressful? According to psychologists Arnold Lazarus and Susan Folkman (Lazarus, 1968, 1991; Lazarus & Folkman, 1984), people who confront a new or shifting environment move through a series of stages (see Figure 5-3). The first step is **primary appraisal**, the assessment of an event to determine whether its implications are positive, neutral, or negative. If people determine that the implications are negative, they appraise the event in terms of how harmful it has been in the past, how threatening it appears for the future, and how likely it is that the challenge can successfully be addressed.

The next step is **secondary appraisal,** the assessment of whether one's coping abilities and resources are adequate to overcome the harm, threat, or challenge posed by the potential stressor. During this stage, people seek to determine whether their personal resources are sufficient to meet the dangers posed by the situation.

According to Lazarus and Folkman, the experience of stress represents the outcome of both primary and secondary appraisal. When the potential harm, threat, and challenge produced by circumstances are high, and coping abilities are limited, stress will be experienced.

For example, consider a student who receives a lengthy reading list at the beginning of a term. First the student engages in primary appraisal, analyzing the implications of the list regarding how much time it will take to do the reading and ultimately how threatening it appears. Next, the student will engage in secondary appraisal, considering whether there is sufficient time to complete the reading. If the answer is yes, then the threat is reduced. But if the student decides that time will be an issue and that there are numerous other time demands during the term, secondary appraisal will result in the perception of stress.

**FIGURE 5-3    Appraisal Leading to the Perception of Stress** According to the Lazarus and Folkman model, potential stressors are assessed using primary and secondary appraisal. If primary appraisal indicates that a potential stressor represents a challenge, and secondary appraisal suggests that the resources available to cope with the potential stressor are inadequate, then the perception of stress will occur.    (*Source:* Figure adapted from Kaplan, Sallis, & Patterson, 1993, p. 123, based on Lazarus & Folkman, 1984.)

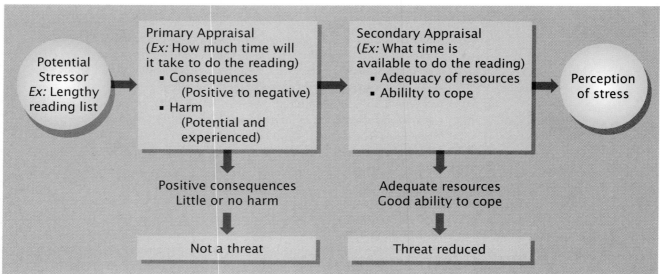

*Stressors: What's Pleasure for You Is Stress for Me*

As the Lazarus and Folkman model suggests, stress is a very personal thing. For some of us, bungee jumping and deep-sea diving would produce high degrees of stress; for others, they simply represent recreational activities that, because of the distractions they represent, may ultimately *reduce* stress.

On the other hand, certain kinds of circumstances produce stress in almost everyone. Social psychologists have identified three main types: cataclysmic events, personal stressors, and daily hassles (Lazarus & Cohen, 1977; Gatchel & Baum, 1983).

**Cataclysmic events** are strong stressors that occur suddenly and affect many people simultaneously. Disasters such as tornadoes, hurricanes, and floods are examples of cataclysmic events that affect literally hundreds of thousands of people at once.

Although cataclysmic events affect many people at the same time, the stress that they produce is often less intense than events that initially are less dramatic. This is because cataclysmic incidents usually have a clear end-point, after which the danger has passed. (One exception: the 1993 Mississippi River flooding, which continued to threaten residents for months.) In addition, the stress of cataclysmic events is lessened because it is shared with many other people. Consequently, no individual feels personally singled out and others may provide social support to those affected (Cummings, 1987).

Still, people who experience cataclysmic events are at risk for posttraumatic stress disorder. **Posttraumatic stress disorder** is a phenomenon in which victims of major incidents reexperience the original stress-producing event and associated feelings in flashbacks or dreams (Wilson & Raphael, 1993). For instance, as many as 60 percent of all Vietnam War veterans may suffer from the condition, although some estimates are much lower. Even soldiers who fought in the Persian Gulf war show signs of the syndrome, which includes sleep problems, drug and alcohol abuse, and high rates of suicide (Pollock et al., 1990; Hobfoll et al., 1991; Peterson, Prout, & Schwarz, 1991; Solomon, 1993; Sutker et al., 1993).

**cataclysmic events**
strong stressors that occur suddenly and affect many people simultaneously.

**posttraumatic stress disorder**
a phenomenon in which victims of major incidents reexperience the original stress-producing event and associated feelings in flashbacks or dreams.

Appraisal determines whether circumstances are seen as stressful. For some people, skydiving produces no stress, while for others it is highly stressful. On the other hand, weaving a basket may produce stress for some, while not being stressful to others.

Uplifts, minor positive events that make people feel good, can counter the negative consequences of daily hassles and reduce overall stress.

**personal stressor**
a major event in an individual's life that has immediate negative consequences.

**daily hassle (or background stressor)**
a minor irritant that produces minor stress to an individual.

**uplift**
minor positive events that make people feel good, even if only temporarily.

A second major type of stressor is the **personal stressor**—a major life event that has immediate negative consequences. The death of a loved one, the termination of an important relationship, or a major school or job failure might all be considered personal stressors. Although the immediate impact of personal stressors can be profound, with time the consequences generally taper off as people learn to adapt.

Finally, there is a third type of stressor, one with which we are all familiar—background stressors or, more informally, daily hassles. **Daily hassles** or **background stressors** are the minor irritants of life that produce minor stress. Although the circumstances that produce daily hassles are not, by themselves, all that aversive, their negative consequences add up and can ultimately produce even more stress than a single, initially more extreme event (Weinberger, Hiner, & Tierney, 1987; Marco & Suls, 1993).

Daily hassles have positive counterparts—uplifts. **Uplifts** are those minor positive events that make people feel good, even if only temporarily. Uplifts range from having a pleasant experience with others, to feeling healthy, to eating out at a favorite restaurant. Uplifts work to counteract the negative consequences of daily hassles and to reduce the stress they cause (Kanner et al., 1981). The most common daily hassles and uplifts are shown in Figure 5-4.

Although the nature of specific stressors varies from one person to another, several broad principles explain when an event will be appraised as stressful. According to social psychologist Shelley Taylor, they include the following (Taylor, 1991):

- *Occurrences that evoke negative emotions are more apt to produce stress than ones that are positive.* For most people, then, planning a wedding is less stressful than planning a funeral.
- *Events that are uncontrollable or unpredictable are more stressful than those that can be controlled or predicted.* For example, people living near airports, who hear airplane takeoffs and landings that occur at seemingly random intervals, report high levels of stress. In comparison, when people feel they have enough control to stop or influence an unpleasant event, stress is likely to be lower.
- *Circumstances that are unclear and ambiguous typically produce more stress than those that are unambiguous and precise.* If an event is not easily understood, people must struggle to comprehend it, rather than dealing with it directly.

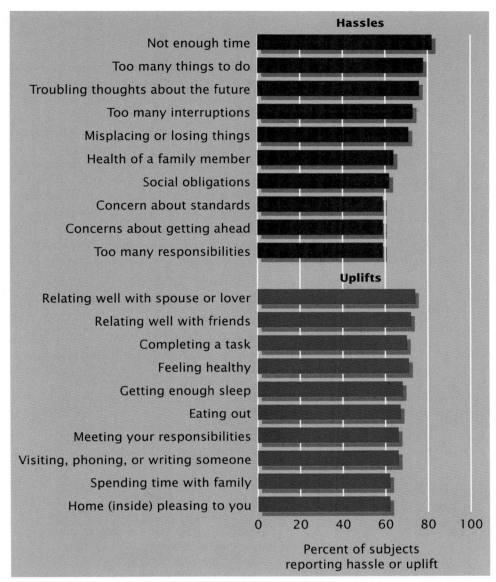

**FIGURE 5-4    Everyday Hassles and Uplifts** These are the most common everyday hassles and uplifts.    (*Sources:* Hassles—Chamberlin & Zika, 1990; Uplifts—Kanner, Coyne, Schaefer, & Lazarus, 1981.)

- *Situations in which a person faces multiple tasks that strain resources are more apt to produce stress than those in which people have fewer things to do.* A person whose to-do list contains many things that need to be accomplished in the same time frame is a prime candidate for stress.

**THE COSTS OF STRESS.** When people do appraise an experience as stressful, the consequences are both physical and psychological. Immediate reactions may be a rise in heart rate and blood pressure, an increase in skin conductance because of sweating, and the secretion of certain hormones by the adrenal glands (Mason, 1975; Selye, 1976; Blascovich & Katkin, 1993). In the short term, such a reaction may be beneficial, because such physiological events produce a burst of energy that may help a person cope with the stressor's immediate threat. For instance, a person may outrun a thief who is attempting to steal a purse.

In the long run, however, the physical changes brought on by stress can be harmful. The ongoing secretion of stress-related hormones may produce deterioration of body tissues such as the blood vessels and the heart. Furthermore, as people's ability to ward off germs declines, they may become more susceptible to disease. For instance, people exposed to stress may experience such common ailments as headaches, backaches, skin rashes, indigestion, chronic fatigue, and colds (Kiecolt-Glaser & Glaser, 1991; Cohen, Tyrrell, & Smith, 1993).

**psychosomatic disorders**
medical problems caused by the interaction of psychological, emotional, and physical difficulties.

In addition, stress may lead to **psychosomatic disorders**—medical problems caused by the interaction of psychological, emotional, and physical difficulties. Ulcers, asthma, arthritis, and high blood pressure, for example, can be psychosomatic disorders, often (although not always) caused or made worse by stress.

Stress has even been linked to severe, life-threatening illnesses. According to some studies, the more stressful events a person experiences over the course of a year, the more likely the person is to have a major illness (see Figure 5-5). Although such research is hardly definitive (not everyone who experiences high stress is destined to become ill), it does suggest the magnitude of physiological reactions produced by stress.

**FIGURE 5-5    Will Stress in Your Life Produce Illness?**

Using the following scale, you can assess the degree of stress in your life (Rahe & Arthur, 1978). To do this, take the stressor value given beside each event you have experienced and multiply it by the number of occurrences over the past year (up to a maximum of four), then add up the scores.

| | |
|---|---|
| 87 | Experienced the death of a spouse |
| 77 | Getting married |
| 77 | Experienced the death of a close family member |
| 76 | Getting divorced |
| 74 | Experienced a marital separation from mate |
| 68 | Experienced the death of a close friend |
| 68 | Experienced pregnancy or fathered a pregnancy |
| 65 | Had a major personal injury or illness |
| 62 | Were fired from work |
| 60 | Ended a marital engagement or a steady relationship |
| 58 | Had sexual difficulties |
| 58 | Experienced a marital reconciliation with your mate |
| 57 | Had a major change in self-concept or self-awareness |
| 56 | Experienced a major change in the health or behavior of a family member |
| 54 | Became engaged to be married |
| 53 | Had a major change in financial status |
| 52 | Took on a mortgage or loan of less than $10,000 |
| 52 | Had a major change in use of drugs |
| 50 | Had a major conflict or change in values |
| 50 | Had a major change in the number of arguments with your spouse |
| 50 | Gained a new family member |
| 50 | Entered college |
| 50 | Changed to a new school |
| 50 | Changed to a different line of work |
| 49 | Had a major change in amount of independence and responsibility |
| 47 | Had a major change in responsibilities at work |
| 46 | Experienced a major change in use of alcohol |
| 45 | Revised personal habits |
| 44 | Had trouble with school administration |
| 43 | Held a job while attending school |
| 43 | Had a major change in social activities |
| 42 | Had trouble with in-laws |
| 42 | Had a major change in working hours or conditions |

**FIGURE 5-5**    *(Continued)*

42    Changed residence or living conditions
41    Had your spouse begin or cease work outside the home
41    Changed your choice of major field of study
41    Changed dating habits
40    Had an outstanding personal achievement
38    Had trouble with your boss
38    Had a major change in amount of participation in school activities
37    Had a major change in type and/or amount of recreation
36    Had a major change in church activities
34    Had a major change of sleeping habits
33    Took a trip or vacation
30    Had a major change in eating habits
26    Had a major change in the number of family get-togethers
22    Were found guilty of minor violations of the law

If your total score is above 1,435, you are in a high-stress category. According to Marx, Garrity, & Bowers (1975), a high score increases the chances of experiencing a future stress-related illness. However, it is important to note that a high score in no way guarantees that you will suffer from a future illness. Because the research on stress and illness is correlational, major stressful events cannot be viewed as necessarily causing illness (Dohrenwend, Dodson, & Shrout, 1984; Lakey & Heller, 1985). Furthermore, other research suggests that future illness is predicted better by daily, ongoing hassles, rather than by the major events depicted in the questionnaire (Lazarus, et al., 1985). In fact, some research has questioned whether the particular values for each event are always appropriate (Birnbaum & Sotoodeh, 1991). On the other hand, too much stress is clearly undesirable, and thus it is reasonable to reduce it where feasible (Marx, Garrity, & Bowers, 1975, p. 97; Maddi, Bartone, & Puccetti, 1987).

Of course, not everyone reacts to stressors identically (Tennen et al., 1991). For example, men and women appear to respond in different ways to certain kinds of stressors. Psychologist Janice Kiecolt-Glaser found that when newlyweds engaged in a 30-minute discussion, women responded more strongly on a physiological level than men at points when their spouse acted negative or hostile (Kiecolt-Glaser et al., in press).

On the other hand, other research finds that although men and women may report different levels of stress from similar stressors, their physiological reactions may be similar. For instance, male victims of Hurricane Andrew in Florida reported more stress than female victims—although careful physiological measurements showed little difference in hormonal levels (Ironson, 1993).

In addition to gender differences in reactions, stress is also related to cultural factors. One of the most extreme examples of this phenomenon is the sudden-death disorder that afflicts male Southeast Asian refugees in the United States. Although the incidence has been low, the consistency—and mysteriousness—of the circumstances under which the deaths have occurred has been puzzling.

In this disorder, apparently healthy males die in their sleep without warning (Lemoine & Mougne, 1983). Victims first make gurgling noises, then thrash about in bed, and then die. Although no cause has been found, one hypothesis is that a combination of physical, psychological, and cultural factors produces death.

Specifically, it may be that an inherited heart defect puts potential victims at risk. When stress is high—due to multiple jobs, family arguments, academic concerns, or some other factor—it is possible that extremely vivid unpleasant dreams can trigger the inherited flaw, leading to death. For instance, some victims reported dreams foretelling their deaths, not long before they died. Because the Hmong, a Cambodian ethnic group who make up most of the victims, place great credence in their dreams, dreams fore-

Reactions to strong stressors can range from active coping to immobilization.

telling death could have produced extremely high levels of stress—leading to the fatal consequence.

**COPING WITH STRESS.**    When faced with potential stressors, some people manage much better than others. We all know people who withdraw and retreat when confronted with even the most minor stressor, and others who appear to thrive under stress, becoming energized and working tirelessly to overcome any challenge.

**coping**
the effort to control, reduce, or learn to tolerate the threats that lead to stress.

   **Coping** is the effort to control, reduce, or learn to tolerate the threats that lead to stress. All of us use habitual coping responses to help deal with stress, although we're not always aware of such responses. For instance, some people use **defense mechanisms**—unconscious reactions to threat that reduce anxiety by distorting or denying the actual nature of the situation. One study examined how students living in a dormitory that was considered vulnerable to earthquakes rated their susceptibility to a future tremor. Compared to students living in a safer dormitory, those who resided in the unsafe one actually rated their personal danger as lower than those in the safer structure (Lehman & Taylor, 1988).

**defense mechanism**
an unconscious reaction to threat that reduces anxiety by distorting or denying the actual nature of the situation.

   But not all coping mechanisms occur in a covert fashion. People also make conscious efforts to cope with stress, with varying degrees of success. For example, some social psychologists suggest that people use one of two alternative strategies: problem-focused coping and emotion-focused coping (Folkman & Lazarus, 1980; 1988). **Problem-focused coping** occurs when a person attempts to manage a stressful problem or situation. People who use problem-focusing coping attempt to directly change the situation to one that produces less stress. They may try to make the people responsible for stress change their behavior, or they may choose to leave the situation altogether. A student who tries to talk a teacher into extending the due date of a paper, or who decides to drop the class, is using problem-focused coping.

**problem-focused coping**
the process of attempting to manage a stressful problem or situation.

   In contrast, **emotion-focused coping** involves the conscious regulation of emotion as a way of dealing with stress. For instance, people who tell themselves they should look at the bright side of a situation or try to cheer themselves up by accepting sympathy from others are using emotion-focused coping.

**emotion-focused coping**
the conscious regulation of emotion as a way of dealing with stress.

Does one type of coping work better than the other? Most research suggests that neither emotion-focused nor problem-focused coping is invariably effective, and that their success may depend on the particular situation (Lazarus & Folkman, 1984). Furthermore, in many cases, problem-focused and emotion-focused coping can be used together (Kaplan, Sallis, & Patterson, 1993). For instance, a person who loses her job may profitably employ both problem-focused coping ("I'll use the want ads to try to find another job") and emotion-focused coping ("I'll try not to make myself feel worse about this by taking it personally").

**social support**
assistance and comfort supplied by a network of caring, interested people.

Another way of coping with stress is to turn to others for support. **Social support**—assistance and comfort supplied by a network of caring, interested people—is a boon to people living under stressful circumstances. Others can provide emotional support—such as listening sympathetically—or concrete support—such as providing tutoring to a student who is floundering academically. The awareness that one is part of a network of relationships can ease the burden of stress (Sarason, Sarason, & Pierce, 1990; Lepore, Evans, & Schneider, 1991; Croyle & Hunt, 1991; Spiegel, 1993).

Coping success also varies as a result of the kind of "coping style" we have, our general tendency to deal with stress in a particular way. For example, people with a "hardy" coping style are especially successful in dealing with stress. **Hardiness** is a personality characteristic associated with a lower rate of stress-related illness.

**hardiness**
a personality characteristic associated with a lower rate of stress-related illness.

Hardiness consists of three components: commitment, challenge, and control (Kobasa, 1979; Gentry & Kobasa, 1984). The commitment component relates to a person's tendency to wholeheartedly engage in activities, bringing energy and passion to bear on each endeavor. The challenge component involves an eagerness to change and to view the world as a place to seek out opportunities for growth. Finally, the control factor is exemplified by the view that we have the ability to cause events to happen, and we are not merely the pawns of forces outside of ourselves.

In sum, hardy people are take-charge sorts of individuals, who revel in life's challenges. It is not surprising, then, that people who are high in hardiness are more resistant to stress-related illness than those who show less hardiness. Hardy people react to potentially threatening stressors with optimism, feeling that they can respond effectively. By

Social support, the assistance and comfort supplied by a network of caring people, aids people in coping. Here, people participate in a workshop designed to cope with stress.

turning threatening situations into challenging ones, they are less apt to experience high levels of stress (Wiebe, 1991).

There is some question as to whether the benefits of hardiness are due to some of the individual components or to the full combination of commitment, challenge, and control. However, the concept has proven to be a useful one for health psychologists (Hull, Van Treuren, & Virnelli, 1987). It is clear that hardiness promotes both physical and psychological well-being (Allred & Smith, 1989).

# THE INFORMED CONSUMER OF SOCIAL PSYCHOLOGY

## COPING WITH STRESS

Stress is part of everyone's life. However, although it is a universal phenomenon, there are no universal formulas for coping with stress, primarily because stress is based on an individual appraisal of how threatening and challenging particular situations are. Still, there are several general approaches that have proven effective in seeking to cope with stress (Holahan & Moos, 1987, 1990; Sacks, 1993; Kaplan, Sallis, & Patterson, 1993). Among them are the following:

- *Attempt to exert control over the situation.* As we've noted, controllable events produce less stress than those that cannot be controlled. One coping strategy, then, is to try to maintain a sense of control. By attempting to exercise control over a situation, one can feel a sense of mastery over the situation, thereby reducing the experience of stress (Taylor et al., 1991; Burger, 1992). For instance, if a paper deadline is looming and causing high stress, it may make sense to negotiate a later due date with a professor. Not only would such a strategy reduce the immediate stress, but it would provide more time to potentially do a better job.

- *Reappraise threatening events as challenging events.* If a stressor cannot be controlled, at least it can be appraised in a different,

| FIGURE 5-6    How to Elicit the Relaxation Response |
| --- |

Some general advice on regular practice of the relaxation response
- Try to find 10 to 20 minutes in your daily routine; before breakfast is a good time.
- Sit comfortably.
- For the period you will practice, try to arrange your life so you won't have distractions. Put the phone on the answering machine, and ask someone else to watch the kids.
- Time yourself by glancing periodically at a clock or watch (but don't set an alarm). Commit yourself to a specific length of practice, and try to stick to it.

There are several approaches to eliciting the relaxation response. Here is one standard set of instructions used at the Mind/Body Medical Institute:

Step 1. Pick a focus word or short phrase that's firmly rooted in your personal belief system. For example, a nonreligious individual might choose a neutral word like *one* or *peace* or *love.* A Christian person desiring to use a prayer could pick the opening words of Psalm 23, *The Lord is my shepherd;* a Jewish person could choose *Shalom.*

Step 2. Sit quietly in a comfortable position.

Step 3. Close your eyes.

Step 4. Relax your muscles.

Step 5. Breathe slowly and naturally, repeating your focus word or phrase silently as you exhale.

Step 6. Throughout, assume a passive attitude. Don't worry about how well you're doing. When other thoughts come to mind, simply say to yourself, "Oh, well," and gently return to the repetition.

Step 7. Continue for 10 to 20 minutes. You may open your eyes to check the time, but do not use an alarm. When you finish, sit quietly for a minute or so, at first with your eyes closed and later with your eyes open. Then do not stand for one or two minutes.

Step 8. Practice the technique once or twice a day.

*Source:* Benson, 1993, p. 240.

less threatening manner. The old truism, "Look for the silver lining in every cloud," reflects social psychological findings that people who discover something positive in otherwise negative situations show less distress and are better able to cope (Silver & Wortman, 1980; Smith & Ellsworth, 1987).

- *Seek out social support.* As we've discussed, other people's social support can provide relief and comfort when we are confronting stress. Consequently, asking for assistance from others can be a means of reducing stress. For instance, friends, family, and even telephone hotlines staffed by peer counselors can be of support.

- *Use relaxation techniques.* If stress produces chronic physiological arousal, it follows that procedures that reduce such arousal might reduce the harmful consequences of physiological wear-and-tear. Several techniques have been developed,

including transcendental meditation, zen and yoga, progressive muscle relaxation, and even hypnosis. One procedure that is simple and effective is relaxation training, which includes the basic components of several other techniques. According to stress expert Herbert Benson, a relaxation response, effective in reducing stress, can be elicited by following the instructions shown in Figure 5-6 (Benson, 1993).

- *Exercise.* Ironically, exercise—which leads to temporary physiological arousal—may ultimately reduce stress. The reason is that regular exercise reduces the body's heart rate, respiration rate, and blood pressure when at rest, as well as releasing chemicals in the brain that can produce a feeling of well-being. If nothing else, exercise provides time off from the circumstances that may be producing stress in the first place (Brown, 1991).

---

## Social Psychological Components of Major Illness

Just two decades ago, most physicians would have scoffed at the notion that social psychological factors were related to major illness. To them, heart disease was solely the result of a temporary loss of oxygen-rich blood to the heart, and cancer was the result of unrestrained multiplication of cells in a tumor.

Today, however, physicians acknowledge that social psychological factors play a role in several kinds of major physical illness. As we'll see, social psychological factors are related both to the cause of major diseases and to their successful treatment.

**TYPE A'S, TYPE B'S, AND CORONARY HEART DISEASE.**  Do you churn when you're forced to wait in a long, slow-moving line at a bank? Do you seethe when a slow-moving vehicle prevents you from driving as fast as you'd like? Are you quick to anger when the book you're looking for in the library is not on the shelves?

If you answer yes to questions such as these, you may have a set of personality characteristics known as the Type A behavior pattern. The **Type A behavior pattern** is characterized by competitiveness, impatience, and a tendency toward frustration and hostility. Type A people appear driven, habitually trying to do better than others, and they are verbally and nonverbally hostile if they are prevented from reaching a goal.

The Type B behavior pattern is essentially the opposite of the Type A behavior pattern. The **Type B behavior pattern** is characterized by noncompetitiveness, patience, and a lack of aggression. Unlike Type A's, Type B's don't have a sense of time urgency, and they are rarely hostile. Although most people are neither purely Type A nor Type B, they usually can be placed into one of the two categories (Rosenman, 1990; Strube, 1990).

**Type A behavior pattern**
a pattern of behavior characterized by competitiveness, impatience, a tendency toward frustration, and hostility.

**Type B behavior pattern**
a pattern of behavior characterized by noncompetitiveness, patience, and a lack of aggression.

People with Type A personalities are characteristically competitive, impatient, and hostile, particularly when prevented from reaching a goal.

The distinction between these two behavior patterns is important, because a good deal of research evidence suggests that they are related to the incidence of coronary heart disease. For instance, some studies have found that men characterized as Type A's have double the rate of coronary heart disease, suffer significantly more fatal heart attacks, and have five times as many heart problems as Type B's (Rosenman et al., 1976). Even when other, potentially confounding factors are experimentally controlled, such as age, blood pressure, smoking behavior, and cholesterol levels, Type A behavior is clearly linked to coronary heart disease (Williams et al., 1988).

What is it about Type A behavior that increases the risks of heart problems? One suggestion is that when Type A's are in stressful situations, they become excessively aroused physiologically. There is an increase in heart rate, blood pressure, and the production of the hormones epinephrine and norepinephrine, causing inordinate wear and tear on the circulatory system—ultimately leading to coronary heart disease (Matthews, 1982).

Although most research has found a link between the Type A behavior pattern and coronary heart disease, there are exceptions. For instance, one study found that the risk for later heart attacks following an initial one may be greater for Type B's than for Type A's (Fischman, 1987; Ragland et al., 1988).

The contradictions in the research are puzzling. Because of the inconsistencies, recent research has tended to focus on the specific components of the Type A behavior pattern that may lead to heart disease. One emerging answer seems to be that hostility and negative emotions—regardless of whether they are manifested through aggressive competitiveness, frustration, anger, or depression—may be the underlying link to coronary heart disease (Wright, 1988; Evans, 1990; Smith, 1992; Suarez & Williams, 1992; Williams, 1993).

If you habitually exhibit behavior associated with the Type A behavior pattern or are often hostile, are you destined to suffer from coronary heart disease? Not at all. For one thing, people can be trained to reduce such behavior. Such training takes the form of teaching people to be more patient, to reduce their competitiveness, and in general to slow down their pace. Research suggests that such training can reduce the risk of coronary heart disease (Williams, 1993). Furthermore, females may be off the hook: The incidence of coronary heart disease is much higher for males than for females, and with a few exceptions (Thoresen & Low, 1990), almost all the results linking Type A behavior with heart disease have been found in studies using men as subjects (Friedman et al., 1984). Until more studies are done using women as subjects, then, the role that the Type A behavior pattern plays in women's heart disease remains uncertain.

CANCER: THE ROLE OF EMOTIONS AND ATTITUDES.    If you're like most people, you probably fear cancer more than any other disease. A diagnosis of cancer is often seen as a sentence to a painful death, preceded by long periods of suffering. Fortunately, the reality is less grim. Many forms of cancer respond to medical therapy, and scientists' understanding of the disease and the range of treatment approaches is rapidly expanding.

One of the most intriguing, although still highly tentative, approaches to cancer suggests that social psychological factors, and emotions and attitudes in particular, affect the course of the disease. For example, one study examined how the type of emotional response cancer patients displayed toward their disease affected their recovery.

In the research, a group of women who had a breast removed due to breast cancer were categorized according to their attitudes—those who felt their situation hopeless or who stoically accepted their cancer, trying not to complain; those who had a "fighting spirit," asserting they would lick the disease; and those who (mistakenly) denied the cancer. Ten years later, when the researchers examined death rates, they found that initial attitude was related to survival. There was a significantly higher death rate among the women who ten years earlier had stoically accepted their cancer or who had felt hopeless.

On the other hand, the death rate was considerably lower for those women who had a "fighting spirit" or who had denied the disease (Pettingale et al., 1985; see Figure 5-7).

Psychologist Sandra Levy and colleagues have also found evidence for a link between a positive mental state and survival (Levy et al., 1988; Levy & Roberts, 1992). In Levy's research, mental resilience and vigor, a set of emotions and attitudes she labeled collectively as "joy," were the best predictor of survival time for a group of patients with recurrent breast cancer. Related studies showed that cancer patients who are characteristically optimistic report less psychological and physical distress than those who are lower in optimism (Carver, 1990; Carver et al., 1993; Scheier & Carver, 1993).

Results of studies such as these suggest that emotional outlook and attitudes may be related to survival rate. But why might this be true? One possibility, of course, is that cancer patients who have positive emotions and attitudes simply are more likely to adhere to the complex, involved medical treatment required by their illness than those who are more negative. As a consequence, the patients who carefully follow their treatment regimens may have better medical outcomes (Holland & Lewis, 1993).

**immune system**
the body's natural line of defense against disease.

Something more may be at work, however. For instance, some health psychologists argue that positive emotions and attitudes benefit the body's **immune system**, the natural line of defense against disease. In this view, the immune system is bolstered by a positive emotional outlook, thereby stimulating the production of natural "killer" cells that can attack cancerous cells. Conversely, negative emotions and attitudes may impair the ability of natural killer cells to fight cancer (Glaser et al., 1986; Kiecolt-Glaser & Glaser, 1991, Kiecolt–Glaser & Kiecolt–Glaser 1993).

Although the relationship between emotions and cancer is far from proven (Office of Technology Assessment, 1990), studies so far suggest that treatment approaches designed to produce more positive emotions and attitudes may be effective in fighting cancer. In fact, some research has found that cancer patients derive several benefits from psychological therapy. In one study, for example, women with advanced breast cancer who participated in psychological group therapy experienced less anxiety, depression, and pain than women who did not participate in therapy. More importantly, on average

**FIGURE 5-7  Attitudes and Survival in Cancer Patients** Women's attitudes about their cancer close to the time of their initial diagnosis were related to the probability that they were alive ten years later. (*Source:* Pettingale, Morris, Greer, & Haybittle, 1985.)

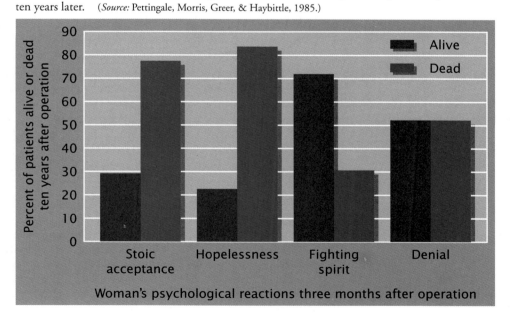

the women in therapy lived 18 months longer than those in the no-therapy group (Spiegel et al., 1989).

In sum, increasing evidence suggests that a link may exist between cancer patients' emotional state and the course of their disease. Still, the research is far from definitive, and, because it is correlational research, it is impossible to draw conclusions about causality. Consequently, it is unreasonable to leap to the conclusion that a positive mental outlook will enable people with cancer to ward off the disease (Smith, 1988; Zevon & Corn, 1990; Holland & Lewis, 1993).

**AIDS: THE TWENTIETH-CENTURY PLAGUE.**    It was only in the early 1980s that the first handful of cases of AIDS were reported. Today, AIDS has grown into one of the major health problems of the twentieth century. Although estimates vary, most health experts project that in the United States there will be well over one million reported cases by the year 2000. Worldwide, around 13 million people had already been infected with the AIDS virus by the beginning of the 1990s; unless a cure is found, all of them will die (World Health Organization, 1993).

**acquired immune deficiency syndrome (AIDS)**
a fatal disease caused by a virus that destroys the body's immune system and that has no known cure.

**Acquired immunodeficiency syndrome**, or **AIDS**, is a fatal disease caused by a virus that destroys the body's immune system, and it has no known cure. The most typical route of transmission is through sexual activity, but it is also spread through blood transfusions and shared needles during intravenous drug use. Although initially the casualties of AIDS in the United States were primarily homosexuals, today the incidence of new cases of AIDS is growing more rapidly among heterosexuals. Minorities have been particularly hard hit: African-Americans and Hispanics account for 40 percent of the cases of AIDs, although they make up only 18 percent of the population.

Reducing the spread of AIDS has proven to be a major challenge. However, because AIDS is communicated through specific types of high-risk activity, it is possible to prevent its spread—if people change their behavior. For instance, health educators such as Kevin Turner (discussed in the chapter prologue) have developed inventories of "safer sex practices"—behaviors that reduce the risk of contracting AIDS during sex (see Figure 5-8). In addition, in some urban areas, intravenous drug users have been provided with sterile needles, thereby reducing the chances they will share used, contaminated needles (Compton et al., 1992).

Unfortunately, efforts to decrease risky behavior and increase safer practices have met with only scattered success. For instance, although reductions in risky behavior have occurred in some groups, such as among gay men, in others little or no change has occurred. Despite increases in knowledge of safer sex practices among high school and college students, the amount of actual behavior change has been relatively minor (Fisher & Misovich, 1990; Catania et al., 1992).

According to a comprehensive review of the programs designed to change AIDS-risk behavior, conducted by social psychologists Jeffrey Fisher and William Fisher

---

**FIGURE 5-8   Safer Sex: Preventing the Transmission of AIDS**

Health psychologists and educators have devised several guidelines to help prevent the spread of AIDS. Among them are the following:

- **Use condoms.** The use of condoms greatly reduces the risk of transmission of the virus that produces AIDS, which occurs through exposure to bodily fluids such as semen or blood.
- **Avoid high risk behaviors.** Such practices as unprotected anal intercourse or the exchange of needles used in drug use greatly increase the risk of AIDS.
- **Know your partner's sexual history.** Knowing your sexual partner and his or her sexual history can help you to evaluate the risks of sexual contact.
- **Consider abstinence.** Although not always a practical alternative, the only certain way of avoiding AIDS is to refrain from sexual activity altogether.

(1992), most interventions have had only limited success. Fisher and Fisher argue that successful reduction of risky behavior is possible only if three factors are taken into account: information, motivation, and behavioral skills.

In their view, *information* refers to people's knowledge about AIDS transmission and ways of preventing the spread of the infection. *Motivation* determines whether people will act on their knowledge. Finally, *behavioral skills* for carrying out prevention are necessary; even informed, motivated people will be unable to engage in less risky practices if they lack the skill to perform the necessary behaviors.

Fisher and Fisher suggest that information and motivation activate behavioral skills, which in turn lead to risk-reduction behavior (see Figure 5-9). Research supports the validity of the sequence: In separate studies of gay men and primarily heterosexual college students, AIDS-preventative behavior was based on information, motivation, and behavioral skills.

Of course, in some cases AIDS prevention is too late, and people develop the disease. How do people cope with AIDS? The question is a difficult one, because the course of the disease varies significantly from one person to another. For instance, some people may carry the virus that produces AIDS for years without showing symptoms, while others quickly become ill.

Although there are only a few studies regarding how people cope with AIDS, the existing research consistently finds that **active behavioral coping**, in which people mobilize to actively fight the illness, results in higher self-esteem, better mood, and increases in perceived social support. In contrast, people who use avoidant coping do not fare as well. In **avoidant coping**, people refuse to think about their illness, and they evade or postpone acting in ways that deal directly with the disease. Avoidant coping leads to depression, anxiety, lower self-esteem, and a weaker sense of social support. Similarly, people with AIDS who have a greater sense of control over their disease and treatment show better coping than those who have a lower sense of control (Nicholson & Long, 1990; Taylor, Helgesen, Reed, & Shokan, 1991).

AIDS presents other social psychological issues (Pryor & Reader, 1993). Should people at risk for AIDS be tested to determine if they carry the virus that produces the disease? How do we reduce the anxiety of people whose contacts with AIDS patients are casual and thus whose fears of catching the disease are groundless? How do people negotiate safer sex practices with their partners? At what point should schools initiate sex education stressing the use of condoms to prevent the spread of AIDS? Does the distribution of condoms and sterile needles promote sexual behavior and drug use? Until a cure is found for the disease, each of these questions—and there are many more—must be answered to deal effectively with the health crisis brought on by AIDS.

**active behavioral coping**
a response to disease in which the victim mobilizes to actively fight the illness.

**avoidant coping**
a response to disease in which the victim refuses to think about the illness and evades or postpones action to deal directly with the disease.

**Figure 5-9    Changing AIDS-Risk Behavior** Behavior that helps prevent the spread of aids is the result of exposure to risk-reduction information, motivation, and behavioral skills. (*Source:* Fisher & Fisher, 1992, p. 465.)

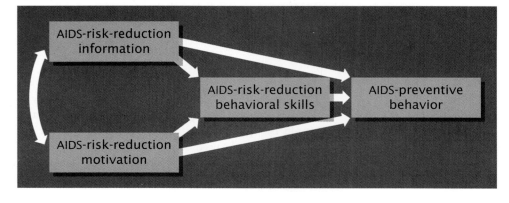

## ► REVIEW & RETHINK

### Review

- Stress is the response to events, known as stressors, that threaten or challenge a person.
- The three major types of stressors are cataclysmic events, personal stressors, and daily hassles.
- Coronary heart disease, cancer, and AIDS all raise social psychological issues.

### Rethink

- Why might it be less stressful if your entire neighborhood were flooded than if only your house were flooded? Is this difference due to primary or secondary appraisal?
- Think of a cultural explanation for the sudden-death syndrome among the Cambodian Hmong. Then think of a biological explanation. Could both explanations be correct?
- Separate the methods for reducing stress that have been described according to whether they are problem-focused coping strategies or emotion-focused strategies.

## PHYSICIANS AND PATIENTS

PATIENT: *I can hardly drink water.*
PHYSICIAN: *Uh huh.*
PATIENT: *Remember when it started? . . . It was pains in my head. It must have been then.*
PHYSICIAN: *Uh huh.*
PATIENT: *I don't know what it is. The doctor looked at it . . . said something about glands.*
PHYSICIAN: *OK. Aside from this, how have you been feeling?*
PATIENT: *Terrible.*
PHYSICIAN: *Uh huh.*
PATIENT: *Tired . . . there's pains . . . I don't know what it is.*
PHYSICIAN: *OK. . . . Fevers or chills?*
PATIENT: *No.*
PHYSICIAN: *OK. . . . Have you been sick to your stomach or anything?*
PATIENT: *(Sniffles, crying) I don't know what's going on. I get up in the morning tired. The only time I feel good . . . maybe like around suppertime . . . and everything (crying) and still the same thing.*
PHYSICIAN: *Uh huh. You're getting the nausea before you eat or after?*
(Goleman, 1988, p. B16).

How would you feel if you were the patient in this scenario? What would you think of the physician, and how likely would you be to follow any suggestions you received?

No matter how good the technical advice that was provided by such a doctor, it would be difficult to walk away from such an exchange (which is an excerpt from an actual case study used to train physicians at Harvard Medical School) feeling that our medical concerns had been properly heard and acknowledged. In fact, when a Harris Poll interviewed people who had changed from one physician to another, most answers involved issues of communication (Harris Poll, 1993; see Figure 5-10).

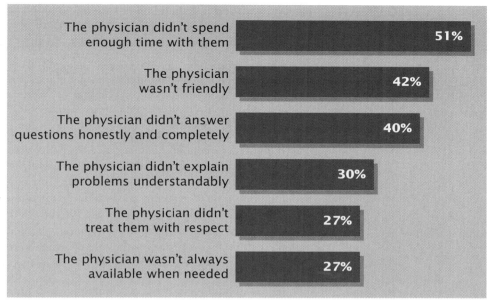

| | |
|---|---|
| The physician didn't spend enough time with them | 51% |
| The physician wasn't friendly | 42% |
| The physician didn't answer questions honestly and completely | 40% |
| The physician didn't explain problems understandably | 30% |
| The physician didn't treat them with respect | 27% |
| The physician wasn't always available when needed | 27% |

**FIGURE 5-10  Reasons for Changing Physicians** Percentages do not equal 100% because respondents could cite more than one reason.   (*Source:* Harris Poll, 1984.)

Clearly, factors other than pure medical competence are required for a successful medical practice. In fact, as we'll see, several social psychological factors play an important role in the success of medical treatment. We'll begin by looking at communication between physicians and patients.

*Patient–Physician Communication*

The manner in which physicians communicate with their patients plays an important role in treatment success.

In order to follow a physician's recommendations, we need to understand exactly what a physician wants us to do. Frequently, however, physicians miscommunicate, and patients misinterpret advice and recommendations.

One important source of miscommunication is the language used by physicians to present information to their patients (Ley, 1982). For instance, when a physician has a druggist indicate on a prescription label that a tablet should be "taken with meals," the instructions may be translated in a variety of ways. Should the pill should be taken before the meal, during the meal, or after the meal? Furthermore, since mealtimes may vary a great deal from patient to patient, the timing of the administration of the drug may vary significantly from one patient to the next, depending on the patient's individualistic interpretation of the instructions.

If the written instructions on medicine containers sometimes prove ambiguous, we might expect that recommendations delivered verbally by a physician might occasionally be even less clear to patients—and this seems to be the case. For instance, some 60 percent of patients in one study misunderstood their physician's verbal directions regarding how they should take their medication (Boyd, Covington, Stanaszek, & Coussons, 1974).

The use of medical jargon and scientific terms by physicians tends to decrease the likelihood that patients will successfully adhere to medical treatments. For example, instead of telling a patient he was "hypertensive" and needed to reduce his "sodium intake," a physician might consider informing him that he had high blood pressure and needed to reduce the amount of salt in his diet (DiMatteo & DiNicola, 1982).

Of course, physicians must walk a fine line between communications that are too technical and those that are overly simplistic. Medical practitioners often underestimate their patients' capacity to understand their medical conditions (McKinlay, 1975; Waitzkin, 1985). Some even use baby talk or exhibit very condescending attitudes with their patients, resulting in patient anger and less attention to medical advice. For example, a physician who said, "Nurse, would you just pop off her things for me? I want to examine her," elicited the following comments from a patient:

> In the hospital, everything is "popped" on or off, "slipped" in or out. I don't think I met a single doctor who, in dealing with patients, didn't resort to this sort of nursery talk. I once heard one saying to a patient, an elderly man, "We're just going to pop you into the operating theater to have a little peep into your tummy" (Toynbee, 1977).

Cultural factors are related to the success with which information is successfully communicated to patients. For instance, to patients for whom English is not the first language, receiving medical recommendations in English may be problematic. Similarly, certain groups are more apt, in general, to act on physicians' recommendations. Male patients and younger patients are less likely to follow health recommendations than female and elderly patients (Samora et al., 1961; Bush & Osterweis, 1978).

In addition, status differences often exist between physicians and patients, with patients perceiving physicians as having a higher status than themselves. Certainly, if income level is the main determinant of status, this perception is often accurate. (See Figure 5-11.)

Because they attribute higher status to their physician, some patients may credit the physician with other abilities. For example, they may believe that their physicians are so adept at making diagnoses that they can recognize patients' problems on the basis of a physical examination alone—in the same way that a good auto mechanic can identify a car problem by examining the vehicle (Leigh & Reiser, 1980; Mentzer & Snyder, 1982). If patients feel that the success of their medical care is the sole responsibility of a high-status, remarkably skilled physician, they may be more passive, less attentive to their health, and less compliant with medical advice.

The manner in which physicians communicate information—sometimes called bedside manner—may be as important as its content. For instance, physicians who are

**FIGURE 5-11**
The view that physicians are high in status is often held by physicians as well.

"It disturbs me that so many of today's young people go into medicine for the money. In my time, the chance to play God was enough."

*© 1992 by Nick Downes; from Science*

perceived as being aloof, antagonistic, or insensitive to patients' needs generally have lower rates of compliance than physicians who are viewed as being interested in their patients' psychological well-being as well as their physical health (Davis, 1968).

On the other hand, in some cases physicians who communicate anger and anxiety in their voice produce greater compliance in their patients. It is possible that signals of tension and anger may emphasize the seriousness of a medical condition, thereby motivating patients to be more compliant to the physician's recommendations (Hall, Roter, & Rand, 1981; Buller & Street, 1992).

## Compliance with Medical Regimens: Following Doctors' Orders

*After a full physical examination of her patient, the physician makes her diagnosis: The patient's symptoms could be significantly relieved by weight loss of at least 20 pounds. The patient nods, agreeing that he understands the problem and that he will go on a diet immediately. He leaves the physician's office, relieved that the problem isn't more serious. On the way home, by way of a little celebration, he stops at a newsstand and picks up a couple of candy bars. "After all," he says to himself, "I can start to diet tomorrow."*

Perhaps you've found yourself in similar circumstances: A physician gives you advice, and—despite your best intentions—you neglect to follow it. Certainly, most of us have been in situations in which we agree wholeheartedly with certain advice, and yet are unable to make ourselves conform.

Failure to comply with medical advice represents a major health problem—one that has long been recognized. Even before modern times, the problem of noncompliance with health-care regimens was recognized. For instance, in the 1600s, the playwright Molière explained his physician's job to the king in this way: "Sire, we converse. He gives me advice which I do not follow and I get better" (Treue, 1958, p. 41, cited in Taylor, 1991).

Not everyone gets better, however. Nonadherence to medical regimens may result in an illness becoming more severe. In the most extreme cases, it can result in death. Furthermore, a physician may not be aware of the degree to which a patient has been noncompliant. As a result, the physician may reach a faulty conclusion about the success or failure of a particular treatment or medicine because of the patient's failure to follow directions.

Noncompliance is widespread. According to various estimates, it ranges from as little as 15 percent to as much as 93 percent. For example, some estimates suggest that of the 750 million prescriptions for medicine written each year, close to 70 percent are not taken as prescribed (Alpert, 1964; Stone, 1979; Rapoff & Christophersen, 1982; Gatchel & Baum, 1983; Becker, 1985; Buckalew & Sallis, 1986; Kaplan, Sallis, & Patterson, 1993).

Noncompliance can take many forms, such as patients not taking medicine at scheduled times or discontinuing its use prematurely. In some cases, patients may not even fill a prescription.

Furthermore, patients are even less prone to follow medical advice that requires deprivation of some sort, or major investments in time and effort. Consequently, physicians' recommendations that require participation in an exercise program or adherence to a strict diet are particularly apt to be ignored. In fact, some studies show that when health recommendations involve changes in personal habits such as eating or smoking, adherence ranges from only 20 percent to 50 percent (DiMatteo & DiNicola, 1982).

In some cases, nonadherence to medical regimes takes a creative turn. Suppose, for example, you regularly took a drug for a particular medical condition. If you believed that you were the person most knowledgeable about your own body's reaction to the drug, wouldn't you be tempted to take matters into your own hands and adjust the dosage of the drug yourself? Many patients modify prescription dosage, figuring that they are more sensitive than anyone else to the way drugs affect them. Such nonadherence to medical regimens has been termed creative nonadherence. In **creative nonadherence**, patients adjust or augment a treatment prescribed by a physician, relying instead on their own medical judgment and experience (Weintraub, 1976; Taylor, 1991).

Creative nonadherence may occasionally work just fine. For instance, patients may be more sensitive to their reactions to medication than anyone else. Diabetics taking insulin can often detect minute reactions to the drug, and they can modify their intake on a continuing basis. Furthermore, one study of children with asthma found that parental modification of prescribed treatment produced better results than strict adherence to physicians' instructions. For instance, parents were more sensitive to their children's specific symptoms and could take into account seasonal changes in allergies (Deaton, 1985).

Unfortunately, creative noncompliance can sometimes be detrimental to a patient's health. In some cases, such noncompliance is produced by extraneous factors. Thus, poor patients may sometimes ration their drug usage, apportioning only a fraction of the prescribed dosage in order to make an expensive drug last longer. In other cases, patients develop inaccurate theories of disease and symptomology. Such noncompliance to prescribed regimens can be injurious (Leventhal, Nerenz, & Leventhal, 1985). For example, a patient with high blood pressure may assume—erroneously—that headaches are a symptom of the disease. Because of this faulty assumption, the patient may conclude that it is necessary to take medication for the condition only when he has a headache, regardless of a physician's prescription to take the medicine daily.

The patient's mistaken medical theory may be reinforced if he measures his blood pressure only on days on which he has a headache—and finds that the pressure is high. Obviously, if he had taken his blood pressure at other times, he probably would have found it high as well, thereby making the inaccuracy of his theory evident. Unfortunately, though, he is less likely to assess his blood pressure at times when he is free of symptoms, and thus his inaccurate theory is likely to persevere.

In some cases, noncompliance is due to psychological reactance. **Reactance** is a disagreeable emotional and cognitive reaction to the restriction of one's freedom that is often associated with medical regimens (Brehm & Brehm, 1981). When people experience reactance, they feel hostility and anger, and as a result, they seek to restore their freedom. Ironically, reactance often motivates people to pursue the restricted behavior with renewed vigor.

Particularly complex, involved medical regimens may unwittingly set the stage for the creation of patient reactance. For example, physicians who order patients to make major lifestyle changes may produce the resentment characteristic of reactance. Similarly, a major illness, by itself, can cause reactance, if patients feel that their lives are restricted by their medical condition.

How do patients deal with psychological reactance? One means is to seek out ways to restore lost freedom. Consequently, patients may choose to behave in a noncompliant fashion. Rather than following physicians' advice, then, patients may act in quite the opposite manner. Obviously, such behavior is self-destructive, but it does help diminish feelings of reactance.

> **creative nonadherence**
> a response to medical regimens in which the patient adjusts or augments treatment prescribed by a physician, relying instead on his or her own medical judgment and experience.

> **reactance**
> a disagreeable emotional and cognitive reaction to the restriction of one's freedom.

## Increasing Compliance with Medical Regimens

We've seen the myriad of social psychological forces that operate to reduce compliance to medical regimens. Even when patients know that a course of action is in their own best interests, they may be unable or—as in the case of reactance—unwilling to follow a treatment prescription.

However, several approaches exist for reducing the level of patient noncompliance that occurs. According to social psychologist Shelley Taylor (1991), several strategies have proven successful in increasing compliance.

- *Changing medical practices: Institutional reform.* The increasing use of prepaid medical insurance, covering all medical expenses, has sometimes led to the depersonalization of medical treatment. Rather than having a particular physician with whom patients develop a personal relationship, they may receive medical care from whomever happens to be available at a given time. When physicians are seen as interchangeable, patients may feel that the health-care provider views them in the same way, and hence is less committed personally to their well-being. Furthermore, patients may have to wait for long periods of time before seeing a physician, which may discourage them from seeking treatment for certain minor ailments. Such depersonalization may reduce compliance to the advice of the physician, who may be a virtual stranger to the patient.

In order to reduce feelings of depersonalization, medical organizations have tried several approaches. One is to permit members of health-care organizations to choose a primary care physician. Rather than being assigned to a provider on a first-come, first-served basis, patients make appointments with a physician of their choice. In addition, improved scheduling procedures can reduce the waiting time for appointments. Finally, some health-care organizations place a special focus on preventive measures. By dealing with patients when they are healthy, they establish an atmosphere of caring that may enhance compliance with medical regimens if and when a person becomes ill.

- *Changing the way medical information is imparted: Cognitive factors.* One reason that patients do not comply with medical regimens is that they simply do not understand them. As a result, one approach to increasing compliance to treatment suggestions is to attempt to maximize patients' ability to understand complex information.

For instance, if patients might become confused by intricate treatment instructions that a medical-care provider delivers verbally, it may be useful to provide the information in written form. When patients have written descriptions of the medications prescribed to them, including possible side effects and dosage levels, they are considerably more compliant (Peck & King, 1982).

Furthermore, patients can be quizzed on their understanding of medical information and their ability to remember its content. The goal is not to make doctors into teachers, but to ensure that patients fully understand and recall the content of their treatment regimen.

- *Improving communication skills of physicians: Emotional issues.* Health-care providers' communications must take into account the delicate emotional balance that exists between providers and patients (Buller & Street, 1992). Because of the importance of health-care providers' communication skills in promoting proper compliance, people in the health-care field need training in ways of interacting with patients. For example, physicians often provide only meager amounts of information to their patients— although they often think otherwise. One study found that while physicians estimated that they spent nearly half of the average 20-minute office visit providing suggestions and recommendations to their patients, the actual figure was about one minute (Waitzkin & Stoeckle, 1976). Another study found that most physicians interrupt their patients during the first 18 seconds when the patients are attempting to explain their problems (Beckman & Frankel, 1984). Naturally, the quality as well as the quantity of physicians' communications with their patients is important. Even rudimentary improvements in physician–patient communication may lead to enhancement of patients' sense of well-being. For instance, physicians who are explicitly taught to be courteous—saying hello, addressing patients by their names, and saying goodbye at the end of a clinical interview—are thought of as warmer and more supportive than physicians who do not follow such procedures (DiMatteo & DiNicola, 1982; Thompson, 1988; Thompson, Nanni, & Schwankovsky, 1990).

- *Using social support to promote adherence.* As we noted earlier in the chapter when we discussed ways of coping with stress, social support can have powerful consequences in terms of stress reduction. Just as social supporters can help an individual withstand the pressure of a group, they can also enhance people's ability to follow a treatment regimen. Social support from friends and family can help people to adhere to medical advice as well as to cope with the stress brought about by illness (Dunkel-Schetter, Folkman, & Lazarus, 1987; Taylor, Buunk, & Aspinwall, 1990; Croyle & Hunt, 1991).

When family members participate in the medical regimens of patients, compliance increases. Such participation can range from simply helping patients remember when to take medicine to actually providing certain kinds of medical treatment or procedures. Social support can also help patients avoid certain behaviors. For instance, refraining from serving a rich dessert to a dieter helps ensure that the dieter will succeed, whereas urging a dieter to sample a piece of cake because it tastes so good just makes it more likely that the dieter will ultimately fail.

The social support of concerned family and friends can also help prevent relapse to unhealthy habits once a health problem has been overcome. For instance, people who have overcome drug addiction can be aided in avoiding lapses through the encouragement and reinforcement of others.

In short, providing social support, as well as promoting institutional reform and taking cognitive and emotional factors into account, can increase compliance with medical regimens. By using these techniques, summarized in Figure 5-12, patients are more likely to follow the recommendations made by those to whom they have entrusted their care.

---

**FIGURE 5-12    Improving Compliance with Medical Treatment**

After surveying the research on patient compliance, social psychologist Shelley Taylor of the University of California, Los Angeles, generated the following list:

1. Listen to the patient.
2. Ask the patient to repeat what has to be done.
3. Keep the prescription as simple as possible.
4. Give clear instructions on the exact treatment regimen, preferably in writing.
5. Make use of special reminder pill containers and calendars.
6. Call the patient if an appointment is missed.
7. Prescribe a self-care regimen in concert with the patient's daily schedule.
8. Emphasize the importance of adherence at each visit.
9. Gear the frequency of visits to adherence needs.
10. Acknowledge the patient's efforts to adhere to the regimen at each visit.
11. Involve the patient's spouse or other partner.
12. Whenever possible, provide patients with instructions and advice at the start of the information to be presented.
13. When providing patients with instructions and advice, stress how important they are.
14. Use short words and short sentences.
15. Use explicit categorization where possible. (For example, divide information clearly into categories of etiology, treatment, or prognosis.)
16. Repeat things where feasible.
17. When giving advice, make it as specific, detailed, and concrete as possible.
18. Find out what the patient's worries are. Do not confine yourself merely to gathering objective medical information.
19. Find out what the patient's expectations are. If they cannot be met, explain why.
20. Provide information about the diagnosis and the cause of the illness.
21. Adopt a friendly rather than a businesslike attitude.
22. Avoid medical jargon.
23. Spend some time in conversation about nonmedical topics.

*Source:* Taylor, 1991, p. 324; based on Haynes, Wang, & da-Mota-Gomes, 1987; and Ley, 1977.

## ► REVIEW & RETHINK

### Review

- Physician–patient communication relies on both the language and the manner of physicians, and can affect patient compliance.
- Nonadherence to medical regimens is widespread and takes many forms, including creative noncompliance and reactance.
- Compliance can be increased through changing medical practices, improving the quality and presentation of medical information, and using social support.

### Rethink

- In recent years the status of physicians has declined somewhat. How might this change affect physician–patient interactions?
- Why is "bedside manner" an important factor in patient compliance?
- Which methods of increasing compliance to medical regimens focus on the physician end of the physician–patient relationship? Which focus on the patient end? Which might be most relevant for convincing a patient to quit smoking?

## LOOKING BACK ◄ ◄ ◄ ◄ ◄ ◄ ◄ ◄ ◄ ◄ ◄ ◄ ◄ ◄ ◄ ◄ ◄ ◄ ◄ ◄ ◄ ◄ ◄ ◄ ◄ ◄

### What are the ingredients of a sense of psychological well-being?

1. Self-complexity—viewing oneself as having many discrepant facets—is linked to a more positive sense of well-being. In contrast, self-discrepancy theory argues that the discrepancy between people's self-concept and their self-guides leads to negative emotions and ultimately lowers psychological well-being.

2. Self-disclosure, in which information about the self is exchanged with others, holds lasting advantages. In fact, confession of past disturbing experiences can provide lasting benefits.

3. Learned helplessness is the belief that no control can be exerted over one's environment, leading people to give up and potentially to develop deep feelings of depression. Those most prone to depression habitually view positive events in their lives as being due to external, unstable, and specific causes. At the same time, they view negative events as being brought about by stable, internal, and global causes.

4. Attribution training replaces inaccurate harmful attributions with more accurate, and beneficial, ones. In contrast, in misattribution training, people are led to replace their accurate, but harmful, attributions with inaccurate, but more beneficial, attributions.

5. Research on illusions has shown that a clear and accurate sense of the world is not always beneficial. Among the most beneficial illusions: holding unrealistically positive evaluations of self, having an exaggerated sense of control over occurrences in one's life, and being unrealistically optimistic.

### What are the determinants and consequences of stress, and what are the strategies for coping with it?

6. Stress is the response to events (known as stressors) that threaten or challenge a person. Circumstances become stressful due to primary appraisal (the assessment of an event to determine whether its implications are positive, neutral, or negative) and secondary appraisal (the assessment of whether one's coping abilities and resources are adequate to overcome the harm, threat, or challenge posed by the potential stressor).

7. There are three basic categories of stress: cataclysmic events, personal stressors, and daily hassles. People who experience cataclysmic events may develop posttraumatic stress disor-

der. Stress can be reduced by uplifts—minor positive events that make people feel good temporarily.

8. Events most likely to produce stress are those that are negative, uncontrollable or unpredictable, unclear or ambiguous, and contain multiple tasks that strain resources. The immediate reaction to stress is physiological arousal, which may be beneficial in the short term. In the long run, however, such arousal may damage the body and lead to psychosomatic disorders.

9. Coping is the effort to control, reduce, or learn to tolerate the threats that lead to stress. Coping may include the use of defense mechanisms, or may involve problem-focused and emotion-focused strategies. Coping success also may be enhanced by the general coping style known as hardiness.

10. Among the means of dealing with stress are attempting to exert control, reappraising threatening events, seeking social support, using relaxation techniques, and exercising.

### What are the social psychological components of coronary heart disease, cancer, and AIDS?

11. The Type A behavior pattern is characterized by competitiveness, impatience, a tendency toward frustration, and hostility. In contrast, the Type B behavior pattern is characterized by noncompetitiveness, patience, and a lack of aggression. The Type A behavior pattern has been linked to an increased likelihood of coronary heart disease, although certain components of the pattern are probably more important than others. For instance, the presence of hostility and negative emotions may be the underlying link to coronary heart disease.

12. The course of cancer has been linked to attitudes and emotions. One reason for the relationship may be that the immune system, the body's natural line of defense against disease, may be bolstered by a positive emotional outlook.

13. Acquired immunodeficiency syndrome, or AIDS, is transmitted by certain risky practices. Successful reduction of unsafe behavior is the result of three factors: information, motivation, and behavioral skill.

### How do patients' interactions with their physicians affect their health and compliance to medical treatment?

14. Physicians may miscommunicate through their verbal language and nonverbal manner, leading to ambiguities in treatment recommendations. Noncompliance is widespread, with some estimates as high as 93 percent. It can take several forms, including creative nonadherence, in which patients adjust or augment a treatment based on their own medical judgment and experience. Reactance can also lead to noncompliance.

15. Among the ways to increase compliance are reforms in the practice of medicine, changes in how medical information is imparted, improving communication skills of physicians, and using social support.

## KEY TERMS AND CONCEPTS

*self-complexity (p. 144)*

*self-discrepancy theory (p. 145)*

*self-disclosure (p. 146)*

*learned helplessness (p. 147)*

*attributional style (p. 148)*

*attribution training (p. 149)*

*misattribution training (p. 149)*

*stress (p. 151)*

*stressor (p. 151)*

*primary appraisal (p. 152)*

*secondary appraisal (p. 152)*

*cataclysmic events (p. 153)*

*posttraumatic stress disorder (p. 153)*

*personal stressor (p. 154)*

*daily hassle (or background stressor) (p. 154)*

*uplift (p. 154)*

*psychosomatic disorders (p. 156)*

*coping (p. 158)*

*defense mechanism (p. 158)*

*problem-focused coping (p. 158)*

*emotion-focused coping (p. 158)*

*social support (p. 159)*

*hardiness (p. 159)*

*Type A behavior pattern (p. 161)*

*Type B behavior pattern (p. 161)*

*immune system (p. 163)*

*acquired immune deficiency syndrome (AIDS) (p. 164)*

*active behavioral coping (p. 165)*

*avoidant coping (p. 165)*

*creative nonadherence (p. 170)*

*reactance (p. 170)*

# FOR FURTHER RESEARCH AND STUDY

Gordon J. S. (1990). *Stress management.* New York: Chelsea House.

Provides an overview of the consequences of stress and delineates approaches to coping with it.

Goleman, D., & Gurin, J. (Eds.) (1993). *Mind–body medicine.* Yonkers, New York: Consumer Reports Books.

A comprehensive guide to the relationship between psychological and medical issues. Written by experts but geared for the layperson, the book is fascinating and presents careful, clear-headed suggestions.

Kaplan, R. M., Sallis, J. F., Jr., & Patterson,

T. L. (1993). *Health and human behavior.* New York: McGraw-Hill.

Taylor, S. (1991). *Health psychology.* (2nd ed.). New York: McGraw-Hill.

These two books review the scientific literature on issues related to the social psychology of health, as well as other health-related issues.

Pennebaker, J. W. (1990). *Opening up: The healing power of confiding in others.* New York: Morrow.

An extended discussion of the psychological and health-related benefits of confession.

# EPILOGUE

In this chapter and the previous one, we've considered what social psychologists know about the self. In Chapter 4, we saw how we develop and maintain a general sense of the self. We considered how people form an evaluation of themselves and how they attempt to present themselves to the world.

In this chapter, we built upon our earlier view of the self, this time taking a more applied approach. Here, we've considered some of the ways that social psychological factors relate to psychological and physical health. We've looked at the components of psychological well-being, considering the links between how people view the self and their general perception of well-being. We then considered how people cope with stress and how ailments once considered purely physical have significant psychological components. We've also investigated how patients' relationships with their physicians affect the success of their treatment.

The material we discussed in this chapter moved us from psychological domains into the physical realm of illness and disease. However, what should be apparent from these two chapters is the close connection between these two worlds. Our understanding of how people perceive themselves is enhanced by examining both the psychological and physical aspects of the self and of well-being. The mind and body work interdependently, jointly creating our experience as humans.

# How Do People Develop and Maintain Relationships with Others?

Our passage through the field of social psychology continues as we enter the territory of relationships. Beginning with the initial contact between two individuals, we'll proceed through the development of relationships, moving from the first stirrings of liking, and building up to the deep intimacy that can occur in long-time friendships and passionate love affairs. We also look at the opposite pattern, in which once-viable relationships begin to deteriorate and dissolve.

In Chapter 6, we focus on interpersonal attraction, those factors that lead us to determine that we like another individual. We consider the factors that propel us toward liking others, and discuss the particular personal characteristics that we find attractive. Then, in Chapter 7, we examine the rise—and potential fall—of relationships. We look at how relationships develop, how people fall in love, and the different types of relationships. ■

### CHAPTER SIX

# INTERPERSONAL ATTRACTION

## OUR LIKING FOR OTHERS

# PROLOGUE: THE RUEHL OF FRIENDSHIP

We first met, two girls with ambition, at the College of New Rochelle a lengthening while ago. You could tell I intended to go places, because I wore only black and I had a real knack for reciting snippets of poetry. You could tell my friend was headed somewhere special by the way she introduced herself, with the kind of flair that would, as she was wont to say, make your liver quiver. Tall, bony, beautiful, she would extend an elegant hand. Her voice was deep, sonorous. "Mercedes, as in Benz," she'd say, "Ruehl, as in golden." She always had an audience . . . .

She wanted to be an actress and I wanted to be a writer, so when I became editor of *Tatler*, the school weekly, I made a point of reviewing her performances, praising the dark truths conveyed in her resonant alto. She auditioned for every part she could at the school's Little Theatre, including the boy roles, which at a girls' school were reasonably plentiful. My first image of her onstage is as Captain Hook, with a chortle so mean and authentic that to this day, when we're sitting in a restaurant about to order, I'll turn to her with this moony look of lamentation for those lost school days, and I'll say in my most cajoling voice, "C'mon, Merce. Pretend to be Hook when you ask for the coffee. Please."

Walking across the leafy campus, with its turreted buildings—including one actually called Leland's Castle, where the nuns lived their mysterious black-robed lives of the spirit—we plotted a future in which the world would hail us with the same fervor as we hailed it (Blais, 1993, p. 50, 52).

Mercedes Ruehl and Madeleine Blais

## LOOKING AHEAD

▶ ▶ ▶ ▶ ▶ ▶ ▶ ▶ ▶ ▶ ▶ ▶ ▶ ▶ ▶ ▶ ▶ ▶ ▶ ▶ ▶ ▶ ▶ ▶ ▶ ▶ ▶ ▶

These two friends plotted well. With a Pulitzer Prize and an Oscar between them, actress Mercedes Ruehl and writer Madeleine Blais remain close confidantes, united by bonds forged during their first year at college.

For most of us, friendships are a central component of our lives. But how do we make the transition from stranger to friend? In this chapter, we consider the forces that lead to **interpersonal attraction**—the degree of liking that people have for one another. We begin by examining the roots of attraction: our need for affiliation and our desire to be in the presence of others.

Next, we turn to some of the specific components of liking for others. We look first at situational factors such as our proximity to specific individuals, as well as how we may grow to like people merely because they become more familiar. And finally, we consider how people's personal characteristics—including their qualities, physical attractiveness and similarity to us—lead to liking.

In sum, reading this chapter will answer these questions:

- What are the origins of interpersonal attraction?
- How do situational factors such as proximity and familiarity lead to liking?
- What are the primary personal qualities that lead people to be liked by others?
- What strategies for making friends do the principles of interpersonal attraction suggest?

**interpersonal attraction**
the degree of liking that people have for one another.

179

## AFFILIATION: THE ORIGINS OF ATTRACTION

*When Terry Anderson, the last American hostage to be freed in Lebanon, looked back at his life in captivity, the companionship of others was one of the few bright spots during seven years of captivity. As he wrote when he was freed:*

*"All of the nine men I shared cells with at various times helped me, and I hope I helped them. We talked, endlessly and about everything. We played chess, and cards. (Secretly at first with homemade decks—cards are forbidden by the strict fundamentalists who held us. Later, they conceded us the privilege.) We made a Monopoly set, and a Scrabble game. We taught each other things—agriculture, economics, education, journalism, literature. Mostly, we depended on each other"* (Anderson, 1992, p. A-10).

People need not be held hostage to realize the importance of others in their lives. Along with other species, humans are social creatures, and most find companionship to be a central and essential component of life.

Although the motivation to be with others is a fundamental aspect of human life, theoretically this state of affairs does not have to be the case. Consider, for example, the advantages of a solitary existence: You would have no interruptions, you would not need to accommodate the idiosyncrasies of others, and you'd never be asked to listen to someone else's problems, help raise money for charity, or lend your bicycle.

Yet few people would choose to live in total isolation; the vast majority of us prefer to live with others. In fact, people who have experienced long periods of isolation—whether involuntary or voluntary—experience major psychological difficulties. For example, reports of prisoners of war, hostages, religious hermits, and shipwrecked castaways show certain commonalities (Schachter, 1959). First, there is often psychological distress caused by the isolation, and the distress increases as time passes. Eventually, isolated people may come to feel extreme apathy, similar to the state of withdrawal that can occur in people with schizophrenia (Thompson & Heller, 1990; Brodsky & Scogin, 1988).

Few of us voluntarily choose to be isolated from others. In fact, enforced isolation is used as punishment.

In addition, isolated individuals often spend long periods thinking and dreaming about others and may hallucinate about others' presence. Finally, if an isolated person is unable to think about or engage in distracting activities of some sort, the psychological suffering becomes profound. Severe anxiety may ensue (Bell & Garthwaite, 1987).

It is clear, then, that physical isolation from others is usually an unpleasant, aversive experience that most people seek to avoid. But why is the presence of others so powerful? Social psychologists suggest that the answer can be found by examining a fundamental motivational need: the need for affiliation.

## The Need for Affiliation: Reducing Fear and Isolation

Suppose you had agreed to be a subject in an experiment, and these were the instructions that you received from experimenter "Dr. Gregor Zilstein:"

> What we will ask each of you to do is simple. We would like to give each of [you] a series of electric shocks. Now, I feel I must be completely honest with you and tell you exactly what you are in for. These shocks will hurt; they will be painful. As you can guess, if in research of this sort we're to learn anything at all that will really help humanity, it is necessary for our shocks to be intense (Schachter, 1959, p. 13).

Suppose, further, that Dr. Zilstein, who also had provided you with a brief lecture on the importance of research on electric shock, then asked where you wished to wait for the procedure to begin. Given the choice of waiting alone or waiting in the presence of other subjects who were waiting their turn to be shocked, which would you choose?

If you are like most of the actual subjects, you'd be certain to choose to wait with others. In the original, now-classic study, carried out by social psychologist Stanley Schachter (1959), most subjects who were in this high-fear situation chose to wait with others. In contrast, in a control condition in which subjects were threatened with a mild, relatively painless shock, most participants chose to wait by themselves.

To Schachter, the results of his study suggested that affiliation needs could be aroused by fear. At least two reasons explain why this might be the case. For one thing, subjects expecting a strong shock may have anticipated that the presence of other people could provide direct reduction of their anxiety by offering comfort, consolation, and reassurance.

A second factor, however, relates to social comparison processes. As you may recall from our discussion in Chapter 4, **social comparison** is the need to evaluate one's own behavior, abilities, expertise, and opinions by comparing them to those of other people. According to social comparison theory, people are dependent on others for information about the world around them, and they use the behavior and views of others to evaluate their own behavior, abilities, expertise, and opinions. People need to do this, the theory suggests, because the objective reality of a situation is often ambiguous or simply unknowable.

**social comparison**
the need to evaluate one's own behavior, abilities, expertise, and opinions by comparing them to those of other people.

In the case of Schachter's subjects, social comparison processes may have led fearful subjects to attempt to understand and control their own emotions by comparing themselves to others in the same situation. By seeking out the company of others, subjects may have tried to better understand the meaning of their emotions and feelings (Wills, 1981; Morris et al., 1976).

Regardless of the specific reason for subjects' preference to be with others when they were afraid, Schachter argued that the results of his study illustrated the need for affiliation. The **need for affiliation** is the desire to establish and maintain relationships with other people. Although the strength of this need varies from one person to the next and from one situation to another, everyone holds some degree of a basic desire to forge associations with others.

**need for affiliation**
the desire to establish and maintain relationships with other people.

Of course, people don't pursue relationships with others indiscriminately. For instance, Schachter's later research showed that individuals fearful of receiving a shock in his experiment didn't just seek out *any* company. Instead, they pursued the presence of others who were in a position similar to their own. Specifically, subjects who thought that they would receive a severe shock were likely to choose to affiliate with others, but only if they knew the others were also expecting to be shocked. Apparently, those who were not going to receive a shock provided none of the solace of those who were similarly afflicted. According to Schachter, then, misery does not love just any company; it loves only miserable company.

It turns out, however, that Schachter was only partially correct. Subsequent research demonstrates that it is not critical for others to be equally miserable in order for their presence to be comforting. Instead, what counts is that other people face similar circumstances, not necessarily that they feel exactly the same way about those circumstances. Hence, it is the similarity of the situation that makes their presence desirable (Bell, 1978).

The reason people seek out others who are in a similar situation is that the presence of these others helps clarify the situation they face, providing a clearer definition and more information that may be useful in reducing their own anxiety. Consequently, the presence of others provides information about what to expect. Therefore, it is not always necessary for others to feel miserable themselves in order to provide useful information (Shaver & Klinnert, 1982).

There are some instances in which the level of misery is so strong that people avoid the presence of others. When circumstances provoke very strong negative emotions, people avoid others. For example, when President John Kennedy was assassinated, people who felt the most upset by his death typically wanted to be alone (Sheatsley & Feldman, 1964).

It may be that when people are deeply distressed, they fear that exposure to the unhappiness or depression of others will increase their own unhappiness. Moreover, when emotions are so strong as to be unambiguous, there is little need to obtain additional information about the situation (Wheeler, 1974). Consequently, at times of deep emotional turmoil, people may forgo contact with others.

## Attachment: The Roots of Affiliation

**attachment**
the positive emotional bond that develops between a child and a particular individual.

The importance of others in our lives begins from the moment of birth. Anyone who has seen children smiling at the sight of their mother or father has seen graphic evidence of the importance of the early affiliative bonds that exist between children and their caregivers.

**Attachment** is the positive emotional bond that develops between a child and a particular individual (Ainsworth et al., 1978). According to social psychologist Phillip Shaver and colleagues, attachment serves two primary functions. First, attachment provides children with a sense of security due to the presence of the person with whom they are attached. When faced with an anxiety-producing situation, children can turn to this individual for support and comfort. Secondly, the person can provide information about

Although we typically seek out others, we may prefer to be alone when we experience strong negative emotions.

Attachment, the positive emotional bond that develops between child and parent, provides children with a sense of security and can provide information about the world.

**secure attachment**
a style of attachment that characterizes a positive, healthy relationship between a child and an adult, based primarily on trust in the adult's comfort and love.

**avoidant attachment**
a style of attachment that characterizes relationships in which the child appears relatively indifferent to caregivers and avoids interactions with them.

**anxious–ambivalent attachment**
a style of attachment seen in children who show great distress when separated from their caregivers, but who appear angry on their return.

the situation. In an unfamiliar situation, the child can look to this person for hints about how to respond (Shaver & Klinnert, 1982).

Three major styles of attachment have been found in infants. **Secure attachment** characterizes a positive, healthy relationship between a child and an adult, based primarily on trust in the adult's comfort and love. In contrast, **avoidant attachment** characterizes relationships in which the child appears relatively indifferent to caregivers and avoids interactions with them. Finally, **anxious–ambivalent attachment** is seen in children who show great distress when separated from their caregivers, but who appear angry on their return (Bowlby, 1969; Ainsworth, 1979; Ainsworth, 1985).

The specific person to whom infants become attached is not always the same. Initially, researchers speculated that the bond between mother and infant was the most critical. However, more recent research shows that children can be simultaneously attached to both their mother and father, although the nature of attachment is not always identical. For instance, it is possible to be securely attached to the mother and insecurely attached to the father (Lamb, 1982; Belsky, Garduque, & Hrncir, 1984).

The type of attachment style that people develop during infancy may well determine their behavior with others for the rest of their lives (see, Erickson, Egeland, & Sroufe, 1985; Shaver, Hazan, & Bradshaw, 1988). Adults can be classified into the same set of attachment categories by asking them the questions shown in Figure 6-1, and the category into which they fall characterizes their adult relationships.

---

**FIGURE 6-1   What Is Your Attachment Style?**

Which of the these three statements best describes you?

**1.** I find it relatively easy to get close to others and am comfortable depending on them and having them depend on me. I don't often worry about being abandoned or about someone getting too close to me.

**2.** I am somewhat uncomfortable being close to others; I find it difficult to trust them completely, difficult to allow myself to depend on them. I am nervous when anyone gets too close, and often love partners want me to be more intimate than I feel comfortable being.

**3.** I find that others are reluctant to get as close as I would like. I often worry that my partner doesn't really love me or won't want to stay with me. I want to merge completely with another person, and this desire sometimes scares people away.

The choice you make suggests you fit into one of three types of attachment styles. A choice of statement 1 suggests a secure attachment style; a choice of statement 2 suggests an avoidant attachment style; and a choice of statement 3 is considered anxious–ambivalent. However, it is important to keep in mind that such a minimal, one-time assessment is open to variation and should not be taken as unerring or infallible.

*Source:* Shaver, Hazan, & Bradshaw, 1988.

Typically, just over half of all adults agree with the first statement, suggesting they are securely attached. About one quarter of adults say that the second statement is the most appropriate description, suggesting an avoidant attachment style. Finally, approximately 20 percent fall into the third category, which describes an anxious–ambivalent attachment style.

## Loneliness: Alone in a Social World

**loneliness**
the inability to maintain the level of affiliation one desires.

**emotional isolation**
a situation in which a person feels a lack of deep emotional attachment to one specific person.

**social isolation**
a situation in which a person suffers from a lack of friends, associates, or relatives.

If you have ever felt lonely, you are not alone: More than one quarter of people polled in a national survey stated that they had felt "very lonely or remote" from others during the prior few weeks. In fact, if you are an adolescent or an adult in your early twenties, you belong to the age segment of society that reports being the loneliest of any group. In spite of the conventional wisdom that it is the elderly who are most apt to be lonely, loneliness actually declines with increasing age—at least until activities must be restricted because of poor health or other problems (Weiss, 1973; Peplau & Perlman, 1982; Schultz & Moore, 1984).

**Loneliness** is the inability to maintain the level of affiliation one desires. It is a subjective state: A person can be alone and not feel lonely, or be in a crowd and feel lonely. Loneliness occurs only when the actual level of affiliation does not correspond with the desired level of affiliation.

At least two distinct forms of loneliness exist—emotional isolation and social isolation (Peplau & Perlman, 1982). In **emotional isolation**, a person feels a lack of deep emotional attachment to one specific person. By contrast, people who experience **social isolation** suffer from a lack of friends, associates, or relatives.

The two types of loneliness often do not go hand in hand. For example, an individual may have many friends and acquaintances and a large, extended family, yet lack any single person with whom to share a deep relationship. Similarly, people who frequently go to parties or eat in a crowded cafeteria with many others may still experience a sense of loneliness if they feel emotionally detached from the people who surround them. Although they might not feel socially isolated, in such cases as these, they may experience emotional isolation (Russell et al., 1984; Weiss, 1973).

**FIGURE 6-2    Attributions Leading to the Experience of Loneliness**

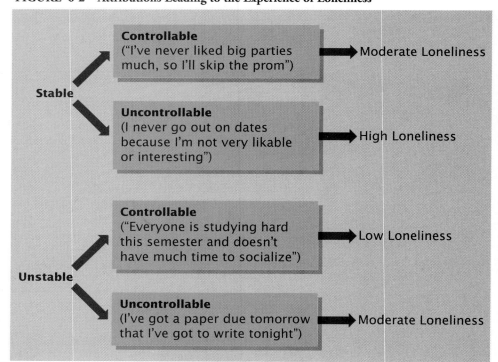

Any architectural feature that brings people together, such as a dormitory lounge, aids in the formation of friendships.

Of course, being alone is not invariably a bad thing. Many people crave time by themselves. What is critical in producing loneliness, then, are the attributions we make regarding the experience of being alone.

Those who view isolation as largely produced by unstable, controllable factors ("Everyone is studying hard this semester and poeple don't have much time to socialize") are less likely to experience loneliness. On the other hand, people who attribute isolation to their own stable, uncontrollable personal shortcomings ("I'm by myself because I'm not very likable or interesting") are much more likely to experience loneliness (Cutrona, 1982; Peplau, Micelli, & Morasch, 1982). Finally, as might be expected, a combination of controllable and stable causes—or uncontrollable but unstable, temporary causes—produces an intermediate degree of loneliness (see Figure 6-2).

## SITUATIONAL INFLUENCES ON ATTRACTION

If people were concerned in life only with fulfilling their general need for affiliation, it probably wouldn't matter much who met those needs. Anyone might fill the bill. Of course, people are considerably more discriminating than that. Some people become friends and lovers, and others develop into enemies and antagonists. We will now examine the factors that underlie attraction to specific individuals, considering what makes individuals like (and dislike) particular people.

*Proximity: The Architecture of Attraction*    Circumstances of geography determine friendships. Consider, for example, who your closest friends were when you were growing up. In most cases, they were probably children who lived close to you.

The same phenomenon often occurs in college dorms; students are often friendliest with people whose rooms are nearby, and least friendly with those who are assigned to rooms farthest away (Newcomb, 1961; Hays, 1985). Perhaps more surprisingly, a similar situation occurs with more intimate relationships, such as marriage. For example, one study of marriage license applications in a city during the 1930s showed that one third of the couples consisted of people who lived within five blocks of one another, and that the number of licenses declined as geographical distance increased (Bossard, 1932). And these findings do not include the 12 percent who shared the same address before they were married!

One of the classic studies in the field of interpersonal attraction highlighted the influence of the architectural configuration of buildings in determining friendships. Social psychologists Leon Festinger, Stanley Schachter, and Kurt Back (1950) carefully scrutinized friendships in a housing complex for married college students. They found that particular architectural features of the buildings in the complex—each of which contained ten apartments—were related to the development of friendships.

For example, they found a close association between friendships and the proximity of apartments to one another. Couples who lived one door apart were more likely to be friends than those living two doors apart; those living two doors apart were more likely to be friends than those living three doors apart; and so on. In addition, people who lived near mailboxes or stairways had more friends in the building than those who lived farther from such architectural features. In fact, any architectural feature that involved heavy traffic conferred greater popularity to those living nearby.

We might wonder, of course, whether the fact that proximity is related to attraction results from the fact that people who like one another may choose to live close to each other. However, this does not seem to be the case: People who are assigned living quarters show the same effects of proximity on liking. For instance, a study in which police trainees were assigned classroom seats and rooms alphabetically according to last name found a clear proximity pattern: The closer together in the alphabet two trainees' last names were, the more likely they were to become close friends (Segal, 1974).

On the other hand, proximity does not guarantee that people will grow to like each other. Crime statistics show that robberies often are perpetrated against people who are either acquainted with or related to the thieves. Even murders are most often kept in the family: One third of all homicides occur during family quarrels. Research also finds that although most of our closest friends may be physically proximate, the people we grow to dislike the most may also be physically close (Ebbesen, Kjos, & Konecni, 1976).

Clearly, proximity provides the opportunity for friendship to develop, although it does not ensure that it will. Why should proximity so often be a forerunner of liking? One explanation is that people can obtain social rewards—in the form of companionship, social approval, and help, at relatively little cost—from those who are nearby. Conversely, the costs involved in building and maintaining a friendship with someone physically distant may be considerably higher. Consequently, people are more apt to develop and maintain friendships with those with whom it is relatively more rewarding and less costly—those who are in close physical proximity.

## Personal Space: Come and Get a Little Closer

**personal space**
the area around a person's body which others may not enter.

How would you react if a stranger sat down next to you on a bus and leaned so close that you felt the side of his body pressing against yours?

Most of us would pull away, and our feelings of interpersonal attraction would hover near zero. The reason is that we have a well-defined sense of **personal space**—the area around a person's body which others may not enter. This space is like a bubble that surrounds people, psychologically "protecting" them from intrusions by others.

The bubble analogy is a bit too simple, however. The area that we protect extends into three dimensions, taking into account that different areas of the body may have different spatial requirements. According to the model shown in Figure 6-3, personal space is greatest for the top half of the body, but tapers below the waist toward the floor. Furthermore, personal space is not rigid; it grows and shrinks according to the situation, the people with whom we are interacting, and one's personality characteristics.

Interpersonal attraction is related to just how much we allow others to intrude on our personal space. Generally speaking, the more we like someone, the closer we permit that person to come. In fact, there are well-defined standards for spacing, depending on the intimacy of the interaction. According to anthropologist Edward Hall (1966), mid-

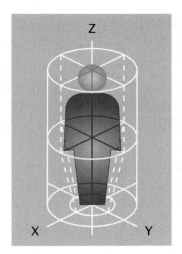

**FIGURE 6-3   Personal Space** A personal space zone surrounds a person three-dimensionally, "protecting" him or her from the intrusion of others.
*(Source:* Hayduk, 1978.*)*

dle-class Americans tend to interact with one another at a distance of 18 inches or less for the most intimate interactions. Casual interactions with friends are held at 18 inches to 4 feet, and people tend to space themselves from 4 to 12 feet apart when conducting impersonal business. Finally, there is a "public zone," which extends from 12 feet to the limits of hearing, generally about 25 feet. Formal occasions, such as lectures and judicial proceedings, occur at this distance.

People use distance to draw inferences about how much others are attracted to them (Mehrabian, 1968a, 1968b). For instance, one experiment found that people who were asked to imagine that another person was standing three feet away thought that they would be liked significantly more than when the other person was imagined to be seven feet away. Another experiment, in which subjects were asked to space themselves as if they liked (or disliked) another person, found that subjects chose to stand considerably closer to the person they liked (Mehrabian, 1968, 1968b). Of course, such data suffer from a methodological drawback: Subjects' perceptions of how they space themselves might be quite different from what they would do when interacting with an actual person (Love & Aiello, 1980).

Furthermore, extremes of closeness are not always related positively to interpersonal attraction. If the interaction is basically positive, increased proximity is related to enhanced liking. But if the interaction is initially negative, nearness can lead to increased negativity on the part of the interactants (Schiffenbauer & Schiavo, 1976). Ultimately, then, increased proximity may not lead to enhanced attraction between two people.

One of the intriguing findings related to interpersonal spacing is that different cultures have very divergent standards regarding the appropriate distance to maintain when conversing. For instance, Arabs tend to sit closer to one another than Americans do when conversing (Watson & Graves, 1966). In fact, Arabs tend to converse casually at a distance of just one foot—whereas Americans tend to hold conversations with non-intimate friends at distances of 18 inches to 4 feet, as mentioned earlier. It is not hard to imagine the discomfort that a newly acquainted American and Arab would feel conversing with each other, each trying to maintain an "appropriate" distance. As the Arab tried to edge closer, the American would be likely to try to back away. Unless some equilibrium were reached, interpersonal attraction between the partners would likely suffer.

*Familiarity: Growing Accustomed to Your Face*

When students in social psychologist Rick Crandall's classes arrived each day, they glimpsed a few strange, non-English words written in the corner of the chalkboard. Although these words were clearly not part of the lesson at hand, they became an accepted, unremarkable part of the backdrop of the class.

What was not obvious to the class was that the words were varied in a systematic way over the course of the term—some words appeared only once, while others appeared

The distance people seek to maintain between each other during the course of their interactions varies from one culture to another. Cross-cultural communication can suffer as a result.

as many as 25 times. At the end of the term, students in the class were surprised to be given a questionnaire to assess their rating of favorability of a list of words. Embedded in the list were all the words that had appeared on the chalkboard at one time or another during the term.

When the ratings were tabulated, the results were clear: The more frequently a word had appeared on the chalkboard, the higher its favorability rating. Increasing exposure to the words led to increased positivity toward them (Crandall, 1972).

The study conducted in Crandall's class demonstrated what became a well-established finding known as the mere exposure effect. The **mere exposure effect** is the phenomenon that repeated exposure to any stimulus increases the positivity of its evaluation. Contrary to conventional wisdom that "familiarity breeds contempt," experimental evidence suggests that the more often people are exposed to something, the more likely they are to like it (Zajonc, 1968; Bornstein, 1989).

Mere exposure results in increased liking not only for frequently seen words, but for other stimuli as well. The more people are exposed to a particular stimulus, be it animal, mineral, or vegetable, the more they are apt to like the stimulus, even if they are unaware of their exposure (Bornstein & D'Agostino, 1992).

For instance, people tend to enjoy musical passages and pieces of art as they become increasingly familiar. They like politicians more the more they are exposed to them. The most favored words in the English language are those that are encountered most often (Zajonc, 1968; Harrison, 1977; Grush, 1980).

Furthermore, humans are not the only species vulnerable to the mere exposure effect. Even rats exposed to pieces of music enjoy them more if they have had prior experience with them. In one study, for example, experimenters exposed rats to selections written either by eighteenth-century composer Mozart or by the contemporary composer Schoenberg (Cross, Halcomb, & Matter, 1967). Twelve hours a day for a two-month period, the rats heard the same composers' selections. Then, after a 15-day period of silence, the rats' musical preferences were tested by allowing them to activate a switch to play the music of either Mozart or Schoenberg.

The newly cultured rats were clear in their choices: They preferred the music with which they were familiar. And we should note that the specific musical selections played during the testing period were not the same as the ones played during the two-month period. Hence, the animals' preferences involved not specific familiar pieces but styles of music—pretty impressive, considering that we are talking about rats.

Given the universality of the mere exposure phenomenon, it is not surprising that the principle operates in the domain of interpersonal attraction. The more one person is exposed to another, the greater the attraction to that person—all other factors being equal. The phenomenon occurs when seeing photographs of someone, when simply exposed to someone's name, and—most important—when actually meeting the person.

As with other things in life, however, there can be too much of a good thing. Increased exposure does not bring about increased attractiveness indefinitely. For

**mere exposure effect**
the phenomenon that repeated exposure to any stimulus increases the positivity of its evaluation.

People who live and work together, such as these Amish women, may develop close personal ties simply due to the mere exposure effect.

instance, repeated exposure to the same commercial can become increasingly irritating, as can hearing the same song over and over. Clearly, then, the effects of mere exposure are not indefinitely more and more positive. In fact, after some optimal level of exposure is reached, liking can decline with repetition. Further, *sexual* attraction does not increase with familiarity. Research carried out on both humans and animals suggests that as familiarity between sex partners grows, sexual attraction declines (Dewsbury, 1981; Rosenblatt & Anderson, 1981).

Despite these exceptions, increasing exposure most often results in people and other stimuli becoming increasingly attractive. Unfortunately, the ubiquity of the phenomenon has not led to a clear understanding of *why* it occurs. Several factors may be at work. For instance, people may experience positive feelings of recognition when they encounter stimuli they have frequently seen in the past. These positive feelings may become associated with the stimulus itself, causing increasing attraction (Birnbaum & Mellers, 1979).

Another possibility is that the more people are exposed to a stimulus, the more they learn about it and whatever interesting, novel aspects it possesses (Berlyne, 1970; Stang, 1973). Because learning is a positive experience, increased exposure leads to increased positive feelings. This also explains why attraction may decrease after too much exposure: After overexposure to a stimulus, the stimulus no longer presents any novel aspects. Learning grinds to a halt, boredom sets in, and feelings toward the stimulus become less positive.

Finally, the mere exposure phenomenon may have its roots in evolution. Preference for the familiar—and, in all likelihood, the consequently safer—may have permitted our prehistoric human ancestors to live longer than those who preferred stimuli that were strange and unfamiliar (and perhaps consequently more dangerous). As a result, those preferring the familiar were more likely to reproduce, passing on this adaptive trait. Although speculative, such an evolutionary argument does help account for the mere exposure phenomenon (Bornstein, 1989).

It is still not certain what underlies the mere exposure phenomenon. What is clear is that repeated exposure, in and of itself, generally results in enhanced attraction. If you are trying to decide whether your absence or your presence will make the heart of your desired grow fonder, you had best opt for your continuing—and repeated—presence.

## ▶ REVIEW & RETHINK

### Review

- The mere presence of others is rewarding, for several reasons.
- Attachment in infancy has lasting effects throughout people's entire lives.

*Continued on next page*

- Loneliness is the inability to maintain a desired level of affiliation.
- Proximity, appropriate personal spacing, and familiarity lead to liking.

*Rethink*

- Why might the presence of others be important for humans?
- Compare the mere exposure effect with the need for affiliation phenomenon. How can the mere exposure effect account for the pleasure associated with being socially active?
- What are the three primary parent–child attachment styles? What becomes of these interaction styles as people grow older?
- What age group suffers the most from loneliness? Is this the age group that is most often alone? Explain any discrepancy in your answers to these two questions.
- "Absence makes the heart grow fonder," but "Out of sight, out of mind." How would a social psychologist evaluate these two opposite maxims?

# OTHER PEOPLE'S PERSONAL CHARACTERISTICS

*As Jon met his new roommate for the first time, he began peppering him with the most obvious questions: Where did he come from? Was it a small or big town? What did he plan to major in?*

*But as Jon heard the answers to his first questions, his anxiety level—already soaring—rose even further. His roommate could hardly have been more different. Jon, an African-American midwesterner who had lived on a farm all his life, would be living with a Hispanic-American raised in downtown New York. Jon had gone to a high school with just 60 kids in his graduating class; his roommate had gone to a huge urban high school ten times the size.*

*After a while, though, Jon began to feel a little better. They shared several significant similarities: a passion for Italian food, rap music, and film. They even expected to have the same major. As they discovered more and more commonalities, Jon began to feel at ease. They were going to get along just fine, he decided.*

Why did Jon end up feeling positively about his new roommate? Although it is unlikely that any single factor accounted for his conclusion, his discovery that they did in fact share several important similarities was probably no small consideration. We turn now to a discussion of similarity and its effects on liking, along with several other ingredients of interpersonal attraction.

*Similarity: Do Birds of a Feather Flock Together?*

If folk wisdom is used as a guideline for determining if similarity is associated with liking, we'd be faced with mixed messages. We are told that birds of a feather flock together, but we're also told that opposites attract.

Social psychologists have been able to make a clear choice between these two conflicting proverbs: With only a few exceptions, people like others who are similar to them. Regardless of whether the considerations are attitudes, values, or personality traits, similarity between two people can kindle interpersonal attraction.

**ATTITUDE AND VALUE SIMILARITY.**    Probably the clearest examples of the relationship between similarity and interpersonal attraction reside in the area of attitude and value similarity. For instance, since the early 1900s, researchers have found that people who like one another tend to share similar attitudes (Schuster & Elderton, 1907). The more

Similarity of beliefs, attitudes, and values, based on similar experiences and background, leads to interpersonal attraction.

challenging issue for researchers became a chicken-and-egg question: Does discovering shared attitudes with another person lead to liking that person? Or does attraction to another person influence the development of similar attitudes? (To complicate matters further, there's yet another possibility: that some additional factor led to both the attraction *and* the attitude similarity.)

By experimentally manipulating the perceived degree of agreement between two people, researchers discovered that similarity of attitudes can, in fact, produce interpersonal attraction (Gold, Ryckman, & Mosley, 1984; deWolfe & Jackson, 1984). In the prototypical experiment used to demonstrate this principle, subjects are asked to respond to a series of questions regarding their attitudes toward various topics, such as school and politics. The experimenter then collects the results, and under the guise of ascertaining subjects' impressions of a stranger, provides information regarding the "stranger's" supposed responses. The responses, which are actually bogus and contrived by the experimenter, can then be manipulated to produce various degrees of agreement with the subject's own attitudes. In the last step in the study, the experimenter assesses the subject's attraction to the confederate. Although quite simple and straightforward, this experimental paradigm allows for some elegant hypothesis testing. For instance, experimenters can vary the absolute number of perceived agreements and disagreements (for example, comparing the effects of agreement on 8 versus 5 versus 3 statements). On the other hand, experimenters can vary the proportion of agreement and disagreement (30 percent versus 50 percent versus 70 percent agreement, for example). In addition, they can also vary the specific nature of attitudes.

Results of a long line of studies indicate that one of the most critical factors underlying the attitude similarity–attraction relationship is the proportion of agreements, and not the absolute number of agreements. For instance, we would tend to like a person more who was thought to agree with one on three out of four attitudes (75 percent) than a person who was similar on five out of ten attitudes (50 percent), even though the absolute number of agreements is greater in the second case. In fact, if we were to graphically summarize the relationship between attraction and the proportion of perceived attitude similarity derived from many studies, we would find a remarkably consistent result: As the proportion of similar attitudes rises, so does attraction (Byrne, 1971; see Figure 6-4).

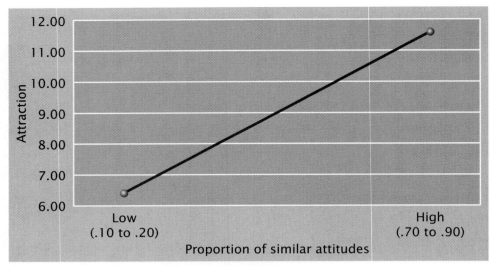

**FIGURE 6-4    Attraction and Attitude Similarity** As this summary of several studies indicates, the greater the proportion of similar attitudes, the more attraction is experienced for others. *(Source:* Byrne & Clore, 1966.*)*

**interpersonal repulsion**
the desire to escape from another's presence; the opposite of interpersonal attraction.

While it seems clear that attitude similarity leads to attraction, social psychologist Milton Rosenbaum has raised a plausible alternative hypothesis (Rosenbaum, 1986). Rejecting the view that similarity leads to attraction, he suggests instead that attitudinal *dis*similarity leads to interpersonal repulsion. **Interpersonal repulsion** is the desire to escape from another's presence—the opposite of interpersonal attraction.

According to Rosenbaum, attitude similarity is not particularly important or even noticed when people interact. Instead, they focus on dissimilarities, which are considerably more interesting psychologically because they are surprising and unexpected. The more dissimilarities people find, the more apt they are to avoid an individual, since they assume that interacting with that person will be unpleasant.

It is not certain whether people focus on attitudinal similarity (which then leads to interpersonal attraction), or on attitudinal dissimilarity (which produces interpersonal repulsion). However, both explanations make the same prediction—that a positive relationship exists between attitude similarity and attraction. It is the underlying explanation that is in dispute (Smeaton, Byrne, & Murnen, 1989; Drigotas, 1993).

Social psychologist Donn Byrne and colleagues suggest that both processes may be at work, although occurring at different stages of the process of developing attraction to another person (Byrne, Clore, & Smeaton, 1986). In their view, when we make new acquaintances we first do an initial screening in which we check out how dissimilar others are from us. If they are too different, we avoid them altogether. But if they pass this initial test, we then take into account attitude similarity, linking best those people whose attitudes are most similar to ours. In this way, both attitude similarity *and* attitude dissimilarity are considered in determining how attracted we are to another individual (see Figure 6-5.)

Because similarity of attitudes leads so clearly to interpersonal attraction, it should come as no surprise that similarity of values is also associated with liking. For instance, college roommates who *chose* to live together had significantly greater similarity in terms of fundamental values pertaining to such subjects as religion and politics than those who had been *assigned* to be roommates (Hill & Stull, 1981). In addition, the greater the degree of value similarity measured at the start of the fall term, the greater the likelihood that the pair would remain roommates in the spring term, suggesting that value similarity enhances liking.

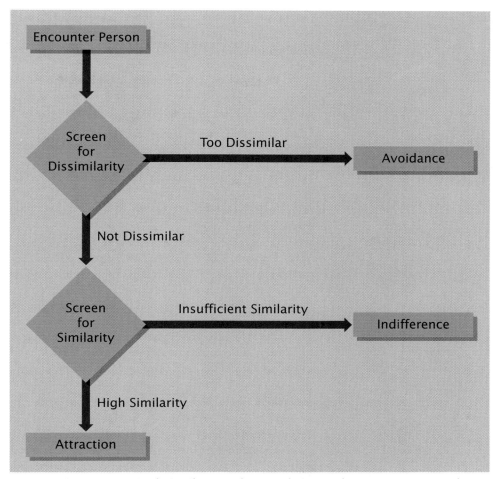

**FIGURE 6-5  How Attitude Similarity and Dissimilarity Produce Attraction** According to a model of interpersonal attraction proposed by Byrne, Clore, and Smeaton (1986), we first screen others to determine their attitudinal dissimilarity and then consider their similarity.

**SIMILARITY OF PERSONALITY TRAITS.**  If you are introverted, low in sociability, and timid, you'll probably be attracted to people who are . . . introverted, low in sociability, and timid.

At least that's the conclusion from research suggesting that people like others who have personalities relatively similar to their own (Reader & English, 1947; Boyden, Carroll, & Maier, 1984; Neimeyer & Mitchell, 1988). However, although the relationship between personality and liking is generally positive, it is considerably less strong than the relationship between attitude similarity and attraction. The reason for the difference is that almost everyone finds certain personality traits attractive—such as warmth and intelligence—whether or not they have those traits themselves.

We might also assume that in certain cases, *dissimilarity* of personality may lead to increased interpersonal attraction—if those differences allow one person to better fulfill the needs of another. Such reasoning reflects the **need complementarity hypothesis**— the notion that individuals are attracted to others who have significantly different personalities but whose needs complement theirs.

The need complementarity hypothesis has been applied primarily in terms of marriage partners, who in some cases appear to have radically different personalities from one another. The hypothesis argues that husbands and wives are most compatible when the needs of one spouse are fulfilled through the needs of the other (Winch, 1958). For

**need complementarity hypothesis** the notion that individuals are attracted to others who have significantly different personalities but whose needs complement theirs.

instance, a dominant wife may get along best with a submissive husband; or a husband and wife may differ in the degree to which they hold the same personality traits (a high-dominant husband with a low-dominant wife). In either instance, the needs of each fit together in the total context of the relationship.

The need complementarity hypothesis makes intuitive sense, reflecting folk wisdom such as this statement cited in a book on marriage: "I've known a lot of couples where the rocks in *her* head seemed to fit the holes in *his*." Folk wisdom aside, however, the research on the need complementarity hypothesis has not been especially successful in garnering experimental support. Despite some early research, which found that married partners did demonstrate complementary needs (Kerckhoff & Davis, 1962), later research has been unsuccessful in supporting the concept (e.g., Levinger, Senn, & Jorgensen, 1970; Meyer & Pepper, 1977; Aron et al., 1989). As is the case in other relationships, married partners tend to be attracted to one another more on the basis of similarity than difference.

**WHY SIMILARITY LEADS TO ATTRACTION.**    Whether on the basis of attitudes, values, or personality, similarity consistently relates to interpersonal attraction. But why?

Four possibilities help explain the relationship. First, similarity may be directly reinforcing. For example, individuals may have learned through prior experience that people with attitudes similar to their own are associated with rewarding circumstances or situations (Hendrick & Seyfried, 1974). Second, the fact that another person has attitudes or qualities similar to your own may confirm your view of the world. For example, if you believe that global warming should be prevented by controls on industrial production, you may be particularly attracted to someone who shares your views, because—in a very real sense—that agreement validates your opinion. Moreover, as we discussed earlier in terms of social comparison, similar others permit you to evaluate your abilities and opinions more readily than dissimilar others.

The third explanation for the relationship between similarity and liking is that learning the attitudes and values another person holds helps us to form a more complete impression of that other individual. We are apt to form positive impressions of similar people, because their similarity means they share traits with us that they value. According to this view, then, we like people who are similar because we infer that they have positive traits, and not directly because of similarity per se (Ajzen & Fishbein, 1980).

Finally, people may like similar others because they assume that *they* will be liked by those others. As we'll see next, knowing that someone likes you generally attracts you to that person. Hence, similarity may lead to inferences that the other person is attracted to you, and consequently your level of attraction increases.

Keep in mind that none of these explanations (summarized in Figure 6-6) is sufficient to explain the similarity–attraction relationship by itself (Huston & Levinger, 1978; Berscheid, 1985). Further, there are times when dissimilar others will be liked just

---

**FIGURE 6-6    Similarity and Interpersonal Attraction: Four Explanations**

| | |
|---|---|
| Similarity is directly reinforcing. | We learn through prior experience that people with similarities are associated with rewarding circumstances or situations. |
| Similarity confirms our worldview. | People who are similar validate our understanding of the world and are useful for purposes of social comparison. |
| Similarity provides knowledge of others' traits. | Learning that others hold similar, positive traits gives information about others' personality, which leads to liking. |
| Similarity leads to inferences that others will like us. | We assume that similar others are going to like us in return, making them more attractive. |

as much as those who are similar. For example, you may find that someone dissimilar can teach you something important, and this discovery may lead you to be attracted to that person (Kruglanski & Mayseless, 1987). Nonetheless, more often than not, perceived similarity will lead to greater interpersonal attraction.

## Reciprocity of Liking: I Like You Because You Like Me

**reciprocity of liking**
a situation in which you like those who like you.

It doesn't much matter how we find out. Whether it is demonstrated by subtle glances, or by deeds, or directly spoken, when we learn that another person likes us, we will tend to like that person in return. One of the most powerful and consistent social psychological findings is that of **reciprocity of liking**, which states that you like those who like you. And the phenomenon goes even further: When you like someone, you tend to assume that they like you in return (Metee & Aronson, 1974; Condon & Crano, 1988).

The consequences of learning that someone likes you are immediate and striking. For example, in one experiment, subjects overheard a confederate, with whom they had just spoken, telling an experimenter that they either liked or disliked the subject. When the confederates and subjects were then required to work together, the subjects' nonverbal facial expressions differed according to what they had overheard. When subjects heard that the confederate liked them, they were more nonverbally positive than when they heard the confederate disliked them. Further, subsequent written ratings showed that liked subjects were much more attracted to the confederate than those who thought they were disliked. Other research demonstrates similar findings: People act more positively toward, and hold more positive attitudes toward, those who they think like them (Feldman, 1976; Curtis & Miller, 1986).

The reciprocity-of-liking phenomenon would come as no surprise to Dale Carnegie, who long ago noted in his famous book *How to Win Friends and Influence People* that the best way for people to acquire friendship was to be "hearty in their approbation and lavish in their praise." However, before we rush to lavish praise on others in order to win their friendship, we should consider situations in which expressions of friendship may not invariably result in liking.

**ingratiation**
a deliberate effort to make a favorable impression, often through flattery.

One exception to the reciprocity-of-liking rule occurs when we suspect that others are saying positive things about us in order to ingratiate themselves. As we first discussed in Chapter 4, **ingratiation** is a deliberate effort to make a favorable impression, often through flattery (Jones, 1964; Jones & Pittman, 1982). But a student who tells his social psychology professor how much he likes her and her class risks being viewed as having an ulterior motive. As a consequence, the professor may end up with an unfavorable impression of the student—hardly the intended consequence.

Another exception to the reciprocity-leads-to-liking sequence occurs for people with exceptionally low self-esteem (Shrauger, 1975). For people in this category, who don't much like themselves, finding that someone likes them is at odds with their own self-concept. In such a case, they may consider a person who likes them as insensitive or undiscerning, and dislike them as a consequence. It is also possible that the inconsistency between our own view of ourselves and the view of us held by another person is unpleasant or uncontrollable. Whatever the reason, inconsistency between one's own view of oneself and that of another is unlikely to produce attraction, regardless of how genuine or enthusiastic the other's liking is.

## Personal Qualities: Who Do You Like?

It is not surprising that people with positive qualities are liked more than those with disagreeable qualities (Aron et al., 1989). For example, a survey of some 40,000 individuals found that such qualities as the ability to keep confidences, loyalty, warmth and affection, and supportiveness were most valued in people identified as friends (Parlee, 1979; see Figure 6-7).

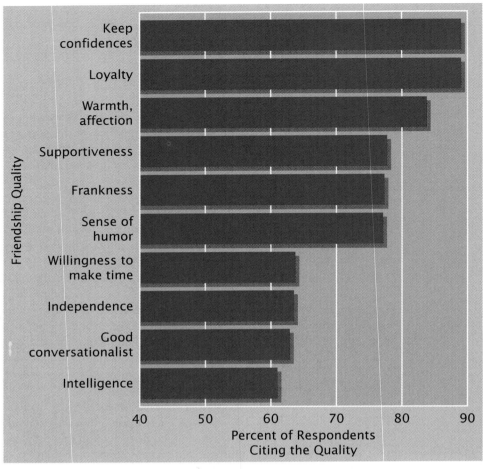

**FIGURE 6-7  What Makes a Friend?** According to a survey of some 40,000 people, these are the primary qualities in a friend.    *(Source:* Parlee, 1979.*)*

But the sheer number of positive qualities is not the whole story. Sometimes people prefer those who display positive qualities that are a bit tarnished by negative ones over those who are seemingly flawless. An example of this phenomenon was found in an experiment in which either a very competent person or an average person clumsily spilled a cup of coffee (Aronson, Willerman, & Floyd, 1966). After the mishap, liking for the competent person increased after the mishap, while attraction toward the average individual fell. Hence it seems that very competent people who commit a blunder become more human and approachable—and consequently more attractive. On the other hand, average people gain little from social blunders; they are already seen as human enough.

In addition to personality characteristics, interpersonal attraction is associated with gender and racial factors. For example, women and men show different kinds of friendship patterns. Although close to 80 percent of all men say that they have casual friendships with other males, just 20 percent report that they are have a close relationship with another man (Rubin, 1985).

In contrast, women are more likely than men to report having close friends and being able to confide in them. Furthermore, they tend to have a wider network of people they call friends than do males (Grambs, 1989; Lewittes, 1988).

Race, too, plays a role in interpersonal attraction. For example, African-American and white adolescents tend to select friends of the same race, and even when they report having a close friend of the other race in their school, they are not likely to socialize with such a friend outside of school (Hallinan & Williams, 1989; DuBois & Hirsch, 1990; Clark & Ayers, 1992).

The nature of friendship patterns differs between women and men. Although most men say they have casual friendships with other males, they are considerably less likely to report having a close relationship with a same-sex friend. In contrast, women are more apt to have close friends and to confide in them.

## ▶ REVIEW & RETHINK

### Review

- Similarity in terms of attitudes, values, and personality traits is related to interpersonal attraction.
- The reciprocity-of-liking phenomenon suggests that people like those who like them.
- Personal qualities relating to personality characteristics, gender, and race are associated with interpersonal attraction.

### Rethink

- Is the similarity–attraction relationship stronger in the domain of attitudes or of personality traits? Why might this be the case?
- How does Rosenbaum's interpersonal repulsion hypothesis differ from the traditional similarity–attraction hypothesis? If the repulsion hypothesis is correct, what strategies would you suggest to someone attempting to make a good impression?
- Describe two notable exceptions to the general tendency for people to reciprocate interpersonal attraction.
- How might the tendency to like people with positive qualities explain the similarity–attraction relationship?

*Physical Attractiveness and Liking: Beauty Beats the Beast*

If Michelle Pfeiffer and Mel Gibson were ugly, would you still like them?

In our supposedly egalitarian and democratic society, most people would agree that people should be judged for what they are and what they do, rather than for what they look like. Yet, despite general agreement with the old adage "Beauty is only skin deep," it turns out that most people act as if physical attractiveness is a good measure of likability. However unwarranted such a bias may be, physical appearance represents an important aspect of how people view others.

With startling consistency, people who are physically attractive are liked more than unattractive people, beginning with nursery-school-age children and continuing into old age (Berscheid & Walster, 1974; Hatfield & Sprecher, 1986). In fact, not only are physically attractive individuals liked more, but people make more positive interpretations of their behavior than of the behavior of the physically unattractive.

For example, social psychologist Karen Dion (1972) presented adults with a description of instances of mild or severe misbehavior by a seven-year-old and asked them to judge the typicality of the child's behavior. Included with the descriptions were a photo of either an attractive or an unattractive child. When the misbehavior was mild, no effects due to the appearance of the child were detected. But when the misbehavior was severe, the physical attractiveness of the child determined how the behavior was interpreted. Subjects viewed attractive children's misbehavior as temporary, atypical incidents, unlikely to be repeated. Hence, one subject described in this way an attractive girl who threw a rock at a sleeping dog:

> She appears to be a perfectly charming little girl, well-mannered, basically unselfish. It seems that she can adapt well among children her age and make a good impression . . . She plays well with everyone, but like anyone else, a bad day can occur. Her cruelty need not be taken seriously.

In contrast, similar incidents committed by unattractive children were judged considerably more harshly, and were seen as examples of chronic misbehavior, symptomatic of an underlying behavior problem. For instance, one unattractive girl who threw a rock at a sleeping dog was perceived like this:

> I think the child would be quite bratty and would be a problem to teachers. . . . She would probably try to pick a fight with other children her own age. . . . She would be a brat at home—all in all, she would be a problem.

Obviously, the same behavior was judged in very different ways, depending on the physical attractiveness of the transgressor.

The consequences of physical attractiveness and unattractiveness persist and well beyond childhood. Numerous experiments in the 1960s and 1970s used the guise of "computer dating," a craze in which people completed questionnaires that were then fed into computers. The computers were programmed to identify a person's "ideal" date.

In a series of experiments, researchers altered the computer programs and matched dates on a completely random basis. By then looking at the success of the matches, they were able to determine what personal factors were most important. In study after study, the most influential factor in determining attraction was the physical attractiveness of one's date. Neither attitudes, values, personality traits, or intelligence were more important in determining liking (Walster et al., 1966; Tesser & Brodie, 1971).

Why was physical attractiveness so important in these situations? One answer is that most of the dating experiments involved only the initial encounters between a man and a woman. In such a situation, we would expect that societal expectations about interpersonal attractiveness would be particularly pronounced. In fact, one of the most widely held societal stereotypes is relevant to dating: the "beautiful-is-good" stereotype.

**beautiful-is-good stereotype**
the belief that physically attractive people have a wide range of positive characteristics.

**THE BEAUTIFUL-IS-GOOD STEREOTYPE.**    Society in general has a widespread beautiful-is-good stereotype regarding physical attractiveness. According to the **beautiful-is-good stereotype**, physically attractive people have a wide range of positive characteristics.

Research on the stereotype finds that these perceived traits include higher sociability, greater dominance, and better social skills. In addition, the physically attractive are thought to be more intelligent, sexually warmer, and in better mental health than the less physically attractive (Romano & Bordieri, 1989; Feingold, 1992).

How accurate is the beautiful-is-good stereotype? According to a large-scale review of the research literature carried out by psychologist Alan Feingold, not very accurate (Feingold, 1992a). For example, some basic personality dimensions such as emotional stability, self-esteem, and dominance are unrelated to physical attractiveness. Further, intelligence and academic ability show no correlation with attractiveness (thereby helping to dispel the myth of the "dumb blonde"; the attractive are neither smarter nor less intelligent than the unattractive).

On the other hand, several personality characteristics related to people's social life were associated with physical attractiveness. Good-looking people do have better social skills, and they report less loneliness and lower social anxiety than do less attractive people. In addition, their greater popularity translates into greater sexual permissiveness and more actual experience in a variety of sexual activities.

Obviously, the beautiful-is-good stereotype has its limitations, especially given that attractive and unattractive people differ relatively little in terms of basic personality traits. Why, then, is the stereotype so pervasive in our society? Several reasons may explain it (Feingold, 1992b).

For one thing, the entertainment media, particularly television and film, portray a world in which the key players are exceptionally attractive. Both male and female leading actors are unusually handsome or beautiful, and they are also charming and sensual. In addition, other actors surrounding the stars are often relatively unattractive, and they frequently play bumbling, socially inept roles. (The television show Cheers is a good example of this phenomenon.) Based on what the media presents, it is little wonder that society expects the physically attractive to also have exceptionally good personalities.

The fundamental attribution error, which we first discussed in Chapter 2, provides another explanation for the pervasiveness of the beautiful-is-good stereotype. It is possible that the primary reason attractive people receive preferential treatment is due to the stereotype. However, when others see them afforded such exceptional treatment, the fundamental attribution error, in which dispositional causes for behavior are overemphasized, may lead to the erroneous assumption that the preferential treatment is due to dispositional factors (their wonderful personalities). At the same time, people may underestimate the contribution of situational factors (the behavior of the other people in the situation) to the preferential treatment of attractive people. The fundamental attribution error, then, may lead to the perpetuation of the beautiful-is-good stereotype.

Finally, there is emerging evidence that the beautiful-is-good stereotype in part may be the result of inborn, genetic factors. Although most researchers have traditionally assumed that the standards of beauty were established within a society, recent evidence suggests that this conclusion may not be entirely accurate (Singh, 1993). For example, in one study, psychologist Judy Langlois and colleagues showed six- to eight-month-old infants pairs of photos—one of a woman judged attractive by adults and the other of a woman judged unattractive (Langlois et al., 1987). The infants spent a significantly greater amount of time looking at the attractive face than at the unattractive one—suggesting that the attractive faces were of greater interest.

Other research concludes that infants show greater social responsiveness to the physically attractive. In one study, one-year-olds interacted with a stranger who wore a mask that was professionally constructed to simulate either an attractive or an unattractive face. When the stranger wore an attractive mask, the infants showed more positive emotions and played more than when the stranger wore an unattractive mask. Furthermore, other studies show that infants play more with dolls that have attractive faces than with those with unattractive faces (Langlois, Roggman, & Rieser-Danner, 1990).

It is unlikely that the babies in these studies had already learned societal standards for attractiveness (Adams & Crane, 1980). Instead, the results argue that there is some sort of genetic predisposition toward a certain kind of beauty, and that faces of particular dimensions and conformations provide socially useful information that had adaptive value for our ancient ancestors. (Also see the accompanying Social Psychology at Work feature.)

---

# SOCIAL PSYCHOLOGY AT WORK

## THE PROPORTIONS OF BEAUTY

Have you ever encountered people who look as if they need to be nurtured and taken care of?

If you looked closer, you might find that they had relatively large eyes and small noses—characteristics that can be labeled as babyishness. According to social psychologists Michael Cunningham and Leslie Zebrowitz, babyishness plays an important role in determining our reactions to others (Zebrowitz & Montepare, 1990; Cunningham, 1990). The more that people have facial features similar to those of a baby, the greater the impression of childlike innocence. At the same time, if these characteristics are not offset by more mature features, such as large cheekbones and chin, they may also convey powerlessness, submissiveness, and social incompetence. The impact of babyishness is so strong that it is found across different cultures, throughout the life span, and even in different species (Keating, 1985; McArthur & Berry, 1987).

In research conducted by Cunningham and colleagues that supports these conclusions, groups of adult men and women indicated their attraction to men's faces. In the research, subjects were shown photos of men's faces and asked to judge how attractive they were on an eight-point scale ranging from extremely unattractive to extremely attractive. Each of the photos was then carefully examined to determine both the absolute size of the facial features and the relationships among the various features (Cunningham, Barbee, & Pike, 1990).

Using the ratings and the measurements, researchers could then determine the characteristics of the preferred male face. For example, judges preferred prominent cheekbones and a large chin, considered to be indications of maturity. But they also included large eye height and width and a small nose, associated with a baby face. Hence, preferred faces seemed to contain a combination of mature and babylike fea-

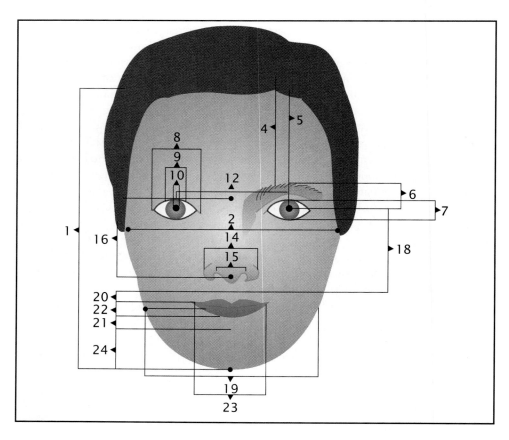

**FIGURE 6-8  Facial Proportions That Relate to Liking** Ratings of preferred female faces show surprising uniformity in the ratios of the various measures of facial configuration shown here. For instance, preferred faces had a chin length that was one-fifth the height of the face. (*Source:* Cunninghamn, 1986.)

tures, conveying a combination of ruggedness and cuteness. Cunningham speculates that such features elicit a combination of respect and nurturing tenderness.

Other research has examined the preferred female face, using judgments made by men (Cunningham, 1986). This work has found that the preferred female face has large eyes, a small nose, high cheekbones and narrow cheeks. In addition, calculations of the precise configuration of facial features, using the different measures illustrated in Figure 6-8, shows great uniformity in judgments. For instance, preferred faces had an eye width (#12 in the figure) that was three tenths the width of the face at the level of the eyes (#2). Similarly, the

distance from the center of the eye to the bottom of the eyebrow (#6) was one tenth the height of the face (#1).

We need to keep in mind, of course, that these proportions represent composite preferences, and not those particular dimensions found in any single person (Alley & Cunningham, 1991). (In other words, don't start measuring how far your eye is from your eyebrow in order to assess your own attractiveness.) Moreover, facial configuration is only one of the factors that enter into judgments of physical attractiveness, and attractiveness is only one of several factors that enter into interpersonal attraction.

On the other hand, many of society's standards of beauty have undergone significant change over the course of time, and beauty standards vary from one culture to another. For example, the women who were considered the most attractive in nineteenth-century Hawaii were the ones who were the most overweight. Similarly, even within U.S. society, there have been significant shifts in society's view of the "ideal" weight. For instance, one survey of the exemplary figure, as depicted in models in fashion magazines, showed that the standard of slenderness in vogue today is matched historically in only one other period: the mid-1920s. For most of the rest of the century, the ideal female figure was relatively full (Silverstein et al., 1986; see Figure 6-9).

Furthermore, the beautiful-is-good stereotype is troubling in terms of the message it sends to members of minority groups. Because the idealized image of female beauty has typically been a Caucasian one, African-American women are put in the position of

**FIGURE 6-9 Historical Changes in Preferred Female Body Types** During the course of the twentieth century, norms regarding women's body types have changed significantly. This graph shows the mean "bust-to-waist" ratio, a measure of full-figuredness, of models appearing in *Vogue* and *Ladies' Home Journal* during the course of the twentieth century. As depicted in women's magazines, slenderness has been in style in only two periods: the mid-1920s and in recent decades. In other times, societal standards supported relatively full figures. *(Source: Silverstein et al., 1986.)*

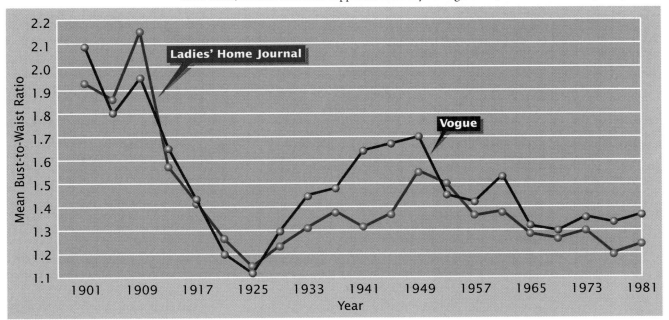

Contemporary standards of physical attractiveness clearly differ from those employed by the seventeenth-century artist Rubens.

seeking to appear Caucasian in order to match this artificial standard. Even the few advertisements that include African-American models often use women who are light-skinned, slender, and young—similar in many ways to the ideal portrayed by the media for whites. Although there have been efforts to promote the message that "black is beautiful," African-American women sometimes report being rejected by African-American men because of their dark skin. A similar situation, in which Caucasian standards of beauty are forced on women without regard for ethnic differences, is found in some Asian countries, where some women have surgery on their eyelids to make them look more westernized (Unger & Crawford, 1992; Freedman, 1986; Chapkis, 1986).

Despite the negative ramifications of the beautiful-is-good stereotype, it remains pervasive. Yet, although it is important, physical attractiveness is hardly the full story in determining interpersonal attraction. For instance, although physical attractiveness may be preferred in the abstract and during initial encounters, evidence indicates that people tend to use a somewhat different standard in longer-term relationships. For example, the **matching hypothesis** suggests that people are attracted to others who have a level of physical attractiveness similar to their own (Berscheid & Walster, 1974; Feingold, 1988).

A good deal of evidence supports the matching hypothesis: During courtship and marriage, the level of physical attractiveness of couples tends to correspond fairly closely. In fact, there is even some evidence that married couples come to look more similar to one another the longer they live together (Zajonc et al., 1987).

It's not just romantically linked couples who show attractiveness matching. People who are friends correspond to each other's level of physical attractiveness. There is also a gender difference, with pairs of male friends corresponding more closely to one another than pairs of female friends (Feingold, 1988; McKillip & Riedel, 1983). Consequently, rather than turning to a mirror to get a sense of how physically attractive you are, you might just take a look at your friends!

**THE DOWNSIDE OF PHYSICAL ATTRACTIVENESS.**    Consider the following scenario:

> *Let's say the list of candidates for a key executive position has narrowed to just two people. Both have very similar backgrounds and exemplary track records. On paper, it's a toss-up. One is a good-looking man, the other a very attractive woman. Who gets the nod? (Schellhardt, 1991, B1)*

The answer is not so pretty: the attractive man. The reason is that attractive women are viewed as gentle, soft, and indecisive, whereas attractive men are considered to be tough, competent, and decisive.

Given the bulk of the research findings, most people would probably wish to be physically attractive, if they had the choice. Certainly, given the amount of money and

**matching hypothesis**
the hypothesis that people are attracted to others who have a level of physical attractiveness similar to their own.

## DOONESBURY by Garry Trudeau

time spent on clothing, makeup, physical fitness, and plastic surgery, physical attractiveness seems a goal to which many aspire.

Yet there is a downside to physical attractiveness, and some research suggests that the expected social rewards of beauty can be illusory. For example, beauty can produce less positive impressions of women in work-related situations. Attractive women may call to mind a common, although totally unfounded, stereotype that successful, attractive women attained their positions as a result of their looks rather than their abilities (Schellhardt, 1991).

Similarly, other research shows that physical attractiveness can be overrated. For instance, consider the results of one study that examined the relationship between women's physical attractiveness in college and their adjustment and happiness twenty years later (Berscheid, Walster, & Campbell, 1974). The results showed that, contrary to what might be expected, women who had been attractive in college tended to be *less* happy and *less* well-adjusted in their later lives than those who had been relatively unattractive in college. It may be that the normal process of aging is more devastating to someone who was initially very attractive than to someone less attractive early in life.

Findings such as these reinforce an important point: Although the significance of physical attractiveness is undeniable, many other factors help determine interpersonal attraction. For example, a pleasant facial expression brings about ratings of greater physical attractiveness than an unpleasant or neutral expression. One experiment found that people who were smiling were not only thought to be more attractive than people in an unsmiling control group, but were also considered to be more sincere, sociable, and competent (Reis et al., 1990).

---

*Theories of Attraction*

Why is it that such factors as similarity, reciprocity-of-liking, and physical attractiveness lead to liking? Researchers have focused their explanations on two main theoretical families: learning theory approaches and cognitive theory approaches.

**LEARNING APPROACHES.**   You are more apt to like someone who provides you with rewards, and you are apt to dislike those who are punishing. Such straightforward propositions grow out of one of the most basic approaches to interpersonal attraction—learning theory (Byrne & Clore, 1970; Byrne, 1971; Byrne & Murnen, 1988). According to the **reinforcement-affect model**, for instance, liking follows the basic principles of learning embodied in classical and operant conditioning. This model suggests that the positive emotions people experience in the presence of someone rewarding lead to attraction, while negative emotions lead to reductions in attraction.

**reinforcement-affect model**
the premise that liking follows the basic principles of learning embodied in classical and operant conditioning.

Specifically, classical conditioning—which you may remember from your introductory psychology course in connection with the experiment on Pavlov's dogs—may occur when other people's presence becomes associated with rewarding or punishing circumstances. Subsequently, individuals transfer feelings about the circumstances to the people themselves. In other words, they respond in a way that is analogous to the response of a dog that learns to salivate at the sound of a bell that in the past has been associated with the presence of food (Lott & Lott, 1974).

Analogously, people may come to learn that specific aspects of other people are reinforcing—such as their rewarding behavior toward us, their rewarding traits, or the access they provide to particular rewards. This reinforcement may lead to attraction through the operation of operant conditioning, in a manner analogous to the way a pigeon learns that pecking a key will produce an edible reinforcer.

**cognitive approaches (to interpersonal attraction)**
an approach that focuses on how people perceive the nature of a relationship they hold with others.

**COGNITIVE APPROACHES.**    **Cognitive approaches to interpersonal attraction** focus on how people perceive the nature of a relationship they hold with others. Unlike learning theories, which examine the absolute degree of rewards and punishments provided by others, cognitive approaches consider how people's thoughts, beliefs, attitudes, and perceptions determine their liking for others.

**comparison level theories**
the theory that suggests that attraction to others is based on comparison to some hypothetical baseline.

For instance, **comparison level theories** suggest that attraction to others is based on comparison to some hypothetical baseline (Thibaut & Kelley, 1959). This baseline, known as a comparison level, is a kind of summary of the past outcomes that have been experienced or that are prominent in a given situation. If the rewards received from the relationship are above the person's comparison level, that person will be satisfied with the relationship; if the rewards fall below it, the person will be dissatisfied. However, whether an individual seeks to maintain a relationship also depends on the alternatives that are available. As a result, one may maintain an unsatisfactory relationship with someone if no better alternatives are available (Black et al., 1991).

**equity theory**
the theory that suggests that people not only take into account their own outcomes, but also the outcomes that are perceived to be attained by others.

**Equity theory** takes comparison level theory a step further, suggesting that people not only take into account their own outcomes, but also the outcomes that are perceived to be attained by others (Walster, Walster, & Berscheid, 1978; Walster, Walster, & Traupmann, 1978). According to this view, people try to maintain a balance between the rewards and costs experienced and those experienced by a friend or partner in a relationship. If your partner is seen as receiving more (or less) than his or her just due, you will likely experience distress and try to restore equity, potentially by modifying our perception of what you are getting out of the relationship or by modifying your feelings for your partner. If you feel that you are putting an undue amount of effort into a friendship—perhaps by always being the one to arrange for various social activities—you may experience feelings of inequity and reevaluate your liking for the friend.

**balance theory**
the theory that people strive for consistency, or balance, in their thoughts, feelings, and attitudes toward others.

One final cognitive approach to interpersonal attraction is represented by balance theory. According to **balance theory**, people strive for consistency, or balance, in their thoughts, feelings, and attitudes toward others (Heider, 1958). Balance theory suggests that people will be attracted to others who hold attitudes similar to their own and who like the same things and people. In contrast, the theory suggests that people are predisposed to dislike those who hold dissimilar attitudes and who like people they don't like.

**THE TWO THEORIES IN PERSPECTIVE.**    As is often the case in social psychology, neither learning nor cognitive approaches alone provide a full explanation of interpersonal attraction. Similarly, no single factor related to attraction—similarity, reciprocity of liking, physical attractiveness, or any of the other components of liking—is sufficient to explain attraction.

On the contrary, whether an initial encounter between two people results in interpersonal attraction depends on a complex set of ingredients. And, as we'll see in the next chapter, whether such attraction blossoms and grows into a deeper relationship is the result of an even more intricate web of social psychological forces.

# THE INFORMED CONSUMER OF SOCIAL PSYCHOLOGY

## MAKING FRIENDS

A quick perusal of the self-help section of any bookstore suggests that the ability to make friends is a source of concern for many people. Even if they don't seek out self-help books on the topic, making friends is one of the most basic and common concerns that people have.

Although no simple formula exists for making friends, the work of social psychologists points to several approaches worth considering. Among them are the following:

- *Let other people know that you like them.* As we've seen, reciprocity of liking is one of the most powerful phenomena in the area of interpersonal attraction. We like those who like us. Consequently, if you want someone to like you, show that you like him or her. Although such honesty can produce feelings of vulnerability—with good reason—it also may pay to take the risk of demonstrating your liking for another person.

- *Reveal yourself.* It is hard for someone to feel they are similar to you if they know little about you. In order for many of the factors that have been discussed in this chapter to be effective (such as similarity of values and attitudes, for example), others need to know where you stand. Don't assume that others will somehow know or guess what you think about things; let them know how you feel. Also, self-disclosure, in itself, can produce interpersonal attraction as we discussed in Chapter 5. By honestly communicating your own ideas and feelings, you can help others learn about the commonalities that you share with them. Of course, there can be too much disclosure : Revealing significant personal facts about yourself too early in a relationship can actually impede its progress.

- *Take part in shared activities.* The research showing the close correlation between proximity and friendship suggests another strategy for making friends: Take part in shared activities. As we'll see in the next chapter, relationships evolve over time, and engaging in mutual activities may set the stage for the development of lasting friendships.

## ► REVIEW & RETHINK

### Review

- People who are physically attractive are liked more than those who are less attractive.
- The beautiful-is-good stereotype suggests that physically attractive people have other positive qualities.
- Learning and cognitive approaches have both been used to explain interpersonal attraction.

### Rethink

- List some of the more common stereotypes that our society holds about attractive people. Do any of these stereotypes have any basis in truth?
- What evidence suggests that attraction to people with certain physical features is innate?
- What disadvantages may result from physical attractiveness? What would the matching hypothesis suggest about the dating success of extremely attractive individuals?
- Describe and differentiate the two main approaches to explaining the interpersonal attraction literature.

## LOOKING BACK ◄ ◄ ◄ ◄ ◄ ◄ ◄ ◄ ◄ ◄ ◄ ◄ ◄ ◄ ◄ ◄ ◄ ◄ ◄ ◄ ◄ ◄

### What are the origins of interpersonal attraction?

1. We seek out the companionship of others for several reasons. The presence of others can provide the direct reduction of anxiety and can permit social comparison, allowing us to evaluate our own abilities, expertise, and opinions by comparing them to others. We also

have a need for affiliation—the desire to establish and maintain relationships with other people.

2. The roots of affiliation can be found in attachment—the positive emotional bond that develops between a child and a particular individual. Attachment provides children with a sense of security and with information about a given situation. There are three major attachment styles: secure attachment, avoidant attachment, and anxious-ambivalent attachment.

3. Loneliness is the inability to maintain the level of affiliation we desire. Among the types of loneliness are emotional isolation, in which a we feel a lack of deep emotional attachment to one specific person, and social isolation, in which we lack friends, associates, or relatives.

### *How do situational factors such as proximity and familiarity lead to liking?*

4. Proximity is a powerful factor in producing interpersonal attraction. For relatively little cost we can obtain social rewards—in the form of companionship, social approval, and help—from others who are nearby. Consequently, we are more likely to develop and maintain friendships with those with whom it is relatively more rewarding and less costly—that is, people who are in close physical proximity. Similarly, appropriate personal spacing is related to interpersonal attraction.

5. The mere exposure effect is the phenomenon that repeated exposure to any stimulus increases the positivity of its evaluation. One explanation for this effect is that we may experience positive feelings of recognition when we encounter stimuli that we have frequently experienced in the past, which then rub off on the stimulus itself. Another possibility is that the more we are exposed to a stimulus, the more we learn about its interesting, novel aspects. Because learning is a positive experience, increased exposure leads to increased positive feelings. Finally, the mere exposure phenomenon may have its roots in evolutionary factors.

### *What are the primary personal qualities that lead people to be liked by others?*

6. We are attracted to those who are similar to us. Among the types of similarity that produce liking are attitude similarity, value similarity, and similarity of personality traits. Similarity may lead to attraction because it is directly reinforcing, it confirms our views of the world, it permits us to form an impression of others' traits, and it allows us to assume that the similarity will produce liking in return.

7. Reciprocity of liking is a strong determinant of interpersonal attraction: We like those who like us. However, exceptions occur in the case of ingratiation and for people with exceptionally low self-esteem. In addition, we like others who have positive qualities, although sometimes people prefer others who have at least a few negative qualities to those who are seemingly flawless. In addition, gender and race are related to attraction.

8. People who are physically attractive are liked more, and more consistently, than unattractive people. One reason is the beautiful-is-good stereotype, which suggests that physically attractive people hold a range of other positive characteristics. However, the stereotype is not entirely accurate. Further, physical attractiveness is most important during initial encounters, and the matching hypothesis suggests that we are attracted to others who are similar to our own level of physical attractiveness.

9. The two main families of explanations for interpersonal attraction are learning approaches and cognitive approaches. Learning approaches state that liking follows the basic principles of learning embodied in classical and operant conditioning. Cognitive approaches focus on people's thoughts, beliefs, attitudes, and perceptions to determine their liking. Comparison level theory and equity theory are examples of cognitive approaches.

### *What strategies for making friends do the principles of interpersonal attraction suggest?*

10. Among the strategies for making friends are to let others know that you like them, to reveal yourself to others, and to take part in shared activities.

# KEY TERMS AND CONCEPTS

*interpersonal attraction (p. 179)*

*social comparison (p. 181)*

*need for affiliation (p. 181)*

*attachment (p. 182)*

*secure attachment (p. 183)*

*avoidant attachment (p. 183)*

*anxious–ambivalent attachment (p. 183)*

*loneliness (p. 184)*

*emotional isolation (p. 184)*

*social isolation (p. 184)*

*personal space (p. 186)*

*mere exposure effect (p. 188)*

*interpersonal repulsion (p. 192)*

*need complementarity hypothesis (p. 193)*

*reciprocity of liking (p. 195)*

*ingratiation (p. 195)*

*beautiful-is-good stereotype (p. 198)*

*matching hypothesis (p. 202)*

*reinforcement-affect model (p. 203)*

*cognitive approaches to interpersonal attraction (p. 204)*

*comparison level theories (p. 204)*

*equity theory (p. 204)*

*balance theory (p. 204)*

# FOR FURTHER RESEARCH AND STUDY

Derlega, V. J., & Winstead, B. A. (Eds.) (1986). *Friendship and social interaction.* New York: Springer-Verlag.

Contains an interesting series of chapters on friendships, including research on interracial friendships and the development of social interaction.

Hatfield, E., Sprecher, S. (1986). *Mirror, mirror . . . The importance of looks in everyday life.* Albany, NY: SUNY Press.

This book focuses on one of the primary determinants of interpersonal attraction: physical appearance.

Duck, S. (1988). *Relating to others.* Chicago, IL: Dorsey.

Duck, S. (1990). *Personal relationships and social support.* Newbury Park, CA: Sage.

Two clearly written overviews regarding our first encounters with others, including a good deal of discussion of interpersonal attraction.

Kleinke, C. L. (1986). *Meeting and understanding people.* New York: Freeman.

A worthwhile volume with considerable guidance on the factors that cause people to be liked.

# EPILOGUE

In this chapter we've traced the development of liking, discussing why people seek out others and how the roots of attraction develop. In looking at attraction, we've concentrated on the forces that bring people together in the first place, such as situational factors and other people's personal characteristics.

What we haven't done, however, is to look at the way initial attraction leads to close, long-term relationships. In the next chapter we take this leap, moving from the origins and first stirrings of liking to the development of full-blown close relationships. We'll see how people form and maintain associations with one another, and consider the reasons why some relationships falter and sometimes end entirely. As we discuss love, marriage, and several other varieties of enduring relationships, we'll see how the work that we discussed in this chapter has paved the way for our understanding of close relationships.

### CHAPTER SEVEN

# CLOSE RELATIONSHIPS
## THE NATURE OF INTIMATE RELATIONS

# PROLOGUE: ON THE RELATIONSHIP ROAD

It took Amy Stewart a week to break the news to her parents: She and her boyfriend of six months, Chad Johnston, were planning to spend the summer touring with Lollapalooza, a traveling show that included some of the most popular rock-and-roll groups.

Amy Stewart and Chad Johnston.

The tour proved to be a challenge to their fledgling relationship. Working together at a midway booth, they sold hand-made bracelets and braided hair for concert-goers wishing to adopt a Rastafarian look. Although they made money, it wasn't easy work, and laboring side by side for 18-hour days didn't make things easier. As Amy noted, "It strains a relationship to be together this intensely. We agreed that from now on, he'll tell me when I'm being crabby and I'll tell him when he's being a jerk."

Ultimately, though, both their job and their relationship prospered. After some rocky times—such as the evening Amy criticized Chad's driving, he got furious, and they stopped speaking for 24 hours—they came to a realization. Amy said to Chad, "We're like an old couple, always nit-picking at each other. Is that why we went on Lollapalooza, to become our parents?"

Chad replied no, and later said the conversation had marked a watershed in their relationship. He said he had spoken to Amy "as if for the first time . . . . I'm learning to talk. And to listen. And to really hear what she's trying to tell me instead of just nodding my head and saying, 'Uh-huh.' What I finally heard her say was 'Tell me what's really going on in your brain.' O.K., I'll try."

Soon after, the couple realized that they had come to something of an understanding of one another. Chad said, "I've learned you have try to if you're in love." After a pause, he continued: "I can honestly say I'm not getting sick of Amy." Amy's reply was swift. As she kissed Chad on the nose, she said, "You better not sucker. Because I'll get you." (Karlen, 1993, p. V1, V9)

## LOOKING AHEAD

▶ ▶ ▶ ▶ ▶ ▶ ▶ ▶ ▶ ▶ ▶ ▶ ▶ ▶ ▶ ▶ ▶ ▶ ▶ ▶ ▶ ▶ ▶ ▶ ▶

We don't know what will happen with Amy Stewart's and Chad Johnston's relationship. Will they stay together? Become engaged? Married? Or will their relationship break up, perhaps terminating because of a fight or because they just lose interest in one another?

In this chapter, we consider the dynamics of close relationships, such as the relationship between Amy and Chad. We begin by considering the characteristics and range of close relationships, examining how people build them and develop increasing degrees of interdependence and intimacy.

We then consider love—characteristic of our most important relationships, and one of the most difficult subjects to study scientifically. We examine several approaches to the phenomenon of love, including categorizations of different types of love.

We next turn to several varieties of close relationships. Although we focus in particular on marriage, we also consider less traditional alternatives, including staying single and gay and lesbian relationships. We discuss the qualities that people seek out in potential partners, as well as the sources of satisfaction and discontent.

Finally, we look at the breakdown and ending of relationships, discussing the decline of relationships and considering the phases through which relationships pass on the route to termination.

After reading this chapter, then, you will be able to answer these questions:

- What are the factors that lead to the development of close relationships, how do these relationships evolve, and what roles do intimacy, self-disclosure, and sexuality play?
- What are the different categorizations of love?
- What are the varieties of relationships?
- What factors lead to the decline of close relationships?

# BUILDING RELATIONSHIPS

Acquaintance. Associate. Friend. Relative. Partner. Intimate. Lover.

Each of these labels represents a very different sort of relationship. But what specifically determines whether a relationship can be considered close? According to social psychologist Sharon Brehm (1992), **close relationships** (which she also refers to as "intimate relationships") are relationships characterized by at least one of three factors: emotional attachment, need fulfillment, and interdependence. Emotional attachment relates to typically positive (although sometimes negative) feelings for another person. Need fulfillment suggests that partners help fulfill significant psychological or physical needs in a partner. Finally, the interdependence criterion presumes that people involved in a close relationship have an impact on one another.

Clearly, such a formulation of close relationships is a broad one, and it encompasses a wide variety of different sorts of relationships, both traditional and unconventional. For instance, it covers such common relationships as marriages and engagements. But it also includes less-traditional types of relationships, such as committed heterosexual couples living together without marriage and gay and lesbian relationships.

One of the key factors that distinguish close relationships from others is the degree of interdependence between the two individuals in the relationship (Miller, 1986; Kelley, 1991; Clark & Reis, 1988). **Interdependence** is the degree of influence two people have over each other and the quantity of activities in which they jointly engage. If two individuals' behaviors, emotions, and thoughts are mutually interconnected, they are interdependent and have a close relationship (Kelley et al., 1983).

To measure the strength of relationships objectively, social psychologist Ellen Berscheid and colleagues developed the **Relationship Closeness Inventory** (Berscheid, Snyder, & Omoto, 1989a, 1989b). As you can see from the sample items presented in Figure 7-1, the questionnaire investigates the nature of interactions with a particular individual. Specifically, it asks how long the two were together and what they were doing. In addition, the inventory asks about the kind of influence the other person has over emotions, thinking, and behavior in areas such as social life, financial decisions, and educational decisions.

Using the Relationship Closeness Inventory, social psychologists have found that people are remarkably similar in the manner in which they perceive their close relationships (Berscheid, Snyder, & Omoto, 1989b). For example, men and women express the same degree of closeness in their relationships; they also view romantic relationships as closer than those with family and friends. In fact, when asked to indicate the one person with whom they felt closest, 47 percent chose a romantic partner, while 36 percent chose a friend. Only 14 percent named a family member, and the remaining 3 percent identified someone else altogether.

The Relationship Closeness Inventory also provides information about how various kinds of relationships develop. For instance, the road of romantic relationships is the most likely to be seen as having twists and bends and—sometimes—dead ends. People perceive the possibility of clear and often-abrupt terminations to romantic liaisons that they don't envision happening in friendships and family relationships. Instead, they perceive relationships among friends and family members as continuing, even when little actual contact occurs between the individuals. When relationships between friends and family members do begin to deteriorate, they are more likely to end with a whimper than a bang (Aron et al., 1989; Berscheid, Snyder, & Omoto, 1989b).

**close relationships**
relationships characterized by at least one of three factors: emotional attachment, need fulfillment, and interdependence.

**interdependence**
the degree of influence two people have over each other and the quantity of activities in which they jointly engage.

**Relationship Closeness Inventory**
a system used to objectively measure the strength of relationships.

## Levels of Relatedness

According to social psychologist George Levinger (1974), relationships should be considered not only in terms of specific types (such as relationships between friends, lovers, or relatives) but in terms of their underlying level of relatedness. He suggests three basic lev-

**FIGURE 7-1    Relationship Closeness Inventory**

What kind of relationship do you have with a particular person? The following sample items, drawn from the Relationship Closeness Inventory (Berscheid, Snyder, & Omoto, 1989a), provide examples of the kinds of questions you might ask yourself in order to assess the closeness of your relationship.

For the following items, indicate which activities you did *alone* with the particular individual:

_____ did laundry

_____ prepared a meal

_____ watched TV

_____ went to an auction/antique show

_____ went to a restaurant

_____ went to a grocery store

_____ went for a walk/drive

_____ discussed things of a personal nature

_____ attended class

_____ went on a trip (e.g., vacation or weekend)

For each of the following items, indicate the amount of influence the same individual, labeled "X" here, has on your thoughts, feelings, and behavior. Use a 7-point scale, with 1 = I strongly disagree and 7 = I strongly agree.

1. _____ X will influence my future financial security.
2. _____ X does *not* influence everyday things in my life.*
3. _____ X influences important things in my life.
4. _____ X influences which parties and other social events I attend.
5. _____ X influences the extent to which I accept responsibilities in our relationship.
6. _____ X does *not* influence how much time I spend doing household work.*
7. _____ X does *not* influence how I choose to spend my money.*
8. _____ X influences the way I feel about myself.
9. _____ X does *not* influence my moods.*
10. _____ X influences the basic values that I hold.

(*Items with asterisks are reverse-scored—a 1 is considered 7, 2 becomes 6, 3 becomes 4, and so on.)

Finally, indicate the degree to which your future plans and goals are affected by X. Use a 7-point scale, with 1 = not at all and 7 = a great extent:

1. _____ my vacation plans
2. _____ my marriage plans
3. _____ my plans to have children
4. _____ my plans to make *major* investments
5. _____ my plans to join a club, social organization, church, etc.
6. _____ my school-related plans
7. _____ my plans for achieving a particular financial standard of living.

Because these are sample items, it is not possible to obtain a fully accurate score. However, in general, the higher your score, the closer the relationship.

els of relatedness; unilateral awareness, bilateral surface contact, and mutuality (see Figure 7-2).

**unilateral awareness**
the level in which individuals view others in terms of their outward characteristics.

**Unilateral awareness** is the level in which individuals view others in terms of their outward characteristics. Those who are perceived at this level are not even aware that they are being observed or judged. For instance, although you may remember the checkout staff at the grocery store at which you shop, to them you might be just one of hun-

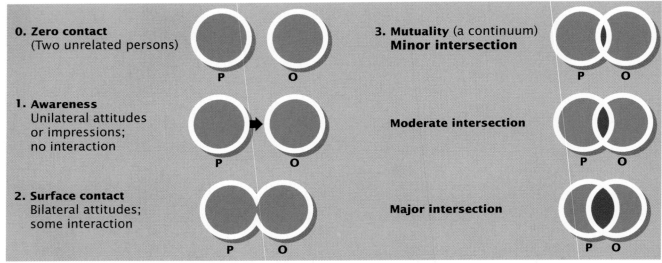

**FIGURE 7-2    Levels of Relatedness** George Levinger suggests that there are three basic levels of relatedness between two individuals (here labeled "P" and "O").    *(Source:* Levinger, 1974.*)*

dreds of customers they see each day. Most of our relationships occur at such levels of unilateral awareness.

**surface contact**
the second level of pair relatedness, in which both people are aware of each other.

With **surface contact**, the second level of pair relatedness, both people are aware of each other. Each forms attitudes and impressions of the other, as well as beliefs and affects regarding the relationship itself. Most daily interactions with others fall into this category. Even though we frequently see the same people—grocery clerk, bus driver, building custodian, or bank teller—the depth and closeness of those relationships are relatively minor.

**mutuality**
a situation in which the individuals in a relationship share knowledge of each other, experience a sense of responsibility for the other person, and develop a set of personal norms informally regulating their relationship.

When relationships reach the third stage, that of mutuality, they become truly personal. In **mutuality**, the individuals in a relationship share knowledge of each other, experience a sense of responsibility for the other person, and develop a set of personal norms informally regulating their relationship. At the mutuality stage, interactions are no longer merely transitory or fixed with a restricted role relationship (such as with a clerk–customer interaction).

**minor intersection**
the early stages of mutuality in which people are hesitant to disclose information about themselves.

The mutuality stage of relationships is itself subdivided into three stages. During the early stages of mutuality, referred to as **minor intersection** in Figure 7-2, people are hesitant to disclose information about themselves. The degree of self-disclosure increases as the relationship progresses to the level of **moderate intersection**, an intermediate stage of relationship development, and then to **major intersection**, a strong, binding relationship. The partners increasingly reveal intimate and important attitudes and feelings about themselves. Further, they learn the sources of the other person's happiness and satisfaction, and they begin to behave in ways that make the relationship rewarding to the other person. Such behavior maintains and strengthens the relationship.

**moderate intersection**
an intermediate stage of relationship development in which the degree of self-disclosure increases.

**major intersection**
the stage of a strong, binding relationship in which the partners increasingly reveal intimate and important attitudes and feelings about themselves.

One of the transformations that can occur during the course of relationships is a change from exchange relationships to communal relationships. According to social psychologist Margaret Clark, **exchange relationships** are associations based on an economic model of interaction, in which people seek to maximize their benefits and minimize their costs (Clark, Mills, & Corcoran, 1989; Clark, Mills, & Powell, 1986; Clark & Mills, 1979; Clark & Reis, 1988). Exchange relationships are characterized by reciprocity: If someone provides something positive to a partner within an exchange relationship, some return benefit is expected. Thus, people who give presents to mail carriers or trash collectors during the December holidays typically do so to receive the benefit of good service during the following year—not because they hope to establish a close friendship.

**exchange relationships**
associations based on an economic model of interaction in which people seek to maximize their benefits and minimize their costs.

The levels of relatedness in relationships spans unilateral awareness, bilateral surface contact, and mutuality.

In sum, they expect any costs will be compensated by future benefits. We tend to have exchange relationships with first-time acquaintances and in business relationships.

Communal relationships are a different story (Clark & Mills, 1993). In a **communal relationship**, the participants feel mutual responsibility for each other, and they provide benefits according to the other's needs or in order to exhibit concern for the other person. For example, we might bring some flowers from our garden to a neighbor, not because we expect a gift in return, but because we value the friendship and like the recipient. Unlike exchange relationships, communal relationships occur most often with romantic partners, family members, and friends.

There are dramatic differences in behavior between exchange and communal relationships. For example, in exchange relationships, people expect that a favor will be repaid fairly quickly. However, in communal relationships people may view rapid repayment of a favor in a negative light, interpreting it as an indication that the partner may view the relationship in exchange terms, rather than as a more desirable communal relationship (Clark & Mills, 1979, 1993).

Furthermore, when people help individuals with whom they have an exchange relationship, they keep careful track of the input, and expect to receive compensation at some time in the not-too-distant future. However, in communal relationships, people provide aid based on the needs of the other person, even when they know full well that they are not likely to receive specific reimbursement for that aid. The goal, then, is not

**communal relationship**
a relationship in which the participants feel mutual responsibility for each other, and provide benefits according to the other's needs or in order to exhibit concern for the other person.

to be directly compensated for the efforts, but to provide benefits to a partner for the sake of the continuing relationship and without thought of future reward (Clark, 1984).

Of course, one could argue that although people in communal relationships do not keep a running psychological balance sheet, tallying the costs and benefits on an ongoing basis, they still have an ultimately self-serving goal in mind: the long-term maintenance of the relationship. After all, we would not expect a relationship to last over the long term if one partner consistently provided benefits and the other partner never reciprocated. Consequently, it is possible that although people in communal relationships forgo an accounting of rewards and benefits in the short run, their expectation is that rewards and costs will be balanced over the long term. This issue is a thorny one (Batson, 1993), and a question to which we will return in Chapter 8, when we discuss whether truly altruistic helping behavior exists.

## Intimacy: Opening Up to Others

**intimacy**
the process in which a person communicates important feelings and information to another through a process of self-disclosure.

One of the key factors that differentiate various types of relationships is intimacy (Reis, 1990). In a social psychological sense, **intimacy** is the process in which a person communicates important feelings and information to another through a process of self-disclosure. When we discussed self-disclosure earlier in Chapter 5, it was in terms of its benefits to the person revealing information. However, self-disclosure provides another advantage: it enhances the sense of intimacy in a relationship (Derlega et al., 1993). As a result of self-disclosure, people come to feel understood, cared for, and validated by the partner in a relationship (Reis & Shaver, 1988; Reis, 1990; Clark & Reis, 1988).

There are many varieties of self-disclosure, of course; revealing your student identification number is quite different from discussing your sexual fantasies. One of the key distinctions between different types of self-disclosure, then, concerns descriptive self-disclosure versus evaluative self-disclosure (Morton, 1978). In **descriptive self-disclosure**, people share *facts* about their lives. Revealing your place of birth and your parents' professions are examples of descriptive self-disclosure. In contrast, **evaluative self-disclosure** communicates information about personal *feelings*. Expressing shame—an emotion—over a past misdeed is an illustration of evaluative self-disclosure.

**descriptive self-disclosure**
a situation in which people share facts about their lives.

**evaluative self-disclosure**
a situation in which an individual communicates information about personal feelings.

The two types of self-disclosure occur in different contexts and result in different degrees of intimacy. For example, in one study subjects were told in one condition to seek out accurate information about a partner during discussion; in another condition, subjects were told to create a favorable impression during a discussion (Berg & Archer, 1982). In the information-seeking condition, the rates of descriptive self-disclosure and evaluative self-disclosure on the part of subjects were about equal. On the other hand, when subjects were trying to make a good impression on a partner, they used significantly more evaluative self-disclosure.

Further information about oneself is sometimes offered tentatively in limited amounts, in order to test the reaction of one's partner. For example, a student may make a joking comment about the difficulty of an upcoming exam in order to judge the listener's reaction. If the comment is met with sympathy, the student may then make a fuller disclosure regarding the strong anxiety that actually underlies the anticipation of the exam. On the other hand, if no sympathy or reciprocal self-disclosure is forthcoming, the topic may be dropped (Miell & Duck, 1986; Duck, 1988).

**theory of social penetration**
a theory by Altman and Taylor that suggests that relationships gradually progress through increasingly deeper intimacy.

According to social psychologists Irving Altman and Dalmas Taylor (1973), self-disclosure, in general, increases as partners become better acquainted. In their **theory of social penetration**, they suggest that relationships gradually progress through increasingly deeper intimacy. Initially, people reveal relatively little about themselves, providing partners with only superficial information through descriptive self-disclosure. However, as the relationship becomes more intimate, the level and degree of disclosure increase. The information becomes broader, encompassing more areas of a person's life; and it becomes deeper, embodying more delicate, hidden material that is revealed through evaluative self-disclosure (Hornstein & Truesdell, 1988).

Although self-disclosure continues to be an important factor throughout the life of a relationship, it may reach its highest level as early as six weeks into the development of a new relationship (Hays, 1984, 1985). At that point the rate of disclosure tends to level off.

Although self-disclosure generally yields positive results and leads to increased intimacy within a relationship, in some cases self-disclosure has negative consequences. If people disclose that they actually don't like their partner much, then self-disclosure may be harmful. For example, reports of self-disclosure in faltering marital relationships show that the depth of self-disclosure actually increases in couples under these circumstances. Unfortunately, what is revealed are the dimensions of displeasure over the relationship. While the depth of disclosure increases, the breadth of disclosure declines, as partners focus on communicating their discontent with the relationship (Tolstedt & Stokes, 1984).

## Reciprocity of Self-Disclosure

**reciprocity of self-disclosure**
a situation in which people who are the recipients of intimate information respond in kind.

Altman and Taylor's theory of social penetration also suggests that the deepening degree of intimacy of ongoing relationships is marked by the phenomenon of reciprocity of self-disclosure. In **reciprocity of self-disclosure**, people who are the recipients of intimate information respond in kind. Within Western cultures, norms of reciprocity lead people to attempt to match the level of self-disclosure provided by new acquaintances. As relationships progress, that norm continues to operate—but only up to a point. In well-established relationships, precise reciprocity is less likely to occur (Won-Doornick, 1979).

One of the puzzling questions regarding reciprocity of self-disclosure concerns the issue of cause and effect. Do people show reciprocity within relationships because individuals who usually disclose equivalent amounts of information tend to prefer one another? Or, alternatively, do people show reciprocity because of the nature of their own particular relationship with one another?

The answer seems to be that reciprocity of self-disclosure has its roots in the particular kind of relationship that develops between two individuals (Miller & Kenny, 1986; Miller, 1990). People don't seek out others who are similar in their levels of self-disclosure in order to form relationships. Instead, people within relationships jointly determine their own specific level of reciprocal self-disclosure.

One of the most researched characteristics affecting self-disclosure is gender. Theoreticians have traditionally argued that norms regarding masculine behavior inhibit self-disclosure in men, because society encourages males to be objective and unemotional and discourages self-awareness and insight (Jourard, 1971; Shaffer, Pegalis, & Cornell, 1991, 1992; Dolgin, Meyer, & Schwartz, 1991).

Most research has supported this hypothesis. Overall, women tend to self-disclose slightly more than men, although the differences are relatively small (Rubin, Hill, Peplau, & Dunhel-Schetter 1980; Derlega et al., 1993). In addition, the nature of the material men and women disclose varies. For example, one study found that women were more apt to disclose information about feelings and negative emotions, while men disclosed more factual and more emotionally positive information (Rubin et al., 1980; see Figure 7-3).

Gender differences in disclosure are more pronounced in same-sex interactions than in mixed-sex interactions. The reciprocity principle helps explain these findings: Because of women's inclination to disclose more than men, their high self-disclosure may induce their partner to self-disclose even more. On the other hand, because men disclose less than women, their low rate of self-disclosure may discourage their partner's self-disclosure (Dindia & Allen, 1992).

Regardless of gender differences in self-disclosure, one thing is certain: Disclosure of important information leads the partners in a relationship toward greater levels of intimacy (Jones, 1991; Camerena, Sarigiani, & Petersen, 1990; Derlega, 1988). In some cases, this intimacy steers people into deeper and deeper relationships.

| FIGURE 7-3    Sex Differences in Self-Disclosure |
| --- |

Female students self-disclose more information than men about:
    Feelings toward parents
    Feelings toward closest friends
    Feelings toward classes
    The things in life they are most afraid of
    Their accomplishments

Male students self-disclose more information than women about:
    Their political views
    The things about themselves that they are most proud of
    The things they like most about their partners

*Source:* Rubin, Z., Hill, C. T., Peplau, L. A., & Dunkel-Schetter, C., 1980.

## Stages of Relationships

We've examined several of the building blocks of relationships, such as interdependence, intimacy, levels of relatedness, and self-disclosure. Yet relationships are hardly ever static. As two people become increasingly involved with one another, the nature of their feelings, thoughts, and behavior evolves, and their interactions change.

Do relationships develop in particular patterns? According to some researchers, relationships pass through a series of stages. For instance, the following general patterns can be seen in relationships as people become increasingly attached to one another (Burgess & Huston, 1979; Berscheid, 1985):

- The partners interact with each other more frequently and for longer periods of time. In addition, the range of settings increases.
- The two individuals increasingly seek out each other's company.
- They open up to each other more and more, disclosing secrets and sharing physical intimacies. They are more willing to share both positive and negative feelings, and they are more apt to offer criticism as well as praise.
- Their goals for the relationship become compatible, and they show greater similarity in their reactions to situations.
- They begin to sense that their own psychological well-being is tied to the success of the relationship, viewing it as unique, precious, and irreplaceable.
- Their behavior changes: They begin to act as a couple, rather than as two separate individuals.

Social psychologist Bernard Murstein views these developments through the lens of what he calls stimulus-value-role theory (Murstein, 1976, 1986, 1987). According to **stimulus-value-role (SVR) theory**, relationships proceed in a fixed order through a series of three stages. In the first phase, the stimulus stage, relationships are built on external characteristics such as physical qualities. Typically, this represents just the first encounter.

The second step, the value stage, often occurs from the second to seventh contact. In the value period, the focus in the relationship changes to similarity of values and beliefs. Finally, during the final period, dubbed the role stage, the relationship is based on specific roles played by the participants, such as boyfriend–girlfriend or husband–wife.

It is important to note that although stimulus, value, and role factors predominate at particular points in the relationship, they may be at least somewhat influential at other junctures, as you can see from the relationship illustrated in Figure 7-4.

Not everyone agrees with stage approaches. For example, although SVR theory suggests that the stages in a relationship occur in a fixed, invariant sequence, it is not entirely clear that this is logically true. Why couldn't a relationship be initiated on the

**stimulus-value-role (SVR) theory** the theory that relationships proceed in a fixed order through a series of three stages.

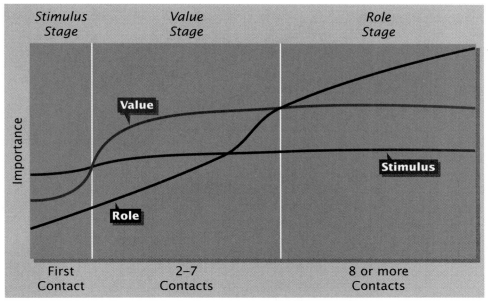

**FIGURE 7-4   Stages of Relationships According to Stimulus-Value-Role Theory** Depending on the stage of the relationship, stimulus, value, or role factors predominate.   *(Source:* Murstein, 1987.*)*

basis of similarity of values, and then develop in terms of stimulus attributes? Moreover, in some cultures, such as those in which arranged marriages are the rule, relationships begin in terms of role considerations (Gupta & Singh, 1982; Sternberg, 1986). Stimulus attributes and values come into play only at some later point, contrary to SVR theory.

In sum, stage theories do not always accurately describe or explain the development of any one particular relationship. However, they do summarize how relationships in general develop over time.

*Sexuality and Relationships*

Some of the most pressing questions faced in any relationship revolve around sexuality. Both heterosexual and homosexual couples face issues regarding if and when sex should take place.

**THE DOUBLE STANDARD.**   Until the 1960s, societal standards provided clear standards for heterosexual couples. According to the traditional view, sexual intercourse should not occur until marriage—a dictum that has traditionally been more rigid for women than for men. Women were warned that "nice girls don't do it," while men were allowed to "sow their wild oats." The view that premarital sex was permissible for men but not for women came to be known as the **double standard** (Ussher, 1989, 1990; Espin, 1986).

**double standard**
the view that premarital sex was permissible for men but not for women.

However, societal views have undergone a dramatic shift in the last few decades. As can be seen in Figure 7-5, the percentage of people who feel that sexual intercourse prior to marriage is wrong has declined significantly. In fact, by the late 1980s, more people thought it was permissible than not (Gallup Poll, 1987).

As societal standards have become more permissive, the actual rate of heterosexual premarital intercourse has increased. For example, just over one half of women between the ages of 15 and 19 report having had premarital sexual intercourse. Men's rate is higher: By the time they reach the age of 20, 80 percent of men have had sex (Arena, 1984; CDC, 1992).

Do these figures suggest that the double standard has disappeared? Most experts agree that it has, although it has been replaced with a new standard: permissiveness with

| **FIGURE 7-5   Is Sexual Intercourse Prior to Marriage Wrong?** | | | |
|---|---|---|---|
| The percentage of people who responded to the question, "Do you think it is wrong for a man and woman to have sex relations before marriage or not?" | | | |
| | **1969** | **1978** | **1987** |
| Yes, it is wrong | 68% | 50% | 46% |
| No, it is not wrong | 21% | 41% | 48% |
| Don't know | 11% | 9% | 6% |

*Source:* Gallup Poll, 1969, 1978, and 1987.

**permissiveness with affection standard**

the view that premarital intercourse is permissible for both men and women it if occurs within a long-term, committed, or loving relationship.

affection. According to psychologist Janet Hyde (1990), the **permissiveness with affection standard** represents the view that premarital intercourse is permissible for both men and women if it occurs within a long-term, committed, or loving relationship (Reiss, 1960; Hyde, 1990).

On the other hand, remnants of the double standard remain, with women frequently being held to stricter sexual standards than men. For instance, college students suggest in surveys that men's and women's behavior should be judged by different standards. Men who were involved in considerable sexual activity were seen as more attractive than men who engaged in little activity, while the opposite was true for women (Moffat, 1989; Breay & Gentry, 1990). (Interestingly, the same double attitudinal double standard holds for married men and women. Surveys have found that men consider it more permissible for a man to engage in extramarital affairs than for a woman to do so [Margolin, 1989]).

Substantial cultural differences exist in the incidence and timing of premarital sexual intercourse. In Japan, for example, premarital sex is much less frequent than in the United States for both men and women. In contrast, in Mexico, rates of intercourse are much lower for females than for males. Even in the United States, subcultural differences are found. For instance, on average, African-American males are likely to have sexual intercourse some two years earlier than their Caucasian counterparts (Liskin, 1985; Moore & Erickson, 1985).

Does the generally higher incidence of premarital sexual intercourse today lead to happier relationships? Most evidence suggests that sexual behavior, per se, is not crucial in determining the long-term ultimate success of a relationship. For instance, although one study found that heterosexual college students who had sexual relationships were more apt to still be dating three months after they were first contacted than those who didn't have a sexual relationship (Simpson, 1987), the long-term effects of premarital sex appear either neutral or slightly negative (Bentler & Newcomb, 1978; Markman, 1981; Glenn, 1990).

On the other hand, sex within marital relationships is positively related to the success of a relationship. Sexual satisfaction is correlated with overall satisfaction with a marriage (Tavris & Sadd, 1977). On the other hand, frequency of sexual intercourse is not associated with marital happiness (Goleman, 1985). At least among married couples, apparently quality of sex is more important than quantity.

**RELATIONSHIPS AMONG GAY AND LESBIAN COUPLES.**   By far, most of the data on relationships has examined heterosexual couples. However, an increasing amount of research has looked at gay and lesbian couples, finding basic similarities between heterosexual and homosexual couples.

For example, gay males describe successful relationships in ways similar to those of heterosexuals—they see them as involving more appreciation for the partner and the couple as a unit, less conflict, and more positive feelings toward the concept of love (Jones & Bates, 1978). Similarly, lesbian women were high in attachment, caring, intimacy, affection, and respect (Peplau & Cochran, 1990; Caldwell & Peplau, 1984). One survey showed that 82 percent of lesbians questioned were currently involved in a relationship , and the majority of women said that having a permanent relationship was either very important or the most important thing in their lives (Peplau, Padesky, & Hamilton, 1982). In sum, increasing evidence suggests that the psychological aspects of male and female homosexual relationships may be more similar than different from those in heterosexual relationships (Dailey, 1979; Kurdek, 1991; Peplau & Cochran, 1990).

▶ # REVIEW & RETHINK

## Review

- Three key elements in close relationships are emotional attachment, need fulfillment, and interdependence.
- Relationships may be communal or exchange.
- Intimacy is the process in which a person communicates important feelings and information to another through self-disclosure.
- Sexual behavior may be an important component of relationships.

## Rethink

- How do exchange relationships differ from communal relationships? What type of relationship is likely to operate in each of Levinger's three levels of relatedness?
- Explain how norms of reciprocity effect the level of intimacy in female–female, male–male, and female–male interactions. Would norms of reciprocity of self-disclosure be stronger in exchange or in communal relationships?
- How would you characterize the type of self-disclosure that predominates at the beginning of a relationship? How does this type of disclosure differ from the self-disclosure of healthy and unhealthy long-term relationships?

# LOVE RELATIONSHIPS

For something that "makes the world go 'round," as the old song goes, love is one of the most elusive phenomena in our everyday lives. We aspire to love, we are overjoyed to be in love, and we seek to establish a permanent relationship with those we love, but understanding love has proven to be a daunting task.

Love has always seemed a difficult topic to understand. For instance, social philosopher H. T. Finck (1902) said, "Love is such a tissue of paradoxes, and exists in such an endless variety of forms and shades, that you may say almost anything about it that you please, and it is likely to be correct" (p. 224). More recently, one United States senator argued that research on love was unnecessary: "I believe that 200 million other Americans want to leave some things in life a mystery, and right at the top of the things we don't want to know is why a man falls in love with a woman and vice versa" (Proxmire, 1975).

Until some 25 years ago, many social psychologists would have agreed that love was an inappropriate topic of study, although for different reasons (Rubin, 1988). The study of romantic love was considered to be unscientific, primarily because the phenomenon was so difficult to observe in a systematic way. More recently, however, social psychologists have modified this stance, and they have offered a number of significant theories to explain love (Hendrick & Hendrick, 1986; Sternberg, 1986, 1987; Shaver & Hazan, 1987, 1988). Given the importance love plays in people's most intimate relationships, as well as its influence on marriage and divorce, understanding love better may prove to be of crucial concern to society.

*Passionate and Companionate Love: Two Terms of Endearment*

**passionate (or romantic) love**
the representation of a state of intense absorption in someone that includes intense physiological arousal, physiological interest, and care for the needs of another.

**companionate love**
the strong affection we have for those with whom our lives are deeply involved.

When social psychologists first sought to understand love, they attempted to identify the factors that distinguished loving from mere liking (Sternberg, 1987). Taking this approach, they argued that love is not simply liking in a greater quantity, but a qualitatively different psychological state (Walster & Walster, 1978). For instance, love—at least in its early stages—includes a relatively intense physiological arousal, an all-encompassing interest in another person, recurring fantasies about the other person, and relatively rapid swings of emotion. As opposed to liking, love includes elements of closeness, passion, captivation, and exclusivity (Hendrick & Hendrick, 1989).

Of course, not all love is the same. There is a difference in the way one loves a spouse, a girlfriend or boyfriend, a clandestine lover, a sibling, a best friend, a parent. Consequently, we can distinguish between two main types of love: passionate love and companionate love (Hatfield, 1988; Hendrick & Hendrick, 1992). **Passionate (or romantic) love** represents a state of intense absorption in someone. It includes intense physiological arousal, physiological interest, and caring for the needs of another. In comparison, **companionate love** is the strong affection that we have for those with whom our lives are deeply involved. Although passionate love may evolve, over time, into companionate love, the two differ in fundamental ways (Hatfield, 1988).

**PASSIONATE LOVE.**    When poets and lyricists sing the praises of love, they are usually referring to passionate love. Societal norms are rather specific in their definitions of love; most people feel if they are truly in love, their hearts ought to beat faster at the sight of their love, they should experience intense desire for each other, and they must forgive each other's shortcomings and focus on their strong points.

Actually, such a view is not all that far removed from what people actually report they feel during the early stages of a romantic relationship. People who are in love don't just *think* about their partner; they physically *experience* intense passion. In contrast to simple liking, which develops more gradually, passionate love often has a swift onset. It can be more volatile: Love's greater intensity may lead to a roller-coaster pattern of ups and downs. Finally, passionate love involves an exclusivity that may preclude interest in other people (Walster & Walster, 1978).

Although there is general agreement on the nature of the characteristics that distinguish superficial attraction from deeper passionate love, they remain somewhat difficult to quantify and specify in scientific terms. One approach is a questionnaire devised by social psychologist Zick Rubin, who developed two independent scales to measure liking and loving (Rubin, 1973). Each scale consists of a series of items in which the respondent fills in the name of someone to whom he or she is attracted and then indicates agreement with each statement on a nine-point scale. For instance, the love scale items include the following:

- I feel that I can confide in _____ about virtually everything.
- I would do almost anything for _____.
- I feel responsible for _____'s well-being.

The more you can agree with each item, the greater the love you are experiencing. In contrast, consider the following questions, also drawn from Rubin's scale:

- I think that _____ is unusually well adjusted.
- I think that _____ is one of those people who quickly wins respect.
- _____ is one of the most likable people I know.

Items such as these tap liking, not love. The more you agree with them, the more you like the individual you have in mind when answering.

As we would expect, couples who score high on the love scale differ substantially from those with lower scores. For instance, high scorers gaze at each other more, and their relationships are more apt to be intact six months later than those who score lower (Rubin, 1973).

Although the scale helps distinguish between loving and liking, it does not explain why passionate love is so different from relationships in which the people merely like one another. Moreover, it does little to explain why people fall in love.

According to one theory that seeks to address such issues, negative emotional responses such as jealousy, anger, and a fear of rejection by another person may help convince people that they are in love. In social psychologists Elaine Hatfield and Ellen Berscheid's **labeling theory of passionate love**, people experience romantic love when two events occur together: intense physiological arousal and situational cues that indicate that "love" is the appropriate label for the feelings they are experiencing (Berscheid & Walster, 1974). Building on Schachter's theory of emotion labeling, which we first discussed in Chapter 4, the theory suggests that when physiological arousal is labeled as being due to "falling in love" or "she's so wonderful" or "he's just right for me," the experience can be labeled "romantic love." The source of the physiological arousal can be sexual arousal, excitement, or even negative emotions such as fear, jealousy, or anger.

**labeling theory of passionate love**
the theory offered by Hatfield and Berscheid in which people experience romantic love when two events occur together: intense physiological arousal and situational cues that indicate that "love" is the appropriate label for the feelings they are experiencing.

The labeling theory of passionate love is particularly useful because it explains why a person who keeps being hurt or rejected by someone else can still feel love for that person. Such negative emotions can produce strong physiological arousal. If an individual labels that arousal as love-related, attraction to another person will be maintained and perhaps even heightened by these circumstances.

Several experiments support this two-factor theory of love (Walsh, Meister, & Kleinke, 1977). However, most of the evidence has been indirect, focusing on the notion that arousal of any sort can lead to the intensification of attraction. For example, in one intriguing study, social psychologists Donald Dutton and Arthur Aron stationed an attractive, college-age woman at the end of a dangerous, swaying, 450-foot suspension bridge that spanned a deep, rocky canyon (Dutton & Aron, 1974). The woman supposedly was conducting a survey, and she asked men who had just managed to make it across the bridge a series of questions. She then offered to give the subjects more information about her survey if they desired, and wrote her telephone number on a small piece of paper so they could get in touch later. In a control condition, the same female was at the end of a safe and sturdy bridge only ten feet off the ground.

The experimenters reasoned that the danger of the suspension bridge would lead to physiological arousal, and that subjects would interpret this arousal as attraction in the presence of the attractive woman. As predicted, of the subjects who contacted the woman later, many more had crossed the dangerous bridge than the safe one. The results supported the notion that subjects associated the increased physiological arousal that likely occurred when they crossed the dangerous bridge with attraction to the woman. Their fear, then, had led to attraction.

**Romeo and Juliet effect**
the phenomenon in which couples who experience strong parental interference in their relationships report greater love for one another than those with little interference.

The labeling theory of passionate love suggests an explanation for what has been called the "Romeo and Juliet effect" (Driscoll, Davis, & Lipitz, 1972). The **Romeo and Juliet effect** is the phenomenon in which couples who experience strong parental interference in their relationships report greater love for one another than those with little interference. Consistent with the two-factor theory, parental interference may raise the general level of arousal between two lovers. They may interpret this heightened physiological arousal as due to enhanced passion for one another.

However, what the labeling theory of passionate love does not do is tell us why people come to interpret physiological arousal as love. One explanation comes from our cultural norms about love. In order for someone to label their arousal as indicative of passionate love, he or she must live in a culture that communicates the concept of passionate love. We need to know that passionate love is a possible, acceptable, and desirable response—something our culture understands, appreciates, and does with gusto (Dion & Dion, 1988).

In our society, no one can dispute that passionate love is portrayed as a worthy state, not only in TV soap operas, love ballads, and romance novels. We are told that love leads to happiness, companionship, and sexual fulfillment. Our culture places love on a pedestal, suggesting that a lack of passionate love in one's life has catastrophic implications.

Interestingly, not all societies hold such a view of passionate love. In several cultures, for instance, love is not a particularly important concept. Even today, in many parts of the world, marriages are arranged by parents on an economic basis or for reasons relating to politics and status (Xiaohe & Whyte, 1990). In fact, even within Western culture, our notion of love is a relatively recent phenomenon. For instance, prior to the Middle Ages, love in its current forms did not exist. The ancient Greeks saw love as a form of madness. When our current conception of love as leading to marriage was originally put forward by social thinkers in the Middle Ages, it was meant to serve as a more desirable alternative to raw sexual desire (Lewis, 1958).

Still, within Western cultures today, passionate love is seen as the cornerstone of relationships. This cultural notion of love allows us to interpret (or, in some cases, misinterpret) physiological arousal as signifying love.

**COMPANIONATE LOVE.**    Although love in its passionate form probably comes closest to societal ideals about love, in reality companionate love is the more frequent and steadfast type. Most people don't experience the ups and downs of passionate love when it comes to the love they feel for their parents, siblings, other relatives, or best friends. Instead, companionate love is relatively stable and invariant (Brehm, 1988).

Perhaps because it is less electrifying than passionate love, companionate love has received somewhat less attention from social psychologists. Yet companionate love lies at the heart of people's most treasured relationships. The partners in such relationships care deeply for one another, and their own happiness depends in part on the happiness of their partner. Companionate love, then, is a communal, rather than an exchange relationship.

The partners in a companionate relationship hold a high degree of trust in one another. Such trust is actually of two types: reliability and emotional trust (Johnson-George & Swap, 1982). Reliability is the expectation that partners will do what they have said they will do. Emotional trust exists when people feel that their partner is tied to them emotionally and that the emotional lives of the two people are linked (Hatfield, 1988).

In some circumstances, companionate love can develop into passionate love. For instance, filmgoers who saw the movie *When Harry Met Sally* may recall how the long-

Even today, marriages in many cultures are arranged by parents, and love is not considered a necessity for marriage. For instance, this seven-year-old girl and eleven-year-old boy are celebrating their marriage in India in the early 1990s, despite laws against such practices.

standing friendship between the Meg Ryan and Billy Crystal characters turned into passionate love. Likewise, passionate love can shift to companionate love, as when a love affair breaks up and the two parties remain confidants. The shift from passionate love to companionate love is eased if the people held companionate love for one another prior to entering the passionate love relationship (Metts, Cupach, & Bejlovec, 1989).

## Sternberg's Love Triangle: The Eight Faces of Love

**intimacy component**
(of Sternberg's love model) the component of love that encompasses feelings of closeness, affection, and connectedness.

**passion component**
(of Sternberg's love model) the component of love that is made up of the motivational drives relating to sex, physical closeness, and romance.

**decision/commitment component**
(of Sternberg's love model) the component of love that embodies both the initial cognition that one loves another person and the longer-term determination to maintain that love.

For psychologist Robert Sternberg, two-sided love is not enough. Sternberg argues that the traditional apportionment of love into companionate and passionate love misses the mark. Instead, he suggests that love is actually composed of three components: intimacy, passion, and decision/commitment (Sternberg, 1986, 1988). The **intimacy component** encompasses feelings of closeness, affection, and connectedness. The **passion component** is made up of the motivational drives relating to sex, physical closeness, and romance. This factor is exemplified by intense, physiologically arousing feelings of attraction. Finally, the third aspect of love, the **decision/commitment component**, embodies both the initial cognition that one loves another person and the longer-term determination to maintain that love.

By jointly considering whether each of the three components is present or absent in a relationship, we can form eight combinations. As shown in Figure 7-6, one kind of love is nonlove, which includes relationships with people with whom we have only casual interactions during the course of our lives. Friendships form the second type of love, in which only the emotional component of love is present. This type of love is actually closer to liking than to love.

A third kind of love is infatuation, in which passion exists without intimacy or decision/commitment. "Love at first sight" falls into this category. The fourth type of love, called empty love, has only the decision/commitment component and lacks intimacy and passion. Long-term relationships that have grown stagnant and lack zest are representative of empty love.

Romantic love contains both intimacy and passion, but it is lacking in decision/commitment. Couples who are romantically in love are drawn together physically and emotionally, but they do not necessarily see their relationship as continuing over the long term.

Companionate love, according to Sternberg, is the result of intimacy and decision/commitment without passion. Companionate love can be seen in long-lasting marriages in which physical passion has ceased, but the bonds between partners remain strong, or in long-lasting, close friendships. In contrast, fatuous, or mindless, love has components of passion and decision/commitment but lacks intimacy. Relationships built

**FIGURE 7-6    The Kinds of Love**

| | COMPONENT* | | |
|---|---|---|---|
| | **INTIMACY** | **PASSION** | **DECISION/COMMITMENT** |
| Nonlove | − | − | − |
| Liking | + | − | − |
| Infatuated love | − | + | − |
| Empty love | − | − | + |
| Romantic love | + | + | − |
| Companionate love | + | − | + |
| Fatuous love | − | + | + |
| Consummate love | + | + | + |

*+ = component present; − = component absent.
*Source:* Sternberg, 1986, Table 2.

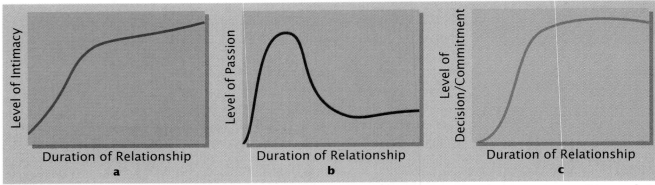

**FIGURE 7-7    The Changing Ingredients of Love** The three components of love vary in strength over the course of a relationship. *(Source:* Sternberg, 1986.)

on fatuous love may not be lasting, because no emotional bond between the partners is present.

Finally, the eighth kind of love is consummate love. In consummate love, all three components of love are present. While it is tempting to consider consummate love as representing the ideal love, such a view is not necessarily accurate. Many gratifying, lasting relationships are maintained with one or even two components only minimally present or not present at all.

The importance of each of the three components tends to vary over the course of a relationship, with each component following a specific trajectory (see Figure 7-7). For instance, in strong, loving relationships the level of commitment peaks and then remains stable. Passion, on the other hand, peaks quickly, and then declines and levels off comparatively early in a relationship.

In Sternberg's view, then, love is a dynamic, changing process rather than a static, invariant state. Over time, the various components may change in intensity and in terms of their relationship to one another. As circumstances and people change, so do the underlying ingredients of love.

## The Rainbow of Love

**eros**

Lee's term for intense, emotional, and passionate love.

**ludos**

Lee's term for playful love, in which the partners view the relationship as a kind of game-playing situation.

**storge**

Lee's term for love in which friendship and companionship prevail.

If Sternberg's classification of love strikes you as too paltry a number to delineate the full range of love, you may be attracted to—and perhaps even love—psychologist John Lee's (1977) multifaceted view of love. According to Lee, love should be thought of as the colors on a painter's palette. Three basic kinds of love are analogous to the primary colors; these are used to form secondary types of love, similar to the way in which combinations of colors can be formed from the primary ones. Beyond these primary and secondary types of love, still other kinds of love exist—just as more and more combinations of colors can be derived starting from only a few basic colors.

What are the primary types of love? Lee suggests three main kinds, based on Greek terminology: eros, ludos, and storge. **Eros** is intense, emotional, and passionate love. In contrast, **ludos** is playful love, in which the partners view the relationship as a kind of game-playing situation. Finally, **storge** is love in which friendship and companionship prevail (Lee, 1974, 1977).

Similarly, Lee identifies three secondary categories of love: mania, agape, and pragma. In mania, love is possessive and demanding, and jealousy is common. Agape is selfless love, in which partners put their lover's welfare before their own. Finally, in pragma, practical concerns underlie love. Lovers seek out partners who meet the "right" criteria according to age, religion, and other pragmatic concerns (Lee, 1977).

Other types of love can be derived from these six. Because there are so many possible varieties of love, relationships can easily become complex, as the two partners may have differing goals and aspirations for the relationship. Further, the intensity of love, the commitment of the partners, and the expectancies about the relationship may vary drastically, further complicating loving partnerships (Borrello & Thompson, 1990).

*Prototypes: Understanding the Concept of Love*

Quick: When you hear the word "love," what examples come to mind?

Your responses to this question provide important insights into the way you understand the concept of love, according to one relatively new approach to the study of love. In the view of several contemporary researchers, one of the most fruitful ways of understanding love is through consideration of how people naturally describe, think about, and categorize the concept of love.

Thus, rather than identifying two, eight, or more kinds of love or the characteristics that differentiate love from other forms of interpersonal attraction, some researchers are seeking to identify how people commonly conceptualize and define love. This approach grows out of the work on prototypes and social cognition that we first discussed in Chapter 2 (Fehr, 1988; Forgas & Dobosz, 1980).

For example, psychologists Beverley Fehr and James Russell sought to understand love from the perspective of prototypes, asking subjects which of 20 types of love were the most representative of the general concept of love. The results, shown in Figure 7-8, formed a pattern that was in some ways surprising. In contrast to approaches to love that emphasize its passionate aspects, subjects considered that the best examples of love were *not* romantic in nature. Instead, the most typical concepts of love related to familial love and friends, with maternal love, parental love, and friendship topping the list (Fehr & Russell, 1991).

| FIGURE 7-8    Prototypicality Ratings for 20 Types of Love | |
| --- | --- |
| **TYPE OF LOVE** | **PROTOTYPICALITY** |
| Maternal love | 5.39 |
| Parental love | 5.22 |
| Friendship | 4.96 |
| Sisterly love | 4.84 |
| Romantic love | 4.76 |
| Brotherly love | 4.74 |
| Familial love | 4.74 |
| Sibling love | 4.73 |
| Affection | 4.60 |
| Committed love | 4.47 |
| Love for humanity | 4.42 |
| Spiritual love | 4.27 |
| Passionate love | 4.00 |
| Platonic love | 3.98 |
| Self-love | 3.79 |
| Sexual love | 3.76 |
| Patriotic love | 3.21 |
| Love of work | 3.14 |
| Puppy love | 2.98 |
| Infatuation | 2.42 |

*Prototypicality ratings were based on a scale ranging from 1 (extremely poor example of love) to 6 (extremely good example of love).* Source: *Adapted from Fehr & Russell, 1991.*

The major prototypes of love include familial love, parental love, and love between siblings.

In fact, the idea of love seemed to be formed from several major prototypes. These include love of a parent for a child, love between romantic partners, love between old friends, and love between siblings. The layperson's conception of love, then, is a broad one, encompassing a variety of types of love on which more traditional approaches do not focus.

The advantage of such a descriptive analysis of the way in which people understand love is that it permits us to better conceptualize how love regulates people's understanding of events. For example, the way judges comprehend the concept of love may guide their decisions about whether a father or mother should have custody of children in divorce proceedings. Similarly, a mother's concerns about whether she provides sufficient love for her child, and questions about whether one is really in love, can be addressed, in part, by the nature of the prototype of love. Thus, prototypic analysis of love complements approaches that categorize love into various types.

## ▶ REVIEW & RETHINK

### Review

- Love can be divided into two types: passionate (or romantic) and companionate.
- Sternberg's categorizations of love suggests it has three basic components: intimacy, passion, and decision/commitment.
- The prototype approach to love considers love in terms of people's cognitions about the concept.

### Rethink

- Is love qualitatively different from liking or merely quantitatively different? How would Rubin answer this question? How would Sternberg answer it?
- Given that cultures differ in their view of what love is or ought to be, is it possible that individuals within a culture differ with respect to their view of love? Is there any evidence that males and females hold differing concepts of love?
- Discuss how each of the following approaches to understanding love would address cultural differences in views of love: Rubin's loving versus liking; Hatfield and

Berscheid's labeling theory; Sternberg's triangle theory; and Fehr and Russell's prototype theory.

- Even psychologists who study love will admit that it is not an easy phenomenon to understand. Why do you think love is such a difficult subject to study? Is it an appropriate topic for scientific investigation?

# VARIETIES OF RELATIONSHIPS

*On Monday, Corporal Floyd Johnson, 23, and Mary Ellen Skinner, 19, total strangers, boarded a train at San Francisco and sat down across the aisle from each other. Johnson didn't cross the aisle until Wednesday, but Skinner later said, "I'd already made up my mind to say yes if he asked me to marry him." Thursday the couple got off the train in Omaha with plans to be married. Because they would need the consent of the bride's parents if they were married in Nebraska, they crossed the river to Council Bluffs, Iowa, where they were married Friday. (San Francisco Chronicle, cited by Burgess & Wallin, 1953, p. 151)*

Talk about whirlwind courtships: from stranger to spouse over the course of five days.

For most of us, the transition across different types of relationships takes considerably more time and presumably involves more deliberation and analysis than in this example. But, in fact, how do people come to view particular relationships as exclusive and so important that they celebrate them in public ceremonies?

In contrast to social psychologists who study the development and typologies of love (a state that cuts across different types of relationships), some researchers have chosen to focus on specific, important types of relationships (Smadi, 1991; Buss et al., 1990; Johnson et al., 1992). We'll consider several varieties, including marriage and cohabitation.

*Choosing a Partner: The Search for the Right Person*

Love is the most important factor in choosing a spouse.

If you believe this statement, you're not alone—at least if you live in the United States. Survey results typically place love at the top of any list of reasons why people choose a particular spouse.

But if you lived in a host of other cultures, love wouldn't be quite so important. For instance, consider the results of a cross-cultural survey in which college students were asked if they would marry someone they did not love. As you can see in Figure 7-9, if you lived in the United States, you'd be unlikely to agree to such a marriage. On the other hand, residents of Pakistan and India might consider it (Levine, 1993).

Congruent results come from research conducted by psychologist David Buss, who conducted a survey of close to 10,000 people from around the world. The survey found that the characteristics sought in a mate differed considerably from country to country (see Figure 7-10). Whereas people in the United States said that love and mutual attraction were the primary characteristics, in China men ranked good health as most important, and women rated emotional stability and maturity as most critical. In contrast, in South Africa men of Zulu culture ranked emotional stability first, and women rated dependable character of most concern (Buss et al., 1990).

Despite such variations in desired qualities across cultures, commonalities did occur. For example, love and mutual attraction were—if not at the top of many cultures' list—highly valued by almost all cultures. In addition, such traits as dependability, emotional stability, pleasing disposition, and intelligence were highly valued as well.

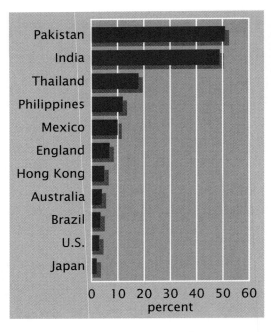

**FIGURE 7-9 Choosing a Partner** Do love and marriage go together like a horse and carriage? Not everywhere, as this graph indicates. It shows the percent of college students who say they would marry someone they did not love. *(Source:* Adapted from Levine, 1993.*)*

There were also commonalities across cultures in terms of differences between what men and women sought in a potential spouse. For example, men more than women preferred mates who are physically attractive. Women, more than men, preferred marriage partners who show ambition and industriousness and other indications of earning potential (a finding supported by later research of Sprecher, Sullivan, and Hatfield, 1994).

**FIGURE 7-10    Rank Ordering of Desired Characteristics in a Mate**

| | CHINA | | SOUTH AFRICAN (ZULU) | | UNITED STATES | |
|---|---|---|---|---|---|---|
| | **MALES** | **FEMALES** | **MALES** | **FEMALES** | **MALES** | **FEMALES** |
| Mutual Attraction—Love | 4 | 8 | 10 | 5 | 1 | 1 |
| Dependable Character | 6 | 7 | 3 | 1 | 3 | 3 |
| Emotional Stability and Maturity | 5 | 1 | 1 | 2 | 2 | 2 |
| Pleasing Disposition | 13 | 16 | 4 | 3 | 4 | 4 |
| Education and Intelligence | 8 | 4 | 6 | 6 | 5 | 5 |
| Good Health | 1 | 3 | 5 | 4 | 6 | 9 |
| Sociability | 12 | 9 | 11 | 8 | 2 | 8 |
| Desire for Home and Children | 2 | 2 | 9 | 9 | 3 | 6 |
| Refinement, Neatness | 7 | 10 | 7 | 10 | 10 | 11 |
| Ambition and Industriousness | 10 | 5 | 8 | 7 | 11 | 7 |
| Good Looks | 11 | 15 | 14 | 16 | 7 | 14 |
| Similar Education | 15 | 12 | 12 | 12 | 12 | 12 |
| Good Financial Prospects | 16 | 14 | 18 | 13 | 16 | 10 |
| Good Cook and Housekeeper | 9 | 11 | 2 | 15 | 13 | 15 |
| Favorable Social Status or Rating | 14 | 13 | 17 | 14 | 14 | 13 |
| Similar Religious Background | 18 | 18 | 16 | 11 | 15 | 16 |
| Chastity (no prior sexual intercourse) | 3 | 6 | 13 | 18 | 17 | 18 |
| Similar Political Background | 17 | 17 | 15 | 17 | 18 | 17 |

*Source:* Buss et al., 1990

Buss interprets these results in evolutionary terms. He argues that the similarities found across different cultures suggest that human beings, as a species, seek out specific characteristics that will strengthen the overall quality of the gene pool. Males, in particular, are genetically programmed to seek mates who have traits potentially indicative of high reproductive capacity. Thus, they view physically attractive, younger women as more desirable mates, since they may be seen as more capable of having children.

In contrast, females are more apt to value characteristics signaling the potential to acquire scarce resources in order to help ensure the survival of their offspring. Thus, they seek out partners who are most likely to demonstrate high economic capabilities and potential (Feingold, 1992).

Although Buss' evolutionary hypothesis is intriguing, it is equally plausible that the cultural similarities found in men's and women's preferences merely reflect commonalities in social learning across cultures and have nothing to do with evolution. Furthermore, the differences in valued characteristics between cultures—such as the importance of good looks for U.S. males—clearly suggest that individual cultures socialize specific values.

Although survey results such as these help identify the qualities that are most desired in a mate, they do not explain how these factors translate into the identification of a specific individual who fills the bill for another individual. One answer comes from a filtering model developed by Louis H. Janda and Karen E. Klenke-Hamel (1980). They suggest that people seeking a mate screen potential candidates through successively finer-grained filters, just as we sift flour in order to remove objectionable material (see Figure 7-11).

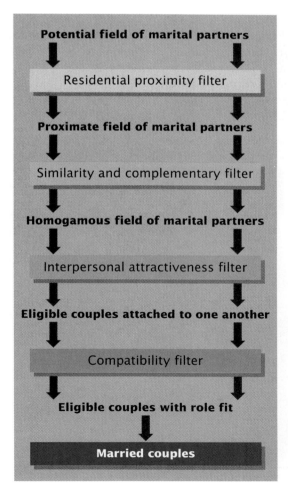

**FIGURE 7-11  The Filtering Model of Partner Selection** According to this model, potential marriage candidates are screened through a series of successively finer-grained filters. *(Source:* Janda & Klenke-Hamel, 1980.*)*

Potential field of marital partners

Residential proximity filter

Proximate field of marital partners

Similarity and complementary filter

Homogamous field of marital partners

Interpersonal attractiveness filter

Eligible couples attached to one another

Compatibility filter

Eligible couples with role fit

Married couples

As you can see from the model, an individual first filters for factors relating to the broad determinants of interpersonal attraction, such as proximity and similarity. Once a potential partner has passed these early screens, more refined criteria are employed, such as those related to level of physical attractiveness. The final filters relate to compatibility of expectations and a concept of the roles a potential partner will play in a relationship. Obviously, as each successive screen is passed, fewer and fewer people make it through.

Once a particular person is identified as a potential partner, one frequent consequence is an idealization of one's partner. People who have settled on a marriage partner and who are in love focus on the positive, seeing primarily their partner's good qualities and minimizing or ignoring any negative ones. The relationship is seen in such positive terms that it encourages "sentiment override," in which negative aspects are ignored or disregarded. People's motivation for coming to terms with conflicts is therefore minimized—an unfortunate consequence that, as we will discuss later, can lead to future marital difficulties (Weiss, 1980; Brehm, 1988; Holmes & Boon, 1990).

## The Course of Marriage: Love Is Not Enough

Following marriage, couples enter into what is expected by themselves and society to be a life-long enterprise. Yet most marriages usually follow not a straight, unvarying path, but a twisting, sometimes bumpy route.

For example, an early transition that often occurs is that romanticized, idealized images of one's partner are replaced by a more realistic view. One factor responsible for this transition is that whereas during courtship people try to put their best foot forward, as time goes on they are more likely to permit their true nature to appear. Such changes in behavior may result in an eye-opening transformation, and as a consequence, two years after marriage couples are usually less satisfied (and less affectionate) with one another than they were as newlyweds (MacDermid, Huston, & McHale, 1990).

Furthermore, research by social psychologists Ted Huston and Anita Vangelisti suggests that expressions of negativity are related to declines in marital satisfaction, whereas (somewhat surprisingly) sexual interest is relatively unimportant to marital satisfaction (Huston & Vangelisti, 1991).

Some research suggests that marital satisfaction reaches its lowest point following the birth of a couple's children and doesn't begin to increase until the last child has left home.

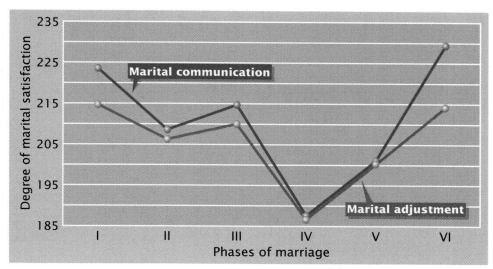

**FIGURE 7-12.    The Patterns of Marriage**  Marital satisfaction for many couples falls and rises in a U-shaped configuration. It begins to decline after the wedding and continues to fall until it reaches its lowest ebb following the births of the couple's children. Satisfaction doesn't begin to increase until the youngest child leaves home.    *(Source: Figley, 1973.)*

Husbands and wives differed significantly in terms of reactions to expressions of negativity. Whether communicated by the husband or the wife, negativity was related to declines in wives' martial satisfaction, but not to declines in husbands' satisfaction. The explanation for the difference in reaction to negativity may be that husbands tend to react to expressions of negativity by psychologically "turning off" and withdrawing from the relationship. Wives, on the other hand, react to negativity by remaining psychologically engaged and involved in the relationship, but they find their experience within the marriage to be less satisfying.

The study's finding that sexual affection was relatively unimportant to marital satisfaction may be attributable to the fact that the research examined only newlyweds. As we discussed earlier in the chapter, over the long run sex is associated with marital satisfaction.

Over the long run, marital satisfaction for many couples falls and rises in a U-shaped configuration. As you can see in Figure 7-12, marital satisfaction begins to decline after the wedding, and continues to fall until it reaches its lowest ebb following the births of the couple's children. Satisfaction doesn't begin to increase until the youngest child leaves home (Figley, 1973). Eventually, though, satisfaction reaches the same level that it did at the start of the marriage.

Does this finding mean that children lie at the heart of marital dissatisfaction for couples whose marital satisfaction follows the U-shaped pattern? Probably not, because most couples state that they want children, they enjoy their children, and they are glad they had children (Luckey & Bain, 1970). It does suggest, however, that no matter how welcome children are, they are a source of stress for husbands and wives. Moreover, this increased stress is likely to cause a decrease in marital satisfaction (Steinberg & Silverberg, 1987; Schlesinger, 1982).

Changes in marital satisfaction do not occur in the same way for all couples. The overall decline in marital satisfaction during child-raising tends to be moderate for most couples, never reaching significant levels of dissatisfaction. In fact, some couples report an increase in marital satisfaction during these years. This is particularly true for couples who hold realistic expectations regarding the extent of child-rearing effort and other household responsibilities they face upon the arrival of children (Cowan & Cowan, 1988; Belsky et al., 1989; Hackel & Ruble, 1992).

One marital transition occurs when the romanticized, idealized image of one's partner is replaced by a more realistic, down-to-earth view.

## Cohabitation: The ABCs of POSSLQs

**cohabitation**

the state in which an unmarried couple choose to live together.

**POSSLQs**

persons of the opposite sex sharing living quarters—the term given by the U.S. Department of the Census to couples who cohabitate.

Although surveys show that most heterosexuals prefer marriage to being single, a significant number of couples choose to live in unwedded bliss, in a state known as **cohabitation**. The U.S. Department of the Census calls them **POSSLQs**—persons of the opposite sex sharing living quarters.    The number of people cohabitating has increased dramatically over the past 30 years (U.S. Department of the Census, 1992; see Figure 7-13). Most people who cohabitate are young, with almost 40 percent under the age of 25. Surveys show that some one quarter of undergraduate college students have cohabitated, and an addition 50 percent say that under certain circumstances they would cohabitate. There are also subcultural differences, with African-Americans more likely to cohabitate than whites (Bianchi & Spain, 1986; Spanier, 1983).

Couples offer several reasons for cohabitating. Some are practicing for marriage, while others are not ready to make a lifelong commitment and see cohabitation as a prelude to a possibly longer obligation. In addition, although married people still report a level of happiness higher than that of unmarried people, married individuals—especially women—are less happy than they once were, while never-married individuals—especially men—report being relatively more happy (Glenn & Weaver, 1988).

Although the number of POSSLQs has grown significantly over the last few decades, the United States actually has a lower proportion—just 4 percent of all couples—than many other countries. For instance, in Sweden, about a quarter of all couples

**FIGURE 7-13  Cohabitation in the United States** There has been a dramatic rise in the number of individuals classified as "POSSLQs" by the U.S. Census Bureau since the 1960s.

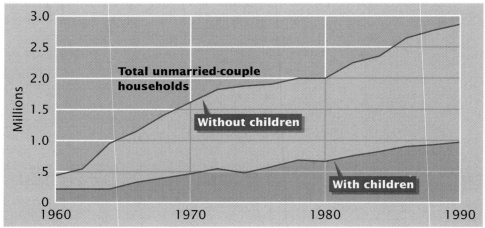

cohabitate, and cohabitation is almost as respected a social institution as marriage (Popenoe, 1987).

There are several reasons why marriage remains a more popular alternative than cohabitation in our society. For one thing, most people still view marriage as the culmination of a loving relationship, the end point in a series of steps that lead to greater closeness and intimacy. Furthermore, for some people, marriage formalizes the several roles that spouses can fulfill (Nass, 1978). For example, spouses play a therapeutic role, in which they provide advice or act as a sounding board. In their recreational role, spouses share pastimes and engage in leisure-time activities, and in their economic role, they may provide economic security and contribute to the couple's financial well-being.

Husbands and wives also play a sexual role. For those who view marriage as the only morally acceptable avenue for sexual activities, a spouse provides the only means of obtaining sexual fulfillment. And even for people who approve of premarital sex, marriage can still provide a frequency of sexual activity that may be less likely in nonmarital situations.

Finally, marriage partners play a child-rearing role. Even today, when attitudes toward having a child out of wedlock are substantially more relaxed than in previous periods, marriage still provides the most socially acceptable environment for having and raising children.

In sum, marriage has several important attributes that may make it preferable to some than cohabitation. Still, for many people, cohabitation offers distinct advantages.

*Staying Single: I Want to Be Alone*

For some people, neither marriage nor cohabitation is a preferred option. To them, living alone represents a path, consciously chosen, through life.

People who choose not to marry or live with a partner give several reasons for their decision. For instance, a survey of elderly women cited the importance of autonomy, freedom, and independence (Simon, 1987). Some reported that they simply had never found anyone they wanted to settle down with, although they were not opposed to the idea.

Despite society's stereotype that unmarried women are lonely "old maids" with no social life, the truth is different. For instance, the women in the survey led full lives with many friends, they were involved with their families, and many had been professionally quite successful.

In sum, for many people, living alone, outside of a permanent relationship, is a viable option. And it is one that many people experience at least some time in their lives because, as we discuss next, many relationships are far from permanent.

United States Attorney General Janet Reno, has chosen a life that does not include marriage.

# ENDING RELATIONSHIPS

*"Al, I don't love you any more. I want a divorce."*

*I couldn't believe my ears. A divorce! . . . My mind was spinning. Everything was a jumble, fragmentary images of what we were and what Jean was saying. This couldn't be. This couldn't be the same Jean, the Jean I had known and loved all those years. I couldn't find words to answer immediately. My mind and my voice were in two different places. Finally, I half cried and half choked, "You can't mean that. Why? What for? What about us? What about the kids?"* (Martin, 1975, pp. 5–7)

In fairy tales, after the beautiful maiden is swept off her feet by the handsome prince, they go off into the sunset and live happily ever after. However, if fairy tales were

---

**FIGURE 7-14    Marital Instability and Divorce**

**FACTORS ASSOCIATED WITH AN INCREASED PROBABILITY OF DIVORCE**

Urban background

Marriage at a very young age (15–19 years old)

Short acquaintanceship before marriage

Short engagement or no engagement

Parents with unhappy marriages

Relatives' and friends' disapproval of the marriage

General dissimilarity in background

Membership in different religious faiths

Failure to attend religious services

Disagreement of husband and wife on role obligations

**FACTORS ASSOCIATED WITH A LOWER PROBABILITY OF DIVORCE**

Rural background

Marriage at average or older ages

Acquaintanceship of two years or more prior to marriage

Engagement of six months or more

Parents with happy marriages

Relatives' and friends' approval of the marriage

Similarity of background

Membership in same religious faith

Regular attendance at religious services

Agreement of husband and wife on role obligations

*Source:* Goode, 1976, pp. 537–538.

---

given a contemporary twist, the couple might ultimately separate and divorce, going their separate ways.

*The Roots of Divorce*     Statistics tell the story: 60 percent of all first marriages end in divorce, and 40 percent of children will experience the breakup of their parents' marriage before they are 18 years old (Scott, 1990; Cherlin et al., 1991). As high as the divorce rate may seem, it has actually declined from the early 1980s.

What lies at the root of such dismal numbers? There is no single trigger that leads to divorce; instead, the disintegration of a marriage represents the culmination of a complex process that may begin in the very earliest stages of a relationship (Kalb, 1983). Several factors increase the possibility that a divorce will occur, while others lower the likelihood of divorce. (See Figure 7-14 and the accompanying Social Psychology at Work feature.)

## SOCIAL PSYCHOLOGY AT WORK

# ASKING THE RIGHT QUESTIONS: PREDICTING WHICH RELATIONSHIPS ARE DOOMED TO FAILURE

Given the high rate of divorce, all it takes is the toss of a coin to predict with 50 percent accuracy which couples' marriages are apt to hit the rocky shoals of divorce. However, according to recent research conducted by psychologist John Gottman and colleagues at the University of Washington, the odds of predicting which couples are most likely to divorce can be improved dramatically by asking the right kinds of questions (Gottman, Buehlman, & Katz, 1992; Gottman, 1993).

In fact, Gottman asserts that responses on an oral history questionnaire and observations during a 15-minute discussion can be used to predict with more than 90 percent accuracy which married couples will be divorced four years later. His claim is based on a sample of 56 couples, all of whom had somewhat higher-than-normal levels of marital satisfaction at the beginning of the study. Four years later, seven marriages had ended, and each of these breakups had been predicted by the questionnaire and the 15-minute observation.

The technique was not infallible, however. Three of the couples it had predicted would be divorced were still together. Still, the predictive power of the method appears to be superior to that of any other current means of identifying distressed marriages prior to their breakup (Brody, 1992).

Several kinds of questions were most helpful in identifying distressed couples. Among the most critical dimensions were the following:

- Affection displayed toward the spouse
- Amount of negativity communicated to the spouse
- Expansiveness or expressivity in communicating information about the relationship
- A sense of "we-ness," or perceiving oneself as part of an interdependent couple, rather than being two separate, independent individuals

- Traditionality in sex roles
- Volatility regarding the intensity of their feelings in conflict situations
- A sense of control over one's life, as opposed to feelings of chaos
- Pride in successfully getting through previous difficulties in the relationship
- Disappointment and disenchantment with the marriage.

When divorce was likely, husbands tended to be low in fondness, "we-ness," and expansiveness, while simultaneously high in negativity and disappointment. For wives, the best predictors of divorce were low "we-ness" and high disappointment scores. Overall, the very best single predictor of divorce was the degree of disappointment the husband held about the marriage.

The ability to predict divorce more accurately holds important practical promise. For example, couples identified as likely to divorce may participate in premarital counseling, in which they can learn more constructive behavior and interactional patterns. In this way, potential threats to a marriage can be reduced before they become so severe that divorce is the inevitable outcome.

Although enumerating the factors associated with divorce does not explain the psychological processes that lead to the deterioration of relationships, several lines of research in recent years have identified some of these underlying processes.

One of the primary factors now seen as promoting the success or failure of a relationship is the nature of the attributions made by husbands and wives (Fincham & Bradbury, 1993). There is a clear difference in the kinds of attributions made by partners in distressed, as compared to successful, relationships. Spouses in distressed marriages attribute negative events to their partner. When bad or unpleasant things then happen, these things are seen as the spouse's fault and as due to qualities in the spouse that are relatively enduring and unchangeable. For example, if a wife fails to give her husband an important message, the husband might attribute that failure to the irresponsibility of his wife, which is viewed as an enduring, relatively unvarying trait (Fincham & Bradbury, 1992; Bradbury & Fincham, 1992).

In solid marriages, however, negative events are explained by causes that minimize the spouse's responsibility. The causes are viewed as situational and as due to a particular set of circumstances. In the same example, for instance, the wife's failure to pass on the message might be seen as the result of temporary forgetfulness, due, perhaps, to her unusually busy schedule (Bradbury & Fincham, 1990).

Although it is clear that more negative attributions are made in distressed marriages than in satisfactory ones, it is not clear whether such negative attributions are the cause or the result of the distress (Bradbury & Fincham, 1992). It may be that negative attributions simply reflect the reality of a spouse's unpleasant behavior. Some husbands and wives do, in fact, have negative personality characteristics that make them difficult to live with (Kelly & Conley, 1987; Buss, 1991).

On the other hand, it is also possible that spouses who characteristically make negative attributions do so with even the most benign and innocent behavior on the part of their partner. Such an unforgiving attributional style may actually be the cause of marital distress. After all, if you had a spouse who tended to consider your personality flaws as the source of many of life's disagreeable events, you might well react negatively—thereby

**THE FAR SIDE**    By GARY LARSON

"The problem, as I see it, is that you both are extremely adept at pushing each other's buttons."

increasing marital distress for both yourself and your partner. As a result, consistent negative misattributions tend to cause resentment that grows with each occurrence and gradually poisons the relationship.

Other aspects of communication between partners hold important keys to understanding marital discord. Distressed and successful marriages differ also in terms of the nature of both verbal and nonverbal communications. For example, although people in unhappy marriages often misinterpret the meaning of their partner's nonverbal behavior, they are unaware of their misinterpretation. In fact, they are often overconfident that they have correctly perceived nonverbal emotional messages from their spouse, and they erroneously feel certain that any message they intend to convey has been communicated effectively—even if it has not (Noller, 1992).

Similar patterns of miscommunication characterize verbal messages. Distressed couples often show patterns of negativity, in which one partner complains about the other's failings, triggering an attack by the other partner. At the same time, the underlying concerns that led to the initial complaint are never addressed (Duck, 1988).

As miscommunication in a relationship escalates, judgments about the meaning of a partner's behavior undergo a shift. For example, behavior that was once seen as "charming forgetfulness" becomes perceived as "uncaring indifference," and the partner becomes less valued as a result (Levinger, 1983). Ultimately, a person may begin to solicit criticism of a partner from individuals outside the relationship and may begin to look to others for the fulfillment of needs that were once met by the partner.

*The Stages of a Deteriorating Relationship*

Social psychologist Steven Duck suggests that a deteriorating relationship proceeds through a series of stages, in much the same way that developing relationships tend to

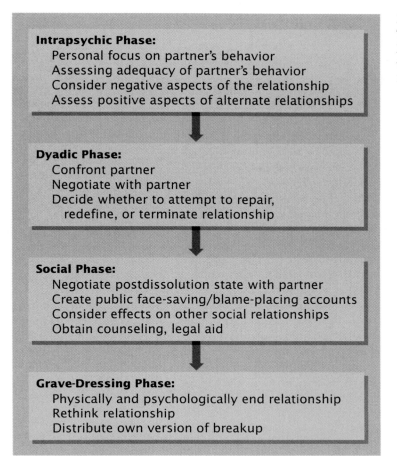

follow a general pattern (Duck, 1982; 1988; see Figure 7-15). In his view, the first phase occurs when a threshold is reached in which a partner feels he or she can no longer tolerate participation in the relationship. This feeling results in an "intra-psychic phase" in which the partner privately considers whether to withdraw from the relationship.

If another threshold is reached in which the partner feels justified in leaving the relationship, the intrapsychic phase is followed by a "dyadic phase," in which the partner confronts and the other person negotiates about the fate of the relationship. If these negotiations are unsuccessful, and a decision to terminate the relationship is reached, the person moves into the "social phase." In the social phase, public acknowledgment is made that the relationship is being dissolved, as friends and family are informed. A public accounting is made regarding the events that led to the termination of the relationship.

Finally, the last stage is a "grave-dressing" phase, in which the major process is to physically and psychologically terminate the relationship. The partners may reconsider the entire relationship, rewriting its history and making what occurred appear reasonable and consistent with their perceptions of the breakup.

Although declining marital relationships often cycle downward in a seemingly inevitable pattern through the stages described by Duck, not all do. In some cases, people can repair relationship difficulties. For example, people can be taught to make different types of attributions about their partner's behavior, or they can learn to act more responsively to a spouse (Reis & Shaver, 1988; Holmes & Boon, 1990). In other cases—as we discuss next—they can learn to handle discord in a manner that ultimately strengthens their relationship.

# THE INFORMED CONSUMER OF SOCIAL PSYCHOLOGY:

## FIGHTING THE GOOD FIGHT

Frequent arguments and fights are a sure sign of a declining relationship.

Although such a statement might represent common sense, in fact it is wrong. According to a growing body of research, the number of arguments is less important than the nature of their content in determining whether a marriage will decline or flourish. Such findings contradict conventional wisdom, which has traditionally suggested that couples who were more likely to fight with one another were the least satisfied with their marriage (Crohan, 1992; Markman, 1991).

However, it turns out that certain types of arguments actually can improve certain relationships. The kinds of arguments in which partners are free to express their anger, while keeping a rein on the intensity of their feelings, are the most apt to solve problems and lead to improved relationships in the future. In contrast, fights in which partners become defensive or stubborn, whine, or repress their anger are more likely to be detrimental to the health of the relationship. The most destructive behaviors are those in which partners make excuses for their behavior, rather than taking responsibility. In addition, acting stubborn, insulting the partner, whining and complaining, or focusing on what the partner should stop doing rather than what they should do more of, were among the behaviors in arguing that were least constructive (Gottman & Krokoff, 1989).

What makes for a good fight? Experts suggest several strategies for maximizing the positive outcomes from an argument, including the following (Goleman, 1989):

- Make explicit complaints, avoiding vague generalities. Charging a partner with being "a slob" not only conveys the information that you are upset, but it is a threatening message as well. A better strategy is to say, "It would help me feel that the housecleaning is not just my responsibility if you rinsed your dishes after you have a snack." Instead of blaming the problem on your partner's personality, then, suggest that your concern is over a changeable behavior.

- Don't state your disagreement with something your partner has said by accusations such as, "You are completely wrong." Instead, paraphrase what you hear your partner say, and try to find a solution. Saying "I'm hearing you criticizing my neatness and it makes me feel bad" is better than the accusatory "Why are you saying I'm sloppy?"

- Show that you are listening to your partner. Say, for instance, "I hear your concern about helping with the garden, and I know that we should talk about it." Acknowledge that your partner may have a point, or at least that the issue is worthy of discussion. Don't fire back with a countercharge every time your partner makes a new complaint.

- Acknowledge that you are angry, if that is how you are feeling. You can say, "I'm getting pretty angry about this issue." Don't pretend that something doesn't bother you if it really does. Ultimately, relationships in which the partners gloss over their anger may be at greater risk than those that air their problems.

Although strategies such as these won't guarantee to take the sting out of arguments, they can go a long way in helping to prevent some of the most destructive consequences of arguing.

---

## ► REVIEW & RETHINK

### Review

- In choosing marriage partners, people across disparate cultures value love and mutual attraction.
- Marriages typically cycle through several transitions.
- Alternatives to marriage include cohabitation and living alone.
- Relationships decline in part due to faulty attributional patterns and to verbal and nonverbal miscommunication.

### Rethink

- What is the relationship between sexual satisfaction and marital satisfaction? How would you explain this relationship?
- What is the general relationship between marital satisfaction and child-rearing? Considering the exceptions to the general rule, what factors do you think are responsible for this relationship?
- Consider the negative correlation between negative attributions and marital satisfaction. Give three possible explanations for this observed correlation.

• According to Duck, what stages does a deteriorating relationship pass through as it declines? Recall the triangle theory of love proposed by Sternberg. How might the eight different types of love differ with respect to the path that their breakups take?

# LOOKING BACK

◄ ◄ ◄ ◄ ◄ ◄ ◄ ◄ ◄ ◄ ◄ ◄ ◄ ◄ ◄ ◄ ◄ ◄ ◄ ◄ ◄ ◄ ◄ ◄ ◄ ◄

## What are the factors that lead to the development of close relationships; how do these relationships evolve; and what roles do intimacy, self-disclosure, and sexuality play?

1. Close relationships are characterized by emotional attachment, need fulfillment, and interdependence. The three basic levels of relatedness are unilateral awareness, surface contact, and mutuality. The mutuality stage of relationships is itself subdivided into three stages.

2. Exchange relationships are associations based on an economic model of interaction, in which people seek to maximize their benefits and minimize their costs. In contrast, in a communal relationship, the participants feel mutual responsibility for each other, and they provide benefits according to the other's needs or in order to exhibit concern for the other person. Exchange relationships occur most often with first-time acquaintances and in business relationships; communal relationships occur most often with romantic partners, family members, and friends.

3. Intimacy is the process in which a person communicates important feelings and information to another through self-disclosure. As a consequence of this self-disclosure, the person comes to feel understood, cared for, and validated by the partner in the relationship. Self-disclosure can either be descriptive or evaluative in nature.

4. According to the theory of social penetration, relationships gradually progress through increasingly deeper intimacy. This increasing intimacy leads to reciprocity of self-disclosure, in which people who are the recipients of intimate information respond with increasing disclosure.

5. Research suggests that relationships may pass through a series of stages. For example, stimulus-value-role (SVR) theory suggests that relationships proceed in a fixed order through three stages: the stimulus stage, the value stage, and the role stage.

6. Sexuality is a key issue in many close relationships. Although the double standard suggested that premarital sex was permissible for men but not for women, in recent years it has been supplanted by the permissiveness with affection standard. Still, attitudes regarding sex are still more liberal towards men than towards women. In addition, there are cultural and subcultural differences in sexual patterns, although heterosexual and homosexual relationships are more similar than different from one another.

## What are the different categorizations of love?

7. One model of love suggests that there are two types. Passionate (or romantic) love represents a state of intense absorption in another person, including intense physiological interest and arousal and caring for the needs of the other. In comparison, companionate love is the strong affection that individuals have for those with whom their lives are deeply involved. According to the labeling theory of passionate love, people experience romantic love when two events occur together: intense physiological arousal and situational cues that indicate "love" is the appropriate label for the feelings they are experiencing.

8. According to Sternberg's model, love is composed of three components: intimacy, passion, and decision/commitment. The various combinations of these components produce eight different types of love. Finally, Lee suggests that love is analogous to the primary colors on a painter's palette, which can then be combined into other types. The three primary types of love as defined by Lee are eros, ludos, and storge.

9. According to prototypes approaches, love should be considered in terms of how people naturally describe, think about, and categorize the concept. Among the major prototypes of love are love of a parent for a child, love between romantic partners, love between old friends, and love between siblings.

### *What are the varieties of relationships?*

10. Although there is considerable variation across cultures in desired qualities in marriage partners, there are commonalities almost all cultures value, such as love and mutual attraction. There are also consistent gender differences in desired qualities for husbands and wives, suggesting the possibility that certain traits are important in evolutionary terms.

11. In long-term relationships such as marriage, several transitions occur with time. For example, romanticized, idealized images of one's partner are replaced by a more realistic view.

12. Cohabitation refers to unmarried persons of the opposite sex living together. Although there has been a large increase in the number of people cohabitating in the last 30 years, the proportion of people cohabitating is relatively small. Other people choose to remain single, and, despite stereotypes to the contrary, lead full lives.

### *What factors lead to the decline of close relationships?*

13. In some cases, long-term relationships decline. Among the factors related to declines are changes in expressions of affection, and negativity on the part of spouses. Although some research suggests that marital satisfaction follows a U-shaped pattern, being highest during the early and late years and lowest during the child bearing years, some couples find greatest satisfaction while they are raising their children.

14. Most people prefer being married to being single. However, although most people still aspire to marriage, it is only one of many types of relationships that can bring satisfaction.

15. Some 60 percent of all first marriages end in divorce, and 40 percent of all children will experience the breakup of their parents' marriage before they are 18 years old. In addition to certain demographic factors related to divorce, there are also significant psychological processes. For example, the nature of partners' attributions and their verbal and nonverbal communication are related to divorce. In addition, relationship dissolution passes through a series of stages.

16. The types of fights and arguments that couples have are related to the ultimate success or failure of their relationship. Among the strategies for fighting in a way that can improve a relationship are making explicit complaints, stating disagreements constructively, showing that you are listening, and acknowledging anger.

---

# KEY TERMS AND CONCEPTS

*close relationships (p. 210)*

*interdependence (p. 210)*

*Relationship Closeness Inventory (p. 210)*

*unilateral awareness (p. 211)*

*surface contact (p. 212)*

*mutuality (p. 212)*

*minor intersection (p. 212)*

*moderate intersection (p. 212)*

*major intersection (p. 212)*

*exchange relationships (p. 212)*

*communal relationships (p. 213)*

*intimacy (p. 214)*

*descriptive self-disclosure (p. 214)*

*evaluative self-disclosure (p. 214)*

*theory of social penetration (p. 214)*

*reciprocity of self-disclosure (p. 215)*

*stimulus-value-role (SVR) theory (p. 216)*

*double standard (p. 217)*

*permissiveness with affection standard (p. 218)*

*passionate (or romantic) love (p. 220)*

*companionate love (p. 220)*

*labeling theory of passionate love (p. 221)*

*Romeo and Juliet effect (p. 221)*

*intimacy component (of Sternberg's love model) (p. 223)*

*passion component (of Sternberg's love model) (p. 223)*

*decision/commitment component (of Sternberg's love model) (p. 223)*

*eros (p. 224)*

*ludos (p. 224)*

*storge (p. 224)*

*cohabitation (p. 232)*

*POSSLQ (p. 232)*

# FOR FURTHER RESEARCH AND STUDY

Derlega, V. J., Metts, S., Petronio, S., & Margulis, S. T. (1993). *Self-disclosure.* Newbury Park, CA: Sage.

This volume focuses on the role of self-disclosure in close relationships, discussing how people use self-disclosure to create intimacy in their interactions with others.

Hendrick, S. S., & Hendrick, C. (1992). *Romantic love.* Newbury Park, CA: Sage.

An up-to-date view of what social psychologists know about a topic of concern to almost everyone.

Rubin, L. B. (1985). *Just friends: The role of friendship in our lives.* New York: Harper & Row.

Provides a clear account of the ups and downs of friendship.

Brehm, S. S. (1992). *Intimate relationships.* New York: McGraw-Hill.

A lively, well-written introduction to the field of close relationships.

Gottman, J. M. (1993). *What predicts divorce? The relationship between marital processes and marital outcomes.* Hillsdale, NJ: Erlbaum.

Although technical, the book highlights some of the most interesting research on the determinants of both marital happiness and divorce.

# EPILOGUE

In this chapter and the previous one, we've sought to answer the question of how people develop and maintain their relationships with others. We began in Chapter 6 by considering the roots of interpersonal attraction, considering how particular characteristics and traits—both our own and those of other people—lead us to be drawn to particular people. In this chapter, we continued the discussion by looking at deeper sorts of relationships. We considered how we build relationships, how we move from liking to loving, and ultimately to the processes involved in lasting relationships.

Although it may seem that these two chapters ended on a pessimistic note, as we considered the decline and failure of relationships, in fact most of the work done by social psychologists has an optimistic foundation. By seeking to understand the dynamics that lie behind interpersonal attraction and relationships, social psychologists are looking towards a future in which people are better able to get along with one another and form deeper, more meaningful relationships that can raise the quality of life.

### PART V

# WHAT ARE THE SOURCES AND CONSEQUENCES OF KINDNESS AND CRUELTY?

As we continue our traversal of the field of social psychology, our route leads us toward two conflicting fundamental human behaviors: helping and hurting. In this pair of chapters, we consider both the origins of human kindness and the roots of aggressive behavior, ultimately seeking ways to promote a more socially responsible world.

In Chapter 8 we discuss prosocial behavior, considering what factors lead us to help others. We also examine aggression, discussing its causes and consequences. In Chapter 9 we turn to the promotion of more socially responsible behavior, considering how aggression can be curbed and helping can be encouraged. ■

### CHAPTER EIGHT

# PROSOCIAL BEHAVIOR AND AGGRESSION

## HELPING AND HURTING

# PROLOGUE: SUBWAY SAMARITAN

It was 2:15 A.M., and Charles Falzon found himself lost in the sprawling Canal Street subway station. It was there that he felt someone's hand encircling his chest.

Hearing a man muttering, "No, no, no," he came face to face with a stranger carrying a knife with a blade eight inches long.

Charles Falzon's life-and-death encounter took place in this lonely subway station.

Falzon fought back, grabbing at the knife, which cut his hand. He thought he was being punched, but he was actually being stabbed, at least four times.

Then Falzon, an officer at the State Supreme Court, pulled out his licensed revolver and shot his assailant three times, critically wounding him.

At that point, things began to take an unusual turn. The assailant, near death, begged Falzon to help him. As Falzon described it the next day, "He told me not to leave him. He told me to help him. He looked scared. I asked him his name. He told me it was George. I said, 'OK, George, I'm going to get you some help'" (Fisher, 1992).

Despite the blood spurting from his own wounds, Falzon moved George off of the subway tracks, where they had been struggling only a few seconds earlier. He propped up the wounded man and tried to locate help for him. However, despite Falzon's efforts to help, it was too late: The assailant died before medical attention could be found. "I could hear the life was draining out of him. That was it," Falzon said (Fisher, 1992, p. A-33).

## LOOKING AHEAD

▶ ▶ ▶ ▶ ▶ ▶ ▶ ▶ ▶ ▶ ▶ ▶ ▶ ▶ ▶ ▶ ▶ ▶ ▶ ▶ ▶ ▶ ▶ ▶ ▶ ▶ ▶ ▶ ▶

In this one episode, we see people at their best, at their worst, and at their most complex. We glimpse the assailant's attack; Falzon's initial aggressive response; and ultimately his compassion to the assailant.

In this chapter we examine the two sides of a social psychological coin that helps explain these complexities of human conduct—prosocial behavior and aggression. **Prosocial behavior** is helping behavior that benefits others. The help may be trivial, such as helping a stranger pick up a dropped paper, or it may be substantial, such as rescuing a child who has fallen through the ice in a partly frozen pond. It may be premeditated and thoughtful, as when volunteers collect money for charity, or it may be impulsive, as in the heroic act of rushing into a burning building to save a screaming child. The common thread tying prosocial behaviors together is the benefit that flows to others from an individual's helping actions.

**prosocial behavior**
helping behavior that benefits others.

The other, and darker, side of this coin is aggression. As we'll discuss more fully later, **aggression** refers to doing intentional injury or harm to another person. It may be as commonplace as a parent's swat of a child's hand, or as extreme as the act of murder. As with prosocial behavior, aggression may be thoroughly calculated, as in a mobster's plan to hire a hit man to kill someone. Conversely, it can be as spontaneous as a child who flies into a violent rage when his sister teases him mercilessly. The common link: behaviors whose purpose is to intentionally hurt another individual.

**aggression**
intentional injury or harm to another person.

245

In this chapter, we first consider the roots of helping behavior. We begin by examining prosocial behavior in emergencies. We then turn to altruistic behavior, in which helping requires self-sacrifice. We inquire whether any helping behavior can be entirely altruistic, or whether there is always some reward inherent in helping. We also consider whether some people have an altruistic personality that leads them to be helpful in different situations, and how empathy for a victim leads to greater helping. Finally, we look at the relationship between emotions, moods, and helping, and at societal standards that promote helping.

We then turn to aggression. After discussing the difficulties in developing a satisfactory definition, we consider different theories that seek to explain why people are aggressive, ranging from biological to social explanations. We examine the link between frustration and aggression, and some of the situational factors that lead to aggression. Finally, we identify the ways victims of aggression can be recognized.

In sum, after reading this chapter, you will be able to answer the following questions:

- What is prosocial behavior, and how is it exhibited in emergencies?
- What factors lead people to help in an emergency?
- Are there personality characteristics that lead to helping?
- How do empathy, emotions, and norms affect helping?
- What is aggression?
- What are the roots of aggressive behavior?
- What social and situational factors lead to aggression?

# PROSOCIAL BEHAVIOR AND ALTRUISM

- Miep Gies, a resident of Holland, risked her life every day for more than two years to feed and provide a place to hide Anne Frank and her family during the Nazi Holocaust.
- Lenny Skutnik repeatedly jumped into the freezing Potomac River to rescue victims of a plane crash. "I just did what I had to do," explained Skutnik later.
- Hundreds of people of all ages rushed to help residents of low-lying areas along the Mississippi place sandbags on levees during the flood of the century in 1993. Although their own homes were safe, many felt compelled to help strangers who lived hundreds of miles away.

What makes people like these so helpful? Social psychologists have long pondered the question, and they have come up with a variety of answers. We'll investigate the major considerations that go into helping, beginning with the ways in which people react during emergency situations.

*Dealing with Emergencies: Would You Help a Stranger in Distress?*

Suppose you were in an experiment, talking to a small group of students over an intercom, and you suddenly heard one of them say the following:

> I-er-um-I think I-I need-er-if-if-could-er-er-somebody er-er-er-er-er-er-er give me a little-er give me a little help here because-er-I-er-I'm-er-er-h-h- having a-a-a real problem-er-right now and I-er-if somebody could help me out it would-it-would-er-er s-s-sure be-sure be good . . . because-er-there-er-er-a cause I-er-I-uh-I've got a-a one of the-er-sei——er-er-things coming on and-and- and I could really-er-use some help so if somebody would-er-give me a little h-help-uh-er-er-er-er-er c-could somebody-er-er-help-er-us-us-us [choking sounds]. . . . I'm gonna die-er-er-I'm . . . gonna die-er-help-er-er-seizure-er- [choking sounds, then silence]. (Latané and Darley, 1970, p. 379)

Most of us would probably guess that if we were in such a situation, we'd rush to the aid of the victim, trying to see what help we could give.

Unfortunately, most of us would be wrong. According to the results of a landmark study carried out by social psychologists Bibb Latané and John Darley, and a long series of experiments that followed, the poor victim would probably have been better off with just a single companion, rather than with a group.

**DIFFUSION OF RESPONSIBILITY: WHERE MORE IS LESS.**    As we discussed in Chapter 1, Latané and Darley's research confirmed that the *greater* the number of people present in a situation requiring help, the *less* likely it is that any one person will provide it—a phenomenon they labeled diffusion of responsibility. **Diffusion of responsibility** is the tendency for people to feel that responsibility for acting is shared, or diffused, among those present. The greater the number of people who are present in an emergency, then, the lower is any one individual's sense of responsibility—and the less likely it is that a person will feel obligated to help. In contrast, the fewer people present to share the responsibility for helping, the more likely it is that help will be provided by any one person (Darley & Latané, 1968; Latané & Darley, 1970; Latané & Nida, 1981).

Such reasoning has been proven sound in literally hundreds of experiments. For example, in the experiment using the seizure "emergency" described above—which was, in reality, staged by the experimenter to test the theory—Latané and Darley found clear evidence for the diffusion of responsibility phenomenon. In the study, subjects were placed in groups of either two, three, or six people, and heard the faked seizure over the intercom. As predicted, the more people who supposedly could overhear the seizure, the less likely it was that any one person would provide help. Specifically, when there were just two people present (the bystander and the "victim"), 85 percent of the subjects helped; when two bystanders and the victim were present, 62 percent provided aid; and when five bystanders and the victim were present, only 31 percent helped (Darley & Latané, 1968).

The concept of diffusion of responsibility helps explain—although not pardon—a considerable number of everyday incidents that exemplify "Bad Samaritanism." For instance, perhaps you recall the true events depicted in the Jodie Foster movie *The Accused,* in which a New England woman was savagely raped on a pool table in a bar as dozens of onlookers stood by idly. Police accounts describe her crying and begging for help, and not one person coming to her aid. While she was being repeatedly raped by several men, one customer did try to call the police; but he dialed a wrong number and gave up. Finally, she broke away from the rapists and fled the bar, dazed and half-naked. A passing motorist stopped and drove her to a telephone, where she called for help.

The concept of diffusion of responsibility allows us to speculate on the social psychological situation that permitted the rape to proceed without intervention. Because the bar was crowded, each of the patrons could feel little individual responsibility for helping the victim. Instead, the obligation for helping was shared with the many people present, lowering the likelihood that any one person would be sufficiently moved by the victim's plight to help her. Ironically, if fewer people had been in the bar, the victim's pleas might well have been answered.

**HELP IN EMERGENCIES: A MODEL.**    Although the diffusion of responsibility phenomenon explains part of what goes into making the decision to help, it is just one of the factors that account for helping in emergency situations. As illustrated in Figure 8-1, several distinct decision-making points must be cognitively traversed in order to determine whether or not helping will occur:

- *Noticing a person, event, or situation that potentially may require help.* In order for even the potential for helping to exist, an individual must notice the circumstances that may require assistance of some sort.

- *Interpreting the event as one that requires help.* Simply noticing an event is no guarantee that someone will provide help. If it is ambiguous enough, the onlooker may decide that it really isn't an emergency at all (Shotland, 1985).

**diffusion of responsibility**
the tendency for people to feel that responsibility for acting is shared, or diffused, among those present.

The terrorist bombing at the World Trade Center in New York City involved an indisputable emergency situation. Do you think victims were more or less likely to receive help because it occurred in a large population center with many bystanders?

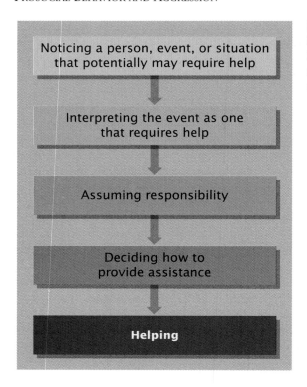

**FIGURE 8-1 Model of Helping in an Emergency** According to the Latané and Darley model, the decision to help is made in several steps. *(Source:* Latané & Darley, 1968.*)*

People are often motivated to decide that a situation is not an emergency. Defining the situation as a routine non-emergency means that no further psychological (and physical) effort is required. We may thus be primed to discount information that the situation is an emergency and be especially attentive to information suggesting that there is no emergency (Wilson & Petruska, 1984).

Similarly, viewing other bystanders who are not themselves intervening may help bolster the interpretation that the event is not an emergency. We may convince ourselves that if it were really an emergency, others would be jumping in to help. Such a mind-set is due to pluralistic ignorance (Taylor, 1982).

**pluralistic ignorance**
a situation that occurs when bystanders in an emergency use the behavior of others to determine whether help is actually required.

**Pluralistic ignorance** occurs when bystanders in an emergency use the behavior of others to determine whether help is actually required (Miller & McFarland, 1987). When others are not helping, their inaction is erroneously perceived as indicating that help is not necessary. As a result, no one intervenes, because each person in the situation mistakenly assumes, based on the behavior of the others, that help is not necessary.

In such a case, the reality may be quite different. Like us, the other people present may feel uncertain of what to do, and they may be looking to others to figure out what to do. But when all the people in a situation see each other not responding, they make the same, erroneous attribution, and everyone becomes immobilized. If they were able to move beyond pluralistic ignorance and understand the true motivation of the others present, they would be more likely to intervene. Obviously, in an ambiguous situation communication with others helps end the state of pluralistic ignorance.

- *Assuming responsibility.* If the first two steps—noticing an event and determining that it is an emergency—are satisfied, a major decision point is reached. It is here that people ask themselves if they should take responsibility for helping. This is the point at which diffusion of responsibility may occur; if there are many others present, the burden of helping is seen to be shared, and helping is less likely to occur.

Of course, diffusion of responsibility is not the only reason that people may not be helpful in an emergency. Sometimes, people don't take responsibility because they don't know what they ought to do; they lack the expertise to intervene effectively. For instance, if someone with apparent medical expertise were present when a medical emergency occurred, it is unlikely that a person without medical training would feel compelled to offer aid. More likely, that person would defer to the specialist.

One study, conducted on the subways of New York, illustrated this point nicely. In the experiment, researchers arranged for a bogus crisis to occur, in which a passenger appeared to collapse, with blood trickling out of the corner of his mouth. Other passengers were considerably less likely to intervene when an apparent medical school "intern" was present than when no such person was present. Not unreasonably, those without medical training readily deferred to the expertise of the intern (Piliavin & Piliavin, 1972).

Ironically, fear of unwanted legal ramifications may prevent experts from becoming involved in providing emergency medical assistance. For example, physicians have been successfully sued for providing unsuccessful medical intervention in emergencies. To prevent such suits from occurring, many states have passed "Good Samaritan" laws, which protect medical and other professionals from being sued for unsuccessfully providing assistance in an emergency (Rosenberg, 1992; Taylor, 1990; Northrop, 1990).

Even without special expertise, those furnishing emergency help may be viewed with suspicion by onlookers. A person who is providing aid may be seen by late-arriving onlookers as the possible source of the harm that befell the victim—a phenomenon dubbed confusion of responsibility (Cacioppo, Petty, & Losch, 1986). In **confusion of responsibility**, observers assume that a person who is actually aiding a victim is in some way responsible for the emergency situation. Awareness of the confusion of responsibility phenomenon may suppress willingness to provide aid during an emergency.

**confusion of responsibility**
a situation in which observers assume that a person who is actually aiding a victim is in some way responsible for the emergency situation.

- *Deciding how to provide assistance.* If people reach this step in the sequence, they must choose from a variety of potential forms of assistance. Call 911? Provide medical assistance? Ask another bystander to get help?

Because the potential choices for helping vary so widely, helpers must weigh the costs and benefits from each potential action, employing a kind of psychological calculus. In an emergency, people quickly tally both the actual and psychological costs of providing particular kinds of aid. For instance, indirect forms of aid, such as getting others to help, are less costly than providing direct aid. At the same time, various types of help

"Look, Joanna, I've told you over and over—I don't have time for sharing and caring when I'm moving and shaking."

bring different kinds of rewards. You can expect to receive more gratitude and approval when you leap into a pond to save a drowning child than when you help an elderly person cross the street.

Many experiments have confirmed that as the costs of helping increase, relative to the rewards, helping is less likely to occur. One example comes from a classic study involving theology students who were on their way to give a talk either on the Good Samaritan parable—which emphasizes the importance of helping—or on a subject having nothing to do with helping (Darley & Batson, 1973). To control the cost of helping, the researchers manipulated the degree to which the students were late arriving to give their talk.

On the way to give their talk, subjects passed a confederate, planted by the experimenters, who was slumped on the ground in an alleyway, coughing and groaning. Would the theology students help?

The answer depended on whether the subjects were late or not. Subjects who were late (which corresponded to a greater cost for helping) were less likely to provide help than subjects who had ample time. Ironically, the topic of their talk had no effect on their helping behavior; subjects about to speak on the virtues of helping were no more likely to provide help than those who had rehearsed a speech on another subject.

On the other hand, we should not sink into despair over the unwillingness of the tardy theology students to help the confederate. Subsequent research suggested that their lack of help may have been induced by their perception that the "greater good" would be fulfilled by arriving at the talk on time, thereby helping a larger number of people, rather than by helping the lone person who was in need (Batson et al., 1978).

It is clear, then, that the kind of assistance a person chooses to provide in an emergency situation is governed in part by an assessment of the personal rewards and costs of helping. Tallying the rewards and costs of various types of helping, people make a decision about what kind of assistance to provide.

- *Helping in the emergency—the final step.* After weighing the rewards and costs for intervening in an emergency situation, people finally reach the stage of action. However, their intention to help does not guarantee that their help will be effective. For instance, if bystanders decide to phone 911 for help, they may find that route blocked: They might not be able to find a phone, they may not have change to make the call, or the phone may be broken. Even if they decide to intervene directly, they may be frozen with fear and unable to act. The decision to help, then, does not guarantee that those in need will receive the aid they require.

## *Altruism: Disregarding the Rewards and Costs of Helping*

Although Latané and Darley's model emphasizes the rational weighing of the rewards and costs of helping, in some cases a logical analysis of the benefits and expenses of helping does not satisfactorily explain why helping occurred. For example, a cost–reward analysis does not convincingly explain why a medic would risk his own life during fierce combat just to retrieve the body of a dead soldier so that it can be sent back to the family.

To explain such situations, some social psychologists have suggested that one form of helping behavior is altruism. **Altruism** is helping behavior that is beneficial to others but requires clear self-sacrifice. In altruism, no expectation of receiving rewards exists, and helpers expect no condemnation from others if they don't provide help (Eisenberg, 1986; Batson, 1990a, 1991).

**altruism**
helping behavior that is beneficial to others but requires clear self-sacrifice.

Many forms of helping can be considered altruistic: running into a burning house to rescue a stranger, sheltering Jews in Nazi-occupied countries during World War II, adopting a baby born with AIDS. In each of these cases, the costs (or potential costs) to the helper are significant, far outweighing the possible rewards.

However, rewards–costs analyses may not fail altogether. If we analyze supposedly altruistic situations closely, it is often possible to identify potential rewards even in

Oscar Schindler, shown here in 1963, saved the lives of hundreds of Jews during the Holocaust, without receiving any discernible reward. Such behavior fits the definition of altruism.

behavior that at first seems completely altruistic. For instance, a helper may gain greater self-esteem and may receive praise from others; and the victim may express enormous gratitude and a sense of obligation to the helper. Hence, psychological rewards may lie in seemingly altruistic behavior (Batson, 1990b).

Although the concept of altruism and the question of whether a behavior can be totally altruistic—harboring no rewards for the help-giver—remains a difficult one for social psychologists, it has not been abandoned. For instance, some investigators have focused on altruism, and helping in general, as a type of personality trait. The concept of an **altruistic personality** suggests that certain individuals have enduring personality characteristics that consistently lead them to help. We encounter this notion throughout classical literature, which provides depictions of unfailingly altruistic individuals.

Despite the appeal of the notion that some people are invariably helpful, evidence for the existence of a stable altruistic personality type has not been found. Most research suggests that people are not invariably helpful or, for that matter, unhelpful. Instead, whether particular individuals act in a prosocial manner depends on a combination of personality factors *and* on the specifics of the situation (Carlo et al., 1991; Knight et al., 1994.).

On the other hand, some groups of people are more helpful than others. For instance, men and women differ somewhat in their levels of helpfulness, with men showing slightly higher helpfulness, in general, than women (Eagly, 1987). However, the greater helpfulness of men may be more apparent than real, and may depend largely on the type of situation in which it has been studied. For instance, men show particularly high levels of helping when they are being watched and when the victim is a woman (Eagly & Crowley, 1986). Such results suggest that men may be motivated as much by their desire to exhibit their strength and mastery as by altruistic motives.

Cultures, too, show differences in helping behavior, although in this case the differences are more pronounced than gender differences. For instance, people living on Israeli collective farms—kibbutzim—tend to show greater helpfulness and even different

**altruistic personality**
a trait suggesting that certain individuals have enduring personality characteristics that consistently lead them to help.

**FIGURE  8-2   Helping in Different Cultures**

The number of helpful acts that occur during children's play varies according to culture. In a 1975 survey, children in the Philippines, Kenya, and Mexico showed higher levels of helpfulness than children in Japan, the United States, and India.

| COUNTRY | NUMBER OF HELPFUL ACTS |
| --- | --- |
| Philippines | 280 |
| Kenya | 156 |
| Mexico | 148 |
| Japan | 97 |
| United States | 86 |
| India | 60 |

*Source:* Whiting & Whiting, 1975.

reasoning about morality than members of the dominant culture in the United States (Mann, 1980; Fuchs et al., 1986).

Differences in altruistic behavior seem to be linked to the way in which children are raised. For instance, one cross-cultural study found that children's helping behavior, as judged from observations made while they were playing, varied substantially in different cultures (see Figure 8-2). Children in the Philippines, Kenya, and Mexico were most altruistic, while children in the U.S. scored among the lowest. These differences appeared to be related to children's degree of involvement with family obligations. In those cultures in which children had to cooperate with other people in their family to do chores or to help in the upbringing of younger children, altruism was greatest. In contrast, when a culture promoted competition—as in the United States—altruism was lower (Whiting & Whiting, 1975; Whiting & Edwards, 1988).

## Empathy: The Heart of Altruism

**empathy**
an emotional response corresponding to the feelings of another person.

**empathy–altruism hypothesis**
the notion that empathy lies at the heart of altruistic behavior.

**egoism**
behavior that is motivated by self-benefit.

**negative state relief model**
an explanation of helping that suggests that helping is based on an effort to end unpleasant emotions produced by observing a victim's need.

Despite the evidence against the existence of consistent altruistic behavior, not all investigators have abandoned the issue. For instance, according to C. Daniel Batson and colleagues, at least some helping behavior is motivated solely by the goal of benefiting someone else, and thus represents what could be described as altruistic behavior. But he argues that our altruism is limited to certain cases: It occurs only when we experience empathy for the person in need (Batson 1990b).

**Empathy** is an emotional response corresponding to the feelings of another person. When we see a person in distress, we feel that person's suffering; when we encounter a person who is sad, we experience his or her sadness. According to Batson's **empathy–altruism hypothesis**, it is empathy that lies at the heart of altruistic behavior. As can be seen in the bottom half of Figure 8-3, experiencing true empathy motivates people to reduce other people's distress.

In contrast, people may help only because helping reduces their own personal distress or produces pleasure over meeting the other's needs. In this case (illustrated in the top half of Figure 8-3), they are acting with **egoism**—behavior motivated by self-benefit (Batson & Oleson, 1991; Batson, 1991).

Finding support for the empathy–altruism hypothesis is tricky; separating altruistic from egoistic motivation requires assessment of underlying motives that can be only indirectly inferred from behavior. However, researchers have come up with some ingenious experimental solutions.

For example, support for Batson's reasoning comes from a study that directly compared the empathy–altruism hypothesis with the **negative state relief model**, which suggests that helping is based on an effort to end unpleasant emotions that come from observing the victim's plight. In the experiment, subjects listened to an account of a female college student who was having difficulty completing an important assignment

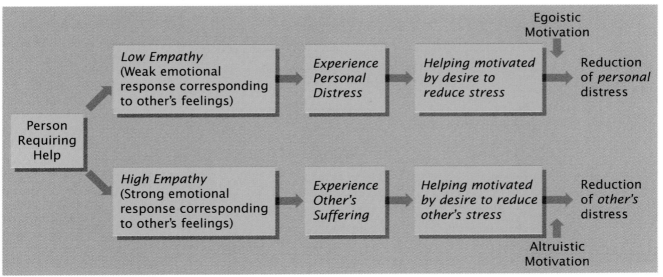

**FIGURE 8-3    The Empathy–Altruism Hypothesis** According to Batson's empathy–altruism hypothesis, experiencing empathy motivates people to reduce others' distress. In contrast, egoistic motivation leads to helping due to a desire to reduce one's own personal distress.    *(Source:* Batson, 1991.*)*

because of illness, and then were given the opportunity to help (Dovidio, Allen, & Schroeder, 1990).

The experimenters manipulated the degree of empathy for the woman by telling subjects either that they should imagine how the woman felt, thereby inducing high empathy, or that they should simply observe the circumstances being described, inducing low empathy. In addition, subjects were given the opportunity to help the woman either on the specific problem that they heard about, or on a different problem.

The researchers reasoned that if empathy were the source of helping, subjects would be motivated to relieve the student's immediate, particular problem—not to solve her problems in general. Consequently, if the empathy–altruism hypothesis were valid, subjects in the high-empathy ("imagine") condition would show high levels of helping on the same problem, and low levels of helping on a different problem. On the other hand, if the negative-state relief model were valid, helping should occur regardless of whether the problem were the same or different, since the goal of the egoistic motivation would be to reduce the helper's negative emotions, which could be accomplished by helping on any task.

As you can see from Figure 8-4, the empathy–altruism prediction was supported. Helping levels varied according to whether subjects could help on the same or a different problem. When helping was possible on the same problem, subjects who were asked to identify with the woman's feelings were more apt to volunteer than those who had been asked to merely observe. On the other hand, the difference in helping between high- and low-empathy conditions was not significant for a different problem.

While the results of this study, and many others, support the empathy–altruism hypothesis, there is still no final word on the ultimate validity of the hypothesis. Plausible alternatives to the hypothesis abound (Hoffman, 1981; Warren & Walker, 1991; Wallach & Wallach, 1991; Cialdini, 1991). For instance, one recent suggestion is that helping is motivated not by selfless altruism but by the potential "empathic joy" one experiences when helpfulness is provided (Smith, Keating, & Stotland, 1989).

Although a plausible hypothesis, the empathic joy explanation remains one of several reasonable hypotheses. To date, no experiment has unequivocally supported any of the alternatives.

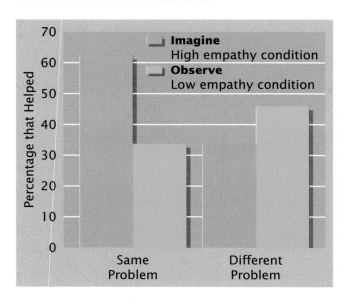

**FIGURE 8-4 Empathy Leads to Helping** Supporting the empathy–altruism hypothesis, the results of the Dovidio, Allen, & Schroeder (1990) study showed that the degree of helping varied according to whether subjects could help solve a current problem or a different one. When helping was possible on the current problem, subjects who were asked to identify with the woman's feelings— the high empathy condition —were more apt to help than those who had been asked to merely observe. On the other hand, helping did not differ significantly between high- and low-empathy conditions when a different problem was involved. *(Source:* Based on Dovidio, Allen, & Schroeder, 1990.*)*

### *Attributions, Emotions, and Mood: The Feelings of Helping*

You're walking down a busy city street, and an unshaven, disheveled man, wearing dirty clothes and carrying a sign that says, "I'm homeless," comes up to you. In a loud voice, he asks for some spare change to buy some food.

What do you feel at that moment?

According to several explanations of helping, your decision to help may well be based on your emotions and mood and the interpretation that you give to them.

**attributional model of helping and emotions**
a model suggesting that the nature of an attribution for a request for help determines a person's emotional response and the nature of the help provided.

**ATTRIBUTIONS AND EMOTIONS.**    According to the **attributional model of helping and emotions**, you may experience any one of a number of emotions at that moment: sadness over his plight, annoyance at being accosted on the street, disgust that the government has not been able to solve the problem of homelessness, happiness that you have a job and don't have to beg for food, fear that he may be deranged and about to rob you. The specific emotion you experience may well determine whether you'll agree to his request or refuse it.

The attributional model suggests that when you initially are approached by the stranger, your general physiological arousal increases due to the uncertainty of the situation. In order to understand and label the arousal, you initiate an attributional assessment process in which you analyze the cause underlying the person's need for help. If you attribute the cause to internal, controllable causes—he's lazy or he's a drunk—the emotion will likely be a negative one. On the other hand, if you attribute the cause to external causes that the victim is unable to control—he's been trying to find a job for months and hasn't been able to find one because the economy is bad—your emotions will be more sympathetic and positive (Weiner, 1980; Meyer & Mulherin, 1980). (See Figure 8-5.)

Ultimately, the emotion you experience determines the degree to which you will provide help. According to this attributional model, if the emotion the person evokes is positive, you'll be more apt to help. On the other hand, a negative emotional response is likely to result in an unwillingness to provide aid.

**MOOD AND HELPING.**    The attributional model we've just examined assumes that we approach helping situations on a fairly even keel, in an emotional state that is not already

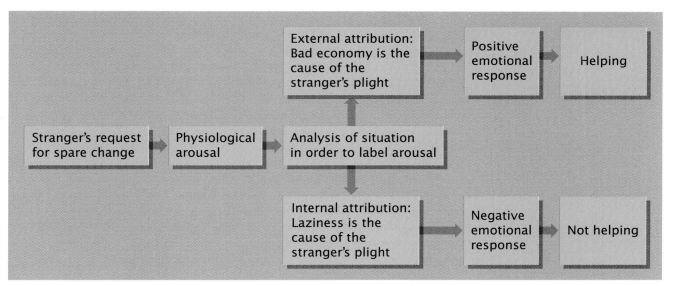

**FIGURE 8-5    An Attributional Analysis of Helping** The attributional model of helping suggests that the way in which people attribute their physiological arousal determines whether helping will occur.    *(Source:* Based on Weiner, 1980; Meyer & Mulherin, 1980.*)*

positive or negative. But suppose it's been a great day, and you feel on top of the world. Are you more likely to help when in such a good mood than at the end of a long, upsetting day, when you are in an awful mood?

Most definitely. People who are in a good mood are considerably more apt to help than those who are not (Carlson, Charlin, & Miller, 1988; Eisenberg, 1991). And it doesn't take much to bring on a good mood: Something as simple as finding a dime in a pay phone is enough to make someone more likely to help others in need (Isen & Levin, 1972). Even a sunny day is enough to put people in a good enough mood to make them more helpful (Cunningham, 1979).

But if you plan to put these findings to use by waiting until your boss is in a good mood before asking for a raise, you'd better move quickly. Good moods don't last too long, and helpfulness drops off after only a few minutes (Isen, Clark, & Schwartz, 1976).

Several possibilities explain why being in a good mood improves the chances of someone's helping. For one thing, the circumstances that put people in a good mood to begin with may lead them to focus their attention on themselves. Because of this, we may be reminded of the societal standards that we have learned as children about the importance of helping, thereby leading to greater helpfulness. Similarly, a whole network of positive memories may be activated by the good mood, leading to recollections of previous favorable experiences in which helping occurred. Finally, people may want to maintain their good mood, and acting helpfully toward another person may allow them to sustain their good feelings (Carlson, Charlin, & Miller, 1988; Salovey & Rodin, 1985; Salovey & Rosenhan, 1989).

If good moods lead people to behave more prosocially, does it follow that being in a bad mood will lead to a lower likelihood of helping? It depends.

Bad moods do often foster lower levels of helping than neutral moods. However, they also sometimes lead to more helping, and in other cases make no difference (Carlson & Miller, 1987; Cialdini, Kenrick, & Baumann, 1982). One explanation for this confusing state of affairs is provided by the negative state relief model proposed by social psychologist Robert Cialdini (Cialdini et al., 1987; Cialdini & Fultz, 1990).

The negative state relief (NSR) model seeks to explain the relationship between bad mood and helping behavior by considering the consequences of prosocial behavior for the help *provider*. The model suggests that people in a bad mood will be helpful if they think their own mood will be improved by helping. For instance, we might help a fellow student study for an exam if we thought that our own bad mood might be improved (Manucia, Baumann, & Cialdini, 1984; Schaller & Cialdini, 1990).

On the other hand, if people perceive that helping will do nothing to benefit their mood—or, even worse, if helping will make them feel bad—they will do nothing to provide aid. In support of such reasoning, studies show that younger children, who haven't yet learned the rewards of helping, are less apt to be helpful if they're in a blue mood than adults (Cialdini & Kenrick, 1976).

Others argue that the NSR model does not provide the full story regarding the relationship between negative mood and helping. One alternative explanation suggests that negative mood influences what people think about. If the mood arouses inward-focused thoughts such as despair, helplessness, and personal inadequacies, they are unlikely to help others. On the other hand, if their mood leads them to look outward, such as to the unfortunate plight of the person who needs help, a negative mood can increase the incidence of helping (Salovey, Mayer, & Rosenhan, 1991; Rogers et al., 1982; Pyszczynski & Greenberg, 1987; Wood, Saltzberg, & Goldsamt, 1990).

It is also possible that a negative mood changes the feelings of responsibility that people have for the welfare of others (Gibbons & Wicklund, 1982; Aderman & Berkowitz, 1983). If a bad mood leads people to feel less responsibility for others, then helping will be inhibited. On the other hand, if the unpleasant mood *increases* their sense of responsibility—perhaps because it raises their level of guilt—then it will be associated with more helpfulness.

**MOOD REGULATION AND HELPING.**   The relationship between mood and helping is not a one-way street. Although we've been considering how good and bad moods affect helping, we can also view helping in terms of how helping effects mood.

According to social psychologist Peter Salovey, people may provide help for others precisely in order to regulate their moods over the long term. Helping may do more than give them a momentary emotional boost: It also may bolster their spirits over long periods of time. Over time, people's awareness that they have been helpful in the past may permit them to view themselves more positively in the future. Ultimately, their self-concept may rise due to their prior helpfulness (Salovey, Mayer, & Rosenhan, 1991).

Considering the long-term benefits to mood from helping provides a way to at least partially understand some of the more extraordinary instances of help-giving, in which the immediate consequences are quite negative. For example, Christians who helped Jews escape from the Nazis during World War II put themselves at substantial risk, while probably feeling little immediate satisfaction from their actions. In the long run, however, they could look back at their behavior with pride, thereby uplifting their mood. In fact, interviews with rescuers and their relatives show that they experienced pleasure from their actions long after the war had ended (Oliner & Oliner, 1988).

---

*Norms and Helping: Standards of Aid*

**norms**
general standards or expectations regarding appropriate behavior.

The United Way, the largest charity in the United States, frequently employs a formula to suggest how much money people should contribute on a regular basis. Called the "Fair Share," it implies that people ought to donate a fixed percentage of their income in order to shoulder their part of the burden of caring for the needy.

The ability of the Fair Share concept to produce large donations—which, it turns out, it does quite impressively for the United Way—rests on societal norms about helping. **Norms** are general standards or expectations regarding appropriate behavior. When people are taught, "Do unto others as you would have them do unto you," "Kindness is its own reward," and "He who helps others helps himself," they are learning the norms that society holds dear.

The norm of social responsibility suggests that people have a societal obligation to aid those in need. During this flood on the Mississippi River, people from all over the United States volunteered their services to help local residents.

**NORMS OF SOCIAL RESPONSIBILITY.**    One of the most fundamental societal norms that encourage helping behavior is the norm of social responsibility. The **norm of social responsibility** suggests that people should respond to the reasonable needs of others, and that all people have a societal obligation to aid those in need (Fisher et al., 1981; Fellner & Marshall, 1981; Rutkowski, Gruder, & Romer, 1983).

> **norm of social responsibility**
> the norm that suggests people should respond to the reasonable needs of others, and that all people have a societal obligation to aid those in need.

The norm of social responsibility is particularly influential when those requiring help are seen to be dependent, or to lack the capacity to help themselves (Berkowitz, 1972). Thus, obligations to children, who are considerably vulnerable, are felt especially keenly.

On the other hand, the norm of social responsibility is so broad that it can be interpreted in ways that sometimes permit people to *sidestep* helping others. Thus, people might justify not giving change to a panhandler by rationalizing that social responsibility lies in not encouraging begging. In this way, they might reason that they are working to rid the streets of vagrants, and thereby helping the majority of society.

**NORMS OF RECIPROCITY.**    If you agree with the adages "Tit for tat" or "An eye for an eye," the norm of reciprocity is at the basis for your beliefs. The **norm of reciprocity** asserts that we should help others because they have helped us in the past or may help us in the future.

> **norm of reciprocity**
> the norm asserting that we should help others because they have helped us in the past or may help us in the future.

Reciprocity norms are found in almost every culture (Gouldner, 1960). We see them manifested when a student lends his car to his roommate with the expectation that the roommate will let him borrow his compact disc player at some point in the future. Similarly, people may donate to charity with the understanding that if they ever lost their job and needed help, they would have the right to ask for charity because of their prior contributions.

The norm of reciprocity is powerful. Indeed, people not only reciprocate help to specific individuals who have helped them in the past, but they are more likely to give help to other people as well. However, their help may not be as generous to those others as it would be to the specific person who provided them help initially (Staub, 1978; Lerner & Meindl, 1981).

**PERSONAL NORMS.**    Sometimes the most potent norms are not the general ones handed down to us by society. Instead, they are our **personal norms**—our own personal sense of obligation to help a specific person in a specific situation.

> **personal norms**
> our own personal sense of obligation to help a specific person in a specific situation.

Consider, for example, the case of a girl whose parents die in an auto crash and who is subsequently raised by an elderly uncle. When she is older, her sense of obligation to help her uncle may be profound—but it is not necessarily accompanied by a sense of responsibility regarding aid to the elderly in general. Indeed, it may be that the woman expends most of her resources on her uncle and has little sense of obligation to society as a whole.

Personal norms also help explain devotion to particular political causes. For instance, in the 1960s, strongly committed civil rights workers often displayed an unusually strong sense of identification with their parents, whom they viewed as holding high moral standards. In raising their children, these parents taught a philosophy that included an emphasis on the rights of others and the obligation to help others. Rather than adhering only to broad, general societal norms, then, the civil rights workers viewed themselves as following a set of more personal standards (Rosenhan, 1970).

**NORMS THAT DETER HELPING.**    Perhaps you've seen photos of people carefully skirting a person sprawled face down on the sidewalk of a city. This lack of care for someone so obviously in need reflects what has been called a **norm of noninvolvement**—a standard of behavior that causes people to avoid becoming psychologically (and physically) entangled with others.

**norm of noninvolvement**
a standard of behavior that causes people to avoid becoming psychologically (and physically) entangled with others.

The norm of noninvolvement is sometimes adopted by urban dwellers, who face so much stimulation that they may attempt to distance themselves from nonacquaintances (Milgram, 1977b). Furthermore, people in cities may experience insecurity about contact with individuals very different from themselves. Adopting a norm of noninvolvement permits them to remain detached from the needs of these others (Fischer, 1976; Matsui, 1981).

Norms that act to deter helping provide an understanding of one of the nagging problems found in our cities: the reluctance of people to act prosocially. Consistent with the stereotype of the cold-hearted, unfriendly city dweller, people living in urban areas are less prone to help others than people living in rural areas—whether the help required is direct or indirect, whether bystanders are present or not, and regardless of the age or gender of the victim (Steblay, 1987).

Intriguingly, it is not true that people raised in rural areas are inherently more helpful; when living in a city they too begin to act less helpfully. City life seems to bring out the worst in people—at least when it comes to the likelihood of behaving prosocially.

The norm of noninvolvement, the standard that allows us to avoid becoming psychologically and physically entangled with others, permits people to remain detached from the very real needs of others.

► ## REVIEW & RETHINK

### Review

- Prosocial behavior is helping behavior that benefits others.
- The question of whether truly altruistic behavior exists is a difficult one.
- Empathy, emotions, and norms affect helping behavior.

### Rethink

- What is the relationship between the number of bystanders present during an emergency and (a) the odds of any one bystander providing aid, and (b) the odds of aid being provided by someone?
- How is the likelihood that a situation will be interpreted as an emergency affected by social comparison processes? What might motivate a person to misinterpret emergency situations?
- What effects does helping another have on a person's mood? Can this phenomenon explain altruistic behavior? What aspects of a helping situation affect whether a person in a bad mood will help?
- Explain how personal norms and societal norms differ. How might the self-monitoring construct (discussed in Chapter 4) help determine which type of norm was more powerful for a given individual?

## AGGRESSION

*"Wilding (verb): The self-described activity of a frenzied group, focused on vandalizing, assaulting, and robbing victims at random, and described by participants as 'fun.'"*

*Although most people's familiarity with this curious leisure-time activity is limited, wilding came to represent the central moment of one jogger's life. One day, as she jogged through a New York park, a group of wilding young men jumped her. They savagely attacked her, hitting her with a pipe and brick; they sexually assaulted her, and left her for dead. She lost three quarters of her blood and suffered permanent brain damage from the attack.*

Unfortunately, wilding is only one form of extreme, unacceptable aggression that people may encounter during the course of their lives. The media report one form of physical aggression after another, be it from war, murder, or mugging. Parents and, in a few U.S. states, teachers, use physical punishment to induce good behavior. And aggression is not only physical: Many of us frequently confront verbal aggression and anger, whose sting may be as painful as physical pain.

*Defining Aggression: An Elusive Concept*

The fact that aggression is so common and widespread does not make it easy to define. Why? Consider the following circumstances:

- A soldier bayonets an enemy soldier, causing horrible pain and eventual death.
- A physician carries out an emergency operation on a choking woman in a restaurant, cutting a hole in her throat to allow her to breathe. It causes excruciating pain, although it saves her life.

"Wilding"—frenzied vandalization, assault, and robbery—became a new word in the vocabulary of many city-dwellers after a horrific attack on a jogger, who was left nearly dead.

- A police officer tortures a person to extract information about terrorist plans to ignite a bomb in a religious shrine, which would kill hundreds of innocent people.
- A mother slaps her child's face after he purposely knocks down his younger sister.
- In a fit of anger, a parent tells his child that she is a failure and that it would have been better if she had never been born.

Although each of these incidents involves a degree of injury inflicted on another person, most of us would probably agree that not all represent aggressive behavior. For example, even though a physician may cause as much pain as a torturer, most people would be unwilling to label the physician's behavior as aggressive. However, some social psychologists disagree, arguing that it is ultimately impossible to make fine distinctions between various types of injury. Consequently, social psychologist Arnold Buss (1961) suggests that aggression is any behavior that harms or hurts someone else. Using this definitional approach makes it simple to identify which of the five incidents described above are aggressive: According to Buss, all would be expressions of aggression.

However, most experts on aggression pursue a different path in defining aggression. They suggest that the *intent* of a person's behavior must be considered in determining whether a given action is or is not aggressive (Linneweber et al., 1984; Carlson, Marcus-Newhall, & Miller, 1989; Lysak, Rule, & Dobbs, 1989).

It is easy to see the drawback with a definition in which "intent" plays a central role: How can anyone clearly establish a person's "intention," which is an unobservable, hypothetical state that can be guessed at only indirectly from that person's overt behavior? How can we ever know that an observer's inference about intent is the appropriate one? Further, if we wish to construct a broad definition of aggression that applies to both humans and other species, intention is not a terribly practical concept, given the difficulties of establishing—and verifying—intent from the actions of animals.

Despite such conceptual difficulties, the notion of intent remains central to most contemporary definitions of aggression. Following their lead, we'll consider aggression as intentional injury or harm to another person (Berkowitz, 1974; Carlson, Marcus-Newhall, & Miller, 1989).

Using this definition unravels several knotty questions. Is a physician who causes untold pain to save someone's life aggressive? No; a physician hardly wishes to hurt the patient. Is a soldier whose goal is to kill the enemy acting aggressively? Yes—because his intention is to hurt the enemy. Is a parent whose anger leads her to wish to wound

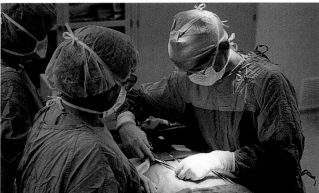

Are these both aggressive acts? The answer depends on the definition of aggression we employ.

her children with her words aggressive? Yes, because her intention is to hurt her children.

On the other hand, such a definition does not solve all our definitional problems. For example, a person who tortures a terrorist is aggressive—the torturer intends to inflict pain—although in some ways the ultimate goal of saving many lives is a noble one. Clearly, the labeling of behavior as aggression is a matter that sometimes resides in the eye of the beholder.

Even the best of definitions, however, doesn't explain the causes of aggression. Given the widespread existence of belligerence and combativeness, probably even in your own life (see Figure 8-6), we need to consider how aggression comes to play such a prominent role in the social world.

*The Roots of Aggression*    The fact that aggression is so common, both in the human and animal worlds, suggests that aggression has its roots in the same primeval chemical stew that brought forth the origins of life itself. Such a notion, in fact, has been mirrored for centuries in the writings of philosophers and other observers of human nature. Philosopher Thomas Hobbes, writing in the 1600s, called the human species *Homo lupus,* or "human wolf," expressing his view that people were little more than savage animals, restrained only by a veneer of civilization.

| FIGURE 8-6   **Are You Aggressive?** | | |
|---|---|---|

To learn how your level of personal aggression stacks up against that of others, answer the following questions:

| | | |
|---|---|---|
| 1. Once in a while I cannot control my urge to harm others. | Yes _____ | No _____ |
| 2. I can think of no good reason for ever hitting anyone. | Yes _____ | No _____ |
| 3. If somebody hits me first, I let him have it. | Yes _____ | No _____ |
| 4. Whoever insults me or my family is asking for it. | Yes _____ | No _____ |
| 5. People who continually pester you are asking for a punch in the nose. | Yes _____ | No _____ |
| 6. I seldom strike back, even if someone hits me first. | Yes _____ | No _____ |
| 7. When I really lose my temper, I am capable of slapping someone. | Yes _____ | No _____ |
| 8. I get into fights about as often as the next person. | Yes _____ | No _____ |
| 9. If I have to resort to physical violence to defend my rights, I will. | Yes _____ | No _____ |
| 10. I have known people who pushed me so far that we came to blows. | Yes _____ | No _____ |
| 11. When I disapprove of my friends' behavior, I let them know it. | Yes _____ | No _____ |
| 12. I often find myself disagreeing with people. | Yes _____ | No _____ |
| 13. I can't help getting into arguments when people disagree with me. | Yes _____ | No _____ |
| 14. I demand that people respect my rights. | Yes _____ | No _____ |
| 15. Even when my anger is aroused, I don't use strong language. | Yes _____ | No _____ |
| 16. If somebody annoys me, I am apt to tell him what I think of him. | Yes _____ | No _____ |
| 17. When people yell at me, I yell back. | Yes _____ | No _____ |
| 18. When I get mad, I say nasty things. | Yes _____ | No _____ |
| 19. I could not put someone in his place, even if he needed it. | Yes _____ | No _____ |
| 20. I often make threats I don't really mean to carry out. | Yes _____ | No _____ |
| 21. When arguing, I tend to raise my voice. | Yes _____ | No _____ |
| 22. I generally cover up my poor opinion of others. | Yes _____ | No _____ |
| 23. I would rather concede a point than get into an argument about it. | Yes _____ | No _____ |

To determine your score for physical aggression, give yourself one point for each of the following questions to which you responded with a "yes": 1, 3, 4, 5, 7, 8, 9, and 10. To find your score for verbal aggression, give yourself one point for each of the following questions to which you responded with a "yes": 11, 12, 13, 14, 16, 17, 18, 20, and 21. To compare yourself with others, look at how close you are to the average scores for men and women listed below:

Physical aggression:    Men's average = 5.1, women's average = 3.3

Verbal aggression:    Men's average = 7.2, women's average = 6.8

Keep in mind that these averages were determined several decades ago and might well be somewhat different if measured today. Still, your answers give you a chance to contemplate how aggressive you might be in a variety of situations.

*Source:* Buss & Durkee, 1957; Biaggio, 1980.

Not everyone holds such a dim view of humanity, however. The sixteenth-century philosopher John Locke argued that we enter the world as a *tabula rasa*, or "blank slate." To Locke, people are taught aggressive behavior by the people and environment they encounter as they grow up. In this view, learning and experience are at the heart of aggression. Furthermore—as we'll discuss further in Chapter 9—people can be taught to be less aggressive (Goodwin & Mahoney, 1975).

In important ways, social psychologists' major schools of thought about the origins of aggression mirror the notions held by the early philosophers. For instance, a central question regarding aggression is whether it is caused more by nature—the inherited, innate attributes of human beings—or by nurture—environmental influences. We'll consider how each side of the argument is supported as we look into the sources of aggression.

**AGGRESSION AS INSTINCT: THE NATURE SIDE OF THE NATURE–NURTURE DICHOTOMY.** When Sigmund Freud surveyed the world in the second decade of the 1900s, he saw battlefields on which hundreds of thousands of soldiers had been killed. World War I had come and gone, and to Freud it proved that people were instinctively prone to behave aggressively.

Freud's view, which grew out of his psychoanalytic theory, was that humans have a primitive instinct he called **thanatos**, or a death drive (Freud, 1920). Freud thought that the energy of thanatos drove people toward aggression and hostility, most often channeled toward others.

**thanatos**
Freud's view that humans have a primitive instinct he called a death drive.

Freud's gloomy view of aggression was shared in important respects by a second major advocate of the aggression-as-instinct model, Konrad Lorenz. However, Lorenz approached the problem from a different orientation. As an ethologist—an expert on animal behavior—he argued that aggression is adaptive, in contrast to Freud's view of aggression as representative of basically destructive impulses.

Lorenz (1966, 1974) believed that animals—including humans—share a fighting instinct that serves a number of critical functions. For one, aggression allows animals to preserve their own territories, thereby assuring a steady supply of food. Aggression also serves to weed out weaker animals, allowing only the strongest and most fit to live to reproduce. Aggression, then, provides long-term evolutionary benefits to the species.

Although Lorenz's research focused on animals, he extended his theorizing to include human behavior. This extension created considerable controversy. He suggested that humans, unlike almost all other species, kill each other because of a breakdown in the primeval "fight-or-flight" reaction to danger. He noted that animals who have relatively little natural means of defending themselves (humans being a prime example) tend to flee at the sign of danger. Species that are better able to defend themselves are more apt to fight it out when threatened.

At the same time, animals who usually flee at the first sign of danger have few inhibitions regarding the use of aggression, since aggression against members of one's own species will be relatively ineffective. In the case of humans, however, the pattern has gone awry. Because humans originally reacted to danger with flight, their innate inhibitions against aggression are relatively weak. But because their superior brainpower permitted them to develop weapons of great destruction, humans are uninhibited in their use of aggression.

**catharsis**
the process of discharging aggressive energy that is continually built up within people.

Lorenz coupled his ideas about the readiness of humans to act aggressively with an even more controversial notion: that aggressive energy is built up continually within people until it is finally discharged in a process called **catharsis**. The longer the energy is bottled up, the greater will be the magnitude of aggression when it is finally discharged. Lorenz suggested that society, to protect itself, should encourage participation in acceptable forms of aggression, such as sports and games. These means would allow people to discharge their pent-up aggression.

Konrad Lorenz argued that people, as well as nonhumans, have an instinct to behave aggressively.

**sociobiology**
*a new field of study that considers the biological roots of social behavior.*

The most recent advocates of instinctual explanations of aggression place their arguments within the context of a relatively new field called **sociobiology**, which considers the biological roots of social behavior. Focusing on how organisms pass on their genes to future generations, sociobiologists suggest that aggression facilitates the goal of strengthening the species as a whole. Consequently, the ultimate goal of aggression is not personal survival, but survival of one's genes to pass on to future generations (McKenna, 1983; Reiss, 1984).

The sociobiological point of view helps explain why aggression is not a consistent pattern of behavior; after all, no species acts aggressively all the time. Instead, people and other species take time for care of their young and for courtship; and they engage in organized, cooperative activities. To the sociobiologists, then, a species must regulate aggressive behavior in order to achieve the ultimate goal of transmitting its genes to future generations (Wilson, 1975, 1978).

Although Freud, Lorenz, and the sociobiological approaches to aggression make intuitive sense, most social psychologists feel that they are incomplete (Bandura, 1978). For one thing, they are based more on animal behavior than on human behavior, and they ignore the higher cognitive abilities of human beings. Furthermore, instinct theories provide little in the way of specific guidance about when and how people will act aggressively, other than contending that aggression is an inevitable part of human behavior.

Most damning to instinct explanations of aggression, however, is the lack of experimental support. In some cases, such support is impossible to obtain (how, for instance, does one measure the energy produced by the hypothetical drive of thanatos?), while in other cases, the research evidence is clearly not supportive, as we will see later. Finally, instincts do not provide scientific explanations that are completely satisfying: "People aggress because they have an aggressive instinct, which we know because they act aggressively." Clearly, such a circular analysis of aggression does not take us very far in understanding *why* people behave aggressively.

Social psychologists, then, have largely focused on other approaches. Still, as we see in the accompanying Social Psychology at Work feature, it is wrong to dismiss entirely the notion that aggression is produced partly by instinctual and biological factors.

---

## SOCIAL PSYCHOLOGY AT WORK

# THE BIOLOGICAL BASIS OF AGGRESSION: ARE AGGRESSION AND HORMONES LINKED?

When Charles Whitman climbed the Texas Tower, a landmark in the center of the University of Texas campus, no one could know that his action would end with the deaths of 16 people. Had he not been killed by police, the toll could have been higher, as he randomly shot at passersby below with a long-range rifle.

After Whitman's death, an autopsy revealed that he had a brain tumor in his skull the size of a walnut. Although no one will ever know for sure, Whitman's aggressive behavior might well have been caused by this biological abnormality. Indeed, several kinds of biological factors are related to aggressive behaviors, both in animals and humans. For example, stimulation of particular parts of the brain produces aggression in animals, suggesting that there is an "aggression center" that controls aggressive behavior (Delgado, 1969). Furthermore, chemical imbalances in the body, such as high or low

blood sugar levels, may result in aggression (Benton, Kumari, & Brain, 1982).

Recent findings suggest another possible source of aggressive behavior: the level of the male hormone testosterone. Beginning with the fact that, throughout the animal kingdom, males typically display higher levels of aggressive behavior than females, some scientists have argued that the presence of testosterone might well lead to heightened aggression (Olweus, 1986). As confirmation, they point to studies that show relatively high levels of testosterone in prison inmates convicted of committing violent crimes and in those who engage in criminal activity early in life (Dabbs et al., 1987; Kreuz & Rose, 1972).

Of course, because such findings are based on unusual, atypical populations—people who have already been convicted of criminal and delinquent activity—we don't know whether they apply universally. To address this question in a wider, more representative population, social psychologist James Dabbs, Jr., and colleagues took a close look at a group of almost 4,500 U.S. Army veterans who had been extensively tested as part of a large-scale study on the effects of military service. The veterans were divided into two groups: a high-testosterone group (the top 10 percent) and a normal-testosterone group (the remaining 90 percent) (Dabbs & Morris, 1990).

As the researchers suspected, veterans in the high-testosterone group were at greater risk for a variety of aggressive and antisocial behaviors. For instance, they had a history of greater childhood and adulthood delinquency, were more apt to engage in drug use, and were more likely to have had multiple sexual partners. On the other hand, the relationship between antisocial behavior and testosterone level was not universal across all subgroups of subjects; subjects at lower socioeconomic levels were most apt to show a link (Dabbs & Morris, 1990). Specifically, the relationship between testosterone and aggression was strongest for the subjects who were low in socioeconomic status. Furthermore, subjects high in socioeconomic status generally had lower overall testosterone levels than poorer subjects, suggesting that high levels of testosterone may perhaps place people at risk for economic failure.

The link between antisocial behavior and testosterone may be related to research showing that men who are domineering and highly competitive may have higher-than-average levels of testosterone. For example, one study of nearly 2,000 men living in metropolitan Boston showed that men with higher levels of testosterone showed relatively aggressive behavior patterns (Gray, Jackson, & McKinlay, 1991). According to John B. McKinlay, one of the researchers, "The picture we get is of a man who attempts to influence and control other people, who expresses his opinions forcefully and his anger freely, and who dominates social interactions" (Goleman, 1990, p. C6).

Of course, it is important to keep in mind that the findings linking testosterone and aggression are correlational. We don't know if testosterone levels directly cause assertive, aggressive, and antisocial behavior. It is possible that participation in habitual aggressive or antisocial behavior raises an individual's level of testosterone, due, perhaps, to a consistently high level of physiological arousal from involvement in active or risky behaviors.

Moreover, the research only accounts for aggressive behavior in men; little research on aggression has been conducted on women, in part because the level of women's aggression typically is substantially lower than that of men (Berkowitz, 1993). Still, there are hints that women's aggression may also be linked to hormones. For example, psychologist June Reinisch examined a group of 11-year-old children whose mothers had received a synthetic hormone, progestin, during their pregnancies (Reinisch, 1981). Although progestin is administered to reduce the risk of miscarriage, it sometimes has the side effect of masculinizing developing fetuses before birth.

To determine whether the progestin had lasting effects on aggression, Reinisch administered a survey to the children whose mothers had taken the hormone. The survey presented a series of scenarios in which conflict occurred, and the subjects were asked to indicate how they would respond. The results were clear: In comparison to the responses of their brothers and sisters who had not been exposed to progestin prior to birth, the exposed children were more likely to choose a physically aggressive response to conflict (see Figure 8-7).

While not definitive (we don't know, for instance, whether the children's survey results represented their actual behavior), such results are intriguing. They certainly add weight to the notion that aggressive behavior is linked in important ways to biological factors. When we speak of humans as "social animals," then, sometimes the emphasis might well be placed on "animal."

**FIGURE 8-7 Aggression in Children Exposed to Progestin Before Birth** In comparison to children who were not exposed to progestin (a masculinizing hormone) prior to birth, the exposed children were more likely to choose a physically aggressive response to a conflict situation. *(Source:* Adapted from Reinisch, 1981.)

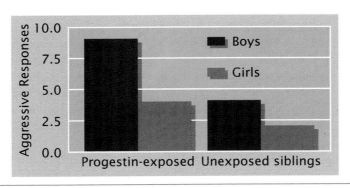

**AGGRESSION AS A CONSEQUENCE OF LEARNING: THE NURTURE SIDE OF THE NATURE–NURTURE DICHOTOMY.** Nine-year-old Billy watches a cartoon in which G.I. Joe shoots at an enemy with his rifle, whirls around, and then swings his gun at another enemy soldier, who is about to sneak up on him from behind. The next day, Billy picks ups a stick, pretends to shoot his younger sister, and then swings the stick at her.

Is there a connection between the two events? Your answer would be yes, if you believe that aggression is largely a learned behavior. Learning approaches to aggression suggest that aggression is based on prior learning. In order to understand aggressive behavior, then, we should look at the rewards and punishments found in an individual's environment.

**social learning theory**
the theory that emphasizes how aggression is learned through the observation and imitation of the behavior of others.

**Social learning theory** emphasizes how social behavior (such as aggression) is learned through the observation and imitation of the behavior of others. The theory suggests that the primary mechanism for learning aggressive behavior is direct reinforcement and punishment. Children learn that they can play with the most desirable toys in preschool if they respond aggressively to classmates' requests for sharing. Hit men know that they get paid only if they successfully murder their victims.

But reinforcement for aggression also comes in indirect ways. Social psychologist Albert Bandura is one of the strongest advocates of social learning explanations of aggression. He suggests that a primary means of learning aggressive behavior comes from models (Bandura, 1973, 1983). **Models** are people whose behavior can be imitated and who provide a guide to appropriate behavior.

**models**
people whose behavior can be imitated and who provide a guide to appropriate behavior.

A long roster of experiments has demonstrated that exposure to an aggressive model leads observers to exhibit heightened aggression, especially if the observers are angered, insulted, or frustrated. For instance, Bandura demonstrated the power of models in a classic study of nursery-school-age children (Bandura, Ross, & Ross, 1963). One group of children watched an adult play violently and aggressively with a Bobo doll (a large, inflatable plastic dummy that always returns to an upright position after being pushed down). In contrast, children in another condition watched an adult play sedately with a set of Tinker Toys.

Later, the children were permitted to play with a number of toys, which included both the Bobo doll and the Tinker Toys. But first the children were made to feel frustration by being refused the opportunity to play with a favorite toy. As social learning theory would predict, the children modeled the behavior of the adult. Those who had seen the violent model play with the Bobo doll were considerably more aggressive than those who watched the placid model playing with Tinker Toys.

Subsequent research has shown that people are most likely to imitate aggression when models are seen to be rewarded for their aggressive behavior (Bandura, 1973). And even if they don't immediately exhibit the same aggressive behavior they have just observed, they learn something about the permissibility of violence in society (Donnerstein & Donnerstein, 1978). Consequently, as we'll discuss in detail in Chapter 9, media portrayals of violence, whether actual or fictionalized, can have a powerful impact on the subsequent behavior of viewers of aggression (Liebert, 1975; Wood, Wong, & Chachere, 1991).

The upside of the social learning approach to aggression is that observation of *non*aggressive models can *reduce* aggression. We don't learn from others only how to be aggressive; we can also learn ways of avoiding confrontations. Similarly, we can directly teach nonviolence. Hence, just as social learning theories of aggression suggest that rewards and punishments are at the heart of aggressive behavior, they also suggest that these same factors are central to nonaggression.

**REJECTING THE NATURE–NURTURE DICHOTOMY.**  It is tempting to try to attribute the causes of aggression to either nature or nurture. It is also wrong.

Just as it is overly simplistic to suggest that aggression stems solely from an instinct to behave aggressively, it is also unlikely that all aggressive behavior is learned. Instead, the truth lies somewhere in between. Inborn, genetic factors—nature—certainly may lead us to behave aggressively in certain situations. Whether or not we actually do so, though, depends in part on what we have learned about the appropriateness of aggressive displays within a given context. Further, society teaches us how to restrain our aggression. The degree to which we've learned such lessons factors into whether or not we'll act aggressively in a particular situation. In sum, both nature and nurture work as partners in determining our aggressive behavior (Nelson, 1974; Reiss, 1984).

We'll turn now from the consideration of the origins of aggression to some specific situational factors that affect aggression.

---

## ▶ REVIEW & RETHINK

### Review

- Aggression is a difficult concept to define.
- Instinctual and sociobiological approaches to aggression consider aggression to have innate components.
- Social learning approaches suggest that aggression is learned through the observation of models.

### Rethink

- Consider the five acts described in our initial discussion of how to define aggression. Identify which ones you would intuitively classify as aggressive. How difficult would it be to reach a consensus with your classmates on a definition of aggression?
- Why is the notion of intent important for definitions of aggression? What difficulties does the notion of intent pose for research psychologists?
- How might philosopher John Locke explain the observed relationship between hormones and aggression? How would Thomas Hobbes explain this relationship?
- Many theories of aggression are based in part on the behavior of animals other than humans. What dangers does this methodology carry? On the other hand, why is this type of research necessary?

---

*The*
*Frustration–Aggression*
*Link*

You've stopped at a traffic light that seems never to change. The day is unbearably hot, without a sign of a breeze at all, and the trip home, which is supposed to take ten minutes, has turned into a 45-minute ride in stop-and-go traffic. Finally, the light turns green, and as you're about to proceed through the intersection, another car cuts you off. You slam on your brakes, and the car behind you nearly smashes into you. As you inch forward, the light turns red again, and you have to wait at the light all over again. You reach the breaking point, and start swearing. You turn on your radio, and you turn the knob so hard that it comes off. That's it: You take the knob and throw it out of the car window as hard as you can.

For anyone who has ever been in this kind of situation, there is little need to explain what you feel: extreme frustration. And it is also not hard to guess how close to physical violence such frustration brings you.

**frustration–aggression hypothesis**
the notion that frustration always leads to aggression of some sort, and that aggression is always the result of some form of frustration.

**frustration**
the thwarting or blocking of some ongoing behavior directed toward a desired goal.

**THE FRUSTRATION–AGGRESSION HYPOTHESIS.**    According to one of the most influential and durable explanations for human aggression, your frustration would likely boil over. As initially formulated, the **frustration–aggression hypothesis** states that frustration always leads to aggression of some sort, and that aggression is *always* the result of some form of frustration (Dollard et al., 1939). In this context, **frustration** refers to the thwarting or blocking of some ongoing behavior directed toward a desired goal.

The frustration–aggression hypothesis has largely stood the test of time, although—as you'd expect with a formulation more than 50 years old—it has undergone considerable revision. Most importantly, we now know that the links between frustration and aggression are much weaker than originally proposed: Frustration does not inevitably produce aggression, and aggression is not invariably preceded by frustration (Berkowitz, 1989).

**AGGRESSIVE CUES AND AGGRESSION.**    What frustration does lead to is a readiness to act aggressively, due to the presence of anger that is produced by frustration. Whether or not an individual responds aggressively depends on the presence, or absence, of aggressive cues that trigger the actual aggressive behavior. **Aggressive cues** are learned stimuli that have previously been associated with aggression (Berkowitz, 1984; Carlson, Marcus-Newhall, & Miller, 1990).

How might aggressive cues lead to aggression? One answer comes from a clever study in which subjects met a confederate who in one condition deliberately angered them, or in another condition acted neutrally toward them (Berkowitz & Geen, 1966). Subjects then watched an excerpt from the movie *Champion*, a violent boxing film starring Kirk Douglas. Following this interlude, the subjects were led to believe that they could give shocks of varying numbers to the confederate, as part of a procedure designed to study learning processes.

The major experimental manipulation came in the form of the confederate's supposed name: In one condition, he was named "Bob," while in the other he was called "Kirk." These names were not chosen at random. Instead, the confederate named Kirk was meant to act as an aggressive cue because of the name's association with Kirk Douglas, the boxer in the film. "Bob," on the other hand, was designed to be a neutral cue, unrelated to the aggression in the film.

If the modified frustration–aggression hypothesis were correct, we would first expect to see a difference in aggression displayed toward the confederate based on whether the subject had first been angered, and this was the case. Subjects who had been first angered by the confederate gave him considerably more shocks than those who had not been first angered.

But a second finding helped clarify that aggressive cues can be crucial in bringing about aggression: When the confederate was named Kirk, he acted as a lightning rod for aggression, receiving significantly more shocks than when he was named the neutral Bob. (Kirks of the world, beware.)

More vivid reminders of aggression than hearing a name associated with prior aggressive behavior may be significantly more potent aggressive cues. For instance, the mere sight of weapons may function as an aggressive cue (Berkowitz & LePage, 1967; da Gloria et al., 1989). Research supports the contention that people become more aggressive after viewing a gun, even if the gun is simply sitting on a shelf, unused. Furthermore, studies have shown that even the anger produced by viewing a sports team losing an important game is enough to produce aggression. Homicides rise abruptly and disproportionately in cities whose professional football team has lost a playoff game. The apparent reason: The loss of the game produces frustration, which leads to a readiness to aggress. Because urban environments contain abundant aggressive cues, the readiness to aggress boils over into actual aggression of the most deadly variety (White, 1989).

**COGNITIVE ASSOCIATIONS: THE THOUGHTS BEHIND AGGRESSION.**    The most recent reinterpretation of the frustration–aggression model suggests that frustration produces aggression only to the extent that the frustration produces negative feelings. According to Leonard Berkowitz, it is not frustration per se that leads to aggression; instead, it is the negative affect that the frustration evokes (Berkowitz, 1989, 1990).

In his **cognitive neoassociationistic model**, Berkowitz argues that aversive circumstances produce negative affect in the form of anger, hostility, or irritation. These feelings then activate particular patterns of cognitions or memories related to prior experiences with aggression, as well as the physiological reactions associated with them.

The result of all this cognitive activity? It depends. If environmental cues support aggressive action—such as the presence of weapons or others who are acting aggres-

**aggressive cues**
learned stimuli that have previously been associated with aggression.

**cognitive neoassociationistic model**
the argument put forth by Berkowitz that aversive circumstances produce negative affect in the form of anger, hostility, or irritation.

sively—thoughts and memories conducive to aggression may be brought to mind, and aggression may result. On the other hand, a network of thoughts may be aroused that is inconsistent with aggression, by cues such as the presence of people who are acting peacefully. In such a case, the network of thoughts aroused can lead to a reduction in aggression.

## Facets of the Social Environment That Lead to Aggression

If you saw the movie *Body Heat*, you know that a central theme of this evocative film is the murderous aggression that lies just beneath the surface of the suffocatingly hot Florida climate. Do high temperatures, in fact, lead to aggression? And do other factors of the environment, both physical and social, result in aggression? We'll consider several possibilities.

**PHYSICAL AROUSAL AND AGGRESSION: DOES SWEAT LEAD TO SWAT?**  What do exercise, sexual arousal, anger, and fear have in common? Under the right circumstances, each of them can lead to aggression, for the same reason: physical arousal. According to the **excitation transfer model**, physiological arousal acts to intensify subsequent emotional experiences, even if they are unrelated to the initial arousal (see Figure 8-8). Thus, if people are angered or frustrated while in a state of physiological arousal, these experiences

**excitation transfer model**
a situation in which physiological arousal acts to intensify subsequent emotional experiences, even if they are unrelated to the initial arousal.

**FIGURE 8-8   Excitation Transfer Model** According to the excitation transfer model, physiological arousal acts to intensify subsequent emotional experiences. However, the extent to which the arousal will lead to aggression depends on what the arousal is attributed to.   *(Source:* Based on Zillman, 1983.*)*

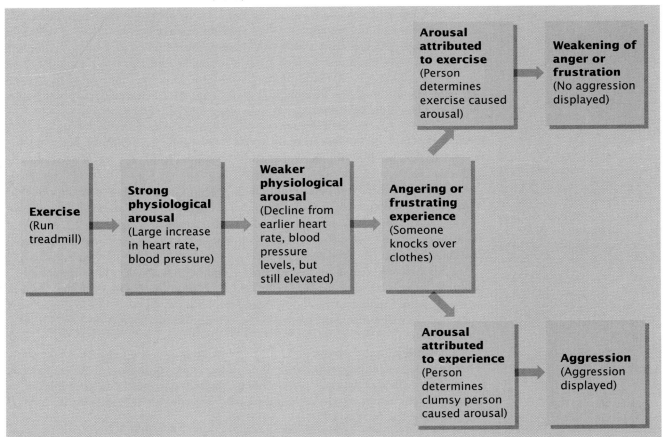

are apt to make them lash out with higher levels of aggression than if they are not in a state of arousal. However, such arousal will intensify aggression only to the extent that arousal is attributed to the angering or frustrating experience. If the arousal is attributed to an initial, neutral source, then aggression is unlikely (Zillman, Hoyt, & Day, 1974; Zillman, 1983, 1988).

Consider the consequences of exercise, for instance. After exercising, people experience a number of dramatic physiological changes. Their heartbeat rises, their respiration rate increases, and they sweat more, for starters. Although these physiological responses begin to calm following exercise, they don't disappear immediately. Instead, there is a residue of arousal, which may last for many minutes until the body has returned to its prearousal state.

It is during this period of mild arousal that people are susceptible to aggression. For instance, if someone frustrates or angers them and they attribute their arousal to the source of the anger, they will be predisposed to act aggressively. However, if they attribute the arousal to its true source—the earlier exercise—they'll be unlikely to behave aggressively. Moreover, if they are not angered in the first place, the arousal will simply dissipate, and no aggression will occur (Zillman, Katcher, & Milavsky, 1972; Zillman, 1988).

For example, suppose you've just completed a rigorous exercise routine at the health club and are now dressing in the locker room. Someone clumsily knocks your clothes on the floor and into a puddle of water. Your heightened physiological arousal due to the exercise may well turn your anger into aggression, but only if you attribute the arousal to the clumsy person. If you are aware that your heightened arousal is due to the previous exercise, you'll be less likely to act aggressively.

Sexual arousal seems to have a similar effect on aggression, although the relationship is more complex. Mild forms of sexual arousal result in relatively little aggression, primarily because the arousal acts as a pleasant distraction from angering or frustrating events. In fact, mild sexual arousal sometimes leads to lower levels of aggression than when there is no arousal present. However, stronger levels of sexual arousal can result in heightened aggression, consistent with other findings from the excitation transfer model.

In sum, very low and very high levels of sexual arousal result in the most aggression, while mild levels of arousal produce less aggression. The links between sex and aggression are not simple, as we will discover in Chapter 9 when we discuss pornography and aggression (Zillman, 1984).

**ENVIRONMENTAL STRESS: THE HEAT OF AGGRESSION.** The term "heat of anger" reflects the widely held belief that high temperatures are related to the display of aggression. Is this notion well founded?

Partially. According to social psychologist Robert Baron's **negative affect model of aggression**, high temperatures, as well as other aversive stimuli in the environment, can lead to higher aggression—but only up to a point (Baron & Ransberger, 1978). When the weather gets too hot, people become either immobilized or flee to cooler surroundings. Aggression becomes too costly to pursue.

Although appealing as a theory, Baron's model has not always been supported by experimental research. For instance, one field study that investigated the incidence of aggressive crimes such as rape and murder over a two-year period in Houston, Texas found that the higher the temperature, the more crime occurred (Anderson & Anderson, 1984; Anderson, 1989). There was no hint of a decline in aggression when it became intolerably hot (and the weather in Houston provides quite a few instances of extremely hot weather). Similarly, another field study showed that during major league baseball games the number of baseball players hit by pitches—an indication of aggression—increased as the temperature rose, with no sign of decline in even the hottest weather (Reifman, Larrick, & Fein, 1991).

**negative affect model of aggression**
Baron's notion that high temperatures, as well as other aversive stimuli in the environment, can lead to higher aggression, but only up to a point.

Crowding and other aspects of the social environment may lead people to behave aggressively. For instance, the frenzied atmosphere at European soccer matches makes violence a fairly common occurrence.

Despite the mixed experimental support for Baron's negative affect model, it does seem reasonable that eventually the temperature will rise so high that aggression—or any other behavior involving physical activity—is unlikely. In sum, we have probably not heard the last word on the relationship between heat and aggression (Anderson & De-Neve, 1992; Bell, 1992).

Other environmental factors have been implicated in aggression. Crowding produces higher levels of aggression, both in humans and in animals (Fisher, Bell, & Baum, 1984). Similarly, subtle modifications in air quality, such as changes in the level of negative ions in the air, can promote the display of aggressive behavior (Baron, Russell, & Arms, 1984). In fact, air pollution in general produces a rise in aggression (Rotton & Frey, 1985).

**PROVOCATION AS A SOURCE OF AGGRESSION: HURT ME AND I'LL HURT YOU.**    During an NCAA basketball playoff game, Duke University star Christian Laettner deliberately stepped on the chest of an opponent who had fallen to the ground. Although the reason for his behavior remained something of a puzzle—Laettner said it was just part of the game—we can guess the feelings of the player at the receiving end of the aggression: an urge to strike back at Laettner.

Indeed, physical aggression often begets a physical response. When people are physically hurting, they respond with aggression toward the source of the pain. Further, as social learning theory predicts, they tend to match their level of retaliatory aggression to the level of pain they have received (Taylor & Pisano, 1971; Jaffe & Yinon, 1979). The same kind of norm of reciprocity that we discussed earlier in reference to helping behavior may be operating here: People feel that it is permissible to reciprocate aggression that is directed toward them (Dengerink & Covey, 1983).

In some cases, people even carry out anticipatory aggression if they believe that someone is planning to be aggressive toward them at some future time (Greenwell & Dengerink, 1973; Donnerstein & Donnerstein, 1977). Obviously, people's aggression toward those who provoke them is not just an automatic, unthinking response. Instead, they may think through and carefully engineer their aggression in advance. It is clear that members of our society take seriously the Biblical dictum "an eye for an eye, a tooth for a tooth."

# THE INFORMED CONSUMER OF SOCIAL PSYCHOLOGY:

## DEALING WITH ANGER

When angry, count ten before you speak; if very angry, count to one hundred.
—Thomas Jefferson
When angry, count four; when very angry, swear.
—Mark Twain

Whether you count to ten, one hundred, or four (or swear, for that matter), anger is a psychological state with which most people have to deal. Indeed, most adults experience the emotion of anger considerably more often than they express overt aggression (Wyer & Srull, 1993).

Although you may suspect that the best response to anger is to ignore it, a considerable amount of data suggest otherwise. As we discussed in Chapter 5, people who consistently suppress their anger may develop a variety of adverse reactions—physical illness, self-condemnation, and psychological dysfunction (Julius, 1990; Pennebaker, 1990).

If unexpressed anger has such negative consequences, what is the best way to deal with the emotion effectively? According to psychologists who have studied the issue, several approaches are useful (Pennebaker, 1990; Zillman, 1993). These are among the strategies that you can follow:

- *Fantasize.* One safety valve is to act out in your mind your hostilities toward others. By thinking through what you might do, you at least are able to cognitively experience the satisfaction you might feel if you let yourself go and showed your true feelings.

- *Empathize with the people who are producing the anger.* By trying to see a situation from their point of view, you may come to understand their behavior better, thereby dissipating your anger.

- *Diminish the importance of the situation.* Anger often occurs when you overrate how vital a situation is. Does it really matter that someone cut in front of you in a line or took a parking place for which you were waiting? By placing a situation into perspective, you may reduce the anger you experience.

- *Write about your feelings.* People who write about unexpressed negative emotions such as anger avoid the unpleasant outcomes of emotional repression. Keeping a journal, in which you describe your feelings of anger, may be helpful in preventing some of the negative consequences of anger.

- *Express your anger—appropriately.* Although screaming at the source of your anger may make you feel better temporarily, such a display of anger rarely has lasting effects. Instead, a better strategy is to use constructive anger, in which you express anger in a way that takes into account the self-respect of the person provoking you. By calmly informing someone in a nonthreatening manner that their actions make you feel angry, you stand a chance of changing their behavior—and reducing your own anger at the same time.

## ► REVIEW & RETHINK

### Review

- The frustration–aggression hypothesis suggests that frustration leads to a readiness to act aggressively.
- The excitation transfer model argues that aggression may be heightened by physical arousal.
- Negative affect can result in aggression.

### Rethink

- In what ways is the nature–nurture dichotomy in the study of aggression misleading? How might this way of looking at causes of aggressive behavior still be useful?
- What is the relationship between anger and aggression, and between frustration and anger?
- Explain the frustration–aggression hypothesis as originally developed some 50 years ago. Compare this hypothesis with the cognitive neoassociationistic theory.
- Violent crime rates are much higher in the summer months than in any other season. How might the excitation transfer model explain this phenomenon? What explanation does the negative affect model provide?

# LOOKING BACK    ◄ ◄ ◄ ◄ ◄ ◄ ◄ ◄ ◄ ◄ ◄ ◄ ◄ ◄ ◄ ◄ ◄ ◄ ◄ ◄ ◄ ◄ ◄ ◄ ◄ ◄ ◄

### *What is prosocial behavior, and how is it exhibited in emergencies?*

1. Prosocial behavior is helping behavior that benefits others. Although diffusion of responsibility—the tendency for people to feel that responsibility for acting is shared among those present—discourages helping, other factors do lead people to help. Among the steps that take place in helping in emergencies are: noticing a person, event, or situation that potentially may require help; interpreting the event as one that requires help; assuming responsibility; deciding how to provide assistance; and actually helping.

2. One source of debate is whether altruism—helping behavior that is beneficial to others but requires self-sacrifice—actually exists. Rewards–costs analyses of helping suggest that there may always be some reward inherent in any act of helping.

### *Are there personality characteristics that lead to consistent helping behavior?*

3. The question of whether some people have an altruistic personality—a set of dispositional characteristics that lead them to consistently act helpfully—is also an open one. However, most research suggests that people do not behave invariably altruistically, although there are gender and cross-cultural differences in helping behavior.

### *How do empathy, emotions, and norms affect helping?*

4. Although some researchers suggest that people are largely egoistic, or motivated by self-benefit, some suggest that altruism can occur when people experience empathy for needy persons. Empathy is an emotional response corresponding to the current emotions of another person. According to the empathy–altruism hypothesis, experiencing empathy motivates us to help the needy person in order to reduce his or her distress, rather than in order to reduce our own personal concerns.

5. The attributional model of helping and emotions suggests that uncertainty related to a person in need leads to an increase in arousal. When people attribute the need for help to internal, controllable causes, it will result in negative emotions; when they attribute the need to external, uncontrollable causes, the emotion will be positive. Negative emotions discourage helping, while positive ones increase the possibility of helping.

6. People in a good mood are more likely to help than those in a neutral mood. On the other hand, being in a bad mood does not necessarily produce a decrease in helping. According to the negative state relief model, people in a bad mood may be helpful if they think that their mood will be improved by helping. In contrast, if they perceive that helping will not improve their mood, they will be unmotivated to help.

7. Underlying helping behavior are several norms, societal standards or expectations regarding appropriate behavior. The norm of social responsibility suggests that people should respond to the reasonable needs of others. The norm of reciprocity states that we should help others because they have helped us in the past or may help us in the future. Finally, individuals have personal norms, their own sense of obligation to help a specific person in a specific situation. Some norms deter helping, such as the norm of noninvolvement.

### *What is aggression?*

8. Although some experts on aggression reject a definition based on intention, most suggest that aggression is most usefully viewed as intentional injury or harm to another individual.

### *What are the roots of aggressive behavior?*

9. Several approaches seek to identify the roots of aggression. For example, Freud and Lorenz saw aggression as instinctual. The most recent advocates of instinctual views of aggression are sociobiologists, who examine the biological roots of aggression. In contrast, social learn-

ing theorists suggest that aggression is largely learned through the observation and imitation of aggressive models. Most experts on aggression reject the either–or view of the nature–nurture argument, suggesting that both factors work together to produce aggression.

**10.** One of the most enduring explanations of aggression is the frustration–aggression hypothesis. Originally, it suggested that frustration always leads to aggression of some sort, and that aggression is always the consequence of frustration. More recent formulations suggest that frustration leads to a readiness to act aggressively; if aggressive cues are present, the aggression is more likely to actually occur. The cognitive neoassociationistic view suggests that frustration produces aggression only to the extent that the frustration produces negative feelings.

### What social and situational factors lead to aggression?

**11.** According to the excitation transfer model, physical arousal may intensify later emotional experiences. Consequently, if people are angered or frustrated while in a state of physiological arousal, aggression may be higher due to the earlier arousal.

**12.** The negative affect model of aggression suggests that high temperatures (as well as other unpleasant features of the environment) can lead to aggression, at least up to a point. However, if conditions become too extreme, aggression becomes too costly a behavior in which to engage. Although the experimental support for the model is mixed, other environmental factors, such as crowding, air quality, and noise, foster the display of aggression.

**13.** Physical aggression directed toward a person is often met with retaliatory aggression. In some cases, people even carry out anticipatory aggression if they believe that they will be the targets of future aggression.

# KEY TERMS AND CONCEPTS

*prosocial behavior (p. 245)*

*aggression (p. 245)*

*diffusion of responsibility (p. 247)*

*pluralistic ignorance (p. 248)*

*confusion of responsibility (p.249)*

*altruism (p. 250)*

*altruistic personality (p. 251)*

*empathy (p. 252)*

*empathy–altruism hypothesis (p. 252)*

*egoism (p. 252)*

*negative-state relief (NSR) model (p. 252)*

*attributional model of helping and emotions (p. 254)*

*norms (p. 256)*

*norm of social responsibility (p. 257)*

*norm of reciprocity (p. 257)*

*personal norms (p. 257)*

*norm of noninvolvement (p. 258)*

*thanatos (p. 263)*

*catharsis (p. 263)*

*sociobiology (p. 264)*

*social learning theory (p. 266)*

*models (p. 266)*

*frustration–aggression hypothesis (p. 267)*

*frustration (p. 267)*

*aggressive cues (p. 268)*

*cognitive neoassociationistic model (p. 268)*

*excitation transfer model (p. 269)*

*negative affect model of aggression (p. 270)*

# FOR FURTHER RESEARCH AND STUDY

Berkowitz, L. (1993). *Aggression: Its causes, consequences, and control.* New York: McGraw-Hill.

Two excellent overviews of the topic of aggression, both interesting and complete.

Latané, B., & Darley, J. M. (1970). *The unresponsive bystander: Why doesn't he help?* Englewood Cliffs, NJ: Prentice Hall.

A classic, covering the program of research that is central to our understanding of helping in emergency situations.

Hunt, M. (1990). *The compassionate beast: What science is discovering about the humane side of humankind.* New York: Morrow.

Baron, R. A., & Richardson, D. R. (1994). *Human aggression* (2nd ed.). New York: Plenum.

Kohn, A. (1990). *The brighter side of human nature: Altruism and empathy in everyday life.* New York: Basic Books.

Two journalists write about the positive side of human behavior.

Staub, E. (1989). *The roots of evil: The origins of genocide and other group violence.* Cambridge, England: Cambridge University Press.

The author analyzes the forces that lead efforts to systematically exterminate various groups of people.

# EPILOGUE

As we've seen, the roots of helping and of aggression are multifaceted. In considering the variety of complex explanations for these behaviors, it is clear that both helping and aggression are brought about not just by one simple cause, but by a variety of factors operating jointly. Indeed, some of the same social psychological processes underlie both aggression and helping. For instance, social learning theory can be employed to explain both how we learn to be helpful and how we learn to act aggressively.

If the same underlying processes can lead to such very different outcomes, we're left with a vexing question: How do we, as members of society seeking to build a better world, promote desirable social behaviors such as helping and, at the same time, deter unwanted aggressive behavior? We'll consider that issue in the next chapter, which seeks to explain what social psychologists know about how to foster and promote socially responsible behavior.

# CHAPTER NINE

# PROMOTING SOCIALLY RESPONSIBLE BEHAVIOR

## INCREASING HELPING AND REDUCING AGGRESSION

# PROLOGUE: HIDDEN VIOLENCE

O. J. and Nicole Simpson

Were it not for the person accused of killing her, the murder of Nicole Brown Simpson would probably have gone unnoticed by the public at large. She merely would have been one of the almost 5,000 women who are murdered each year in the United States, about one-third at the hands of their boyfriends or husbands.

However, because football and movie star O.J. Simpson was accused of her murder, her death became the focus of world-wide attention. The case received enormous publicity, and the picture of domestic violence that apparently was a part of the Simpsons' life was not a pretty one. Nicole Simpson had called the police eight times, alleging that she had been beaten. Simpson pleaded "no contest" to striking and threatening to kill his wife in 1989, accepting a fine of $700 and performing community service. On one occasion when his wife had called the police, O.J. Simpson urged that they leave, saying that the alleged violence was a "family matter."

## LOOKING AHEAD

▶ ▶ ▶ ▶ ▶ ▶ ▶ ▶ ▶ ▶ ▶ ▶ ▶ ▶ ▶ ▶ ▶ ▶ ▶ ▶ ▶ ▶ ▶ ▶ ▶ ▶

The ugly violence that took the life of Nicole Simpson represents just one of thousands of murders that occur in the United States each year. Moreover, such aggression is just the tip of the domestic iceberg: Violence occurs in some 25 percent of all marriages nationwide, and almost 15 percent of marriages include chronic, intense aggression.

The presence of such violence raises many questions. Why does aggression occur so often in our culture? Is violence an inevitable part of American society? Can aggression be supplanted with conduct that is more prosocial, behavior that improves, rather than detracts from, the quality of human interaction that people experience on a routine basis?

In this chapter, we consider the ways that aggression and helping behavior are reflected in our everyday lives. We discuss how the violence of our society impacts on our day-to-day experiences, and how such aggression and its consequences can be reduced and eliminated. In addition to examining how to curb aggression, we consider how to increase the incidence of prosocial behavior in our daily lives.

In our discussions, we'll be using both the terms aggression and violence. Although in many cases they are employed interchangeably, the formal definitions are slightly different. As you'll recall from Chapter 8, **aggression** refers to doing intentional injury or harm to another person. According to this definition, the injury or harm can be either physical or psychological. In contrast, **violence** is a deliberate attempt to carry out serious physical injury (Berkowitz, 1993). Violence, then, is solely physical.

We first discuss the effects of exposure to media violence, examining the extraordinary amounts of aggression to which most people are exposed. We then turn to a related issue: the consequences of exposure to media content that is both violent and sexually explicit.

Next, we examine violence that occurs behind the closed doors of people's homes. We look at the surprisingly high incidence of spouse abuse, and then focus on the factors that lead to child abuse. We consider how aggression is perpetuated from one generation to the next through a cycle of violence, and we consider sexual aggression in the form of

**aggression**
intentional injury or harm to another person.

**violence**
the deliberate attempt to carry out serious physical injury.

rape. We also examine large-scale, societal aggression considering collective violence, terrorism, and war.

Finally, we consider practices that are designed to increase prosocial behavior. We discuss how rewards and helpful models bring about increased prosocial behavior. We also speculate on the adequacy of methods for directly teaching moral behavior and moral reasoning.

In sum, after reading this chapter, you will have answers to these questions:

- Does exposure to media violence and pornography produce aggression in viewers?
- What is the incidence of family violence and rape?
- How can we reduce aggressive behavior?
- What are the factors that lead to societal-level aggression such as riots, terrorism, and war?
- How can we increase prosocial behavior?

## AGGRESSION IN EVERYDAY LIFE

At 8:00 P.M. on a typical Tuesday evening in a typical U.S. city, a person who wants to watch a movie on TV can choose from the following selection:

8 P.M. (WFXT) *Bad Boys*. A scar-faced street fighter becomes king of reform school and spots the guy who assaulted his girlfriend.

8 P.M. (WHLL) *The Contender*. A small-town Oregonian quits college to become a boxer.

8 P.M. (WNDS) *Sword of Gideon*. Five commandos avenge the massacre of Israeli athletes by terrorists at the 1972 Munich Olympics.

8 P.M. (WGOT) *Charley Hannah*. A Florida policeman befriends a wayward runaway boy while tracking down a band of killer teens. (*TV Week*, 1992)

This sampling provides a telling commentary about the state of the airwaves in the United States. It is hard for people to insulate themselves from aggression, whether real or fictitious. As we'll discuss, whether aggression is viewed through the lens of the media, or is observed in real-life situations such as in cases of family violence, exposure to aggression has a profound impact on people's lives.

*Media Aggression: Visions of Violence*

Between the ages of five and fifteen, the average American child is exposed to no fewer than 13,000 violent deaths on television. Almost two thirds of prime-time fictional dramas involve violence. Even Saturday morning shows, designed specifically for children, sport such titles as *G.I. Joe* and *Robo Cop* and contain lengthy sequences of aggression (Liebert & Sprafkin, 1988).

In fact, a study of children's television in the early 1990s showed that the number of violent acts per hour on children's programs averaged 32 per hour, and 74 percent of the characters were victims of violence (see Figure 9-1). Although there is some indication that there has been a decline in the amount of violence, the absolute level remains extraordinarily high (Gerbner et al., 1978; Freedman, 1984; Waters, 1993; Gerbner, Morgan, & Signorielli, 1993). Acknowledging this, the major TV networks have taken to providing a warning that alerts viewers when an upcoming program contains significent contains violence.

What are the consequences of viewing such heavy doses of violence? There is no simple answer, because of several complicating factors. For one thing, it is nearly impossible to design an experiment that would accurately determine the consequences of watching the massive amounts of media aggression to which children are exposed. Ideally, an experimenter would seek to compare children who are placed in a condition in which they watch large amounts of violence over a long period of time to those in a control condition in which the children are led to watch media violence in smaller doses. Obviously, though, such an experiment is both impractical and unethical, particularly if the hypothesis underlying the research is that exposure to media violence yields aggression.

Given the difficulties in conducting an actual experiment, investigators have turned to correlational studies, in which they assess and compare television viewing and aggressive behavior. Such studies are able to determine whether there is a relationship between viewing violent shows and subsequent aggression. However, like all correlational research, they cannot show that media violence *causes* later aggression. An alternative explanation is equally plausible—for example, that a person's interest in viewing aggressive media and subsequent aggressive behavior are both caused by some other factor,

**FIGURE 9-1  Violence on Television** Violence in television programs targeted for both children and adults occurs at high levels.    *(Source: George Gerbner, University of Pennsylvania.)*

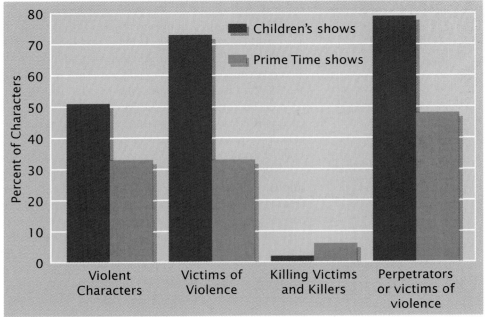

Although it is impossible to show unequivocally that viewing media depiction of aggression produces later aggressive behavior, correlational studies clearly show a significant link between observation of violence and later aggression.

such as educational level or socioeconomic status. Furthermore, the consequences of viewing media depictions of violence may be circular, with observation of violence affecting subsequent aggression, and aggressive individuals increasingly choosing to watch aggressive television shows and movies (Eron, 1982; Gunter, 1983; Huesmann, Lagerspetz, & Eron, 1984).

Despite their inability to demonstrate unequivocally that viewing media depictions of aggression produces subsequent aggressive behavior, correlational studies clearly show a significant link between observation of violence and later aggression. For example, one long-term project (dubbed the "Rip Van Winkle" study) extended for more than two decades. The study found that children who had watched more televised violence in their grade-school years showed relatively higher levels of aggression in adulthood then children exposed to lower levels of televised aggression (Eron et al., 1972; Eron & Huesmann, 1984).

However, the findings were far from universal: Some adults' aggression was unrelated to their early viewing patterns; and the findings were more accurate in predicting the behavior of males than of females. In addition, other researchers have found contradictory results, showing that early exposure is unrelated to later aggression (Milavsky et al., 1982). Overall, however, the correlational work, coupled with the experimental research on social learning of aggression conducted in laboratory settings (discussed in Chapter 8), leads to the conclusion—albeit still controversial—that a causal relationship between exposure to media violence and later aggression exists (Berkowitz, 1993; Comstock & Strasburger, 1990; Pierce, 1984; Huesmann & Miller, 1994).

Because of the difficulty of establishing causal relationships from correlational studies, researchers have begun to turn their experimental spotlights toward more focused questions. Rather than asking whether viewing violence leads to aggression, they have been attempting to discover the circumstances under which media violence is translated into actual aggression, and the specific causes that might produce a link between the observation of aggression and the enactment of aggression.

**WHY DOES OBSERVATION OF AGGRESSION PRODUCE AGGRESSION?**    What has become increasingly clear is that aggression following media exposure is not just a matter of simple imitation of aggressive acts. Rather, several mechanisms may be involved. For exam-

**normative approach (to media aggression)**
the notion that viewing media depictions can lead people to assume that aggression is a socially acceptable behavior.

ple, a **normative approach** to media aggression suggests that viewing media depictions can lead people to assume that aggression is socially acceptable behavior (Gunter, 1988; Thomas & Drabman, 1978). In some cases, observing aggression may actually teach people how to be aggressive in a particular manner. In one dismaying case, for instance, a group of men raped a young girl with a soda bottle, apparently in imitation of a similar incident in a television movie that had aired four days earlier. It seems unlikely that the perpetrators would have attempted such an unusual and specific act without having seen the movie (Phillips, 1982).

The normative approach suggests that people learn "scripts" for aggressive behavior. After a script has been learned—presumably through exposure to media violence—it may be recalled in some future situation, providing a guide for behavior. Individuals, then, may come to see aggression as a legitimate response within the context of a particular situation (Huesmann, 1986).

Why are aggressive scripts triggered in particular situations? Leonard Berkowitz's cognitive–neoassociationistic model, discussed first in Chapter 8, suggests an explanation. You will recall that this model proposes that aggressive stimuli may prime, or bring to mind, other thoughts and emotions that are linked to aggression (Berkowitz, 1984, 1993). In turn, these aggressive cognitive and emotional reactions to observed violence may ultimately lead to increased aggression on the part of the viewer (Bushman & Geen, 1990; Rule & Ferguson, 1986).

One example of this is the finding that even socially sanctioned violence—in this case, observation of a prize fight—may lead to increased aggression of other sorts. Specifically, one analysis of national homicide statistics found that during the period immediately following a nationally televised championship prize fight, the homicide rate bumped up slightly. (Nationally, about 12 more homicides occurred following each bout.) Although several explanations are possible, the results are consistent with the suggestion that observation of the fight led to thoughts and emotions related to violence, making viewers more prone to subsequent aggression (Phillips, 1986).

Further support for the notion that observation of violence begets violence comes from a five-nation study. Because different cultures have very different views of aggression, it seems reasonable that viewing violence might have different consequences depending on the country. To study this hypothesis, researchers conducted a three-year investigation in Australia, Finland, Israel, Poland, and the United States. Although the impact of observed aggression was not consistent, overall the most aggressive children tended to watch more television in general, were more likely to prefer violent programs, and were more likely to think that the violence on television was more lifelike (Huesmann & Eron, 1986).

But there were also some cultural differences. For example, TV viewing was minimally associated with children's aggression in Australia. Similarly, there was no relationship in Israel, at least for children who lived on a collective farm—a kibbutz. Although it is not certain why the Australians showed a less-pronounced link between media aggression and actual aggression, it seems plausible that the Israeli kibbutz-dwellers' lower aggression was due to the fact that they watched relatively little TV. Furthermore, when they did watch violent shows, there was apt to be a group discussion regarding the implications of aggression for society—something that occurred regularly in no other society. Clearly, then, the cultural context regarding aggression plays an important role in determining the effects of aggression.

In addition to fostering societal norms about displays of aggression, observation of aggression may also produce another result: an inaccurate view of the world and a consequent rise in concern about one's own personal safety (Morgan, 1983). For instance, frequent violence on television and in the movies may make people feel that their environment is more violent than it actually is (Wober, 1978). Indeed, children who watch higher-than-average levels of television tend to overestimate the number of violent crimes that actually occur. By creating the impression that a climate of violence exists, the media may actually cause higher levels of aggression to occur.

**attributional approach (to media aggression)**
the explanation that suggests that the conditions to which people attribute the aggression they observe have a significant effect upon their subsequent aggression.

Another explanation for the effects of observing media violence is attributional. The **attributional approach** to media aggression suggests that the conditions to which people attribute the aggression they observe have a significant effect upon their subsequent aggression. If people believe that a particular instance of aggression that they observe is justified, they are more likely to act aggressively than if they assume the aggressive act is unjustified or random (Berkowitz & Powers, 1979). For instance, in one experiment, subjects were shown actual news footage of a North Vietnamese soldier being stabbed to death by South Vietnamese soldiers (Meyer, 1972). Researchers varied the context of the killing: Some subjects were told that it represented retaliation for the victim's earlier atrocities against innocent civilians, while others were told it was a cold-blooded killing of a prisoner of war. Subjects were subsequently given the opportunity to behave aggressively. Those who thought the aggression represented legitimate retaliation were more aggressive than those who viewed it as unjustified.

**disinhibition hypothesis**
the suggestion that exposure to media violence reduces people's normal inhibitions against behaving aggressively.

Another explanation for the consequences of media aggression relies on the phenomenon of disinhibition. According to the **disinhibition hypothesis**, exposure to media violence reduces people's normal inhibitions against behaving aggressively (Drabman & Thomas, 1974). For instance, having previously viewed a film in which a mother slaps her child, a mother may feel less inhibited in acting out her own aggressive impulses when she has been frustrated and angered by her child. If she had not viewed the film, it is possible that the typical societal restraints that work to inhibit the enactment of violence would have been sufficiently strong to prevent her aggressive behavior.

**desensitization**
a reduction in the negative reaction to aggressive stimuli.

Finally, frequent exposure to media violence can produce **desensitization**—a reduction in the negative reaction to aggressive stimuli (Thomas et al., 1977; Geen & Donnerstein, 1983; Griffiths & Shuckford, 1989). After people consume a steady diet of brutality, the kind of stimuli that earlier might have repelled or disgusted them (and thereby diminished the likelihood of their acting aggressively) may eventually come to produce little or no reaction. One classic experiment confirmed this process: Viewers of a series of graphic puberty rites carried out in a primitive culture showed a marked decrease in stress by the time they viewed the fourth cut in a young boy's genitals (Lazarus et al., 1962). In the same way, soldiers often become accustomed to the death and injury that they encounter during the heat of battle; the violence eventually produces little reaction. As people become less sensitive to the meaning and consequences of aggression, it is logical to assume that they may feel more free to act aggressively themselves.

In sum, several explanations support the conclusion that observation of media violence is linked to subsequent aggression (summarized in Figure 9-2). However, regardless of the reason—and it is likely that there are multiple causes at work—it is clear that a

**FIGURE 9-2    Explanations for the Link Between Observation of Media Violence and Subsequent Aggression**

*Social Learning*

Aggressive behavior is imitated because of rewards the model receives.

*Normative Approach*

Viewing media depictions of aggression leads to the assumption that violence is socially acceptable.

*Attributional Approach*

The attributions regarding the reasons behind observed aggression are crucial. If aggression is seen as justified, it is more likely to be modeled.

*Disinhibition*

Exposure to media violence reduces people's normal inhibitions against behaving aggressively.

*Desensitization*

Observing aggression diminishes the negative reaction to aggressive stimuli.

steady diet of observed aggression has potentially severe consequences. And as we discuss next, when the media contain elements that are both aggressive and sexually explicit, the situation becomes even more complex.

**SEX AND AGGRESSION: THE CONSEQUENCES OF VIEWING VIOLENT PORNOGRAPHY.**   Consider the following scene:

> On a chilly Sunday evening as most of San Francisco settles in for supper, Annette Haven is sprawled across a desk in an unheated sound stage, naked and shivering. Haven and costar Jamie Gillis are entwined in the third sex scene of *A Coming of Angels—the Sequel.* The atmosphere is hardly erotic: a 35-mm camera on a dolly tracks the couple's labors from three feet away. A boom mike hovers inches above. After two hours of filming from every conceivable angle, the director is winding down. "Tight shot on your face, Jamie, and then we'll need a reaction from Annette," he calls out. "And, cut! Thank you very much, that's beautiful music." (Friendly, 1985, p. 62)

And so goes the filming of another in the hundred or so feature-length pornographic movies that are made each year. Each week, people purchase approximately two million tickets to X- or XXX-rated films. Moreover, movies are just one source of pornographic images; sexually explicit magazines and books have widespread distribution throughout the world.

The omnipresence of media depictions of sexual activity in our society raises several important issues. What are the results of exposure to pornographic material? Can the viewing of pornography result in aggression? Does the specific content of sexually explicit material lead to particular kinds of outcomes?

In attempting to answer these questions, social psychologists have found themselves in the midst of a thicket of issues, many of which are more political and moral than scientific. For instance, in the mid-1980s several social psychologists found themselves at odds with the findings of a commission on pornography formed by the U.S. attorney general (*Attorney General's Commission on Pornography,* 1986). In publishing rebuttals to the commission's findings—whose primary recommendation was to strengthen obscenity laws—the researchers argued that the focus ought to be on depictions of violence and aggression in all types of media, not only in pornography (Linz, Donnerstein, & Penrod, 1987).

In order to judge the issue ourselves, let's look at the research. Recall, as we discussed in the previous chapter, that viewing some types of sexually arousing material has been linked to increases in aggression. The excitation transfer model suggests that heightened physiological arousal can lead to higher levels of aggression. Because pornography can lead to sexual arousal, sexually explicit pornographic materials can lead to heightened aggression, depending on the level of arousal that the material produces (Zillman, 1984).

However, it turns out that a more critical factor in determining whether pornography produces aggression is whether the pornography links sexual material with violence. The evidence clearly suggests that violence against women portrayed in pornography leads to increased aggression (Demare, Briere, & Lips, 1988; Hui, 1986). For instance, in an experiment conducted by Edward Donnerstein and Leonard Berkowitz (1981), male participants were angered by either a male or female confederate and then were exposed to one of four different films. One depicted a neutral talk-show interview; one was a purely erotic film that contained no aggression; a third was a positive-outcome, aggressive, erotic movie (in which a woman was slapped and sexually attacked by two men but ended up smiling and apparently enjoying the experience); and the fourth was a negative-outcome, aggressive, erotic film (similar to the positive-outcome movie except for the ending, in which the woman appears to be suffering). After the film, subjects were given the opportunity to behave aggressively toward a male or female confederate.

The amount of aggression subjects later displayed toward women was clearly affected by the film that they had first viewed. Although aggression toward the male confederate differed little according to the film the subjects had seen, for subjects who had a female target, the story was different. The purely erotic film produced no more aggression than the neutral film; exposure to either the positive- or negative-outcome film produced a significant increase in aggression toward the female confederate. In sum, it was the combination of sex and aggression toward women that produced the most potent subsequent aggression.

Other research shows that long-term exposure to violent and sexually degrading depictions of women leads to emotional and physiological desensitization. For instance, people who were shown a series of R-rated violent "slasher" movies later showed less anxiety and depression when exposed to violence against women, and they demonstrated less sympathy toward victims of rape than people who saw a series of nonviolent films (Linz, Donnerstein, & Penrod, 1987; Linz, Donnerstein, & Adams, 1989).

Similarly, viewing films containing sexual violence against women leads to inaccurate attitudes and beliefs about rape. For instance, men exposed to violent pornography are more apt to subscribe to the dangerous (and completely misguided) myth that women enjoy being the victims of violent sexual assault (Malamuth & Check, 1985).

The data are clear in suggesting, then, that observing pornography that includes violent content increases the likelihood of actual aggression on the part of viewers. Furthermore, exposure to such material produces beliefs and attitudes that support the concept that sexual violence against women is permissible.

Do the links between pornography and aggression argue in favor of banning erotic material? The answer is complex, since it involves constitutional rights of free speech. One obstacle to finding a reasonable answer is the difficulty of defining what constitutes pornography and obscenity—a problem that has confounded lawmakers and courts for decades (Linz, Donnerstein, & Penrod, 1987). Another complication is the issue of who will be the judge of the vast array of sexually explicit material that is produced each year.

An even more important consideration is that the most negative consequences of exposure to erotic materials comes from those materials that contain a mixture of sex and violence. And such sexual, violent images are seen not only in pornography, but also in more common, easily accessible films, tapes, and books (Sherman & Dominick, 1986). For instance, one review of the covers of detective magazines revealed that three quarters of them showed women being dominated, and that more than one third showed women in bondage situations (Dietz, Harry, & Hazelwood, 1986). Such magazines are not usually considered pornographic or obscene in the traditional sense.

Similarly, it appears that explicit, hard-core pornographic films may represent less danger than the more common R-rated movies, which are often shown on cable television stations. In one recent analysis, R-rated films (which are restricted in movie theaters to those who are at least 17 years old unless accompanied by a parent) were compared with X- and XXX-rated movies (to which no one under age 18 is admitted). Not surprisingly, the percentage of sexual behaviors was far higher in the X-rated and XXX-rated movies (Yang & Linz, 1990).

However, the amount of violence was proportionately much greater in the R-rated movies than in those with X and XXX ratings (see Figure 9-3). More critically, the incidence of combinations of sex and violence was virtually the same in R-, X-, and XXX-rated movies. In addition, a careful analysis of the films found that, although sexually violent episodes lasted longer in X-rated movies, the percentage of aggressive, sexually explicit violence that was directed specifically toward women was higher in the R- than in the X-rated films. As a result, the unfavorable consequences of viewing depictions of sexual violence against women may be greater in R-rated movies than in X-rated films.

In sum, banning pornographic material, even that which contains violence, would make only a dent in the public's exposure to violent, sexually oriented material. Rather than trying to ban broad categories of material, a more practical approach may be to focus on measures that neutralize or reduce the impact of the almost inevitable exposure to media sexual violence (Donnerstein & Linz, 1986).

The negative consequences of viewing sexual violence may be greater from viewing R-rated films than X-rated movies, given that R-rated films contain higher levels of violence towards women.

One step in this direction has come from the television networks themselves, who recently began to broadcast warnings at the start of unusually violent programs. Similar alerts are now included in newspaper and magazine television listings. The warning, like those found on packages of cigarettes and in advertisements, states that "Due to some violent content, parental discretion is advised" (Waters, 1993).

Although the warning is mild, it may help parents deter their children from viewing programs that are particularly violent. At the same time, in many cases children watch television without parental supervision, and it is unlikely that children will be terribly motivated to turn off a show just because of such a warning.

In the end, the best approach to offsetting the effects of media violence is for parents and schools to teach their children to understand that media aggression is not real aggression. Furthermore, children need to be reminded that violence has real, harmful consequences, and that aggression is not the best way to deal with the frustrations of life—as we'll discuss later in the chapter when we consider ways of reducing aggression.

**FIGURE 9-3    Sex and Violence in R-rated, X-rated, and XXX-rated Movies** Although the proportion of sexual behavior was much higher in the X-rated movies than in the R-rated ones, violence was proportionately much higher in the R-rated movies. Furthermore, the proportion of sexual violence was similar across all three movie ratings.    *(Source:* Based on Yang & Linz, 1990.*)*

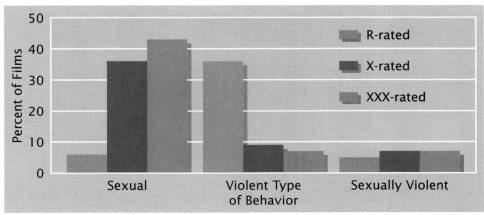

*Family Violence: At Home with Aggression*

She was a competent, articulate professional. A lawyer, she was known for the brilliant, vigorous arguments she made on behalf of her clients. Yet a few things were amiss: She wore long-sleeved, high-collared clothing in even the hottest weather. She also claimed to be unusually accident-prone, reporting that she sometimes tripped and bumped into doors and walls, bruising or scraping her face. Her apparent clumsiness became something of an office joke.

The truth, however, was no laughing matter. The lawyer was a victim of spousal abuse. She was terrorized by her husband, who, when drunk, lashed out at her brutally. She rationalized his behavior, saying that she loved him, and that he was perfectly well behaved most of the time. She blamed his aggression on his drinking and on her inability to meet his exacting standards. If only she could be a better wife, he wouldn't hit her so often.

One of the ugliest truths about family life is the prevalence of domestic violence. As many as two-thirds of high school and college students report that they have been the victims of some form of violence (Gelles & Cornell, 1990). The particular form of violence they have experienced runs the gamut from childhood sexual abuse, to parental beatings, to rape. No one is safe from abuse within the family—men and women, young and old, wives and husbands, children and parents.

**ABUSE OF SPOUSES AND CHILDREN.** Violence occurs in one quarter of all marriages, and between 20 and 30 percent of women who require emergency surgical interventions need it because of violence sustained at home. The presence of severe, continuing violence is characteristic of close to 15 percent of all marriages in the United States (Straus, Gelles, & Steinmetz, 1980; Straus & Gelles, 1990).

Spousal abuse occurs throughout all segments of society; no social class, race, ethnic group, or religious persuasion is immune to the possibility of violence at home. There are, though, certain factors that increase the likelihood of abuse. Lower socioeconomic status, a high level of verbal aggression, large family size, economic worries, and having grown up in a violent family are all associated with an increased risk of spousal violence (Straus & Gelles, 1990; Hampton et al., 1993).

The risk factors for abuse against spouses are not all that different from those involved in another form of family violence: child abuse. Child abuse is most common within families living in stressful environments, in lower socioeconomic classes, in single-parent families, and in families in which higher-than-average marital conflict occurs. It is also related to the presence of violence between spouses (Dodge, Bates, & Pettit, 1990; see Figure 9-4).

**FIGURE 9-4   Child Abuse** Types of child abuse.   *(Source:* American Humane Association, 1991.*)*

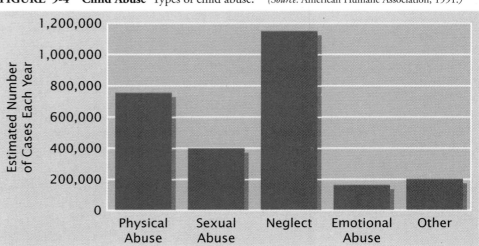

But certain characteristics of the child are also related to a higher incidence of child abuse. Children who are fussy, resistant to control, and have trouble adapting to new situations are more likely to be the recipients of abuse than those who show more relaxed, adaptable temperaments (Gil, 1970). This does not mean, of course, that such children somehow bring on the abuse and are deserving of it. Instead, such findings suggest that children with such characteristics are more at risk of being at the receiving end of familial violence.

Why are parents abusive? Most parents certainly don't intend to hurt their children. In fact, most abusers are surprised and dismayed at their own behavior, having unintentionally crossed the line into child abuse.

Part of the problem is the fuzzy demarcation between physical violence that our society deems permissible and that which is not. Society tells us that spanking a child is not only legal and acceptable, but even necessary at times, while beating a child is illegal and unacceptable. But the line between spanking and beating is typically not a clear one. (For indications of when child punishment crosses the line into abuse, see Figure 9-5).

Interestingly, other societies do not attempt to make such distinctions between different forms of violence. In Sweden, for instance, any form of physical punishment directed toward a child is illegal. Furthermore, in many countries—China is one example—physical punishment of children is rare (Kessen, 1979). In contrast, the U.S. culture, which values privacy and personal freedom, tolerates a high level of violence and creates a social climate in which child abuse occurs at very high levels (Steinberg, Belsky, & Meyer, 1991).

**THE CYCLE OF VIOLENCE.**    Does violence breed violence? Quite often, the answer is yes. Child abusers have often themselves suffered from abuse as children, leading to the notion that a cycle of violence exists. The **cycle of violence hypothesis** suggests that abusing and neglecting suffered by children lead them to be predisposed as adults to abuse and neglect their own children (Widom, 1989; Dodge, Bates, & Pettit, 1990).

According to the hypothesis, victims of abuse have learned from their childhood experiences that physical violence is an appropriate and acceptable form of discipline. In accordance with social learning theory, then, the cycle of violence is perpetuated as each generation learns to behave abusively through its participation in an abusive, violent family (Straus, Gelles, & Steinmetz, 1980; Feshbach, 1980).

**cycle of violence hypothesis**
the hypothesis suggesting that abuse and neglect suffered by children lead them to be predisposed as adults to abusing and neglecting their own children.

---

**FIGURE 9-5    What Are the Warning Signs of Child Abuse?**

Since child abuse is typically a secret crime, identifying the victims of abuse is particularly difficult. Still, there are several signs that indicate that a child is the victim of violence:

- Visible, serious injuries that have no reasonable explanation
- Bite or choke marks
- Burns from cigarettes or immersion in hot water
- A child who is in pain for no apparent reason
- A child who appears afraid of adults or care providers
- A child who is dressed inappropriately in warm weather (long sleeves, long pants, high-necked garments), thereby possibly concealing injuries to the neck, arms, and legs
- A child whose behavior is extreme—extremely aggressive, extremely passive, extremely withdrawn
- A child who is afraid of physical contact

If you suspect that a child is a victim of aggression, it is your responsibility to act. Call your local police or city or state department of social services. Talk to a teacher or clergyman. Remember that by acting decisively, you may literally save someone's life.

*Source:* Robbins, 1990.

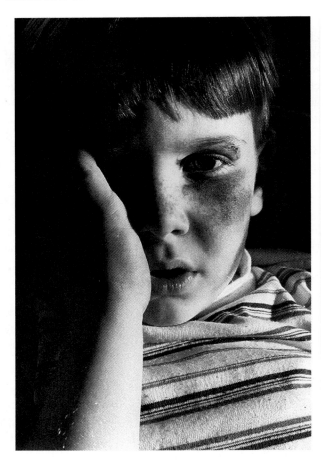

One of the causes of child abuse is the ambiguous message U.S. society sends about whether violence toward children is permissible. In other countries, such as Sweden, the line is clear: *any* physical punishment directed toward a child is illegal.

As the cycle of violence hypothesis would suggest, parents who have abused their children often have been raised in homes in which physical abuse occurred. On the other hand, being abused as a child does not inevitably lead to abuse of one's own children. In fact, statistics show that only about one third of those people who were abused or neglected as children abuse their own children; the remaining two thirds of abusers were not themselves abused as children. Clearly, then, we need to look at additional factors, beyond a history of abuse, to account for parents' violence toward their children (Kaufman & Zigler, 1987).

Even if victims of child abuse do not invariably act abusively to their own children, they do show a higher incidence of aggression in general. For example, psychologist Kenneth Dodge and colleagues examined a group of 46 children who had suffered abuse during some point of their lives prior to entering kindergarten (Dodge, Bates, & Petitt, 1990). In comparison to a group of nonabused peers, the abused children showed greater aggressive behaviors, as judged by their parents and their teachers. Even their classmates thought these children were more aggressive, classifying them as more likely to start fights, get angry, and act mean to others. Figure 9-6 shows the results of three separate measures of aggression: teacher ratings of aggression, peer perceptions of aggression, and direct observations of aggressive behavior.

In addition, the children who had been abused showed significant differences in the way they viewed the world. When considering social situations, they were more apt to attribute hostile intentions to others. They also devised less-acceptable solutions to social problems than children who had not been abused. In sum, abused children appeared less socially competent.

Clearly, living through the victimization of child abuse brings about numerous grim outcomes. Abuse goes far beyond immediate physical pain and injury; the harmful psychological effects can last a lifetime.

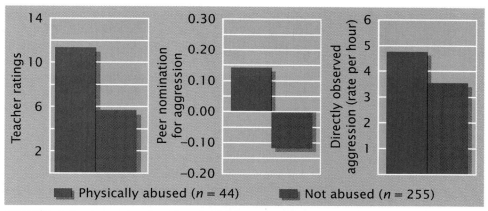

**FIGURE 9-6    Aggression in Abused Children** In comparison with a group of nonabused peers, abused children showed greater aggressive behaviors, as judged by their parents and their teachers.    *(Source:* Adapted from Dodge, Bates, & Petitt, 1990.*)*

*Rape: A Crime of Aggression*

**rape**

the act of one person forcing another to submit to sexual activity such as intercourse or oral-genital sex.

**date rape**

the act of rape that occurs on a first date, casual date, or involves a romantic acquaintance.

If you assume that rape is a crime involving sexual passion, think again: Rape has far less to do with sex than it does with aggression.

**Rape** occurs when one person forces another to submit to sexual activity, such as intercourse or oral-genital sex. Although typically it consists of a male assaulting a female, in fact the act may involve members of either sex.

Although rape is usually thought of as relatively rare and an act that is carried out by a stranger, the reality is different. Rape occurs fairly often, and statistically it is more likely to be committed by an acquaintance than by a stranger. For example, in one national survey conducted at 35 universities, one out of eight women reported having been raped. Of that group, about half said the rapists were first dates, casual dates, or romantic acquaintances—something that has come to be known as **date rape** (Sweet, 1985; Koss et al., 1988). Overall, a woman has a 26 percent chance of being raped at some time during her lifetime (Russell & Howell, 1983).

Women in certain segments of society appear to be more at risk for rape than others. For instance, in one survey, 25 percent of the African-American women reported being the victim of sexual assault at least once, while 20 percent of white women reported being victims of such assaults (Wyatt, 1992). Other ethnic groups also experience sexual assault at differing incidence levels, probably in part because of differences in cultural views of women and what is permissible sexual conduct (Sorenson & Siegel, 1992).

Who commits rape? In a survey of close to 3,000 college men, psychologist Mary Koss and colleagues found that more than 4 percent admitted to behaviors that fit the

Overall, one out of four women are victims of sexual assault during their lifetime.

legal criteria of rape, 3.3 percent said they had attempted rape, 7.7 percent said they had sexually coerced a woman, and more than 10 percent said they had forced or coerced sexual contact. Overall, some 25 percent of college men acknowledged that they had engaged in some form of sexual aggression (Koss et al., 1988).

Rape is often motivated not by sexual needs but as a way of demonstrating power and control over the victim. In other cases, the primary motivation is anger, often directed at women in general (Lisak & Roth, 1988; Gelman, 1990).

Rape is also motivated by the myth that it is both appropriate and desirable for men to seek out sex, and that sexual aggression is acceptable behavior. In this view, sex is a battle, with winners and losers, and violence is one way to obtain sex (Mosher & Anderson, 1986; Hamilton & Yee, 1990).

The groundless view that sexual coercion is acceptable is surprisingly widespread. For instance, in one study, high school students were given a list of circumstances and asked whether it was acceptable, under those conditions, for a man to hold a woman down and force sexual intercourse. Just 44 percent of the females and 24 percent of the males considered that no situation warranted forced sex; the remainder felt that under some conditions rape was acceptable, as can be seen in Figure 9-7 (Mahoney, 1983; White & Humphrey, 1991).

**FIGURE 9-7   OK to Rape?**   High school students felt it was permissible to force a woman to have sex under particular circumstances. Only a minority of men and women felt it was never permissible to use force.    *(Source:* Mahoney, 1983.*)*

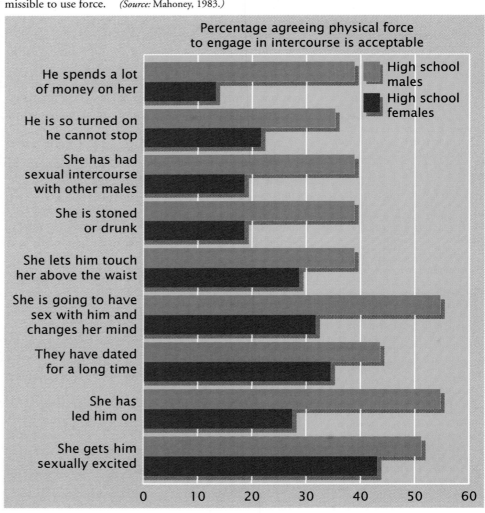

Misattributions can also explain some instances of rape, particularly in dating situations. For instance, the erroneous and harmful societal belief that a woman who says no to sex really doesn't mean it may result in misinterpretations that ultimately lead to rape (Muehlenhard & Hollabaugh, 1988). For example, consider these two perspectives on a case of date rape, reflecting very different explanations for the events:

> BOB: Patty and I were in the same statistics class together. She usually sat near me and was always very friendly. I liked her and thought maybe she liked me, too. Last Thursday I decided to find out. After class I suggested that she come to my place to study for midterms together. She agreed immediately, which was a good sign. That night everything seemed to go perfectly. We studied for a while and then took a break. I could tell that she liked me, and I was attracted to her. I was getting excited. I started kissing her. I could tell that she really liked it. We started touching each other and it felt really good. All of a sudden she pulled away and said "Stop." I figured she didn't want me to think that she was "easy" or "loose." A lot of girls think they have to say "no" at first. I knew once I showed her what a good time she could have, and that I would respect her in the morning, it would be OK. I just ignored her protests and eventually she stopped struggling. I think she liked it but afterwards she acted bummed out and cold. Who knows what her problem was?

> PATTY: I knew Bob from my statistics class. He's cute and we are both good at statistics, so when a tough midterm was scheduled, I was glad that he suggested we study together. It never occurred to me that it was anything except a study date. That night everything went fine at first, we got a lot of studying done in a short amount of time, so when he suggested we take a break I thought we deserved it. Well, all of a sudden he started acting really romantic and started kissing me. I liked the kissing but then he started touching me below the waist. I pulled away and tried to stop him but he didn't listen. After a while I stopped struggling; he was hurting me and I was scared. He was so much bigger and stronger than me. I couldn't believe it was happening to me. I didn't know what to do. He actually forced me to have sex with him. I guess looking back on it I should have screamed or done something besides trying to reason with him but it was so unexpected. I couldn't believe it was happening. I still can't believe it did. (Hughes & Sandler, 1987, p. 1)

Clearly, the two explanations reflect significant misinterpretations of the meaning behind the other person's behavior—with disastrous consequences. However, as we discuss next, there are several ways of reducing the risk of date rape.

---

# THE INFORMED CONSUMER OF SOCIAL PSYCHOLOGY

# REDUCING THE RISK OF DATE RAPE

Several guidelines, developed by university counseling centers, health services, and women's and men's groups, suggest ways in which men and women can form more accurate impressions and make more appropriate attributions about their dates' behavior. They include (American College Health Association, 1989; Goleman, 1989; Warshaw, 1988; Unger & Crawford, 1992; Hughes & Sandler, 1987):

- Set clear sexual limits. You should clearly articulate what your sexual limits are, and they should be communicated early on.
- Don't give mixed messages. Don't say "no" when you don't mean "no." Say "yes" if you mean "yes."

- Be assertive if someone is pressuring you. Don't worry about politeness. Remember that passivity may be taken for a sign of assent to further sexual activity.
- Be aware of risky situations. Remember that others may make unwarranted interpretations regarding your form of dress or behavior. Never assume that everyone holds the same sexual standards that you do.
- Remember that alcohol and drugs are often associated with date rape.
- Trust your feelings. If a situation seems dangerous or risky, or if you feel that you are being pressured, leave the situation or confront your date.

> # REVIEW & RETHINK

## Review

- A substantial link exists between observation of violence in the media and later aggression.
- Explanations for media effects on aggression include social learning, normative, attribution, disinhibition, and desensitization approaches.
- In addition to the cycle of violence hypothesis, other factors also account for violence in the family.
- Rape is a crime of aggression.

## Rethink

- What is the relationship between viewing televised violence and behaving aggressively? How can this relationship be explained?
- Why aren't social psychologists more certain about the long-term consequences of watching television and movie violence? What methodological difficulties do they face? What political difficulties do they face?
- Briefly describe the attributional, normative, and desensitization approaches to understanding the effects of being exposed to media portrayals of violence. Are any of these views mutually exclusive?
- What theory suggests that exposure to sexually explicit images is sufficient to increase aggression? According to this theory, would R-rated or X-rated movies incite more aggressive behavior by viewers?
- What family characteristics are related to a higher incidence of violent behavior within the family? Does the identification of personality traits associated with the likelihood of being abused justify the actions of the abusive parents?

# REDUCING AGGRESSION

*It hadn't been an easy day for eighth-grader Darryl Johnson. He had done poorly on his history midterm—much worse than he expected—and the girl he liked told him she would rather go shopping this weekend than go to the football game with him. To top it off, Darryl's boss at his part-time job had given him a harsh dressing-down the day before, telling him if he was late one more time, he'd be out of a job.*

*Consequently, when Jack Bobbin bumped into him in the hall—it wasn't clear whether it was on purpose or a mistake—Darryl was primed to retaliate. Unthinkingly, he turned on Jack, and punched him in the stomach. As Jack fell to the ground in pain, a teacher grabbed Darryl by the shoulder and took him to the principal, who promptly called his parents. "This isn't the first time Darryl's hit another student," the principal said. "Somehow, we've got to get his aggression under control."*

Similar scenes take place every day in schools throughout the United States. Dealing with aggression represents one of the major challenges facing not only educational institutions but society at large.

*Catharsis and Punishment*   Although no single means of controlling aggression has proven invariably effective, the various explanations of the phenomenon we discussed in Chapter 8 provide a guide to potential solutions to Darryl's aggression. Consider, for instance, an approach based on the notion of catharsis. As noted previously in discussions of the work of psychoanalyst Sigmund Freud and ethologist Konrad Lorenz, the notion of catharsis proposes that people experience a continual buildup of aggressive energy. The theory argues that if this pent-up energy is not discharged through some socially acceptable means—such as through physical exercise—it paves the way for undesirable episodes of aggression (Baron, 1983).

In theory, catharsis can occur in several ways. Some theorists, taking a psychoanalytic approach, suggest that hitting others with foam-covered bats, which actually produce no pain or injury to the victim, may have therapeutic results. The assumption underlying this therapy is that the tendency toward actual aggression will be reduced following such a session (Bach & Wyden, 1968; Feshbach, 1984; Tachibana, Ohgishi, & Monden, 1984).

Following the catharsis approach, we might suggest that Darryl participate in some sports activity that involves a good deal of violence, such as football or hockey. Additionally, we might recommend that Darryl be encouraged to watch violent films, which potentially could release his pent-up aggression in a more acceptable manner.

The idea of catharsis is appealing, because it suggests that permitting people to "let off steam" can reduce their subsequent penchant for violence. Despite its appeal, though, results of experiments investigating catharsis do little to buttress the claims of theorists (Quanty, 1976; Geen & Quanty, 1977; Fehr, 1979; Warren & Kurlychek, 1981). For example, studies have shown that high school football players are *more* aggressive after the football season than prior to it. Similarly, observation of sporting events is no guarantee of reduced aggression: One study of Canadian and American spectators of hockey, football, and wrestling matches found that people showed more hostility after viewing a contest than before it (Arms et al., 1979; Russell, 1983, 1985). In sum, little evidence exists supporting the catharsis notion.

Of course, social psychologists have identified other tactics that may be employed to control aggression. Consider, for example, the use of punishment. Punishment is actually one of society's favorite means for controlling aggression: Convictions for assaults, muggings, and rape lead to long prison terms, and in most parts of the world

Although the notion of catharsis suggests that participation in societally approved aggression can permit people to "let off steam," the research evidence suggests just the opposite. People are often more aggressive following participation in aggressive activities.

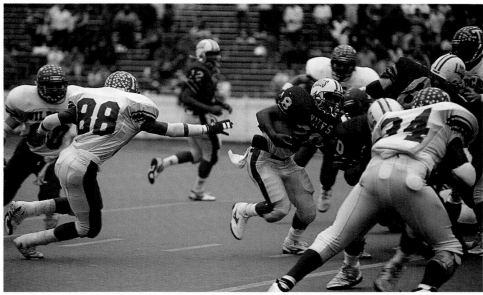

murder is punishable by death. On a lesser scale, it was not long ago that corporal punishment (the use of physical pain) was common in schools in the United States, and it is still legal in some jurisdictions. Spankings remain an established, and largely socially acceptable, child-rearing practice (Grasmick, Bursik, & Kimpel, 1991; Greydanus et al., 1992; Medway & Smircic, 1992; Graziano et al., 1992).

Despite the prevalence of punishment as a deterrent to aggression, its long-term effectiveness is highly questionable (Henson, 1985; Cryan, 1987; Mathis & Lampe, 1991). For one thing, physical punishments are likely to arouse anger in the recipient, and such anger is often a cause of aggression (as we discussed in the last chapter). In addition, the people who mete out the punishment might be perceived as aggressive models themselves, and thereby increase the likelihood of future aggression in others who are witnesses.

Furthermore, to those who administer punishment, it may seem to have positive results, since it usually leads to at least a temporary cessation of the aggressive behavior that is being punished. Consequently, people administering the punishment may become more likely to act aggressively themselves in the future—escalating the climate of violence.

Finally, the consequences of punishment are typically transitory. While punishment may temporarily prevent future violence, the decrease usually does not last (Sulzer-Azaroff & Mayer, 1991).

## Social Learning Approaches to Controlling Aggression

If aggressive models can lead observers to act aggressively, might not the observation of nonaggressive models produce a decline in aggression?

This reasonable question has received a clear, affirmative answer from a host of laboratory studies: The observation of nonaggressive models can, in fact, lead to a reduction in aggression. When people have seen a model act nonaggressively, they are subsequently less aggressive than if they have seen a model act aggressively (Baron & Kepner, 1970; Donnerstein & Donnerstein, 1977).

Despite the promise of these findings, however, the unfortunate reality is that the number of nonaggressive models present is often minimal in situations in which aggression is a likely response. Furthermore, the actions of aggressive models are considerably more conspicuous than the inactions of passive, nonviolent models. Because their behavior is relatively restrained and subdued, people who are behaving unaggressively are likely to be less prominent and eye-catching than those who are behaving aggressively. Thus, the likelihood is greater that the focus of attention will be on the aggressive models (Gunter & Furnham, 1986).

In spite of these obstacles to producing social learning from the behavior of nonaggressive models, this theoretical approach has spawned several powerful by-products with potential for reducing the impact of aggression (Hoberman, 1990). One of the most promising has been a program developed by social psychologists Rowell Huesmann and Leon Eron (Huesmann et al., 1983). Their basic strategy for reducing the influence of aggressive models is to modify how observers perceive the meaning and interpretation of aggressive acts.

Their procedure is straightforward and ingenious. Rather than being concerned with whether a model is behaving aggressively or nonaggressively, they teach observers that media violence represents an unrealistic portrayal of life. They also teach viewers that aggressive behaviors do not have the same degree of acceptability in the real world that they have on television and on film. Finally, they provide the message to viewers that modeling the aggressive behavior demonstrated by television and film characters is neither an appropriate nor warranted response to grievances. In sum, the clear, unmistakable message is that violence is an unsatisfactory way of behaving.

Is this message conveyed successfully? According to the results of several studies, trained observers of media violence do, in fact, come to modify their attitudes regarding aggression. For example, one experiment studied a group of first- and third-grade children who reported viewing high amounts of television aggression (Huesmann et al., 1983). In the initial phase of the study, the children attended three training sessions designed to teach that the behavior of the characters on violent shows does not represent the behavior of most people, that camera techniques and special effects provide only the illusion that aggression is occurring, and that most people use alternatives to aggression to solve their problems.

Nine months later, the children attended an additional training session. In this part of the study, they were explicitly taught that watching television violence was undesirable. The experimenters emphasized the importance of avoiding the imitation of the aggression.

The experimental program was a great success. Compared with a control group of children who received training on issues unrelated to aggression, those subjects taught to reinterpret the meaning of aggression were rated by their classmates as showing significantly lower aggression. In addition, the attitudes of program participants toward watching television aggression became decidedly more negative.

In sum, altering people's attitudes and interpretation of the meaning of observed aggression is an effective way to decrease the consequences of exposure to violence. Still, social learning theory suggests an even more direct way to reduce aggression: limiting exposure to aggressive models. If television and other media were to reduce the violent content of their programming, it seems reasonable to think that aggression on the part of viewers could be reduced.

## SOCIETY AND AGGRESSION: RIOTS, TERRORISM, AND WAR

*"They're robbing the market!" The news seared along The Block. A hundred manic looters surged past the Vermont Square Shopping Center. Some swung axes, others crowbars; some had lock cutters. They smashed the windows at the ABC Supermarket. They snapped the lock at Sunny Swap Meet. They piled into a pickup and tried to bash through the steel shutter at the Best Discount housewares store. Then they plunged into Tong's Tropical Fish store and ran out with boa constrictors, fish—even the turtles. When it was all over, one observer, eyes glinting, walked up to a Korean merchant studying the ruins. "Get out of here, motherf—," he shouted. "I'll burn your motherf— ass. I'll bring 'em back to burn your ass a second time!" (Hammer, 1992b, p. 40).*

Pure rage was unleashed in Los Angeles during the 1992 riots. Tearing the fabric of the city apart, causing dozens of deaths and hundreds of millions of dollars in property damage, the riots followed the announcement of a "not guilty" verdict for the white police officers accused of brutality in beating African-American Rodney King in Los Angeles. As we first discussed in Chapter 1, the jury's unexpected verdict, which confounded public anticipation of a guilty verdict, unleashed a wave of seemingly random violence that enveloped the city for days.

We live in a world that contains many forms of large-scale violence. Whether it be in the form of riots, terrorism, or all-out war, aggression appears to be a universal aspect of the human condition.

Or is it? Is senseless societal violence something we are destined to live with? We turn now from consideration of aggression on a personal level and turn instead to aggression on a more depersonalized, societal level. We'll consider three types of large-scale aggression that plague society—riots, terrorism, and war—discussing what social psy-

The riots that followed the acquittal of policemen who beat Rodney King left dozens of people dead and produced hundreds of millions of dollars in property damage.

chologists have learned about them and considering some of the ways that we might reduce their threat.

*Mobs and Rioting: Collective Violence*

**riot**
a violent public disorder created by groups of people.

**collective behavior**
a situation that occurs in groups of people who are relatively unorganized, yet hold a sense of unity and may work toward similar goals.

**emergent norm perspective**
the norm suggesting that a group definition of appropriate behavior arises in violent mobs.

**deindividuation**
the reduction of a person's sense of individuality and the corresponding increase in the willingness to engage in deviant behavior.

**Riots**, like the one that occurred in Los Angeles, are violent public disorders created by groups of people. Although riots initially appear to be composed of chaotic, unrelated acts of violence, their seemingly haphazard nature is only surface deep. The reality is that riots are considerably more organized than they at first appear. According to social psychologists who study large groups, rioting represents an example of **collective behavior** that occurs in groups of people who are relatively unorganized, yet who hold a sense of unity and may work toward similar goals.

One leading explanation of such collective behavior is known as the emergent norm perspective. The **emergent norm perspective** suggests that a group definition of appropriate behavior arises in violent mobs (Aguirre, Quarantelli, & Mendoza, 1988). Specifically, this theory suggests that when crowds form they are initially made up of heterogeneous people who do not necessarily share similar motivation and behavior. However, once in the situation people develop norms regarding appropriate behavior, and these norms are communicated to the other crowd members, as they observe others' conduct. Because of implicit pressures to conform to the norm, crowd members may behave in ways that are quite at odds with their typical conduct (Killian, 1980).

According to this explanation, rioting crowds in Los Angeles were not uniformly composed of individuals who were habitually aggressive and violent. Instead, rioters may have been everyday citizens who were vulnerable to the apparent emergent norm of violent behavior. How might such a norm emerge? Presumably, it would take only a few conspicuous acts of violence to provide the impression that a norm was developing in which aggressive acts were legitimate and permissible.

On the other hand, the emergent norm perspective does not explain why other norms—such as those supporting prosocial behavior—do not arise or prevail in crowd situations (McPhail, 1991). For example, a few conspicuous examples of heroism occurred during the Los Angeles riots. In one well-publicized case, several onlookers helped a truck driver, who had been pulled from the cab of his truck and beaten senseless by members of an angry mob. Their help enabled the driver to reach the safety of a hospital. It is unclear why these helpful models would not in turn create an emergent norm of helpfulness and nonaggression in the same way that the aggressive behavior triggered the norm of violence.

The shortcomings of the emergent norm perspective have led to the development of alternative explanations for mob violence (Mann, Newton, & Innes, 1982). According to the deindividuation approach, participation in crowds reduces individuals' concerns about being evaluated by others and about maintaining a positive social image. **Deindividuation** is the reduction of a person's sense of individuality and the corresponding increase in the willingness to engage in deviant behavior (Diener, 1980; Zimbardo, 1970).

According to the deindividuation approach, members of large groups feel anonymous and do not think of each other as individuals. Furthermore, their self-awareness becomes reduced as they focus on others and on events occurring around them.

In a sense, then, people in violent crowds lose a sense of themselves, and their internal norms and values regarding appropriate and nonviolent conduct do not come into play. Because these norms of social control and violence, which would otherwise keep their behavior in check, are not operating, people are more willing to engage in antisocial and violent behavior (Prentice-Dunn & Rogers, 1982, 1983; Prentice-Dunn, 1990).

Finally, deindividuation predicts a decline in people's sense of accountability for their actions. If many others are engaged in antisocial acts such as looting, any single individual may feel that the probability of getting caught by the authorities is relatively minimal. Therefore, the potential costs of such violent behavior may be viewed as relatively low. Such reasoning can lead to an increase in unrestrained, violent behavior (Prentice-Dunn & Rogers, 1982).

The deindividuation perspective suggests several ways of preventing the violence that may grow out of mob behavior. One method is to attempt to reduce deindividuation by making people feel personally accountable for their actions. For instance, a visible police presence may enhance an individual's self-awareness and also increase the perceived riskiness of participation in violent, unlawful acts.

Efforts along these lines were made to stave off the Los Angeles riots: A well-publicized church service was held just after the Rodney King verdict was announced. At the service, community leaders urged citizens to engage in peaceful demonstrations that would show their inner strength and peacefulness. Translated into social psychological terms, they were encouraging norms of social responsibility and discouraging those relating to violence.

Unfortunately, the rioting began even before the service was over, and calls for calm went unheeded. The result: Dozens of people were killed, and hundreds of millions of dollars in property damage was sustained.

## Terrorist Violence: The Weapon of Fear

**terrorism**
the use or threat of violence against particular or random targets for the purpose of achieving political aims.

When Beirut hostage Terry Anderson was released from his imprisonment after spending almost seven years in confinement, his liberation was hailed as a step forward in the fight to end terrorism. Yet it is not unreasonable to question whether his release, which was accomplished after literally years of delicate negotiations, marked an end to this form of terrorism, or just a way-station on the road to future terrorist incidents.

**Terrorism** is the use or threat of violence against particular or random targets for the purpose of achieving political aims. Although we often think of terrorism in terms of international politics, terrorism oriented around domestic issues exists as well. For example, the bombing of abortion clinics by antiabortion demonstrators represents an act of terrorism (Gibbs, 1989a; Wilson & Lynxwiler, 1988).

One of the central goals of terrorism is to obtain publicity for a particular cause. Terrorists often justify their violence with the rationale that terrorism offers the only means to communicate their message to the world. This rationale accounts for the eagerness of groups to claim responsibility for specific terrorist acts. Members of terrorist organizations fervently believe that the ends justify the means, and that terrorism represents their single opportunity for achieving their goals—which they typically feel are moral and just (Lee, 1983; McCauley & Segal, 1989).

In sum, terrorists' attributions for their own behavior are very different from those of people outside the terrorist situation. The people who triggered a massive explosion at the World Trade Center in New York City, killing or injuring dozens of people, saw themselves as freedom fighters; to their victims, they were terrorists.

Over the past two decades, the number of acts of political terrorism has risen dramatically. In particular, the taking of innocent hostages has increased drastically. Political

Dealing with terrorism has proven to be a difficult issue for governments throughout the world. Should force be used to attempt to free hostages? Should a government negotiate with terrorists? Should news of terrorist activities be withheld from the public?

groups learned through experience that hostage taking offered immense publicity for their particular cause. At the same time, it provided a sense of personal martyrdom and heroism for themselves, and adulation from their followers. Most of all, though, imprisonment of a hostage bestowed a potent bargaining chip.

The question of how to deal with terrorists holding hostages has represented an important issue for governments throughout the world (Reich, 1990). Several schools of thought exist. One approach is to ignore terrorists and to refuse to negotiate with them. According to this perspective, dealing with terrorists simply provides them with political legitimacy and increases the value of the hostages to the terrorists, thereby making their early release less likely. Moreover, holding negotiations increases the likelihood that terrorism will occur in the future, because terrorists who achieve some gain act as models who are rewarded for their aggression.

Refusal to negotiate with terrorists represents the official policy of the United States. However, the policy only rarely has been followed. The reality is that negotiations have often taken place, albeit out of the public eye. For instance, Terry Anderson's release could not have occurred without months of previous negotiations between his captors and the U.S. government.

Another approach to dealing with terrorism is to use force to free the hostages. For example, in the 1970s, Israeli commandos rescued a group of airplane passengers at Uganda's Entebbe airport. The drawback of such an approach, of course, is that the risks of failure are high (as evidenced by the unsuccessful military effort to free the American hostages in Iran during the presidency of Jimmy Carter). In most cases, then, the risks of injuring heavily guarded hostages are so great that using force is not an attractive option.

A final process for dealing with terrorists is to enter into negotiations with them. For instance, despite the U.S. policy to refrain from negotiating with terrorists, such bargaining has sometimes occurred. The danger, of course, is that the very act of negotiating may reinforce terrorist behavior and lead to an increase of terrorism in the future.

One way to circumvent such a problem is to hold negotiations in total secrecy. When a news blackout is in force, terrorists cannot become salient models of aggressive behavior to others (Rubin & Friedland, 1986). Furthermore, widespread publicity about the punishment of terrorists who are eventually caught, placed on trial, and sent to prison sends a message to would-be terrorists that the risk is high and the disadvantages outweigh the benefits of hostage taking.

It is unlikely that we have seen the last of terrorism, since it provides a means for small political groups with minimal resources to have their message heard by the world. Dealing with terrorists represents an obviously difficult and delicate exercise for negotiators—and an indescribably torturous experience for the terrorists' victims.

*War and Peace*  Despite the dissolution of the former Soviet Union, world peace has not broken out. Whether one lives in Afghanistan, the former Yugoslavia, the Middle East—or, for that matter, the United States—war remains a reality to many peoples of the world. Two areas relating to war have received particular attention from social psychologists: how we perceive (and misperceive) our enemies, and how people judge the threat of war.

**PERCEIVING OUR ENEMIES.**   When you think of Saddam Hussein, the Iraqi leader the United States and its allies fought in the Gulf War, do the words "diabolic," "fiendish," and "wicked" seem appropriate?

If you hold such a view, you may be falling victim to a common trap. According to social psychologist Ralph White, our views of our political enemies often become slanted and warped. In fact, the perceptions that the citizens and leaders of a country hold of another country may become so skewed that they entirely misrepresent reality.

For example, when White analyzed perceptions prevalent during the Vietnam War, he found that the degree of distortion was great. Specifically, several narrow, unsubstantiated, and downright false views predominated (White, 1984):

- An image of a diabolical enemy. The North Vietnamese were seen as deceptive, enigmatic, and crafty, capable of horrific atrocities.
- A virile self-image. At the same time, the United States was seen as strong, determined, and invariably correct.
- A lack of empathy for the enemy. Deaths and injuries to the enemy gave rise to sterile accountings and "body counts." The enemy was not seen as experiencing grief or even having a coherent notion of why it was fighting.
- Selective inattention. Military leaders consistently ignored information that might have led to a change in U.S. policy. For instance, the undemocratic policies and rampant corruption of the South Vietnamese government were largely disregarded, on account of its alliance with the U.S.
- A moral self-image. The U.S. government viewed itself as morally just. By extension, virtually any action it took was viewed by some leaders as moral.

Of course, it was not just the war in Vietnam that produced such perceptions; the same sorts of misperceptions are applicable to other disputes. Furthermore, enemies often hold **mirror-image perceptions**—views that duplicate those held by one's opponent. Consequently, each side may see itself as moral and just, and the enemy as amoral, unscrupulous, and unjust (Hunter, Stringer, & Watson, 1991; Robinson et al., 1991).

**mirror-image perceptions** views that duplicate those held by one's opponent.

These World War I posters sought to persuade citizens to support the government's war efforts.

Clearly, such mirror-image perceptions impede efforts to bring about peace. Just as people in the United States came to view Saddam Hussein as the personification of evil, citizens of Iraq were told that the United States was the "evil empire." In such an environment, it is difficult to envision a reduction in tension between the two countries.

**ASSESSING THE THREAT OF WAR.**    Consider the following situation:

> *My friend has cancer. She has reason to believe that she has a 1–in–3 chance of dying from it. Although she understands this diagnosis, her possible death remains somewhat hypothetical to her. She imagines her death mostly in the abstract, and she talks about missing the city and her occasional trips into the country. Strangely, she does not talk so much about missing the people in her life. She also believes she cannot do anything to change her odds. She does not worry about the cancer very often. . . . She goes on about her normal life. Some people say she is marvelous, remarkable, life-affirming, brave, and adaptable. Other people say she is suppressing her fear, denying reality, and becoming desensitized to her own death—to such an extent that she avoids taking the measures that might save or extend her life (Fiske, 1987, p. 207).*

The friend?—the average United States citizen. Her cancer: the risk of nuclear war.

When social psychologist Susan Fiske drew this analogy, she was attempting to dramatize the way most citizens react to the threat of nuclear war. During the 1980s, the percentage of people who believed that a nuclear war was likely was between 10 and 50 percent, depending on the survey in which they were queried. Although these worries peaked in the first half of the decade and then declined, people's concerns about nuclear war remained substantial (Fiske, Pratto, & Pavelchak, 1983; Tyler & McGraw, 1983; Schatz & Fiske, 1992).

And so they should: Arms experts suggest that the risk of nuclear war remains almost as great a threat to the earth's survival as it did during the Cold War. Increasing numbers of countries are feverishly working to develop the technology to launch a nuclear attack against their potential adversaries.

When people do envision the results of nuclear war, their perceptions are justifiably bleak. They expect that the world's population will be annihilated, although their focus is on physical damage and not on the deaths of specific individuals. Most people believe that they personally would not survive a nuclear war.

Despite this belief that nuclear war is a real possibility, most people don't spend much time thinking about it. This seems surprising: Even if you thought you had only a 10 percent chance of contracting a disease such as cancer and dying from it, you would probably think long and hard about the possibility and how to prevent it. You'd likely try to ward off the illness by taking preventive measures. Surprisingly, though, most people report that they do nothing to help stop the threat of nuclear destruction, which threatens the survival of the world's population as well as themselves.

Why don't people act more emphatically, more assertively to end the threat of war? One reason is that the threat of a nuclear war is so frightful that people are unable to deal with it on a conscious level, and consequently they may repress their fears to an unconscious level. Another explanation is that individuals often feel little personal control over broad governmental policy. And rightly so: The unfortunate truth shown by research is that even a large group of citizens working together has only a minor influence on decisions made by governments.

People may also be immobilized because they lack a coherent strategy for minimizing the danger of nuclear war. Several strategies have been developed, some of which are contradictory. For example, consider the following governmental policies for reducing the risk of nuclear war:

**nuclear freeze**
a situation in which the world's nuclear powers pledge to build no new nuclear weapons.

- Nuclear freeze. In a **nuclear freeze**, the world's nuclear powers pledge to build no new nuclear weapons. After the freeze is in place, the nuclear powers could presumably hold talks regarding the reduction of the number of arms, since sufficient weapons already exist to incinerate the world many times over (Plous, 1988).

**deterrence**
the strategy that the threat of large-scale retaliation against an enemy attack is the best method of preventing an initial attack.

- Deterrence. **Deterrence** is the strategy that the threat of large-scale retaliation against an enemy attack is the best method of preventing an initial attack. According to this perspective—which runs counter to the freeze strategy—the best defense against nuclear war is a continued arms buildup, in which a country continually seeks to modernize its weapons. By amassing an enormous arsenal, a particular country would have the capability to completely destroy an enemy that attacked it. This concept is known, quite aptly, as "MAD"—mutually assured destruction (Morgan, 1977; Jervis, Lebow, & Stein, 1985).

Which of these two strategies is most effective? We have little comparative evidence, primarily because there are so few examples of the implementation of nuclear freezes. However, there is evidence regarding the effectiveness of deterrence, and what we see is not particularly impressive (Lebow & Stein, 1987). Historical records over the past 2,000 years show that countries that added to their arms stockpiles in order to deter wars were more likely to go to war subsequently than those that had not armed themselves (Naroll, Bullough, & Naroll, 1974). It appears that the accessibility of weapons actually makes military action an option that is likely to be chosen by governmental leaders.

In sum, history teaches us that the presence of weapons can lead to a self-fulfilling prophecy: The initial expectation that weapons are necessary results in a decision to employ them.

## ▶ REVIEW & RETHINK

### Review

- Although catharsis and punishment have not been shown to reduce aggression, exposure to nonaggressive models, and altering attitudes and interpretations of aggression, have proven useful.
- The emergent norm perspective and deindividuation provide explanations for rioting and other forms of collective behavior.
- Terrorism is the threat of violence to bring about political aims.
- People's perceptions of the enemy, and their view of the risk of war, are often not accurate.

### Rethink

- Explain how the concept of catharsis has been used to attempt to reduce violent behavior. According to social learning theorists, why might catharsis-based techniques generally be unsuccessful?
- Members of an angry crowd are more likely to imitate violent than peaceful behavior of other people in the crowd. How do social learning theorists explain this phenomenon? How is it explained by deindividuation theorists?
- Which approach to reducing aggressive behavior has been most successful?
- Why don't people who fear nuclear war do anything to reduce the odds of its occurrence? People often lobby for government policy changes. What are some possible reasons for their inaction in this particular policy domain?

## INCREASING PROSOCIAL BEHAVIOR

*You realize you left your wallet on the bus and you give up hope of ever seeing it again. But someone calls that evening asking how to return the wallet to you.*

*Two toddlers are roughhousing when one suddenly begins to cry. The other child rushes to fetch his own security blanket and offers it to his playmate.*

*Driving on a lonely country road, you see a car stopped on the shoulder, smoke pouring from the hood. The driver waves to you frantically, and instinctively you pull over to help, putting aside thoughts of your appointments as well as your own personal safety (Kohn, 1988, p. 34).*

Our focus so far in this chapter on the alleviation and prevention of aggression should not prevent us from recognizing that helping behavior is as central an aspect of human behavior as aggression. Indeed, instances of prosocial behavior are part of most people's everyday lives—acts as simple as holding the door for a stranger or picking up and replacing a package that has toppled from a grocery store shelf. In the remainder of this chapter, we consider some social psychological findings that suggest ways of increasing helping behavior.

*Rewarding Prosocial Behavior*

If you've ever received a reward for good conduct, you know the potency of reinforcement. We learn at an early age that acting prosocially brings rewards. At the most basic level, for example, parents reward children for sharing and behaving generously and they punish them for selfish behavior. But, as social learning theory suggests, we also learn to be helpful by observing others' behavior, vicariously experiencing the rewards and punishments that others receive. Ultimately, we model the behavior of those who have been rewarded (Bandura, 1974, 1977, 1978).

At first, prosocial behavior is guided through direct reward and punishment. One early experiment showed that when candy was provided to four-year-old children when they shared marbles, their sharing behavior increased (Fischer, 1963). But as children become older, verbal reinforcement becomes equally effective. In another study, 12-year-

Positive reinforcement from sharing increases the likelihood that children will be helpful in the future.

old children's donations to charity increased following verbal approval (Midlarsky, Bryan, & Brickman, 1973).

Just as positive reinforcement can promote increases in helping, negative reinforcement and punishment diminishes the likelihood of future helping behavior. For instance, in one study, a confederate on a street corner in Ohio asked subjects for directions (Moss & Page, 1972). To some subjects, she offered thanks for the help she received, while to others she said, "I can't understand what you're saying. Never mind, I'll ask someone else."

Further down the street, subjects encountered a second confederate, who dropped a small bag, but continued walking, pretending not to notice the dropped bag. Subjects who had received the verbal punishment from the ungrateful confederate were less likely to provide help to the second confederate than those who had received thanks earlier. The moral: Verbal gratitude for helpful deeds is apt to increase helping, while verbal punishment is likely to lead to declines in helping behavior.

*Modeling and Helping*    Just as Columbia University was about to begin a major fund-raising drive, it announced a gift of $25 million by John W. Kluge, a 1937 graduate of Columbia and chairman of the Metromedia Company.

The announcement was hardly coincidental. It reflected the belief—well supported by a wealth of social psychological research—that the example of a generous model can nurture the generosity of others. In both adults and children, the observation of someone behaving prosocially leads to increased prosocial behavior on the part of the observer (Kim & Stevens, 1987; Spivey & Prentice-Dunn, 1990). The reverse holds true, as well: If a model behaves selfishly, observers tend to act more selfishly themselves (Staub, 1971; Rushton, 1975; Grusec, 1991).

Social psychologists James Bryan and Mary Ann Test demonstrated the importance of a helpful model in a classic study almost three decades ago (Bryan & Test,

One way that we learn to be helpful is by imitating the behavior of others.

1967). In the field experiment, people driving along a busy Los Angeles highway passed a woman whose car seemed to have a flat tire, but who was receiving help in changing it from an apparent passerby. Coincidentally, a quarter mile down the road, another woman seemingly had a flat tire.

In actuality, the entire scene was an elaborate hoax, designed to determine how many people driving by would stop and help the (second) woman in distress. The rate at which people stopped was compared to another condition, in which passersby did not first see a helpful model. The results were clear. In the no-model condition, just 35 out of 4,000 passersby stopped, while in the helpful model condition, more than twice as many (98) people stopped to offer aid. (We might note, of course, that in neither condition was the incidence of helping terribly impressive.)

Later research confirms that the consequences of viewing a helpful model are powerful and lasting (Grusec, 1982; 1991). But why do helpful models lead to greater prosocial behavior on the part of observers? There are several reasons. For one thing, if we see models being rewarded for their helpfulness, we learn through the basic processes of social learning that prosocial behavior is a desirable behavior. In addition, though, models act as salient reminders of society's norms about the importance of helpfulness. They show us, in a concrete way, how socially desirable behavior may be enacted in a particular situation, thereby paving the way for our own prosocial behavior. In other words, they make it easier to do what we know we should do.

Thus, modeling goes beyond simply mimicking the behavior of others, and it plays a particularly significant developmental role as we move through childhood into adulthood. As we get older, we build general rules and principles in a process called **abstract modeling**. Rather than always modeling other's specific behaviors, we begin to draw generalized principles that underlie the behaviors we have observed. Hence, after observing several instances in which a model is rewarded for acting in a prosocial manner, we initiate a process in which we infer and learn the meaning of such acts, and we build and internalize our own model of behaving in an altruistic fashion. (For another sort of reward that helping brings, see the accompanying Social Psychology at Work feature. )

**abstract modeling**
The tendency, as one gets older, to build general rules and principles, and rather than always modeling others' specific behaviors, to draw generalized principles that underlie the behaviors we have observed.

---

## SOCIAL PSYCHOLOGY AT WORK

# GETTING A HELPER'S HIGH

If you are a long-distance runner, you may experience a physical "high" during or after the run. Such a runner's high typically consists of feelings of well-being, calmness, and sometimes euphoria.

Surprisingly, recent work suggests that similar physical responses may occur as a result of something much less exhausting—helping other people. According to the results of a large-scale survey of women who had helped others in some way, the majority reported feeling an actual pleasant physical sensation while they were helping (Luks, 1988). In fact, those who engaged both in helping and physical exercise frequently reported that the positive sensations were quite similar to one another.

As you can see in Figure 9-8, the actual response to helping differed among respondents. Approximately half reported feeling "high" in some way, while more than 40 per-

cent said that helping made them feel stronger or more energetic. A significant proportion said they felt "warm" or "calmer and less depressed," while almost one fifth said they felt greater self-worth and experienced fewer aches and pains as a result of their prosocial behavior.

The positive feelings that arose from helping lingered beyond the actual period of helping behavior. Most respondents said they experienced these feelings whenever they remembered their helping activities.

These findings are consistent with intriguing research that has been done on reactions to donating blood. According to the research of social psychologist Jane Piliavin and collaborators, people who habitually give blood may begin to feel stronger and stronger positive reactions following each donation. The positive emotional response leads habitual givers to become, in a very real sense, psychologically addicted to the

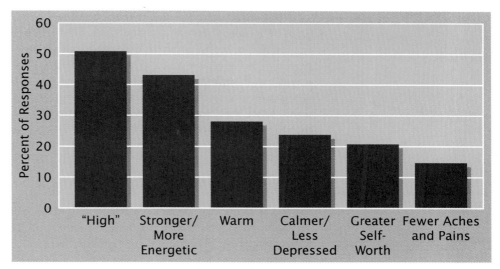

**FIGURE 9-8    How Does It Feel to Help?** Most people report that helping provides a kind of physical "high." *(Source: Luks, 1988.)*

donation process, and it increases the frequency with which they will give blood (Piliavin, Evans, & Callero, 1984; Piliavin & Callero, 1991).

In sum, prosocial behavior may bring its own special reward—a helper's high.

*Teaching Moral Behavior: Do as I Say, Not (Necessarily) as I Do*

Despite emphatic intentions to avoid it, more than one parent has fallen back on the adage, "Do as I say, not as I do." The old dictum tends to emerge when a child points out some inconsistency between the parents' prior behavior and what they are now telling their child to do.

When such an admonition occurs, parents are engaging in a fundamental form of moral education. People often use moral exhortations and preaching in an effort to promote altruistic and prosocial behavior. It turns out, though, that such an approach is not a terribly effective one. For example, in comparison to models who *act* generously, a model who merely *preaches* generosity is considerably less effective in eliciting donations (Grusec & Skubiski, 1970).

On the other hand, not all exhortations to behave in a prosocial manner are doomed to failure. One key to the success of moral prompts is the nature of the attribution made by the targets if they do behave in a prosocial manner. Specifically, the effectiveness of preaching depends on the degree to which the preaching suggests that the enactment of moral behavior is related to someone's moral character, instead of simply representing a reaction to external pressure. For example, exhorting people to do good because of their underlying positive qualities ("Underneath we're all good") is more effective than telling people to help in order to receive an external reward ("Other people will owe you a debt of thanks").

Consequently, when people are led to believe that moral behavior demonstrates that they have high personal moral standards, they will be more likely to behave altruistically in the future. On the other hand, to the extent that they are led to attribute their altruistic actions to external, situational pressures, they will be less apt to behave helpfully in the future (Lepper, 1983a; Grusec & Dix, 1986; Grusec, 1991).

Attributional approaches suggest that steering people toward the development of internal attributions for their prosocial behavior is an effective means of promoting more helping in the future. It is quite consistent with techniques used by charitable organizations, which sometime engineer future large donations by attempting to obtain only tiny ones at first.

For instance, one slogan that has been used with great success is "Even a dollar will help." The slogan represents a double-barreled strategy. First, once we have given even a small amount, we are likely to experience the positive reinforcements that a charity dispenses to any giver—a thank-you note, a membership card, and an explanation of how useful the contribution will be to the cause. Second, the donation of even a small amount of money may be sufficient to allow us to modify our attributions about ourselves. Once we've given a donation in the past, we may come to see ourselves as donors motivated by an internal trait of generosity, as opposed to being motivated by external prompts. For both reasons, then, we may increase the size of our donations when asked for contributions in the future (Carducci & Deuser, 1984; Dillard, 1991).

## Values Clarification and Moral Reasoning: Instruction in Morality

When the United States initiated formal public schooling in the nineteenth century, one of the primary goals was to provide education in moral values. Slowly, however, educational objectives changed, and today the teaching of moral values occurs only rarely. In fact, the teaching of values is a highly politically charged notion, associated with particular political ideologies.

On the other hand, certain basic prosocial values are universal, regardless of people's political orientation. For example, few people would dispute the general importance of helping others. In order to instill the value of prosocial behavior, educators have developed several approaches (Damon, 1989). Among the primary methods they identify are values clarification techniques and the teaching of moral reasoning.

**values clarification**
a procedure in which students are encouraged to examine their values.

**Values clarification** is a procedure in which students are encouraged to examine their values. Instead of endorsing any particular set of values, the goal is to make students aware of their current values. In addition, students are led to consider how their values have been formed and how their values may differ from those of other people.

Although there are several values clarification techniques currently in use, one of the most prevalent is the "either–or forced choice" (Simon, Howe, & Kirschenbaum, 1972). In this procedure, teachers ask questions that highlight two conflicting underlying values, such as, "Do you identify more with a Honda Civic or a Mercedes?" By being forced to choose and explain one of the two alternatives, students find that their underlying values come to the surface. In addition, by producing cognitive conflict between particular values, the method may provide insight into the assumptions about prosocial behavior that students hold.

Of course, there are potential drawbacks to the values clarification method. For one thing, although it does make people aware of their values, it doesn't provide them with a means to resolve underlying conflicts. Furthermore, it really isn't designed to teach new values; it only provides a framework for understanding existing values.

A more direct means for promoting prosocial values in schools is through increasing the level of sophistication of moral reasoning used by students. The underlying assumption here is that by improving their reasoning powers, students will ultimately behave in more prosocial ways.

One procedure for increasing moral reasoning is through discussion of moral dilemmas. Students forced to articulate their moral reasoning and hear the conclusions reached by others are better able to come to grips with the complexity of the issues. Furthermore, the cognitive conflict created by class discussion can lead students to a better understanding of others' logic and perspectives. Through the process of discussion, then, students' reasoning abilities may increase to higher, more sophisticated levels (Reimer, Paolitto, & Hersh, 1983).

Assuming that these techniques are successful in raising the level of moral thinking, does this translate into behavior that is more socially responsible? The answer is decidedly mixed. Some research does find that moral judgments are related to prosocial behavior (Candee & Kohlberg, 1987). In contrast, other studies suggest that the relationship between moral judgments and behavior is more tenuous. It is not clear that understanding the difference between right and wrong leads people to behave invariably in a moral fashion (Darley & Schultz, 1990).

We should not think, then, that it is easy to convey in the classroom the values inherent in prosocial behavior. But the possibility is real that people can be taught to better understand the merits of helping others, and that their own conduct will improve as a consequence.

## ▶ REVIEW & RETHINK

### Review

- Positive reinforcement and observation of helpful models are effective in increasing helping behavior.
- Moral admonitions are not terribly effective.
- Values clarification and increasing the sophistication of moral reasoning can lead to greater helpfulness.

### Rethink

- What operant conditioning technique has been used to increase prosocial behavior? According to attribution theorists, what danger exists in this strategy?
- What is abstract modeling, and how does it relate to prosocial behavior?
- Compare the effectiveness of moral exhortation with that of modeling in increasing prosocial behavior.
- Describe the values clarification approach to increasing prosocial behavior. Under what conditions would such an approach be most successful?

## LOOKING BACK ◀ ◀ ◀ ◀ ◀ ◀ ◀ ◀ ◀ ◀ ◀ ◀ ◀ ◀ ◀ ◀ ◀ ◀ ◀ ◀ ◀ ◀ ◀ ◀ ◀

### Does exposure to media violence and pornography produce aggression in viewers?

1. Given the high level of exposure to media depictions of aggression by the average person, the question of whether observation of violence leads to subsequent aggression is an important one. Correlational studies clearly show a significant link between observation of violence and later aggression, although they have been unable to demonstrate unequivocally that viewing media depictions of aggression produces subsequent aggressive behavior.

2. Several approaches seek to explain the link between observation of media aggression and later violence. Social learning theory suggests that the observation of models who act aggressively teaches aggressive behavior. The normative approach suggests that viewing media depictions of aggression leads people to assume that aggression is socially acceptable. The attributional approach suggests that the nature of viewers' attributions regarding the causes of viewed aggression determines whether they will behave aggressively. Disinhibition approaches suggest that exposure to media violence reduces people's normal inhibitions against behaving violently. Finally, frequent exposure to media violence can produce desensitization, a reduction in the negative reaction to aggressive stimuli.

3. Observing pornography that includes violent content results in an increased likelihood of actual aggression on the part of viewers. In addition, exposure to such material produces beliefs and attitudes that support the concept that sexual violence against women is permissible.

### What is the incidence of family violence and rape?

4. As many as two thirds of high school and college students report that they have been the victims of some form of violence. The particular form of violence they have experienced

ranges from childhood sexual abuse, to parental beatings, to date rape. Both men and women are the victims of abuse.

5. The cycle of violence hypothesis suggests that abuse and neglect suffered by children leads them to be predisposed as adults to be abusive and neglectful of their own children. However, being abused as a child does not inevitably lead to abuse of one's own children.

6. Rape, which occurs when one person forces another to submit to sexual activity, is a crime of violence. Rape is surprisingly common; as many as one of eight college women say they have been raped. Rape is often motivated not by sexual desire but by power and control needs, anger, or the myth that it is acceptable to be sexually aggressive.

### How can we reduce people's aggressive behavior?

7. Approaches to reducing aggression through catharsis and punishment have been suggested, but there is little evidence to demonstrate that either technique is effective. In contrast, exposure to nonaggressive models—a procedure suggested by social learning theory—is a promising approach. Furthermore, altering people's attitudes toward and interpretation of the meaning of observed aggression can decrease the consequences of exposure to violence.

### What are the factors that lead to societal-level aggression such as riots, terrorism, and war?

8. Rioting is an example of collective behavior—behavior that occurs in groups of people who are relatively unorganized, yet who hold a sense of unity and may work toward similar goals. The emergent norm perspective of collective behavior suggests that initially heterogeneous crowds develop norms that permit violent behavior. An alternative explanation suggests that being in a crowd brings about deindividuation, the reduction of a person's sense of individuality and a willingness to engage in deviant behavior.

9. Terrorism is the use of threats of violence against particular or random targets for the purpose of achieving political aims. Among the approaches for dealing with terrorism are refusal to negotiate, the use of force, or negotiation while maintaining a news blackout.

10. Misperceptions of the enemy can interfere with an appropriate understanding of enemies and to mirror-image perceptions. In addition, several techniques have been developed to minimize the danger of nuclear war. These include a nuclear freeze and deterrence.

### How can we increase prosocial behavior?

11. One means of increasing prosocial behavior is to provide direct positive reinforcement, rewarding instances of helping behavior. Another is through the observation of helpful models, since the observation of someone behaving prosocially leads to increased prosocial behavior on the part of the observer. The reverse also holds true: If a model behaves selfishly, observers tend to act more selfishly themselves.

12. A less effective technique is to use moral admonitions, urging people to behave prosocially. However, in comparison with models who act helpfully, a model who preaches helpfulness is considerably less effective. Attributional approaches suggest that steering people toward the development of internal attributions for their prosocial behavior is an effective means of promoting more helping in the future.

13. One other technique for producing increased prosocial behavior is values clarification, a procedure in which people are encouraged to examine their values. The notion behind the technique is that students will become aware of their current values and perhaps reexamine them. In addition, attempts have been made to increase the sophistication of moral reasoning through discussion of moral dilemmas. However, it is not clear that changes in reasoning capabilities about moral issues result in increased helping behavior.

# KEY TERMS AND CONCEPTS

*aggression (p. 277)*

*violence (p. 277)*

*normative approach (to media aggression) (p. 281)*

*attributional approach (to media aggression) (p. 282)*

*disinhibition hypothesis (p. 282)*

*desensitization (p. 282)*

*cycle of violence hypothesis (p. 287)*

*rape (p. 289)*

*date rape (p. 289)*

*riot (p. 296)*

*collective behavior (p. 296)*

*emergent norm perspective (p. 296)*

*deindividuation (p. 296)*

*terrorism (p. 297)*

*mirror-image perception (p. 299)*

*nuclear freeze (p. 301)*

*deterrence (p. 301)*

*abstract modeling (p. 304)*

*values clarification (p. 306)*

# FOR FURTHER RESEARCH AND STUDY

Liebert, R. M., & Sprafkin, J. (1988). *The early window: Effects of television on children and youth* (3rd ed.). New York: Pergamon.

A comprehensive, clear view of the consequences of television on viewers.

Oliner, S. P., & Oliner, P. M. (1988). *The altruistic personality: Rescuers of Jews in Nazi Europe.* New York: Free Press.

What motivated people to help Jews during the Nazi domination of Europe in World War II? This book helps shed light on the rescuers.

Damon, W. (1989). *The moral child: Nurturing children's natural moral growth.* New York: Free Press.

In this volume, Damon summarizes current work on the teaching of values and moral reasoning.

# EPILOGUE

In the last two chapters, we've considered the positive and negative sides of human behavior. Beginning with a discussion of the theoretical roots of helping and aggression, we turned to ways in which we might encourage socially responsible behavior.

In our travels through the field, you may have noted that we have not addressed a larger issue about helping and aggression: the question of whether human behavior is basically good or bad.

This hasn't been an oversight. Instead, it reflects the orientation of social psychology and, to a large extent, the field of psychology as a whole. Most social psychologists argue that such a question is best answered by other disciplines, such as theology or philosophy. Still, scratch the surface of most social psychologists, and you will find someone who is an optimist regarding the existence of at least the potential for human goodness. For in exploring the kinds of issues that social psychologists address, it is nearly impossible to avoid the practical implications of their research. Hence, even the most theoretical explanations of helping and aggression have, in some ways, provided hints and suggestions about ways of improving the human propensity for caring, socially responsible behavior—an admirable, albeit ambitious, goal.

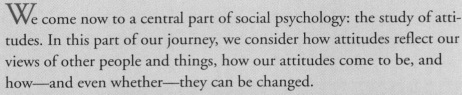

### PART VI

# HOW ARE ATTITUDES FORMED, MAINTAINED, AND MODIFIED?

We come now to a central part of social psychology: the study of attitudes. In this part of our journey, we consider how attitudes reflect our views of other people and things, how our attitudes come to be, and how—and even whether—they can be changed.

In Chapter 10 we discuss the origins of attitudes, their basic functions, and how they relate to our behavior. Then, in Chapter 11, we turn to persuasion, discussing the conditions under which attitudes can be altered. ■

### CHAPTER TEN

# ATTITUDES
## APPRAISING OUR SOCIAL WORLD

# PROLOGUE: CLASSIC COKE

The makers of Coca-Cola thought it was time for a change. Tinkering with the soft drink's 99-year-old formula, they came up with a sweeter, less tangy version, which they called "New Coke." After investing $4 million dollars in taste tests, they learned that people liked the new formula a bit better than the old one, and—perhaps even more important—-preferred the new one over chief rival Pepsi. With great fanfare, they introduced "New Coke" and withdrew the older version from the market.

What the Coca-Cola decision-makers hadn't considered, however, was the intensity of their customers' attitudes toward the original Coke. For many of them, the original Coke was part of their childhood and evoked fond memories of the past. For others, their attitude toward Coke was formed from the omnipresent advertisements touting the benefits that came from drinking the beverage. Even people who hadn't given much thought to their attitudes toward Coke suddenly found themselves taking sides against the manufacturer of the drink.

The company was shocked at the outpouring of anger against the change. According to the head of the company, Roberto Goizueta, "We knew some people were going to be unhappy, but we could never have predicted the depth of their unhappiness."

To express their anger, members of the public boycotted "New Coke" and turned to rival soft drinks. The original formula Coke suddenly became valuable, and people hoarded cases of it in their basements.

After just six weeks, Coke officials relented. They announced that the original Coke—now dubbed "Coke Classic"—would be back on supermarket shelves. The attitudes of the public had been heard, loud and clear (DeMott, 1985).

When the manufacturers of Coca-Cola introduced "New Coke," they did not take into account the intensity of the public's attitudes toward the original Coke.

## LOOKING AHEAD

▶ ▶ ▶ ▶ ▶ ▶ ▶ ▶ ▶ ▶ ▶ ▶ ▶ ▶ ▶ ▶ ▶ ▶ ▶ ▶ ▶ ▶ ▶ ▶

The public's reaction to the introduction of "New Coke" does not surprise social psychologists. To them, attitudes represent one of the major ingredients in people's social worlds and must be taken into account in order to fully understand human behavior.

In this chapter, we examine attitudes. We first consider the various approaches that social psychologists take to defining the concept. Despite (or perhaps because of) the fact that attitudes play such an important role in our everyday social lives, there is little agreement regarding how best to formulate the concept. We explore how attitudes are formed and several of the major vantage points from which to view them. We also examine the origins of attitudes and the various functions they serve, and the ways in which they can be measured.

Finally, we consider how attitudes are related to behavior. We discuss how people strive for consistency among attitudes and how they resolve inconsistencies. We conclude by exploring some strategies for evaluating reports of public polls about attitudes.

In sum, after completing this chapter, you'll be able to answer these questions:

- How are attitudes most accurately defined?
- How are attitudes formed, and what functions do they serve?
- Are our attitudes internally consistent? How do we strive to maintain consistency?
- How is behavior related to attitudes?
- What factors should we consider in evaluating the results of attitude surveys?

# THE ABC'S OF ATTITUDES

Japan. Abortion. The president of the United States. Smoking. The economy. Your social psychology instructor.

It's unlikely that you are completely neutral about anything in this list. Instead, as you read through these items, each one probably rings at least one mental bell of recognition.

The very mention of abortion, for instance, may conjure up your thoughts and beliefs about the topic, your opinion about whether or not it should be legal, and perhaps the recollection of participating in a demonstration about it in the past or planning to engage in some activity relating to abortion in the future. Your response to the word "abortion," as well as to each of the other items on the list, stems from the attitudes that you hold.

## *Defining Attitudes: Formulating an Approach*

Despite the fact that attitudes are a central concept in social psychology—or perhaps *because* they are so pivotal—social psychologists have not reached agreement on any one single definition. We'll consider the three primary candidates: attitudes as evaluations, attitudes as memories, and the three-component model of attitudes.

**attitudes**
learned predispositions to respond in a favorable or unfavorable manner to a particular person, object, or idea.

**ATTITUDES AS EVALUATIONS.** **Attitudes** are learned predispositions to respond in a favorable or unfavorable manner to a particular person, object, or idea. According to this definition, attitudes represent primarily a positive or negative evaluation of an individual, behavior, belief, or thing (see Fishbein & Aizen, 1975; Eagly & Chaiken, 1993; see Figure 10-1).

Although most social psychologists agree that evaluations lie at the core of attitudes, several other definitions of the term have evolved, reflecting different emphases

One reason the abortion issue raises such strong reactions is that it is related to a broad spectrum of thoughts and beliefs about the topic.

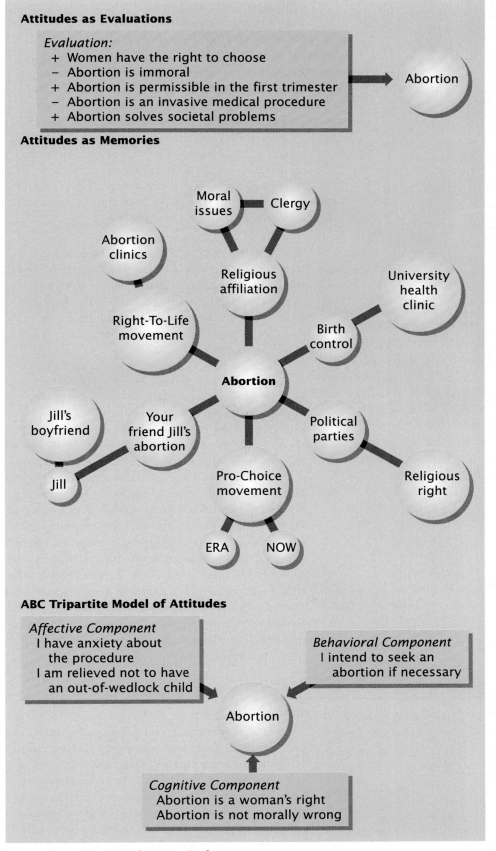

**FIGURE 10-1    Approaches to Attitudes**

and theoretical issues. These alternatives stress the relationship of evaluations to other aspects of attitudes, such as relevant cognitions and behaviors. For instance, one alternative approach emphasizes the way that attitudes are stored in memory.

**ATTITUDES AS MEMORIES.**  Focusing on the cognitive aspects of attitudes, some researchers consider attitudes as a set of memories linking cognitions regarding the topic about which the attitude is held to evaluations of the topic (see Fazio, 1989, 1990; Tesser & Shaffer, 1990; Judd et al., 1991; see the third panel of Figure 10-1).

According to this view, an attitude is composed of a set of interrelated memories about a particular person, object, or idea. Such memories exist about different kinds of information—some about beliefs, others about feelings, and still others about behavior concerning the subject of the attitude. When a stimulus in the environment triggers one of these memories, it activates an entire mental network of related memories having to do with the topic of the attitude.

**ABC tripartite model**
the notion that attitudes are composed of three components: an affective component, a behavioral component, and a cognitive component.

**THE ABC TRIPARTITE MODEL.**    A third approach to attitudes focuses on their underlying structure. According to the **ABC tripartite model**, attitudes are composed of three components: an affective component, a behavioral component, and a cognitive component (Rajecki, 1989; Ostrom, 1969; Breckler, 1984; see the bottom third of Figure 10-1). The affective component encompasses the emotional reactions—positive or negative. For instance, many people harbor strong positive or strong negative emotions regarding abortion.

The behavioral component of the attitude consists of a predisposition or intention to act in a way that reflects the attitude. For example, this part of the attitude would include your intention to join a pro- or anti-abortion rally, or your willingness or unwillingness to consider having an abortion.

Finally, the cognitive component of an attitude refers to the beliefs and thoughts about the object of the attitude. In reference to abortion, we might hold strong moral or religious beliefs that shape our views of the legitimacy of the practice.

Of course, no one of these components is entirely independent of the others; rather they are all three interrelated. Our emotional reactions are likely to affect our behavioral intentions, just as our beliefs will influence our emotions. For example, if a woman believes that abortion is immoral (the cognitive component), and if the thought of abortion produces a strong negative reaction (the affective component), she is unlikely to intend to seek an abortion (the behavioral component).

On the other hand, if the woman believes that abortion is an appropriate moral choice and considers it a matter of a woman's choice (the cognitive component), and if she reacts favorably to abortion as an option (the affective component), she is considerably more likely to intend to participate in a pro-choice rally or even to seek out an abortion herself (the behavioral component). In sum, the A, B, and C of the tripartite model often are consistent with one another.

## Reconciling the Approaches

We've encountered three approaches to attitudes: one that focuses on evaluative aspects, a second that concentrates on the basis of attitudes in memory, and a third that emphasizes the three interrelated components of attitudes. Which of these three approaches provides the most accurate description?

Actually, the three approaches are less contradictory than they may seem at first: To a large extent, they represent not different views but different areas of focus. The evaluative approach concentrates on likes and dislikes; the view of attitudes as memories embraces the notion that memories can represent affective, cognitive, and behavioral intentions; and the ABC tripartite model concentrates on several aspects of an attitude, including likes and dislikes. Hence, the three approaches share many common elements.

When United States intervention in Somalia was presented in terms of relief for hungry children, the public's attitudes were largely favorable. But when the mission proved quite hazardous, attitudes shifted, and the U.S. soldiers soon left Somalia.

Although these different emphases direct researchers to different theoretical and research paths, all three approaches assume that there is a structure to attitudes and that attitudes cannot be considered in isolation from one another. Finally—and perhaps most important—all three agree on the fundamental importance of attitudes in shaping human behavior.

## THE ORIGINS AND FUNCTIONS OF ATTITUDES

You were not born loving rap music, disliking Saddam Hussein, or feeling so-so about Ivory soap. Somewhere in your past, you developed an attitude about each of them. Where did these attitudes come from?

From the time of birth, we are deluged with stimuli that generate attitudes. Parents, friends, the media, teachers—anyone or anything can provide information that may lead to attitude formation. Whether or not this information is translated into an attitude depends, to a large extent, on the basic principles of learning.

*Classical Conditioning of Attitudes: Turning Saddam Hussein into Hitler*

Each time you eat broccoli you get sick to your stomach—apparently the result of an allergic reaction. Is it any surprise that you grow to hate the vegetable?

The process that led you to develop your negative attitude toward broccoli was classical conditioning. You probably remember the work of Pavlov and his dogs. Pavlov discovered that by pairing two stimuli, such as the sound of a bell and meat, hungry dogs learned to respond—in this case to salivate—not only when the meat occurred in conjunction with the bell sound, but even when the bell was sounded alone (Pavlov, 1927).

The key to Pavlov's process was stimulus substitution, in which a previously neutral stimulus that didn't naturally bring about a response was paired with a stimulus that did evoke a response. Repeatedly presenting the two stimuli together resulted in the second stimulus taking on the properties of the first, in effect substituting the second stimulus for the first.

Attitudes can be learned in the same fashion (Cacioppo et al., 1992). In the instance of broccoli aversion, the repeated pairing of broccoli with an upset stomach eventually might produce a strong negative affective reaction to the broccoli alone—without having to go through the trouble (and consequences) of eating it. This negative reaction, according to learning theory, would be the attitude.

The American Dairy Association seeks to build positive attitudes toward milk by associating, through classical conditioning, the concept of "wholesomeness" with milk.

Not only unpleasant physical reactions can produce the kind of experiences that result in classical conditioning. For example, President George Bush repeatedly equated Saddam Hussein with Adolf Hitler in connection with the occupation of Kuwait and the Persian Gulf War. Over and over, Bush portrayed the Iraqi leader as the modern-day Hitler, and Americans were told of routine executions and torture at Hussein's behest (*U.S. News & World Report*, 1991). It is no surprise that ultimately the attitudes people held about Saddam Hussein took on the same (negative) qualities as those they held toward Hitler.

Classical conditioning of a more covert nature helps explain, at least in part, the origins of prejudice in the form of negative attitudes toward members of particular racial, religious, ethnic, and gender groups. For example, consider children who repeatedly overhear their parents discussing members of a particular group in negative terms ("The Irish drink too much, Turks are cruel, Arabs are devious, women are overly emotional"). These children clearly are at risk for learning the same associations between the group and the negative evaluations inherent in the adjectives of lazy, drunken, devious, overly emotional—regardless of their own experiences with members of these groups (Staats & Staats, 1958; Riordan & Tedeschi, 1983).

*Operant Conditioning: In Praise of Attitudes*

Great idea. Perfect. You're right.

Forget it. That's the dumbest opinion I ever heard. Not on your life.

If you've ever been in the position of hearing such replies to a comment of yours, you know the power of praise—and condemnation. In fact, one of the central ways our attitudes are formed and shaped is through response to the compliments and critiques of others.

Once again, it is basic learning theory that provides an explanation for this form of attitude formation. In this case, however, the specific process is operant conditioning, growing out of the work done by the behavioral psychologist B. F. Skinner (1957; 1983). According to operant conditioning approaches, when we are rewarded, or reinforced, for expressing certain attitudes, we are more likely to voice similar attitudes in the future. On the other hand, when punishment follows our expression of a particular view, we are less likely to state it in the future (Insko, 1965; Singer, 1961; Hildum & Brown, 1956).

One early demonstration of the power of reinforcement comes from a study in which subjects held a conversation with an experimenter. As the conversation progressed, participants made an increasing number of statements of opinion when the experimenter expressed increasing agreement with the subject. Conversely, in conditions in which the experimenter expressed disagreement, the rate of opinion statements declined (Verplanck, 1955).

It is not just pleasant or unpleasant verbal responses that lead us to develop positive or negative attitudes toward particular objects. We also respond to the deeds of others. A professor who gives you an "A" in the course is providing the kind of reinforcement that may well lead to the development of positive attitudes about the course.

**Social learning theory** (or **observational learning**), a derivative of operant conditioning, also helps explain attitude acquisition. According to social learning explanations, people learn attitudes through the observation and imitation of the behavior of others. Children who observe others acting aggressively and being rewarded for the aggression are apt to imitate that aggression if placed in similar circumstances. Furthermore, they learn the lesson—and come to hold the attitude—that aggression is a permissible behavior (Bandura, Ross, & Ross, 1963; Bandura, 1977). As we discussed in the previous chapter, social learning is one of the central reasons for concern over the high levels of aggression depicted in the media (Gerbner et al., 1978; Liebert & Sprafkin, 1988).

On the other hand, it is not just negative behaviors that are learned through observation. For example, in one experiment, children who held extremely unfavorable attitudes toward dogs, harboring strong fears about them, watched a model (dubbed the "Fearless Peer") who was happily playing with a dog. After seeing the model, the fearful children who had seen the model were much more likely to play with a strange dog than were those who hadn't been exposed to the model (Bandura, Grusec, & Menlove, 1967).

**social learning theory (or observational learning)** the theory that people learn attitudes through observing and imitating the behavior of others.

*Attitude Acquisition: Why Bother?*

Could we lead our lives without attitudes?

Although the work on attitude acquisition that we have discussed shows that several learning processes help account for how attitudes are acquired, we have not yet addressed what is perhaps a more fundamental question: Why do we develop attitudes in the first place?

Social learning theory explains how children learn their attitudes through the observation and imitation of the behavior of others. In this case, a girl watches as her father gives a Nazi salute at a Ku Klux Klan rally in the early 1990s.

The question is not a trivial one. It is possible to argue, for instance, that society would be considerably better off if we were not predisposed to like or dislike particular individuals or objects on the basis of previously acquired attitudes. We might wish instead that people would make judgments on a case-by-case, moment-by-moment basis and not on the basis of a set of evaluations that color the way they view the world.

It turns out, however, that attitudes play several critical psychological roles. The two main roles have been called knowledge functions and self functions (Greenwald, 1989; Pratkanis & Greenwald, 1989; Shavitt, 1989).

**knowledge function of attitudes**
the aspect of attitudes that permits people to organize and make sense of the world.

The **knowledge function of attitudes** refers to those aspects of attitudes that permit us to organize and make sense of the world. They provide us with clues about why people behave as they do, and they allow us to summarize our understanding of people and events in the world. They also help us organize and recall new information to which we are exposed. For example, people holding strongly positive attitudes toward sports often possess a wide array of detailed information about particular athletes and games. Their positive attitude helps them learn and remember information concerning athletic topics.

**self function of attitudes**
the aspect of attitudes that enables people to create and maintain a positive self-image.

In addition to knowledge functions, attitudes also serve self functions. The **self function of attitudes** rests on the desire to create and maintain a positive sense of one-self. For instance, by holding attitudes that are shared by people who are important to us, we may hope to gain their esteem and liking, leading us to feel more positively about ourselves.

Similarly, we may gain self-esteem by embracing (and expressing) a particular set of attitudes. Hence, a person who values freedom of choice may gain self-esteem by demonstrating in favor of abortion rights for women.

One further self function of attitudes relates to their ability to permit us to identify with social institutions that are important to us, such as religious organizations or professional groups. Specifically, by holding attitudes that support such groups, we may experience a greater sense of belonging.

In sum, we form attitudes for two basic reasons. First, they serve a knowledge function by helping us summarize and cognitively package the world around us. They also play another role: In their self function, attitudes help us maintain our self-esteem and foster a positive sense of ourselves as individuals.

# TAKING THE MEASURE OF ATTITUDES

**hypothetical constructs**
abstract concepts that cannot be directly observed.

Although we're all acquainted with the concept of attitudes, none of us has actually ever seen or heard one. The reason is that attitudes are **hypothetical constructs**—abstract concepts that cannot be directly observed. This creates a dilemma for social psychologists who wish to study attitudes: What is the best way to approach something that cannot be directly observed? To solve this dilemma, social psychologists use both direct approaches and covert, more indirect approaches.

*Direct Measurement of Attitudes*

If you want to know someone's attitudes toward the use of drugs, just ask them.

At least that's the theory behind direct measurement techniques of attitudes, in which people straightforwardly are asked to identify their attitudes about a particular person or issue. Typically, it involves translating an abstract attitude into some sort of numerical scale (see Figure 10-2 for examples of different kinds of scales).

**Likert scale**
an approach to the measurement of attitudes in which objects are rated on the basis of a numbered evaluative response scale.

**THE LIKERT SCALE.**    The Likert scale, named after the person who originated it, Rensis Likert, is probably the most direct and simple way to measure attitudes (Likert, 1932). In a **Likert scale** measure of attitudes, a researcher asks a question about the object of an attitude and supplies a rater with a numbered evaluative response scale. Suppose, for example, you wished to know people's attitudes toward sexual harassment. Using the Likert technique, you might present a statement such as, "Sexual harassment usually is primarily a woman's issue." To respond, raters indicate their level of agreement using a 4-point scale ranging from "agree strongly" to "disagree strongly" (see Figure 10-2).

By having raters respond to a series of such statements, researchers can obtain a summary score for a general attitude. Researchers can also vary the number of categories; there are five-category Likert scales, which provide general information; and there are 100-category Likert scales, which potentially provide more refined information.

**SEMANTIC DIFFERENTIAL MEASURE OF ATTITUDES.**   Another approach to the study of attitudes is to assess specific aspects of attitudes. For example, we might want to directly target the evaluative aspect of an attitude. To do this, researchers often employ a semantic differential measure (Osgood, Suci, & Tannenbaum, 1957). In the **semantic differential**, an object is rated on a pair of adjectives, which are opposites. For instance, a researcher could ask someone to rate "welfare" along such dimensions as good–bad, attractive–unattractive, valuable–worthless, and fair–unfair.

The advantage of the semantic differential is that it allows researchers to target the evaluative component of the attitude. In addition, it permits researchers to obtain attitudes toward general, broad concepts, rather than very specific ones.

**semantic differential**
an approach to the measurement of attitudes in which objects are rated on the basis of a pair of adjectives that are opposites, such as good/bad, attractive/unattractive.

---

**FIGURE  10-2   Examples of Direct Measures of Attitudes**

**LIKERT SCALE**
**Some Items from the Short Form of the**
**Attitudes Toward Women Scale**

The statements listed below describe attitudes toward the role of women in society that different people have. There are no right or wrong answers, only opinions. You are asked to express your feeling about each statement by indicating whether you (A) agree strongly, (B) agree mildly, (C) disagree mildly, or (D) disagree strongly. Please indicate your opinion by indicating either A, B, C, or D for each item.

1. Swearing and obscenity are more repulsive in the speech of a woman than of a man.
2. Women should take increasing responsibility for leadership in solving the intellectual and social problems of the day.
3. Both husband and wife should be allowed the same grounds for divorce.
4. Intoxication among women is worse than intoxication among men.
5. Under modern economic conditions with women being active outside the home, men should share in household tasks such as washing dishes and doing the laundry.
6. There should be a strict merit system in job appointment and promotion without regard to sex.
7. Women should worry less about their rights and more about becoming good wives and mothers.
8. Women earning as much as their dates should bear equally the expense when they go out together.
9. It is ridiculous for a woman to run a locomotive and for a man to darn socks.
10. Women should be encouraged not to become sexually intimate with anyone before marriage, even their fiancés.
11. The husband should not be favored by law over the wife in the disposal of family property or income.
12. The modern girl is entitled to the same freedom from regulation and control that is given to the modern boy.

*Continued on next page*

---

*Source:* These items were presented by Spence, Helmreich, and Stapp (1973, pp. 219–220) and reprinted in Eagly & Chaiken, 1993.

| FIGURE 10-2 | *(Continued)* |
| --- | --- |

## SEMANTIC DIFFERENTIAL MEASURE

Americans

| | | |
| --- | --- | --- |
| Good \_\_\_\_:\_\_\_\_:\_\_\_\_:\_\_\_\_:\_\_\_\_:\_\_\_\_ Bad |
| Unattractive \_\_\_\_:\_\_\_\_:\_\_\_\_:\_\_\_\_:\_\_\_\_:\_\_\_\_ Attractive |
| Valuable \_\_\_\_:\_\_\_\_:\_\_\_\_:\_\_\_\_:\_\_\_\_:\_\_\_\_ Worthless |
| Ugly \_\_\_\_:\_\_\_\_:\_\_\_\_:\_\_\_\_:\_\_\_\_:\_\_\_\_ Beautiful |
| Fair \_\_\_\_:\_\_\_\_:\_\_\_\_:\_\_\_\_:\_\_\_\_:\_\_\_\_ Unfair |
| Wise \_\_\_\_:\_\_\_\_:\_\_\_\_:\_\_\_\_:\_\_\_\_:\_\_\_\_ Foolish |

## GUTTMAN SCALE
### Items from a Guttman Scale of Attitudes Toward Handgun Control

1. Institute a waiting period before a handgun can be purchased, to allow for a criminal records check.
2. Require all persons to obtain a police permit before being allowed to purchase a handgun.
3. Require a license for all persons carrying a handgun outside their homes or places of business (except for law enforcement agents).
4. Require a mandatory fine for all persons carrying a handgun outside their homes or places of business without a license.
5. Require a mandatory jail term for all persons carrying a handgun outside their homes or places of business without a license.
6. Ban the future manufacturing and sale of non-sporting-type handguns.
7. Ban the future manufacturing and sale of all handguns.
8. Use public funds to buy back and destroy existing handguns on a voluntary basis.
9. Use public funds to buy back and destroy existing handguns on a mandatory basis.

*Discarded items*

A. A crackdown on *illegal* handgun sales.
B. Strengthen the rules for becoming a commercial handgun dealer.
C. Require a mandatory prison sentence for all persons using a handgun to commit a crime.
D. Ban the manufacturing and sale of small, cheap, and low-quality guns like the "Saturday Night Special."

*Source:* These items were presented by Teske and Hazlett (1985, p. 375) and reprinted in Eagly & Chaiken, 1993.

**GUTTMAN SCALES.**  If you know how to figure out that $(15 \div 3) \times 5 = 25$, you're sure to know that $5 \times 5 = 25$. That's the logic behind the Guttman scale of attitude measurement. **Guttman scales** (see Figure 10-2) present a gradation of attitudes, ranging from the least extreme to the most extreme. The scale assumes that people completing the scale will be able to endorse all the items up to a certain a degree of extremity, but beyond that will no longer be able to endorse the rest (Guttman, 1944).

In the example depicted in Figure 10-2, for instance, people who agree that the manufacturing and sale of non-sporting-type handguns should be banned would also agree with statements that occur earlier in the list. At the same time, if they don't agree with that statement, they wouldn't be expected to agree with the more extreme statement suggesting there should be a ban on the manufacture and sale of *all* handguns.

**Guttman scale**
a measurement that presents a gradation of attitudes, ranging from least extreme to the most extreme.

*Covert Measures of Attitudes*

Although the Likert scale, semantic differential, and Guttman scale permit a direct assessment of attitudes, they suffer from the same drawback: They are susceptible to subject self-presentational motives. Even the most prejudiced college students would likely pause before admitting their prejudice on a questionnaire; even the bigoted are likely to

Errors in the findings of election exit polls sometimes occur because people wish to present themselves in a socially acceptable manner and thus disguise for whom they really voted. Consequently, covert measures of attitude change may be more accurate.

be aware of the range of socially acceptable responses on a college campus and would likely be reluctant to admit that they hold views that are not "politically correct."

Similarly, although exit polls showed that African-American Douglas Wilder would defeat his white opponent by a wide margin in a Virginia election for governor, he actually won by only the slimmest of margins. The reason for the discrepancy: White voters apparently were reluctant to admit that they would actually be voting against Wilder for fear of being thought of as racially prejudiced (Traugott & Price, 1991).

The problem of self-presentation becomes particularly acute when comparing responses on attitude scales across different cultures. For example, people in some cultures routinely give more extreme ratings on Likert scales than others, in part due to differences in concerns about social desirability (Moghaddam, Taylor, & Wright, 1993).

**covert measure of attitude**
an approach to the measurement of attitudes in which the measurement technique is disguised.

Because people are responsive to social desirability in their questionnaire responses, social psychologists have turned to covert measures of attitude. In a **covert measure of attitude**, the measurement technique is disguised in some way. For example, researchers may assess subtle, nonverbal measures of attitudes. Specifically, as we discussed in Chapter 4, facial expressions reflect emotional response, and some researchers have inferred attitudes on the basis of facial expression (see, for example, Feldman & Rimé, 1991; McHugo, Lanzetta, & Bush, 1991).

However, people can manipulate their facial expressions to conceal their feelings and attitudes (as any of us know who have smiled as we opened a disappointing gift in front of the giver). Consequently, researchers have devised subtler physiologically based measures to assess attitudes. For example, different patterns of changes in certain facial muscles seem to differentiate both positive and negative attitudes, as well as the intensity of attitudinal reactions (Cacioppo, Petty, Losch, & Kim, 1986; Cacioppo & Tassinary, 1990; see Figure 10-3).

Another covert approach to the measurement of attitudes is through the examination of patterns of brain waves. Advertising agencies, which have more than a passing interest in ensuring that consumers react positively to their advertisements, have begun to investigate whether the right or left hemisphere of the brain is more involved in the processing of information.

One such study found that commercials appealing primarily to logic are processed largely by the left hemisphere of the brain. In contrast, commercials with an emotional

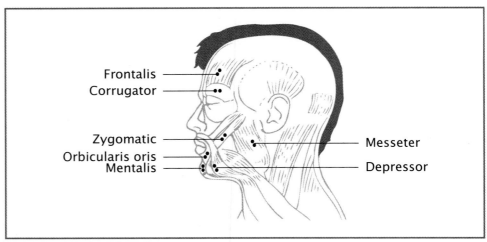

**FIGURE 10-3  Facial Muscles That Reflect Attitudes** Patterns of changes in certain facial muscles appear to differentiate  both positive and negative attitudes, as well as the intensity of attitudinal reactions.

message are processed primarily by the right hemisphere. Such results suggest that the type of initial cognitive processing may influence the nature of attitudes that ultimately develop. In turn, this knowledge may permit advertisers to craft ads that evoke the desired attitude. Although this approach to measuring attitudes has not been sufficiently validated, it does suggest a promising avenue of research (Weinstein, Weinstein, & Drozdenko, 1984; Price, Rust, & Kumar, 1986).

► **REVIEW & RETHINK**

*Review*

- Attitudes can be defined as evaluations, as memories, and in terms of the ABC tripartite model.
- Classical and operant conditioning underlie attitude acquisition.
- Attitude measurement techniques include direct and indirect procedures.

*Rethink*

- What are the three components in the tripartite model of attitudes? Which component would be most reflected in a semantic differential scale measurement?
- How are attitudes formed? Might the way in which an attitude is formed be related to specific attitudes?
- What important functions do attitudes serve? Which function would expedite a shopping trip to the grocery store?
- What advantage do "direct" scaling techniques (such as the Likert and semantic differential scales) afford? What is the main disadvantage of such techniques? What techniques have been effective in overcoming this problem?

# THE CONSISTENCY OF ATTITUDES

*Put yourself in Marian Keech's living room. It is approaching midnight—December 21—the time when Keech, a self-proclaimed psychic, has predicted the arrival of a group of aliens calling themselves the Guardians. Over the past months, you've become convinced that Keech is able to receive messages from the Guardians, who have warned her that they are going to destroy Earth with a cataclysmic flood.*

*But you're one of the lucky ones: Because of your association with Keech, you will be picked up by the Guardians and flown away to safety, just before the flood is about to occur. You've quit your job, packed your bags, discarded the zippers from your clothing (metal and flying saucers do not mix, according to Keech), and you're ready to start your adventure.*

*Midnight comes and goes with no sign of the Guardians. To your horror, you realize that Keech is wrong, and you are trapped on the soon-to-be-destroyed Earth.*

Fortunately, Keech was also wrong about something else: the end of the world did not come, and no flooding occurred (Festinger, Riecken, & Schachter, 1956).

Imagining yourself in that situation, you might think that you would be more than a bit annoyed with Keech. But the true believers who sat in Keech's living room that evening reacted very differently from what you might expect. They saluted Keech as a hero when she announced that, because of the prayers and great faith of her small band of believers, God had decided to spare the Earth.

Within the next few days, the people who had waited with Keech in the room became even more convinced of her powers to foresee the future, firmly believing that one day the Guardians would indeed come for them. Their attitudes toward Keech, which were positive to begin with, became even more positive than they had been prior to the night of the 21st (Festinger, Riecken, & Schachter, 1956).

This curious but true scenario, described in the classic book *When Prophecy Fails*, illustrates the importance people place on maintaining consistency. In order to maintain consistency between their attitudes and their behavior, the group members attempted to justify their actions. They could not simply admit they were wrong, thereby making themselves look awfully foolish for quitting their jobs, selling their homes, alarming their family and friends, and engaging in other irreversible acts that led up to the night of December 21st. Instead, they sought to justify what they had done by intensifying their allegiance to Keech and her prediction. The more they became committed, the more justification they were able to muster for their actions.

## Cognitive Consistency and Attitudes

As the case of Marian Keech and her followers illustrates, consistency—at least in attitudes—is a powerful influence in behavior. In fact, the hypothesis that we strive to maintain consistency, both in terms of the individual components of an attitude and between various attitudes, is supported by a great deal of evidence.

**cognitive consistency**
an approach to attitudes that focuses on the ways in which people strive to maintain consistency within and between attitudes and how they manage to reconcile inconsistencies of which they are aware.

**Cognitive consistency** approaches to attitudes focus on the ways people strive to maintain consistency within and between attitudes, as well as how they manage to reconcile inconsistencies of which they are aware. Such approaches assume that people are reasonably rational and thoughtful and strive to make sense out of what they think, feel, and do. The natural outcome of these cognitive efforts to behave reasonably and rationally, according to consistency theories, is that people actively construct and interpret the world in order to make consistent what is inconsistent (Eisenberg, et al., 1989).

All cognitive consistency approaches to attitudes share the basic principle that inconsistency is a psychologically uncomfortable state that prompts people to seek ways to reduce the inconsistency. Several kinds of inconsistencies can trigger such an effort.

For example, inconsistency can exist between the cognitive and affective aspects of an attitude ("Drinking is bad for people; but I sure enjoy doing it"). Or the affect felt toward an individual can be inconsistent with that person's position on a particular issue ("I really like Jake, but he is the worst sexist I know"). Finally, there can be inconsistencies among cognitions and behavioral intentions ("I know that safe sex is important, but I don't need to practice it because I have sex only with harmless partners"). Whatever the nature of the inconsistency, cognitive consistency approaches suggest that people are motivated to reduce the discrepancy.

*Cognitive Dissonance Theory*

*You've just spent an hour as a subject in an experiment, participating in an excruciatingly boring task consisting of placing spools on a tray and twisting a series of square pegs around and around. "Why in the world did I ever agree to do this?" you ask yourself as you finally finish. Just as you're about to leave, though, the experimenter, with a sheepish look on his face, makes an unusual request.*

*The experimenter says that due to a scheduling problem, he needs the services of a confederate for the next subject, and asks if you might be willing to help out by preparing a subject for the task you just completed. (The experiment you've just done is actually concerned with the effects of motivational preparation on task performance. You did the task with no advance preparation, but other subjects were provided with information about the task before starting.)*

*Further, the experimenter asks if you would consider being "on call" to participate as a confederate to prepare subjects in future experiments.*

*The next subject is due to arrive at any minute. You ask what kind of information you need to provide this person prior to participation in the experiment. Simple, according to the experimenter: You just say that the task is fun, fascinating, and exciting. For this, you'll be paid $1.*

If you agree to the experimenter's request and tell the next subject how interesting the task will be, receiving $1 for your trouble, something you never expected will probably happen: Your attitude toward the initial task will change and you'll come to feel more positively toward it. Even more surprisingly, your attitudes toward the task will undoubtedly be more favorable than if the experimenter had offered you $20 to be his confederate (Festinger & Carlsmith, 1959).

The explanation for this surprising state of affairs is found in one of the most influential theories ever put forward in the field of social psychology—cognitive dissonance theory (Festinger, 1957). According to the theory, **cognitive dissonance**, a state of psychological tension, is aroused when a person simultaneously holds two ideas or thoughts—cognitions—that contradict one another. For example, most smokers know that smoking is linked to lung cancer. In the language of cognitive dissonance theory, the cognition "I am a smoker" does not fit psychologically with the cognition "Smoking causes lung cancer," consequently creating the state of psychological tension referred to as dissonance.

**cognitive dissonance**
a state of psychological tension that is aroused when a person simultaneously holds contradictory cognitions.

When we experience dissonance, we are motivated to reduce it. We can do this in a variety of ways. (1) We can modify one (or even both) of the cognitions—"I smoke so little that it hardly counts as smoking." (2) We can change the perceived importance of one of the cognitions—"The evidence that links smoking to lung cancer is inconclusive." (3) We can add new cognitions to the cognitive equation—"My vegetarian diet and exercise regime compensate for the cigarettes I smoke." (4) We can deny that the two cognitions are related to one another—"I don't believe that smoking will lead to lung cancer." No matter what method we use, the result is the same: a reduction in dissonance (see Figure 10-4).

Dissonance theory provides the explanation for the results of the situation described earlier, in which participants were offered either $20 or $1 to act as confederates. The scenario was employed in an actual experiment conducted in the late 1950s that proved to be a groundbreaking demonstration of the validity of cognitive dissonance theory (Festinger & Carlsmith, 1959).

According to a dissonance theorist's point of view, the $20 that subjects were paid to tell someone things they didn't believe provided ample justification for the deception

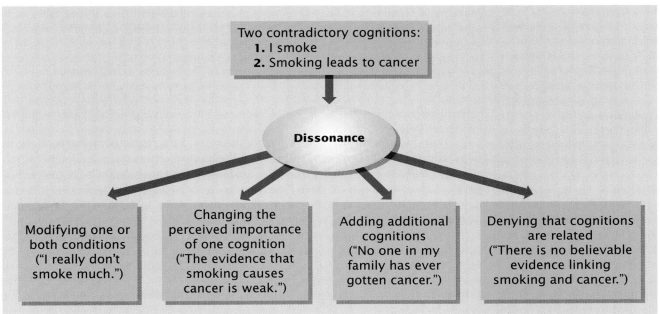

**FIGURE 10–4    Dissonance Produced by Smoking** The two contradictory cognitions that 1. I smoke, and 2. Smoking leads to cancer, produce cognitive dissonance, which may be reduced in several ways.

in which they were engaged. (Taking inflation into account, $20 at the time the experiment was run was the equivalent of close to $100 today.) Little dissonance would be expected to arise.

But consider the subjects who were offered only $1 to say something they didn't believe. For them, **insufficient justification** existed, a situation in which people perform, for a minimal inducement, a behavior that is discrepant with their true attitude. Subjects in this insufficient justification condition were left holding two contradictory cognitions:

*Cognition 1:* I believe the task is boring.
*Cognition 2:* I'm telling others the task is interesting, with little justification.

How could these subjects reduce the dissonance? It was hard to deny that they had agreed to tell others that the task was an interesting one (the second cognition), since that flew in the face of reality. On the other hand, the first cognition was more easily changed—the route most subjects followed. When asked how much they enjoyed the initial task, subjects in the $1 condition stated that they enjoyed the peg-turning significantly more than did those who were paid $20.

**insufficient justification**
a situation in which people perform, for a minimal inducement, a behavior that is discrepant with their true attitude.

One of the most striking features of this result is that it disagrees with what other theoretical approaches might predict. If we were to take a strict learning theory approach (or even just rely on common sense), we might well reason that someone paid a larger sum would come to hold more positive attitudes than someone paid a lower amount. After all, presumably the reinforcement value of the money would be greater when more, rather than less, money is offered. But this was not the case at all, thus supporting the validity of cognitive dissonance theory.

Festinger's initial work on cognitive dissonance theory marked the beginning of a decades-long search for the conditions that arouse dissonance and lead to attitude change. Dissonance, it turns out, is readily aroused, and the circumstances under which it occurs are many.

Consider, for instance, something as straightforward as purchasing a new stereo. You go to the store, and the salesperson shows you two models that fit your needs: Hitech and Goodsound. The Hitech model is state-of-the-art; it has lots of fancy buttons, an obscure feature called parallel sound, and some terrific-looking graphic tone gauges. Goodsound, on the other hand, is a reliable old standard. It's been around for years and has a good reputation. It doesn't look as sharp or have as many features as the Hitech brand, but it delivers fine sound.

After much anguish, you finally choose Goodsound. As you hand over your credit card, though, and ponder whether you made the right choice, you experience an uneasy feeling: dissonance!

Your discomfort is not surprising: Suddenly you hold two sets of discrepant cognitions. For one set of cognitions, you have all the positive qualities of the rejected Hitech model (it looks so good) and the negative qualities of the Goodsound model you've chosen (its lack of features), combined into one cognitive package. The second cognition is the major, and inescapable, fact that you're in the midst of buying the Goodsound model.

Happily, though, dissonance reduction processes come to the rescue. You can't very well deny that you've bought the Goodsound model, since the clerk is boxing it up right before your eyes. But you can turn to the other set of cognitions and try to maximize the

A car salesman may emphasize the economy features of an expensive car. This tactic may help reduce the dissonance a person may experience when purchasing a costly luxury model. Consequently, the cognition that the car is extravagant could be altered into a cognition that the car gets such good mileage that the owner will save a considerable amount on gas.

positive features of your purchase and minimize its negative qualities. You can ask the clerk to describe how some of the features of your model operate, or you can ask how often it needs repair, certain what the answer will be.

**post-decision cognitive dissonance**
a phenomenon following the resolution of cognitive dissonance in which the chosen alternative becomes more positive and the unchosen one becomes more negative.

Choosing from several alternatives, then, brings about a recasting of attitudes due to post-decision cognitive dissonance. In **post-decision cognitive dissonance**, the chosen alternative becomes more positive, and the unchosen one becomes more negative. This phenomenon has been demonstrated repeatedly in laboratory experiments (Brehm, 1956; Younger, Walker, & Arrowood, 1977; Bazerman, Giuliano, & Appelman, 1984).

**selective exposure**
a phenomenon that occurs when people seek out information that supports a choice they have made and avoid information that is inconsistent with the choice.

Post-decision dissonance has another consequence: It may lead to selective exposure. **Selective exposure** occurs when people seek out information that supports a choice they have made and avoid information that is inconsistent with that choice (Frey & Wicklund, 1978; Sweeney & Gruber, 1984; Frey, 1986). For instance, after purchasing the Goodsound model, you may read every word of an advertisement about that brand, while avoiding a friend who recently bought a Hitech stereo and likes nothing better than to talk about how great it is.

For a theory that is now approaching its fourth decade, cognitive dissonance has held up surprisingly well. But not unlike what happens to people who find themselves approaching middle age, certain limitations have become apparent.

In the case of dissonance theory, those limitations suggest that although the basic tenets of the theory are quite accurate, dissonance is aroused only under certain conditions. According to Joel Cooper and Russell Fazio (1984), dissonance occurs only when people feel that they have personal responsibility for their actions.

For example, if subjects in the Festinger and Carlsmith (1959) study believed they had no choice but to act as the experimenter's confederate (perhaps the experimenter was also their unprincipled introductory psychology professor, and they suspected that their class grade was vulnerable), they would likely experience little or no dissonance. Consequently, if subjects in the Festinger and Carlsmith (1959) experiment felt no remorse about persuading a fellow student to participate in a boring experiment because of their lies, they would probably have felt little dissonance in the study. (Although, in actuality, subjects in the study *were* induced by the experimenter to agree to act as confederates, at least the illusion existed that the choice to participate or not participate was theirs—leading them to experience dissonance.)

Finally, in order for dissonance to be experienced, some degree of physiological arousal must occur. Although Festinger was never terribly explicit about the specific underpinnings of the state of dissonance, it has become apparent that the unpleasantness of dissonance is brought about by actual changes in physiological arousal (Joule, 1987; Elkin & Leippe, 1986; Croyle & Cooper, 1983). Of course, for the dissonance to have any effect on attitudes, it is also necessary to be able to attribute that arousal to dissonant cognitions. If we think the discomfort we feel is due to having just jogged six miles or having taken No-Doz, for example, it is unlikely that we will be motivated to change our attitudes (Zanna & Cooper, 1974; Frey, Fries & Osnabrugge, 1983).

*Alternatives to Cognitive Dissonance Theory: Is Dissonance the Right Route to Attitude Change?*

Although the ravages of time—and experimental investigation—have largely been kind to cognitive dissonance theory, a significant note of dissent does exist. Few social psychologists argue that the experimental findings and results of dissonance experiments are in error, but some have developed fundamental misgivings about explanations that rest solely on the phenomenon of cognitive dissonance. Rather than finding flaws in the patterns of results coming from experimental work designed to confirm dissonance theory, they suggest that the findings have very different implications from the ones arrived at by dissonance theorists. In other words, no one questions the results, but some question the lessons to be learned from the results. We turn now to some of the alternatives to cognitive dissonance explanations.

**SELF-PERCEPTION: THE RATIONAL OBSERVER LOOKS INWARD.**    Return once again to the Festinger and Carlsmith (1959) study and put yourself back in the place of the subject. You might argue to yourself that $20, thank you, is ample justification to say that the experiment is fascinating, regardless of your own personal beliefs. There's clearly no need to look inward and figure out why you're doing what you're doing.

But suppose you agreed to the experimenter's request for a mere $1. Here, as you examine your motivations, things are a bit more puzzling. Why did you agree to his request? In order to solve this little problem, you try out the perspective of an outside observer who might be watching the experimental scene play out. By taking this approach you are able to come up with a solution: You reason that, from a logical point of view, your agreement to make positive statements for so little justification must mean that you really did enjoy the task. Consequently, when asked what your attitude is about the task, you shift to a more positive response.

It's important to recognize that the ultimate result is the same as that suggested by cognitive dissonance theory: Attitudes shift more when the justification is low (the $1 condition), and they change little when the justification is strong (the $20 condition). What changes, however, is the underlying explanation, which is embodied in an approach known as self-perception theory.

According to **self-perception theory**, championed by social psychologist Daryl Bem (1967, 1972) and first discussed in Chapter 4, people come to be aware of their own dispositions, emotions, attitudes, and other internal states in the same way that they learn about those of other people—through observation of behavior. Consequently, to the extent that our attitudes are ambiguous or unclear, we look inward at ourselves and our own behavior—analogous to the way we use other peoples' behavior to infer what their attitudes are. Based on what we encounter, we rationally determine our attitudes.

In a test of self-perception theory, Bem (1967) carried out what he referred to as an "interpersonal replication" of the Festinger and Carlsmith (1959) experiment in which he presented a detailed description of the original study. He asked subjects to predict the attitude that an imaginary subject would hold at the end of the study.

Bem's findings corresponded to those of the original study quite precisely: The observers guessed that the subjects in the $1 condition would hold more positive attitudes than those in the $20 condition. Bem reasoned that when the external inducement is low (the $1 condition), the observer takes the behavior as an indication of the subject's true attitude. More crucially, he argued that the subjects themselves went through the same logical process, inferring their attitude on the basis of their behavior. Consequently, dissonance theory predictions to the contrary, no arousal due to dissonance was necessary to produce a shift in attitude. What produced the change were the rational, logical powers of deduction of the subjects.

It makes sense. However, you may begin to see a flaw in Bem's reasoning—one that his critics were quick to identify. Despite the fact that the results of an interpersonal simulation match those of an original experiment, no guarantee exists that the underlying psychological processes that produce the two sets of results are identical. Furthermore, because both dissonance and self-perception theories make the same predictions about attitudes, there appears to be no reason to choose one over the other.

The fact that both theories make identical predictions was provocative, and it caused researchers to redouble their efforts to identify which of the two provides the most accurate explanation. The results were basically a draw between the two possibilities, although certain situations may favor one theory over the other (Ronis & Greenwald, 1979; Leary, 1979; Greenwald, 1975; Fazio, Zanna, & Cooper, 1977).

According to a careful review of the literature by Russell Fazio and colleagues (Fazio, Zanna, & Cooper, 1977), cognitive dissonance theory best accounts for situations in which people are induced to behave in ways that strongly contradict their attitudes. For instance, when with little justification you say you love something that you

**self-perception theory**
the notion that people come to be aware of their own attitudes, dispositions, emotions, and other internal states by observing their own behavior.

actually hate, you are likely to experience the disagreeable arousal that dissonance theory predicts.

On the other hand, mild discrepancies between attitude and behavior are unlikely to produce arousal and dissonance. For instance, unenthusiastically saying that you like something when in fact you're actually unsure about it creates just a minor discrepancy between attitude and behavior ("I'm not sure how I feel about the tie, but I just told Bill it looks OK"). In such low-discrepancy situations, dissonance is unlikely to be aroused, and you will be more likely to act like the rational observer of your own behavior that self-perception theory predicts.

**SELF-AFFIRMATION: ELIMINATING THE STING OF DISSONANCE.** According to social psychologist Claude Steele (1988), it is not so much the inconsistency between two cognitions that brings about the disturbance of dissonance. Instead, it is the threat that the inconsistency poses to our self-concept (Steele & Liu, 1981, 1983; Steele, 1988).

Consider, for instance, what may happen when people who smoke are confronted with the knowledge that they are engaging in an unhealthy activity. In classic dissonance theory, the means of remediating the inconsistency consists of changing one (or both) of the cognitions regarding the act of smoking. By altering their cognitions, they are able to bring the cognitive situation back in synch.

In Steele's view, on the other hand, another process may account for how people resolve the dissonance. According to his **self-affirmation theory**, people who experience dissonance may deal with it by seeking to assert their adequacy as individuals. To affirm their self-worth, they may engage in activities that have little or nothing to do with smoking—such as aiding the homeless, working harder in their academic or occupational pursuits, or trying to be a better parent to their children. The dissonance between cognitions still exists; people are well aware that their smoking and the health consequences of the behavior are dissonant. However, what has changed is that with enhanced self-esteem the dissonance has lost its sting.

Several experiments demonstrate the link between dissonant cognitions and self-affirmation. In one, for example, Steele identified a group of students at the University of Washington who were strongly opposed to an impending tuition hike (likely not hard to find!) (Steele, 1988). When these students came to the laboratory, they were told that the experiment in which they were to participate involved writing essays for a "legislative survey" about tuition increases. Because of a supposed oversupply of essays against the tuition rise, they were asked to write one in favor of the hike—an activity designed to arouse dissonance between their cognitions (against the hike) and their behavior (writing an essay in favor of the hike).

In order to influence the degree of dissonance, the experimenters led the subjects to believe they had varying degrees of choice in writing the essay. Subjects in one condition were given essentially no choice in the matter and were told they were required to complete the questionnaire, thereby producing relatively little dissonance. Subjects in the other condition, however, were maneuvered into thinking that they had ample choice in writing the essay. These subjects, of course, experienced considerable dissonance.

As we would expect, subjects in the high dissonance condition who were asked their attitudes about the tuition hike just after they wrote the essay expressed more favorable attitudes toward the impending hike than those who were in the low dissonance condition. (See the first two bars in Figure 10-5). Such a result is entirely consistent with classic dissonance theory.

Remember, though, that the experiment was designed to test self-affirmation theory. In order to do this, it was necessary to give subjects the opportunity to affirm an important aspect of their self-concepts just prior to having their attitudes assessed. In so doing, any dissonance produced would potentially be less aversive, consequently producing less threat to self-esteem.

---

**self-affirmation theory**
the notion that people deal with dissonance by seeking to assert their self-adequacy as individuals.

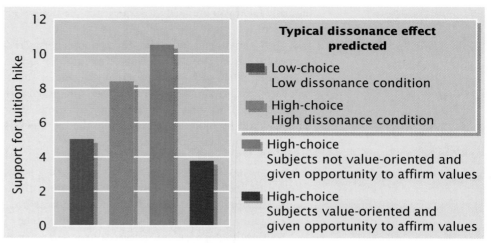

**FIGURE 10-5  Dissonance as Self-affirmation** Higher numbers indicate more support for the tuition hike, reflecting more dissonance-reducing attitude change. In the first two conditions, the typical dissonance effect was found: Low choice led to low dissonance (and hence no attitude change), while high choice led to high dissonance (and therefore attitude change). In contrast, for subjects in the last two conditions, who were given the opportunity to affirm their economic-political values, dissonance (and consequently attitude change) occurred only for subjects who held such values weakly. In contrast, for those who held the values strongly, the opportunity for self-affirmation reduced dissonance (and consequent attitude change).    *(Source:* Steele, 1988.*)*

In order to provide a group of subjects with the opportunity to affirm their self-concepts, Steele identified two subgroups of subjects opposed to tuition hikes. One group consisted of those who held a set of strong economic–political values, and the other did not hold this orientation. According to the theory, if the subjects with the strong values were given the opportunity to display or affirm this aspect of themselves, dissonance would be less likely to produce a change in attitudes. But for those subjects who did not hold such a value orientation, providing them the opportunity to assert their economic–political values wouldn't matter; they would experience dissonance and would be expected to show attitude change.

This is just what happened, as you can see in the third and fourth bars in Figure 10-5. When subjects with strong economic–political values were given the opportunity to complete a questionnaire about their values just after writing the essay (and therefore being unable to assert an important part of their self-concept), they were much less likely to become more favorably disposed toward the tuition increase. Apparently, dissonance was not aroused. On the other hand, subjects who did not hold strong economic–political values showed the typical consequences of dissonance: They were likely to show more favorable attitudes after writing the essay, because they had had no opportunity to affirm their self-worth.

**THE THREE FACES OF DISSONANCE.**    Few theories have spawned as much research and theorizing as cognitive dissonance theory. As we have seen in the three explanations for dissonance-related phenomena, there is little argument regarding the basic tenets of the theory. Holding discrepant or contradictory cognitions often does lead to shifts in attitude. However, it is the specific nature of the underlying phenomenon that is in question.

According to classic dissonance theory, dissonance is an unpleasant, aversive state. It leads to actual physiological arousal that people are motivated to eliminate. On the other hand, self-perception theory maintains that attitude change comes about because of the inferences that people make about their own behavior. Finally, self-affirmation theory suggests that dissonance need not be an unpleasant state that motivates people to change their attitudes—*if* the means exist for affirming our self-worth.

The difficulty in choosing among the three explanations is that all of them rely on the same basic principle: A discrepancy in cognition leads to efforts to make our attitudes consistent with our behavior. The success of all three approaches suggests that although there may be different routes to reaching such consistency, it is something to which we aspire.

On the other hand, success in attaining consistency sometimes eludes us. Indeed, as we see next, the question of how closely attitudes and behavior match up is one that has proven to be one of the most important—and sometimes vexing—questions confronting social psychologists who study attitudes.

## ▶ REVIEW & RETHINK

### Review

- People strive to maintain consistency, both in terms of the individual components of attitudes and among attitudes.
- Cognitive dissonance theory proposes that a state of psychological tension is aroused when a person simultaneously holds to cognitions that contradict one another.
- Self-perception theory and self-affirmation theory are alternatives to cognitive dissonance explanations.

### Rethink

- According to the book *When Prophecy Fails*, what is the typical reaction of cult followers when confronted with evidence suggesting their leader may be a fraud? Using cognitive dissonance theory, explain other possible reactions to this scenario.
- According to self-perception theory, would you enjoy a task more if you were paid $10 or $5 for completing it? Compare this prediction with that made by learning theory.
- What would cognitive dissonance theory suggest about the possibility of using operant conditioning with attitudes? Describe an attempt to use operant conditioning on an attitude that would be unlikely to succeed, and one that would be likely to succeed.
- Why are social psychologists unable to ascertain which of the three competing explanations for the dissonance literature is correct? Is it possible that more than one theory is correct? Defend your answer.

## ATTITUDES AND BEHAVIOR: WHAT ARE THE LINKS?

*It's the 1930s, and prejudice against Asian-Americans is widespread and blatant. You're the owner of a small hotel, and one day a well-dressed Asian-American couple, accompanied by a Caucasian, asks to spend the night. Despite the strong prejudice against Asian-Americans, you say without hesitation, "Of course. We have several rooms available. Just sign the guest register here."*

*A few months later, you receive a letter requesting a reservation. The letter notes that the people needing a room are Asian-American. Without even bothering with the courtesy of a reply, you throw the request in the trash.*

People observing your behavior in both instances probably would be perplexed. The negative attitudes implied in your failure to reply hardly seem to fit with your ready

Although Catholics may subscribe to the general teachings of the Catholic Church and the Pope, their behavior relating to certain issues—such as the use of birth control—may be inconsistent with their overall attitudes.

**correspondence (between attitude and behavior)**
the similarity between an individual's attitude and his or her relevant behavior.

acceptance of the Asian-American couple when they stood in front of you. The most plausible conclusion: Attitudes and behavior are not linked.

In fact, this was the reasoning used by Richard LaPiere, who in the 1930s conducted a study that has become a classic. LaPiere accompanied a Chinese couple on a three-month, 10,000-mile trip, stopping at some 250 hotels and restaurants. In every establishment but one, he and the couple received service (LaPiere, 1934).

A few months later, LaPiere sent a letter to every place they had stopped, asking whether the establishment would serve patrons of Asian ancestry. About 50 percent of the establishments didn't even bother to respond. Of those who did reply, almost 92 percent flatly said "No"; the rest said "Maybe."

LaPiere concluded that attitudes and behavior were unrelated—reasoning that was embraced by social psychologists for several decades. Still, it seemed puzzling: If one of the components of attitudes was an intention to behave in a particular way, and if people strive to maintain consistency, why weren't attitudes and behavior linked?

Part of the answer, it turns out, comes from the methodological difficulties that were later found to have flawed LaPiere's study. For example, there is no way of ascertaining whether the individuals who answered LaPiere's letter (and remember that only 50 percent even took the time to reply) were the same ones who actually permitted the Chinese couple to stop at their establishment. Furthermore, the Chinese couple may have received subtle signs of prejudice and disapproval, such as unpleasant service or nonverbal indicators of displeasure, even though they were allowed into the establishment. In sum, the actual **correspondence**, or similarity, between attitude and behavior might have been more apparent if the study had employed a more sensitive measure.

With these serious shortcomings, it is no wonder that the study was incapable of establishing a link between attitudes and behavior. Moreover, had LaPiere's study been the only one unable to find evidence for a link, the idea would have quickly died. Instead, dozens of studies followed supporting the conclusion that attitudes and behavior were not linked. By 1969, after thoroughly sifting through the existing research literature, social psychologist Allan Wicker suggested that the weight of the evidence showed that only a minimal link existed between attitudes and behavior (Wicker, 1969).

*The Right Answer to the Wrong Question*

However, Wicker's review was not to be the last word. In fact, in some ways it provided the right answer to the wrong question. Wicker's review focused on the issue of whether attitudes were related to behavior, and when he summarized many studies, he found that the average correlation between measures of attitudes and measures of behavior was an extremely modest 0.30.

However, the question should not have been *whether* attitudes and behavior were associated with one another. Instead, the more appropriate question is: Under *what circumstances* are attitudes and behavior linked? When social psychologists began to investigate this issue, their understanding of how attitudes and behavior are related took a giant step forward (Petty & Krosnick, in press).

Why would attitudes be linked to behavior at some times and not at others? The answer is that many times our behavior is influenced by factors inherent in the situation, and at such times our personal attitudes are less influential in governing our behavior.

For instance, a teenager may have a positive attitude toward music videos, but she may not watch MTV much because her parents are firmly opposed to it (and are in charge of the television). A bigoted white restaurant owner in San Antonio may hold a negative attitude regarding Latinos, but he still serves them because it is illegal not to do so or because he would be hurt economically if he didn't. You may love to eat red meat, but you order tofu burgers in the presence of your vegetarian friends in order to avoid offending them.

In sum, holding a particular attitude is no guarantee that it will determine our behavior in a given situation. The question we need to address, then, is this: Under what circumstances are attitudes and behavior related?

*When Attitudes and Behavior Are Linked*

Imagine an unmarried woman who holds a generally negative attitude about abortion. To her dismay, she learns that she is pregnant, and she tries to decide what to do. She considers the options, and, ultimately, decides that abortion is her best option. Is her behavior unrelated to her attitude?

In order to answer the question, several factors must be taken into account—including the relevance of the attitude to the behavior, the strength and stability of the attitude, and factors relating to the specifics of the situation (Lord, Lepper, & Mackie, 1984; Doll & Ajzen, 1992).

**RELEVANCE OF THE ATTITUDE TO BEHAVIOR.**    Before we can expect to find a link between an attitude and behavior, we need to be certain that the attitude being assessed is one that is relevant, or pertinent, to the specific attitudinal object of interest (Ajzen & Fishbein, 1977). For instance, when LaPiere asked in his letter whether an Asian couple would be welcomed at an establishment, he most likely elicited an attitude regarding Asian-Americans in general, stereotypical terms—and not one having to do with well-dressed Asian-Americans accompanied by a Caucasian.

Similarly, although common sense might suggest that a woman's negative attitude regarding abortion would prevent her from having one, we need to consider if other attitudes might be more relevant, given the specifics of the situation. For instance, attitudes regarding the difficulties of unwed motherhood or fears of embarrassing her own parents may be the more relevant attitudes in such a situation.

**STRENGTH AND STABILITY OF ATTITUDES.**    Obviously, the stronger the attitude, the more likely that it will influence behavior. For instance, if your attitude about abortion is grounded in strong religious and moral beliefs, you are considerably more likely to act in a manner congruent with the attitude than if your attitude is relatively weak. Similarly, a person with firm attitudinal convictions regarding a political candidate would be considerably more likely to vote for the candidate than someone who was unsure and wavering in attitudinal support for the candidate.

Furthermore, attitudes that are relatively stable and enduring are more likely to affect behavior than those that are relatively recent in origin (Doll & Ajzen, 1992). A lifelong Democrat is less likely to be swayed by the rhetoric of a Republican candidate than is someone whose only brush with the Democratic Party was during the previous election (Davidson & Jaccard, 1979; Kallgren & Wood, 1986).

**ATTITUDES, BEHAVIOR, AND THE SITUATION.**    You know it's important to floss your teeth. You even feel pretty good when you floss, knowing that you've potentially spared yourself a lecture on dental hygiene on your next visit to the dentist. You have good intentions, too; you always aim to floss your teeth. All three components of an attitude are in place: cognition, affect, and behavioral intention. So why don't you floss more?

The answer to the apparent incongruence between attitude and behavior rests on the specific aspects of the situation that is related to the attitude and that requires action or behavior of some kind. You may feel too tired to floss. You may have run out of floss. You may think that you've brushed your teeth with such vigor that you don't need to floss. You may decide you have no time to floss.

As this example illustrates, several attributes of a situation may conspire to prevent people from demonstrating behavior that is consistent with the attitude that they hold. Exhibiting behavior congruent with an attitude may entail certain costs—effort, time, material, equipment. Lacking any one or a combination of these may all produce an apparent discrepancy between attitude and behavior.

**theory of planned behavior** the notion that suggests that the likelihood that a person will behave in a way that is congruent with an attitude depends on a measured, rational decision-making process in which a combination of several factors is considered.

The role of situational factors plays a central part in an influential theory originally proposed by social psychologists Martin Fishbein and Icek Ajzen (pronounced "I-zen"), and reformulated by Ajzen in the mid 1980s (Ajzen & Fishbein, 1980; Ajzen, 1985; Madden, Ellen, & Ajzen, 1992; Doll & Ajzen, 1992). The **theory of planned behavior** suggests that the likelihood that someone will behave in a way that is congruent with an

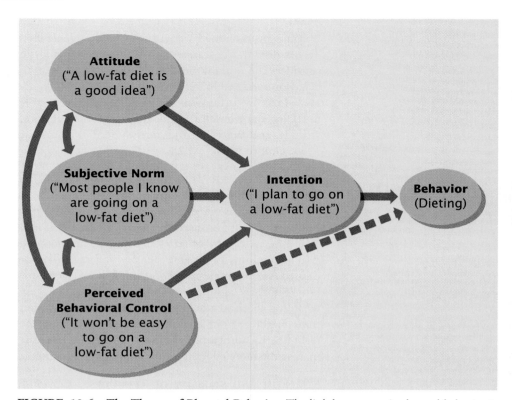

**FIGURE 10-6  The Theory of Planned Behavior**  The link between attitudes and behavior is not a direct one. According to the theory of planned behavior, behavior is the result of an intention to behave in a particular way. However, the intention is a result of an attitude, subjective norm, and perceived behavioral control.  *(Source:* Based on Ajzen, 1987, p. 46.*)*

attitude depends on a measured, rational decision-making process in which a combination of several factors are considered (see Figure 10-6).

The most influential and immediate determinant of behavior is, not surprisingly, a person's behavioral intention. A **behavioral intention** reflects people's plan or resolve—their intent—to engage in a behavior that is relevant to the attitude. For example, you might intend to begin a low-fat diet in order to lower your risk of heart attack and lose weight.

How do behavioral intentions arise? As you can see in the figure, an individual's behavioral intention to do something is in part a consequence of particular attitudes that person holds about the behavior and related topics. In the model, attitudes (for example, feeling positively toward a low-fat diet) are considered primarily in terms of evaluations of particular behaviors.

In addition to the attitude, though, two additional, equally important factors result in behavioral intention: subjective norms and perceived behavioral control. A **subjective norm** is the perceived social pressure to carry out the behavior, while **perceived behavioral control** is the perceived ease or difficulty of carrying out the behavior, based on prior experience and anticipated barriers in performing it.

For instance, a subjective norm about low-fat diets may be that many friends are going on similar diets and that it is an admirable thing to do. Similarly, perceived behavioral control might be manifested as the idea that such a diet would be hard to maintain and that there are many obstacles to staying on such a diet. Subjective norms directly affect behavioral intention, while perceived behavioral control has an impact both on behavioral intention and actual behavior.

In sum, only by jointly considering a person's attitude, subjective norms, and perceived behavioral control relevant to the attitude can we understand behavioral inten-

**behavioral intention**
the probability that people place on the likelihood that they will engage in a behavior that is relevant to a held attitude.

**subjective norms**
the factor in behavioral intention that takes into account the perceived social pressure to carry out the behavior.

**perceived behavioral control**
the factor in behavioral intention that takes into account the ease or difficulty of carrying out the behavior, based on prior experience and anticipated barriers in performing it.

tions, which in turn lead to actual behavior. The model suggests, then, that attitudes and behavior are related—but the linkage is not a direct one.

Does the model of planned behavior provide an accurate account of attitude–behavior links? The vast majority of research evidence suggests that the basic model is, in fact, quite precise. Although its precision is dependent on the accuracy with which each component of the model is measured—something that is not always simple, as suggested by the work reported in the accompanying Social Psychology at Work feature—in general the model is quite accurate. Furthermore, it has been applied to a wide variety of settings in such diverse attitudinal arenas as those involving the purchase of an automobile, engaging in safer sex, studying, behaving prosocially, and exercising (see Ajzen, 1987, 1988; Sheppard, Hartwick, & Warshaw, 1988; Vallerand et al., 1992).

## SOCIAL PSYCHOLOGY AT WORK

## PRIVATE ATTITUDES AND PUBLIC STANDARDS: HOW MISPERCEPTIONS OF OTHERS' ATTITUDES LEAD TO PLURALISTIC IGNORANCE

How closely do your private attitudes about drinking match the attitudes of your classmates?

If you're like many college students, your estimate may well be wrong. At least that's the implication of a series of studies conducted by social psychologists Deborah Prentice and Dale Miller at Princeton University.

In a series of studies, Prentice and Miller (1993) examined the relation between college students' own attitudes toward the use of alcohol and their estimates of the attitudes of their peers. What they found was widespread pluralistic ignorance. Pluralistic ignorance occurs when individuals

assume (erroneously) that others acting similarly to themselves have a different reason for *their* behavior than the individual does (Miller & McFarland, 1987, 1991).

For instance, although students' private attitudes about alcohol use may be relatively negative, they may look around them and see evidence of high alcohol consumption on the part of classmates. Rather than assuming that others hold negative attitudes, they may assume—erroneously—that other people hold more positive attitudes about alcohol. Because others, as well as themselves, are simultaneously making the same assumption, pluralistic ignorance takes hold.

Pluralistic ignorance about others' true attitudes—such as those regarding drinking—may lead people to discard their own more supportive views and adopt the more positive attitudes they assume (erroneously) that others hold.

*Continued on next page*

People assume that almost everyone else has positive attitudes toward alcohol, while they themselves are part of a minority that holds negative attitudes about drinking.

In their research, Prentice and Miller found clear evidence for pluralistic ignorance. For example, when subjects were asked to compare their own comfort with alcohol to that of other students, most subjects perceived that they were much less comfortable with alcohol consumption patterns on campus than was the average student. They even thought their private attitudes toward drinking were more negative than those of their college friends. In sum, the average subject believed that everyone else was more comfortable with drinking than he or she was—a classic case of pluralistic ignorance.

What are the consequences of such pluralistic ignorance? One prediction is that people's private attitudes will ultimately shift to be closer to the perceived group standards. If such a hypothesis is correct, the longer a student is on campus, the fewer private misgivings about alcohol use he or she would have. In other words, students' private attitudes should converge with their perception of the public norms about drinking.

In fact, further research showed this prediction to be true—but only for men. Over the course of the semester, male students' private attitudes toward alcohol consumption became more positive. On the other hand, women's views did not change; they remained negative over the course of the

semester. In fact, the female subjects appeared increasingly alienated from apparent campus norms regarding the use of alcohol.

Why should men and women differ? One possibility is that alcohol consumption is more central to men's social lives than to that of females. If this is true, then men may feel greater pressure to change attitudes to be congruent with apparent norms, while women may come to view norms about alcohol as less important.

Although it is not clear why men and women showed different consequences of pluralistic ignorance over time, what is apparent is that both had attitudes regarding alcohol that were more negative than they (erroneously) felt that others held on campus. This phenomenon has practical implications for programs designed to reduce alcohol consumption on college campuses. For example, one effective technique might be to permit students to speak privately, in small groups, with others. In an airing of views, pluralistic ignorance regarding the real attitudes that others have about alcohol may be dispelled, thereby changing perceived norms about alcohol usage.

In sum, if you think that your attitudes toward alcohol, or anything else for that matter, differ significantly from those of your fellow students, you might want to think again. You could be the victim of pluralistic ignorance.

---

*Attitudes Without Awareness: When Rationality Stumbles*

Although the theory of planned behavior is largely successful in predicting behavior from attitudes, not everyone agrees with its basic presumption that people typically act on a rational basis. On the contrary, some recent approaches reject the notion that people thoughtfully consider behavioral alternatives on the basis of attitudes and then act on the choices they've rationally made. Instead, they suggest that people's behavior is sometimes based on attitudes below conscious awareness—and that in some cases, that behavior may be entirely unrelated to attitudes.

Consider smoking, for example. People who smoke may continue to do so long after the attitudes that gave rise to the behavior initially (such as the desire to act cool or to fit in with peers) have completely vanished. Indeed, you may know smokers who readily state that their attitudes toward smoking are entirely negative, that they hate the mess, the cost, and the fact that it offends other people. But nonetheless, they continue to smoke, because the behavior has become habitual and occurs without conscious thought (Ronis, Yates, & Kirscht, 1989). As a result, in "automatic" behaviors such as smoking, attitudes and behavior may be completely independent of one another.

**accessibility**
the degree to which an attitude can be brought to mind.

In other cases, attitudes do guide our behavior—but without our awareness. Specifically, attitudes vary in their degree of **accessibility**—the degree to which an attitude can be brought to mind (Roskos-Ewoldsen & Fazio, 1992; Fazio, Powell, & Williams, 1989; Fazio, Blascovich, & Driscoll, 1992). Some attitudes are readily accessible from memory, and just mentioning them immediately brings their evaluative component to mind. (Two good examples of highly accessible attitudes are those that relate to the president of the United States and to one's mother.) On the other hand, other attitudes are relatively low in accessibility; the evaluative component is not readily triggered, and the memory connections between the object of the attitude and our evaluation are not particularly strong. (Consider your attitude toward "toothpicks" as one example of an attitude likely to be low in accessibility.)

The more accessible an attitude, the more likely it is to color our behavior when the attitude is brought to mind. Even more important, we need not be aware of this process to be influenced by the attitude—a point brought home by a series of experiments carried out by social psychologist Russell Fazio and colleagues (Fazio, 1990). For instance, in one of these experiments, participants were presented with a target object about which they had a positive or negative attitude (Fazio et al., 1986). This initial presentation was meant to prime participants, arousing the memory network that contained the attitude and the particular evaluations associated with the object.

In the next part of the experiment, the experimenter presented the participants with a list of adjectives, some of which were positive and some of which were negative. When asked to indicate as quickly as possible which of the adjectives were positive and which were negative—by pressing a key marked "good" or "bad"—they answered more quickly when the adjective was congruent with the attitude that had been primed.

For example, participants who had been primed first by seeing the word "cockroach" (about which, like most of us, they held a negative evaluation) were quicker to identify adjectives such as "disgusting" as "bad" adjectives. This effect was most pronounced for attitudes that were highly accessible—those attitudes having strong links between the target of the attitude and the target's evaluation in memory (Fazio et al., 1986).

In summary, it is now clear that our behavior can be influenced by our attitudes in subtle ways, even when we are unaware that the attitude has relevance to the situation or that the attitude has been activated. Although the research demonstrating this phenomenon is not extensive at this point (see Fiske & Taylor, 1991), the implications are profound. For instance, if people hold particular attitudes toward members of minority groups, those attitudes may alter or bias their behavior toward members of the group—even if they are not aware that their behavior is being affected. Hence, the route from attitude to behavior is an important one.

---

# THE INFORMED CONSUMER OF SOCIAL PSYCHOLOGY:

# EVALUATING ATTITUDE SURVEYS

- The President's popularity rating has fallen to an all-time low.
- Forty-two percent of Americans believe that hunting for seal skins should be banned.
- Seven in ten college students say that they regularly practice safe sex.

Anyone who reads a newspaper or watches the nightly news is familiar with assertions such as these. The attitudes of the American people are assessed regularly on topics ranging from airline safety to the treatment of zoo animals.

What we typically don't learn from these news stories, however, is just how accurate such survey results are. Like any measures, summary statements derived from surveys are only as good as the data on which they are based. To evaluate such results, we need to consider several questions:

1. Was a carefully chosen, representative sample used? If a survey assesses attitudes only from voters living in Iowa, the results should not be generalized to voters across the country.

2. What was the specific question asked of survey respondents? Consider, for instance, a question that asks whether a person agrees or disagrees with the following statements:

> "Because everyone is entitled to quality health care, a national health care system is necessary."
>
> "Because the quality of health care in the United States is the best in the world, a national health care system is unnecessary."

In both of these sentences, the introductory clause would be expected to move respondents toward agreeing with both statements. Similarly, use of emotionally loaded phrases such as "police brutality" or "the president's policy" might unduly influence respondents' responses (Oskamp, 1977).

3. Did the social desirability needs of the survey respondents bias the results? People who are surveyed usually want to be helpful and not show their ignorance. Therefore, they may state that they agree with a policy even when they know little or nothing about it ("I think the government's passport policy is pretty good").

4. Finally, are the results statistically meaningful? As we discussed in Chapter 1, in order for differences to be real, they

*Continued on next page*

must meet certain statistical criteria that help rule out the possibility that the differences are due simply to chance. Just knowing that 47 percent of Democrats approve a policy while only 43 percent of Republicans approve of it is not very informative. In order to interpret the four percent difference, we need to know whether it represents a statistically significant difference—a formal standard that can only be determined mathematically, not by merely eyeballing the data.

In sum, be very cautious when considering the results of everyday attitude assessments. Sometimes the results of such surveys are far less than meets the eye.

---

## ▶ REVIEW & RETHINK

### Review

- The degree to which attitudes are related to behavior depends on several factors, including the degree of correspondence, the relevance of an attitude, its stability and strength, and the situation.
- According to the theory of planned behavior, the major determinant of behavior is a person's behavioral intention.
- Social cognitive approaches suggest that behavior is sometimes based on attitudes of which we have no awareness.
- Several factors must be taken into account when evaluating a survey.

### Rethink

- The very definition of an attitude implies that they strongly affect behavior. What evidence led Allan Wicker to conclude in 1969 that attitudes only weakly affected behavior? Was he correct?
- When are attitudes most likely to influence behavior? What characteristics of the attitude affect the attitude–behavior relation? What characteristics of the situation affect this relation?
- According to Ajzen, what hypothetical construct is most predictive of future behavior? What factors influence this construct?

---

# LOOKING BACK ◀◀◀◀◀◀◀◀◀◀◀◀◀◀◀◀◀◀◀◀◀◀◀

### How are attitudes most accurately defined?

1. The predominant definition considers attitudes as learned predispositions to respond in a favorable or unfavorable manner to a particular person, object, or idea. However, two other major approaches exist. A more cognitive approach to attitudes considers them as a set of interrelated memories about a particular person, object, or idea. According to the ABC tripartite model, attitudes are composed of three components: an affective component, a behavioral component, and a cognitive component.

### How are attitudes formed, and what functions do they serve?

2. Several factors help explain the formation of attitudes. Among the basic processes are classical conditioning and operant conditioning, with social learning being of particular importance.

3. Regardless of how they are formed, attitudes serve two main functions. The knowledge function of attitudes refers to those aspects of attitudes that permit people to organize and make sense of the world. In contrast, the self function of attitudes permits people to create and maintain a positive sense of themselves.

4. Attitudes are hypothetical constructs and thus cannot be observed directly. Among the procedures used to directly measure them are Likert scales, the semantic differential, and

Guttman scales. In addition, covert measures can be used; these include facial expressions, changes in facial muscles, and brain wave patterns.

### *Are our attitudes internally consistent? How do we strive to maintain consistency?*

5.  Cognitive consistency approaches to attitude focus on the ways people strive to maintain consistency within and between attitudes, as well as how they manage to reconcile inconsistencies.

6.  One of the most influential theories of cognitive consistency is that of cognitive dissonance. Cognitive dissonance is a state of psychological tension aroused when a person simultaneously holds two ideas or thoughts—cognitions—that contradict one another. When people experience dissonance, they are motivated to reduce it through several means.

7.  Several alternative explanations exist for phenomena explained by cognitive dissonance theory. Self-perception theory suggests that people form and maintain attitudes by observing their own behavior. Self-affirmation theory contends that people who experience dissonance may seek to deal with it by asserting their self-adequacy or worth as individuals.

### *How is behavior related to attitudes?*

8.  The extent to which attitudes affect behavior depends on several factors, including the degree of correspondence between attitude and behavior, the relevance of an attitude to a behavior, the strength and stability of an attitude, and situational factors.

9.  The theory of planned behavior proposes that the likelihood that someone will behave congruently with an attitude depends on a measured, rational decision-making process. The major determinant of behavior in this process is an individual's behavioral intention. In turn, behavioral intention is produced by a combination of attitude, subjective norms, and perceived behavioral control.

10. Recent social cognitive approaches to attitude suggest that our behavior is sometimes based on attitudes without our awareness, and that in some cases our behavior is entirely unrelated to our attitudes. One of the most critical factors determining when an attitude will affect behavior is its accessibility.

### *What factors should be considered in evaluating the results of attitude surveys?*

11. To evaluate the results of a survey, these questions need to be addressed: Was a carefully chosen, representative sample used? What was the specific question asked of survey respondents? Did the social desirability needs of the survey respondents bias the results? Finally, are the results statistically meaningful?

# KEY TERMS AND CONCEPTS

*attitudes (p. 314)*

*ABC tripartite model (p. 316)*

*social learning theory (observational learning) (p. 319)*

*knowledge function of attitudes (p. 320)*

*self function of attitudes (p. 320)*

*hypothetical constructs (p. 320)*

*Likert scale (p. 320)*

*semantic differential (p. 321)*

*Guttman scale (p. 322)*

*covert measure of attitude (p. 323)*

*cognitive consistency (p. 325)*

*cognitive dissonance (p. 326)*

*insufficient justification (p. 327)*

*post-decision cognitive dissonance (p. 329)*

*selective exposure (p. 329)*

*self-perception theory (p. 330)*

*self-affirmation theory (p. 331)*

*correspondence (between attitude and behavior) (p. 334)*

*theory of planned behavior (p. 335)*

*behavioral intention (p. 336)*

*subjective norms (p. 336)*

*perceived behavioral control (p. 336)*

*accessibility (p. 338)*

# FOR FURTHER RESEARCH AND STUDY

Rajecki, D. W. (1989). *Attitudes* (2nd ed.). Sunderland, MA: Sinauer.

A readable, up-to-date overview of the field of attitudes, with good coverage of attitude formation and how attitudes relate to behavior.

Zimbardo, P. G., & Leippe, M. R. (1991). *The psychology of attitude change and social influence.* New York: McGraw-Hill.

This volume includes a lively introduction to the field of attitudes.

Eagly, A., & Chaiken, S. (1993). *The psychology of attitudes.* Fort Worth, TX: Harcourt Brace Jovanovich.

A definitive overview of attitudes. Although technical, the book is well-written and clear.

# EPILOGUE

As we've seen throughout this chapter, the concept of attitudes is not a simple one. Social psychologists have yet to agree upon a single definition of attitudes, and researchers still struggle to specify the circumstances under which attitudes and behavior are linked.

At the same time, though, the variety of the approaches seeking to explain attitudes has led to significant advances in the field of social psychology. As we'll discuss in the next chapter, social psychologists have developed quite a few ways to change people's attitudes, identifying how persuasion takes place most effectively. Without doubt, this work, which has considerable practical value, could not have taken place without the achievements in our theoretical understanding of attitudes that we have discussed in this chapter. Once again, social psychologist Kurt Lewin's dictum, first mentioned in Chapter 1, applies: There is nothing so practical as good theory.

# CHAPTER ELEVEN

# PERSUASION
## CHANGING ATTITUDES

# PROLOGUE: THE SMOKING CAMEL

He's a natty dresser. He's a cool dude. He's fun-loving, shooting pool, and scuba diving. He's just one of the boys.

He's also on the hit list of the U.S. Surgeon General and the American Medical Association, who would like to see him permanently banished.

According to the U.S. Surgeon General and the American Medical Association, the Joe Camel advertising campaign is targeted to children.

He is Joe Camel, the cartoon character used by the R. J. Reynolds Tobacco Company in its advertisements for Camel cigarettes. In ads shown around the world, Joe Camel is portrayed as the kind of guy you'd like to get to know and invite to your parties. Always ready for a good time, Joe is the embodiment of "cool."

The trouble is, of course, that Joe's basic message is a deadly one: Smoke cigarettes. And, according to the Surgeon General and the American Medical Association, that message is one that is targeted largely to children.

According to these authorities, the cartoonish characteristics of Joe make him appealing mostly to kids, and his message that smoking is cool is apt to be persuasive mostly to children. As the Surgeon General, Antonia Novello, said, "In years past, R. J. Reynolds would have us walk a mile for a Camel. Today, it's time that we invite old Joe Camel himself to take a hike" (Elliott, 1992, p. A-1).

Both the Surgeon General and the AMA called for R. J. Reynolds to cancel the advertising campaign, for stores to remove signs touting Joe Camel, and for magazines and newspapers to refuse ads in which Joe Camel was depicted. They cited surveys that show Joe's appeal is high among youngsters and that children as young as six identified Joe Camel as readily as they could identify the Mickey Mouse logo of the Disney cable television channel.

The R. J. Reynolds Corporation denied the charges, stating they had no desire to promote smoking among children. Joe Camel, they claimed, was intended to persuade only adults to purchase Camels. And in this respect, it turns out, Joe Camel has done quite well: Camel's share of the cigarette market among smokers age 18 to 24 has risen some 80 percent since Joe was introduced, and Camels are now the sixth largest-selling brand of cigarettes (Lipman, 1992).

## LOOKING AHEAD

▶ ▶ ▶ ▶ ▶ ▶ ▶ ▶ ▶ ▶ ▶ ▶ ▶ ▶ ▶ ▶ ▶ ▶ ▶ ▶ ▶ ▶ ▶ ▶ ▶ ▶ ▶ ▶

Joe Camel is just one of tens of thousands of advertisement figures designed to persuade us to use a particular product. If you are like the average U.S. citizen, you probably are exposed to close to 50,000 commercials each year, each one of them designed to change or reinforce your attitudes.

Of course, it is not just commercials that communicate messages of persuasion. Politicians, teachers, family, friends, and even foes attempt to change our attitudes. The messages come in conversation, through the airwaves, in the mail, on billboards and bumper stickers, and on the Levi's tag on the back of your roommate's jeans.

In this chapter, we consider what social psychologists have learned about the processes that underlie persuasion. We discuss the way persuasive information is perceived and processed cognitively, and how various types of processing can be primed through the use of particular kinds of persuasive messages.

We also examine the source of persuasive messages and how characteristics of the person delivering the message affect its reception. Then we consider the message itself,

345

focusing on such aspects as how much information should be presented and how often it should be repeated for maximum persuasive impact. We also look at personal characteristics of individuals that may predispose them to be susceptible to persuasion.

Finally, we focus on persuasion in the marketplace, examining how advertisers attempt to persuade consumers through their advertising messages, the kinds of appeals that are used in ads, and how advertisers determine who are the most likely persuasive targets. But we also describe ways we can beat persuaders at their own game, focusing on how people can resist persuasion and remain independent.

In sum, in this chapter you'll find the answers to these questions:

- What are the cognitive paths to persuasion?
- What characteristics of the message source produce the greatest persuasion?
- How do messages differ in their ability to persuade?
- What personal characteristics are associated most with persuasion?
- How do advertisers devise effective persuasive messages?

# CENTRAL OR PERIPHERAL? PURSUING THE ROUTE TO PERSUASION

Who was the most significant figure of the 1988 presidential campaign? In some ways, it was neither of the two candidates, George Bush and Michael Dukakis. Instead, it was Willie Horton.

Horton was the star of what was widely seen as the most influential political commercial of the campaign. In the ad, the Bush campaign told Horton's story. He was an African-American prisoner in a Massachusetts jail, convicted of murder. During his prison term, he was released for the weekend on a furlough program, during which he bolted the state and raped a white woman.

The point of Bush's ad: not only was Dukakis soft on crime in general, but he showed poor judgment in supporting the furlough program. Indeed, the ad implied that Dukakis was somehow responsible for permitting Horton to leave for the weekend and commit the rape (Pratkanis & Aronson, 1991).

Why was the advertisement so successful in placing Dukakis in a negative light and persuading the electorate to vote against him? The answer can be found in the discovery that there are two paths to persuasion, according to attitude experts Richard Petty and John Cacioppo (1986a, b).

*The Elaboration Likelihood Model: Two Paths to Persuasion*

**central route persuasion**
route to persuasion based on the logic, merit, or strength of the arguments.

**peripheral route persuasion**
route to persuasion based on factors unrelated to the nature or quality of the content of a persuasive message.

**elaboration likelihood model**
the notion that central route persuasion occurs when the recipient carefully considers arguments and

Petty and Cacioppo argue that persuasion follows one of two routes: the central route and the peripheral route. In **central route persuasion**, persuasion occurs on the basis of the logic, merit, or strength of the arguments. People are swayed in their judgments because of the soundness and sense of the position being put forward.

In contrast, **peripheral route persuasion** occurs when people are persuaded on the basis of factors unrelated to the nature or quality of the content of a persuasive message. Instead, they are influenced by factors that are irrelevant or extraneous to the topic or issue—factors such as who is providing the message or how long the arguments are.

In a theory summarizing their position, called the **elaboration likelihood model**, Petty and Cacioppo suggest that central route persuasion occurs when the recipient carefully considers arguments and expends a cognitive effort in elaborating the meaning and implication of a message. When central route persuasion occurs, people process information relatively thoroughly, considering the content of the message. In short, they think about the topic.

In contrast, peripheral route persuasion takes place when people don't take the

Photos of a fearsome-looking Willie Horton, a convicted murderer who raped a woman while on prison furlough, were included in advertisements for the 1988 presidential campaign of George Bush, and designed to make his opponent look soft on crime.

expends a cognitive effort in elaborating the meaning and implication of a message.

time, or make the effort, to consider the content or meaning of a persuasive message. Instead, they focus on aspects of the message that are immaterial to its content.

The Willie Horton ad is a good example of a persuasive message that was designed to produce attitude change via the peripheral route. Nowhere in the message is there a measured discussion of the furlough system—its value and its deficiencies—or of candidate Bush's potential merits and how he would solve the problem the furlough program was designed to address. Instead, the message evoked and highlighted raw emotions regarding a killer-turned-rapist. In addition, the fact that Horton was an African-American who had raped a white woman added racial overtones to the message content.

Of course, it could have been possible to produce an advertisement that promoted central route processing. The ad might have focused on the role of furloughs in prison reform or on the demographics of prison populations. Such an ad also might well have produced a collective yawn among viewers. Consequently, the makers of the Willie Horton ad—as well as many other types of advertising—avoided a measured, reasoned discussion of the topic.

On the other hand, providing a particular type of message does not ensure that a certain kind of cognitive processing will automatically occur. Just because a message emphasizes peripheral concerns (such as racial issues or candidate Dukakis's image as "soft on crime" in the case of the Horton ad) does not mean that peripheral processing will necessarily take place. A viewer motivated to be critical might well invoke central route processing and see the fallacies of the argument. Similarly, just because a message emphasizes the merits of an argument does not ensure that central route processing will take place. Instead, an inattentive or bored message recipient might well focus on irrelevant cues—such as the misfit of a speaker's jacket or the extraordinary good looks of the advocate—and engage in peripheral route processing.

**heuristics**
principles or "rules of thumb" that permit people to make decisions on the basis of limited information and with relatively little cognitive effort.

One of the important determinants of whether central or peripheral route processing occurs is the availability of heuristics. **Heuristics** are personal principles or rules of thumb that permit us to make decisions on the basis of limited information and with relatively little cognitive effort (Chaiken, 1987).

For example, we might hold the heuristic that "longer arguments are better than shorter ones" or that "people with Ph.D.'s know more than people without them." By

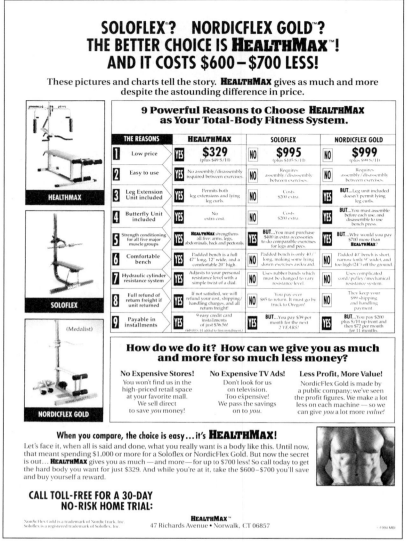

Advertisements like this, which focus on the benefits of using the product, aim for central route persuasion.

invoking such heuristics, we avoid evaluating arguments on their merits, thereby employing peripheral processing.

## The Ideal Route to Enduring Attitude Change

Does peripheral route processing or central route processing produce the greater degree and the greater persistence of attitude change?

The answer is clear and straightforward. The most lasting and persistent attitude change is brought about by central route processing. If people have the opportunity to consider and elaborate upon an argument, they can begin to understand the argument's merits and potentially even come up with a few more supportive arguments of their own. As a result, the greater the intensity of cognitive work, the more likely that attitude change will be enduring.

Conversely, although peripheral route processing can sway attitudes, the degree of change is not as likely to be as strong nor as lasting as when central route processing is employed. People who do not expend the cognitive effort to consider and cognitively amplify the issues involved in a topic are less likely to have long-term attitude changes.

Clearly, central route persuasion techniques seem preferable to peripheral route techniques. Why, then, do politicians, advertisers, salespeople, and other professional persuaders invariably employ persuasive communications that promote peripheral route processing?

The reason is that central route processing is considerably more difficult to elicit than peripheral route processing. Two conditions must be met in order for central route processing to proceed. First, people must be sufficiently *motivated* to expend the cognitive effort to think about the issue. They need to have sufficient interest in the topic to warrant the effort it takes to elaborate upon the message. However, most of us have neither the time, the energy, nor the inclination to consider every message to which we are exposed. Consequently, central route processing may never take place, or may readily fall by the wayside if the motivation to think about the issue is not present.

The second key to determining whether central or peripheral route processing is employed relates to a message recipient's *ability* to process it. No matter how carefully crafted a message about the possibility of a nuclear meltdown, the physics involved may be so mysterious that we might not able to understand the core of the communication. Similarly, if we are distracted by activities in the midst of the message—as when the dog leaps on the couch while we're watching a television commercial—central route processing is unlikely to occur.

In sum, central route processing promotes longer-lasting attitude change than peripheral route processing, but recipients' motivation and ability to consider a persuasive communication determines whether central or peripheral route processing will occur.

The nature of the processing employed by the recipient of a message, however, is only part of the story in determining how attitudes are changed. We also need to consider the origin of a persuasive message and various characteristics of the recipients of that message in order to get a full picture of the process of persuasion.

# THE MESSAGE SOURCE: THE ROOTS OF PERSUASION

Are you more likely to be persuaded to use a particular toothpaste by the president of the United States or by the president of the American Dental Association? No matter how much you like the U.S. president or how appealing his smile, it is highly unlikely that his views on toothpaste will lead you to change your brand. The president of the American Dental Association is another story; the views of that individual are likely to carry some weight.

As this example illustrates, the source of a message is apt to play an important role in its persuasiveness. Among the most important factors are the expertise and trustworthiness of communicators and their attractiveness and likability (Roskos-Ewoldsen & Fazio, 1992; Kassin, 1983; McGarry & Hendrick, 1974).

*Communicator Credibility: Expertise and Trustworthiness*

When a newspaper wishes to identify a source whose name may be unknown to its readership, it often says, "X, an expert on. . . ." Instant credibility is thereby bestowed on the individual.

People place great stock in the opinions of experts (Hass, 1981; Maddux & Rogers, 1980). We are much more likely to be swayed by a theory of why the dinosaurs became extinct when it is presented by an award-winning biologist than when it is put forward by a junior high school student. Furthermore, experts have credibility even in areas in which their expertise is questionable (Aronson & Golden, 1962).

For example, William Shockley, a Nobel-prize-winning physicist who helped invent the transistor, developed a theory that African-Americans had lower intelligence than whites due to genetic factors. Although his hypothesis had no basis in reality—it was roundly refuted by critics in the field of psychology—it did attract a fair amount of attention, largely because of Shockley's Nobel credentials. The fact that expertise in physics does not translate into expertise in psychology was lost on some recipients of Shockley's message.

On the other hand, experts are not invariably credible. If we believe that an expert has an ulterior motive, for instance, we are less prone to be swayed by his or her message (Eagly, Wood, & Chaiken, 1978). For instance, a physician in the employ of a drug company who asserts that the company's new drug is entirely safe is considerably less credible than an employee of the U.S. Food and Drug Administration making the same argument.

Experts, then, must be trustworthy in order to be credible. If we feel they are not completely honest, or are simply telling us what we want to hear, we are less apt to be persuaded by their arguments, no matter how compelling and carefully crafted.

Of course, the opposite is also true: The more it appears that experts are arguing *against* their own best personal interests, the higher their credibility. A politician who makes a pro-environmental speech to a company accused of polluting the atmosphere will be considered to be more credible than one who takes a pro-environmental position in a speech to the Sierra Club (Eagly, Wood, & Chaiken, 1978).

Even message sources with little credibility, however, are not without their persuasive resources—a point illustrated by a phenomenon called the sleeper effect. The **sleeper effect** is an increase in the degree of persuasiveness of a message that occurs with the passage of time (Hovland & Weiss, 1951; Allen & Stiff, 1989; Heslin & Sommers, 1987).

**sleeper effect**
the notion that the persuasiveness of a message increases with the passage of time.

The sleeper effect was discovered in a study conducted some 40 years ago. In the study, a group of American soldiers watched a pro-U.S. film (Hovland, Lusdaine, & Sheffield, 1949). Five days after viewing the movie, they showed little attitude change. But nine weeks later, the soldiers were more apt to show more positive attitudes than a control group of soldiers who had never viewed the film. Obviously, between day five and week nine something had happened to bring about attitude change, and that something was dubbed the sleeper effect.

To explain the sleeper effect, the investigators turned to the credibility of the message source. Because the soldiers viewed the original message as questionable—they held the U.S. Army in low regard and saw its messages as biased—the message had little initial credibility. Consequently, they tended to discount the message of the film. However, after several weeks had gone by, the source of the information was forgotten, while the content of the message had been retained. This explanation came to be known as the "discounting cue hypothesis," and it rests on the notion that we store information about the message differently from the way we store information about the message source, and we recall these kinds of information with different degrees of success.

Over the years, the sleeper effect has proven to be elusive; sometimes investigators were able to demonstrate its existence, and other times they were not (Pratkanis et al., 1988; Cook et al., 1979). Frustration reached a peak in the 1970s, when attitude researchers Paulette Gillig and Anthony Greenwald (1974) wrote a paper asking, "Is it time to lay the sleeper effect to rest?"

Fortunately, the research community answered the question with a resounding "No." In fact, recent studies have not only demonstrated the reality of the sleeper effect but also pinpointed the conditions under which it occurs.

For instance, in one experiment, all subjects were exposed to persuasive information arguing against a four-day work week, suggesting that it reduced employee satisfaction and created several other kinds of difficulties (Pratkanis et al., 1988). In some conditions, subjects also received several additional bits of data meant to act as discounting cues. Specifically, the discounting cues raised serious objections to the message content, indicating that new evidence contradicted the conclusion that the four-day work week was unsuccessful. However, the timing of the discounting cues differed for different groups of subjects: Some learned of it prior to reading the information about the four-day week, others were exposed to it after reading that information, and some didn't receive the discounting cues at all. In addition, a control group of subjects received no message.

The results of the study showed that subjects who received the message alone (without the discounting cues) were swayed by the information initially, but showed little effect after six weeks had passed. For those who received the discounting cues prior to reading the information, there was little attitude change over the course of the six weeks. But those subjects who received the discounting cues after reading the information displayed the sleeper effect: Their attitudes were more influenced by the information six weeks later than just after reading the message (see Figure 11-1).

These results suggest that the sleeper effect is alive and well, but only under certain conditions. For one thing, discounting cues—messages contradicting the initial message—must follow the persuasive message. If they come before, they influence the way a message is initially evaluated and learned. When this happens, any attitude change is likely to reflect both the discounting cues and the information itself, and both kinds of information are likely to be recalled to the same extent when the attitude is assessed after the passage of time. Hence, there would be little difference between immediate measures of recall and later ones.

In contrast, information that is initially presented by itself might be learned in one way, while the subsequent discounting cue is learned in another way. In this case, the two sets of data would be stored in memory separately and might well be forgotten at separate rates. Although the two kinds of information would be expected to be recalled equally well during immediate measures of attitudes, only the information in the message may linger in memory, while the discounting cue may be forgotten. When this occurs, the information in the message would be influential after the passage of time.

How might you use this information about the sleeper effect in practice? Suppose you are a politician presenting information about yourself in a magazine ad, trying to convince voters to support your candidacy. Keeping the sleeper effect in mind, you might strive to disguise your message, making it appear to be part of the magazine's text,

**FIGURE 11-1    The Sleeper Effect** When a message opposing a four-day work week was read aloud, it produced some initial attitude change, but six weeks later had little effect. When the initial message was preceded by discounting cues, attitudes changed little over time. But when the message was read first and then followed by the discounting cues, a sleeper effect occurred in which initial attitude change was low, but subsequent attitude change was high.
(*Source:* Pratkanis, Greenwald, Leippe, & Baumgardner, 1988.)

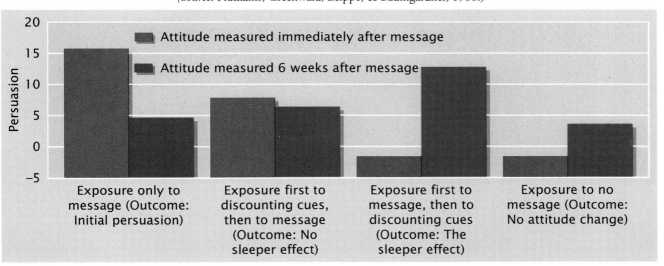

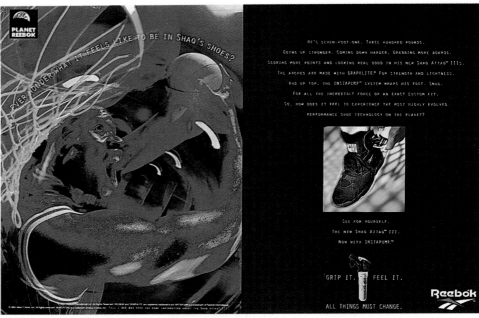

Shaquille O'Neal

---

**FIGURE  11-2    Celebrity Pitches: Stars of the '90s**

The most popular entertainers and athletic product, ranked according to product appeal:

| ENTERTAINERS | PRODUCTS |
| --- | --- |
| Candice Bergen | Sprint |
| Bill Cosby | Jell-O |
| Cher | Equal |
| Cindy Crawford | Revlon |
| Burt Reynolds | Florida Citrus Commission |
| Regis Philbin | Ultra Slim-Fast |
| Susan Lucci | Ford |
| Sally Struthers | Christian Children's Fund |
| Ray Charles | Diet Pepsi |
| Kathie Lee Gifford | Carnival Cruise Lines, Ultra SlimFast |

| ATHLETES | PRODUCTS |
| --- | --- |
| Michael Jordan | Nike, McDonald's, Hanes, Wheaties |
| Bo Jackson | Nike |
| Tommy Lasorda | Ultra SlimFast |
| Earvin "Magic" Johnson | Converse, Pepsi, Kentucky Fried Chicken |
| Joe Namath | Flex-All, The Wiz |
| Bob Uecker | Miller Lite |
| Joe Montana | Diet Pepsi |
| Nolan Ryan | Advil |
| Hulk Hogan | Right Guard |
| Arnold Palmer | Jiffy Lube, Hertz, Sears |

*Source:* Video Storyboard Tests Inc., cited in Lipman, 1991 and in Goldman, 1993.

and not an advertisement. Only in the last paragraph of the "article" would you admit that the text was actually an advertisement.

Although the recognition that the "article" was actually an advertisement might cause the readers temporary annoyance (and increase the possibility that they will discount the ad initially), the end result may be in your favor. The sleeper effect suggests that after a certain amount of time has gone by, the discounting information will be forgotten, and only the favorable information about your candidacy may be remembered—and accepted by the reader. (Magazines are not unaware of this phenomenon, by the way, and most require that advertisements be prominently identified as such on each page.)

*Communicator Attractiveness and Likability*

You'd probably be startled to find an advertising campaign featuring the recommendations of Jeffrey Dahmer, the admitted serial killer of a dozen people in Milwaukee, Wisconsin. Instead, commercials tend to feature the likes of entertainment stars and prominent athletes such as Candice Bergen, Paula Abdul, and Michael Jordan (see Figure 11-2).

The use of celebrities to pitch products stems from the fact that the attractiveness of a communicator is a key factor in determining how persuasive the message will be. For instance, physical attractiveness clearly plays a role in a person's ability to persuade others; people tend to be more persuaded by those who are good-looking than those who are less so (Chaiken, 1979). Furthermore, it is not just physical attractiveness that produces greater persuasion; general social attractiveness—such as that found in famous, but not-necessarily-handsome sports stars—is enough to provide greater persuasibility on the part of a communicator (Chaiken, 1980; Mills & Aronson, 1965; Roskos-Ewoldsen & Fazio, 1992).

Happily, the link between attractiveness and persuasibility is not ironclad; we are not destined to slavishly follow what the attractive wish us to do. Indeed, in some cases the use of celebrity endorsements backfires. Consider, for example, the case of Ringo Starr, who plugged Sun Country wine coolers just before he reputedly was treated for alcohol abuse. In such a situation, Starr's value as a communicator certainly became questionable (Lipman, 1991).

Furthermore, communicator attractiveness has considerably less impact in instances when people are led to use central route, as opposed to peripheral route, processing. For example, in one experiment, subjects were presented with a message communicated either by famous and admired sports figures or by anonymous, middle-aged people from Bakersfield, California (Petty, Cacioppo, & Schumann, 1983). When the subjects were relatively uninvolved and unmotivated to consider the message content (and therefore used peripheral route processing), the celebrity endorsers made a difference, producing greater attitude change. But when the subjects were involved and motivated to pay attention to the message—and therefore employed central route processing—the attractiveness of the communicators had no effect (Petty, Cacioppo, & Schumann, 1983).

▶ REVIEW & RETHINK

*Review*

- According to the elaboration likelihood model, persuasion takes place through either the central or peripheral route.

*Continued on next page*

- Expertise and trustworthiness, characteristics of message credibility, are a major source of a message's effectiveness.
- A communicator's attractiveness and likability also are related to persuasiveness.

*Rethink*

- If you were to devise a message designed to relate to peripheral route processing, what characteristics would it have?
- What factors affect perceptions of source credibility? Is the trust afforded experts always logical?
- Aside from credibility, what characteristics of a message source affect persuasibility? Recall the "beautiful-is-good" stereotype discussed in Chapter 6. Explain how this stereotype relates to source persuasibility.

# THE MESSAGE: CRAFTING THE COMMUNICATION

*Illinois Power was in trouble.* 60 Minutes *had just done a story that charged that the nuclear power company had seriously mismanaged its finances, to the point of running up thousands of dollars in cost overruns. In this age of corporate public relations, the company knew it had to do something. One solution was to write a press release that described all of the positive accomplishments the company had made in the areas of nuclear power and financial management. Another possibility was to take on* 60 Minutes *directly by developing a message that outlined each of the charges by* 60 Minutes *and then explained why each charge was false. If you were working for Illinois Power, which message strategy would you select? (Perloff, 1993, p. 166).*

The answer to the question (which we'll come back to a bit later) is provided by years of research on whether one- or two-sided messages are most persuasive. Indeed, issues regarding how to best formulate an argument are central to the study of persuasion.

If an audience is motivated and able to use central route processing, the way in which arguments are crafted and presented play a primary role in determining how well others are influenced by the message. In following the central route, people consider and pay attention to how big the hole in the ozone layer is, or why one automobile is safer than another, or why they should vote in the primary. In these circumstances, whether they heed a speaker's call, however, depends on the quality of the arguments they hear and how the arguments are presented.

*The Amount and Type of Information*

The old 1950s television show *Dragnet* was clear on the kind of information detective Joe Friday wanted: "Just the facts, ma'am." But how many facts make for a persuasive argument?

In formulating a persuasive message, more is sometimes—but not always—better. If the arguments are equally strong and valid, then the more the merrier. This is true regardless of whether recipients employ central or peripheral processing. If central route processing occurs, the strong arguments provide support for the position that is being promoted. And if peripheral route processing is being employed, people fall back on the heuristic that "a longer argument must be a better argument," without carefully evaluating the message (Stasson & Davis, 1989; Petty & Cacioppo, 1984, 1986b).

On the other hand, if additional arguments are relatively weak, then they should be used only if peripheral processing is taking place. In the peripheral route, the quality of the arguments doesn't particularly matter, since the message recipient isn't paying close attention. But if central route processing is occurring and the arguments are being evaluated on their merits, then weak arguments detract from the overall message and may even raise counterarguments in the mind of the listener. A speaker's general point may be diluted if the additional arguments are weak, suggesting that a speaker is better off presenting fewer, but more solid, arguments if central route processing is occurring (Petty & Cacioppo, 1984; Calder, Insko, & Yandell, 1974; Harkins & Petty, 1987).

*Point and Counterpoint: One or Both Sides of the Coin?*

During every political campaign, candidates ponder the effect of negative advertising, in which they not only present their own side of an argument, but simultaneously attack their adversary's position. Although negative advertising permits a politician to attack an opponent, it also implicitly suggests that the adversary's position has enough merit to warrant a response. Furthermore, it raises the unwelcome possibility that someone observing the attack will find the opponent's position more convincing. If this occurs, clearly it would have been better not to mention the opponent's position in the first place and merely to present one's own.

To social psychologists, this issue has been considered in the more general terms of identifying whether communicators are better off sticking with their own side of an issue, or whether it makes more sense to also present the other side of the argument and then refute it. The answer is that it depends largely on the target audience of the message.

If the audience is relatively well educated, disagrees with the intended message, is aware that there are many different perspectives on an issue, and is likely to be exposed to subsequent information, a communicator is better off presenting both sides of an issue. On the other hand, audiences who are less well educated, who are initially favorable to the speaker's point of view, and who themselves see the issue as one-sided are more likely to be influenced by one-sided presentations than by two-sided communications (Hovland, Lumsdaine, & Sheffield, 1949; Perloff, 1993).

Given the complexity of these findings, what advice might a social psychologist give to a candidate about to enter the fray of political battle? The best counsel would be to tailor each message to the specific audience that will hear it. When speaking to the party faithful, who are likely to already agree with the broad outlines of the candidate's position, stick to a one-sided message in order to reinforce and strengthen the audience's commitment. But when reaching out to uncommitted voters, a candidate should take a more measured approach, providing both sides of the argument and refuting the opposition's position.

In the case of Illinois Power, executives of the company assumed that viewers of *60 Minutes* would be reasonably well educated; they would probably agree with the *60 Minutes* charges, but would also be aware that there was more than one perspective on the issue. This set of conditions suggested that a two-sided presentation would be best, in which each of the allegations would be rebutted.

Was Illinois Power correct in its assessment? Research suggests that it was. The company produced a videotape containing a two-sided message and distributed it across the country. Research on its effectiveness suggested that, compared with individuals who saw only the *60 Minutes* presentation, people exposed to the tape found that the *60 Minutes* presentation was less believable and the power company more credible (Clavier & Kalupa, 1983; Perloff, 1993).

*Repeating the Message*

"You got the right one baby, uh huh. Uh huh. Uh huh."

How many times must people hear this slogan before they forget that it is a grammarian's nightmare and begin to yearn for a sip of Pepsi? And is there a moment when they've heard it one time too often, and their feelings for Pepsi drift toward the negative?

As we discussed in Chapter 6 when we considered interpersonal attraction, generally familiarity breeds not contempt, but attraction. The greater our acquaintance with a person or object, the more likely we are to hold positive attitudes toward them.

Congruent with these conclusions, the amount and persistence of attitude change increases for at least the first several times we are exposed to a message. After that, there can be too much of a good thing: Increasing numbers of repetitions of a message add only a little, and may even decrease its effectiveness in producing attitude change (Cacioppo & Petty, 1979; Calder & Sternthal, 1980).

How quickly a message wears out its welcome depends, in part, on its complexity. More complex messages can benefit from increased repetitions, as there is more to learn and retain. Simple messages, such as slogans, can be heard only so many times before they become tedious and unpleasant. Professionals in the advertising field call this "wear-out."

To avoid wear-out, advertisers sometimes resort to repetition-with-variation. In this procedure, the basic message is presented repeatedly, but it undergoes subtle transformations each time it is delivered. For example, advertisements may display a closeup of a bottle of dishwasher detergent from the front, side, or rear; or a driver is shown sitting behind the wheel of a Honda while driving through the city, country, or suburbs. The message is basically the same, although the context varies slightly.

Repetition-with-variation is effective in promoting positive attitudes—as long as people don't think too much about the message. When people engage in peripheral route processing, they're apt to find that the variations relieve the boredom that might be expected from unvaried repetition. On the other hand, if they are processing in the central route, their increased scrutiny of the message may lead to boredom, even if it is presented with variation, or they may engage in more critical thinking about the content of the message (Schumann, Petty, & Clemons, 1990).

Advertisers, of course, can rest easy: few people scrutinize advertisements very thoughtfully. Their repetition-with-variation strategy, then, is likely to be effective.

## Fear Appeals: Raising the Stakes

If you have unprotected sex, you might well get AIDS and die.

Few appeals for safer sex make such blatant statements. Why? Not because the statement is untrue. Quite the contrary: It is an accurate prediction in the age of sexual freedom and the AIDS epidemic.

**fear appeals**
messages regarding attitude change that are designed to produce apprehension and anxiety if the message is not followed.

The reason we are not likely to encounter such statements is related to a long history of research on **fear appeals**—messages regarding attitude change that are designed to produce apprehension and anxiety if the message is not followed. According to this accumulated research, strong fear appeals—by themselves—do not produce significant attitude change. Instead, they produce so much distress that they are more likely to arouse people's defenses. Instead of accepting and following the message, listeners are more likely to ignore the message because it is so unpleasant (Mewborn & Rogers, 1979; Natarajan, 1979).

For example, when people see a video that graphically illustrates what happens to one's lungs after contracting lung cancer from smoking, the likely result is not a reduction in smoking but rather a sense of disgust over the film. Similarly, when people are told to wear bike helmets to protect them from horrible brain damage if they are in a crash, they are unlikely to follow the advice, since it may be so threatening that they repress the gist of the message. In some cases, then, milder fear appeals may produce greater attitude change than stronger fear appeals (Janis, 1967; Dziokonski & Weber, 1977).

On the other hand, strong fear appeals can be effective—if they are accompanied by specific, precise recommendations for actions to avoid the danger. For instance, rather than simply suggesting that smoking leads to frightful lung cancer, a message needs to

There is a proven connection between sun exposure and skin cancer, as well as premature wrinkling. If you must be in the sun, use sunscreen and common sense.

AMERICAN CANCER SOCIETY®

The use of fear appeals, such as raising the specter of the illness can be effective—if the message includes specific recommendations. Here, the advice for avoiding getting cancer is straightforward: stay out of the sun.

communicate specific ways in which a person can stop smoking (Maddux & Rogers, 1983). Similarly, to persuade people to wear bike helmets, it would be useful to pair the fear-evoking message with information on what kind of helmet works best and where they can be purchased (Leventhal, 1970; Axelrod & Apsche, 1982).

The key to successful fear appeals is to make people feel they are vulnerable to a threat, but that there are actions they can take in order to overcome the threat—and that they have the capability of taking those actions (Rogers, 1983).

For instance, suppose your goal were to reduce the incidence of breast and testicular cancer by persuading people to carry out self-examinations to check for lumps—a simple and effective procedure. To do this, you might first begin by making people feel vulnerable, perhaps by revealing that each year, 40,000 women die of breast cancer and 6,000 men of testicular cancer.

After creating this sense of vulnerability, the message would need to show that corrective actions can be taken to avoid these kinds of cancer, and that any individual is able to carry out those actions. Hence, an effective message would incorporate specific information regarding how to carry out a self-examination.

Although social psychologists have considered fear more than any other emotion, they have also investigated the use of appeals that inspire other emotions. For a study of how emotional appeals are affected by their context, see the Social Psychology at Work feature on the next page.

## SOCIAL PSYCHOLOGY AT WORK

# SHOULD ADS BE HAPPY OR SAD? IT DEPENDS ON THE CONTEXT

At the height of the war in the Persian Gulf, many advertisers pulled their carefully crafted ads off the airwaves. They took this drastic step because they feared that in the face of the grim news about the war's destruction, their messages would be ineffective.

According to the results of at least one study, however, if the advertisements had a sad mood, they might well have gotten their message across. In fact, the grim circumstances might even have increased the impact of such ads. The reason for this phenomenon: Ads that make viewers feel sad are more persuasive when placed in the context of sad programming than when shown in the context of a happy program (Kamins, Marks, & Skinner, 1991).

In the study, participants were shown one of three types of advertisements: a happy ad, a sad ad, and a neutral ad. They viewed these ads in the context of three types of programming—happy, sad, and neutral. Researchers learned that viewers' response to the ads depended on the context in which they were seen.

Sad ads had the most pronounced reaction in the midst of sad programming, while happy ads were most effective in the context of happy programming. Specifically, a sad ad placed in a sad program was some 40 percent more effective than a happy ad seen in the sad program, and 15 percent more effective than a sad ad in a happy program. Surprisingly, the sad ad placed within the context of a sad program was more powerful than a happy ad shown in the context of a happy program.

What is the explanation behind the study's conclusion? The researchers hypothesize that viewers who already are in a particular emotional state as a result of watching the program are going to feel more empathy to the message of an ad that is congruent with their current mood. In contrast, a happy ad placed in the context of sad programming or a sad ad in a happy program may be so jarring that its message is lost.

According to these findings, upbeat ads for messages relating to vacation travel, tennis racquets, or gym shoes might best be shown during comedies. On the other hand, if advertisers are hawking life insurance, drug treatment centers, or air bags, they might well run their ad during a documentary about homelessness or cancer in order to make sure their message is heard (Hinge, 1991).

When shown on television, upbeat ads like this work best when presented in the context of "happy" programming.

# THE TARGET OF PERSUASION: RECEIVING THE MESSAGE

When politicians go out on the stump, they don't give the same speech to the National Evangelical Association and to a group of rock video producers. Honda won't run the same ad in both *Rolling Stone* magazine and the *New York Times.*

Even though their respective goals are the same—vote for me, or purchase a Honda—the persuasive approach takes into account the identity and character of the audience. For good reason: Targets of persuasive messages react quite distinctly according to their specific characteristics.

The early research on the relationship between persuasion and receiver attributes sought to identify personal characteristics that consistently led people to be easy or difficult prey for persuasive messages (Hovland & Janis, 1959). Were unintelligent people more easily persuaded than intelligent ones? Were men influenced more readily than women? Did people with low self-esteem respond more to persuasive messages than those high in self-esteem?

As it turned out, the exercise was futile. Very few people were invariably easy marks; nor were many always immune to persuasion. Instead, people's reactions to persuasive messages depend on a combination of the kind of message that is being communicated, its source, their own personal qualities, and even their emotional state (McGuire, 1985). We'll consider how two such factors (a person's characteristic level of thoughtfulness or cognitive activity, and the person's mood) relate to attitude change.

## *The Need for Cognition*

**need for cognition**
a person's habitual level of thoughtfulness and cognitive activity.

Look at the statements presented in Figure 11-3. Which ones do you agree with?

People who agree with the first two statements, and disagree with the rest, have a relatively high need for cognition. **Need for cognition** is a person's habitual level of thoughtfulness and cognitive activity. If you enjoy pondering and philosophizing about the world around you, it is likely that your need for cognition is relatively high. On the other hand, if you become impatient when forced to spend too much time thinking about things, your need for cognition probably is relatively low.

---

**FIGURE 11-3   The Need for Cognition**

Which of the following statements apply to you?

1. I really enjoy a task that involves coming up with new solutions to problems.
2. I would prefer a task that is intellectual, difficult, and important to one that is somewhat important but does not require much thought.
3. Learning new ways to think doesn't excite me very much.
4. The idea to rely on thought to make my way to the top does not appeal to me.
5. I think only as hard as I have to.
6. I like tasks that require little thought once I've learned them.
7. I prefer to think about small, daily projects rather than long-term ones.
8. I would rather do something that requires little thought than something that is sure to challenge my thinking abilities.
9. I find little satisfaction in deliberating hard and for long hours.
10. I don't like to be responsible for a situation that requires a lot of thinking.

*Scoring:* The more you agree with statements 1 and 2, and disagree with the rest, the greater the likelihood that you have a high need for cognition.

*Source:* Cacioppo & Petty, 1982.

When exposed to a persuasive message, people who are high in the need for cognition tend to produce a greater number of responses to the message—in other words, they think more about it. However, this thinking does not invariably lead to either an acceptance or a rejection of the message. Instead, it depends on the specific content of the message. A high-quality, multiple-argument, detail-laden message is likely to produce attitude change, while a weak message, containing low-quality, undetailed, and relatively few arguments, is likely to produce little attitude change (Cacioppo et al., 1983; Cacioppo et al., 1986).

But what of people low in the need for cognition? What kind of arguments are most effective with them? It turns out that for individuals who are low in the need for cognition, the quality of the argument matters very little. The reason is that people low in the need for cognition tend to stick to the peripheral processing route. Relying on heuristics—those handy rules of thumb that make peripheral route processing so effortless—people low in the need for cognition tend to be influenced by factors other than the quality and detail of the message content (Chaiken, 1987).

We should not think, however, that people high in cognition are necessarily more adept at evaluating messages to which they are exposed. Both those high and low in need for cognition are susceptible to persuasive evidence—but that evidence must be demonstrated in different ways for high-cognition people than for low-cognition people. For example, subjects in one experiment read details of a murder case and watched a 45-minute interrogation of a defendant, whose answers were rather ambiguous regarding her guilt (Kassin, Reddy, & Tulloch, 1990). Subjects also heard a summary of the case presented by her defense attorney and the prosecutor. In some cases, they first heard the defense attorney and then the prosecutor; for others, the order was reversed.

The reactions of the subjects, who were asked to judge the validity of the defendant's story, varied according to whether they were high or low in need for cognition, as well as to the order of presentation. Subjects high in need for cognition were more swayed by the person they heard first—a phenomenon known as the primacy effect. Apparently, they carefully evaluated what the first speaker had to say, and found that evidence convincing. The later presentation did not sway them.

The result was different for those subjects low in cognition. They showed a recency effect, being influenced most by whomever they heard last. Having the last word consequently made the greatest impact on the low-need-for-cognition individuals (see Figure 11-4).

In sum, the degree to which we habitually think about the world and process information—our need for cognition—has an important impact on the kind of persuasive material that influences us most. Remember that it is not people who are either high or low in need for cognition who are invariably more or less easy to influence. Instead, the degree to which they can be persuaded depends on the kind of persuasive message they receive and the circumstances at the time they receive it.

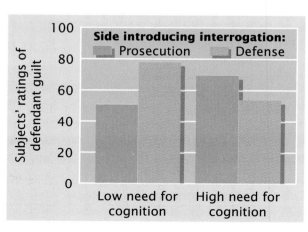

**FIGURE 11-4 Guilty or Innocent?** When mock jurors were asked to rate the validity of the defendant's story, their ratings of guilt varied according to their need for cognition and whether the prosecution or the defense presented arguments first. (*Source:* Kassin, Reddy, & Tulloch, 1990.)

*Moods: Happy to Be Persuaded?*

If you'd just won the lottery, you know you'd be in a good mood. Would that also make you more susceptible to persuasion?

Probably. According to research carried out by social psychologists Diane Mackie and colleagues, placing people in a good mood makes them more apt to change their attitudes (Mackie & Worth, 1991; Schwarz, Bless, & Bohner, 1991; Petty et al., 1993).

For example, subjects in one study were led to believe they had unexpectedly won a prize—placing them in a good mood. These subjects, along with others who had not won and were therefore in a neutral mood, were then exposed to a supposedly unrelated persuasive message regarding acid rain. The message was supposedly written by either an expert or a nonexpert, and included either nine strong arguments or nine relatively weak arguments.

As can be seen in Figure 11-5, subjects' mood affected their responses. For people in a good mood, it didn't much matter whether the arguments were strong or weak; attitude change was quite similar. But for people in a neutral mood, the nature of the arguments did make a difference. For them, strong arguments were considerably more persuasive.

Mood also affected responsiveness to expert and nonexpert sources. Here, subjects in a positive mood were more apt to change their attitude when the message was written by an expert than by a nonexpert; but for neutral-mood subjects, the expertise of the writer had no effect.

What accounts for these results? If you think back to our earlier discussion of central and peripheral route processing, you'll recall that the quality of the arguments was related to central route processing, while expertise was related to peripheral route processing.

This distinction provides a handy explanation for these results. What appears to be happening is that placing someone in a good mood is distracting, increasing the likelihood of peripheral route processing. Consequently, factors associated with peripheral route processing—such as expertise—would be expected to have a significant impact on attitude change. In contrast, factors such as argument strength, which relate to central

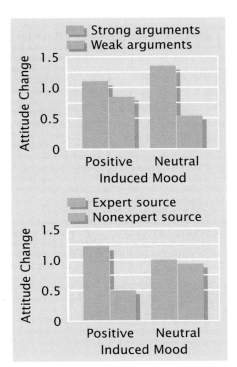

**FIGURE 11-5  Mood and Attitude Change** For people in a good mood, it doesn't matter substantially whether the arguments are strong or weak. But for people in a neutral mood, the nature of the arguments makes a significant difference. Mood also affects responsiveness to the source of a message. People in a positive mood are more apt to change their attitude when the message is communicated by an expert, but the expertise of the communicator has little effect for people in a neutral mood. *(Source:* Adapted from Mackie & Worth, 1991.*)*

route processing, would be less likely to affect attitude change in people who are feeling good.

In sum, people in a positive mood are apt to be distracted, perhaps thinking about their good fortune, and therefore more likely to engage in peripheral route processing. As a result, experiencing a good mood may lead someone to be happier, but also more gullible.

> ## REVIEW & RETHINK

### Review

- The amount and type of information in a message affects persuasion.
- Depending on the circumstances, one- or two-sided messages are more appropriate.
- Fear appeals may be useful if they are accompanied by specific, precise recommendations.
- A message recipient's need for cognition and the recipient's mood are associated with ease of persuasion.

### Rethink

- Under what circumstances are two-sided arguments more effective than one-sided arguments? Would you recommend using a two-sided argument in a television ad for a soft drink? Why or why not?
- During which program would a fear ad be most effective: a situation comedy, a dramatic series, or the nightly news?
- What target characteristics did Hovland and his colleagues investigate in connection with persuasion?
- Describe the relationship you would expect to find between need for cognition and the following aspects of persuasion: source credibility, amount of message information, quality of message information, and repetition with variation.

## PERSUASION IN THE MARKETPLACE

*It's late December, and for the last few weeks you've been subjected to a media blitz by Ed McMahon telling you about the American Family Publishers Sweepstakes. You've seen friendly, trustworthy Ed introducing a past winner of $1 million. You've seen the letter on TV. Finally, it arrives, your "LAST CHANCE! Million Dollar Document" warning you, "Don't Throw Away! This is the letter you just saw on TV!" . . . .*

*You now open the big envelope. On the large, official-looking document, you find your name throughout the text at least 20 times in various sizes of type. The first large print catches your eye: There's your name preceding ". . . SHALL BE PAID A FULL ONE MILLION DOLLARS." In contrasting color in the upper margin is the constant reminder, "LAST CHANCE!" A little farther down, there's your name again with nine—count 'em—nine Personal Prize Claim Numbers . . . .*

*The next piece of paper has a color picture of Ed, more instructions, and photos of a Mercedes, a mink coat, a cabin cruiser, and a beautiful home. "Become a Multimillionaire and Treat Yourself to the Things You Want Most!" you're told.*

*After extensive reading you finally figure out what to paste where to enter the contest. You also have a big page of colorful, perforated, sticky stamps that can*

> *be pasted on the entry blank to purchase any of a variety of magazines. Another full-color sheet from Ed tells you, "You can take it from me—THERE ARE NO LOWER PRICES AVAILABLE ANYWHERE TO THE GENERAL PUBLIC. American Family values are GUARANTEED UNBEATABLE!" There is also a list of selected magazines that offer Free Bonus Gifts, such as watches and desk clocks. You decide a Money-Manager Calculator would be useful—so you order* Newsweek, *which will keep you better informed for school. Besides the good price, you don't have to pay now, because you'll be billed in the future. Also there's a money-back guarantee if you don't like the subscription—and, as it says, "You risk nothing!" So, you get the calculator,* Newsweek *at a great price, and maybe . . . just maybe . . . BIG, BIG BUCKS!!! (Peter & Olson, 1987, pp. 305–306)*

Unless you've spent the last few years on a desert island, you're probably familiar with messages such as this one. Each year, just after Christmas, the airwaves are saturated with the news that the mail will soon bring you your chance to win millions, while also enjoying the opportunity to purchase subscriptions to your favorite magazines.

It is not pure chance that brings these sales pitches after the Christmas season. Research carried out by advertisers has shown that at this time of year consumers are most receptive to messages that promise the chance to win a big jackpot (Peter & Olson, 1987). After all, the bills for all those expensive holiday presents are coming due, and who couldn't use a sudden windfall to help pay them off?

Probably the most sophisticated use of the basic principles of persuasion that has been identified by social psychologists is found in the study of consumer behavior. The exploration of **consumer behavior** focuses on understanding buying habits and the effects of advertising on buyer behavior. Social psychologists specializing in consumer behavior explore how consumers are affected by particular kinds of advertising, and how they make decisions to purchase (or forgo) specific products.

**consumer behavior**
buying habits and effects of advertising on buyer behavior.

You are most likely to get an invitation to enter a sweepstakes after the Christmas holiday season, when the chance of obtaining quick cash may be particularly appealing.

*Persuasive Advertising: Changing Consumers' Collective Minds*

**informative advertising**
advertising designed to introduce new products, suggest new ways of using an existing product, or correct false impressions about a product in a way that produces demand for a particular class of products.

**selective demand advertising**
advertising designed to establish or modify attitudes about a particular brand of product or service, compared with other brands of the same kind of product or service.

If you are like the average American, you watch more than 700 advertisements on television each week. In that same week, you may be exposed to several hundred additional commercials on the radio and in newspapers and magazines (Aaker & Myers, 1987).

All those advertisements may seem pretty much alike to you, passing by in a blur. However, although all advertisements are designed to promote the purchase of some product or service, they actually have several different purposes (Kotler, 1986). For instance, the primary purpose of some advertisements is informative. **Informative advertising** is designed to introduce new products, to suggest new ways of using an existing product, or to correct false impressions about a product. In this sort of advertising the goal is to generate demand for a class of products. For instance, the insurance industry runs advertisements in which the general objective is to promote the idea that everyone needs some sort of life insurance.

In contrast, **selective demand advertising** is designed to establish or modify attitudes about a particular brand of product or service, compared with other brands of the same kind of product or service. Selective demand ads build preferences for particular products or brands, advocate switching brands, or attempt to persuade customers to buy a certain product immediately, rather than at a later date (Aaker & Biel, 1993).

Some kinds of selective demand advertising also make straightforward or indirect comparisons between different brands. For instance, in Avis's well-known advertising campaign, the company admitted that although they were "number two" in the field, they "tried harder." Such an advertisement made implicit comparisons between Avis and its major competitor, Hertz, the largest car rental company. Other comparisons are even more subtle, as when an ad for Scope mouthwash stated that it fought bad breath without giving purchasers "medicine breath." The unstated message: One acquires objectionable "medicine breath" from the use of Scope's major competitor, Listerine.

In contrast to selective demand and reminder advertising, informative advertising is meant to introduce new products or to provide facts about existing products.

**reminder advertising**
advertising designed to keep consumers thinking about a product or to reinforce the message that preferring a brand is appropriate.

Finally, the third major type of advertising is reminder advertising. In **reminder advertising**, the goal is to keep consumers thinking about a product or to reinforce the message that preferring a brand is appropriate. For example, when Hallmark sponsors television's *Hallmark Hall of Fame,* its purpose is largely to remind people of the brand name "Hallmark." Similarly, some advertisements seek to assure consumers that they have made an appropriate decision in already having purchased a product. Hence, commercials showing satisfied customers are designed not only to persuade potential purchasers to buy the product, but also to assure those who have already made a purchase that they made the right choice—making it more likely that the same product will be purchased in the future (Batra, Lehmann, & Singh, 1993).

## *Advertising Messages: Relating Consumers and Products*

Regardless of the particular goals of an advertising campaign, the most effective persuasion takes place when the advertisement takes into account the relationship between consumers and products. For instance, one aspect of this relationship is the extent to which consumers understand the product and are involved with it with (Berger, 1986; Homer & Kahle, 1990; Andrews, Durwasula, & Akhter, 1990).

As Figure 11-6 illustrates, involvement is one major dimension relating to consumer attitudes about products. Involvement pertains both to the amount of prior experience and the degree of consumer interest in a product.

The second major dimension centers on the nature of the knowledge, meaning, beliefs, and thoughts that are activated when consumers consider a product. Some products are considered primarily in terms of their cognitive aspects—the rational, thoughtful associations of the product. When considering a product in cognitive terms, the functions of the product are primary. Consequently, when we think of insecticides or cameras, we consider them primarily in functional, cognitive terms.

In contrast, we consider other products more in emotional and affective terms. We think of products of this type primarily in nonlinguistic terms consisting of visual images or their sensory aspects. For example, most of us conceive of perfume in terms not of its chemical composition but of its fragrance and its potential use in social situations. Similarly, items such as favorite foods or flashy automobiles may evoke primarily emotional reactions and images.

According to social psychologist David Berger, a product's location on the grid shown in Figure 11-6 points to the best way to devise advertising for the product (Berger, 1986). For instance, products that are located toward the emotional end of the cognitive–emotional dimension are advertised in ways that are considerably different from products that are more cognitive in nature. Thus, perfume—a product with strong emotional connotations—is best promoted through advertisements that evoke the emotional aspects of the product. In practice, this results in advertisements that emphasize the sexual implications of the use of perfume. Perfume advertising also pioneered the use of "scent strips," which are samples of the product that can be placed in magazine or mail advertisements. By actually incorporating the perfume's fragrance with the written message, ad writers aim to establish a classically conditioned association (Gubernick, 1986).

In some cases, advertising attempts to shift the location of a product on the grid. For example, a South American manufacturer was faced with a problem. It had produced thousands of unattractive green refrigerators that lacked many features. Meanwhile, the manufacturer's competition was promoting refrigerators that contained substantially more features, such as built-in icemakers. The manufacturer's dilemma: Consumers view refrigerators primarily in cognitive terms, and these particular refrigerators had relatively little to recommend them in terms of their cognitive aspects.

The solution? The advertising agency devised an ad campaign to shift the refrigerator from the cognitive quadrant of the grid to the emotional/affective quadrant. Their advertisements displayed Venezuelan beauty queens along with the refrigerators, now

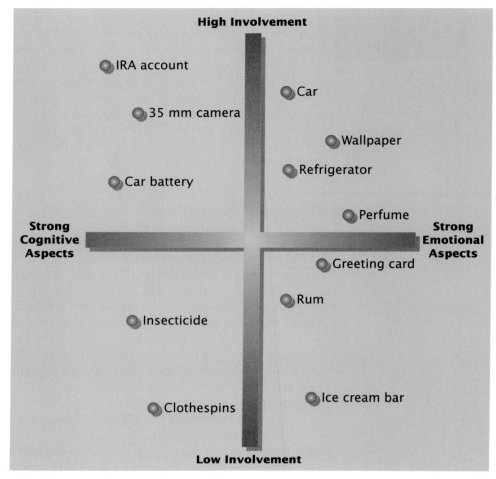

**FIGURE 11–6   Consumer Product Characteristics** As this graph indicates, consumer products can be placed on a grid with two dimensions. The first dimension is involvement, reflecting prior experience and interest in the product. The second reflects whether a product is strong in cognitive or emotional aspects. For example, a camera is relatively high in involvement and in cognitive aspects. In contrast, an ice cream bar is low in involvement and has strong emotional aspects.    *(Source:* Adapted from Berger, 1986.*)*

identified as "another Venezuelan beauty." All five thousand refrigerators sold in just three months (Berger, 1986).

In sum, by analyzing the way consumers perceive a product, advertisers are able to create ad campaigns tailored to consumers' relationship with the particular product. Furthermore, not only can advertising try to persuade consumers to purchase particular products, but it can strive to change the more fundamental nature of the consumer–product relationship.

*The Appeal of Advertising:*
*Hard Sell, Soft Sell*

Consider these advertising claims:

No aspirin cures headaches better.
This is the best auto on the market.
The strongest stain remover ever sold.

Now, compare the phrases above to these:

This ad, which ran in fashion magazines, was impregnated with the smell of the cologne. (If you're sniffing now, don't: the fragrance is not included in this book!)

You'll brighten your day with this coffee.

People will say you're in love when you use this deodorant.

You'll say that happy days are here when you eat these hot dogs.

Clearly, these two sets of statements are very different in tone. Those in the first set are more direct, focusing on the qualities of the products. Those in the second set are much more tranquil, evoking positive images about the product but saying relatively little about what it can accomplish.

The two sets of phrases actually exemplify the two major strategies used by advertisers (Fox, 1984; Snyder & DeBono, 1989). The first approach is the **hard sell** strategy, an advertising approach that focuses on the qualities of the product itself. When using the hard sell, advertisers focus on the function of the product, how the product performs, its taste, or its effect on the life of the consumer. For example, when the electronics manufacturer Zenith claims that "The quality goes in before the name goes on," they are using a hard sell approach.

In contrast to hard sell approaches, **soft sell** techniques strive to link a product with a pleasant image related to the product's use. In using a soft sell approach, advertisers attempt to suggest that potential product purchasers can project or achieve a desirable image through the use of the product.

Hence, when an ad for Close-up toothpaste reminds you that "Tartar isn't sexy," its goal is to link the use of Close-up (and its destruction of tartar) with the presumably

**hard sell**
an advertising strategy that focuses on the qualities of the product itself.

**soft sell**
an advertising strategy that links a product with a pleasant image related to the product's use.

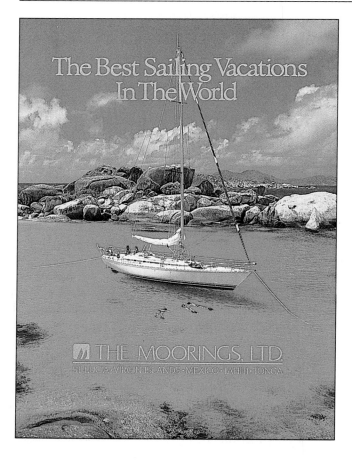

*The Best Sailing Vacations In The World*

THE MOORINGS, LTD.
ST. LUCIA · VIRGIN ISLANDS · MEXICO · TAHITI · TONGA

By focusing on the qualities of the product itself, the Rogaine ad represents a hard-sell strategy. In contrast, the Moorings advertisement is an example of a soft-sell strategy, because it highlights the product's positive image.

desirable consequences of sexiness. Similarly, when men see the Marlboro man, the embodiment of robust masculinity, advertisers want them to feel that they will also personify such qualities if they merely smoke Marlboro. (Women have their own soft sell role models: Virginia Slims cigarette advertisements include attractive, slender females projecting a sophisticated, elegant image.)

In some cases, both hard and soft sell approaches are consolidated into a single advertisement. Consider the BMW automobile advertisement that states, "BMW meets the demands of the 90s with its spirit intact" and "A safe car needn't be a boring one." By touting the safety benefits of the BMW (a hard sell approach) while still claiming that its "spirit" is unbroken and that it isn't boring (a soft sell approach), BMW tries to offer the best of both worlds.

Neither the hard sell nor the soft sell is invariably persuasive to consumers. In fact, their effectiveness depends in part on the personality characteristics of the consumer exposed to the advertisement. One particularly relevant factor is the characteristic level of self-monitoring employed by a potential purchaser.

**self-monitoring**
a regulating of one's behavior in order to meet the demands of a situation or the expectations of others.

As we noted first in Chapter 4, **self-monitoring** is the regulating of one's behavior to meet the demands of a situation or the expectations of others. High self-monitors adjust their behavior from one situation to another in an effort to present themselves effectively and well. They are concerned about the image they project to others, and they are likely to display significant variations in their behavior from one social situation to another. Social chameleons, they easily relate to very different kinds of social settings.

In contrast, people low in self-monitoring are relatively insensitive to the social demands of a given situation. Their behavior is more consistent from one setting to another, and their behavior is more apt to mirror their own attitudes, beliefs, and values. In contrast to high self-monitors, they don't make an effort to blend into social settings (Snyder, 1987).

How do high and low self-monitors differ in their reactions to hard and soft sells? We might expect that high self-monitors, who are most sensitive to issues of image and to presenting themselves optimally, would be more likely to respond to soft sell ads. In contrast, low self-monitors, who are less concerned with image, might be most persuaded by messages that relate to issues of product quality and usefulness—that is, to advertisements that use the hard sell approach (Snyder & DeBono, 1985; Johar & Sirgy, 1991; DeBono & Telesca, 1990).

Support for this reasoning was found by social psychologists Kenneth DeBono and Michelle Packer, who exposed groups of subjects to bogus advertisements that used either hard or soft sell techniques (DeBono & Packer, 1991). In the experiment, subjects who were high or low self-monitors viewed either an image-oriented advertisement (the soft sell) or a quality-oriented advertisement (the hard sell) for a cola or cassette tape. For instance, the image-oriented, soft sell cola ad exhibited cans of cola in an office and on a mountain, under a headline that stated, "In the office . . . or great outdoors, Brand X cola helps you climb to the top." In the hard sell ad emphasizing quality, a picture of the cola can was shown, followed by an equals sign and a dollar sign, stressing the equation between the product and value.

After seeing one of the advertisements, subjects were asked to drink a sample of cola, which was actually an everyday brand sold in supermarkets, and rate how much they liked it. The results are shown in Figure 11-7: high self-monitors felt that the product had higher quality when they had seen the image-oriented ad than when they saw the quality-oriented ad. In contrast, low self-monitors thought just the opposite; they felt that the product was of higher quality when they had seen the quality-oriented advertisement than when they saw the image-oriented advertisement.

In sum, there is probably no persuasive advertisement that is universally effective and will appeal to all consumers. Instead, advertisers must tailor their ads to people with particular kinds of characteristics. Indeed, there is a growing tendency to take into

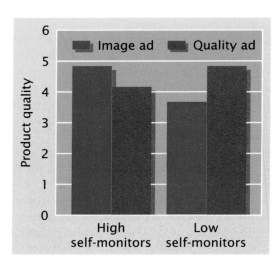

**FIGURE 11-7 Judgments of Product Quality by High and Low Self-Monitors** High self-monitors judge a product to be of higher quality after being exposed to an image-oriented advertisement than after being exposed to a quality-oriented advertisement. In contrast, low self-monitors responded in just the opposite way, judging a product to be of higher quality after seeing a quality-oriented ad as opposed to an image-oriented ad. *(Source:* DeBono & Packer, 1991.*)*

account a variety of personality and demographic characteristics when designing persuasive messages, as we see next.

*Psychographics: The Demography of Advertising*

Who are the people most likely to buy Peter Pan Peanut Butter?

Although this question may not be a particularly pressing one to you, to the makers of the product it most certainly is crucial. Without knowing who the potential customers are, it is impossible to target advertising to the people most likely to purchase the product.

Fortunately—at least from the perspective of the makers of Peter Pan Peanut Butter—researchers have been able to identify the buyers quite precisely: In the New York metropolitan area, the heaviest consumers tend to live in suburban and rural households, have children, and be headed by 18- to 54-year olds. They tend to rent home videos frequently, go to theme parks, watch television at rates below the national average, and listen to radio at rates above the national average (McCarthy, 1991).

The manufacturers of Peter Pan Peanut Butter have come to their understanding of who their potential purchasers are through the technique of psychographics. **Psychographics** is a method for dividing people into lifestyle profiles that are related to purchasing patterns (Rice, 1988). These profiles group people according to factors such as race and ethnic background, marital status, and educational levels, and also according to the kinds of activities that potential buyers participate in. By using psychographics, professional persuaders can analyze consumers' values, needs, attitudes, and motivation to purchase particular items.

**psychographics**
a method for dividing people into lifestyle profiles that are related to purchasing patterns.

Probably the most widely used blueprint for classifying consumers is the "Values and Lifestyles" system, or VALS for short (Mitchell, 1983). VALS stems from clinical psychologist Abraham Maslow's hierarchy of needs, which represents people's progression of motivational needs from the most basic, physiological level to higher-order needs such as esteem and self-actualization (Maslow, 1987).

According to VALS, consumers can be considered as belonging to four major groups: need-driven, outer-directed, inner-directed, and combined outer–inner directed. Need-driven consumers purchase goods in order to satisfy fundamental, basic needs. Outer-directed consumers are motivated by the wish to impress and influence others. Inner-directed consumers make purchases largely for psychological reasons, by trying to increase their own self-awareness. The fourth set of consumers consolidate the needs of inner- and outer-directed purchasers, combining social needs and self-needs. These four groups of consumers are summarized in Figure 11-8.

Within each of the four broad levels of VALS, there are several subcategories. Among need-driven consumers, for example, some are elderly and poor, and their basic

## FIGURE 11-8  VALS Nine American Lifestyles.

### Need-Driven Consumers

*Survivors* (4 percent of the U.S. adult population) These consumers are elderly and intensely poor. They are often widowed and living only on Social Security income. Some have been born into poverty and never escape it; others have slipped to this lifestyle because of bad luck, lack of enterprise, or the onslaughts of old age. Entertainment consists of watching television; basic staples are purchased with an emphasis on low price.

*Sustainers* (7 percent of the U.S. adult population) These consumers are angry, distrustful, anxious, combative, and live on the edge of poverty. Unlike Survivors, Sustainers have not given up hope; they try for a better life. They are careful shoppers and cautious buyers for their large families.

### Outer-Directed Consumers

*Belongers* (38 percent of the U.S. adult population) These consumers typify what is generally regarded as middle-class America. Traditional, conservative, and old-fashioned, these consumers prefer the status quo or the ways of the past and do not like change. These consumers want to fit in rather than stand out, and they follow the rules of society. They value their home and family and seek security.

*Emulators* (10 percent of the U.S. adult population) These consumers are intensely striving people, seeking to be like those they consider richer and more successful. They are more influenced by others than any other lifestyle group and are ambitious, competitive, and ostentatious. Many have attended technical school; few have college degrees. Emulators are in a turbulent transition stage; most of them will not make it to Achiever status. They are conspicuous consumers.

*Achievers* (20 percent of the U.S. adult population) These consumers are the driving and driven people who have built "the system" and are now at the helm. They are effective corporate executive, skilled professionals such as doctors, lawyers, and scientists, adroit politicians, money-oriented athletes and entertainers, and successful artists. They live comfortable, affluent lives and in so doing they have set the standard for much of the nation. They are major consumers of luxury and top-of-the-line products.

### Inner-Directed Consumers

*I-Am-Me* (3 percent of the U.S. adult population) These consumers are young and in a transition period from an outer-directed to an inner-directed way of life. Many have come from Achiever parents and the transition to new values is full of turmoil and confusion of personal identity. Most are students in their 20s and have very energetic, active lives. Clothes and other purchases may be made to differentiate these consumers from their parents and establishment values.

*Experientials* (5 percent of the U.S. adult population) Many of these consumers passed through the I-Am-Me stage a few years earlier. They tend to be artistic, liberal, and to seek vivid, direct experiences with other persons, things, and events. They are highly educated, very energetic, and engage in social activities ranging from outdoor sports to wine tasting. Most are in their late 20s and prefer natural products.

*Societally Conscious* (11 percent of the U.S. adult population) These consumers are well educated, prosperous, politically liberal, and deeply concerned with social issues. They are approaching 40 years of age and are the leaders of movements for improving consumer rights, reducing environmental pollution, and protecting wildlife. Many ride a bike or drive an economy car, insulate their home or install solar heating, and eat only foods grown without pesticides and prepared without additives.

### Combined Outer- and Inner-Directed Group

*Integrateds* (2 percent of the U.S. adult population) These consumers are psychologically mature and find both outer direction and inner direction good, powerful, and useful. They have an unusual ability to weigh consequences and to solve difficult problems. They tend to be open, self-assured, self-expressive, keenly aware of nuance, and command respect and admiration. They tend to be middle-aged or older.

*Source:* Adapted with the permission of Macmillan Publishing Company from Arnold Mitchell, *The Nine American Lifestyles: Who We Are & Where We're Going,* New York: Macmillan Publishing Company; and The Values and Lifestyles Program, SRI International, Menlo Park, California. Copyright © 1983 by Arnold Mitchell.

objective is simply to sustain themselves. Termed "Survivors," they are of relatively little interest to advertisers.

More interesting to advertisers are consumers who have the financial ability to make discretionary purchases beyond the necessities of life. For instance, the largest VALS category is comprised of "Belongers"—outer-directed consumers who are hard-working, responsible, blue-collar or service industry employees. Relatively conservative politically, they conform fairly rigidly to the rules of society.

One fifth of consumers fall into the "Achievers" category, and they are typically successful managers or professionals. They relish symbols of prestige such as expensive homes, automobiles, and vacations.

Although there are several other categories (described in the accompanying table), the pinnacle of consumer success is left for just a few individuals—the "Integrateds." Analogous in some ways to Maslow's notion of self-actualization, consumers who fall into the "Integrateds" category are both achievement-oriented and socially aware.

Consumers generally make purchases in a pattern that is congruent with their VALS category (Mitchell, 1983). For instance, Achievers are likely to be attracted to extravagant luxury cars, while Belongers are more likely to buy family-sized vehicles (they're the ones driving the family station wagons). In contrast, people in the Societally Conscious category tend to purchase small, energy-efficient vehicles, and the Experientials are most apt to purchase showy and powerful sports cars.

---

*Culture and Consumers*    Members of various racial and ethnic groups don't respond uniformly to advertising strategies—a fact of which advertisers, as well as social psychologists, are becoming increasingly aware (Piirto, 1991).

For example, research comparing African-Americans, Hispanics, and whites shows that their purchasing decisions differ significantly. For instance, African-Americans are

Ads such as this are designed to appeal to a particular racial or ethnic group.

more loyal to national brand names than whites, and Hispanics purchase more juice and beer than other groups (Engel & Blackwell, 1982; Boone & Krutz, 1986; Aaker & Biel, 1993).

In some cases, manufacturers of consumer products have attempted to target ads to specific populations—with mixed results. For instance, one ad about telephone service, targeted to Hispanics, involved a Puerto Rican actress telling her husband to "run downstairs and phone Mary. Tell her we'll be a little tardy." Unfortunately, the ad was not successful because it did not take into account two characteristics of Hispanic culture. First, because the culture is relatively male-oriented, the scenario of a wife telling her husband so directly what he should do is implausible. Furthermore, because Hispanic culture has more relaxed, less rigid norms about time, running a little late would not be a cause for concern (McGrath, 1988; Englis, 1993).

In some cases, targeting ads and products to particular populations takes a questionable turn. For instance, the R. J. Reynolds Tobacco Company—which makes the Joe Camel ad campaign we discussed at the start of the chapter—also briefly contemplated distributing a brand of cigarettes called "Uptown." When it became obvious that the brand was targeted toward African-Americans, the product was condemned by the Secretary of the U.S. Department of Health and Human Services. Eventually, the brand was discontinued (Quinn, 1990).

---

# THE INFORMED CONSUMER OF SOCIAL PSYCHOLOGY

## RESISTING THE POWERS OF PERSUASION

We are continually the targets of persuasion. Not only are we bombarded with media communications, but our family, friends, and even foes are constantly presenting information suggesting that their point of view is the correct one.

In this age of omnipresent forces of persuasion, it is not easy to maintain independent decision making. Still, it is possible to retain one's own point of view and resist being a pawn of persuaders. Social psychologists have devised several strategies for maintaining independence and considering persuasive messages in a cool and rational manner. Among the most effective:

- **_Inoculation._** Medical researchers learned long ago that if we expose people to a weakened form of smallpox germs, they will produce antibodies that will later be able to repel a subsequent full-scale onslaught of the disease.

  In an analogous way, social psychologist William McGuire (1964) suggested that people could be made resistant to persuasive appeals by "inoculating" them with counterattitudinal information *prior* to a full-scale attack on their attitudes. Specifically, McGuire suggested that people's attitudes were especially vulnerable to attack when they had rarely heard contradictory arguments. This is especially the case for cultural truisms, such as "It is important to brush your teeth after every meal."

  Indeed, when faced with arguments contrary to cultural truisms, people tend to change attitudes fairly readily. On the other hand, if previously they have been exposed to at least

some arguments opposing the truism, and also provided the means to refute the opposition (the social psychological equivalent of a shot in the arm), they are considerably more likely to resist the persuasive attack (Burgoon & Miller, 1990).

In sum, one way of counteracting persuasive messages is to prepare yourself for an upcoming persuasive onslaught. By inoculating yourself before exposure, you'll be able to resist the persuasive efforts of others (McAlister et al., 1980).

- **_Taking the role of devil's advocate._** A devil's advocate is someone who takes a certain position not necessarily from conviction but more for the sake of argument. According to social psychologists Anthony Pratkanis and Elliot Aronson, one constructive technique for retaining your independence is to adopt the role of devil's advocate. Specifically, put yourself into the shoes (and mind) of the source of the persuasive message, and ask yourself questions such as:

What does the source of the information have to gain?

Why are these choices being presented to me in this manner? Are there other options and other ways of presenting those options?

What would happen if I chose something other than the recommended option? What are the arguments for the other side? (Pratkanis & Aronson, 1991, p. 213.)

By asking yourself—and answering—questions such as these, you're in a considerably better position to understand the underlying intent of the message. Ultimately, such knowledge

*Continued on next page*

will better permit you to make up your own mind, rather than unwittingly being persuaded by the information being communicated to you.

- **Forewarning.** Forewarned is forearmed. "Brace yourself: You're about to be the recipient of a persuasive message." Is a warning such as this—explicitly stating that you will soon encounter a communication intended to influence you—sufficient to allow you to keep your independence?

In many cases, yes. If the issues at hand are important and you have a reasonable amount of knowledge about them, knowing that you are the target of persuasion will increase the possibility that you can remain independent.

Two reasons account for the forewarning effect. First, the knowledge that you are about to be persuasively attacked permits you to spend some time thinking about supportive arguments for your own position and counterarguments against the persuader's position. And second, such awareness may raise your defenses; you may become obstinate and attempt to resist the persuasive attempt. In some cases, in fact, forewarning produces a boomerang effect: After learning that you may be the target of persuasion, you become even more committed to your initial position (Hass & Grady, 1975; Cialdini & Petty, 1981).

None of these methods is foolproof; all of us, at times, are going to fall prey to the powerful clout of persuasive messages. However, the use of these techniques can give us at least a fighting chance to ward off unwarranted persuasion and maintain our independence.

---

## ▶ REVIEW & RETHINK

### Review

- Types of advertisements include informative, selective demand, and reminder advertising.
- Consumer involvement and understanding of a product are associated with advertising effectiveness.
- Psychographics groups people according to lifestyle profiles.

### Rethink

- Identify and define the three broad classes of advertisements. What approach would be most appropriate for a company that enjoys the largest market share within its retail area?
- Would hard or soft sell tactics be more effective in promoting a brand of cigarettes? Suggest both a soft sell and a hard sell ad that could be used in a campaign to convince people to quit smoking. Which do you think would be more effective?
- Why is the concept of the high self-monitor of interest to advertisers? Why might an ad that combined both hard and soft sell tactics influence product purchase more among low self-monitors than among high self-monitors?
- How does VALS enable advertisers to increase the effectiveness of their ads? What type of advertising would you use to persuade "outer-directed" consumers? Briefly describe an ad that would appeal to "Survivors."

---

# LOOKING BACK ◀ ◀ ◀ ◀ ◀ ◀ ◀ ◀ ◀ ◀ ◀ ◀ ◀ ◀ ◀ ◀ ◀ ◀ ◀ ◀ ◀ ◀ ◀

### *What are the cognitive paths to persuasion?*

1. Persuasion follows one of two paths, the central route and the peripheral route. In central route persuasion, persuasion occurs on the basis of the logic, merit, or strength of the arguments. Peripheral route persuasion occurs when people are persuaded on the basis of factors unrelated to the nature or quality of the content of a persuasive message. Instead, they respond to irrelevant or extraneous factors such as who is providing the message or the length of the arguments.

2.  The most lasting and persistent attitude change is brought about by central route processing. Although peripheral route processing can sway attitudes, the degree of change is not as likely to be as strong or as lasting as when central route processing is employed.

3.  Two conditions must be met in order for central route processing to proceed. First, people must be sufficiently motivated to expend the cognitive effort to think about the issue. Second, they must have the ability to process the information.

### *What characteristics of the message source produce the greatest persuasion?*

4.  The credibility of a message source, relating to the source's expertise and trustworthiness, is a major determinant of a message's ability to be persuasive. Even message sources with little credibility can be persuasive, as illustrated by the sleeper effect. The sleeper effect is an increase in the persuasibility of a message that occurs with the passage of time.

5.  Another important factor related to the message source's persuasive abilities is the communicator's attractiveness and likability. Celebrities are often used to persuade consumers to use products, even when the celebrity has no special expertise regarding the product.

### *How do messages differ in their ability to elicit persuasion?*

6.  The amount and kind of information contained in a message affects persuasion. If additional arguments are equally strong and valid, then more information results in greater persuasion. If the additional arguments are weak, then their effectiveness depends on the presence of peripheral route processing.

7.  Whether the message should present only one side of an issue or both sides depends on the nature of the target audience. In addition, repetition of a message, up to a point, produces greater and more persistent attitude change. The success of repetition depends on the message's complexity.

8.  The success of fear appeals—messages regarding attitude change that are designed to produce apprehension and anxiety if the message is not followed—depends on their accompaniment by specific, precise recommendations for actions to avoid the danger. If no such information is provided, strong fear appeals may be ignored because they arouse so much anxiety.

### *What personal characteristics are associated most with persuasion?*

9.  Early research was unable to identify personal characteristics that consistently lead people to be easy or difficult to persuade. More recent research suggests that people's reactions to persuasive messages depend on a combination of the kind of message that is being communicated, its source, and specific personal qualities of the target.

10. Need for cognition—a person's habitual level of thoughtfulness and cognitive activity—is associated with persuasibility, although it depends on the specific content of the message. Mood, too, is related to persuasion. For instance, being in a good mood leads to an increased likelihood of peripheral route processing.

### *How do advertisers devise effective persuasive messages?*

11. Informative advertising is designed to introduce new products, to suggest new ways of using an existing product, or to correct false impressions about a product. In contrast, selective demand advertising is designed to establish or modify attitudes about a particular brand of product or service, compared with other brands of the same kind of product or service. Finally, in reminder advertising, the goal is to keep consumers thinking about a product or to reinforce the message that preferring a brand is appropriate.

12. The degree of consumer involvement with and understanding of a product are associated with the effectiveness of various types of advertising. In addition, ads differ in whether they use a hard sell approach (focusing on the qualities of the product) or a soft sell approach (which focuses on linking a product's use with pleasant images).

13. Psychographics is a method for dividing people into lifestyle profiles that are related to purchasing patterns. Among the most frequently used classification techniques is the "Values

and Lifestyles" system, or VALS. Consumers' purchases are related to their VALS category, as well as to their racial and ethnic group membership.

14.    Several techniques are available to help people resist persuasive messages. Among the most successful are inoculation, taking the role of devil's advocate, and forewarning.

---

# KEY TERMS AND CONCEPTS

*central route persuasion (p. 346)*

*peripheral route persuasion (p. 346)*

*elaboration likelihood model (p. 346)*

*heuristics (p. 347)*

*sleeper effect (p. 350)*

*fear appeals (p. 356)*

*need for cognition (p. 359)*

*consumer behavior (p. 363)*

*informative advertising (p. 364)*

*selective demand advertising (p. 364)*

*reminder advertising (p. 365)*

*hard sell (p. 367)*

*soft sell (p. 367)*

*self-monitoring (p. 369)*

*psychographics (p. 370)*

---

# FOR FURTHER RESEARCH AND STUDY

Perloff, R. M. (1993). *The dynamics of persuasion*. Hillsdale, NJ: Erlbaum.

Everything you wanted to know about persuasion, in a readable, lively form. Filled with interesting examples and case studies.

Zimbardo, P. G., & Leippe, M. R. (1991). *The psychology of attitude change and social influence*. New York: McGraw-Hill.

A good overview of the methods people use to bring about attitude change.

Pratkanis, A., & Aronson, E. (1991). *The age of propaganda: The everyday use and abuse of persuasion*. New York: Freeman.

With an emphasis on real-world cases of persuasion, this book provides a handy introduction to the world of attitude change.

---

# EPILOGUE

In the past two chapters, we've traveled through the world of attitudes. Beginning with the theoretical foundations of attitudes, their origins, structure, and functions, we discussed ways of measuring this abstract concept and addressed the question of how attitudes and behavior are linked. We then progressed into more applied territory, considering how attitudes could be changed.

As we've made this journey, we've once again seen how the theoretical foundations of the discipline can be built upon to derive exceedingly practical outcomes. In starting with an abstract, unseen hypothetical construct—that of attitudes—we've moved into the gritty real world of advertisements and political campaigns. We hope this journey has provided the tools to help you make more knowledgeable, informed judgments about the many persuasive efforts of which all of us are continually targets.

### PART VII

# WHY AND HOW ARE PEOPLE SUSCEPTIBLE TO THE INFLUENCE OF OTHERS?

No member of society is immune from the influence of others, and no society can function without at least some degree of social control over its members. Whether this social influence is subtle or is as unmistakable as a direct command, such control has an enormous influence over what we think and do. Understanding why people are susceptible to the influence of others represents one of the central questions addressed by social psychologists.

In Chapter 12 we consider the most basic forms of social influence, ranging from conformity to compliance and obedience to authority. We then look, in Chapter 13, at how society formally influences and governs our behavior through the legal system and political processes. ■

### CHAPTER TWELVE

# CONFORMITY, COMPLIANCE, AND OBEDIENCE

## FOLLOWING THE LEAD OF OTHERS

Ethnic cleansing. This chilling term, used in the war fought in the fragments of the former Yugoslavia, was employed by Serbian leaders to explain the need to root out people of non-Serbian ances-

try. The leaders' argument: Their country required purification in order to protect the majority from the presumed offenses of the minority.

The chilling term "ethnic cleansing" has been used to justify the death and displacement of tens of thousands of people.

To others, it was an excuse for genocide, a policy in which a national, ethnic, racial, or religious group is destroyed. It was a justification that had its roots in the unbridled hatreds of the Nazi regime in Germany. There, millions of Jews, gypsies, homosexuals, and other minorities were sent to concentration camps and murdered.

Serbian soldiers conducted the ethnic cleansing with a vengeance. They burned homes, murdered, and carried out systematic rapes of Muslim and Croat women—all under the command of their superior officers. And for many of the soldiers who participated, it was their superior officers who provided them with the excuse for their conduct. When asked how they could participate in the ethnic cleansing, they said they had no choice—they were only following orders.

## LOOKING AHEAD

▶ ▶ ▶ ▶ ▶ ▶ ▶ ▶ ▶ ▶ ▶ ▶ ▶ ▶ ▶ ▶ ▶ ▶ ▶ ▶ ▶ ▶ ▶ ▶ ▶ ▶ ▶ ▶

It would be comforting to view the war in Bosnia as an example of a singular, grotesque bit of historical lunacy. After all, how could normal people follow the dictates of leaders who recommended actions so inhumane?

Unfortunately, the forces that led Serbian soldiers to follow their leaders' orders are not all that different from those we encounter in our everyday lives. How often do we follow the mandate of a teacher, or employer, or parent—even if we don't agree with it? How often are we influenced by the latest clothing or music fad? And how often do we go along with other people not because we agree with them but because we want to be accepted by the group?

In this chapter, we consider the topic of social influence. **Social influence** is the area of social psychology that explores how people are affected by the real or imagined pressure of other individuals or of a group. The influence may be intentional, as in the case of the Serbian leaders, who ordered their army to conduct ethic cleansing. On the other hand, social influence may be unintentional, as when a group's majority induces a minority to adhere to its position through fear of potential embarrassment or ridicule. Either way, the outcome is the same—a change in behavior as a result of real or imagined pressure from others.

We will consider a variety of social influences in this chapter, ranging from indirect, implicit social influence to direct, overt pressures (see Figure 12-1). We begin with a discussion of conformity, which occurs when people change their behavior or attitudes out of a desire to follow the beliefs or standards of others. We discuss the underlying rea-

**social influence**
real or imagined pressure from others that results in a change in behavior or attitude.

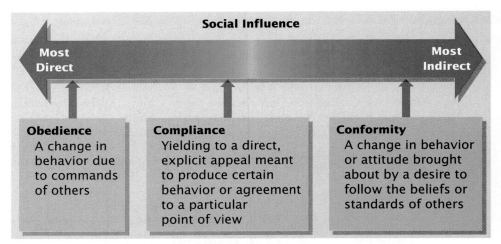

**FIGURE 12-1**    **The Varieties of Social Influence**

sons that people conform, and the factors that permit a person to maintain independence in the face of group pressures. We also examine the ways in which a group minority can exert social influence on a group majority.

Our discussion then turns to compliance—yielding to direct, explicit appeals to change one's behavior or point of view. A more explicit form of social pressure than conformity, compliance, as we will see, can be sought by means of several distinct strategies.

Finally, we examine obedience—social pressure that is the result of direct commands. We consider historical situations in which blind obedience has occurred; then we turn to experimental studies of the phenomenon, which help explain the dynamics of obedience.

After reading this chapter, then, you will be able to answer these questions:

- Why do people conform to the views and behavior of others?
- What factors promote independence from conformity pressures?
- What strategies can be employed to make others compliant, and how can such pressures be resisted?
- Why are people so readily obedient to authority figures?

# CONFORMITY

*You are sitting at a table with a group of five fellow students, participating in what seems to be a pretty straightforward experiment. The researcher has explained that he is studying perception, and that he'll be showing you a series of cards on which lines are printed. Your job is simple: Along with the other subjects, you are to announce in turn which of three lines is similar in length to a fourth line, which he calls the "standard."*

*At first, nothing seems amiss. The other subjects in the experiment look at the lines, and make the obvious response, identical to your own. But on the third set of lines, you are startled when the first subject to respond seems to make a mistake. Even more surprising, the second subject makes the same error. When the third, fourth, and fifth subjects make the same mistake, you are in turmoil. How can they all be wrong? Is there something about the lines they see and you don't? Are your eyes failing you? What explains this mysterious coincidence?*

The military makes explicit use of conformity pressures in order to maintain discipline.

By now, you probably have an inkling about what is happening in this experiment, being well aware of the length to which social psychologists will go in order to study social behavior. The other subjects in the study were actually confederates of the experimenter, trained to give a unanimous, erroneous response.

But consider the plight of an individual unschooled in the ways of social psychology. For the average person, the situation is baffling. When others in the study all respond with what seems to be the same wrong response on such an easy task, the subject must make a choice between his or her own sensory judgment or going along with the group.

This situation, devised by social psychologist Solomon Asch, has become a classic in the investigation of conformity. **Conformity** is a change in behavior or attitudes brought about by a desire to follow the beliefs or standards of others. As we might suspect in the situation above, conformity may involve public acceptance but private disapproval of a group's position. Sometimes, however, actual persuasion occurs, and a person's private opinion actually changes as well (Van Knippenberg & Wilke, 1988; Hall, Varca & Fisher, 1986).

How do subjects respond to the plight into which the Asch study casts them (see Figure 12-2)? In many cases, they go along with the group. Specifically, in about one third of the trials subjects conformed to the unanimous but erroneous group decision, choosing an alternative that was clearly in error.

But there are also significant individual differences: Some subjects conform all the time, while others remain totally independent of the pressure. Nonetheless, more than three quarters of the subjects in the experiment conformed at least once to the others' judgments (Asch, 1951).

**conformity**
a change in behavior or attitudes brought about by a desire to follow the beliefs or standards of others.

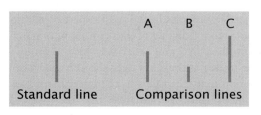

**FIGURE 12-2 Asch's Conformity Task** In Solomon Asch's classic study, subjects were shown a standard line and asked to state out loud which of the three other lines matched the standard length. An easy task—until confederates began unanimously choosing the wrong answer.

*Normative and Informational Social Pressure*

**normative social influence**
pressure that reflects expectations regarding appropriate behavior held by those belonging to groups.

**informational social influence**
pressure to conform that emanates from our assumption that others have knowledge we lack.

**autokinetic effect**
the illusion that occurs when a small, stationary light in a darkened room appears to move.

To understand why people conform to group pressure, social psychologists have distinguished between two types of social pressure: normative social influence and informational social influence (Deutsch & Gerard, 1955; Kaplan & Miller, 1987; Campbell & Fairey, 1989). **Normative social influence** is pressure that reflects group norms, which are expectations regarding appropriate behavior held by those belonging to groups. Normative social pressure operates because of our desire to meet the expectations of a group.

One reason people conform, then, is because experience has shown that transgressors of group norms are punished in some way by the other members of the group. An individual may appear to agree with a majority in order to avoid anticipated unpleasant consequences of violating group standards. Hence, in Asch's experiment, subjects may conform in order to avoid the anticipated retaliation of the other subjects for defying the majority response.

But we are influenced by group members not only through normative social influence. In many cases we must rely on the perceptions, experience, and knowledge of others because we are unable to experience firsthand certain aspects of the world. How many of us have measured the distance between New York and California, for example? As a result, we need to rely on other people to provide us with information about the world. **Informational social influence** is pressure to conform that emanates from our assumption that others have knowledge that we lack.

We conform to informational social influence because we think that group members have information about the situation that we are lacking. Subjects in Asch's experiment may be prone to conform if they feel that the other subjects have some sort of special insight into the situation. Similarly, we may be influenced by a majority position on an environmental issue such as the necessity of recycling because we feel that those in the majority simply know more about the issue.

When we consider why people are influenced by informational social pressure, it becomes apparent that viewing conformity as an invariably objectionable or morally deficient behavior is unwarranted. Other people do know more about certain things than we do; and we can't always verify certain pieces of information on our own.

Further, even when we do try to rely on our own senses to make a judgment, we are not always accurate. For instance, one of the earliest examinations of conformity relied on a visual illusion called the autokinetic effect. The **autokinetic effect** is the illusion that a small, stationary light in a darkened room appears to move.

The autokinetic effect is especially amenable to social influence because of the ambiguity of the phenomenon. When people make judgments without others present they vary widely in how much they estimate the stationary pinpoint light is moving, with judgments ranging from less than an inch to more than a foot.

Interestingly, though, when the same people are later brought together in groups and asked to announce their judgments aloud, their estimates begin to converge. After a relatively short time, subjects in a group end up with similar reports about how much the light has moved (Sherif & Sherif, 1969; MacNeil & Sherif, 1976). Even more important, when people are subsequently separated once more and again asked to make judgments alone, their estimates are similar to those they made while part of the group.

In sum, both informational and normative social influence produce conformity. Furthermore, it is likely that under most circumstances, neither type functions by itself. Instead, informational and normative social influence work in tandem in most situations.

For example, subjects in the Asch experiment who conformed likely did so out of a desire to avoid contradicting group norms and potentially being laughed at, embarrassed, or punished in some other way by the group—a response to normative social influence. At the same time, though, subjects' conformity may have been predicated on their assumption that the others in the experiment had greater experience in the task or perceived something in the situation that they were missing—a response to informational social influence.

## Factors Producing Conformity: The Fine Points of Accommodating to a Group

Although any group situation holds the potential for normative and informational social pressures to produce conformity, people do not invariably conform to the behavior of others. Why is it that people conform slavishly in some situations, but are able to maintain independence in others? To answer that question, we need to take a look at several factors that social psychologists have identified as critical in intensifying or weakening conformity (Allen, 1965; Tanford & Penrod, 1984; Nail, 1986).

The strength of the ties between the individual and the group is one determinant of how likely that person is to conform to the group's position. For instance, the more a person is attracted to a group and its members, the more likely that person is to conform to the group's standards (Hogg & Hardie, 1992; Brehm & Mann, 1975). Consequently, members of a popular, high-status sorority are likely to produce high levels of conformity pressures on the members who value highly the perceived prestige of the group. At the same time, however, those members who find the group unattractive are less likely to yield to the pressure to conform to its standards. If you dislike the sorority and the type of people who populate it, you'll be unlikely to experience much desire to conform to the group norms.

**status**
the evaluation or a role or person by the group.

Within a group, the status of a person's position also affects his or her susceptibility to conformity pressures. **Status** is the evaluation of a role or person by the group. In general, lower-status people conform more than higher-status individuals (Williams, 1984; Larsen et al., 1979). However, in some cases high-status group leaders may conform more to group norms than people in nonleadership roles. Leaders may conform in order to maintain and bolster their leadership positions by going along with the other group members (Nagata, 1980).

Finally, pressures to conform are greatest in groups in which the members are similar to one another. This explanation relates to our earlier discussion in Chapter 4 about people's need for social comparison, in which they use comparisons with others to judge their own abilities, attitudes, and behavior. The more similar others are to ourselves, the more apt we are to use them for comparison purposes. As a consequence, their social influence on our own behavior is likely to be greater (Insko, Sedlak, & Lipsitz, 1982).

## The Mathematics of Conformity: The Opposition Doesn't Always Count

Suppose you find yourself in a meeting whose purpose is to decide whether to offer passenger-side air bags as a standard feature for your company's forthcoming new car model. You strongly favor the option, but everyone else argues that it will be too expensive, that the passenger seat is occupied infrequently, and that the safety data don't support their installation. Will you be more likely to conform to the majority opinion if there are three people opposing you or if there are ten?

It seems reasonable to assume that the more people who are aligned against the position we hold, the more likely we would be to cave in to the majority position. However, such an assumption would be both right and wrong: Up to a point, the presence of more people does lead to greater conformity. But after the number in the majority

The more attractive we find group membership, the more apt we are to conform to the group. For instance, dressing in this distinctive manner indicates members' allegiance to this Texas Shriner's group.

reaches a critical—and, it turns out, surprisingly modest—point, conformity levels off. In fact, in some cases conformity may decrease slightly when more people are added to the majority. Specifically, most research has found that conformity increases as the size of a united majority grows to around four or five people, but then conformity levels off (Rosenberg, 1961; Gerard, Whilhelmy, & Conolley, 1968; Tanford & Penrod, 1984; Stang, 1976).

According to social psychologists Bibb Latané and Sharon Wolf, the decreasing influence of increasing majorities can be explained by social impact theory (Latané & Wolf, 1981; Wolf & Latané, 1983; Wolf, 1985). **Social impact theory** suggests that the effect of a majority on a minority rests on three basic factors—the majority's strength, immediacy, and number. The strength of a majority relates to its status, competence, and general relationship to a target of influence. Immediacy refers to the physical proximity of an influence source. And number relates to the quantity of individuals in the majority.

To explain why simply increasing the sheer number of members of the majority does not lead to a corresponding increase in conformity, Latané and Wolf use the analogy of lighting a room. They note that when a room is in total darkness, turning on a light of any brightness appears to make an enormous difference. But once the brightness reaches a level that permits one to see enough to navigate around the furniture, each subsequent increase in lighting has a successively smaller impact. In a similar fashion, social impact theory suggests that as a unanimous majority increases in size, each additional person provides relatively less influence than the previous person—a prediction that characterizes a good deal of research on the topic (see Figure 12-3).

Although social impact theory provides one explanation for the leveling-off in the impact of increasingly large majorities, it is not the full explanation (see Jackson, 1986; Mullen, 1986; Clark & Maass, 1990). For example, as the size of a majority aligned against us increases, we may come to feel increasingly under siege. We may think we are the targets of a concerted effort to get us to conform, and that the majority members may not even share the view they are expressing. Ironically, we may come to assume that the majority is less unanimous and uniform in its views than it appears to be. As a consequence, we may be able to withstand the influence of a large majority more readily than a small one (Wilder, 1977).

**social impact theory**
the notion that the effect of a majority on a minority rests on three basic factors—the majority's strength, immediacy, and number.

## Social Support: Discovering a Partner in Disunity

**social supporter**
a person holding a position similar to one's own.

It always helps to have an ally who shares our views, but never more so than when we are facing a majority unanimously aligned against us. In fact, having even a single **social supporter**—a person holding an opinion similar to one's own—typically allows an individual to remain independent of the group (Allen, 1975; Boyanowsky et al., 1981; Wilder & Allen, 1977).

For instance, in Asch's classic studies, when a social supporter was present confor-

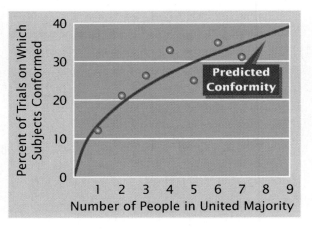

**FIGURE 12-3 Social Impact Theory** As the number of people in a united majority increases, their social impact declines. Consequently, conformity increases sharply initially but begins to level off as more people join the majority. (*Source:* Latané, 1981, p. 344.)

mity was reduced to 15 percent of what it was when a partner was not present (Asch, 1952, 1955). The effect of having a social supporter is so powerful that the competence of the supporter doesn't even matter much.

In one study, for example, subjects were told that the purpose of the experiment was to make visual judgments in a group situation (Allen & Levine, 1971). However, one of the supposed other subjects—the person who would later turn out to be the subject's social supporter—appeared to be completely incompetent at the visual task, miserably failing a vision test administered at the start of the experiment. Nonetheless, this same individual later made visual judgments that were surprisingly accurate. These judgments provided the subject with a potential social supporter against the rest of the group's supposed judgments, which, on most trials, were unanimously incorrect. Even though the social supporter apparently had impaired vision, making his correct answers seemingly due to chance, subjects' conformity to the group dropped significantly compared to another experimental condition in which no social supporter was present.

In sum, standing alone in a group and maintaining an unpopular position is decidedly difficult. However, the presence of even one ally who agrees with our stand is enough to allow us to elude the grip of conformity pressures.

## Gender and Cultural Differences in Conformity

Are certain groups more susceptible to conformity pressures than others? We can address the question from two distinct vantage points: whether there are gender differences in conformity, and the nature of cultural differences.

**GENDER AND CONFORMITY: DO WOMEN OR MEN YIELD MORE?**    Less than 30 years ago it was stated as an unequivocal fact: Women conformed more than men. For instance, one early, influential review of the literature noted, ". . . difference in amount of conformity for males and females has been repeatedly demonstrated, with females generally conforming more than males" (Allen, 1965, p. 159).

Subsequent research began to chip away at the assertion. Partially as a reaction to the growing women's movement of the 1960s and 1970s, social psychologists began to take a second look at gender differences. They found a picture considerably more complicated than they anticipated.

For example, one major review of the conformity literature, conducted by social psychologists Alice Eagly and Linda Carli (1981), did confirm that in group settings, women generally conformed more than men. However, upon closer examination, a potentially biasing factor was found: the sex of the researcher. Almost 80 percent of the influenceability studies were carried out by males, and these male researchers tended to obtain greater female conformity than female researchers did. In fact, experiments conducted by female researchers tended to show no gender differences.

Why should this be the case? One possibility is that male and female experimenters make different decisions about which of their findings they seek to publish. It is conceivable that female experimenters may be more likely than male experimenters to chose to publish findings of "no difference" between men and women in conformity. Consequently, given that there were more studies conducted by men, the findings of a difference in conformity would be more apt to be reflected in the literature than studies that found no difference.

A more likely explanation may lie in the choice of topics used in the typical conformity experiment. If researchers tend to use topics of a stereotypically "masculine" nature in their studies, such as discussions of football or warfare, women may conform more than men because of their perceived lack of expertise in the subject matter. Conversely, if the topic is more familiar to women than to men, then we might expect greater conformity on the part of men. Because most conformity studies had been conducted by male experimenters, it is possible that the topics they employed in their studies reflected more "masculine" subjects than "feminine" ones—-leading to the appearance of greater conformity on the part of female subjects (Eagly & Carli, 1981).

The possibility that the topical area used in an experiment affects the experimental outcome is not farfetched. According to one study that directly tested the possibility, the kinds of items used to elicit group pressure had a predictable effect, depending on whether the items were more familiar to men or to women, or were neutral (Sistrunk & McDavid, 1971). Males conformed most on the "feminine" items; females most on the "masculine" items; and there was no difference between males and females on the items that were equally familiar to both sexes.

After the publication of Eagly and Carli's review, the prevailing opinion among social psychologists was that the differences between conformity in males and females that had been found in the past might well be largely attributable to research problems and experimental misinterpretations. Gender differences, then, appeared to be minor, unreliable, and not terribly important.

But this conclusion was not to be the last word. Current thinking has come full circle, suggesting that sometimes women do indeed conform more than men—but only under certain circumstances. In public, face-to-face clashes in which they can be observed by others, women are more apt to hide their true feelings and go along with the group than when they are not being observed. Conversely, when men are in such public situations where their behavior is under the scrutiny of others, they are less likely to conform to the group than when they are alone (Eagly & Chravala, 1986; Tuthill & Forsyth, 1982).

The roots of the differences in conformity between men and women may be traced to differences in the salience of gender roles in public and private situations. When people are in a public, confrontational setting, they are concerned about how well they are representing themselves and how closely their behavior adheres to what people expect of them. The traditional female gender role emphasizes relationship maintenance and getting along with others, while the traditional male role is more confrontational and assertive.

As a result, in order to meet the expectations of others, both males and females are more likely to present their behavior in a way that is congruent with their own traditional sex roles, but only when in public settings. In private, they can be themselves—and hence, differences between men's and women's conformity behavior diminish (Eagly, 1987; Eagly, Wood, & Fishbaugh, 1981).

Of course, there are other explanations for gender differences in conformity. For instance, because of societal barriers, women may hold positions of lower status than men in some groups. It is possible that the fact that they occupy a lower status position makes women in such situations more apt to conform in public. In sum, it may be status factors, and not gender, that lead to public conformity (Unger & Crawford, 1992).

Both gender role and status explanations of conformity differences in men and women suggest that if changes occur in gender roles and status, the nature of conformity differences may also change. Hence, the ending of the story of gender differences in conformity has yet to be written.

**CULTURAL DIFFERENCES IN CONFORMITY.**    When Mahatma Gandhi mobilized his followers in India, he did so by making an emotional appeal to manufacture salt and weave one's own cloth (Sinha, 1990, cited in Moghaddam, Taylor, & Wright, 1993). Although such encouragement sounds rather odd to the ear of a resident of North America, in fact it was quite effective in rallying supporters to his cause.

Clearly, conformity to social norms depends on the content of social norms. Moreover, the degree to which conformity is typical and valued varies from one culture to another. For instance, findings from a large-scale cross-cultural study found clear differences in how highly parents desired independence and self-reliance in their children, compared with obedience to their parents. Parents in the United States felt that it was most important for their children to be independent; parents in less-industrialized countries such as Indonesia and Turkey placed far less emphasis on independence and more on conformity to their parents' wishes (Kagitcibasi, 1984).

Given these differences in values, it is not surprising that various cultures show different patterns of conformity. For example, in experiments in conformity using variations of the Asch experimental technique, some groups, such as Brazilians, Chinese, and Fijians, show similar levels of conformity to North Americans, while others, such as the Bantu of Rhodesia, demonstrate more conformity (Chandra, 1973; Milgram, 1992; Matsuda, 1985; Whitaker & Meade, 1967).

On the other hand, some people are less conforming in Asch-type situations than people in North America, including subjects in Germany and Japan (Frager, 1970; Timaeus, 1968). Although such findings may be surprising in the light of stereotypes about the high levels of conformity of Germans and Japanese, it might be that the Asch situation, which involves conformity to strangers and not to people of authority, might evoke relatively low conformity in the laboratory (Moghaddam, Taylor, & Wright, 1993). If such an explanation is valid, it highlights the difficulty in drawing conclusions from experimental procedures developed in one culture and imported to others.

Other research suggests, surprisingly, that the nature of food accumulation in a society is related to conformity. The explanation goes like this: Societies in which food-accumulation depends on hunting and fishing require individual initiative and effort, while those that depend more on agriculture require greater cooperation and community activities. We might expect, then, that people in cultures that depend on hunting and fishing would show greater independence and less conformity, while people in cultures that rely on agriculture would show greater conformity.

To test out the hypothesis, psychologist John Berry compared two societies: the Temne of Sierra Leone in Africa, and the Inuit of Baffin Island in Canada. The Temne rely primarily on agriculture for food, while the Inuit generally employ hunting to gather food. As would be predicted, the Temne people showed more conformity than members of the Inuit culture (Berry, 1966, 1967).

## Individual Influence over the Group: When One Can Overcome Many

When Sigmund Freud first developed his psychoanalytic theory in the early 1900s, he was met with skepticism and derision. The concepts of unconscious processes, infant sexuality, and libido were seen as absurd and even subversive. According to one biographer of Freud, he and his disciples were thought of as "not only as sexual perverts but also as either obsessional or paranoid psychopaths, and the combination was thought to be a real danger to the community" (Jones, 1961, p. 299).

How did Freud respond to this attitude? Never retreating from his lone position of dissent from the majority view of the scientific community, he instead reiterated, refined, and expanded his theory. He unrelentingly advocated for his convictions, and he presented a consistent (and persistent) view to the world.

We all know the outcome: Freud's theories have far outlasted his harshest critics. His work has had enormous influence not only in terms of the treatment of abnormal behavior but on Western intellectual thought in general.

Although most cases illustrate majorities influencing minorities, there are a fair number of historical examples of single individuals influencing majority thinking. Consider, for instance, such influential figures as Charles Darwin, Susan B. Anthony, and Martin Luther King, Jr., all of whom faced initial skepticism but remained firm in their position long enough to bring a majority around to their way of thinking. Such examples lead to an important question: What are the circumstances under which a single member or minority in a group can influence and change the opinions held by the majority?

Freud's technique of remaining consistent suggests a general strategy of engaging in a consistent demonstration of the minority's beliefs and behavior. In fact, some social psychologists have suggested that unvarying consistency is the key to minority influence.

Biologist Charles Darwin and voting-rights advocate Susan B. Anthony exemplify Moscovici's strategy for influencing a majority: maintaining a consistent viewpoint.

Others, however, have suggested that a more effective strategy for influencing a majority is for the minority to conform first and then to deviate from the group. As we will see, each approach has garnered substantial experimental support.

**MINORITY CONSISTENCY: THE NO-WAFFLE POSITION.** Social psychologist Serge Moscovici, working in laboratories in Europe, argues that the key to successful minority social influence over a majority is consistency (Moscovici & Faucheaux, 1972; Moscovici & Mugny, 1983). He suggests that a minority's unyielding insistence on its own point of view creates a conflict that prevents the smooth functioning of a group. In turn, this conflict may cause the majority to rethink its position and eventually be swayed by the minority's position.

One of Moscovici's initial experiments quite clearly illustrates the effect that a consistent minority can have on a majority (Moscovici, Lage, & Naffrechoux, 1969). In the study, groups of six female subjects were told that they would be making judgments about the color of a group of 36 slides. Unbeknownst to the subjects, all the slides were blue in color—although they did vary in the intensity of the blue. In addition, the subjects did not know that two of the group members were confederates, who had been instructed to answer on every slide that the color was green (a clearly incorrect response). There was also a control condition, which consisted of groups of six actual subjects and no confederates.

After taking a public test for colorblindness, the subjects were shown the series of 36 slides. For each slide, subjects answered sequentially and aloud. The results showed a clear influence of the (erroneous) minority upon the majority. In comparison to the control condition, in which one quarter of one percent of the responses were erroneous, more than eight percent of the responses in the groups with confederates responded incorrectly by identifying the color they saw as green. In fact, about one third of the experimental subjects answered incorrectly at least once.

Even more intriguing is the subsequent finding that the consistent minority influenced the majority even after their part in the experiment had ended. After they had finished responding in their group of six, each subject was taken individually to another room and shown a series of 16 disks, which this time did vary in color—from very green, to blue-green, to very blue. Subjects were told to categorize each disk as blue or green but were not given the opportunity to make compromise judgments such as "blue-green."

The most interesting finding from this post-experiment task were judgments for the blue-green disks. Subjects exposed to the consistent minority were more likely to say "green" than "blue" for the blue-green disks, indicating that the effects of the minority persisted beyond their physical presence. And it turned out that those most likely to be affected by the group during the post-experimental phase were those who had been least susceptible to the influence of the consistent minority during the experiment itself. Consequently, even those subjects who appeared at first to remain independent of the minority were apparently influenced by the minority's unfluctuating responses.

How does the consistency of the minority influence the majority? We have already considered one possibility: that a consistent minority chips away at the group consensus that group members try to maintain in order to have a smoothly functioning group. In turn, that disruption may lead the majority to rethink its position.

But another factor, going beyond the motivation to maintain a well-oiled, smoothly functioning group, may be at work. Moscovici suggests that the minority, due to its persistence, is likely to be perceived by the majority as holding an intense, strong position. The minority is also likely to be seen as quite confident in its views, as it continues to be unyielding in the face of the implicit group pressure to conform.

This apparent certainty of the minority may lead the majority to question its own point of view, and any lack of confidence on the part of the majority will be increased. In this way, the consistent minority can exert influence over, and potentially modify, the majority's position. In fact, for generations, such a tactic has been used by minority political parties and religions—with some degree of success (Mugny & Perez, 1991).

**CONFORM FIRST, THEN DEVIATE: A MINORITY BAIT-AND-SWITCH TACTIC.** Members who deviate from the group typically face a potential problem. As we mentioned earlier, they are often disliked, and frequently group members try to exclude from future group activities those whose opinions and actions diverge from the majority (Schachter, 1951; Levine, 1989; Kruglanski & Webster, 1991).

Given this possibility, Moscovici's strategy of unyielding consistency for modifying the majority view places a minority in real peril. Rather than trying to understand the minority's position, the majority may simply reject it and ignore the minority members. In some cases, then, minority consistency may fail.

According to social psychologist Edwin Hollander (1980), a more effective strategy exists. He suggests that when a minority initially conforms to the established group majority position, its initial period of conformity establishes the "credentials" of the minority. Furthermore, initial conformity provides status within the group. Once the group member's credentials and status have been proven, the member is then able to deviate from the group majority.

**idiosyncrasy credit**
a psychological "currency" that permits deviation from the group.

The mechanism underlying a person's ability to espouse an unpopular view is referred to as idiosyncrasy credit. **Idiosyncrasy credit** is a psychological "currency" that permits deviation from the group. Like money, idiosyncrasy credit can be earned and later spent (Hollander, 1958; Hollander, Julian, & Haaland, 1965).

A group member can accumulate idiosyncrasy credit by demonstrating to the group competence and the ability to fulfill the expectations of the group regarding appropriate behavior. When the person has built up sufficient credit, he or she can make a withdrawal, which occurs when that person deviates from the group's majority position. Through the use of such credit, a deviate is able to dodge the group majority's sanctions or rejection, which might otherwise have occurred. Of course, eventually the idiosyncrasy credit will be depleted, and anyone espousing a minority position must resume adherence to the majority position in order to maintain a firm standing in the group (Lortie-Lussier, 1987).

| FIGURE 12-4   **Comparing Methods of Minority Influence** | | |
| --- | --- | --- |
| **THEORY** | **PROCESS** | **EXPLANATION** |
| Moscovici's Consistency Theory | Minority is consistent in presenting its point of view | Unyielding insistence creates conflict, which may cause majority to rethink its position and eventually be swayed |
| Hollander's Idiosyncrasy Theory | Minority accumulates idiosyncrasy credit by initially maintaining majority position, then expends idiosyncrasy credit by deviating from the majority position | The use of idiosyncrasy credit will allow the minority to avoid the majority's sanctions or rejection, which might otherwise have occurred |

Clearly, the notion of idiosyncrasy credit suggests a very different technique for influencing a group majority from Moscovici's consistency approach (see Figure 12-4). For example, if Freud had taken the idiosyncrasy credit approach at face value, he would have used quite a different tack from the one he did. Instead of unyieldingly maintaining his position, Freud would initially have conformed to the predominant views of his era. Then, once he had established his credentials as a follower of the status quo, he would have been free—at least for a time—to present his deviant perspective. (In one sense, Freud followed such a scenario, since his early life was somewhat conventional, such as his early acceptance of standard medical practice just after he graduated from medical school.)

Hollander's process for gaining idiosyncrasy credit actually is a not-too-distant relative of the "bait-and-switch" technique that deceptive advertisers sometimes employ. In bait-and-switch, potential buyers are lured into a store on the basis of unusually low prices. Then, when they arrive at the store, salespeople steer them toward a more expensive item that the advertiser was actually trying to sell. Similarly, in the idiosyncrasy approach to individual influence, a minority member who at first conforms to the majority's view in order to be in a better position later to make a persuasive case is—in a sense—laying out a lure for the majority, who may later be more willing to bite at the minority's position.

**CONSISTENCY VERSUS BAIT-AND-SWITCH: WHEN IS ONE PREFERABLE TO THE OTHER?**
Given that Moscovici's consistency approach and Hollander's idiosyncrasy credit perspective suggest quite different tactics on the part of would-be minority influences, it is logical to ask under what conditions one of the two techniques is more effective than the other. At this point, however, the answer to such a query is ambiguous.

Experimental evidence supports both approaches (Maass & Clark, 1984; Lortie-Lussier, 1987; Clark & Maass, 1988, 1990). Moreover, few direct comparative tests of the two theories exist, and those that have been done often show inconsistent results. For instance, one study directly comparing the two found that the idiosyncrasy credit explanation was supported when only male subjects were examined, but when the behavior of female subjects was examined the results supported both theories (Bray, Johnson, & Chilstrom, 1982). In sum, the jury is still out on which of the two approaches provides the best description of how minorities can influence a majority.

The work on minority influence raises a broader question: Are the processes and principles under which minority influence operates identical to those used by majorities to influence minorities in groups?

**single-process approach**
an approach to social influence that suggests that both majorities and minorities employ similar influence techniques.

Two schools of thought provide competing answers. According to the **single-process approach**, majorities and minorities both employ similar influence techniques. According to theoreticians and researchers in this camp, little difference exists between the ways in which a majority and a minority use social influence in group situations. Although influence pressures from a minority may differ from pressures from the majority in their magnitude, they are qualitatively similar (Tanford & Penrod, 1984; Wolf, 1985). For support of the single-process approach, researchers point to work using computer simulations of group behavior, as well as to direct experimental evidence.

**dual-process approach**
an approach to social influence that suggests that minority influence differs in degree and in kind from majority influence.

However, a significant number of social psychologists support a dual-process approach. The **dual-process approach** argues that minority influence differs from majority influence not just in degree but also in kind.

In arguing for a dual-process approach, social psychologist Charlene Nemeth (1986) contends that majorities and minorities exert their influence in very different ways. When people succumb to a majority position, then, it is because of strong pressure, which produces temporary but often superficial conformity. Often, no lasting change in position occurs.

In contrast, when a minority is able to bring about a change in the majority's position, the change tends to be more genuine and enduring. Minority dissension forces the majority to consider the issue at hand from a variety of perspectives, only one of which may be the view proposed by the minority. Because the majority's thinking becomes broader and more complex, their ultimate decision is of a higher quality, and therefore is likely to be more lasting (Nemeth, 1986; Nemeth, Mayseless, Sherman, & Brown, 1990; Maass & Clark, 1983).

It is still too early to say for sure whether majority and minority pressures represent single or dual processes (see Nemeth & Kwan, 1985; Mackie, 1987). Probably, the truth lies somewhere in between, with single processes operating in some kinds of situations, and dual processes operating in others (Chaiken & Stangor, 1987; Kruglanski & Mackie, 1989). What is clear is that social influence is not a one-way street. Both majorities and minorities can influence each other, making groups a rich tapestry of competing sources and targets of social influence.

## ▶ REVIEW & RETHINK

### Review

- Conformity is a change in behavior or attitudes brought about by a desire to follow the beliefs or standards of others.
- Normative and informational social pressure produces conformity, and both situational factors and gender and cultural factors are related to conformity.
- Minorities may use several strategies to remain independent from a majority.

### Rethink

- What evidence suggests that subjects in Asch's experiments were influenced by normative social pressure? What evidence suggests they were influenced by informational pressure?
- Which type of conformity pressure might be stronger in groups whose members are very similar and in groups whose members are proud of their membership?
- If you were to conduct the Asch study today, would you expect to find gender-related effects in your data?
- Which technique for influencing the majority would be most effective for producing normative pressure and which for producing informational pressure?

## COMPLIANCE

*It's taken days of searching, but you've finally found the new car of your dreams. You've fallen in love with it, and the salesperson informs you that you could be behind the wheel in just two days.*

*Continued on next page*

*Because you think of yourself as a savvy consumer, you've read an article on negotiating prior to shopping for the car. You're quite pleased with yourself because, after a good deal of dickering, the salesperson has agreed to what looks like a great price.*

*After you fill out a batch of forms, the deal seems almost complete. The salesperson says the only thing left is the OK from his manager. He goes into a back office and is gone for several minutes. However, when he returns, he has a pained expression on his face. "I'm really embarrassed," he says, "but my manager won't approve the deal. He told me that at the price we agreed to, the dealership would actually end up losing money.*

*"But look," he continues, "rather than kill the deal, I was able to get him to agree to a price that's just $500 more than the figure we originally agreed to. We're still taking a beating, but I want your business badly. I know it's more than you wanted to pay, but it's the only way he'll OK the deal."*

*You mull it over a short time, and you come to a decision: You'll take the new deal. After all, $500 more is just a drop in the bucket on a transaction that costs thousands of dollars, and you're still getting a good price on the car. Besides, while the salesperson was talking to his manager you were picturing yourself driving the car and showing it to your friends. You smile and tell the salesperson you agree to the new price.*

Your smile might be a little less bright if you realized the true facts about the situation: You've been had. As we will discover, you have been the victim of a carefully-thought-out procedure designed to nudge you into compliance with a higher price, without your feeling much distress in the process.

We turn now to a consideration of compliance. **Compliance** consists of yielding to direct, explicit appeals meant to produce certain behavior or agreement to a particular point of view. Whereas the pressures on a person to conform are generally implicit and not in the form of direct requests or demands, compliance pressures are more overt. In compliance, there is little ambiguity in the social pressure that is brought to bear—a car salesperson urges you to accept a deal, a jewelry store clerk offers the opinion that the purchase of a bigger diamond offers better value, or a store sells compact discs in a 2-for-1 sale. As we will see, social psychologists have identified a variety of strategies that produce compliance.

**compliance**
yielding to direct, explicit appeals meant to produce certain behavior or agreement to a particular point of view.

## The Foot-in-the-Door Technique: Asking for a Little to Gain a Lot

At one time, the Fuller Brush Company salesperson was a staple of American life. In an era when most women were home during the day, Fuller Brush representatives went door to door in neighborhoods throughout the country, selling cleaning supplies. Housewives welcomed Fuller Brush salespersons because of a distinctive characteristic: They always arrived with a small but useful gift.

The gift was hardly just a nice gesture on the part of the Fuller Brush Company. Instead, it represented a social influence tactic designed to increase the probability of a sale. The salesperson first requested a small, no-cost favor (accepting the free gift), and then went on to ask for a bigger favor (purchasing cleaning supplies). It was a tactic that led to greater sales.

The success of the tactic rests on a principle of social influence called the foot-in-the-door technique. According to the **foot-in-the-door technique**, a target of social influence is first asked to agree to a small request, but later asked to comply with a more important one. It turns out that if the person agrees to the first request, compliance with the later, larger request is considerably more likely.

The foot-in-the-door phenomenon was first demonstrated in a study by social psychologists Jonathan Freedman and Scott Fraser, who had experimenters go door to door in a neighborhood asking residents to sign a petition in favor of safe driving (Freedman & Fraser, 1966). Almost everyone complied with such a small, mild request.

**foot-in-the-door technique**
a technique of social influence in which the target is first asked to agree to a small request, but later asked to comply with a more important one.

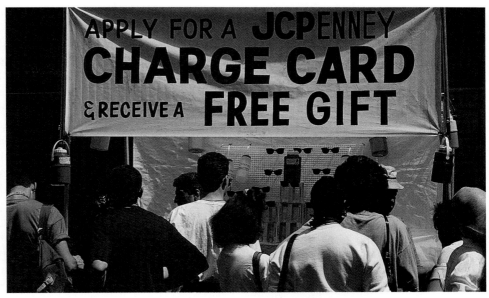

That "free gift" may actually have a price attached to it: one's future compliance. In an example of the foot-in-the-door technique, a target of social influence is first asked to agree to a small request, such as accepting a small, but free, gift. Later, though, the target is asked to agree to a larger request—such as completing an application for a charge card—and is much more likely to comply.

However, a few weeks later, a different experimenter recontacted the residents and made a much larger request, bordering on the outrageous—that they erect on their front lawn a huge sign that said "Drive Carefully." Surprisingly, more than half of those who had signed the initial petition agreed to the second request. In comparison, only 17 percent of a group of people who had not been asked to sign the initial petition were willing to place a sign on their lawn.

Subsequent research not only has confirmed these initial findings regarding the foot-in-the-door technique, but has added this additional principle: The larger the initial request, the greater the subsequent compliance that can be expected. Although the foot-in-the-door technique is not always as powerful as in the Freedman and Fraser experiment, it is real (Beaman et al., 1983; Dillard, Hunter, & Burgoon, 1984; Dillard, 1991). But why is the strategy effective?

Several explanations can be suggested. For one thing, involvement with the small request may result in the development of an explicit interest in an issue. Taking an action, even the most trivial, makes a person more committed to the issue, thereby increasing the likelihood of future compliance.

Another reason for the success of the foot-in-the-door procedure relates to self-perception theory. Agreement to the initial, small request begins a process in which people come to redefine themselves in certain ways that are consistent with their initial behavior. For instance, they may start to see themselves as social activists with an interest in safe driving (as in the Freedman and Fraser experiment), or they may come to view themselves as a person who uses Fuller brushes. Such a change in self-perception may increase their willingness to comply with later, larger requests.

*The Door-in-the-Face Technique: Asking for a Lot to Get a Little*

You've always had an interest in campaigns to end world hunger, and you've even attended some lectures and occasionally passed out literature on your college campus. So you're not all that surprised when you get a call from the campaign asking for a donation. You're stunned when you hear the size of the request, though: $100. You immediately refuse, saying that such an amount is out of the question. But when the fund raiser then asks for a $35 donation instead, you think for a minute, and then agree. You usually wouldn't donate so much, but, after all, it is an important cause.

**door-in-the-face technique**
a technique of social influence in which a large request, whose refusal is expected, is followed by a smaller one.

You've just encountered the **door-in-the-face technique,** a procedure in which a large request, whose refusal is expected, is followed by a smaller one. By employing a strategy that is virtually the opposite of the foot-in-the-door, the expectation is that the initial, outlandishly large request makes targets of persuasion more receptive to the subsequent smaller request (Reeves et al., 1991; Dillard, 1991).

The utility of the door-in-the-face procedure is illustrated by a field study carried out by social psychologist Robert Cialdini (Cialdini et al., 1975). In the study, college students were approached by researchers posing as representatives of a youth counseling program. The students were asked to make a substantial commitment—act as unpaid counselors for juvenile delinquents for two hours a week for a minimum of two years. Unsurprisingly, no one agreed to such a substantial request.

Later, though, when they were asked to agree to the much smaller (although not insubstantial) favor of taking a group of delinquents on a two-hour trip to the zoo, half of those approached agreed. In comparison, only 17 percent of a control group, who had not first been asked the larger favor, agreed to chaperone the delinquents.

The door-in-the-face technique is common, and you've probably used it at some time in your life. Perhaps you asked your parents for a giant raise in your allowance, hoping that they would settle for a smaller amount. In the same way, television writers have been known to sprinkle their scripts with obscenities that they know that network censors will remove, in order to preserve other key phrases that otherwise might be questionable (Cialdini, 1988).

The door-in-the-face procedure is effective largely due to the exchange of reciprocal concessions between the person making the request and the target of persuasion. In **reciprocal concessions,** requesters are seen to make a compromise (by reducing the size of their initial request), thereby inviting a concession on the part of those who initially refused the request. The consequence is that people are more willing to comply with the smaller request. Obviously, the principle of reciprocal concession stems from the norm of reciprocity, which—as we discussed in Chapter 8—asserts that we help those who have helped us in the past.

**reciprocal concessions**
a technique of social influence in which requesters appear to make a compromise (by reducing the size of their initial request), thereby inviting a concession on the part of those who initially refused the request.

Other reasons, besides the principle of reciprocal concessions, contribute to the effectiveness of the door-in-the-face technique. For instance, self-presentational factors may be at work (Pendleton & Batson, 1979). People who refuse the first request, even when the request is unreasonable, may fear that they may be seen by others as inflexible, inconsiderate, and unhelpful individuals. When the second—and more reasonable—request comes along, they feel compelled to comply in order to avoid being characterized by the unfavorable labels.

Finally, the effectiveness of the door-in-the-face technique may stem from perceptual factors. If you think back to your introductory psychology class, you probably learned about a phenomenon known as perceptual contrast when you studied sensation and perception. Perceptual contrast works like this: After exposure to a very powerful stimulus (say, a bright light), a new stimulus (such as a dimmer light) appears even less potent than it would if presented by itself.

Applying this principle to the door-in-the-face phenomenon, exposure to the initial, large request may make the second request seem more modest in comparison. Consequently, a person's willingness to agree to it will be higher (Cantrill & Seibold, 1986; Shanab & O'Neill, 1979).

## The That's-Not-All Technique: Discounter's Delight

"The price for this dress is $80. But that's not all: If you buy it right now, I'll be able to give it to you for just $70."

You've probably heard similar sales pitches. But did you know that you'll be much more likely to make the purchase than if you were told from the start that the regular price was $70?

In the **that's-not-all technique,** a customer is offered a deal at an initial, often inflated, price. But just after making the initial offer, the salesperson immediately offers

**that's-not-all technique**
a technique of social influence in which the salesperson offers a deal at an initial, often inflated price, then immediately offers an incentive, discount, or bonus to clinch the deal.

an incentive, discount, or bonus to clinch the deal. Although the technique seems transparent, it is quite effective.

For example, in one experiment, researchers sold cupcakes at a campus fair. In one condition, the cupcakes were peddled at the regular price of 75 cents each. But in another condition, customers were told the price was $1.00, but had been discounted down to 75 cents. You guessed it: The discounted cupcakes sold considerably faster than the regularly priced ones, despite their identical prices (Burger, 1986).

*The Low-Ball: Start Small, Finish Big*

**low-balling**
a technique in which an initial agreement is reached, but then the seller reveals additional costs.

Think back to the car purchase that we discussed earlier, in which the salesperson suddenly jacks up the price at the last minute by claiming that the original deal was not approved by the sales manager. Similar scenarios are routinely played out every day at car dealerships, and they result in consumers' being fleeced out of hundreds of dollars.

The technique is known as low-balling. In **low-balling**, an initial agreement is reached, but then the seller reveals additional costs. Low-balling works because it fits the processes we go through when making a consumer purchase decision. Just prior to committing ourselves to an initial purchase decision, we consider both the advantages and disadvantages of the deal. But when we finally reach a decision, we tend to emphasize the advantages of the deal in order to justify our decision. In fact, we may overemphasize the advantages, due to post-decision cognitive dissonance.

Consequently, while the salesperson is off getting final approval, we're cognitively busy, convincing ourselves of the wisdom of the deal. When the salesperson returns with the news that the deal has become unhinged and that the price must go up, we're ready to leap for the bait. The typical reaction: to tell ourselves that despite the higher price, the deal is still so good that we shouldn't refuse it (Cialdini, 1988).

There's another reason that low-balling may be effective. Good salespersons attempt to make you like them, and they try to instill the sense that the two of you are

Effective salespersons aim to create the impression that they have a personal relationship with a target of social influence. This may lead targets to feel a sense of personal commitment to the salesperson, making them more susceptible to future influence.

in the early stages of building a personal relationship. If that is the case, you may accept the higher-priced deal because you genuinely feel that it is out of the salesperson's hands and the cost increase is due solely to the sales manager's stubbornness. Your sense of personal commitment to the salesperson, then, may propel you toward accepting the deal (Burger & Petty, 1981). For a consideration of the ways in which social influence is used by business organizations, see the accompanying Social Psychology at Work feature.

---

# Social Psychology at Work

## On-the-Job Influence: Bottom-up, Lateral, and Top-down Compliance Tactics

You're a manager in a factory that produces compact discs. You are certain that the company is overproducing the new Barry Manilow collection, and you wish to convince your boss that she should lower the production numbers. What do you do to get her to comply with your point of view?

At the same time, you want to convince the people who work for you that the new production schedule that you've devised is an improvement over the old one. Although you're thoroughly convinced you're right, they aren't so sure. How do you convince them to accept your position?

Finally, you need to borrow some expensive, fragile audiovisual equipment that another manager, who holds the same rank as you, uses in his daily work. How do you get him to help you?

And do you use the same influence tactics in all three of these scenarios—with your boss, with your subordinates, and with your coworker?

Preliminary solutions to all these problems come from studies carried out by industrial psychologists Gary Yukl and Cecilia Falbe. According to their findings, the answer is clear: You'll probably employ very different sorts of social influence techniques, depending on whether you are dealing with a boss, a subordinate, or a coequal.

Yukl and Falbe provided a group of business managers with a list of influence tactics, including the following:

- *Pressure tactics.* The person uses demands, threats, or intimidation to convince you to comply with a request or to support a proposal. ("If you don't complete the report, you'll be fired.")

- *Upward appeals.* The person seeks to persuade you that the request is approved by higher management, or appeals to higher management for assistance in gaining your compliance with the request. ("This request comes straight from the division director herself.")

- *Exchange tactics.* The person makes an explicit or implicit promise that you will receive rewards or tangible benefits if you comply with a request or support a proposal, or reminds you of a prior favor to be reciprocated. ("If you do a good job on this, you'll be in line for the promotion.")

- *Coalition tactics.* The person seeks the aid of others to persuade you to do something or uses the support of others as an argument for you to agree. ("Help me get Hannah to agree to this, will you?")

- *Ingratiating tactics.* The person seeks to get you in a good mood or to think favorably of him or her before asking you to do something. ("You really did a great job on that last task force. That's why I'd like you to be on the new one.")

- *Rational persuasion.* The person uses logical arguments and factual evidence to persuade you that a proposal or request is viable and likely to result in the attainment of task objectives. ("Your knowledge of computers will raise productivity for the entire company.")

- *Inspirational appeals.* The person makes an emotional request or proposal that arouses enthusiasm by appealing to your values and ideals, or by increasing your confidence that you are the right person for the task. ("You're the only one who can do the job right.")

- *Consultation tactics.* The person seeks your participation in making a decision or in planning how to implement a proposed policy, strategy, or change. ("How can we introduce this new policy so people will accept it?") (Based on Yukl & Falbe, 1990, p. 133)

The participants in the study were asked how applicable each of the persuasive techniques would be, according to whether the target of persuasion was a subordinate (downward influence), a peer (lateral influence), or a supervisor (upward influence). As you can see from the results displayed in Figure 12-5, the frequency with which a particular tactic was used varied in most cases according to whether the influence was directed downward, laterally, or upward. For example, pressure tactics were used most often in downward influence attempts and least often in upward attempts.

Further, upward appeals and exchange tactics were less frequent when attempting to gain compliance from a superior than when involved in downward or lateral relationships. Inspirational appeals and consultation tactics were used more frequently in downward than in upward influence situations.

However, some compliance techniques were used frequently, regardless of the kind of target. For instance, appeals based on coalitions and on rational persuasion did not differ in frequency according to the status of the persuasive target.

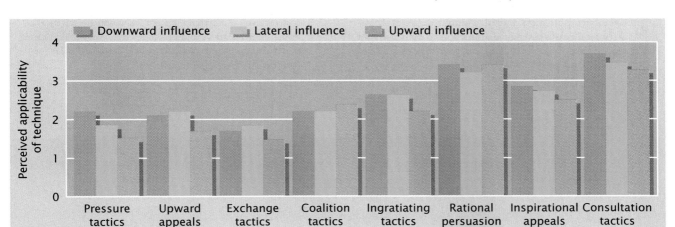

FIGURE 12-5   **Persuasion in the Workplace**  The type of persuasion that business managers thought they would use depended on whether the target of persuasion was a subordinate (downward influence), a peer (lateral influence), or a supervisor (upward influence). *(Source:* Yukl & Falbe, 1990.*)*

These findings reveal which influence techniques managers report using on the job, but they don't indicate how effective they were. Just because people report using particular kinds of techniques doesn't mean they worked. Future research, then, needs to investigate which ones work best on the job. For the moment, though, the research findings give us a start in understanding people's attempts to gain compliance in the business world.

# THE INFORMED CONSUMER OF SOCIAL PSYCHOLOGY

## AVOIDING COMPLIANCE BY JUST SAYING "NO"

By now, you've probably traveled down the road of compliance tactics long enough to develop a healthy skepticism regarding any salesperson you meet. In fact, you may be discouraged, thinking that the average person has few weapons at his or her disposal with which to fend off the attacks of those trying to gain compliance.

Nothing could be further from the truth, however. Your very awareness of the range of compliance techniques makes you less of a mark. Furthermore, there are several counter-compliance techniques that you can employ in order to avoid the label of "patsy." Among those suggested by social psychologist Robert Cialdini, an expert in social influence, are the following (Cialdini, 1993):

- *Redefine the situation.* As we've seen, "free" gifts often have strings attached. But if you don't consider them as no-strings-attached gifts, their power to evoke the rule of reciprocity or to act as the foot-in-the-door will be greatly diminished. Thus, it is critical to look a gift horse in the mouth, and to label freebies for what they are: attempts to make you feel obligated to the giver.

- *Avoid consistency for consistency's sake.* Although we have seen in prior chapters that efforts to maintain consistency (in our

attitudes, behavior, and so forth) are characteristic of our social lives, it doesn't have to be that way. By becoming aware of the self-induced pressures to behave consistently, we can avoid situations in which consistency is actually harmful to our better interests. For instance, it is not logical to maintain a consistent commitment after a deal that we have initially struck has changed significantly—such as with the addition of several hundred dollars to an agreed-upon price.

- *Avoid mindlessness.* According to social psychologist Ellen Langer, people are sometimes in a state of "mindlessness," in which they simply do not think about what they are doing. By relying on mindless scripts, people sometimes move through their daily activities with little thought, alertness, or creativity. The more mundane and commonplace the activity, the more likely a person will use an old script to guide behavior, with an accompanying lack of awareness. Because a state of mindlessness increases one's susceptibility to compliance tactics, we need to be vigilant to the underlying message we are receiving. This means looking beyond what people are telling us and trying to determine their underlying motives (Langer, 1989a, 1989b).

- *Just say no.* No law of human conduct requires you to be agreeable to people who seek your compliance with their

*Continued on next page*

social influence attempts. Indeed, a healthy degree of skepticism is in order whenever anyone attempts to influence your behavior. Even if you are dealing with something like a "Save-the-Planet Foundation" (who could be against saving the planet?), you need to be vigilant whenever anyone tries to convince you of anything. Except when you are certain that others' motives are devoid of self-interest, you should assume that their compliance tactics are being employed more for their benefit than for your own.

---

## ► REVIEW & RETHINK

### Rethink

- Compliance is yielding to direct, explicit appeals.
- The foot-in-the-door, door-in-the-face, and that's-not-all techniques lead to compliance.
- Several strategies can reduce compliance.

### Rethink

- How does compliance differ from conformity?
- The foot-in-the-door and the door-in-the-face techniques suggest exactly the opposite strategies when trying to persuade someone. How can both be correct?
- Explain how cognitive dissonance might contribute to the effectiveness of low-balling techniques.
- What advice would you give to others to help them avoid being duped into buying something they didn't want or paying too much for it?

---

# OBEDIENCE

How would you react if you found yourself in the following situation?

*In a shopping mall, you pass by a stranger in a white laboratory jacket standing at the front of one of the stores. In the store window is a sign that reads, "Research Associates." As you walk by, the man calls out to you, asking for a few minutes of your time. He says he needs your assistance, and he is willing to pay for it.*

*You ask what he wants, and the stranger tells you that he has devised a new way of improving memory, and he wants your help in testing it. He tells you that he'd like you to teach people a list of word pairs, and then to give them a test.*

*The novel part of the procedure, which he wishes to test, is that you must give the learners a shock each time they make a mistake on the test. He shows you a shock generator that you are to use, which contains switches ranging from 30 to 450 volts. The switches are labeled from "slight shock" through "danger: severe shock" at the top level, where there are three red X's.*

*When you express hesitation about administering the shocks, he tells you not to worry: Although the shocks may be painful to the learners, they will produce no lasting damage.*

Would you comply with the stranger's request? You probably are fairly sure that you, like most people, would be quick to balk at the man's strange request. Obviously, it is far from a reasonable scenario, and few people would be inclined to go along with such a request.

But let's modify the scenario a bit. Suppose the man, rather than being an unidentified stranger about whom you had no knowledge, was instead identified as a psychologist conducting an experiment. Or assume that it was your employer, or your professor, or your military commander. Wouldn't you now be more likely to comply with the request for help, despite its improbable, even bizarre, nature?

If you still think it unlikely that you would submit to such a request, you might wish to rethink your response. For as we shall see, a landmark series of studies carried out in the 1960s suggests that you might well be inclined to obey, giving shocks of increasing intensity to a luckless learner.

**obedience**
a change in behavior that is due to the commands of others in authority.

We turn now to the social psychological phenomenon of obedience. **Obedience** is a change in behavior that is due to the commands of others in authority. Unlike conformity and compliance, in which people are gently guided or steered toward a particular position, obedience is the result of a more active approach to social influence. In obedience, direct orders are meant to elicit direct submission.

## Obedience to Authority: Only Following Orders

For many people, the My Lai massacre signified all that was wrong with the Vietnam War. In the massacre, a group of U.S. Army soldiers brutalized, raped, and killed hundreds of civilians in the tiny village of My Lai. Masses of civilians—children, the elderly, women—were herded into drainage ditches and executed. Babies were bayoneted, and one woman was raped right after watching soldiers kill her children. According to one journalist, as soon as they entered the village, troops began to "systematically ransack the hamlet and slaughter the people, kill the livestock, and destroy the crops. Men poured rifle and machine-gun fire into huts without knowing—or seemingly caring—who was inside" (Hersh, 1970, pp. 49–50).

The explanation supplied by the soldiers who participated in the carnage: They were only following orders to rid the area of North Vietnamese Communist enemies.

When details of the My Lai massacre came to light after the Vietnam War, many people saw it as an exceptional event, some awful one-time aberration. But the pages of history tell a different story. Events as varied as the Holocaust, the Iran-Contra scandal, torture in South America, and the Serbian "ethnic cleansing" that we discussed at the beginning of the chapter all testify to this darker side of human behavior.

The people involved in events such as these typically share a common excuse: They simply were following the orders of their superiors. And, as far as it goes, such an explanation is often accurate. People in such situations are often behaving in ways that are consistent with what they are told to do by legitimate authority figures. For instance, soldiers who participated in the My Lai massacre argued that they were following the orders of their superior, Lieutenant William Calley. Calley, in turn, argued that he was simply following the orders of his superiors, in ridding the village of My Lai of supposed Communist sympathizers.

In an analysis of obedience, social psychologist Herbert Kelman and sociologist Lee Hamilton suggest that obedience to authorities is based on three factors: the legitimacy of the system, the legitimacy of the authorities or power holders within the system, and the legitimacy of their demands (Kelman & Hamilton, 1989). The legitimacy of the system refers to the degree to which an authority group that holds sway over a person is seen as appropriate and rightful. The group may be a government; a unit of government such as an army; a religious organization; or even a family. Whatever the explicit nature of the group, it commands obedience because of its position within society and an individual's view of its place in society.

The legitimacy of the authorities or power holders is largely based on the way those individuals come to hold their positions. A winner of a presidential election is a legitimate authority, as is a general who has moved up in the ranks of the army. In contrast, a leader who comes to power through a rigged election or a military revolt may not be seen as having legitimate authority.

Following the Iran-Contra scandal, Oliver North attributed his deception during Congressional hearings to the arguments that he was acting under the orders of President Reagan and for the greater good of the country. His excuse relates to Kelman and Hamilton's three components of obedience: the legitimacy of the system, the legitimacy of the authorities, and the legitimacy of their demands.

Finally, the third factor that affects obedience to authorities is the legitimacy of the authority or power holder's demands. The legitimacy of demands refers to a person's perception that what is being demanded fits within the framework of a valid, justifiable request.

To the extent that a seemingly legitimate demand is seen as emanating from a legitimate authority within a legitimate system, it is likely to be obeyed without question. However, should any one of the three factors (the system, the authority figure, or the demand itself) be seen as less than legitimate, the likelihood of obeying the demand will be diminished.

It is important to keep in mind that Kelman and Hamilton's analysis of obedience to authorities is a social psychological one, resting on the impact of an individual's perception of the legitimacy of a particular demand. It is equally important to consider what the analysis doesn't focus on: personality factors.

The omission is not by accident. For example, it turns out that participants in the My Lai massacre don't seem to have been mentally ill or disturbed or to have had any fundamental personality disorders. Indeed, more than half of a national sample of Americans said in a survey that they would have shot all the inhabitants of a Vietnamese village if so ordered. Such sentiments suggest that the participants in the massacre only did what other Americans think they would do in similar circumstances (Kelman & Lawrence, 1972).

Similarly, there was little that was out of the ordinary about people who participated in the German Holocaust during World War II. Even Adolph Eichmann, who committed some of the most heinous crimes, has been described as "an average man of middle class origins and normal middle class upbringing, a man without identifiable criminal tendencies" (Von Lang & Sibyll, 1983).

Hence, most evidence suggests that people who participate in the long list of bloodbaths and instances of genocide that punctuate world history differ relatively little from the average person (Staub, 1989). But what leads an ordinary individual to cross over the line and commit a deed that in retrospect can only be labeled as abhorrent and repugnant? This is one of the questions that social psychologist Stanley Milgram sought to answer in a pioneering—and controversial—series of studies that he began in the early 1960s.

*Obedience to Authority: The Milgram Studies*

In many respects, Milgram's studies were not too different from the scenario laid out in the opening passage of this section. Subjects were recruited to participate in an experiment that ostensibly dealt with the topic of learning. They were told that the experimenter was testing a way to enhance memorization, and that the basic procedure required that a learner memorize a list of pairs of words. Following the memorization phase, the subjects would test the learners. Each time a learner made an error, a subject administered a shock, using the formidable shock generator pictured in Figure 12-6.

In reality, of course, the real topic of the experiment was obedience to authority. Milgram was seeking to learn the degree to which people would follow the commands of an experimenter, who during the course of the experiment urged that learners be administered shocks of a higher and higher intensity.

On hearing of the study, most people predicted that only a rare, and possibly disturbed, subject would be willing to progress too far in the procedure—a view shared with a group of distinguished psychiatrists. The psychiatrists, who were polled when the experiments were first conducted, surmised that only one in a thousand people would give the highest-level shock. The prevalent opinion was that most people would not go beyond the 150-volt level. Other individuals, without any special training, were even more conservative, with many predicting that none of the subjects would administer shocks.

The reality was quite different. Neither distinguished psychiatrists nor untrained individuals were able to predict accurately how Milgram's subjects would perform. Surprisingly, 65 percent of the subjects who participated in the experiment gave the highest-level shock of 450 volts (Milgram, 1974).

These startling results are tempered by the fact that in all cases the learners were confederates of the experimenter and did not receive any electric shocks. However, this is small solace, because the subjects were unaware of this situation. They presumably thought that they were administering painful shocks at the behest of the experimenter.

Over the course of a decade, Milgram tried a number of variants of his original study. For instance, in one experiment, the physical proximity of the victim to the subjects was manipulated. In one condition (called the "remote condition"), the victims could be neither seen nor heard; in another (the "voice feedback condition"), they could not be seen, but their verbal protestations could be heard from the next room. In the two remaining conditions, the victims were in the same room as the subject. In one case, a learner was positioned just a few feet away (the "proximity condition"). In the final

**FIGURE 12-6 The Milgram "Shock Generator" and "Victim."** This impressive—but bogus—"shock generator" was used to make subjects think that they were giving shocks to a supposed victim, who was connected to the generator by electrodes.

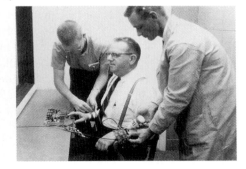

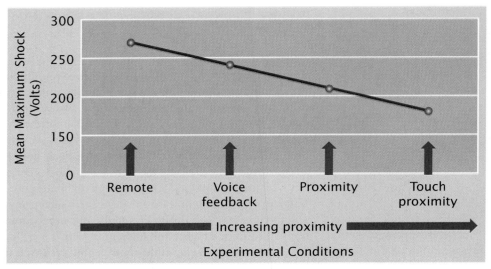

**FIGURE 12-7  Proximity and Obedience** Victims who were physically closer to the subject received less severe shocks than those who were further away.    *(Source:* Milgram, 1974.*)*

case, the subject actually had to place the victim's hand on a shock plate in order to administer the shock (the "touch proximity" condition).

As you might guess, increasing proximity led to decreasing obedience. Figure 12-7 illustrates the mean maximum shock for each of the four conditions. Similarly, the percentage of subjects who were obedient also declined as proximity increased. Still, the absolute level of obedience was high even in the most extreme condition. For instance, even when subjects had to physically take the hand of the victim (who, at the 150-volt level, demanded to be set free and would not voluntarily touch the shock plate), a full 30 percent of the subjects obeyed the experimenter's wishes and gave the maximum shock.

Further studies investigated whether there were significant individual differences between subjects. For example, Milgram speculated that the subjects who gave the highest level shocks might differ significantly in terms of personality or other demographic characteristics from those who refused to obey the experimenter. However, he was unable to identify many distinctions between subjects—a finding that has held up to the present.

For example, research to date has not identified any gender differences; men and women are equally obedient (Blass & Krackow, 1991). Similarly, there do not seem to be any strong, general personality differences that differentiate obedient and disobedient subjects.

On the other hand, some personality factors are implicated in obedience, although they appear to play a relatively minor role. Some evidence suggests that people who characteristically attribute factors external to themselves as the cause of their behavior may be more prone to obedience than those who characteristically attribute their behavior to internal factors (Blass, 1991). Hence, people who attribute their actions to the commands of another (an external attribution) may behave more obediently than people who feel more personally responsible for another's suffering (an internal attribution).

Still, the preponderance of evidence suggests that although personality factors should not be ignored, situational factors play a powerful role in determining obedience. Put any of us in circumstances similar to the one in which Milgram placed his subjects, then, and our behavior probably will be similar to those of the subjects in his experiment.

**THE RETURN OF THE "ONLY FOLLOWING ORDERS" DEFENSE.** Why were so many subjects obedient? Extensive interviews with subjects following their participation in the experiment revealed a theme similar to that utilized by the soldiers in the My Lai massacre: They were only following orders.

In addition, subjects in the Milgram study claimed that they had been obedient because they believed that the experimenter would be responsible for any potential ill effects that befell the learner. The primary justification provided by subjects for their obedience was that they felt little or no personal responsibility for their actions. They claimed any unfavorable ramifications were the responsibility of the experimenter, whose orders they were simply following and who explicitly had told them that he accepted full responsibility for the situation.

In fact, the experimenter had been explicit in accepting culpability. For instance, even when they ended up totally obedient to the experimenter, subjects rarely complied without at least some form of protest. Instead, many broached concerns, albeit sometimes tentatively, about the learner's well-being. When that occurred, the experimenter used a series of standardized prods of increasing intensity, designed to secure the subject's obedience.

At the first protest, the experimenter said, "Please continue." If subjects continued to object, the experimenter moved through these phrases: "The experiment requires that you continue"; then, "It is absolutely essential that you continue"; and finally, "You have no other choice, you must go on." Such statements reinforced the experimenter's initial assertion that subjects should feel no personal responsibility for their actions because he, the experimenter, accepted the complete responsibility.

**WAS OBEDIENCE ILLUSORY? THE CRITICS RESPOND.** The results of Milgram's studies were startling, and they led to a good deal of controversy. Some of the questions that were raised were methodological (Orne & Holland, 1968). Did subjects really believe they were giving shocks to the confederate? Furthermore, could the obedience that was observed in the study be attributable to the fact that subjects knew they were in the protected environment of a psychological laboratory?

After all, the experimental situation was, at best, an unusual and even strange one. A calm, detached experimenter urges a subject to continue giving shocks, even when the learner shouts in protestation. In addition, thoughtful subjects might wonder, even as they are being asked to increase the intensity of the shocks, why they are needed at all. If the study were actually about understanding the effects of punishment on learning, why couldn't the experimenter act as the teacher? What did the subject's presence add to the study?

Such alternative explanations cannot be ruled out entirely. However, the behavior of the typical subject in the experiments makes it appear that participants were taken in by the experiment's cover story. Subjects displayed strong emotional reactions while administering the shocks. They sweated; they stuttered; they bit their lips; they broke into nervous laughter. Many reported feeling anxious and upset after the experiment.

If we accept that subjects were taken in by the experimental procedure—which most social psychologists do—then another troubling question arises: Were the Milgram experiments ethical? Some observers say no. For instance, some social psychologists suggest that it was unethical in the first place to put subjects in a situation in which they were pressed to carry out acts that normally would be unthinkable to them (Baumrind, 1964).

Even worse, according to critics, was the extreme tension subjects displayed during the course of the experiment. In their view, it is plausible that some subjects would show lasting adverse consequences from their experimental participation (see Figure 12-8).

In reply to such criticisms, Milgram claimed that following the experiment a full debriefing eradicated any negative outcomes of participation. Furthermore, long-term follow-ups also indicated no effects due to participation (Milgram, 1977). Nevertheless, the ethical issue cannot be dismissed. It remains an important, if ultimately unresolvable, footnote to Milgram's work.

**FIGURE 12-8    You Be the Judge**

Although critics of the Milgram obedience to authority experiment suggest that subjects were placed under undue stress, Milgram responded that there was no evidence of subjects being unduly pressured in the experiment. The following is a transcript of an actual session with one subject, who ended up giving the highest-level shock. What are your reactions?

*150 volts delivered.* You want me to keep going?

*165 volts delivered.* That guy is hollering in there. There's a lot of them here. He's liable to have a heart condition. You want me to go?

*180 volts delivered.* He can't stand it! I'm not going to kill that man in there! You hear him hollering? He's hollering. He can't stand it. What if something happens to him? . . . I'm not going to get that man sick in there. He's hollering in there. You know what I mean? I mean I refuse to take responsibility. He's getting hurt in there. He's in there hollering. Too many left here. Geez, if he gets them wrong. There's too many of them left. I mean who is going to take responsibility if anything happens to the gentleman?

[*The experimenter accepts responsibility.*]

All right.

*195 volts delivered.* You see he's hollering. Hear that. Gee, I don't know.

[*The experimenter says: "The experiment requires that you go on."*]—I know it does, sir, but I mean—ugh—he don't know what he's in for. He's up to 195 volts.

*210 volts delivered.*

*225 volts delivered.*

*240 volts delivered.* Aw, no. You mean I've got to keep going up with the scale? No sir. I'm not going to kill that man! I'm not going to give him 450 volts!

[*The experimenter says: "The experiment requires that you go on."*]—I know it does, but that man is hollering there, sir . . .

*Source:* Milgram, 1965.

Independent of ethical issues, Milgram's studies reveal an important fact: Authority figures can induce people to perform antisocial acts with relative ease. And while it would be comforting to suggest that Milgram's work reflects past senselessness and that people today are less likely to act obediently, this just isn't so. In a recent analysis of experimental replications and extensions that have been carried out in the three decades since Milgram's work first began, social psychologist Thomas Blass and colleagues found no systematic shift in the magnitude of obedience shown by subjects (Blass & Krackow, 1991).

The real world, too, shows little evidence for a decline in the inclination of people to follow orders, as one can infer from such cases as the Serbian ethnic cleansing that we discussed at the start of the chapter. Obedience remains a very real phenomenon.

We are all obedient to some of the demands of authorities some of the time. The question is, under what conditions will obedience occur, and how extreme will it be.

► **REVIEW & RETHINK**

*Review*

- Obedience is a change in behavior due to the commands of others in authority.
- The perceived legitimacy of the system, of authorities or power holders, and of demands are associated with obedience.
- Milgram's studies showed that many people would be surprisingly obedient to the commands of another person.

*Rethink*

- How does obedience differ from conformity and compliance?
- Consider a soldier at My Lai and a subject in Milgram's original obedience experiment. Identify and compare factors in each situation that affected these individuals' willingness to comply.
- According to Kelman and Hamilton, what three factors determine the likelihood that a request will be obeyed?
- Which of the methods to help resist unwanted pressure to comply that were discussed earlier can be helpful in resisting unwanted pressures to be obedient?

## LOOKING BACK

◄◄◄◄◄◄◄◄◄◄◄◄◄◄◄◄◄◄◄◄◄◄◄◄◄◄◄◄◄◄◄

### Why do people conform to the views and behavior of others?

1. Conformity is one of the basic responses to social influence, in which people are affected by the real or imagined pressure of other individuals or a group. Conformity is a change in behavior or attitudes brought about by a desire to follow the beliefs or standards of others.

2. People conform due to normative and informational social influence. Normative social influence is pressure that reflects group norms, which are expectations regarding appropriate behavior held by those belonging to groups. In contrast, informational social influence is pressure to conform that emanates from the assumption that others have knowledge that we lack.

3. Among the factors that promote conformity are the nature of the relationship a person has to a group, the number of people aligned against an individual, and the presence of a social supporter (a person holding a position similar to one's own). There are also some individual differences, such as gender and cultural background, that are related to conformity, although the relationships are complex.

### What factors promote independence from conformity pressures?

4. Two strategies may be employed by group minorities who wish to remain independent from the group. One, proposed by Moscovici, suggests that a minority will have maximal influence if it displays unvarying consistency. The second, suggested by Hollander, calls for the accumulation of idiosyncrasy credit by first conforming to the group. When enough credit is amassed, deviation from the majority position is possible.

5. One source of controversy is whether majority and minority social influence operate differently. The single-process approach suggests that both majorities and minorities employ similar influence techniques. In contrast, dual-process approaches suggest that majorities and minorities exert their influence in qualitatively different ways. Neither position has been fully upheld.

*What strategies can be employed to make others compliant, and how can such pressures be resisted?*

6.  Several strategies have been developed to produce compliance—yielding to direct, explicit appeals meant to produce certain behavior or agreement to a particular point of view. For instance, in the foot-in-the-door technique, a target of social influence is first asked to agree to a small request, but later asked to comply with a more important one. In contrast, the door-in-the-face technique is a procedure in which a large request, whose refusal is expected, is followed by a smaller one. The door-in-the-face procedure is effective primarily because of the exchange of reciprocal concessions between the person making the request and the target of persuasion.

7.  In the that's-not-all technique, a customer is offered a deal at an initial, often inflated, price. But just after making the initial offer, the salesperson immediately offers an incentive, discount, or bonus to clinch the deal. In contrast, low-balling occurs when an initial agreement is reached, but then the seller reveals additional costs.

8.  Several methods can reduce a person's unwitting compliance. These include redefining the situation, avoiding consistency for consistency's sake, avoiding mindlessness, and just saying no.

*Why are people so readily obedient to authority figures?*

9.  According to Kelman and Hamilton's analysis, obedience—a change in behavior that is due to the commands of others in authority—occurs because of three factors: the perceived legitimacy of the system, the perceived legitimacy of authorities or power holders, and the perceived legitimacy of demands.

10.  Milgram's studies of obedience employed a procedure in which subjects were asked to administer increasingly intense shocks to a victim. Although experts predicted that almost no subjects would give the highest-level shock, 65 percent of the subjects who participated in the basic form of the experiment gave the maximum shock.

11.  Subjects reported that they were obedient because they were following the orders of the experimenter, who they believed would be responsible for any potential ill effects. However, the experiment has been criticized on both methodological and ethical grounds. Some critics claimed that subjects did not really believe that they were giving shocks. Furthermore, some argued that the experiment was unethical and may have produced long-term negative outcomes. Still, Milgram's experiments illustrated that authority figures can induce people to perform antisocial acts with relative ease.

# KEY TERMS AND CONCEPTS

*social influence (p. 381)*

*conformity (p. 383)*

*normative social influence (p. 384)*

*informational social influence (p. 384)*

*autokinetic effect (p. 384)*

*status (p. 385)*

*social impact theory (p. 386)*

*social supporter (p. 386)*

*idiosyncrasy credit (p. 391)*

*single-process approach (p. 392)*

*dual-process approach (p. 393)*

*compliance (p. 394)*

*foot-in-the-door technique (p. 394)*

*door-in-the-face technique (p. 396)*

*reciprocal concessions (p. 396)*

*that's-not-all technique (p. 397)*

*low-balling (p. 397)*

*obedience (p. 401)*

# FOR FURTHER RESEARCH AND STUDY

Milgram, S. (1993). *The individual in a social world* (2nd ed.). New York: McGraw-Hill.

A series of essays and experiments written by the late Stanley Milgram, who made important contributions in several areas of social influence.

Cialdini, R. (1993). *Influence: Science and practice* (3rd ed.). New York: Harper-Collins.

A witty and eye-opening guide to the strategies arrayed against us to produce compliance in our everyday lives.

Kelman, H. C., & Hamilton, V. L. (1989). *Crimes of obedience.* New Haven, CT: Yale University Press.

An fascinating psychological analysis of authority and the reasons people commit illegal acts under the orders of others.

Pratkanis, A., & Aronson, E. (1991). *Age of propaganda: The everyday use and abuse of persuasion.* New York: Freeman.

A series of appealing essays on the ways in which we are targets of persuasive onslaughts.

# EPILOGUE

It is easy to focus purely on the negative sides of conformity, compliance, and obedience, looking at how they guide people to do things that they might not have necessarily wished to do. However, it is important to keep in mind that our social world would not operate very effectively without these phenomena. Indeed, from the moment of birth, caretakers attempt to make children increasingly responsive to social regulation and aware of social norms.

Consequently, in the next chapter, we consider how the law and the political system under which we operate affect our behavior. We look at how we, as citizens, accept that others have legitimate authority over us and over what we do, and what effect that acceptance of the law and the political system has on our everyday social world.

### CHAPTER THIRTEEN

# LAW AND ORDER

## THE LEGAL SYSTEM AND POLITICS

# PROLOGUE: MURDER IN THE FIRST DEGREE?

The killer planned the deed carefully. He sawed off the end of the 20-gauge shotgun in order to more easily conceal it under his jacket. He packed the bullets with candle wax, which made the shotgun even more deadly. After the shooting, he turned himself in to authorities, freely admitting he had done the killing. During his trial, he confessed, "I gave it a lot of thought. . . . I wanted to make sure he would definitely die" (Mitchell, 1976, p. vii). The case brought to trial had all the elements of murder in the first degree.

Yet, after less than three hours of deliberation, a conservative, blue-collar jury of seven men and five women found the defendant not guilty.

A miscarriage of justice? You be the judge. This was no simple murder: The defendant was Lester Zygmaniak, the

Was Lester Zygmaniak guilty of the first-degree murder of his brother George? A jury said no.

brother of the victim. The victim of a motorcycle accident, George Zygmaniak was a quadriplegic, paralyzed from the neck down. He was a total invalid, in constant severe pain. His distress was so profound that he repeatedly begged his brother, in front of other family members, to kill him. In fact, he said at one point, "I want you to promise to kill me: I want you to swear to God." Eventually, after much thought, Lester complied with his brother's wishes. He said it was an act of love for his brother.

To the prosecuting attorney, on the other hand, it was a simple case of murder. Because the criminal code made no provision for "mercy killings," the only possible charge was murder in the first degree. And the only allowable sentence for such a charge was life imprisonment.

In its swift response, the jury took matters into its own hands. Rather than complying with the evidence and the judge's predeliberation legal instructions, which clearly suggested that a "guilty" verdict should be forthcoming, the jury found the defendant innocent. Apparently, the jurors felt that when rendering their verdict they could not ignore the obvious moral issues involved in the case. Lester Zygmaniak was a free man.

## LOOKING AHEAD ▶ ▶ ▶ ▶ ▶ ▶ ▶ ▶ ▶ ▶ ▶ ▶ ▶ ▶ ▶ ▶ ▶ ▶ ▶ ▶ ▶ ▶ ▶ ▶ ▶ ▶ ▶ ▶

Cases like the one described in the Prologue do not always produce the same result. For instance, a less-fortunate defendant, Roswell Gilbert, killed his 73-year-old wife after she begged him to end her suffering from incurable osteoporosis and Alzheimer's disease. After Gilbert complied, a jury found him guilty of murder, and at age 75, he was sentenced to life imprisonment (Associated Press, 1985).

The complexities and contradictions of the law are many. Justice can take many forms, and it is administered through a complex system that takes into account a variety of interests and perspectives, many of which are conflicting. The intricacy of the legal system reflects in part a political process that attempts to take into account the concerns of all citizens. The ultimate goal of the system is to ensure that all are treated in a just manner.

In this chapter, we examine social psychological approaches to the law and politics. We begin by examining several of the major players in the criminal justice system: the defendant, the judge, and the jury. We consider how a defendant's characteristics affect assumptions of guilt or innocence; how judges can influence juries regarding matters of the law; and how a jury's size and makeup produce different types of verdicts. We discuss the social psychology of criminal activity and the kinds of excuses criminals use to explain their failure to comply with the law.

Finally, we consider several issues of concern to social psychologists interested in the broader political system. We concentrate on leadership, examining the factors that lead to people's rise to leadership positions. We also examine manifestations of power, suggesting that power has several distinct bases.

In sum, after reading this chapter, you will be able to answer these questions:

- What are the social psychological factors that affect defendants and judges in criminal trials?
- How do juries reach decisions?
- How do social psychological factors affect criminal activity?
- What steps can be taken to make trials more fair?
- What are the major explanations for leadership?
- On what basis is power acquired, and what are the consequences of wielding power?

# THE LAW AND THE COURTROOM

The cast of characters is well known to devotees of crime and suspense thrillers: the tough, disagreeable defendant, in need of a shave; the attractive, modest victim; the honorable silver-haired judge; the vigorous, self-righteous defense attorney; and the crusading district attorney, eager to add another conviction to a record that is attracting attention in local political circles. And of course, there's also the jury: those twelve nondescript, upstanding citizens who watch the trial, hear the evidence, and retire to the privacy of the deliberation room to render justice in a fair and impartial way.

Those are the stereotypes. The reality, though, is quite different. In actual courtrooms, the cast of characters is much more varied than the stereotypes suggest, matching the range and variability of humanity. Some defendants are guilty, some are innocent. Some victims are amiable and evoke compassion, others are sullen and unpleasant. Some judges are fair, others are dishonest and corrupt. The attorneys—for the prosecution and for the defense—may all be seeking justice, or they may be working to further their own careers at the expense of others. Some jurors may be conscientiously fulfilling their responsibilities as citizens; others may be biased and unfair.

The diversity among the key players in the legal system limits the precision with which the judicial system operates. Despite carefully-thought-out rules and procedures devised over centuries, legal practice is subject to distortions, biases, and errors of judgment. Above all, legal decisions are social decisions, made on the basis of numerous interacting factors of a social psychological nature. To understand some of these factors, we'll consider several of the major players in courtroom settings in order to illustrate how social psychological factors affect judicial decisions.

*The Defendant*     Despite the goal of equal justice for everyone, not all defendants are treated the same. In fact, what should be irrelevant characteristics—such as physical appearance, gender, and race—have a significant influence on jurors' decisions about guilt and innocence.

**PHYSICAL APPEARANCE.**     As we first discussed in Chapter 6, physical appearance plays a powerful role in determining interpersonal attraction. It is not surprising, then, that jurors are influenced by a defendant's attractiveness. In most cases, the influence is positive: Both jurors and judges are more lenient when defendants are physically attractive than when they are less attractive (Landy & Aronson, 1969; Dane & Wrightsman, 1982; Wuensch, Castellow, & Moore, 1991). Not only are attractive defendants more likely to be found innocent, but they also are more likely to receive shorter sentences, and they are less likely to be sent to jail (Stewart, 1980). Even the bail set for attractive defendants is apt to be lower than that set for unattractive defendants (Downs & Lyons, 1991).

On the other hand, attractiveness is not always an asset in the courtroom. For example, if the defendant's physical appearance seems to have been used advantageously during a crime, jurors may give harsher sentences to more attractive than to less attractive defendants.

In an experiment that demonstrated the importance of physical attractiveness, social psychologists Harold Sigall and Nancy Ostrove (1975) conducted a study in which they told subjects acting as mock jurors that a female defendant had been involved in one of two kinds of crimes: a burglary in which $2,200 was stolen, or a swindle in which a bachelor was persuaded to invest the same amount in a nonexistent corporation. One group of subjects was told the defendant was attractive; the other group of subjects was told the defendant was unattractive.

When the crime was burglary, the mock jurors handed out a more lenient sentence to the attractive burglar than to the unattractive one. But when the crime was a swindle, they gave the attractive defendant a slightly harsher sentence than they gave the unattractive one. The reason: The attractive swindler was seen as using her beauty in the service of her criminal activity.

**RACE AND GENDER.** Physical appearance is not the only defendant characteristic that affects the judicial process. Another powerful factor is race. As you might expect, members of racial minorities often receive more severe treatment at the hands of the courts than members of the racial majority. If they are accused of committing a crime, African-Americans are more likely to be convicted than whites. Furthermore, African-Americans receive longer prison terms than whites after convictions for similar crimes (Stewart, 1980; U.S. Department of Justice, 1990; Moses, 1992).

Moreover, the punishment to defendants is related to the race of the victim. An African-American who kills a white is significantly more likely to receive the death penalty than an African-American who kills another African-American.

Gender, too, plays a role in defendants' success at clearing their names in the judicial process. Male and female defendants are not treated identically in the judicial arena. For example, in one experimental simulation, mock jurors heard a case in which the defendant stabbed a victim with a kitchen knife. In one condition, the defendant was described as a woman and the victim as a man, and in the other condition, the defendant was said to be a man and the victim a woman.

Although, except for the gender switch, the descriptions of the incident were identical, jurors were significantly more likely to judge the defendant guilty when identified as a woman rather than a man (see Figure 13-1). Apparently, the woman was more likely to be seen as guilty because her behavior was incongruent with the traditional female gender role. In the eyes of this simulated jury, then, a woman who was accused of acting like a man was probably guilty (Cruse & Leigh, 1987).

In fact, actual crime statistics indicated that serious crime is an activity largely carried out by men. Close to 90 percent of all people arrested for murder, rape, robbery, and assault are male (Department of Justice, 1990). Such statistics are not terribly surprising, given their congruence with the traditional male gender role, which encompasses such characteristics as aggressiveness, lack of emotionality, and toughness.

---

*The Judge*   Wise. Uncompromising. Fair.

If these descriptions match your beliefs about the nature of trial judges, your beliefs may well be in error, for the reality is in many ways inconsistent with this view. Although judges clearly hold the most power in any courtroom drama, like other experts they are susceptible to the same kinds of biases to which people in general are vulnerable (Slovic, Fischhoff, & Lichenstein, 1977).

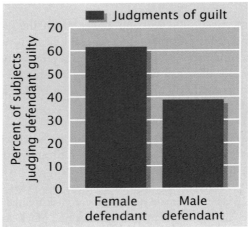

**FIGURE 13-1  Influences on the Processing of Trial Testimony** A female defendant who stabbed a male victim with a kitchen knife was more likely to be judged guilty than a male defendant who stabbed a female victim, apparently reflecting mock jurors' perception that stabbing is incompatible with the traditional female gender role. *(Source:* Based on data reported in Cruse & Leigh, 1987.*)*

One reason for the discrepancy between the "ideal" judge and the reality is that judges' backgrounds are not all that different from that of the average person. Although their educational level and socioeconomic status are often higher than the norm, this difference does not guarantee that they possess special qualities to distinguish their decision-making abilities from those of the layperson. In fact, judges are sometimes elected or appointed for purely political reasons. Consequently, merit may take a back seat to politics or commitment to a particular ideology (such as being pro-choice or pro-life on the abortion issue).

Furthermore, even the best-qualified judge, being human, may fall into attribution and judgmental traps. As a consequence, even the most honest and upright judges may be prone to error—errors which ultimately may introduce bias and a lack of fairness into the courtroom.

Consider, for instance, how judges set bail. Judges have wide latitude in the amount of bail they can require a defendant to pay in order to be free prior to trial, and they are supposed to take into account all relevant information. For instance, a judge typically is supposed to consider such factors as the prosecutor's recommendation, the defense attorney's recommendation, the extent of a defendant's community ties, and the nature of the defendant's prior criminal record.

However, an analysis of actual bail decisions demonstrates that only the prosecutor's and defense attorney's recommendations had a direct, significant effect on judges' decisions (Ebbesen & Konecni, 1982). Community ties and prior criminal record had either an indirect effect or no effect on the decision-making process.

The verbal and nonverbal demeanor of judges also varies significantly. For instance, judges' nonverbal behavior differs in such dimensions as the amount of warmth and confidence they exude in the courtroom, and such behavior affects their judicial performance (Blanck & Rosenthal, 1992; Blanck, 1991). One burglary conviction was overturned when evidence was presented that the trial judge, "hearing the defendant's brother testify that the defendant was at home watching television when the alleged burglary occurred, placed his hands to the sides of his head, shook his head negatively, and leaned back, swiveling in his chair 180 degrees" away from the jury (*State v. Barron*, 1971). In addition, appeals courts regularly consider the "emphatic or overbearing" nature of a judge's verbal and nonverbal behavior (Blanck, Rosenthal, & Cordell, 1985).

Judges also vary widely in terms of the sentences they assign to defendants who have been found guilty by a jury. Even when judges must follow mandatory sentencing guidelines, they still have wide discretion in sentencing. Consequently, a criminal found guilty in one judge's courtroom may receive a sentence that is literally a lifetime longer than someone found guilty in another judge's courtroom (Doob & Beaulieu, 1992; Provorse & Sarata, 1989).

Judges' sentencing behavior may be so extreme that they develop a reputation for either leniency or harshness. For example, one judge became known as "Turn 'Em Loose Bruce" because of his leniency. Another came to be called "Maximum Morphonios" because of her penchant for lengthy sentences, such as the one in which she ordered a defendant to spend 17 centuries in prison. At the sentencing, she caustically noted that the defendant would probably have to serve only half of that time (Wrightsman, 1991).

One reason for the discrepancy in sentencing among judges is the philosophical orientation they bring into the courtroom, relating to their understanding of the underlying causes of crime. One analysis of judges' behavior found that there were two basic types of judges. One type included judges who emphasized the social factors that led people to become involved in crime, such as poverty and difficult childhoods. Such judges emphasized the rehabilitative possibilities of prison. The other type included judges who focused on criminals' personal responsibility for their crime and viewed a prison term as punishment and retribution for the criminals' behavior (Carroll et al., 1987).

As you might expect, judges with these two different perspectives tended to deliver very different kinds of sentences. Judges who held society and circumstances to blame for criminal activity tended to give shorter sentences than those who perceived the criminal as more responsible for the crime.

---

*The Jury*    In most trials, it is the jury that makes the ultimate decision as to the guilt or innocence of a defendant. Is it possible to predict the kind of decision that a jury will make? Increasing evidence from a variety of sources suggests that the answer is a qualified yes, as social psychologists develop increasingly sophisticated and accurate models of the factors that affect jury decision-making processes.

**JURY COMPLIANCE WITH JUDGES' INSTRUCTIONS: FORGET IT.**    Suppose, during the course of a trial, a witness blurts out that she has heard that the defendant who is on trial had several prior convictions. The defendant's attorney immediately jumps up, enters an objection, and asks that the witness's statement be ruled inadmissible. The judge agrees and orders the jury to disregard the information.

If you were part of that jury, how successful would you be in following the judge's instructions? Most jurors find it nearly impossible—not because of outright disobedience, but because they simply cannot erase the memory from their deliberations (Wissler & Saks, 1985).

Social psychologist Daniel Wegner (1989) refers to this as the "white bear" phenomenon. According to Wegner, if someone tells a person to avoid thinking about a particular topic—such as a white bear—it becomes particularly prominent in the person's thoughts. In fact, the more we try to suppress a thought, the more likely it is that we will think about it (Wegner, 1989; Wegner et al., 1990; Wegner et al., 1991).

But there are other reasons why jurors might not comply with a judge's instructions. For example, in some cases, jurors may avoid following judges' instructions simply because they feel that noncompliance with such information results in a more equitable decision—even if it is technically illegal to do so. Jurors in the case described at the start of the chapter behaved in this manner, finding the defendant innocent even though it was clear that he had in fact killed his brother. It is jurors' sense of justice, then, that sometimes leads them to ignore judges' admonitions regarding the use of certain kinds of material (Wissler & Saks, 1985; Diamond, 1993; Borgida, 1982).

Does noncompliance with judges' instructions about the use of certain kinds of information actually affect sentencing? Experimental findings suggests that it does. For example, one experiment provided mock jurors with certain information about a defendant, which they were later informed should not be considered in their deliberations (Sue, Smith, & Caldwell, 1973). Despite these instructions, however, the inadmissible evidence did significantly affect the verdicts and sentence lengths arrived at by the jurors.

**reactance**
a disagreeable emotional and cognitive reaction that occurs to the restriction of one's freedom.

But there is still another reason why jurors do not comply with a judge's instructions: Jurors may resent the instructions because they perceive that their independence is being obstructed (Wolf & Montgomery, 1977; Seguin & Horowitz, 1984). Under these circumstances, feelings of reactance may be aroused among jurors. **Reactance** is a disagreeable emotional and cognitive reaction to the restriction of one's freedom, often resulting in hostility and anger (Brehm & Brehm, 1981). Reactance may lead to a boomerang effect, in which jurors place particular weight on the forbidden fruit of inadmissible evidence, resulting in a decision that runs directly counter to the instructions.

In a series of experiments, social psychologist Eugene Borgida (1982) presented mock jurors with a description of a rape case. Some jurors were explicitly instructed that admissions made by the rape victim regarding her prior sexual experiences should be disregarded because they had no bearing on whether she had, as the defendant claimed, consented to sexual intercourse with the defendant.

However, jurors who received the instructions to ignore the information about the victim's prior sexual history were more likely to find the accused rapist innocent than those who didn't receive the admonition. Apparently, the jurors interpreted the explicit instruction as a threat to their own decision-making freedom and reacted in a way that directly contradicted the judge's admonitions. Sometimes, explicit and precise instructions to a jury may backfire.

**JUROR COMPREHENSION: UNDERSTANDING THE LAW.**    Even when jurors attempt to comply with judges' instructions, they may unwittingly make errors. Although such mistakes can occur at several points in a trial, they most often happen just prior to jury deliberations, when judges typically interpret the laws that are relevant to the case. The manner in which the judge defines the legal issues has a substantial impact on jury behavior (Nagao & McClain, 1983; Smith, 1991a).

In some cases, jurors are simply unable to comprehend what the judge is talking about. In order to make their instructions precise, judges may use technical legal terms, or provide so much detail that their instructions become incomprehensible to a person unschooled in the nuances of the law.

Furthermore, even when jurors think they have understood a judge's instructions, they may misinterpret rules of law. For example, one study found that only about half the jurors in a criminal case grasped the fundamental fact that the burden of proof rests on the prosecution, not the defense—even after they had been explicitly informed (Strawn & Buchanan, 1976). Furthermore, jurors' prior knowledge of the law, gleaned in part from such sources as television shows and novels, influences their deliberations (Smith, 1991b).

Some social psychologists suggest that jurors try to make sense of the evidence they hear during a trial by creating one or more scenarios about what happened. For example, social psychologists Nancy Pennington and Reid Hastie noted that as the jurors listen to the testimony, they develop a story in which they formulate speculative scenarios that include explanations for why the people involved in a certain situation behaved as they did. Then, when judges provide instructions about the law prior to jury deliberation, jurors evaluate these stories they have constructed to see how well they fit the legal criteria of guilt or innocence (Pennington & Hastie, 1992).

Although jurors' understanding of the law is sometimes limited and biased, steps can be taken to help them make more informed decisions. For instance, when judges' instructions are free of legal jargon and expressed in everyday language, the comprehension of jurors is vastly increased (Luginbuhl, 1992).

Furthermore, when information is presented in concrete terms rather than in abstractions, jurors are better able to comply with instructions. For example, when discussing the concept of a defendant's guilt, judges might well discuss the issue in terms of numerical percentages ("You must have an 80 percent certainty of a defendant's guilt") rather than in terms of the traditional, but more vague, standard of "guilty beyond a reasonable doubt" (Elwork, Sales, & Alfini, 1982; Kagehiro, 1990).

**JURY MATH: WHO COUNTS?**    In legal theory, a juror is a juror is a juror. Each has an equal voice in determining the guilt or innocence of a defendant.

The reality is different (Pennington & Hastie, 1990). As in any other group situation, some members of a jury emerge as leaders, exerting a strong influence on the other members, while other jurors fade into the background. Some jurors enter the jury room partial to conviction; others feel that a defendant is probably innocent. What determines which juror's view prevails in such a situation?

One influential factor appears to be the size of the jury. The traditional jury size is twelve—a number inherited from the British legal tradition. The rationale for this figure was that twelve people somehow better represented a cross-section of the citizenry than a smaller number.

In recent years, however, the number of jurors required for a trial has begun to shrink. Beginning in 1970, six-person juries have been ruled legal in all cases except those involving the death penalty. In ruling on the legality of the six-person jury, the Supreme Court pointed to findings from Solomon Asch's work on conformity that we discussed in Chapter 12.

Unfortunately, the Supreme Court didn't do its homework very well (Saks, 1977). Misinterpreting Asch's (1956) work, the Court claimed that Asch's findings suggested that a 1:5 split in a six-person jury was identical to a 2:10 split in a twelve-person jury. To the Court, a single minority juror seemed to be under no more psychological pressure to conform to a five-person majority than two minority jurors would be to conform to a ten-person majority.

The justices erred, though. As you'll recall, Asch found that having a single social supporter allowed a minority group member to remain independent, while having no allies led to considerable conformity. For a minority juror in a 2:10 split, then, the pressures to conform are relatively weak, given that he or she has another person in the minority. In contrast, a minority juror in a 1:5 split is much more likely to experience intense pressures to conform.

Using the conformity research as a guide, then, large juries may be preferable to smaller ones, if the goal is the careful consideration of both minority and majority opinions. Other findings support such a conclusion.

For example, research comparing individual and group decision-making suggests that groups may reach better (although more time-consuming) decisions than individuals. Groups tend to remember information better than individuals. Larger juries are also more likely than smaller ones to represent minority segments of the population , providing the potential of more diversity in jurors' points of view (Vollrath et al., 1989; Forsyth, 1990; Wrightsman, 1991).

In sum, social psychological research points to the superiority of twelve-person juries over smaller ones. However, the evidence is not entirely consistent. Some research, for instance, suggests that the differences in the ultimate verdicts of six- compared with twelve-person juries are not substantial (Saks, 1977). On the issue of jury size, then, the final verdict has yet to be rendered.

## ► REVIEW & RETHINK

### Review

- Several characteristics of defendants, including attractiveness, gender, and race, affect judicial outcomes.
- Judges are also susceptible to biases.
- Among the factors affecting jury decisions are their difficulty in understanding instructions, their disregard of instructions, and the size of the jury.

### Rethink

- How does the beautiful-is-good stereotype affect courtroom proceedings? What other stereotypes influence the jury decision-making process?
- In some states, judges make sentencing decisions, while in others, separate jury trials are held for sentencing. What are the pros and cons of each system?
- Both prosecuting and defense attorneys generally try to avoid having college students put on juries. Yet, research on juries is conducted on many college campuses using students as subjects. Discuss the possible implication of this inconsistency.
- Imagine that you are a defense attorney and that your case is going badly. Based on your knowledge of juror comprehension, what kinds of closing arguments might you make in order to persuade the jury?

**JURY DEMOGRAPHICS.**    Clarence Darrow, the most famous attorney of his time, had this to say about the characteristics of jurors:

*I try to get a jury with little education but with much human emotion. The Irish are always the best jurymen for the defense. I don't want a Scotchman, for he has too little human feelings; I don't want a Scandinavian, for he has too strong a respect for law as law. In general, I don't want a religious person, for he believes in sin and punishment. The defense should avoid rich men who have a high regard for the law, as they make and use it. The smug and ultrarespectable think they are the guardians of the society, and they believe the law is for them. (Quoted in Sutherland & Cressey, 1974, p. 417)*

Apart from the specifics he mentions, was Darrow right in his implicit view that certain types of people are likely to be bring particular kinds of biases into the courtroom? Probably—although the real world is not quite as simple as he made it out to be.

Although some evidence suggests that people of certain nationalities are more prone to favor the prosecution than the defense (Broeder, 1959), such research must be assessed with considerable skepticism. The differences among various national groups identified in these studies are most probably due to other factors. For example, it is likely that socioeconomic differences among various ethnic groups explain their different jury-related behavior, not their membership in a particular ethnic group per se.

In sum, there is little serious evidence to support the views of lawyers such as Clarence Darrow that members of particular ethnic groups respond consistently in jury situations. Instead, it seems that we must consider the particular personal characteristics and traits of jurors, and we must consider them not in isolation but in terms of the specifics of a given trial.

One of the more accurate predictors of jurors' decisions is the degree of similarity between a juror and the defendant in a trial. It is quite clear that the greater the similarity (in terms of attitudes and demographic characteristics) between a juror and the defendant, the greater the leniency toward the defendant (Monahan & Loftus, 1982).

Similarly, particular personality characteristics help predict juror behavior. For example, highly dogmatic or closed-minded jurors, who are intolerant of ambiguity and tend to make extreme judgments of people as a way of resolving uncertainty, are more influenced by judges' instructions than nondogmatic jurors (Kerwin & Shaffer, 1991).

Similarly, juror authoritarianism (a complex mix of rigidity, social and political conservatism, conformity to social norms, and submissiveness to authority) is associated with juror behavior. People high in authoritarianism are more apt not only to convict defendants but also to recommend longer sentences for those they consider guilty (Bray & Noble, 1978; Shaffer, Plummer, & Hammock, 1986; Moran & Comfort, 1986). But not always: If the defendant is an authority figure or someone who was following the orders of an authority figure, jurors high in authoritarianism are more likely to let the defendant off the hook (Hamilton, 1976).

By and large, though, the search for a consistent relationship between personality characteristics and juror conduct has been a fruitless one (Matlon et al., 1986; Reskin & Visher, 1986). However, this has not stopped trial attorneys and prosecutors from searching for a means to choose a group of jurors that will be sympathetic to either the defense or the prosecution. This pursuit of congenial jurors is accomplished prior to the start of a trial during **voir dire** proceedings, in which prospective jurors can be questioned as to their impartiality and background in order to eliminate those who are biased toward or against a particular side.

Turning *voir dire* on its head, a whole industry has developed that seeks to help the legal profession identify jurors sympathetic to one side or the other. Typically, experts hired by the defense or prosecution administer a series of questionnaires to a sample of registered voters in the area in which a trial is being held. By asking pertinent questions about the trial, the defendants, and the prosecution, it may be possible to identify general attitudinal patterns and demographic factors that relate to a predisposition to favor acquittal or conviction in a particular case (Schwartz, 1993; Patterson, 1986).

Subsequently, when a jury is being chosen for the actual trial, attorneys can identify potential jurors who hold attitudes and demographic characteristics similar to those who seem, from the survey results, most prone to acquit or convict the defendant. Using this procedure, defense attorneys can challenge conviction-prone jurors and remove them before they take their places on the jury—resulting in a jury that is presumably inclined to vote for acquittal. In the same way, the prosecution may be able to identify and attempt to remove jurors who are prone to be sympathetic to the defense.

Does it work? Although many lawyers think so, social scientists remain skeptical. There are no special questions that accurately identify either conviction- or acquittal-prone jurors in all instances. Furthermore, when systematic, so-called more "scientific" jury selections are compared with conventional jury selection procedures, neither technique is invariably better at producing a desired result than the other. For the moment, at least, identification of the "perfect" juror remains an unfinished task (Horowitz, 1980; Penrod & Cutler, 1987). (To consider the role that eyewitness memory plays in trials, see the accompanying Social Psychology at Work feature.)

**voir dire**
proceedings at the start of a trial in which prospective jurors can be questioned as to their impartiality and background in order to eliminate those who are biased toward or against a particular side.

# SOCIAL PSYCHOLOGY AT WORK

## RECOLLECTIONS IN THE COURTROOM

*In the end, no one was satisfied with the outcome—not the parents, who suspected that their children had been sexually molested; not the defendants, whose lives were shattered by the accusations; and not the children themselves, who had to testify in court about hazy memories of events that had (or had not) occurred years before.*

*The source of all this dissatisfaction was a 33-week, $15 million trial, the longest and most expensive in U.S. history. After nine weeks of deliberation, the jury acquitted the defendants of 52 counts of child sexual abuse, and announced it was deadlocked on 13 other counts.*

*During the trial, Ray Buckey and his mother, Peggy McMartin Buckey, stood accused of molesting dozens of preschool-age children who attended the exclusive day care center they operated. At the trial, some of the young witnesses—now ten and eleven years old—recited in detail how the Buckeys had abused them while they attended the school, providing vivid details of events that had occurred years earlier.*

*At the same time, though, some of the children's recollections seemed suspect, including bizarre tales of jumping out of airplanes and digging up bodies at a cemetery. In the end, the jurors simply could not accept the validity of the testimony of the children, and the Buckeys were freed.*

The Buckey case illustrates the suggestibility of trial witnesses and the fragility of their memories. Children, in particular, are susceptible to errors. For one thing, their lower level of cognitive sophistication makes them more prone to error. Furthermore, when they are exposed to information subsequent to an event, young children's memories are especially vulnerable to the influence of others. This vulnerability may be particularly strong when an event is highly emotional or stressful (Kassin, Ellsworth, & Smith, 1989; Doris, 1991).

In the Buckey case, there was a huge amount of pretrial publicity, and the children who had supposedly been molested were interviewed repeatedly. During the trial, then, instead of providing an accurate recollection of events, the children may have responded with information to which they had been exposed during the interviewing process (Schindenhette, 1990; Loftus & Ketcham, 1991; Loftus, 1991).

Difficulties in assessing the validity of witnesses's memories are not limited to children (Doris, 1991). Adults, too, are prone to a considerable degree of error. Consider, for

Based on the recollections of young witnesses, Peggy and Raymond Buckey were accused of molesting dozens of preschool children. However, their 33-week trial ended with their release.

**FIGURE 13-2.    The Fallacies of Memory.** In a classic study, subjects were shown a drawing of a subway scene, similar to this one, in which one of the characters was an empty-handed African-American conversing with a white man who was holding a razor. Subjects were asked to describe the picture to another person who had not seen the picture, who in turn recounted it to another person, and so forth. The typical story told by the last person in the chain included, as a major element, an African-American holding a razor.    *(Source:* Allport & Postman, 1945.*)*

instance, an experiment conducted during a New York City television news program (Buckhout, 1975). Viewers saw a twelve-second film of a mugging, and then viewed a six-person lineup that included the actual assailant. Members of the audience were invited to call in to identify the actual assailant. Out of more than 2,000 viewers who phoned, about 15 percent were correct—a figure no different from what would be expected if the viewers had guessed randomly.

Why do eyewitnesses have such problems? One explanation is related to social expectations and stereotypes. The kinds of expectations about the way in which the world operates influences how a person perceives and remembers information. If people hold the stereotype that African-Americans are more prone to criminal activity than whites, they are going to perceive and remember events within this context (Wells, 1993; Loftus, 1993).

For example, in a set of classic studies, subjects were shown a drawing of a subway scene, similar to the one shown in Figure 13-2 (Allport & Postman, 1945). Among the characters in the picture was an empty-handed African-American conversing with a white man who was holding a razor. Subjects were asked to describe the picture to another person who had not seen the picture, who in turn recounted it to another person, and so forth. The typical story told by the last person in the chain included, as a major element, an African-American holding a razor. Clearly, the communication of the description had altered it to match social expectations and stereotypes.

A second major reason that eyewitnesses are prone to error concerns their motivational and emotional state during

a crime. Eyewitnesses may be motivated to remember events in particular ways. For example, the victim of a stabbing may believe that he did not provoke his assailant prior to being stabbed, and as a result he may well forget the angry words that were exchanged before the stabbing.

Similarly, highly aroused, emotional eyewitnesses may be inaccurate in their recollections. Someone witnessing a mugging is apt to be apprehensive, anxious, and concerned about his or her own safety. However, such emotional arousal may not always introduce errors in recall: Sometimes heightened arousal may cause various details to be stored in memory with greater clarity (Christianson, 1992).

The way questions are framed and worded to eyewitnesses also has a significant impact on their responses. For instance, memory specialist Elizabeth Loftus showed subjects a short film of two cars crashing into each other. Some of the subjects were asked, "About how fast were the cars going when they *smashed* into each other?," while others were asked, "About how fast were the cars going when they *contacted* each other?" When the question talked about "smashing" cars, the average estimate was 40.8 miles an hour; but when the question was framed in terms of cars "contacting" each other, the average estimate was only 30.8 miles per hour (Loftus & Palmer, 1974). In addition, when the words "collided," "bumped," and "hit" were used in the question, subjects estimated speeds in between the two extremes of smashed and contacted (see Figure 13-3).

When is eyewitness testimony most suspect? Among the situations most likely to reflect errors or distortions in

*Continued on next page*

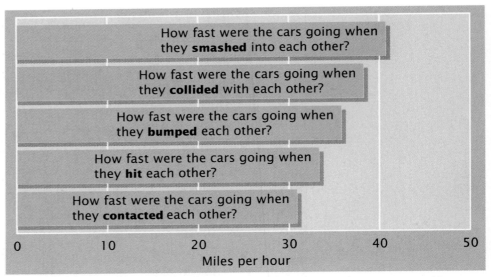

**FIGURE 13-3   Stacking the Deck** After viewing an accident involving two cars, subjects were asked to estimate the speed of the collision. Estimates varied substantially depending on the way the question was worded.    *(Source:* Loftus & Palmer, 1974.*)*

memory are the following (Wall, 1965; Platz & Hosch, 1988; Wrightsman, 1991; Kassin, Ellsworth, & Smith, 1989):

- If witnesses first say they are unable to identify anyone.
- If the defendant was known to the witness before the crime but wasn't originally identified when first questioned.
- If a major discrepancy exists between the witness's first description of the perpetrator of the crime and the actual appearance of a defendant.

- If a witness first identifies someone else and then retracts the identification.
- If the witness and the person identified belong to different racial groups.
- If a long period has elapsed between the crime and the identification of a perpetrator.

Although not every eyewitness recollection is distorted or in error, juries need to remember these human fallibilities when considering the fate of a suspect.

*The Social Psychology of Criminal Behavior*

Most of us, at one time or another, have broken the law. In most cases our offenses have been relatively minor—jaywalking, parking illegally, or underage drinking. Some people shade the truth when they fill out their tax returns, while others engage in outright fraud, hiding income they have received or taking deductions they have not earned. Still others have committed major crimes, such as theft, embezzlement, or murder.

Although compliance with the law represents a major social issue, the field of social psychology has been relatively silent on the subject. Most of the research that has been conducted has concentrated on circumstances that occur after a crime has been committed. However, some social psychologists have taken an innovative tack by concentrating on the prevention of crime. Working with the police, they have developed programs, based largely on social psychological principles, to reduce the occurrence of criminal activities (Winkel, 1991; Fowler, 1981).

**CRIME PREVENTION.**   One example of the joint efforts of social psychologists and the criminal justice system has taken place in a field study conducted in the Asylum Hill section of Hartford, Connecticut, a poor area with a high crime rate. As part of the study, three key changes were introduced in Asylum Hill (Fowler, 1981). First, a police team was assigned permanently to the area. This change permitted the police to develop close social ties with area residents and enabled them to become more familiar with the specific crime problem in the area.

A neighborhood watch sign like this one does more than just notify potential criminals that the neighbors are vigilant. It also increases the shared sense of responsibility among neighbors for reducing crime.

A second major change concerned auto and pedestrian traffic patterns. In order to emphasize the residential nature of the area and provide the residents a greater sense of control over their neighborhood, some streets were closed to vehicular traffic altogether, while others were made one-way.

Finally, neighborhood organizations were formed. These groups had the goal of providing citizen input into the crime reduction plans. Through these organizations, the residents' sense of control was further enhanced, making those who lived in the area feel more responsible for what happened.

The program was a success. Burglary rates in Asylum Hill fell significantly, compared with other parts of the city. Other street crimes also dropped, although to a lesser degree. The psychological consequences were beneficial as well: Residents' fears declined regarding the likelihood that they would be victims of burglary and that burglary was a significant neighborhood problem.

The results of the Asylum Hill program are congruent with other research that shows that making people feel responsible for crime prevention can help reduce criminal activity (Austin, 1979; Klentz & Beaman, 1981). For instance, making people feel that they are personally responsible for helping stop crime increases their sense of involvement in the situation. It also increases the likelihood that they will actively intercede in situations in which intervention is desirable.

Similarly, "Neighborhood Watch" programs, in which residents of an area collectively pledge to keep an eye out for possible criminal activity, also help increase the responsibility felt by individuals living in a given neighborhood. Putting up signs of the sort pictured here fulfills two specific goals. First, it provides a warning to potential criminals that the neighborhood is particularly vigilant. But second, it also reminds residents of their personal responsibility in fighting neighborhood crime.

**EXCUSES: JUSTIFYING CRIMINAL ACTIVITY.** "I didn't do it" is often the first excuse offered by people—adults and children—who have been detected carrying out illicit activities. But it's not the last. Once it becomes clear that a person has in fact committed an offense, a variety of excuses is offered. Typically, one of five justifications is used to explain behavior that violates society's standards of conduct. Gresham Sykes and David Matza (1957) describe these justifications collectively as **techniques of neutralization**:

**techniques of neutralization**
justifications used to explain behavior that violates society's standards of conduct.

- *Denying responsibility.* Although people may admit to an act, they may refuse to accept responsibility for the act. They typically deflect blame from themselves to the ills of society—living in a bad neighborhood, poverty, or poor schooling—as well as to being enticed into an illegal act by others. Basically, people using this technique refuse to acknowledge that they are personally responsible. By shifting the responsibility to some external agent, perpetrators feel they deserve no punishment (Tomita, 1990).

- *Denying harm and injury.* Rather than accepting the reports of authorities that they did real destruction, a perpetrator may try to translate an action into something more benign. Take, for example, a college student who helps knock down the goal posts following a football game. To the university, the student is guilty of damaging expensive university property. To the student, the behavior represents minor mischief, hardly worthy of note (Tomita, 1990).

- *Blaming the victim.* One frequent excuse by perpetrators of criminal acts is that the victim deserved whatever befell him or her. The perpetrator was just giving the victim his or her due, given the circumstances. According to such an explanation, it was a victim's behavior that brought on the perpetrator's actions.

  For example, during the Los Angeles riots that occurred in the wake of the Rodney King verdict (described first in Chapter 1), many stores owned by Korean immigrants became particular targets for mob aggression. By way of justification, rioters later suggested that Korean shopkeepers were guilty of "cheating" patrons and that the presence of their stores had prevented other minorities from opening their own establishments. Hence, the Korean grocers deserved the damage their stores incurred—a classic blame-the-victim explanation.

Following rioting in Los Angeles, some participants attempted to justify their behavior by blaming the victim. They contended that shopkeepers had been cheating customers and therefore deserved to have their stores destroyed.

**victimization**
a justification used by perpetrators of violent actions to claim that the act was the fault of the victim.

**dehumanization**
a justification for illicit activity in which the victim is portrayed as lacking human characteristics and consequently not being worthy of equitable and considerate treatment.

Similarly, perpetrators in rape cases sometimes justify their act by saying that the rape was the fault of the victim—a phenomenon known as **victimization**. For instance, a victim may be said to have dressed in such a provocative manner that she was "asking for it." (Unfortunately, other members of society—including jurors, the public, and even judges—are also susceptible to blame-the-victim biases. For instance, in some cases of rape, judges have agreed with defense contentions that because a woman behaved in a way labeled alluring and seductive, the defendant should receive a relatively light sentence (Drogin, 1992).)

In extreme cases, blaming the victim translates into **dehumanization**—a phenomenon in which the victim is perceived as lacking human characteristics and consequently not being worthy of equitable and considerate treatment. Dehumanization was a frequent justification for Nazi war criminals who participated in the Holocaust, in which Jews and members of other religious, racial, and ethnic groups were targeted for systematic extermination. The excuse was that because members of these groups were somehow less than human, they did not deserve humane treatment; they could be treated no better than an overpopulation of stray dogs.

- *Denouncing authorities.* Another neutralization strategy used by people who have committed criminal acts is to condemn social institutions or authority figures. Saying that the political system is corrupt permits a low-salaried government worker to feel justified in embezzling government money. Similarly, if you feel that the police and judicial system are unfair, it may be easier for you to commit criminal acts because you may feel that no matter what you do, you can't do anything worse than what they do. In essence, the argument is that two wrongs make a right (Mitchell & Dodder, 1983).

  Condemnation of authorities is a manifestation of the norm of reciprocity, which we first spoke about in Chapter 8. As you may recall, the norm of reciprocity suggests that we should treat others as they have treated us. Criminals may justify their acts because others have treated them in ways that they deemed illegal.

- *Invoking higher principles or authority.* Some people who act illegally justify their actions because they consider the goal they seek to achieve more important than the laws they are breaking. Excuses of this type are often given by people who hold illegal demonstrations, for example. Likewise, members of the Mafia may refuse to testify against a fellow Mafioso, even at great personal cost. Their refusal is based on the concept of *omerta,* or code of silence, that they pledge to honor when they become members. The maintenance of *omerta* is seen as representing a higher-order authority than the more conventional control of the legal system (Mitchell & Dodder, 1983).

**THE BENEFITS OF NEUTRALIZATION.**    These five techniques of neutralization—denying responsibility, denying harm or injury, blaming the victim, denouncing the authorities, and the invocation of higher principles or authorities—provide a measure of both psychological and legal relief to perpetrators of crimes. By shifting responsibility away from themselves, perpetrators can maintain a relatively positive self-image and even cast themselves in the role of the victim. In extreme cases, criminal perpetrators can end up feeling that they are worse off than their alleged victims.

Of course, such attributions make later rehabilitation of criminals a difficult task. If people feel no responsibility for their actions, it is unlikely that they will be receptive to attempts to get them to change their antisocial behavior.

It is interesting that the legal system is something of a coconspirator in the maintenance of harmful, maladaptive attributions of responsibility. For instance, criminal perpetrators may be found innocent if they can prove in court that they were the targets of entrapment. **Entrapment** occurs when a person is lured by a law enforcement agent into committing a crime. However, the legal system may be unwittingly setting the stage for future criminal activity by legitimizing the notion that people may not actually hold responsibility for their antisocial activities.

**entrapment**
a justification for illicit activity in which a person is lured into committing a crime by a law enforcement agent.

---

# THE INFORMED CONSUMER OF SOCIAL PSYCHOLOGY

# MAKING CRIMINAL TRIALS FAIRER

We've seen the biases that tend to color the fair and equitable administration of justice. Based on this work, social psychologists have made several suggestions to improve the quality of justice. Among them are the following suggestions by social psychologist Lawrence Wrightsman (Wrightsman, 1987):

- Increase the representativeness of people on juries, by ensuring that all citizens have an equal chance to be on a jury and by keeping to an absolute minimum the number of exemptions from jury duty.

- Decrease the opportunity for defense attorneys and prosecutors to remove particular potential jurors prior to a trial. By preventing "scientific" selection of juries by either side in a

criminal case, potential bias in the outcome would be reduced.

- Videotape trial presentations and edit out unwanted material. Such a procedure would address the difficulty of jurors' forgetting inadmissible testimony, even when instructed to do so.

- Instruct jurors in simple, clear, and direct language, avoiding legal jargon. For example, employing specific probabilities or percentages about guilt and innocence may make it easier for jurors to understand the concepts of "reasonable doubt" (Elwork, Sales, & Alfini, 1982; Kagehiro, 1990).

- Allow jurors access to a videotape of the trial while they deliberate.

---

## ▶ REVIEW & RETHINK

### *Review*

- Although the evidence that juror demographic factors are related to conviction rates is weak, efforts have been made to systematically choose conviction- or acquittal-prone juries.
- Eyewitness recollections are often faulty.
- Several strategies exist for reducing crime.
- Criminals employ several types of justifications for their conduct.

*Continued on next page*

*Rethink*

- Children who testified to being molested by Peggy and Ray Buckey must have believed their own stories. What relationship might you use to increase the accuracy of their recollections?
- Identification of members of different racial groups are more likely to be erroneous than identification of members of one's own racial group. What person perception phenomenon may underlie this bias?
- What techniques can the police use to instill in community members a sense of personal responsibility for crime prevention?
- Discuss the five neutralization techniques in the context of how (a) convicted rapists and (b) income tax evaders might maintain their moral innocence.

# POLITICS, LEADERSHIP, AND POWER

Julius Caesar, Elizabeth I, Catherine the Great, Mahatma Gandhi, President Clinton. Five very different people, with distinct skills and personalities. Yet all fall into the same category: leader. Each inspired and influenced millions of individuals, leading others to accept them as legitimate authority figures, rulers, and advocates for their own interests. Each of these leaders inspired others to place their trust in them.

What factors led to these people being perceived as leaders, capable of influencing and regulating the behavior of others? Are some people "born" leaders? Is there something about a historical situation or set of circumstances that propels a person toward leadership, relatively independently of the characteristics of that person? Or does the truth lie somewhere in between? These questions, raised by philosophers, historians, and political scientists, have also been addressed by social psychologists (Bass, 1990; Chemers & Ayman, 1993). We will examine some of the answers they have found.

*Great Person Approaches to Leadership: Leaders Are Born, Not Made*

"The history of the world is the history of great men." When the well-known historian Thomas Carlyle wrote these words, he was endorsing an approach to leadership that has come to be called the great person theory. (He was also promoting a somewhat restrictive view of history, given that, at least in recent times, it is not just great men but great women who have risen to significant positions of leadership.)

**great person theory of leadership** the notion that certain people are born to lead others.

According to the **great person theory of leadership**, certain people are born to lead (Bass, 1990). The theory proposes that some aspects of a person's personality or character—in other words, traits of greatness—lead that individual to rise naturally to a position of leadership.

The great person theory attracted several generations of theoreticians, for on the surface it seems quite reasonable. It certainly is plausible that great leaders such as Martin Luther King, Jr. and George Washington embodied specific characteristics that set them apart from most other folk. Similarly, even leaders of local organizations, such as college clubs and town mayors, appear to have traits that thrust them into leadership roles.

However, despite the common-sense appeal of the theory, the evidence in support of the great person approach has been minimal at best (Hollander, 1985). While some traits do appear to be associated with leadership, the results are neither very surprising nor very informative.

For instance, there is some evidence that the typical leader is slightly more intelligent than average. Furthermore, leaders tend to be more extroverted and dominant, are slightly better adjusted, are more self-confident, have a higher need for power, and are taller and heavier than nonleaders (Stogdill, 1974; Hollander, 1985; Winter, 1987). (Consider this bit of trivia: Since 1900, in every election except for two, the taller of the two major presidential candidates won. Perhaps Bill Clinton's one-half-inch height advantage over George Bush was the secret of his success in the 1992 presidential election.)

Unfortunately, such findings shed little light on leadership. For one thing, they focus on the differences between leaders and followers and ignore the ultimate success of the leader. Because people who become leaders are not always successful (consider the domestic failings of the Nixon presidency, for example), great person theories need to take into account the distinction between effective and ineffective leaders.

Furthermore, finding that leaders hold particular traits raises a chicken-and-egg question of whether the trait existed prior to the acquisition of leadership or developed as a result of the individual's being thrust into a leadership position. Consider this question: Does the trait of self-confidence lead someone to emerge as a leader, or does self-confidence arise because a person assumes the role of leader? Those who have been elected president of the United States, for instance, find themselves in a world apart from everyday life, with a large, supportive, agreeable, and sometimes subservient staff. Who wouldn't feel more self-confident after experiencing these advantages?

Despite the difficulties with the great person theory, recent evidence suggests that some especially inspiring leaders do have characteristics that differentiate them from nonleaders. In particular, Bernard Bass (1985, 1990) suggests that distinguished, outstanding individuals such as Golda Meir, John Kennedy, and Nelson Mandela are transformational leaders. **Transformational leaders** are leaders who spur their followers into behavior that surpasses their own personal interests. Followers of these leaders are driven less by the promise of individual gain than by the vision of a greater good for a greater number of people. By inspiring others with their vision for a better future and with their ability to get people to look beyond their own immediate best interests, transformational leaders are able to motivate others. Transformational leaders have charisma, a personal magnetism that produces trust and respect. In addition, they are inspiring and intellectually stimulating. Finally, they have the ability to consider others as individuals, making them feel as if the leader has a personal stake in their welfare (Bass & Avolio, 1990).

Some experts in political psychology have suggested taking another route in the search for the critical characteristics of leadership. Presidential scholar James David Barber (1985, 1992) suggests that the most fruitful approach to understanding leadership, at least on the level of the U.S. presidency, is to examine two primary dimensions: vigor and emotion. Classifying presidential vigor on a passive–active dimension and presidential emotion on a positive–negative dimension has permitted Barber to decipher and often predict presidential success.

More specifically, Barber argues that the vigor dimension relates to the degree to which a president, on the one hand, takes a dynamic, energetic role in promoting particular policies (an active president); or, on the other hand, is more reactive to others' proposals (a passive president). The emotion dimension relates to a president's prevalent emotional state. For instance, some presidents are relatively positive, enjoying the political arena, while others are more negative, behaving out of duty and not appearing to enjoy the political fray all that much.

Because the two dimensions are independent of one another, it is possible to classify U.S. presidents into one of the four combinations shown in Figure 13-4. Based on their life histories and experiences, most presidents fall rather neatly into one of the four categories.

For instance, Presidents Nixon and Johnson exemplify the active–negative category. Hard-driving and energetic, at the same time they were focused on their own personal obsessions and negativity. The active–negative category is thought to produce the

**transformational leaders**
leaders who spur their followers into behavior that surpasses their own personal interests.

| FIGURE 13-4 | **Presidential Personality** | |
| --- | --- | --- |
| | **POSITIVE** | **NEGATIVE** |
| *Active* | Franklin D. Roosevelt | Woodrow Wilson |
| | Harry S. Truman | Lyndon Johnson |
| | John F. Kennedy | Richard M. Nixon |
| | George Bush | |
| | Bill Clinton | |
| *Passive* | Warren Harding | Calvin Coolidge |
| | Ronald Reagan | Dwight D. Eisenhower |

*Source:* Barber, 1985; 1992a; 1992b.

most perilous presidencies. The individuals in this category tend to be perfectionists, introspective and rigid. When they are threatened, their predominant reaction is to lash out at enemies, and they find compromise difficult.

Passive–positive presidents, on the other hand, enjoy the affection that the presidency brings to them. However, they are fixed more on themselves than on others, leading them to a passivity in their political behavior. Such presidents, exemplified by Harding and Reagan, are rather easily manipulated by others.

Presidents such as Coolidge and Eisenhower, who typify the passive–negative category, see themselves as disinterested in politics. They feel compelled to enter politics because of their noble, high-minded principles, but they don't enjoy it much. Viewing themselves as above the fray of political life, they don't do much in the way of new policy initiatives.

Finally, we come to the active–positive category. Exemplified by Presidents Truman and Kennedy, the presidents in this category find politics great fun. They enjoy the give-and-take of political action, and they are able to make things happen. Their presidencies are often looked upon as particularly effective. But not always: The dynamism and positive outlook of active–positive presidents may lead them to take unusual risks.

Despite the identification of the transformational leadership pattern and the utility of classifying U.S. presidents along certain dimensions, the great person theory remains largely in disrepute. The central hypothesis of the great person theory—that certain characteristics or personality traits boost a person into a position of leadership—has not been supported. Without considering the specifics of a particular situation, it has proven difficult to identify any single trait or set of traits that differentiates leaders from followers. Similarly, no evidence suggests that certain traits differentiate effective leaders from ineffective ones. We need, then, to turn to characteristics of a particular situation in order to understand the emergence of leadership.

## Situational Approaches to Leadership: Under the Right Circumstances, Anyone Can Be President

One of the enduring cultural beliefs in the United States is that anyone, regardless of background, can grow up to become president of the country. It is a belief supported by the rise to power of such presidents as Jimmy Carter, Ronald Reagan, and Bill Clinton, all of whose origins were, in fact, truly humble.

The rise to power of such individuals suggests that almost anyone can rise to leadership, independent of his or her own personal characteristics, if the situation is one that calls for leadership. For example, Harry Truman unexpectedly was thrust into the U.S. presidency when Franklin Roosevelt died. Truman became a decisive and, some say, a great president. Similarly, Dwight Eisenhower was elected president largely because of his World War II record—not because of inherent leadership skills.

**situational approach to leadership** the notion that people become leaders due to the characteristics of the situation in which they find themselves.

According to the **situational approach to leadership**, people become leaders due to the characteristics of the situation in which they find themselves. In this view, leaders, in general, don't necessarily share any particular personality traits. For instance, the mayor of Peoria, Illinois, the head of the National Rifle Association, and the president of the League of Women Voters would not be assumed to have similar personality traits and characteristics. Instead, it is the situation that requires certain skills in a leader.

The situational approach, then, suggests that a particular person can be a leader in one setting and not in another, because it is the characteristics of the situation and not the person that leads to leadership attainment. In its most extreme form, the situation hypothesis suggests that anyone can become a leader, provided he or she finds the appropriate situation in which to lead.

Despite the romantic appeal of the view that any of us—no matter what our abilities and personality—can rise to a leadership position if the situation were of a certain sort, the research conducted to examine the situational approach has not been supportive. Although studies on leadership in groups have found that certain situations are more likely to produce particular leadership requirements, researchers have been unable to demonstrate that a situation, by itself, determines who becomes leader (Hollander, 1985; Graeff, 1983).

Were leaders such as Martin Luther King, Jr., Golda Meir, and John F. Kennedy born to lead? Or did circumstances thrust them into a leadership role? Or was it a combination of their personal qualities and the situation that led to their effective leadership?

On the other hand, there is a kernel of truth to the situational approach to leadership: Particular kinds of circumstances do seem to thrust individuals into leadership positions. For example, a group structure that presents the opportunity to communicate with others increases the likelihood that the person who is an effective communicator will become the group's leader (Guetzkow, 1968). Specifically, the greater the ability of a person to communicate with others in a group or organization, the more likely that person is to become the leader of the group. Still, reliance on the situational approach to leadership has its drawbacks. Most glaringly, there is little research to support the theory that people ignore personality traits and abilities in determining who becomes and remains a leader.

More fundamentally, the basic premise of the situational approach can be questioned. It seems unlikely, for instance, that anyone can become president of the United States, no matter how favorable the situation is for his or her rise to power. Furthermore, it ignores the possibility that leaders may modify their behavior to fit a particular situation, and that they may alter the situation to fit their behavior. Because of such objections to the situational model, social psychologists have turned to theories of leadership that take both the situation and the leader's characteristics into account: interactional approaches to leadership.

## Interactional Approaches to Leadership: Person + Situation = Leadership

**interactional approach to leadership**
the notion that different situations call for different kinds of leaders.

**contingency model of leadership**
the notion that leader effectiveness is based on three contingencies: the nature of leader–member relations, the task structure, and the leader's power.

According to the interactional approach to leadership, Bill Clinton's victory in the 1992 U.S. presidential race was no accident. Instead, his particular personality traits meshed more closely with the country's desire for change than did those of the other candidates. His election, then, was the result of a unique combination of situational requirements and Clinton's personality.

According to **interactional approaches to leadership**, different situations call for different kinds of leaders. This view holds that in certain types of situations one kind of leader will be likely to emerge and be more effective, while in other circumstances another leader will emerge and be more effective (Hornstein, 1987; Halal, 1974; Fiedler, 1987).

One specific model of leadership, based on the interactional approach, is social psychologist Fred Fiedler's contingency model (Fiedler, 1978; Fiedler & Garcia, 1987). According to the **contingency model of leadership**, leader effectiveness is based on the nature of leader–member relations, the task structure, and the leader's power. The model, which has spawned hundreds of studies, is generally quite effective in identifying the particular type of leader that is appropriate for certain situations.

The model first considers the situational aspects of leadership. According to the Fiedler model, three crucial characteristics of a situation need to be taken into account. First among these is the nature of the relationship between the leader and group members, which can range from positive to negative. The second situational characteristic is the degree of structure in the task the group is attempting to accomplish; tasks can be clear and unambiguous (high structured), or they can be vague and ambiguous (low structured). The third characteristic in Fiedler's model is the power the leader holds over the other group members, which consists of the amount of rewards (and punishments) that the leader is able to control.

By considering jointly these three factors, we can assess the overall favorability of a situation. In the most favorable case, the relations between leader and followers are positive, the task is highly structured, and the power of the leader is strong. In contrast, situations most unfavorable to a leader are those in which relations between leader and followers are poor, the task is unstructured, and the leader's power is weak.

Recall, of course, that because the contingency model takes an interactional approach, we must also consider the personality of the leader. But what is the key characteristic that must be taken into account? According to Fiedler, the most crucial variable is the motivational style of the leader—whether the leader is motivated primarily toward accomplishing the group's task or toward maintaining positive group relationships. Hence, leaders tend to be either task-oriented (in which the completion of the task is of greatest importance) or relationship-oriented (in which the personal relations of the members are weighted more heavily).

In order to measure the leader's motivational style, Fiedler relies on the leader's assessment of the least preferred coworker, or LPC. The **least preferred coworker (LPC)** is the person in a group whom the leader identifies as the one individual with whom it is most difficult to work. Low-LPC leaders, who perceive the LPC relatively harshly, tend to be primarily task-oriented leaders. In contrast, leaders who see even the LPC in a relatively positive light, called high-LPC leaders, are primarily relationship-oriented leaders. (Figure 13-5 illustrates a questionnaire used to determine a group's LPC.)

We are now ready to tackle the central issue of the contingency model—which is determining when particular types of leaders are most effective. According to the contingency model, whether a low- or high-LPC leader is most effective depends on the situation. As you can see in Figure 13-6, the model predicts that situations that are either

**least preferred coworker (LPC)**
the person in a group whom the leader identifies as the one individual with whom it is most difficult to work.

---

### FIGURE 13-5    Example of an LPC Scale

Instructions:

People differ in the ways they think about those with whom they work. On the scale below are pairs of words which are opposite in meaning. You are asked to describe someone with whom you have worked by placing an "X" in one of the eight spaces on the line between the two words. Each space represents how well the adjective fits the person you are describing, as in the following example:

Very neat : _____ : _____ : _____ : _____ : _____ : _____ : _____ : _____ : Not neat

| 8 | 7 | 6 | 5 | 4 | 3 | 2 | 1 |
|---|---|---|---|---|---|---|---|
| Very neat | Quite neat | Some-what neat | Slight-ly neat | Slight-ly untidy | Some-what untidy | Quite untidy | Very untidy |

Now, think of the person with whom you can work least well. The person may be someone you work with now or someone you knew in the past. The person does not have to be the person you like least well, but should be the person with whom you had the most difficulty in getting a job done. Describe this person as he or she appears to you.

| Pleasant | : _____ : _____ : _____ : _____ | _____ : _____ : _____ : _____ : | Unpleasant |
|---|---|---|---|
| Friendly | : _____ : _____ : _____ : _____ | _____ : _____ : _____ : _____ : | Unfriendly |
| Rejecting | : _____ : _____ : _____ : _____ | _____ : _____ : _____ : _____ : | Accepting |
| Helpful | : _____ : _____ : _____ : _____ | _____ : _____ : _____ : _____ : | Frustrating |
| Unenthusiastic | : _____ : _____ : _____ : _____ | _____ : _____ : _____ : _____ : | Enthusiastic |
| Tense | : _____ : _____ : _____ : _____ | _____ : _____ : _____ : _____ : | Relaxed |
| Distant | : _____ : _____ : _____ : _____ | _____ : _____ : _____ : _____ : | Close |
| Cold | : _____ : _____ : _____ : _____ | _____ : _____ : _____ : _____ : | Warm |
| Cooperative | : _____ : _____ : _____ : _____ | _____ : _____ : _____ : _____ : | Uncooperative |
| Supportive | : _____ : _____ : _____ : _____ | _____ : _____ : _____ : _____ : | Hostile |
| Boring | : _____ : _____ : _____ : _____ | _____ : _____ : _____ : _____ : | Interesting |
| Quarrelsome | : _____ : _____ : _____ : _____ | _____ : _____ : _____ : _____ : | Harmonious |
| Self-assured | : _____ : _____ : _____ : _____ | _____ : _____ : _____ : _____ : | Hesitant |
| Efficient | : _____ : _____ : _____ : _____ | _____ : _____ : _____ : _____ : | Inefficient |
| Gloomy | : _____ : _____ : _____ : _____ | _____ : _____ : _____ : _____ : | Cheerful |
| Open | : _____ : _____ : _____ : _____ | _____ : _____ : _____ : _____ : | Guarded |

Source: *Adapted from F. E. Fiedler,* A Theory of Leadership Effectiveness. *New York: McGraw-Hill. 1967.*

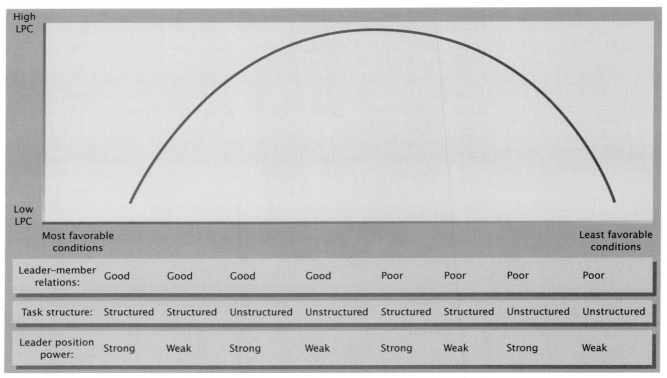

| Leader–member relations: | Good | Good | Good | Good | Poor | Poor | Poor | Poor |
| --- | --- | --- | --- | --- | --- | --- | --- | --- |
| Task structure: | Structured | Structured | Unstructured | Unstructured | Structured | Structured | Unstructured | Unstructured |
| Leader position power: | Strong | Weak | Strong | Weak | Strong | Weak | Strong | Weak |

**FIGURE 13-6   Predictions Relating Situational Favorability and Leader LPC Level** Depending on leader–member relations, task structure, and the leader position power, Fiedler's contingency model predicts that situations that are either relatively favorable or unfavorable for the leader are best handled by a low-LPC leader, who is primarily task-oriented. On the other hand, situations of moderate leader favorability lead to optimum performance on the part of high-LPC leaders, who are more oriented toward maintaining positive relationships with the other members of the group.    *(Source:* Based on Fiedler, 1978.*)*

relatively favorable or relatively unfavorable for the leader are best handled by a low-LPC leader, who is primarily task-oriented. On the other hand, situations of moderate leader favorability lead to optimum performance on the part of high-LPC leaders, who are more oriented toward maintaining positive relationships with the other members of the group.

The underlying logic of the model is straightforward. Under conditions of low leader favorability, leader–member relations tend to be poor, the task is unstructured, and the leader's power is weak. In this case, an assertive, directive, task-oriented leader would clearly be most effective in the group. On the other hand, in very favorable situations, in which leader–member relations are good, the task is unambiguous, and the leader's power is strong, the group is already task-oriented and ready to be led. Consequently, a task-oriented low-LPC leader will be most effective.

However, under conditions of moderate leader favorability, a high-LPC leader will excel. In this instance, the relationship-oriented high-LPC leader, sensitive to the interpersonal needs of the group members, is most likely to succeed.

The contingency model of leadership makes clear, specific predictions. How well have they been supported through research? In some ways, very well. Studies conducted in laboratory experiments show quite consistently that the contingency model predicts leader effectiveness (Fiedler & Garcia, 1987; Peters, Hartke, & Pohlmann, 1985).

Outside the laboratory, however, the picture is more mixed. Some field studies have shown that leadership follows the patterns suggested by the theory. In fact, studies in which leaders are taught techniques for modifying situations to optimize the match with their LPC level have had impressive results. In one field experiment, for instance, West Point platoon leaders were tutored in the basics of the contingency model and were taught how to alter situations so that an optimal match could exist between their leadership style and the group. The training obviously paid off: The platoon leaders who received instruction in the contingency model were more apt to be ranked first or second in their company than those who had not received training (Csoka & Bons, 1978).

On the other hand, some field studies have produced results contrary to predictions of the contingency model, suggesting that the theory needs further refinement in order to provide a more complete account of leader effectiveness (see Peters, Hartke, & Pohlmann, 1985; Schneier, 1978). Still, the contingency model of leader effectiveness remains the best articulated, most comprehensive, and best supported of any interactional model of leadership.

| *Gender and Cultural Patterns in Leadership* | Are males and females similar in the way they lead? Are leadership patterns the same in other cultures? To answer these questions, we turn now to a consideration of gender and cultural factors in leadership. |

**GENDER AND LEADERSHIP.**    Until the twentieth century, the history of world leaders is almost exclusively the history of male leaders. Despite some notable exceptions, such as Golda Meir of Israel, Margaret Thatcher of Great Britain, and Indira Gandhi of India, political leaders have typically been men.

The relative lack of women in leadership roles has led some to presume that certain crucial differences may exist between men and women in terms of their leadership styles or capabilities—differences that may prevent women from rising to leadership positions. Others suggest, however, that the relative rarity of female leaders is due primarily to social stereotypes that prevent women from rising to positions of leadership, and that the actual leadership behavior displayed by men and women differs insignificantly. They point to the large increase in the number of women elected to the U.S. Congress in the past few years, and to the fact that the number of women in corporate leadership positions continues to rise.

To consider this question, social psychologists Alice Eagly and Blair Johnson carefully reviewed the results of more than 150 separate studies of leadership (Eagly & Johnson, 1990). They found that women and men were generally similar in terms of the

Political leaders like California Senator Diane Feinstein remain the exception, rather than the rule.

concern they displayed regarding task accomplishment and the maintenance of personal relationships.

On the other hand, there was a difference in leadership style relating to a democratic, participative style compared with an autocratic, directive style in work and organizational settings: Female leaders favored a more democratic style, while males displayed a more autocratic style. One possible explanation—admittedly speculative—may be that women, who tend to display higher interpersonal skills than men, find it easier than men to work within a democratic framework, which requires a good deal of give and take. Men, in contrast, may feel more comfortable in leading in a more directive manner, in which it is less necessary to deal with the politics of participative decision making.

It is important to note that no evidence suggests that the differences in styles displayed by male and female leaders result in greater or lesser leadership success; both styles seem to be equally effective. However, women who adopt a leadership style more congruent with typical male leadership behavior do run a significant risk in terms of how they are perceived. For instance, female leaders who use the autocratic leadership style typical of males are likely to be underrated and even belittled. Men, in particular, seem to find a woman in an authority position to be threatening. For example, when a woman is encountered who has authority over men of the same age and social class as herself, the typical reaction is to downgrade the view of her subordinates ("What kind of man would work for a woman?"), rather than elevating the woman's status ("Isn't it great that she is in a position in which she has authority over others?") (Denmark, 1980; Brinkerhoff & Booth, 1984; Jacobson et al., 1977; Wiley & Eskilson, 1982).

Similarly, women who hold leadership positions that are viewed as stereotypically masculine—such as business manager—get devalued. When a woman takes on what society traditionally views as the rightful position of a man, then the view of the woman's femininity may suffer (Eagly, Makhijani, & Klonsky, 1992).

The nonverbal behavior of men and women also relates to perceptions of differential status and accomplishment. For instance, there is a surprising degree of similarity between women's nonverbal behavior and that of low-status men. Women show tense posture, do a relatively high amount of smiling, and avert their eyes and watch others. Surprisingly, these are quite similar to the behaviors exhibited by low-status men (see Figure 13-7). Research examining other types of nonverbal behavior, including eye contact and other signs of visual dominance, supports the notion that women's nonverbal behavior is remarkably similar to that of men in low-status, as compared to high-status, positions (Dovidio et al., 1988; Lott, 1987).

In sum, the issue of gender differences in leadership is subtle and complex. Although there are differences between male and female leaders in terms of democratic versus authoritative styles, little or no sex differences exist in terms of emphasis on task accomplishment versus maintenance of interpersonal relationships. At the same time,

**FIGURE 13-7    Powerful Gestures: Examples of Nonverbal Behaviors Related to Power**

| NONVERBAL BEHAVIOR | BETWEEN STATUS NONEQUALS | | BETWEEN MEN AND WOMEN | |
| --- | --- | --- | --- | --- |
| | USED BY SUPERIOR | USED BY SUBORDINATE | USED BY MEN | USED BY WOMEN |
| Demeanor | Informal | Circumspect | Informal | Circumspect |
| Posture | Relaxed | Tense | Relaxed | Tense |
| Personal space | Closeness (option) | Distance | Closeness | Distance |
| Touching | Touch (option) | Don't touch | Touch | Don't touch |
| Eye contact | Stare, Ignore | Avert eyes, Watch | Stare, Ignore | Avert eyes, Watch |
| Facial expression | Don't smile | Smile | Don't smile | Smile |
| Emotional expression | Hide | Show | Hide | Show |
| Self-disclosure | Don't disclose | Disclose | Don't disclose | Disclose |

Source: *Adapted from N. Henley (1977). Body politics: power, sex, and nonverbal communication. Englewood Cliffs, NJ: Prentice Hall.*

women who rise to high-status positions are sometimes devalued by others; the impression that others draw of women in leadership roles may be negative, particularly if they behave in the same way that men in high-status positions behave.

Given the obstacles that society puts in place for women in high-status, leadership positions, it is not surprising that the numbers of women leaders is proportionately small. If societal stereotypes hold that males are more appropriate leaders than females, an invisible barrier, sometimes called the "glass ceiling," may continue to prevent the rise of women to high leadership positions.

CULTURE AND LEADERSHIP.    When we consider leadership in different cultures, we find that several of the factors that appear to be important in theories of leadership in the Western cultures are not universal. For example, Fiedler's contingency model is not fully supported by the results of experiments conducted in several cultures. Specifically, research shows that the most able leaders in bank organizations in the Philippines score low on the LPC scale, while those in Hong Kong score high (Bennett, 1977). Although the most obvious explanation is that the situational contingencies operate differently in the two cultures (Tannenbaum, 1980), such an explanation is not particularly helpful in allowing us to identify just what the particular contingencies are.

One promising approach to understanding differences in leadership styles comes from work comparing cultures that are primarily collectivistic compared with those that are more individualistic. As we will discuss more fully in Chapter 15, collectivistic cultures place greater emphasis on the group's well-being than on that of the individual. In contrast, individualistic societies emphasize personal identity, uniqueness, and individual freedom. In individualistic societies, the emphasis is on accomplishment of one's own goals (Hui, 1988).

Research on leadership in collectivistic and individualistic societies suggests that the meanings that followers attribute to the tasks that leaders carry out are relatively different. For instance, psychologist Peter Smith and colleagues compared perceptions of leaders in two collectivistic cultures (Hong Kong and Japan) and in two individualistic societies (the United States and Great Britain). The researchers found that leaders in the collectivistic cultures were perceived as carrying out a broader range of behaviors and appeared to be less specialized in the tasks they carried out. In contrast, leaders in the individualistic cultures were more apt to be perceived as specializing in activities primarily oriented either to completing the task or to maintaining good social relations within the group (Smith et al., 1990).

Other research shows that leaders in organizational settings have different preferences regarding the behavior of subordinates. For instance, organizational leaders in highly developed Western countries, such as the United States and Great Britain, prefer subordinates to be relatively more active and involved (Barrett & Bass, 1970; Tannenbaum, 1980). In comparison, managers in less-well-developed countries such as Greece and India favor more passive subordinates.

---

*Choosing a Leader: The Politics of Voter Choice*

Backers of Dwight D. Eisenhower were right on target when they came up with the slogan "I like Ike" and printed the phrase on millions of buttons and bumper stickers.

Although they may not have known it at the time, the most important dimension in choosing a leader is often the candidate's likability. In fact, even party affiliation is less critical than how much a voter likes and feels comfortable with a candidate. In most instances, people vote for the person with whom they feel most comfortable (Markus, 1982; Kinder & Sears, 1985).

For political figures, the quality of likability is actually grounded in two kinds of information: the traits candidates are seen to hold, and the emotions that those candidates demonstrate. In terms of traits, competence and integrity are the most important components of liking. For instance, the fact that Dwight D. Eisenhower had played a pivotal role in winning World War II was seen by many as an illustration of his competence, making him a popular candidate.

The emotions that politicians project also have an impact on voter preferences (Kinder, Abelson, & Fiske, 1979). Candidates attempt to produce positive emotions and simultaneously avoid behavior that might kindle negative emotions. For instance, one of Ronald Reagan's strengths as president was his ability to communicate a "good news" message to voters, as illustrated by an effective advertising campaign during his successful quest for reelection that stressed that it was "morning in America." In contrast, when Jimmy Carter talked about a "malaise" affecting the country, his popularity plummeted.

The importance of voter emotions is illustrated by research examining the degree of optimism displayed by candidates. Because an optimistic speech presumably produces positive emotions, we might expect that politicians who behave optimistically might be the most successful at acquiring voter support. In fact, this scenario appears to be true. An analysis of the degree of optimism expressed in presidential candidates' speeches given during their nominating conventions shows a clear distinction between winners and losers: Between 1948 and 1984, the more optimistic candidate went on to win in every election except for one (Zullow & Seligman, 1990):

## The Nature of Power

- A Senate staff member laughs uproariously at his boss's joke, even though it isn't funny.
- A driver of a powerful Porsche stays within the speed limit to avoid getting a ticket.
- A teenager buys Calvin Klein underwear after seeing an ad in which rap star Marky Mark wears it.
- An incumbent politician loses a bitter election, then dutifully agrees to cooperate with the winner's transition team.
- Despite your reservations, you follow the advice of your physician and go on a salt-free diet and begin a vigorous exercise regime in order to lower your blood pressure.
- The president's chief of staff is invited to lunch by a reporter and is pumped for information.

**social power**
the power a person holds based on the ability to control and shape another's behavior.

The common thread in all of these situations? Each represents an example of social power. **Social power** consists of one person's ability to control and shape the behavior of others. Although the political realm represents the most obvious manifestation of power, the concept is useful in understanding behavior in a number of situations. In fact, social psychologists have identified six forms of power, corresponding to each of the above examples (French & Raven, 1959; Raven, 1988, 1992, 1993):

**reward power**
the power a person holds based on the ability to provide rewards.

**REWARD POWER.** One form of power that enables people to influence others is **reward power**—the ability to provide rewards when others comply with their wishes. Employers can give raises, parents can hand out candy bars, teachers can give grades to those who conform to their standards and directions. Of course, such power is highly situation-specific: Although a Senate staffer may laugh uproariously at a senator's joke, the senator's constituents may not feel compelled to respond so heartily to the same jokes—they have the (reward) power to reelect the senator or not (Claes & Rosenthal, 1990; Jurma & Wright, 1990).

**coercive power**
the power a person holds based on the ability to deliver punishments.

**COERCIVE POWER.** **Coercive power** refers to a person's ability to deliver punishments. In some ways the opposite side of the coin from reward power, coercive power can be an effective technique—as those of us know who carefully monitor our driving speed in order to avoid a ticket. However, there are drawbacks, as with any method of social control that uses punishment (Sulzer-Azaroff & Mayer, 1991). People seem to realize the down side of coercive power, and most of us prefer to use reward power instead of coercive power if such a choice is possible (Molm, 1988).

**REFERENT POWER.**    Although rap singer Marky Mark may not be everyone's hero, he's at the top of the list for some people. For those who find him attractive and wish to be like him, he is high in **referent power**—the power a person holds based on the ability to act as a model for the behavior of others.

referent power
the power a person holds based on the ability to act as a model for the behavior of others.

Referent power is held by those we respect, find attractive, and wish to emulate. Such people act as models whom we want to be like. In order to be like them, we mimic the powerful person's behavior, appearance, dress, language, or mannerisms. The source of referent power, then, lies in powerful people ability to mobilize others to act in a way that is similar to the way they act themselves. A parent who tries to get a younger child to follow the example of her older sibling, or leaders who act courageously in order to get their followers to make their own sacrifices, are using referent power (Gold & Raven, 1992).

legitimate power
the power a person holds because of the formal position or role that person occupies.

**LEGITIMATE POWER.**    One kind of power, called **legitimate power**, arises from the formal position or role a person occupies. Legitimate power is often couched in terms of "should's" and "ought's." For example, parents tell their children to obey not on the basis of logical arguments but because children are "supposed" to listen to their parents.

One of the unique characteristics of legitimate power is that its holders do not have to rely on rational arguments in order to convince others of their right to power. Instead, the power flows inherently from the individual's position or role. For example, when a professor announces a long, involved, and difficult assignment, the class dutifully complies, with little or no argument. Moreover, the specific individual holding legitimate power is less crucial than in the other kinds of power. Presidents of the United States come and go, but the legitimate power of the presidency remains high and relatively independent of who is in office at a given time (Yukl & Falbe, 1991).

expert power
the power a person holds because of his or her superior knowledge and abilities.

**EXPERT POWER.**    The dictum "knowledge is power" refers to the influence that experts hold over our lives. **Expert power** derives from a power holder's superior knowledge and abilities. For instance, physicians have the ability to effect radical changes in our lifestyle with their advice. In fact, even when physicians make recommendations that raise misgivings, we are likely to defer to their greater knowledge.

Expert power is specific to a person's special area of expertise. Consequently, no matter how willing we are to comply with our physician's medical advice, we would be considerably less willing to comply with that same person's advice concerning the repair of an automobile (Harrow & Loewenthal, 1992).

informational power
the power a person holds because of the specific content of his or her knowledge.

**INFORMATIONAL POWER.**    The most transitory type of power is informational power. **Informational power** is power related to the specific content of a person's knowledge. People who hold valuable information are sought out and complied with because of their superior knowledge.

Ironically, once the information they hold is communicated, people with informational power lose their clout. For example, a clerk at a college treasurer's office who can tell a student how to get her student loan check issued loses all power as soon as the information is communicated (Eyuboglu & Atac, 1991).

## The Hazards of Power

Power has a bad name. In a society that cherishes the concepts of equality and individuality, the notion that some people wield power over others is suspect.

Yet it is also a fact that many of our societal institutions would operate badly or not at all if there were not at least some execution and distribution of power. Politicians could not govern without the power given to them by constitutions and legal systems. Similarly, teachers could not teach without the power to make assignments or to discipline unruly children. Large organizations would break down if clear lines of authority did not exist.

On the other hand, power, if abused, can corrupt the power holder. According to social psychologist David Kipnis (Kipnis et al., 1976), power may produce four increasingly excessive results. First, the desire for power becomes a need in and of itself, apart from the larger goals that power is intended to fulfill, such as accomplishing the task. Second, the ease in using power encourages power holders to use power to benefit themselves, at the expense of those under their power. Next, power holders receive unwarranted positive feedback—even adulation—from others, thereby producing an inflated sense of self-worth.

Finally, power may lead to the devaluation of others. For instance, in one simulation experiment, managers with substantial power tended to view their subordinates as working only for money (which could be controlled by the managers). In contrast, managers who had less power attributed their subordinates' efforts as due to high internal motivation (Kipnis, 1974; Kipnis et al., 1976). In sum, once people gain meaningful power, they tend to see the worst in others.

**mandate phenomenon**
a situation in which a person with strong support exceeds the group norms and seeks even more power.

Having an inflated view of one's power may also lead power holders to overstep the bounds of appropriateness. For instance, when Franklin D. Roosevelt was elected president by a huge majority, he took several actions that the courts later ruled were unconstitutional. Such behavior exemplifies the **mandate phenomenon**, in which a person with strong support exceeds the group norms and seeks even more power (Clark & Sechrest, 1976; Forsyth, 1990).

**need for power**
a personality characteristic in which an individual has a tendency to seek impact, control, or influence over others, and a need to be seen as a powerful person.

Ultimately, power holders may become absorbed in seeking power, motivated by needs for power. In fact, many people who hold power have a strong **need for power**, a personality characteristic in which an individual has a tendency to seek impact, control, or influence over others, and a need to be seen as a powerful person (Winter, 1973, 1987).

Despite this pessimistic view of the corrupting influence of power, the U.S. political system provides voters with the ultimate opportunity to correct the situation of abuse of power—by voting an incumbent out of office. Power may corrupt, but corrupt power will not necessarily endure.

# ► REVIEW & RETHINK

## Review

- The great person, situational, and interactional approaches seek to explain leadership emergence and effectiveness.
- Likability is a critical factor in voter choice.
- Social power consists of one person's ability to control and shape the behavior of others.
- Holding power has several drawbacks.

## Rethink

- In the question of what separates a person who becomes a leader from a person who does not, which type of explanation has been most successful—personality, situational, or some mix?
- In the question of which leaders will be successful, which type of explanation has been most successful—personality, situational, or some mix?
- Consider Barber's theory of presidential personality in the context of Fiedler's contingency model of leadership. Who would have been a more effective leader during World War II—Lyndon Johnson or Warren Harding? Who would have been a better leader in today's uncertain times?

- No evidence suggests that women are less capable than men of being effective leaders, and social psychologists generally maintain that stereotypes about their ability are (at least partly) to blame. Based on your knowledge of stereotype formation, suggest how this particular stereotype might have developed.
- In the taxonomy of power, how does expert power differ from informational power? How does legitimate power differ from coercive power?

## LOOKING BACK

◄ ◄ ◄ ◄ ◄ ◄ ◄ ◄ ◄ ◄ ◄ ◄ ◄ ◄ ◄ ◄ ◄ ◄ ◄ ◄ ◄ ◄ ◄ ◄ ◄ ◄ ◄ ◄ ◄ ◄

### What are the social psychological factors that affect defendants and judges in criminal trials?

1. Legal decisions are at least in part social ones, based on factors of a social psychological nature. For example, the physical attractiveness of a defendant typically has a positive influence over judgments of defendant innocence. On the other hand, if the defendant's physical attractiveness seems to have been used profitably during a crime, jurors may give harsher sentences to more attractive than to less attractive defendants. Other defendant characteristics, such as gender and race, also play a role in jurors' perceptions of guilt and innocence.

2. Despite judges' greater knowledge and experience with the law, they are susceptible to biases. Furthermore, they exhibit dramatic differences in the setting of bail and in sentencing. Such differences may be based on prior attitudes and judicial philosophy.

### How do juries reach decisions?

3. Jury decisions can be better understood by considering social psychological factors. For example, jurors have difficulty ignoring evidence that they have heard but have been instructed to disregard. In addition, jurors' sense of justice or reactance to instructions may lead them to ignore a judge's instructions. Finally, a jury may simply misunderstand a judge's instructions.

4. Although it is legal for juries to be smaller than the traditional twelve, smaller juries produce different psychological dynamics than larger ones. For example, a 2:10 jury split has different psychological consequences for jurors holding minority positions than a 1:5 split.

5. Although some demographic differences in jury members' willingness to convict have been reported, by and large the results are not compelling. However, some personality factors do seem important, such as dogmatism and authoritarianism. Nonetheless, social psychologists remain skeptical over attempts to systematically choose conviction- or acquittal-prone juries.

6. Eyewitness memories are unreliable, for several reasons. For one thing, social expectations and stereotypes affect the way that people perceive and remember information. In addition, their motivational and emotional state during a crime affects their recall. Finally, the way in which a question is framed and asked affects witnesses recollections.

### How do social psychological factors affect criminal activity?

7. In order to reduce crime, law enforcement authorities have attempted to develop closer social ties with residents of crime-ridden areas, give residents a greater sense of control over their environment, and form neighborhood organizations.

8. The major justifications for criminal behavior, called techniques of neutralization, are denying responsibility, denying the harm or injury, blaming the victim, denouncing authorities, and invoking higher principles or authorities.

### What steps can be taken to make trials fairer?

9. Possible approaches to making the trial process fairer include increasing the representativeness of people on juries; decreasing the opportunity to remove potential jurors from a jury;

videotaping trial presentations and editing out inadmissible material; using simpler language when instructing jurors; and allowing jurors access to videotapes of the trial while they are deliberating.

### What are the major explanations for leadership?

10. The great person theory of leadership proposes that some aspects of a person's personality or character—traits of greatness, in other words—lead that individual to rise naturally to positions of leadership. Although most evidence does not support the theory, some characteristics—such as transformational leadership—are related to leadership.

11. According to the situational approach to leadership, people become leaders because of the characteristics of the situation in which they find themselves. As with the great person theory, there is little consistent supportive evidence that situations bring about leadership.

12. According to interactional approaches to leadership, different situations call for particular kinds of leaders. This view holds that under certain types of situations, one kind of leader will be likely to emerge and be most effective, while under other circumstances another kind of leader might emerge and be more effective. For instance, Fiedler's contingency model suggests that leader effectiveness is a joint consequence of two factors: (1) the overall degree of favorability of the situation to a leader, and (2) the leader's motivational style, which refers to whether the leader is focused primarily on accomplishing the group's task or on maintaining positive group relationships.

13. Both gender and culture affect leadership. For example, although women and men were generally similar in terms of the concern they displayed regarding task accomplishment and the maintenance of personal relationships, female leaders favored a more democratic style, while males displayed a more autocratic style. In addition, there are cultural differences in leadership, such as the difference in perceptions of leaders in collectivistic and individualistic societies.

14. One of the primary factors in determining people's choice of leader is an individual's likability. Likability is based on two types of information: personal traits, and the emotions displayed by the leader.

### On what basis is power acquired, and what are the consequences of wielding power?

15. An individual's ability to lead often rests on his or her social power, which is a person's ability to control and shape another's behavior. The six major bases on which social power rests are reward power, coercive power, referent power, legitimate power, expert power, and informational power.

16. Power may have several negative consequences, such as becoming a need in and of itself, the use of power to benefit the power holder, an inflated sense of self-worth, and the devaluation of others. It can also lead to the mandate phenomenon, in which a person with strong support exceeds the group norms and seeks even more power.

# KEY TERMS AND CONCEPTS

*reactance (p. 416)*

*voir dire (p. 419)*

*techniques of neutralization (p. 423)*

*victimization (p. 424)*

*dehumanization (p. 424)*

*entrapment (p. 425)*

*great person theory of leadership (p. 426)*

*transformational leaders (p. 427)*

*situational approach to leadership (p. 428)*

*interactional approach to leadership (p. 430)*

*contingency model of leadership (p. 430)*

*least preferred coworker (LPC) (p. 431)*

*social power (p. 436)*

*reward power (p. 436)*

*coercive power (p. 436)*

*referent power (p. 437)*

*legitimate power (p. 437)*

*expert power (p. 437)*

*informational power (p. 437)*

*mandate phenomenon (p. 438)*

*need for power (p. 438)*

# FOR FURTHER RESEARCH AND STUDY

Wrightsman, L. S. (1991). *Psychology and the legal system* (2nd ed.). Belmont, CA: Brooks/Cole.

A thorough, wide-ranging summary of the psychological factors involved in the functioning of the judicial system.

Hans, V., & Vidmar, N. (1986). *Judging the jury.* New York: Plenum.

A careful review of the psychological processes related to juries.

Loftus, E., & Ketcham, K. (1991). *Witness for the defense: The accused, the eyewitness, and the expert who puts memory on trial.* New York: St. Martin's.

Elizabeth Loftus, an expert on eyewitness memory, describes her research and experiences in testifying in court.

# EPILOGUE

In the past two chapters, we've considered the conditions under which people are susceptible to the influence of others. Beginning with theoretical approaches to conformity, compliance, and obedience, we saw how people react to implicit and explicit social pressure.

In this chapter, we've discussed social influence in terms of two applied areas: the legal system and politics. We've seen how the rule of the law, codified over centuries, is still susceptible to some very real biases. In essence, even the most fundamental of society's institutions—law and politics—are influenced by social psychological factors.

### PART VIII

# HOW DOES OUR MEMBERSHIP IN SOCIETY AND CULTURE AFFECT OUR SOCIAL LIVES?

In this final part of the book, we consider how our membership in groups, organizations, and society influences our lives. This pair of chapters links the everyday groups to which we belong to the larger institutions of society, moving from our understanding of how people in groups behave to the larger focus of the ways in which organizations, culture, and society relate to our behavior.

In Chapter 14, we discuss groups, defining them and considering their impact on people's behavior. In Chapter 15, we move to a discussion of how groups operate in organizations and the ways in which our culture and society influence our everyday behavior. ■

# GROUPS

## JOINING WITH OTHERS

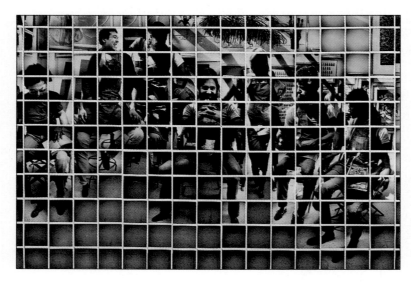

On the Florida coast, the weather, usually balmy, was unseasonably cold, and predictions for the next day were for even colder temperatures. The chilly weather made NASA officials nervous; they had never held a launch in such cold weather. Yet the takeoff of the space shuttle *Challenger* had already been postponed several times, and NASA officials were eager to get the astronauts into space. The presence in the crew of teacher Christa McAuliffe was designed to focus the public's attention on the mission, and as a result the launch was under unusual scrutiny by the press and public.

NASA officials faced a difficult decision: Did the subfreezing temperatures pose a significant risk to the launch? Sufficient to postpone it? To make the decision, NASA convened several groups of experts to review the pros and cons. Some cautionary information was already in hand. Several months before, an engineer involved in the manufacture of the shuttle rocket warned that extreme environmental conditions could make a group of rubber seals so brittle that they could deteriorate. The result, he cautioned, could be a catastrophic failure of the shuttle.

The tragic launch of the space shuttle Challenger.

However, NASA officials largely ignored the warning, along with additional reservations that arose from a group of engineers the night before the launch. Consulted about the low temperatures predicted for the next day, these engineers strongly urged a delay in the launch. They told their supervisors that their firm opinion was that the shuttle could fail in such cold temperatures.

However, NASA officials, who were anxious to get the shuttle off the ground, gave little consideration to the engineers' views. In fact, they ordered the engineers to rethink their recommendation. Ultimately, the person who made the final decision never even learned of the engineers' concerns; subordinate members of the launch team "protected" him from the conflicting information.

As we know today, the engineers' warnings were sadly prophetic. The rocket seals did fail on launch. The shuttle rocket exploded, and all seven astronauts on board died. Despite the input of many individuals, the wrong decision was made.

# LOOKING AHEAD

▷ ▷ ▷ ▷ ▷ ▷ ▷ ▷ ▷ ▷ ▷ ▷ ▷ ▷ ▷ ▷ ▷ ▷ ▷ ▷ ▷ ▷ ▷ ▷ ▷ ▷ ▷ ▷ ▷

With 20/20 hindsight, it is clear that the people involved in the *Challenger* disaster made the wrong decision. But why? Couldn't groups of knowledgeable people avoid such a calamity by rationally making a decision that properly takes into account all relevant factors? Don't group decisions, made by individuals with differing information, expertise, skills and personalities, represent an improvement over those made by solitary individuals?

As we'll see in this chapter, the answers to such questions are not simple (Esser & Lindoerfer, 1989; Moore-Ede, 1993). For almost a century, social psychologists have addressed questions about groups, and one of the first formal social psychological experiments examined the issue of whether individual or group performance is superior. In this chapter we will explore the social psychological perspective on groups.

We begin the chapter by considering how, in a formal sense, a group differs from a mere aggregation of individuals. After examining the criteria that identify a group, we consider the underlying structure of a group. We examine how people in groups play particular roles and are associated with a status that determines how they are evaluated by others. We also consider the standards, or norms, that groups provide, and how groups differ in terms of attractiveness to their members.

In addition, we discuss the benefits and costs of participation in groups. We consider the circumstances under which the presence of others can boost or diminish performance, and we identify some techniques for optimizing group performance.

We then turn to the ways in which groups solve problems and make decisions, examining the stages that groups follow in approaching challenges and the different frameworks that groups may adopt. Finally, we consider the factors that affect the quality of group problem solving and decision making. We discuss how in certain kinds of groups members may be subject to defective thinking, and how to improve decision making in such situations.

In sum, after reading this chapter, you'll be able to answer these questions:

- How can we formally define a group?
- What are the formal characteristics of groups?
- How does the presence of others affect performance, for better or worse?
- What are the processes by which groups strive to solve problems and reach decisions?
- What factors affect the quality of problem solving and decision making?

# WHAT MAKES A GROUP A GROUP?

*You stand at a bus stop, waiting with several others for the next bus to come.*

*You sing "Happy Birthday" with the other guests at your grandmother's 75th birthday party.*

*Along with a troop of teammates, you go door to door, collecting money to support your intramural hockey team.*

*You participate unenthusiastically in weekend military exercises with your ROTC unit, which you joined only to get scholarship benefits.*

If you keep track of your activities for a few weeks, you'll probably find that you spend relatively little time alone. Instead, you'd most likely determine that a good part of your waking hours are spent in the presence of others, participating with other people in group situations.

It doesn't seem all that hard to know what a group is, but that hasn't proven to be the case. Partly because the study of groups has played a central role in the development of social psychology, there are almost as many definitions of "group" as there have been social psychologists.

Consider some of the questions that are raised when we contemplate how to define a group: Does a group exist only when there is interaction between members? Must people consider themselves to be part of a group in order to be part of one? Do group members need to communicate with one another? Do they need to share attitudes or goals? All of these questions, as well as many others, have been addressed and highlighted by particular historical definitions of the concept (Forsyth, 1990).

## Defining Characteristics of Groups

**group**
two or more people who interact with one another, perceive themselves as a group, and are interdependent.

According to many social psychologists, the most useful view of groups is in terms of several basic criteria that all groups seem to share. In this view, a **group** consists of two or more people who (1) interact with one another; (2) perceive themselves as a group; and (3) are interdependent. Let's consider each of the criteria in turn.

**INTERACTION.**    At the most basic level, groups must permit some form of interaction among the members. It need not be physical, face-to-face interaction, however. For instance, written interaction, as can occur in an e-mail network, may suffice.

**PERCEPTION OF GROUP MEMBERSHIP.**    To be part of a group, people must view themselves as group members. For example, an assemblage of people milling about at an airport gate waiting to board a plane would generally not be conceived of as a group because the individuals waiting would probably perceive themselves as being associated with one another in only the loosest sense.

A corollary to the principle of perception of membership is that persons in groups not only perceive themselves as group members, but usually are also perceived by others as being in a group. Consequently, group membership can sometimes be thrust upon people who may not think of themselves as members of a group. Prime examples are ethnic, racial, and religious groups to which a person belongs. For instance, even if individuals believe they are not affected by being a member of a racial minority, it may make a significant difference in how others view them.

**INTERDEPENDENCE.**    A group exists only when the group members are interdependent. Events that affect one group member affect other members, and the behavior of group members has significant consequences for the success of the group in meeting its goals. For instance, if a football team is successful, all members share in the glory; when the team loses, it is a loss for the group as a whole. In sum, each person's outcomes are affected by what others do when members of a group are interdependent.

If we return to the examples described at the beginning of this section and apply these three criteria, it becomes clear that only some represent groups in a social psychological sense. For example, waiting for a bus is hardly a group situation: Interaction is minimal, the perception of group membership is low, and there is little interdependence. On the other hand, your grandmother's birthday party and fund-raising for the intramural hockey team just as clearly are group situations, since interaction is high, the per-

Are these groups? Only if members meet the three criteria: interacting with one another, perceiving themselves as a group, and being interdependent.

ception of being in a group is real, and there is interdependence between the group members.

Finally, your unenthusiastic participation in an Army ROTC unit represents a more difficult definitional problem. Although you obviously engage in interaction, and others may perceive you to be part of the group, the interdependence criterion may or may not be met, depending on the congruence between your goals and motivation and those of the other participants. Whether a group is a group, then, depends in part on the eye of the beholder.

## The Structure of Groups

"Felice, would you mind taking the minutes of the meeting?"

If you are Felice, you might well object—if you think you were asked to take notes primarily because you are a woman.

However, until the last two decades or so, a woman in a group setting would not have found it all that objectionable—or even surprising—to be asked to take minutes of the meeting. The reason? Because the preponderance of secretaries in the world were female, people assumed that women were somehow better suited than men to take notes. As we discussed in Chapter 3, these sexist notions and mistaken assumptions can cause harm as well as errors. What is important for our examination of groups, however, is that they are examples of how people fall into particular patterns of behavior in group situations.

**group structure**
the regular, stable patterns of behavior in groups.

The regular, stable patterns of behavior in groups are known collectively as **group structure**, and they have important consequences for the effective operation of groups. In some cases, the group structure is explicit. For instance, work groups typically have executives, managers, and workers, and each of these has explicit roles attached to the position. In other cases, however, the structure of a group is more informal. For example, some groups have a person who typically is serious and oriented to accomplishing the group's task, while another person may play the role of group clown, constantly cracking jokes but not getting all that much done. We'll consider four major aspects of groups: roles, status, norms, and cohesiveness.

**ROLES: PLAYING OUR PART IN A GROUP.** A person's typical conduct in a group can be considered a role. **Roles** are the behaviors that are associated with and come to be expected of people in a given position. Sometimes roles evolve during the course of group interaction, while in other cases they are assigned to people upon entrance into the group. In either case, roles have a considerable impact on people's behavior in the group.

**role**
the behaviors that are associated with and come to be expected of people in a given position.

Consider, for instance, social psychologist Philip Zimbardo's stunning demonstration of the power of roles (Zimbardo, 1973; Haney, Banks, & Zimbardo, 1973). Zimbardo and colleagues set up a mock prison in the basement of the Stanford University psychology department, complete with cells, solitary confinement cubicles, and a small recreation area. The researchers then advertised for subjects, asking for volunteers to spend two weeks in a study of prison life. Once they identified the study participants, a flip of a coin designated who would be a prisoner and who would be a prison guard. Neither prisoners nor guards were told how to fulfill their roles.

On the first day of the study, prisoners were picked up unexpectedly at their homes and brought, by police car, to the basement "prison." They were given loose-fitting, baggy prison smocks, and chains were clamped to their ankles. The guards received uniforms, nightsticks, handcuffs, and whistles. Apart from a few rules, the guards and prisoners were given little direction on what to do; they had only their conception of what the role of guard and prisoner required of them.

After just a few days, it became apparent that no direction was necessary: Both parties had a clear, and ultimately frightening, conception of the behavior and expectations associated with their roles. The guards became abusive to the prisoners, waking them at odd hours and subjecting them to arbitrary punishment. They withheld food from the prisoners and forced them into hard labor.

The prisoners were initially rebellious, but soon became docile and subservient to the guards. They became extremely demoralized, and one slipped into a depression so severe he was released after just a few days. In fact, after only six days of captivity, the remaining prisoners' reactions became so extreme that the study was terminated—to the disappointment of the guards, who were enjoying their taste of power.

Following a series of intensive debriefing sessions, no lingering negative consequences from participation in the study for either the prisoners or the guards were reported, despite the intensity of the experiment (Zimbardo, 1975). Some critics, however, have faulted the experiment on both ethical and methodological grounds (see, for example, Banuazizi & Movahedi, 1975). Regardless of its shortcomings, however, we can draw a clear lesson from the study: Placing people in a particular role has a powerful effect on their behavior, inducing them to behave in ways that may be incongruent with their more typical modes of behavior.

The way we play a particular role is a consequence of the culture in which we live. Although some aspects of roles are universal (there is no culture in which the role of "woman" does not include child care), other components of roles vary drastically. For example, in traditional societies such as fundamentalist Islam, the role of women revolves around the home and family. Every other aspect of the role is secondary, particularly those that do not involve the family. In contrast, the current definition of the role of woman in Western society reflects the importance of individualism and fulfillment of each person's particular talents and wishes. As a consequence, greater stress is placed on behavior that results in an increase in the equality between the sexes (Moghaddam, Taylor, & Wright, 1993).

**STATUS: EVALUATING OTHERS.**   Not every member of a group is held in similar regard. In work groups, for example, people of greater authority have bigger desks, larger offices, and better views when they look out their window. They may have their own secretary and assistant, and they may even have a separate rest room.

**status**
the evaluation of a role or person by the group.

Such perks reflect differences in status among group members. **Status** is the evaluation of a role or person by the group. People of higher status have greater access to the group's resources, and they have the authority either to tell others what to do directly or

The arrangement of the Supreme Court in this photo is not accidental: It reflects their official status. The Chief Justice is seated in the center, and the other justices are arranged according to the number of years they have served on the Court.

*"Say, Pop, where do you stand in the pecking order?"*

*Drawing by Joe Mirachi; © 1986 The New Yorker Magazine, Inc.*

to wield influence over them indirectly. In contrast, group members of lower status tend to follow the lead of the members of higher status.

What determines the status of a group member? Two factors are central: the magnitude of a person's contribution to the success of the group in achieving its goals, and the degree of power the person wields over others. People who contribute prominently to a group's accomplishments will be viewed by other members as significant group participants, and they will be held in high regard by the other members (Suchner & Jackson, 1976). Consider, for example, the accolades accorded to football stars, whose prowess on the field translates into team victories.

Similarly, people who control the outcomes of the group—those who hold power—are generally held in high regard, primarily because they are able to control the group's limited resources. For instance, in work groups, the ability of managers to determine subordinates' salaries lends them considerable status.

Although holding a particular role or position in a group can determine a person's status, an individual's personal characteristics also play a part. A person who is more intelligent, friendly, and physically attractive, or who has other positively valued characteristics, will typically be of higher status than someone who has fewer valued attributes (Kello & Ruisel, 1979).

**NORMS: FOLLOWING THE RULES.**   In addition to roles and status, a third central facet that underlies group members' conduct are norms. As we discussed in Chapter 10, **norms** are general standards or expectations regarding appropriate behavior. Norms may be written (as in a group's constitution or bylaws), or, in less formal cases, unwritten.

Norms can be prescriptive or proscriptive. **Prescriptive norms** suggest to people the ways they ought to be behave. In contrast, **proscriptive norms** inform people about behaviors they should avoid. When a fraternity member wears a baseball cap because most members of the group do so, he is responding to prescriptive norms; when that same member avoids going to a Barry Manilow concert because of the kidding he'd get, he is responding to proscriptive norms.

Group norms can be so powerful that they override an individual member's self-interest. For example, a classic study conducted in a switchboard manufacturing plant found that there was an informal norm for each worker to produce two switchboards a day, in contrast to management's goal, based on time-and-motion studies, to produce two-and-a-half switchboards a day (Roethlisberger & Dickson, 1939).

**norm**
general standards or expectations regarding appropriate behavior.

**prescriptive norms**
norms that suggest to people the ways they ought to behave.

**proscriptive norms**
norms that inform people about behaviors they should avoid.

Workers who produced either more or less than the informal goal of two per day were subjected to verbal abuse from their coworkers for their transgression. Underproducers were called "chiselers," and overproducers were called "speed kings" and "rate busters." The overproducers were even punished physically, by being punched on the arm by their coworkers. In this way, workers maintained a norm of productivity.

What is most noteworthy about the power of these norms, particularly those that prevented high productivity, is that they conflicted with the workers' own self-interest. Because workers' pay was based on their production, their voluntary restriction on their productivity resulted in a lower paycheck at the end of the week.

Of course, groups may have multiple norms, not all of which are equally important to their members. For instance, while norms relevant to the immediate goals of a group typically exert the greatest influence on a group's activities, other norms may also come into play (Weldon & Weingart, 1993). There is greater tolerance for deviation from these less central norms than from more important norms (Rossi & Berk, 1985).

In some cases, norms condone activities that are blatantly illegal. In one recent case, for example, a major airline company had a problem with thefts—from passenger bags and cargo shipments—that were clearly being carried out by company employees. Despite appeals from company executives for other employees to support solving the problem, employees did not step forward, although it was clear that they had to be fully aware of what was happening. Eventually, the company was forced to offer a large reward of $10,000 in order to overcome employee norms about squealing (Miner, 1992).

**GROUP COHESIVENESS: ATTRACTION TO THE GROUP.**    Just as individuals vary in their attractiveness, so do groups. The extent to which the members of a group find the group attractive is known as **group cohesiveness**. Groups in which the members are committed to the group and are strongly attracted to it are considered to be high in cohesiveness. On the other hand, groups in which there is little attraction on the part of the members are said to be low in cohesiveness.

**group cohesiveness**
the extent to which the members of a group find the group attractive.

Group cohesiveness is produced by a variety of factors. For instance, the more a group is able to attain its goals, the greater will be its cohesiveness (Nixon, 1976). In some cases, though, even unsuccessful groups are high in cohesiveness (Taylor, Doria, & Tyler, 1983).

You may have experienced belonging to a group that is not particularly successful. For instance, you might have worked on a school newspaper that, because of limited resources, was generally unread and was held in low esteem by the student body. Or you might have been in the cast or crew of a play that few people attended. Yet, despite the fact that the formal goals of such groups went unmet, the group may have been highly attractive to you. Why?

One answer resides in the nature of the other group members and of the group's activities. If we find the other members attractive, the inability of the group to meet its formal goals becomes less critical. Instead, the social interactions that the group provides may become increasingly central to the group experience. Hence, if we shift what we wish to attain from the group from producing one particular outcome (such as creating a newspaper that all students read and enjoy) to another (such as enjoying the camaraderie of others), we are more likely to find the group experience a positive one. In these circumstances, group cohesiveness is likely to rise.

When group cohesiveness is high, several consequences are likely. For example, members of highly cohesive groups tend to maintain their membership longer than if cohesiveness is low (Robinson & Carron, 1982). Furthermore, groups that are high in cohesiveness wield more influence over their membership. Members of religious cults and other highly cohesive groups, for example, often share decidedly uniform attitudes and conform to the standards of the group.

For instance, as we discussed in Chapter 2 when we considered the case of David Koresh and his Branch Davidian cult, members cut their ties with friends and family and accepted Koresh's Biblical teachings without question. Members who deviated were

Members of highly cohesive groups share similar attitudes, show considerable conformity to the group's standards, and may see the group as central to their lives.

placed under intense—and quite effective—social pressure to conform to Koresh's teachings.

Membership in highly cohesive groups yields some personal benefits, as well. For instance, members of highly cohesive groups have higher self-esteem and display less anxiety than members of groups with less cohesiveness. Apparently, high cohesiveness leads to greater acceptance and trust of the group's members, which in turn allows each member to feel more secure and develop high self-regard (Julian, Bishop, & Fiedler, 1966; Stokes, 1983; Wheeless, Wheeless, & Dickson-Markman, 1982; Karasawa, 1988; Roark & Sharah, 1989).

Finally, group cohesiveness is related to group productivity, but not in a simple way. We might assume, for example, that cohesive groups, given their tendency to maintain membership and influence members, would represent an ideal means to maintain and even increase productivity in work-related groups. However, it turns out that this is true only in groups in which the norms, or standards, accepted by the group members support high productivity. If the norms favor only minimal productivity (such as doing as little as one can get away with), then high cohesiveness can keep productivity at a minimum (Seashore, 1954; Dorfman & Stephan, 1984).

The manner in which cohesiveness relates to group productivity illustrates a central principle of group behavior: Groups have neither consistently positive nor consistently negative consequences on their members. Instead, membership in groups provides both benefits and costs, as we discuss next.

## ▶ REVIEW & RETHINK

### Review

- Formal groups consist of two or more people who interact with one another; perceive themselves as a group; and are interdependent.
- Group structure includes roles, status, norms and cohesiveness.

### Rethink

- According to the definition of groups proposed in this section, would a dues-paying member of Amnesty International, a charity that works for social justice, be part of a "group"? If you had to reduce the definition of groups down one criterion, what would it be?

- Describe how group roles can influence members' behavior. How is this influence different from that of group norms?

- How does attractiveness relate to status within a group? How does it affect group cohesiveness?

- Explain how group norms, roles, status, and cohesiveness affected subjects in Zimbardo's prison experiment.

# BEHAVIOR IN GROUPS: THE BENEFITS AND COSTS OF MEMBERSHIP

*You wake up with a clear memory of the events of the prior day, although they still don't make too much sense. Why did you get into that stupid argument at the conference? Was it really necessary to get into such a heated debate? Why did your arguments become so extreme that after a while even you had trouble believing what you were saying? When you're in a group, why can't you control your urge to stake out a position and defend it, no matter how persuasive the arguments on the other side? What is it about group situations that prevents you from discussing things in a cool, rational way?*

If you've ever found yourself in a similar situation, you know full well the powerful effect that groups can have on our actions. Sometimes the influence of groups brings out the best in us. At other times, though, in groups we say things and act in ways that reflect poorly on ourselves.

The consequences of group membership, then, are neither invariably positive or negative. Instead, particular group processes result in very different outcomes. We focus now on some of the benefits—and costs—of group participation.

*Social Facilitation*    When are runners most likely to perform their best—when they are running a track alone, or when they are running in a group, competing with others?

If you're a serious jogger, you probably already know the answer to the question. If not, you'll be able to figure out the answer yourself by examining the results of one of the earliest research studies carried out in social psychology.

The work began when psychologist Norman Triplett became interested in the performance of bicycle racers in the late 1800s. As a bicycling buff, Triplett noticed a clear pattern: Racing times were significantly faster for rides made during competition with other riders than when a lone rider tried to beat the best time established for a track. Triplett theorized that the presence of others acted to release riders' "extra energy" and caused them to pedal faster.

To test this reasoning, Triplett carried out an experiment in which children were asked to turn reels like those on a fishing rod that moved a marker around a four-meter course. The reels were set up so that the children could either work alone or compete with another child. Triplett found that children moved the marker significantly faster when competing with a peer than when operating the reel by themselves, thereby confirming the results of the bicycle racers studies. Subsequent research, conducted early in the history of the field, showed that the phenomenon was not restricted to competitive situations; even the presence of others as noncompeting spectators could lead to improved performance (Dashiell, 1930).

**social facilitation**
the phenomenon in which the presence of others leads to improvements in performance.

The results of this early research suggested a clear principle: The presence of others leads to improvements in performance. Indeed, the phenomenon was recognized with a name—**social facilitation**—that focuses on the improvement, or facilitation, of performance that came about when others were present. Activities ranging from running to using a computer all are carried out better when done in the presence of others than when done alone (e.g., Robinson-Staveley & Cooper, 1990).

Only one flaw marred this scientific portrait: The prediction that performance would improve with others present was far from infallible. In fact, it soon became evident from a variety of studies that just the opposite result often occurred. In many cases, the presence of others seemed to lead to reductions in performance. For instance, although the presence of others produced improved performance of simple multiplication problems, refutations of Greek maxims took a turn for the worse when tried in the presence of others (Allport, 1924; Baron, Kerr, & Miller, 1992).

This puzzling state of affairs was unresolved until the 1960s, when social psychologist Robert Zajonc (pronounced "zi-ence," rhymes with "science") came up with a solution that has proved surprisingly durable. Zajonc (1965) suggested that the presence of other people raises our general level of emotional arousal, as indicated by increases in heart rate, perspiration, and hormonal activity. (Think what's it like to perform a solo at a concert or to make an oral report to a class.) Because work from the field of learning psychology has demonstrated that higher levels of arousal lead to better performance of well-learned responses, then performance of well-learned behaviors should be enhanced by the presence of others—the social facilitation effect.

At the same time, learning psychologists have also found that higher arousal leads to declines in performance of poorly learned responses. As a result, the higher arousal caused by the presence of others ought to cause poorer performance in responses that are poorly learned. In sum, the mere presence of others will cause either increases or decreases in performance, depending on whether the behavior in question is well-learned or poorly learned (See Figure 14-1).

Zajonc's simple and elegant solution solved a mystery that had troubled social psychology for decades. But, like a detective who identifies a murderer but does not identify the killer's motive, his explanation, which focuses on the mere presence of others, did not provide a fully satisfying explanation, at least in the view of many researchers. Specifically, the reason why the presence of others leads to arousal has remained a question of some debate. Several possibilities have been put forward.

According to Nicholas Cottrell, it is not just the mere presence of others that leads to facilitation effects. Instead, the presence of others produces arousal because we are apprehensive about how the others are appraising us (Cottrell, 1972). According to the concept of **evaluation apprehension**, the presence of others leads to the inference that the audience is evaluating us, a circumstance that is definitely physiologically arousing.

**evaluation apprehension**
the phenomenon in which the presence of others leads to the inference that the audience is evaluating us, a circumstance that produces physiological arousal.

If this reasoning is correct, social facilitation should occur only when others are paying attention to us; when others are present but are not paying attention, and are therefore unable to evaluate our performance, social facilitation effects should be reduced. And that seems to be just what happens. For example, in one experiment, joggers ran in the presence of a spectator, who was actually a confederate (Strube, Miles, & Finch, 1981). In one condition, the spectator was barely attentive to the jogger, but in the other, the spectator kept close tabs on the jogger, constantly gazing at the jogger and even making eye contact. As an evaluation apprehension explanation would lead us to predict, the attentive spectator led to social facilitation effects: Joggers ran swifter than when they were alone. But the inattentive spectator produced speed no greater than when the jogger was alone.

Yet evaluation apprehension is not the full story behind social facilitation, since the phenomenon frequently occurs under circumstances in which evaluation is, to put it mildly, unlikely to be a factor. For example, even the most committed animal rights advocates would find it implausible that cockroaches feel much in the way of evaluation apprehension. Yet such creatures clearly demonstrate social facilitation effects.

**FIGURE 14-1    Social Facilitation: Explaining How the Presence of Others Changes Performance**

| THEORY | EXPLANATION |
|---|---|
| Mere Presence | The mere presence of others leads to arousal, which enhances the performance of well-learned, simple tasks and causes declines in performance on difficult, complex tasks. |
| Evaluation Apprehension | The presence of others leads to assumptions that performance is being evaluated, leading to heightened arousal. |
| Distraction-Conflict | The presence of others is distracting, causing attention to be divided between the task and the people present, leading to conflict. This conflict leads to higher arousal. |

In one experiment, run-of-the-mill household cockroaches progressed through a simple maze more quickly when in the presence of four observer cockroaches than when they were by themselves (Zajonc, Heingartner, & Herman, 1969). On the other hand, a maze that was more complex for the cockroaches (it required a turn) produced performance that was less quick when observer cockroaches were present. Hence, the classic social facilitation prediction was confirmed—improved performance on simple tasks, and declines in performance on complex ones.

Similar findings have been found employing other species, such as armadillos, chickens, and opossums, who presumably are as little concerned as cockroaches about the evaluation that others of their species make of them. Consequently, social psychologists have suggested explanations based on psychological mechanisms not exclusive to humans and their more sophisticated cognitive abilities.

One alternative is distraction-conflict theory (Sanders, 1983; Baron, 1986). According to **distraction-conflict theory**, social facilitation effects occur because the presence of others is distracting, and our attention becomes divided between the task at hand and the others who are present. This divided attention leads to conflict, which in turn leads to higher physiological arousal. When the task is simple, the interference due to the distraction is minimal, and the increased arousal is strong enough to overcome the distraction and result in superior performance. But when the task is difficult, the

**distraction-conflict theory**
the explanation of social facilitation effects that suggests that the presence of others is a distraction, dividing our attention between the task at hand and the others who are present.

increase in arousal is not large enough to overcome the distraction of the presence of others, leading to a decline in performance.

In sum, distraction-conflict theory, like the other explanations of social facilitation, explains why the arousal due to the presence of others leads to better performance on simple tasks and declines in performance for more complex and difficult ones. What makes distraction-conflict theory unique is the source of the arousal: It stems from the fact that people divide their attention between at least two compelling targets of interest.

We've seen that there are several competing explanations for the social facilitation effect, not one of which has unquestioned experimental support (Geen, 1989). As a consequence, social psychologists have begun to reject the notion that any one particular explanation can fully account for all instances of social facilitation. Instead, current research has been designed to test under what circumstances particular expectations most effectively account for the data.

Although there is disagreement over the explanation of social facilitation, the effects of the phenomenon remain among the longest-established findings in the field of social psychology, and they have produced some important applications. Drawing on the findings, for example, Robert Zajonc has suggested—only in part facetiously—how a savvy student could prepare for an exam:

> Study all alone, preferably in an isolated cubicle, and arrange to take your examination in the company of many other students, on stage, and in the presence of a large audience. The examination results would be beyond your wildest expectations, provided, of course, you learned the material quite thoroughly (Zajonc, 1965, p. 274).

## Social Loafing

We all know that "many hands make light work." Or do we? As we've seen several times before, cultural truisms often contain little truth and are not infrequently contradictory. With this maxim, however, the research securely backs up the contention that having more people work on a problem makes an individual participant's job a little easier.

The issue is not a new one: At the beginning of this century, Max Ringelmann, a French agricultural engineer, provided clear evidence that the more people who work on a task, the less effort each one expends. Ringelmann asked his subjects to pull on a rope as hard as they could. He measured each subject's efforts while pulling alone and with one, two, or seven others. The results were clear: The more people were pulling, the less hard the average individual pulled (Ringelmann, 1913; Kravitz & Martin, 1986).

These results exemplify a phenomenon that has come to be known as social loafing. **Social loafing** represents the decrease in individual effort that occurs when people engage in shared group activity. Such loafing occurs in a wide variety of situations, ranging from performance on tasks involving physical activity to participation in perceptual and intellectual tasks (see, for example, Petty et al., 1980; Szymanski & Harkins, 1987).

**social loafing**
the phenomenon in which individual effort decreases when people engage in shared group activity.

Social loafing has been found in a variety of different cultures, including India, Japan, and Taiwan (Weiner, Pandy, & Latané, 1981; Williams & Williams, 1984; Gabrenya, Wang, & Latané, 1981; Gabrenya, Latané, & Wang, 1983). Indeed, one extreme application of this view might be to attribute the fall of communism to the use of collective industrial and agricultural techniques, which emphasized group productivity rather than individual contributions. Such social norms may have set the stage for social loafing on a grand scale.

In sum, social loafing is a pervasive phenomenon (Williams, Jackson, & Karau, 1992; Karau & Williams, 1993). However, we hardly become lazy in all social situations. For example, if our motivation to succeed is sufficiently great, we may perform at peak levels, regardless of whether we are working with others or alone. Similarly, if we think that our contribution to the group effort can be individually identified, we're considerably more likely to contribute fully to the group effort (see Kerr & Bruun, 1981; Williams, Harkins, & Latané, 1981; Harkins & Szymanski, 1989).

Some observers have suggested that the fall of communism in the Soviet Union (symbolized by this toppled statue of Lenin) is related in part to pervasive social loafing—the decrease in individual effort that occurs when people engage in shared group activity.

The different circumstances in which social loafing does and does not occur has led researchers to suggest several different explanations for the phenomenon. One possibility is that people may perceive others in a group to be less motivated or less skilled than they are, and this conclusion leads them to reduce their own output. If the task is relatively trivial, why bother to work hard, if others aren't? On the other hand, if the task is meaningful, people may expect that their contributions will make a relatively significant difference when others aren't working hard; in this case, social loafing will be minimized as group members engage in social compensation for their weaker coparticipants (Williams & Karau, 1991; Jackson & Harkins, 1985).

A second explanation for the social loafing phenomenon is that group participants choose goals that are less ambitious when others are present than when they are alone. In this case, they may assume that the task will be easier when others are involved. Because of their lowered goals, they may put in less effort (Kerr & Bruun, 1983).

Social loafing may also be a result of the perception of participants that when they are in a group their own efforts are less closely linked to any potential outcomes than when they are alone. If a group member follows such logic, he or she has less reason to expend much energy on the task.

Cultural factors may also influence social loafing. For instance, people from Eastern cultures are somewhat less susceptible to social loafing than those from Western cultures (Karau & Williams, 1993). Why? The reason may relate to the greater concern with group and social orientations common in Eastern cultures, and the greater emphasis on individualism found in Western cultures, which we'll discuss in greater detail in Chapter 15 (Triandis, 1989).

At this point, there is no single, compelling explanation for the phenomenon of social loafing, and we are left with several alternatives, each of which is plausible. Still, despite our current inability to zero in on the cause of the phenomenon, there is no escaping its reality. People working together in group situations are susceptible to slacking off, contributing only a fraction of what they would if they were working independently (Karau & Williams, 1993).

# THE INFORMED CONSUMER OF SOCIAL PSYCHOLOGY:

## REDUCING SOCIAL LOAFING

We've seen how easy it is for people in groups to engage in social loafing. Are there ways to reduce the consequences of social loafing? Can groups be structured to thwart social loafing on the part of individual members and to maximize the output of all members?

The answer from social psychologists is yes. The following guidelines suggest several ways to minimize productivity losses in groups and to magnify the benefits of groups:

- *Increase members' sense of personal responsibility.* Groups should be structured so that each group member is made to feel personally responsible for the outcomes of the group as a whole. One of the best ways to do this is to make sure that each person feels that his or her input is personally identifiable and will not be lost among the other members' contributions (Hardy & Latané, 1986). In addition, the group output should be evaluated on the basis of individual contributions, not only on the success or failure of the group as a whole (Harkins, 1987).

- *Increase feelings of individual self-efficacy.* Group members need to understand that they are capable of making a successful contribution to the joint effort. A sense of self-efficacy and the expectation of success are likely to enhance performance in groups. Consequently, instilling expectations of success will decrease social loafing and lead to optimum output.

- *Make the group's activities involving.* When the group's task is involving, interesting, or challenging, social loafing is mini-

mized (Brickner, Harkins, & Ostrom, 1986; Harkins & Petty, 1982; Zaccaro, 1984). Consequently, one way to reduce social loafing is to ensure that whatever the group is trying to accomplish keeps members engaged.

- *Optimize trust in the other group members.* If you thought that the other members of a group were not working as hard as they could, what would you do? According to social psychologist Norbert Kerr, you might hold yourself back. After all, why give others a free ride, allowing them to share in the rewards of the group, even though their effort is minimal? Kerr suggests that the perception that others are *"freeriders"* —people who put in minimal effort but benefit from the group's rewards—leads the other group members to reduce their own efforts.

  One solution to the free-rider problem is to ensure that group members trust that their fellow members are putting in maximum effort. By making all members feel that everyone is maximizing their efforts, the incidence of free-riding can be reduced (Williams & Karau, 1991).

- *Make each member's contribution highly visible.* If people's contributions to the group task are noticeable and obvious, social loafing will not occur. Consequently, it is worthwhile to recognize and publicize personal achievement (Matsui, Kakuyama, & UyOnglatco, 1987; Price, 1987).

---

## ▶ REVIEW & RETHINK

### Review

- Social facilitation refers to the change in performance that results from the presence of others.
- Social loafing represents the decrease in individual effort that occurs when people engage in shared group activity.
- Several strategies can be employed to reduce social loafing.

### Rethink

- What experimental evidence supports the evaluation apprehension explanation of social facilitation? What evidence refutes this hypothesis? How might you resolve this conflicting evidence?
- What aspect of the presence of others determines whether social facilitation of social loafing processes will result?
- Which suggestions for eluding social loafing can also be applied to increasing social facilitation in work settings? Explain your answers.

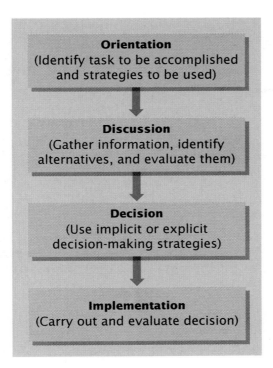

**FIGURE 14-2  The Stages of Decision Making** Groups typically move through four stages in their efforts to reach a decision. *(Source:* Forsyth, 1990.*)*

# GROUP PROBLEM SOLVING AND DECISION MAKING

When "a hundred clever heads join a group, one big nincompoop is the result."

Was the famous therapist and personality theorist Carl Jung correct when he made this observation, straying from his usual realm of abnormal behavior into that of social psychology and arguing that group solutions are inferior to those made by an individual? The issue is a simple one, but the answer has proven to be complex—more so than Jung's response would presume (which also may suggest that experts in abnormal behavior are sometimes better off sticking to their own turf). In some cases, groups arrive at more and better solutions to problems and make better decisions; in other cases, individuals working alone are more effective problem solvers and decision makers. The challenge for social psychologists has been to identify the circumstances under which one type of problem solving and decision making—individual or group—is better than the other.

*The Processes of Group Decision Making: Joining Forces in Groups*

To address the question of whether individuals or groups are *better* at solving problems and making decisions, we first need to know something about *how* groups solve problems—the processes that describe what a group does when confronting an issue (Castellan, 1993).

**TRACING THE COURSE OF GROUP DECISION MAKING.**   When a group must come to a decision, how do the members proceed? Typically, groups move through four stages in their efforts to reaching a decision: orientation, discussion, decision, and implementation (Forsyth, 1990; see Figure 14-2).

In the orientation stage, the group seeks to identify the task it is trying to accomplish and the strategy it will use to accomplish it. The task may be to reach a decision about an immediate, specific problem, or it may be to resolve some long-standing conflict that requires a long-term strategy. For instance, a group seeking to determine a new

© 1994 Charles Barsotti and The Cartoon Bank, Inc.

In decision-making, two heads are not always better than one.

alcohol policy for university functions might decide that it wishes to hold a series of three meetings, one of which will be open to the public.

In most groups, the orientation stage is relatively brief. Most group members typically are motivated to begin immediately on the task itself, rather than spending a great deal of time on the process or strategy the group will use to reach a decision (Varela, 1971; Hackman & Morris, 1975).

The second stage marks the beginning of the actual discussion to solve the problem. Here, groups generally gather information about the problem, identify the alternatives, and evaluate each of them. There is a certain amount of verbal hypothesis testing, as group members suggest ideas and consider how the decision might actually play out. For instance, the alcohol policy group might discuss the legal ramifications of serving alcohol to minors, as well as the reactions of students if liquor is banned outright.

The actual decision is made in the third stage. Using either implicit or explicit decision-making strategies decided upon in the first stage, groups reach a final decision. This stage may include a consolidation period, in which group members try to convince those who harbor doubts about the wisdom of the decision that it is in fact the best one. In our example, for instance, an alcohol policy would actually be adopted by the group during this stage.

The last stage of decision making is implementation. The implementation stage is composed of two aspects: carrying out the decision by ensuring that it gets accomplished, and evaluating the decision. Actually, the evaluation of a decision often marks the reinitiation of the four-stage cycle. If evaluation of the decision establishes that a mistake was made, then the group may seek to come to a better solution, returning to the stages of orientation and discussion. For instance, the alcohol policy group might issue a letter to everyone on campus, informing them of the decisions and explaining why it was adopted. They might also ask for feedback from those affected by the policy, as well as monitoring the success of its implementation.

**THE FRAMEWORK FOR GROUP DECISION MAKING.** In making decisions, groups rely on either explicit or implicit social decision schemes. A **social decision scheme** is the way individual judgments and preferences are combined into a collective decision. Social decision schemes may be explicit (a group's bylaws may stipulate that "the majority rules" or, in the case of juries, a unanimous decision may be required). In other decision-making groups, however, the social decision scheme is never articulated and may remain obscure and even mystifying to some members (Stasser, Kerr, & Davis, 1989).

**social decision scheme**
the way in which individual judgments and preferences are combined into a collective decision.

Social decision schemes vary in two major ways—strictness and distribution of power (Miller, 1989). The strictness of a scheme relates to the degree to which group members must hold similar views in order for a group to reach a decision. A scheme that requires unanimity is relatively strict, since every member must agree with the group decision. In contrast, a majority scheme is much less strict, since a minority of members can disagree and still permit the group to reach a decision.

The second major dimension of social decision schemes relates to power distribution. In some groups, power is spread equally among all the group members. In more authoritarian groups, however, decision-making power resides in a single person.

The strictness and power distribution of social decision schemes play a central role in determining the outcome of decision making. For example, the stricter the decision scheme, the less likely it is that the group will be able to come to a particular decision. Furthermore, if a decision is reached, stricter schemes are apt to result in a compromise (Miller, 1985, 1989).

Stricter schemes and more equal power distributions are likely to lead to greater conflict during group discussions than schemes that are less strict and those in which power lies disproportionately in the hands of particular members. In addition, the degree to which a decision is perceived as fair depends on how much the decision reflects the preferences of group members. Even the decisions of a dictatorship may be viewed as equitable if group members perceive that the decision reflects the group's majority view (Miller et al., 1987).

In sum, the kind of decision scheme used by a group has a critical impact on the nature of group deliberations and on the kind of decision that is ultimately reached. (Figure 14-3 summarizes the impact of the strictness of a decision scheme on group decision making.)

**GUIDELINES FOR GROUP DECISION MAKING.**  In addition to decision schemes, groups also employ social combination rules in their efforts to make decisions and solve problems. According to social psychologist Ivan Steiner, **social combination rules** are the guidelines used by members of groups to decide what needs to be done and how the task should be divided up among group members (Steiner, 1976). Steiner suggests that social combination rules can be thought of as a recipe for group process, analogous to a recipe for baking a cake. In fact, he provides several "recipes" for groups, depending on the kind of task that the group is trying to accomplish (see Figure 14-4).

**social combination rules**
the guidelines used by members of groups to decide what needs to be done and how the task should be divided up among group members.

- *Additive tasks.* An additive task is one in which each person's contribution is added to everyone else's. For instance, shoveling snow is additive: Each person's accomplishments add to the total group's performance. The more people, the more snow is shoveled. The

| FIGURE 14-3   Decision Making in Groups: The Effects of the Strictness of the Social Decision Scheme | | |
| --- | --- | --- |
| | **STRICTER SCHEMES** | **MORE LENIENT SCHEMES** |
| Reaching a decision | Less likely | More likely |
| Reaching a compromise | More likely | Less likely |
| Satisfaction with the decision | More likely | Less likely |
| Duration of discussion | Longer | Shorter |
| Perception of discussion by members | Uncomfortable, difficult, but thorough and adequate | Comfortable, easier but less thorough and less adequate |
| Fairness | Seen as more fair | Seen as less fair |

Source: *Based on Miller, 1989.*

## FIGURE 14-4     Recipes for Group Success

According to social psychologist Ivan Steiner, different tasks require different "recipes" to ensure that the optimal solution will be found. Among the most popular recipes:

| TASK TYPE | DESCRIPTION | EXAMPLE | STRATEGY |
|---|---|---|---|
| Additive | Individual inputs are added together | Shoveling snow | Each member maximizes output, and everyone attempts to coordinate |
| Disjunctive | Group selects best solution from pool of individual members' judgments | Either/or, multiple-choice problems with a correct answer | Identify best/smartest member, use his or her response |
| Compensatory | Group product is average of individual judgments | Averaging estimates or ratings | Calculate the mean response |
| Conjunctive | All group members must contribute | Rock climbing, relay race, class group projects | All members work their hardest |

Source: *Based on Steiner, 1972, 1976.*

recipe here is simple: Each member does as much as he or she can, while members attempt to coordinate their activities with one another.

- *Disjunctive tasks.* Disjunctive tasks require a single choice among several alternatives, one of which is correct and the others wrong. For instance, a group seeking the answer to a newspaper trivia game would be involved in a disjunctive task. The recipe: Identify the most competent member of the group and present that person's solution to the group for approval. If it is not obvious who the most able person is, then all members should work simultaneously on the solution.

- *Compensatory tasks.* Compensatory tasks require the averaging of individual judgments to produce a group product. Members of college admissions committees often make individual judgments about a candidate and then use an averaging process to determine whether or not a candidate should be accepted. The recipe here is a mathematical one in which the decision is made by averaging the judgments of individual group members who devise solutions on their own.

- *Conjunctive tasks.* If you've ever tried rock climbing, you know that you are strapped together with the other climbers in your party during your ascent. You can only advance as quickly as the slowest and least skilled member of your group.

    Rock climbing represents a conjunctive task, in which the group is able to produce an outcome no better than the one the least competent person in the group can make. In dealing with conjunctive problems, group members must adjust their performance to fit the least competent individual.

    Despite the potential frustration involved in carrying out a disjunctive task, there is a way to optimize success: All the members of the group should be encouraged to work their hardest, especially the weakest members. In addition, the stronger members should be encouraged to follow the lead of these weaker members.

Although groups can benefit from Steiner's "recipes," they don't always reach their potential. Often they suffer from **process loss**—aspects of the group's interaction patterns that hinder performance and prevent them from operating at 100 percent proficiency. The interactions of the various members with one another and with the group as a whole may prevent the group from reaching its potential.

**process loss**
the aspects of a group's interaction patterns that hinder performance.

*The Quality of Group Decision Making: Are Many Heads Better Than One?*

We've seen that decision-making groups operate according to regular patterns, moving through a series of stages. But what of the specific nature and quality of the decisions that they make? Are they better than those made by individuals? Do groups overcome the biases of their members and reach decisions that are somehow better than the individuals who make them up?

In additive tasks, such as cleaning up a beach after an oil spill, each person's contribution adds to the total effectiveness of the group activity. In disjunctive tasks, such as students competing in an academic contest, the group must make a single choice from several alternatives. Compensatory tasks—such as judging a contest—require the averaging of individual evaluations. Finally, in conjunctive tasks such as a relay race, the group can do no better than its weakest member.

Resolving the issue of whether groups solve problems better than individuals has proven to be a formidable challenge. The reason the issue has proved so vexing rests in part on the way one phrases the question. For example, if we consider whether groups arrive at more accurate solutions to problems more quickly, then we come up with the answer that groups are better. Groups typically produce more and higher-quality solutions to problems than the same number of people working alone (see Davis, 1969; Laughlin, 1980).

However, if we consider whether it is more efficient to use groups or individuals, we find that although groups reach solutions more quickly, the cost in time expended per individual is greater in group situations. In other words, although groups produce more correct solutions, they do so at a cost of time in the form of total person-hours expended. If you happened to be footing the payroll bill, then your inclination might well be to use individuals acting alone to solve a problem. The cost to you would be smaller—although the quality of solutions might not be quite so high.

In sum, the way in which we can answer the question of whether groups or individuals find better solutions and make better decisions depends in part on the particulars of the situation and our goals in asking the question in the first place. Furthermore, there are several group phenomena that, if operative within a group, can affect its functioning. We consider several, including brainstorming, the composition of the group, group polarization, and groupthink.

**BRAINSTORMING: HELP OR HINDRANCE TO CREATIVITY?**    Brainstorming is a procedure designed to generate ideas in groups. In **brainstorming**, group members are asked to produce as many, and as uninhibited, ideas as they possibly can. Initially, other group members are told to withhold criticism, thereby creating an atmosphere that presumably overcomes evaluation apprehension and produces an environment encouraging the generation of ideas. Only later are the ideas considered and evaluated. The procedure is used widely in business and industry as a way to optimize creativity (Osborn, 1957).

**brainstorming**
a procedure designed to generate ideas, in which group members are asked to produce as many (and as uninhibited) ideas as they possibly can and to withhold criticism in order to optimize creativity.

There's only one problem: Research has never demonstrated the effectiveness of brainstorming. In fact, most research suggests that it is a less effective technique than allowing the same number of group members to generate ideas on their own, independent from any group experience (Diehl & Stroebe, 1987; Mullen, Johnson, & Salas, 1991).

The primary reason for the lack of effectiveness of brainstorming lies in part due to production blocking. **Production blocking** reflects the strongly held social norm that in a group only one person can speak at a given time. Although most of us don't spend much time thinking about it, we automatically obey our society's implicit rule that it is discourteous, as well as impractical, to speak while another person is speaking.

The rule against simultaneous speaking prevents people from blurting out their ideas the moment they think of them. It also does something else: When group members restrict the immediate expression of ideas, they may later forget them, or they may not articulate them because the idea seems irrelevant or less original. Consequently, they ultimately are less likely to express the idea, leading to a definite disadvantage for group brainstorming compared to the generation of ideas while alone (Diehl & Stroebe, 1991; Mullen, Johnson, & Salas, 1991).

Despite the clear evidence that brainstorming is ineffective due to production blocking, the idea that brainstorming is a useful technique for generating ideas remains firmly embedded in everyday beliefs. Why should this be true? According to social psychologists Michael Diehl and Wolfgang Stroebe (Stroebe, Diehl, & Abakoumkin, 1992), one part of the answer lies in what they call the "illusion of group effectivity." This illusion is produced in part because people enjoy working in groups, and their enjoyment makes group production of ideas seem desirable and motivating. In addition, there is an appearance of group superiority—a type of illusory correlational bias of the sort that we first considered in Chapter 2 when we discussed attribution theory. This bias is due to the misleading appearance that more ideas are generated while working in groups than when working alone—even though controlled research does not support such a contention. In sum, although research does not suggest that brainstorming is an optimal procedure, it will probably continue to be employed.

**GROUP MEMBERSHIP: IS THERE AN OPTIMUM GROUP COMPOSITION?**    When President Bill Clinton took office and nominated the members of his first cabinet, he announced that he wanted the cabinet to "look like America." The implicit goal was to create a cabinet that represented the diversity of the United States population, producing a group made up of people with a wide range of diverging views.

Does such heterogeneity of membership produce better problem solving than a more homogeneous group? To answer the question, consider a classic problem used in research on group problem solving (albeit one that a president's cabinet is unlikely to be called on to tackle):

> *A man bought a horse for $60 and sold it for $70. Then he bought it back for $80 and sold it for $90. How much money did he make in the horse business? (Baron, Kerr, & Miller, 1992, p. 39)*

The problem is straightforward, and there is only one correct solution.* Presumably, any group that includes at least one person capable of solving it alone can, as a group, come up with the right answer, since all that one person has to do is to explain it to the others.

However, this simple scenario doesn't always take place. In fact, in one early study that used the problem, one fifth of the groups rejected the correct answer and came up with some other, erroneous solution (Maier & Solem, 1952).

**production blocking**
the process loss that reflects the strongly held social norm that only one person in a group can speak at a given time.

*The answer is $20, in case you're wondering.

The group's rebuff of the correct response underscored the social psychological quality of group behavior. Clearly, group performance depends on more than the ability and skills of the individual members. For example, the status of the person who actually has the correct solution influences the degree to which the group will accept the right answer. People in relatively low-status positions in a group are less persuasive than those of higher status. In fact, persons of low status may be unwilling to present their solution to the group in the first place (Torrence, 1954; Dubrovsky, Kiesler, & Sethna, 1991; Tjosvold & Deemer, 1980). Similarly, a person who is low in self-confidence is less likely to be convincing to the group, and the other members may reject the solution of the less-confident person due to this lack of persuasiveness (Hinsz, 1990).

Gender factors have also been found to be related to group performance, although the differences that have been identified between men's and women's performance have hardly been consistent. For example, some studies have found that men outperform women (see, for example, Hoffman & Maier, 1961); others found that women did better than men (see Kerr, 1983); and still others found little difference between men and women (see Shaw & Harkey, 1976).

A reconciliation of the assorted (and contradictory) findings about gender differences in group behavior finally was accomplished through a careful meta-analysis of the research literature. According to social psychologist Wendy Wood (1987), a review of more than 50 relevant studies showed that two key factors determined whether male or female groups would be superior—the nature of the group's task, and the interaction style of the groups. All-male groups tended to accomplish best those tasks that were stereotypically male-oriented or that tapped skills with which men were apt to be more experienced. Similarly, all-female groups were better at tasks that were stereotypically female-oriented or those with which women were more apt to have experience. For example, male groups were more likely to excel on tasks involving mathematical skill or physical strength, while female groups did better on verbally oriented tasks (Wood, Polek, & Aiken, 1985).

The second factor that explained differences in male and female performance had to do with contrasting interaction styles. Male groups typically use a task-oriented interaction style in which the focus of the interaction is on getting the task accomplished. In contrast, female groups are more interpersonally oriented, tending to be more interested than men in maintaining the social fabric of the interactions. As a consequence, tasks that require high efficiency and productivity tend to be accomplished better by male groups, while those that require cooperation and other sorts of interpersonal finesse tend to be done best by female groups (Wood & Karten, 1986).

In sum, neither male nor female groups are invariably better. Instead, optimum performance occurs when the task is best suited to the particular qualities of the people making up the group.

**GROUP POLARIZATION: GOING TO EXTREMES.**   You're a member of a group charged with determining whether, and how much, student activity fees should be increased. The members of the group start the deliberations with a range of views, a few leaning toward keeping the current fees, others suggesting that at least a 5 percent increase is necessary. As a group, you discuss the issue over the course of several meetings, and finally you vote on the question. To your surprise, the increase to which the members of the committee agree is 7 percent—higher than even the most extreme person's initial suggestion!

You've experienced the phenomenon of group polarization. According to social psychologists David Myers and Helmut Lamm, **group polarization** is an exaggeration of a group's initial tendencies following group discussion (Myers, 1982; Myers & Lamm, 1976).

The principle that group decisions tend to be more extreme following discussion grew out of a finding that captured the imagination of social psychologists during the

**group polarization**
an exaggeration of a group's initial tendencies following group discussion.

1960s and early 1970s. According to a body of research that blossomed during that time, the common sense view that group decision making produced more conservative, less extreme decisions (which were therefore more workable) was wrong. Instead, evidence pointed to just the opposite: that groups often tended to make riskier decisions than individuals solving the same problems on their own.

**risky shift**
the situation in which groups often tend to make riskier decisions than individuals solving the same problems on their own.

The finding of greater riskiness in groups was dubbed the **risky shift**, and the phenomenon spawned literally dozens of experiments designed to explain it. The trouble with all this work was that the risky shift didn't always occur. In fact, there were some situations in which the groups behaved in just the opposite way, making decisions that were less risky in the group than their initial positions.

After examining the seeming inconsistency across various studies, social psychologists figured out the solution. The risky shift was seen as just one part of the broader phenomenon of group polarization. The risky shift occurred when the initial positions of the group tended toward the risky; group decisions became riskier as a result. However, when the initial views of the group members were on the conservative, less risky side, group discussion resulted in a decision that was ultimately more conservative.

Group polarization has been demonstrated in a variety of contexts, ranging from the military and business to terrorist organizations (McCauley & Segal, 1987). For instance, in one study, groups of army officers, ROTC cadets, and non-military-affiliated university students discussed solutions regarding action following a hypothetical international military crisis threatening United States security (Minix & Semmell, cited in Lamm & Myers, 1978). Both student groups were consistently more likely to suggest diplomatic alternatives than the army officers, who tended to recommend military action. More importantly, following discussion with others in their own group category, members of each group showed polarization by becoming more extreme in their attitudes than they were initially. Hence, polarization had occurred as the group's differences became exaggerated.

Why does polarization occur? There are several reasons. One explanation is informational social influence, which we discussed in Chapter 12 in relation to conformity. You will recall that informational social influence rests on our knowledge that others may have more information about an issue than we do. Relating this to polarization, the arguments made during a group discussion tend to support the position that is generally accepted. Because each person within the group is not likely to have thought of all the previous arguments in support of his or her position, these new arguments—which are, after all, supportive of most people's initial view—are likely to reinforce their initial position. As a result, it is this new information that induces the group, as a whole, to take a more extreme position than the individuals making up the group took initially (Mongeau & Garlick, 1988; Lamm, 1988; Isenberg, 1986).

A second explanation rests on the kind of social comparison processes that we considered in Chapter 4. The social comparison view suggests that prior to group discussion, people think the view that they hold is reasonable, appropriate, and perhaps even superior to others' positions. However, when they participate in the group discussion, they may learn that others hold views that are even more extreme—and potentially more "correct"—than their own. In order to maintain their perception of the appropriateness of their own views, then, they shift to a more extreme position in order to make their views agree with, and perhaps even one-up, the positions of the others in the group (Goethals & Zanna, 1979; McGarty et al., 1992; Isenberg, 1986).

The precise explanation for group polarization remains elusive. Still, the phenomenon is real, and numerous real-life examples of extreme (and in retrospect poor) decisions probably reflect polarization. For instance, the decision behind the slow but steady escalation of fighting during the Vietnam War holds all the elements that suggest that group polarization was at work. Similarly, both opponents and supporters of abortion often slip into arguments that are increasingly extreme when they argue the issue.

**GROUPTHINK.**   If you think back to the *Challenger* disaster that we described at the beginning of the chapter, it may seem surprising that the combined minds of so many at NASA and at the space shuttle manufacturer could be so wrong in their assessment of the safety of the launch. However, the decision to launch is not all that surprising in the context of a phenomenon called groupthink (Esser & Lindoerfer, 1989; Moorhead, Ference, & Neck, 1991).

**groupthink**

a type of thinking in which group members share such strong motivation to achieve consensus that they lose the ability to critically evaluate alternative points of view.

According to social psychologist Irving Janis, **groupthink** is a type of thinking in which group members share such strong motivation to achieve consensus that they lose the ability to critically evaluate alternative points of view (Janis, 1972, 1989; t'Hart, 1991). Groupthink has several central characteristics:

- The group develops the illusion that the group is invulnerable and cannot make significant errors.
- Members of the group—individually and collectively—rationalize and discount information that is contradictory to the predominant view of the group.
- The group views other groups stereotypically, enabling it to disregard their opinions.
- Members with views contrary to those of the majority are pressured to adopt the majority view, thereby stifling minority opinions.
- Because group members feel pressure to conform, an illusion of unanimity develops, thereby reinforcing the dominant view.
- "Mindguards" emerge—group members who act to protect the group from divergent or contradictory information.

As we discuss in the accompanying Social Psychology at Work feature, many major historic decisions bear the hallmarks of groupthink. They range from Chamberlain's appeasement of Germany prior to World War II to the Nixon administration's decision to lie about the Watergate break-in.

## SOCIAL PSYCHOLOGY AT WORK

# GROUPTHINK: WHEN GROUPS GO WRONG

They were the best and the brightest. They had experience and were handpicked from among the finest in the country. If they couldn't make the right decision, who could?

When President John F. Kennedy formed a group to evaluate a CIA plan to invade Cuba, he chose people with a proven ability to make the right decision. Yet this group did just the opposite, choosing a course that led to one of the worst foreign policy fiascoes in U.S. history.

Planned and executed by Kennedy and his advisors, the abortive invasion was an immediate disaster. The plan called for a force of about 1,400 Cuban exiles to land at the Bay of Pigs in Cuba and, with the help of the general Cuban populace (who were expected to spontaneously revolt at the start of the invasion), to overthrow the Communist government.

In actuality, things went wrong from the beginning. The exile force was poorly equipped, the Cuban air force was able to mount a strong offensive, and within three days most of the invasion force had been captured by the vastly larger Cuban militia. Just about everything that could have gone wrong did go wrong. In Kennedy's own words, the question was "How could we have been so stupid?"

An answer to this question was provided by social psychologist Irving Janis. According to Janis, Kennedy and his advisors had been subject to groupthink.

Although, in retrospect, groupthink seems to explain a variety of improper decisions, critics have complained that such explanations represent 20/20 hindsight. Specifically, they suggest that the reliance on case studies of selected historical events may lead researchers to overlook aspects of the events that don't correspond to the groupthink hypothesis. Furthermore, because analyses of historical events can be made only in retrospect, no way exists of experimentally and unequivocally testing Janis's formulation.

However, a recent analysis of a series of historical events—some of which were hypothesized to show groupthink and others of which did not—indicates the basic validity of the groupthink formulation. Social psychologist Philip Tetlock and colleagues carefully and objectively examined ten

*Continued on next page*

decision-making historical episodes (Tetlock et al., 1992). In their analysis, judges were provided with a series of pairs of statements, such as "The group leader is insulated from criticism" versus "The group leader is exposed to a wide range of views and arguments." By objectively rating the extent to which such statements were characteristic of each historical episode, the researchers were able to identify objectively particular characteristics of historical events.

Tetlock and colleagues found clear support for several critical aspects of the groupthink formulation. For instance, poor group decisions were related to a lack of appropriate procedures for solving problems. However, not all factors presumed to cause groupthink were shown to be critically important. For instance, group cohesiveness was not, by itself, central to the development of symptoms of groupthink in the historical situations examined.

Given the potential for groupthink to result in defective decision making, is there a way to prevent its occurrence? According to Irving Janis, one approach is to increase the quantity and quality of information available to the group. For example, experts who represent a wide divergence of views can be included in the deliberations of the group. The group can encourage members to play the role of devil's advocate (Janis, 1982).

Furthermore, the group leader might encourage criticism and refrain from voicing an opinion early in group discussions. The group can also develop explicit procedures for presenting and dealing with divergent information. Finally, after a tentative decision has been reached, the group can hold later meetings to air any remaining doubts or to bring up new ideas. By using such techniques, groupthink may be minimized.

However, groupthink does not occur only in high-level corridors of government. For instance, business, school, and religious groups are all susceptible to the phenomenon (Leana, 1985).

**THE BOTTOM LINE ON GROUPS.**   Potential pitfalls in group decision making, such as group polarization and groupthink, might lead us to presume that decisions made in groups are generally inferior to decisions made by individuals. However, such a conclusion is too narrow and too extreme, for several reasons.

For one thing, groups collectively have greater knowledge and more information about a topic than any single individual. Moreover, groups permit a broader perspective to be brought to bear on a topic than individuals. Consequently, people may produce a greater quantity of solutions when they act in groups than when they act alone.

Groups, then, are often more effective in reaching appropriate decisions than individuals working alone. But no group is inevitably successful. Members of groups, then, must tread a cautious path in order to avoid the pitfalls that may occur when making decisions with other people.

## ▶ REVIEW & RETHINK

### Review

- In reaching decisions, groups move through a series of four stages and employ social decision schemes and social combination rules.
- Although groups typically come to more accurate solutions more quickly than individuals, they are less efficient than individuals working alone.
- Group polarization and groupthink affect the quality of decisions.

### Rethink

- What are the steps in group decision making?
- In what type of group is social loafing most likely to occur?
- Would group polarization be more or less extreme in groups characterized by a strict social decision scheme? In groups characterized by little distribution of power? Why?
- Why might group polarization based on informational social influence lead to better decisions? Why might it lead to worse decisions?
- Compare group polarization and groupthink. In what way is the latter an example of the former?

# LOOKING BACK ◁ ◁ ◁ ◁ ◁ ◁ ◁ ◁ ◁ ◁ ◁ ◁ ◁ ◁ ◁ ◁ ◁ ◁ ◁ ◁ ◁ ◁ ◁ ◁ ◁ ◁ ◁ ◁

### How can we formally define a group?

1. In order for an aggregate of people to be considered a group in a formal sense, several criteria need to be met. Specifically, a group consists of two or more people who interact with one another, perceive themselves as a group, and are interdependent.

### What are the formal characteristics of groups?

2. Group structure comprises the regular, stable patterns of behavior that occur in the groups. Among the most important elements of group structure are roles, status, norms, and cohesiveness.

3. Roles are the behaviors that are associated with and come to be expected of people in a given position. The roles people assume exert a powerful influence on their behavior. Roles differ in status—the evaluation of a role or of a person holding a role. The two major determinants of status are the magnitude of a person's contribution to the success of the group in achieving its goals, and the degree of power the person wields over others.

4. Norms are the rules that guide people's behavior in groups. Prescriptive norms suggest ways people ought to behave, while proscriptive norms inform people about behaviors they should avoid.

5. Group cohesiveness is the extent to which the members of a group find the group attractive. High group cohesiveness results in longer maintenance of membership, greater influence over members, and high self-esteem and lower anxiety among members. Cohesiveness also influences group productivity, depending on the nature of the group norms.

### How does the presence of others affect performance, for better or worse?

6. Social facilitation refers to the change in performance due to the presence of others. According to one explanation, the mere presence of others raises the general level of emotional arousal, leading to improved performance in well-learned activities but to declines in performance of poorly learned activities.

7. Other explanations for social facilitation effects suggest that the presence of others leads to evaluation apprehension—the perception that the audience is evaluating us. Alternatively, distraction-conflict theory proposes that social facilitation effects occur because the presence of others is distracting, and our attention becomes divided between the task at hand and the others who are present. This divided attention leads to conflict, which in turn leads to higher physiological arousal.

8. Social loafing represents the decrease in individual effort that occurs when people engage in shared group activity. Among the explanations for social loafing are that group participants perceive decreased effort on the part of others; that group participants choose less ambitious goals; that group participants' efforts are less closely linked to group outcomes.

9. Among the strategies to reduce social loafing are to increase group members' sense of personal responsibility; to increase feelings of individual self-efficacy; to make the group's activities more involving; to optimize trust in the other group members; and to make each member's contribution highly visible.

### What are the processes by which groups strive to solve problems and reach decisions?

10. In reaching decisions, groups generally move through a series of four stages: orientation, discussion, decision, and implementation.

11. To come to decisions, groups use social decision schemes, which are the means by which individual judgments and preferences are combined into a collective decision. Social decision schemes may be explicit or implicit, and they may vary in terms of strictness and power distribution.

12. Social combination rules are the guidelines used by members of groups to decide what needs to be done and how the task should be divided among group members. Optimum

group performance varies according to whether the task is additive, disjunctive, compensatory, or conjunctive. However, process loss, aspects of interaction patterns that hinder performance, may reduce a group's ability to solve a problem effectively.

### *What factors affect the quality of problem solving and decision making?*

13. Although groups typically arrive at more accurate solutions to problems more quickly than individuals, they do so at the expense of efficiency. Based on total number of person-hours, then, groups expend more time than individuals.

14. Brainstorming, in which group members are asked to produce as many ideas as they can without fear of criticism, is a technique intended to optimize creativity. However, research suggests that the method is not particularly effective, as production blocking may reduce the generation of ideas.

15. The composition of a group affects its problem-solving abilities. For instance, members' status influences the degree to which their solutions are accepted by other members. In addition, men and women differ in their contributions to group performance, depending on the nature of the task.

16. Group decisions are often inferior to those made by individuals. One reason is the phenomenon of group polarization—the exaggeration of a group's initial tendencies following group discussion. Group polarization is explained by informational social influence or social comparison processes.

17. Group decisions also may suffer due to groupthink. Groupthink is a type of thinking in which group members share such strong motivation to achieve consensus that they do not critically evaluate alternative points of view.

18. However, group decisions are not invariably inferior. Groups usually have greater knowledge and more information than any one member. In addition, they have a wider perspective. As a consequence, they may produce more solutions than individuals acting alone.

---

# KEY TERMS AND CONCEPTS

*group (p. 447)*

*group structure (p. 448)*

*role (p. 448)*

*status (p. 449)*

*norms (p. 450)*

*prescriptive norms (p. 450)*

*proscriptive norms (p. 450)*

*group cohesiveness (p. 451)*

*social facilitation (p. 454)*

*evaluation apprehension (p. 454)*

*distraction-conflict theory (p. 455)*

*social loafing (p. 456)*

*social decision scheme (p. 460)*

*social combination rules (p. 461)*

*process loss (p. 462)*

*brainstorming (p. 463)*

*production blocking (p. 464)*

*group polarization (p. 465)*

*risky shift (p. 466)*

*groupthink (p. 467)*

---

# FOR FURTHER RESEARCH AND STUDY

Forsyth, D. R. (1990). *Group dynamics.* Pacific Grove, CA: Brooks/Cole.

A fine introduction to groups, comprehensively covering the field.

Baron, R. S., Kerr, N. L., & Miller, N. (1992). *Group process, group decision, group action.* Pacific Grove, CA: Brooks/Cole.

Covers work on group processes, how

groups come to decisions, and how good those decisions are.

Janis, I. L. (1989). *Crucial decisions: Leadership in policy-making management.* New York: Free Press.

A readable book that represents one of the best expositions of how groups are susceptible to groupthink and other factors that affect decision making.

---

# EPILOGUE

In this chapter we've examined what social psychologists have learned about people's behavior in groups. We've looked at such aspects of groups as their structure, the kinds of behavior that occur when groups try to solve problems and make decisions, and the quality of solutions that result.

Throughout this chapter, however, the groups we've considered are fairly small. In fact, the theoretical literature on which our discussions have been based typically employs a relatively narrow range of groups, often consisting of as few as four or five—or sometimes even fewer—individuals.

In the next chapter, we turn to a different species of group—organizations and culture. Although much of the basic material we've covered applies to these larger kinds of groups, the focus and type of analysis that is applied to phenomena in these larger arenas is different. Still, the basic goals of understanding social behavior remain intact as social psychologists expand the scope of their studies.

### CHAPTER FIFTEEN

# ORGANIZATIONS, CULTURE, AND THE SOCIAL WORLD

## LIVING IN SOCIETY

# PROLOGUE: JAPAN COMES TO THE UNITED STATES

The event begins with a series of vigorous group exercises. Clothed in shorts and T-shirts, the participants begin with calisthenics, shouting the cadence in unison. The main events are a series of relay races, tug-of-war games, and similar diversions. People with high-salaried, white-collar jobs team up with blue-collar assembly-line workers. During the event, conversation often centers on such topics as *kaizens*, *muda*, and *nemawashi*.

Although this event may sound like the Japanese equivalent of a Fourth of July observance, that is hardly the case. The locale is Fremont, California, and the occasion is the annual picnic of the New United Motor Manufacturing, Inc., company, or NUMMI for short.

NUMMI is a joint venture formed by General Motors and Toyota, designed to produce Chevrolets and Toyotas. Using a plant abandoned by GM in the early 1980s, the

The Japanese style of management is remarkably different from management in Western organizations.

NUMMI factory is more efficient than almost any other auto-making facility in the United States.

NUMMI's success did not emerge by accident, but due to a conscious decision to adopt a Japanese organizational model. One of the first moves was to discard such perks as reserved parking spaces and a separate dining room for executives. Instead, the distinctions between management and workers were minimized.

NUMMI invested in extensive retraining for the employees, sending hundreds to Japan for specialized instruction. Employees became team members who *nemawashi* (discussed) how to eliminate *muda* (waste) and make continual *kaizens* (improvements). Teams of six to eight members periodically exchange jobs, in contrast to the traditional American model in which the same individual always performs the identical job on an assembly line.

At the same time, though, the cultural infusion from Japan has not been a one-way street. Japanese workers transferred to work in the California plant have also learned a few things. They have discovered, for instance, that workers need not be rigidly devoted to their jobs, and they have loosened up to the point where they will now take a coffee break during the day.

The overall result? According to one observer, "the Americans are working better, and the Japanese are enjoying life more." (Michaels, 1988, p. 14)

---

# LOOKING AHEAD

▶ ▶ ▶ ▶ ▶ ▶ ▶ ▶ ▶ ▶ ▶ ▶ ▶ ▶ ▶ ▶ ▶ ▶ ▶ ▶ ▶ ▶ ▶ ▶ ▶ ▶ ▶ ▶ ▶

The partnership between the U.S. and Japanese cultures that the NUMMI plant represents is just one manifestation of how our globe is continually shrinking. The customs and traditions of different societies increasingly encounter—and sometimes collide with—-one another. Even within the United States, the number and proportion of people representing minorities are increasing at a rapid pace. How people from diverse cultures learn to live and interact with one another represents one of the major challenges of our time.

In this chapter, we move beyond the discussion of groups that we started in the previous chapter to an examination of organizations and culture. We first consider how organizations operate, focusing on business and industrial organizations, since they represent the major area examined by social psychologists specializing in organizations. We then move to an even broader level of analysis—culture—considering the consequences of culture on social behavior.

Specifically, the chapter begins with a discussion of different models of organizations. We will examine how organizations develop their own cultures and how they initiate and socialize newcomers. We also discuss how communications travel through organizations and how the communication system affects productivity and member satisfaction.

Next, we turn to culture. We examine one of the major organizing principles of a culture, the degree of individualism that prevails, and note how it relates to several fundamental social psychological phenomena. We also consider the ways in which interpersonal relationships and competition and aggression differ from one culture to another. Finally, we consider ways suggested by social psychologists for promoting world peace.

In sum, after reading this chapter, you'll be able to answer these questions:

- What models explain the basic structure of organizations?
- How do organizations maintain particular cultures and teach them to the organization's newcomers?
- How is information communicated in organizations?
- What is culture, and does it affect basic social psychological processes?
- What impact does a society's level of individualism and collectivism have on social behavior?
- To what extent are high levels of competitiveness and aggression uniquely American?
- What methods have social psychologists developed to promote world peace?

# ORGANIZATIONS: GROUPS AT WORK

Consider these rules for workers in a Chicago department store in the early 1900s:

1. Store must be open from 6 A.M. to 9 P.M.

2. Store must be swept; counters and base shelves dusted; lamps trimmed, filled, and chimneys cleaned; a pail of water, also a bucket of coal brought in before breakfast; and attend to customers who will call.

3. Store must not be open on the Sabbath day unless necessary and then only for a few minutes.

4. The employee who is in the habit of smoking Spanish cigars, being shaved at the barber shop, and going to dances and other places of amusement will surely give his employer reason to be suspicious of honesty and integrity.

5. Each employee must not pay less than $5 per year to the church and must attend Sunday school regularly.

6. Men employees are given one evening a week for courting and two if they go to prayer meeting.

7. After 14 hours of work in the store, the leisure time should be spent mostly in reading. (Cited in Mitchell, 1982)

If these rules strike you as hopelessly dated and outmoded, consider the plight of workers employed today at a major insurance company. Except for two 15-minute breaks and a lunch hour, workers are tied to computer terminals, processing health claims. Their every keystroke is monitored by both human and electronic supervisors, who tally how rapidly they perform their duties.

Employees never know how big their paychecks will be until they receive their pay envelope at the end of each week. Wages are based on a formula so complicated that it is impossible for employees to keep track of how successful they are. In fact, paychecks may vary by hundreds of dollars from one week to the next (*New York Times*, 1984).

*How Organizations Operate: The Rules of the Game*

Obviously, not all business **organizations** (groups of people working together to attain common goals) operate with such unpleasant working conditions. In fact, there are wide variations in the underlying philosophies of organizations, which are reflected in particu-

Although the specific tasks carried out by auto workers on this early assembly line are very different from those of a modern pool of computer operators, the underlying management styles may not be dissimilar.

**organization**
a group of people working together to attain common goals.

**bureaucratic model (of organizations)**
the organizational model that attempts to achieve success in the workplace organization by applying rationality and efficiency to the functioning of the organization.

lar organizational models. Four basic models exist: bureaucratic models, human relations models, contingency models, and Japanese models (Taylor, 1984).

**BUREAUCRATIC MODELS.**    Both the department store and the insurance company follow what is known as the bureaucratic model of workplace organizations. The **bureaucratic model** represents the attempt to apply rationality and efficiency to the functioning of organizations (Weber, 1952).

According to the bureaucratic model, the ideal organization has explicit rules, regulations, and procedures for every task. There is a rigid division of labor, in which people have well-defined jobs and employees perform the same task repeatedly in order to promote maximum efficiency (Baron & Bielby, 1986).

According to the bureaucratic model, decision making should be centralized and decisions should be passed down along a well-established chain of command. Most typically, communication is rigidly controlled, and messages are communicated only to the position above and below one's own. Are bureaucratic models effective? Anyone who has stood in line at a university financial aid office to pick up a form or who has waited for an hour at a state motor vehicle registry for a license renewal knows the answer. Despite the best of intentions, organizations run on a bureaucratic model are often unproductive, ineffective, and inefficient. As centralization and the number of rules and regulations increase, employees feel alienated from the organization. Worker attitudes contrary to formal management policy often take hold, leading to inefficiency and organizational dysfunction. Because of the emphasis on rules, workers also become quite rigid, a situation that leads to difficulties in solving problems (Mars, 1981; Rojas & Gil, 1989; Magalhaes, 1984).

**human relations model (of organizations)**
the organizational model that emphasizes the social interactions and the psychological state of members of the organization.

**HUMAN RELATIONS MODELS.**    The difficulties with the bureaucratic model led to the development of an alternative framework to shape the workings of organizations: the human relations model. **Human relations models** emphasize the social psychological nature of organizations. Rather than focusing on the structure of an organization, as the bureaucratic model does, the human relations model emphasizes the social context of the organization. In focusing on the social interactions and the psychological state of members of an organization, the human relations model assumes that a pleasant psychological environment will lead to greater organizational success. A happy worker, in this view, is a more productive worker (Taylor, 1984; Macher, 1986).

However, as we noted in Chapter 14, happy workers are not necessarily more productive workers. Organizations with highly cohesive work groups may have higher pro-

Do happy workers equal more productive workers? Although the human relations model suggests that the answer is yes, this is not always the case.

ductivity only if the informal norms support higher production—which often is not the case. Furthermore, human relations models of organizations sometimes have focused so heavily on the nature and quality of social interaction that the ultimate goal of the organization—to accomplish some task—is forgotten in the effort to create a pleasant, psychologically supportive environment (Rastogi, 1987).

**CONTINGENCY MODELS.**    A more recent approach to organizations is to consider them in the context of a system. Instead of focusing on organizational structure (as in the bureaucratic model) or on the network of social relations (as in the human relations model), **contingency models** of organizations focus on how specific features of an organization's environment affect the operation (Tosi, 1991; Tayeb, 1987; Tosi & Slocum, 1984).

**contingency model (of organizations)**
the model that focuses on how specific features of an organization's environment affect its operations

Contingency models emphasize the means by which organizational change can be accomplished in the face of shifting conditions. Customers may change their preferences, new legislation may be passed, or some dramatic, well-publicized event, such as the bombing of the World Trade Center in New York City, may occur, modifying the environment in which an organization operates. In order to adapt to such modifications, the organization must be ready to change and develop. Organizations using contingency models are apt to emphasize problem-solving and analytic skills.

Although the contingency model provides a useful approach to understanding the functioning of organizations, it does not provide the full story. For instance, the model stresses the need for organizations to respond to changing environmental conditions, but does not identify particular ways in which this can be accomplished. Specifically, the contingency model suggests that there is no single way to structure an organization. Although this suggestion is undoubtedly true, it sidesteps the issue of what course of action one should take in designing the optimal organizational structure.

**JAPANESE MODELS.**    An approach to organizations that has attracted much recent attention are Japanese models of organizations. **Japanese models** emphasize decision making by group consensus, shared responsibility, and concern for employee welfare, both on and off the job.

**Japanese model (of organizations)**
the organizational model that emphasizes decision making by group consensus, shared responsibility, and concern for employee welfare.

One typical feature of Japanese models is the regular use of **quality circles**—small groups that meet frequently to solve problems and ensure excellence. The groups contain

**quality circles**
a method originated in Japan in which small groups within a workplace organization meet regularly to solve problems and ensure excellence.

members from many levels within the organization. By using participative methods of decision making and problem solving, in which unanimity and consensus are sought, workers can gain a sense of responsibility for their work. Production appears to be of higher quality as a result of participation in such circles (Ouchi, 1981; Cotton, 1993).

On the other hand, the Japanese approach has been criticized because its emphasis on teamwork may stifle individual creativity. Furthermore, the pledge of lifetime employment, which has been a traditional practice of major Japanese business organizations, may lead to lower levels of motivation. Researchers have even collected survey data indicating that Japanese supervisors had lower satisfaction with their jobs and reported more stress than supervisors in the U.S. (DeFrank et al., 1985). Consequently, most organizational experts now suggest that a combination of Japanese and Western management systems may be most effective—as we discuss in the accompanying Social Psychology at Work feature.

---

## SOCIAL PSYCHOLOGY AT WORK

# WHERE EAST MEETS WEST: BLENDING JAPANESE AND U.S. APPROACHES TO ORGANIZATIONS

They are inflexible. Their bosses are autocratic. They are highly centralized and rigid.

If this sounds to you like the prototype for organizations that fit the bureaucratic model, you're technically right. And given the drawbacks of the bureaucratic model, it might be reasonable to assume that such organizations are anything but successful. In point of fact, however, these are characteristics of some of the most successful organizations in the world—Japanese business organizations.

For many years, the success of Japanese business has been the envy of much of the world. It turns out that this achievement may be traced to several characteristics. Among the most important features:

- Japanese businesses guarantee that individuals they hire will be in the organization for life. Although not a universal feature of employment in Japanese industry, and not one that is made available to women, the guarantee of a lifetime job for their employees is standard procedure for many Japanese companies. Because of this no-layoff policy, people are willing to start in entry-level positions, assured that they will slowly work their way up through the organization. They are also not fearful of technological innovations that might otherwise be seen as a threat to their jobs.

- Reward and responsibility are shared collectively. If the organization does well, everyone is rewarded. Conversely, if the company shows poor results, all members of the organization share in the blame.

- The principle of *kaizen,* the constant search for improvement, underlies organizational activities. The norm of *kaizen* permeates Japanese business organizations, not only in terms of improvements in products, but for employees who are con-

stantly striving to improve themselves (Rehder & Smith, 1986; Wood, 1990).

Although the Japanese organizational model has sometimes been touted as an antidote for all that is wrong with American business organizations, it is not clear that the model represents a solution to organizational difficulties in the United States. For instance, U.S. business organizations are hesitant to make lifetime guarantees of employment. Furthermore, one result of a lifetime employment policy is that there is little opportunity to change jobs once hired, given the stability of an organization's work force. Even if someone is shifted to a new job, he or she typically must start at an entry-level position (and salary) all over again. Consequently, there is little eagerness to change organizations. In sum, there are significant drawbacks to the Japanese organizational model.

Clearly, neither the Japanese nor Western models of organizations represent the single best approach to organizations. In fact, according to organizational expert William Ouchi, the optimum perspective may be a combination of the two (Ouchi, 1981). In what he designates as "Theory Z," Ouchi suggests that the most effective organizations have some of the following characteristics, which represent a combination of Japanese and Western approaches:

- The promise of employment is fairly long term, but not for a lifetime.

- Promotions are made at a slower rate than in the United States, but more quickly than the very slow pattern typical in Japan.

- Decision making is carried out using participation and consensus. Decisions are not made entirely by a single individual,

*Continued on next page*

as is often the case in the U.S., nor are they made solely in groups.

- Concern over employee welfare extends to aspects beyond the job, but does not extend to every aspect of life. In contrast, U.S. approaches largely ignore workers' lives outside the office, while Japanese approaches typically encompass all parts of workers' lives, both in and out of the organization.

By combining the Japanese and Western approaches to organizations, businesses may discover the best of both worlds. In fact, there is some evidence that Japanese organizations may be becoming more like those in the U.S., and those in the U.S. may be adapting various aspects of the Japanese system (Luthans, 1989).

Although the broader culture in which an organization is situated clearly has an effect on its operation, organizations also develop a culture of their own. We turn now to a consideration of how organizations vary in their organizational culture.

## The Culture of Organizations

*A visitor to the Aetna Insurance Company is immediately struck by the neat, orderly cubicles filled with desks, inhabited by neatly dressed people in suits, jackets, and ties. The desks are of a uniform size, and in fact a corporate manual provides strict rules as to the size of the desk in relationship to the position held by the desk's occupant. With a promotion comes an increase in desk size.*

*A tour of Microsoft Corporation, producer of the fabulously successful Windows computer software, yields a very different impression. Coats and ties are rarely seen. You might encounter a group of programmers in bathing suits, playing volleyball. If you listen to the interchanges around you, you might think that you've stumbled onto a set for* Star Trek. *For instance, you are likely to hear such conversational snippets as "He's very high bandwidth," "Your idea has no granularity," "She's hardcore about spreadsheets," and "He went nonlinear on me." (Rebellow, 1992, p. 63)*

**organizational culture**
the dominant pattern of basic assumptions, perceptions, thoughts, feelings, and attitudes held by members of an organization.

The differences between the two companies are not just superficial, but reflect deep differences in organizational culture. **Organizational culture** is the dominant pattern of basic assumptions, perceptions, thoughts, feelings, and attitudes held by members of an organization (Schein, 1990). For instance, organizational psychologist Fred Luthans (1989) gives the example of the U.S. Marine Corps, which strives to teach new recruits the "Marine way." Recruits are taught to think and act as Marines, as they are led to change previous ways of behaving. In a sense, the Marine Corps attempts to modify the very identity of new recruits, indoctrinating an entirely new set of values that reflect the Corps.

Other organizations have their own cultures, although typically they are not as aggressive as the Marines in teaching them to newcomers. Among the most important features of corporate culture are the following (Luthans, 1989):

- *Regularities in behavior.* When people in a particular organization get together, they engage in common rituals and use a similar kind of language and terminology.
- *Norms.* As we discussed in Chapter 14, groups within organizations have standards that guide behavior. These norms permeate group life. For instance, some organizations have informal norms regarding when people take coffee breaks, what they eat for lunch, and where they hang out together after work.
- *Shared values and philosophy.* Members of an organization are expected to share a set of core values and philosophy. It might be something as crass as "Make a profit," or it might be more uplifting, such as "Improve the quality of life for the most people."
- *Organizational climate.* Different organizations have very different climates. The climate is the overall impression one receives upon entering the organization. It is based on physical layout, what the members are wearing, how they speak to one another, and how people interact with outsiders.

Organizational cultures differ significantly from one organization to another. Such cultural standards may affect every aspect of the organization, even encompassing where people eat lunch.

Although all organizations have cultures, they vary widely in how pervasive they are. In some companies, for example, the culture is strong and uniform. Almost all members share the organization's values, and the culture has a major impact on the day-to-day activities of the members. In other cultures, in contrast, the organizational culture is relatively weak, and it has little effect on the operation of the organization.

Furthermore, regardless of whether there is a strong or weak culture, organizations can also harbor subcultures. **Organizational subcultures** are the shared set of assumptions, perceptions, thoughts, feelings, and attitudes that are held by a relatively small minority of members of an organization and that differ from the dominant organizational culture.

**organizational subculture**
the shared set of assumptions, perceptions, thoughts, feelings, and attitudes that are held by a relatively small minority of members of an organization and that differ from the dominant organizational culture.

Subcultures may develop when a group of workers experience particular difficulties, and they often occur within smaller units of a larger organization. For example, in some companies the computer software development group may have norms and values that are very different from those of the larger corporation. This difference may lead to animosity between those subscribing to the dominant culture and those following the subculture.

The specific nature of an organization's culture varies widely from one organization to another. For example, some researchers have suggested that business organizations in the United States fall into one of the broad categories presented in Figure 15-1. Obviously, though, other characterizations of corporate culture are possible.

A company's organizational culture is connected to the larger cultural context of a given society (Tayeb, 1987). For example, comparisons of French and American supervisors show major differences in employee behaviors—which behaviors are considered appropriate cause for concern, and which permit intervention (Inzerilli, 1980). Specifically, French supervisors are less likely than American supervisors to be concerned about the type of clothing an employee wears to work, how much alcohol an employee drinks at lunch, and whether an employee is faithful to his or her spouse. Such differences are likely to reflect broader cultural differences in attitudes.

Whatever the specific nature of an organization's culture, people do not automatically adopt the culture upon joining. As we consider next, there is an initiation period during which newcomers are taught, either explicitly or implicitly, the organizational culture.

*Organizational*
*Socialization*

*It's been a curious month. After being hired for what you thought was the job of*
*your dreams at General Construction, you've spent the first month learning the*
*realities of organization life. Although you knew before you started that working in*
*a large organization would involve dealing with a well-established system, you*
*never expected it would be so different from college. After all, you mastered the col-*

*Continued on next page*

**FIGURE 15-1** Organizational Culture Profiles

| | Tough-Guy, Macho | Work Hard/Play Hard | Bet Your Company | Process |
|---|---|---|---|---|
| *Name of the culture* | | | | |
| *Type of risks that are assumed* | High | Low | High | Low |
| *Type of feedback from decisions* | Fast | Fast | Slow | Slow |
| *Typical kinds of organizations that use this culture* | Construction, cosmetics, television, radio, venture capitalism, management consulting | Real estate, computer firms, auto distributors, door-to-door sales operations, retail stores, mass consumer sales | Oil, aerospace, capital goods manufacturers, architectural firms, investment banks, mining and smelting firms, military | Banks, insurance companies, utilities, pharmaceuticals, financial-service organizations, many agencies of the government |
| *The ways survivors and/or heroes in this culture behave* | They have a tough attitude. They are individualistic. They can tolerate all-or-nothing risks. They are superstitious. | They are super salespeople. They often are friendly, hail-fellow-well-met types. They use a team approach to problem solving. They are nonsuperstitious. | They can endure long-term ambiguity. They always double-check their decisions. They are technically competent. They have a strong respect for authority. | They are very cautious and protective of their own flank. They are orderly and punctual. They are good at attending to detail. They always follow established procedures. |
| *Strengths of the personnel/culture* | They can get things done in short order. | They are able to quickly produce a high volume of work. | They can generate high-quality inventions and major scientific breakthroughs. | They bring order and system to the workplace. |
| *Weaknesses of the personnel/culture* | They do not learn from past mistakes. Everything tends to be short-term in orientation. The virtues of cooperation are ignored. | They look for quick-fix solutions. They have a short-term time perspective. They are more committed to action than to problem solving. | They are extremely slow in getting things done. Their organizations are vulnerable to short-term economic fluctuations. Their organizations often face cash-flow problems. | There is lots of red tape. Initiative is downplayed. They face long hours and boring work. |
| *Habits of the survivors and/or heroes* | They dress in fashion. They live in "in" places. They like one-on-one sports such as tennis. They enjoy scoring points off one another in verbal interaction. | They avoid extremes in dress. They live in tract houses. They prefer team sports such as touch football. They like to drink together. | They dress according to their organizational rank. Their housing matches their hierarchical position. They like sports such as golf, in which the outcome is unclear until the end of the game. The older members serve as mentors for the younger ones. | They dress according to hierarchical rank. They live in apartments or no-frills homes. They enjoy process sports like jogging and swimming. They like discussing memos. |

Source: Adapted from T. E. Deal and A. A. Kennedy, Corporate Cultures: The Rites and Rituals of Corporate Life. © 1982, Addison-Wesley, Reading, MA. Excerpts from Chap. 6. Used with permission.

*lege bureaucracy, and by the time you were a senior you understood the system enough so that you could get done just about anything you wanted.   But General Construction is different. To accomplish the most ordinary task, you've spent a goodly amount of time filling out forms, and as for doing anything innovative, well, forget it. Your fellow employees and even your supervisor discourage you from making waves. All your confidence in your new ideas, and your faith that you would be able to bring about innovative change, are just about gone—and you've only been working at the job for a month. How did your attitudes change so quickly?*

It doesn't take long for employees at both large and small organizations to "learn the ropes." In addition to a formal orientation that occurs in most organizations, the informal communication of appropriate conduct is also accomplished early on in a job.

**organizational socialization**
the process by which an individual comes to behave like and hold attitudes similar to those of others in an organization.

**Organizational socialization** is the process by which an individual comes to behave like and hold attitudes similar to those of others in an organization. In an organizational context, the concept of socialization, first used to explain how children learn customary and acceptable behaviors in a particular culture, considers how people "learn the ropes" in group settings. It relates both to the formal indoctrination and training people receive, and to the informal communication of norms from older members of the organization.

Formal socialization and informal socialization do not always convey the same messages about the operation of the organization. While formal socialization may convey management's ideal view of how employees should behave, with the goal of maximizing profit and minimizing expenses, informal socialization may provide a contradictory message. For example, a company's formal rules may state that long-distance personal phone calls may not be billed to the company. Informally, an employee may learn from a coworker that phone bills are never checked and that long-distance calls may be made without fear of being discovered. In fact, the employee may learn that most employees regard free telephone calls as a perk of the job—a very contradictory message from that provided by the formal management socialization.

Socialization in organizations, as well as in groups in general, proceeds through a series of stages. Illustrated in Figure 15-2, they include the investigation, socialization, maintenance, resocialization, and remembrance stages (Moreland & Levine, 1982, 1988).

- *Investigation stage.* Before you formally commit yourself to membership in a group or organization, you would likely try to find out as much as you could about it. Social psycholo-

Organizational rituals, such as retirement parties, do more than recognize the guest of honor. They also help newer members to socialize.

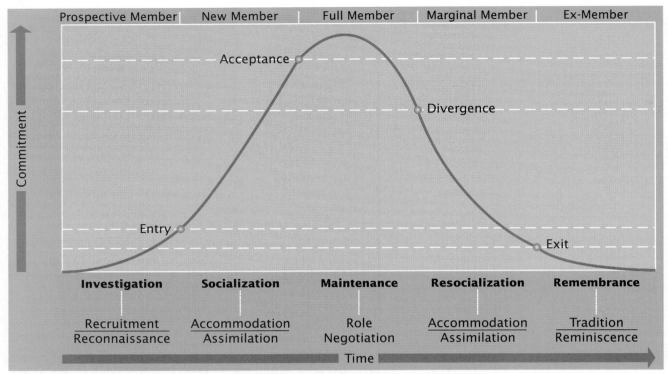

**FIGURE 15-2 A Model of Group Socialization** As time goes by, socialization in a group changes in a regular pattern. *(Source:* Moreland & Levine, 1982.*)*

gists Richard Moreland and John Levine dub this procedure *reconnaissance*, in which people attempt to compare the benefits and costs of membership. At the same time, the organization engages in *recruitment*, gauging the contributions a potential new member might make. If the individual and the organization agree that membership is appropriate, *entry* takes place.

- *Socialization stage.* Following actual entry, a newcomer enters the formal stage of socialization. During this period, the group or organization attempts to indoctrinate the newcomer into existing norms and attitudes, while the newcomer tries to shed incompatible norms and attitudes. This process is not always a one-way street, in which newcomers are forced to modify their views and the organization remains unaltered. Instead, change occurs in a reciprocal context. The organization may be forced to make accommodations to newcomers, particularly when the newcomers enter the organization at higher levels of authority. At the same time, newcomers must formulate changes in their own point of view and position.

  At the point when the socialization phase is complete, there comes a transition point known as *acceptance*. Acceptance marks the time when a newcomer is confirmed and endorsed as a full member of the group or organization. In many cases, acceptance occurs fairly rapidly, while in some cases it never fully occurs. In such a case, both the newcomer and the organization are likely to find the situation objectionable, and the new member leaves the organization.

- *Maintenance stage.* Even after someone becomes a full-fledged member of an organization, socialization is not complete. In fact, socialization forces may become even stronger, as long-time veterans of the organization seek to make new members adhere to the existing norms. However, socialization pressures are also placed on veterans. In addition to adjusting to the presence of new members, they may also face changes in organizational goals or changes in their own standing within the group. For instance, veterans may find themselves under the authority of a new boss, who may seek to modify procedures that have been in place for many years.

The maintenance stage can last indefinitely, although eventually everyone reaches a point at which they leave the organization. Employees retire, and members of student organizations graduate.

In some cases, though, maintenance does not proceed smoothly. Organizational changes may become too extreme for a member to accept and tolerate, or a member's interests, goals, and aspirations may change, making membership less attractive. In other cases, the organization becomes dissatisfied with a member's performance or contribution. When such situations occur, another transition point is reached, known as *divergence*, which leads into the next stage, resocialization.

- *Resocialization stage.* If the member or the group (or both) becomes sufficiently dissatisfied with the situation, the resocialization stage begins. In resocialization, the organization attempts to change dissatisfied members in ways that might help them become more accepting of the group as it currently stands. At the same time, members may try to produce changes that will make the group more acceptable.

  There are two ways resocialization can end. First, resocialization may be successful in increasing a person's commitment to the group (and vice versa), and people may once again be seen as full members of the organization. In such a case, they move back into the earlier stage of maintenance.

  The second way the resocialization stage can end is more negative—people terminate their involvement in the group. This point is known as the *exit point*. If the situation does reach this point, people move into the final stage in the process: remembrance.

- *Remembrance stage.* In the final remembrance stage, both the individual who has left the organization and the remaining members reassess the person's contributions to the organization. Members *reminisce* about their term in the organization, considering how well the group fulfilled their personal needs. Sometimes these reminiscences tend to rewrite history. For instance, attendees at retirement dinners are sometimes astounded to hear about the important contributions made by a former coworker who in reality made only marginal contributions to the group.

**mentor**
an informal instructor who acts as a socialization guide for a newcomer.

---

# THE INFORMED CONSUMER OF SOCIAL PSYCHOLOGY

# SOCIALIZING YOURSELF: EASING YOUR PATH INTO A NEW ORGANIZATION

For some people, socialization into a new group proceeds relatively smoothly, while for others, it is a rocky, and sometimes ultimately impossible, road. How can you make your own socialization into an organization more effective?

In their discussion of strategies used by groups that produce successful socialization, social psychologists Richard Moreland and John Levine (1989) raise several issues relevant to how newcomers to groups can foster their own socialization:

- *Choose the right organization in the first place.* Not everyone belongs in every group or organization. A free-spirited, independent individual might do best in a company with loose regulations, and stumble in an organization with a rigid, hierarchical organization.

- *Take advantage of initiation opportunities.* In some cases, initiations may be informal, as when organization veterans are especially solicitous of new members. In other instances, initiations can be formal and elaborate. For example, new employees of a large bank in Japan go through a set of rigorous activities. During their first three months, they have to meditate and fast at a Zen monastery, carry out basic training exercises at a military base, participate in community service activities, take a 25-mile hike, and vacation together at a Spartan resort (Rohlen, 1973). Whether informal or formal, initiations serve an important purpose, and newcomers should take advantage of every opportunity to participate.

- *Identify a mentor.* Organizational **mentors** are informal instructors who can act as socialization guides for newcomers. Mentors can describe the unwritten, informal norms of an organization and teach newcomers to avoid possible pitfalls. They can also help newcomers by persuading veterans in groups to be more accepting and helpful to the newcomer.

Although these techniques will not guarantee that newcomers in groups and organizations will fit in smoothly, they do optimize their chances of success.

*Organizational Communication: Working Through Channels*

If you have a gripe with the company you work for, to whom should you communicate your concern?

In many organizations, your complaint must be channeled to one person, and one person only—your immediate supervisor. In such a situation, organizational rules will not permit you to mention your difficulty to the company president, even if you see her eating lunch every day in the employee cafeteria. On the other hand, other organizations provide employees with the opportunity to contact the company executives directly. For instance, the chief executive officer of IBM routinely receives electronic mail messages from employees at every level of the company.

How members of an organization can "work through channels" represents a central feature of organizations. Almost all organizations are structured so that communications follow a specific pattern or arrangement. Furthermore, the nature of such patterns can have a direct bearing on the efficiency and satisfaction of the members of the organization.

One of the most critical features bearing on communication is a position's degree of centralization. **Centralization** reflects the degree to which people occupying a position can communicate with others. With greater centralization, certain individuals have greater opportunities to communicate with multiple individuals, but others have relatively little opportunity. In a more decentralized organization, however, all members of an organization have a relatively similar opportunity to communicate with others. In a decentralized organization, then, no single individual holds the advantage when it comes to the ability to communicate with others.

In highly centralized organizations, people with the most opportunities and freedom to communicate have a distinct advantage. For instance, they are most likely to take leadership roles and to be seen as leaders. They are also more likely to be satisfied than those who have only limited opportunities to communicate with others (Leavitt, 1951; Shaw, 1981).

Why do people in centralized positions have such an advantage? One reason is that, as the old saying goes, "Knowledge is power." A person occupying a central position knows more about what is happening in the organization, and this knowledge, in turn, may permit such an individual to more effectively solve problems than a person with less information.

People who occupy central positions in highly centralized groups tend to be relatively satisfied, but peripheral members tend to show less satisfaction. As a consequence, if we consider the group as a whole, the overall level of satisfaction of highly centralized groups tends to be lower than in more decentralized ones (Krackhardt & Porter, 1986).

But the advantages of being in central positions do not extend to every domain. People in central positions may experience **information saturation**—an overload of communications from the other group members. When saturation occurs, people in centralized positions receive and produce so many messages that they are unable to perform their jobs effectively or efficiently.

Because saturation is most apt to occur when the tasks the organization is attempting to accomplish are complex, centralized communication patterns may be inappropriate for intricate, difficult, and complicated tasks. For these circumstances, decentralized communication patterns may be more effective. In contrast, centralized patterns seem to work best for more straightforward, simple, and routine jobs.

**centralization (of communication network)**
the degree to which people occupying a position in an organization can communicate with others in the organization.

**information saturation**
a situation in an organization in which people in central positions experience an overload of communication from other group members.

## ► REVIEW & RETHINK

### Review

- Organizations are groups of people working together to attain common goals.
- The four basic models of organizations are the bureaucratic, human relations, contingency, and Japanese.

- Organizations have characteristic cultures, socialization practices, and communication patterns.

*Rethink*

- Compare the Japanese model of organization with the three Western models. Given the success of the Japanese economy, why don't more Western companies import the Japanese model?
- How does organizational "culture" differ from organizational "climate"? What does the "strength" of the culture within an organization refer to?
- Explain the difference between formal and informal organizational socialization. When these types of sources provide contradictory messages, which is more likely to prevail?
- Describe the concepts of "acceptance" and "divergence" within the process of organizational socialization. What is "resocialization"?
- According to cognitive dissonance theory, what type of initiation would produce the most loyal employees?
- According to contemporary organizational communications theories, what level of centralization would be most effective in running the executive branch of a government? Does the United States use such a level of centralization?

# CULTURE: SOCIAL PSYCHOLOGY AND SOCIETY

- *When eating at the home of an acquaintance in India, you would be well-advised to leave something on your plate and avoid finishing everything. Leaving some food on the plate establishes the generosity of the host, who has provided so much food that the guest becomes full and is unable to eat another bite. In contrast, to finish everything on the plate implies that the host has not provided enough food and that the visitor still may be hungry.*
- *When visiting a marketplace in many parts of Asia, you may find no prices posted. The price a merchant gives may be highly inflated. The visitor is expected to bargain with the merchant and haggle to lower the price. Accepting the initial price would be seen as foolish.*
- *When holding a conversation in some Middle Eastern countries, try to stand close enough so that you can feel the other's breath as you speak—a signal of concern and respect.*

It is obvious that people living in different parts of the world go about their daily lives employing standards and norms that vary in important ways from one another. While people in Western cultures expect that they should finish everything on their plates, that merchandise will have a fixed price (except in car dealerships), and that they should avoid standing so close to others that they feel (and smell) their breath, individuals raised in other cultures feel quite differently.

Were these differences in behavior merely indicative that various cultures have different rules of etiquette, they would not matter very much. However, such variations in daily behavior represent even more fundamental, and important, differences that exist between people of different cultures.

**culture**
the learned behaviors, beliefs, and attitudes that are characteristic of an individual society or population.

**Culture** comprises the learned behaviors, beliefs, and attitudes that are characteristic of an individual society or population. However, it also encompasses the products that people create, such as architecture, music, art, and literature. In sum, culture is created and shaped by people, while at the same time it shapes people's behavior (Moghaddam, Taylor, & Wright, 1993).

Traditionally, social psychology has paid relatively little attention to cultural factors. There are several reasons for this, but the primary one is that social psychologists have sought to identify universal principles, principles that apply across various situations, contexts, and cultures. In taking such a stance, they have suggested that there are broad laws of social behavior that explain all human relationships, just as neurons and the nervous system operate in the same basic way in all humans, regardless of cultural background.

Although a worthy goal, the identification of such broad principles of social behavior has not yet been fully accomplished. Indeed, some social psychologists have argued that the research findings amassed after nearly a century of investigation represent only a snapshot of social behavior in a given historical era and place, rather than illustrating broader principles that are unbound by time or place (Gergen, 1982; Pepitone, 1987; Jahoda, 1986). They argue that research conducted largely on white, middle-class, college-age students may have little relevance for an understanding of the kinds of social behavior that takes place, say, in the plains of Africa or on the crowded streets of China.

Although we can't know for certain how valid such criticisms are, it is clear that as a field, social psychology has begun to place an increasing emphasis on understanding the impact of culture on social behavior. We can consider the influence of culture in several domains.

## Individualism Versus Collectivism: Does the Individual or the Group Prevail?

Are you often influenced by the moods of your neighbors? Do you think people should take their parents' advice in determining their career plans? Would you help a colleague at work if he or she needed money to pay utility bills?

If you answer yes to questions such as these, you may hold a view of the world that is dissimilar from that of most people in the dominant North American culture. Each of these questions, drawn from a questionnaire devised by social psychologist C. Harry Hui, suggests a particular value orientation that is characteristic of many Asian and other non-Western cultures. (More items from the questionnaire are found in Figure 15-3.)

The differing value orientations are known as individualism versus collectivism. Societies supporting **individualism** hold that the personal identity, uniqueness, freedom, and worth of the individual person are central. People in individualistic societies emphasize that their own goals should hold greater weight than those of the groups to which they belong.

In contrast, many cultures support **collectivism**, the notion that the well-being of the group is more important than that of the individual. People in collectivistic cultures emphasize the welfare of the groups to which they belong, sometimes at the expense of their own personal well-being.

Whether a society predominantly supports individualism or collectivism is related to a wide variety of social behaviors. For example, societies with individualistic value systems tend to have strong economic and industrial development. In contrast, industrialization is relatively weaker in more collectivistic societies, such as India (Hofstede, 1980).

Whether a culture is predominantly collectivistic or individualistic influences the kinds of attributions of both one's own and others' behavior. For instance, research comparing attributions made by people living in Japan (a more collectivistic culture) with those made by people living in the more individualistic North American culture have shown pervasive attributional differences.

Specifically, as we first noted in Chapter 2, American students are more likely to attribute their performance to stable, internal causes (such as their native level of intelligence), while Japanese students are more apt to see temporary, situational factors (such as effort or a lack of it) as responsible for their performance. The Japanese view stems in part from Confucian writings about the importance of hard work in realization of one's goals. Japan's collectivistic orientation minimizes individual differences in ability and accentuates the role of hard work and perseverance.

**individualism**
the belief in the worth of personal identity, uniqueness, and freedom.

**collectivism**
the belief that the group's well-being is more important than that of the individual.

---

**FIGURE 15-3    Assessing Individualism and Collectivism**

Agreement with the following items, adapted from a scale devised by C. Harry Hui (1988), suggests whether a person has an individualistic or collectivistic orientation.

### Spouse-related

*Collectivistic orientation:* If I am married, the decision of where to work should be jointly made with my spouse.

*Individualistic orientation:* If I am interested in a job that my spouse is not very enthusiastic about, I should apply for it anyway.

### Parent-related

*Collectivistic orientation:* It is reasonable for me to continue my father's business.

*Individualistic orientation:* I would not share my ideas and newly acquired knowledge with my parents.

### Kin-related

*Collectivistic orientation:* If a relative told me that he/she is in financial difficulty, I would help, within my means.

*Individualistic orientation:* Each family has its own problems unique to itself. It does not help to tell relatives about your problems.

### Neighbor-related

*Collectivistic orientation:* I enjoy meeting and talking to my neighbors every day.

*Individualistic orientation:* I have never chatted with my neighbors about the political future of this state.

### Friend-related

*Collectivistic orientation:* I like to live close to my good friends.

*Individualistic orientation:* I would pay absolutely no attention to my close friends' views when deciding what kind of work to do.

### Coworker-related

*Collectivistic orientation:* Classmates' assistance is indispensable to getting a good grade at school.

*Individualistic orientation:* I have never loaned my camera/coat to any colleagues/classmates.

---

In contrast, Americans are more likely to emphasize the importance of innate intelligence in making causal attributions for school performance. If a student does not do well, he or she is seen as lacking the intellectual abilities that would lead to good performance (Holloway, 1988; Holloway et al., 1986).

For example, one cross-cultural study examined attributions of mothers of fifth-grade children in Japan and the United States. The subjects were asked to apportion responsibility for poor performance in mathematics to each of several different potential causes, such as lack of ability, lack of effort, poor training at school, and bad luck, among other possibilities. As can be seen in Figure 15-4, striking differences between countries emerge. Japanese mothers attributed poor performance in math primarily to a lack of effort. In contrast, explanations by mothers in the United States for poor performance were more evenly divided among several causes, and they considered a lack of ability considerably more influential than the Japanese did (Hess et al., 1986).

Obviously, such differences in attributions regarding the cause of academic performance influence the reaction to poor performance. For Japanese students, poor performance is seen as a temporary state, one that hard work will remedy. American students, on the other hand, react to academic failure with loss of self-esteem, discouragement, and withdrawal from academic endeavors, rather than working to overcome their difficulty (Stevenson, 1992; Stevenson & Stigler, 1992).

The comparative attributional styles of Japanese and American students may explain the differences in educational performance found between the two cultures.

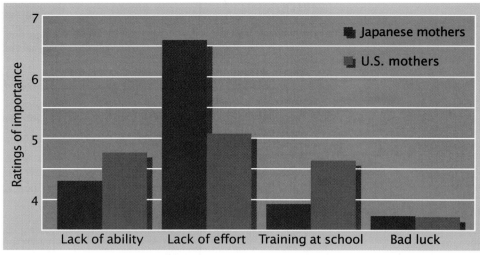

**FIGURE 15-4  Mothers' Attributions for Poor Math Performance** To Japanese mothers, lack of effort is the most important reason for a child's poor performance in math. In contrast, U.S. mothers saw several causes as equally important.    *(Source:* Adapted from Hess et al., 1986, p. 160.*)*

Although in first grade there is relatively little difference between Asian and American students in mathematics performance, by fifth grade Asian students consistently outperform American students on standardized tests of math achievement. Results on reading tests are similar: While Americans actually outperform Asians in reading scores in the first grade, by fifth grade the Asian children have caught up with the Americans (Stevenson & Lee, 1990).

Differences associated with a collectivistic compared with an individualistic orientation can be seen within other contexts. For instance, the way people in a given culture distribute scarce resources, and their helpfulness in general, is related to the kind of value orientation predominant in the culture. People in collectivistic cultures tend to focus on the norm of equality (equal rewards for all, regardless of performance) and the neediness of the recipient when distributing rewards to members of their own group. In contrast, people in individualistic societies tend to distribute rewards on the basis of a norm of equity, in which rewards are commensurate with the quality of performance. On the other hand, cross-cultural differences in how resources are distributed become less pronounced if the person receiving a reward is not a member of the group to which the allocator belongs. Specifically, distribution norms are considerably less powerful when the person who is in need is not a member of the same cultural group as the help-provider—a phenomenon that is particularly true in collectivistic cultures (Leung & Bond, 1984).

*Interpersonal Relationships in a Cultural Context*

If you recall our discussion in Chapters 6 and 7 of liking, loving, and close relationships, the focus of social psychologists was on choice—how people make choices about the particular person with whom to become interpersonally involved. Consequently, the focus of social psychological research has been on those relationships in which choice is present: friends and lovers, who are chosen because of their particular personal qualities and characteristics.

However, personal choice is not the central issue in interpersonal relationships in all cultures. In fact, in many cultures, **kinship relationships**—those involving relatives—are of primary importance. In other cultures, it is one's standing in the community, in reference to the profession or role that one carries out, that determines relationships. And in still other cultures, it is the group to which an individual belongs that determines the nature of interpersonal relationships. For instance, it may be people's race, ethnic background, the language they speak, or their religion that establishes the

**kinship relationships**
relationships involving relatives.

nature of their relationships and determines the person who is their friend, partner, or lover.

Furthermore, in Western cultures relationships tend to be less stable, and Western social psychologists have tended to focus on relationships that are relatively impermanent, such as acquaintances, friendships, and even the rise and fall of close relationships. (The current high divorce rate in Western society hardly argues that even marital relationships should be considered as stable or permanent.)

On the other hand, in many cultures there is a far greater permanence to relationships. In isolated, agriculturally based societies, people tend to play the same role from generation to generation, as when farmers pass their farm down to their children. There is little mobility, so relationships tend to be very stable.

Finally, relationships in Western cultures are more apt to reflect the individualistic values of the society, while those in non-Western cultures are more likely to involve collectivistic considerations. Specifically, in Western cultures, the kind of relationship that two people establish is largely determined by the characteristics of the individuals involved. Consequently, it is their personal beliefs and attitudes and personality factors that determine the course of a relationship.

On the other hand, people in collectivistic cultures are more likely to develop relationships based on membership in a particular kinship or other group. The kind of relationship that two people develop is more affected by factors outside the immediate relationship, such as how the relationship meets the needs of the community at large. Personal needs and desires are far less a factor in initiating and maintaining a relationship than are the needs and wishes of the broader community (Hsu, 1993; Triandis, 1988).

Another way of looking at interpersonal relationships across cultures, one that focuses on the psychological foundations of social relations, has been proposed by social psychologist Alan Fiske (1991). Fiske suggests that four basic models underlie how people throughout every culture make sense of their social world. People operate according to one of four approaches in planning their future actions, anticipating what people in their social worlds will do, and coordinating their activities with others (Fiske, 1991). The four models of social relations are communal sharing, authority ranking, equality matching, and market pricing. They are summarized in Figure 15-5.

**community sharing**
the model of social relations in which group membership and group identity are central.

**authority ranking**
the model of social relations in which different status relationships are primary.

**equality matching**
the model of social relations in which all people are seen as equal and the underlying principle is that everyone should get a fair and equal share of resources.

**market pricing**
the model of social relations in which people interact with others in a "psychological marketplace," attempting to maximize the value of their relationships with others, comparing what they might do with various alternatives, and choosing their course of action according to rational criteria that will maximize their psychological gain.

In **community sharing**, group membership and group identity are central to social relations. People's sense of belonging to the group colors all aspects of their social lives. In contrast, **authority ranking** is a social system in which different status relationships are primary. People are ranked according to their position in a culture, and that position determines the nature of social relationships. In **equality matching**, all people are seen as equal, and the principle underlying societal relations is that everyone should get a fair and equal share of resources. Finally, the **market pricing** model suggests that people interact with others in a kind of psychological marketplace. They attempt to maximize the value of their relationships with others, comparing what they might do with various alternatives and choosing their course of action according to rational criteria that will maximize their psychological gain.

Although the models are fairly abstract, they seem to provide a complete guide to the range of social interactions that occur in a society. To illustrate this point we can use the example of a community deciding how to provide fire protection for its citizens to show how the approaches differ (Fiske, 1991):

- *Communal sharing.* In communal sharing, the community makes a joint decision, reaching a consensus. All members of the group participate in the decision, and the decision is not complete until everyone agrees on a course of action. In a consensus on how best to provide fire protection, no decision is made until a course of action is found that produces agreement.

- *Authority ranking.* Another possibility is for a leader to make the decision about fire protection. The leader may be elected, appointed, or even have taken power through illegitimate means, such as violence. The important point is that people defer the decision to the authority.

**FIGURE 15-5  The Four Elementary Relational Models**

| | COMMUNAL SHARING | AUTHORITY RANKING | EQUALITY MATCHING | MARKET PRICING |
|---|---|---|---|---|
| *Reciprocal Exchange* | People give what they can and freely take what they need from pooled resources. What you get does not depend on what you contribute, only on belonging to the group. | Superiors appropriate or preempt what they wish, or receive tribute from inferiors. Conversely, superiors have pastoral responsibility to provide for inferiors who are in need and to protect them. | Balanced, in-kind reciprocity. Give and get back the same thing in return, with appropriate delay. | Pay (or exchange) for commodities in proportion to what is received, as a function of market prices or utilities. |
| *Distribution (Distributive Justice)* | Corporate use of resources regarded as a commons, without regard for how much any one person uses; everything belongs to all together. Individual shares and property are not marked. | The higher a person's rank, the more he or she gets, and the more choice he or she has. Subordinates receive less and get inferior items, often what is left over. | To each the same. Everyone gets identical shares (regardless of need, desire, or usefulness). | "To each in due proportion." Each person is allotted a quota proportionate with some standard (e.g., stock dividends, commissions, royalties, rationing based on a percentage of previous consumption, prorated strike benefits or unemployment compensation). |
| *Contribution* | Everyone gives what they have, without keeping track of what individuals contribute. "What's mine is yours." | Noblesse oblige: superiors give beneficently, demonstrating their nobility and largesse. Subordinate recipients of gifts are honored and beholden. | Contributors match each other's donations equally. | People assessed according to a fixed ratio or percentage (e.g., tithing, sales or real estate taxes). |
| *Work* | Everyone pitches in and does what he or she can, without anyone keeping track of inputs. Tasks are treated as collective responsibility of the group, without dividing the job or assigning specific individual duties. | Superiors direct and control the work of subordinates, while often doing less of the arduous or menial labor. Superiors control product of subordinates' labor. | Each person does the same thing in each phase of the work, either by working in synchrony, by aligning allotted tasks so they match, or by taking turns. | Work for a wage calculated as a rate per unit of time or output. |
| *Decision Making* | Group seeks consensus, unity, the sense of the group (e.g., Quaker meeting, Japanese groups). | By authoritative fiat or decree. Will of the leader is transmitted through the chain of command. Subordinates obey orders. | One-person, one-vote election. Everyone has an equal say. Also rotating offices or lottery. | Market decides, governed by supply and demand or expected utilities. Also rational cost/benefit analysis. |
| *Social Influence* | Conformity: desire to be similar to others, to agree, maintain unanimity, and not stand out as different. Mutual modeling and imitation. | Obedience to authority or deference to prestigious leaders. Subordinates display loyalty and strive to please superiors. | Compliance to return a favor ("log rolling"), taking turns deciding, or going along to compensate evenly or keep things balanced. | Cost and benefit incentives—contracts specifying contingent payments, bonuses, and penalties. Bargaining over terms of exchange. Market manipulation. Offering a "special deal" or a bargain. |

| FIGURE 15-5 | The Four Elementary Relational Models (continued) | | | |
|---|---|---|---|---|
| | COMMUNAL SHARING | AUTHORITY RANKING | EQUALITY MATCHING | MARKET PRICING |
| *Constitution of Groups* | Sense of unity, solidarity, shared substance (e.g., "blood," kinship). One-for-all, all-for-one. | Followers of a charismatic or other leader. Hierarchical organization (e.g., military). | Equal-status peer groups, e.g., car pool, cooperative, rotating credit association. | Corporations, labor unions, stock markets and commodity associations. |
| *Moral Judgment & Ideology* | Caring, kindness, altruism, selfless generosity. Protecting intimate personal relationships. "Never send to know for whom the bell tolls; it tolls for thee." *Traditional legitimation* in terms of inherent essential nature or karma of group. | What supreme being commands is right. Obedience to will of superiors. *Heteronomy, charismatic legitimation.* | Fairness as strict equality, equal treatment, and balanced reciprocity. | Abstract, universal, rational principles based on the utilitarian criterion of the greatest good for the greatest number (since this calculus requires a ratio metric for assessing all costs and benefits). *Rational-legal legitimation.* |
| *Moral Interpretations of Misfortune* | Stigmatization, pollution, contamination. Isolation as pariah. Feeling of being different, set apart, not belonging. Victims seek and join support groups of fellow-sufferers, among whom the misfortune is a source of solidarity. | Have I angered God? Did I disobey the ancestors? (E.g., story of Job.) | Feeling that misfortune should be equally distributed: "things even out in long run." Idea that misfortune balances a corresponding transgression. | Was this a reasonably expectable risk or calculable cost to pay for benefits sought? Is this too high a price to pay? |
| *Aggression & Conflict* | Racism, genocide to "purify the race." Killing to maintain group honor. Riots based on deindividuation. Equivalence of all "others": terrorists and rioters indiscriminately kill all members of opposed ethnic group. | Wars to extend political hegemony. Execution of people who fail to accept the legitimacy of political authorities or who commit lèse majesté. Also political assassination and tyrannicide. | Eye-for-an-eye feuding, tit-for-tat reprisals. Revenge, retaliation in kind. | Mercantile wars, slaving, exploitation of workers. Killing to protect markets or profits. Robbery and extortion. War strategies based on kill ratios. |

Source: *A.P. Fiske,* Structures of Social Life. © 1991, Free Press, New York.

- *Equality matching.* In some towns, the decision on fire protection may take place through a vote. If every member of the town has an equal opportunity to vote, then the decision is being made by an equality matching model.
- *Market pricing.* An alternative approach to making the decision is through market pricing. In such a scenario—once common in some parts of the United States—people individually arrange for their own fire protection, establishing an understanding with a fire department that should their house catch fire, they will pay for protection. Houses that catch fire are left to burn if their owners have not made this arrangement in advance.

As we can see, the four models of social relations lead to very different approaches to decision making. Furthermore, it is important to keep in mind that several of the models can be used jointly to make the decision. For example, a community could take a vote (equality matching) to decide on the form of fire fighting but then allow officials to determine the details of how the decision will be implemented (authority ranking). In addition, not all aspects of life in a community will follow the same model. For instance, a culture may follow different rules in such domains as work, social influence, moral judgments, and prevention of aggression (see Haidt, Koller, & Dias, 1993).

This four-part model of human relations provides one of the fullest accounts of the fundamental elements of social life. Although it is still largely theoretical, it helps explain the ways in which different cultures approach and solve the problems—and possibilities—inherent in interacting with others.

## ▶ REVIEW & RETHINK

### Review

- Culture comprises the learned behaviors, beliefs, and attitudes that are characteristic of an individual society or population.
- One basic difference between cultures is individualism and collectivism.
- The four basic models of social relations across different cultures are community sharing, authority ranking, equality matching, and market pricing.

### Rethink

- What is culture? Does culture encompass everything we have ever learned? In other words, is culture-free learning possible? To what extent do all people in the United States share the same culture?
- What does it mean to say that a culture is collectivistic? How do collectivistic and individualistic cultures differ with respect to helping behavior?
- The field of social psychology is dominated by Americans. How has this domination affected what topics of human behavior we have and have not chosen to investigate? List two or three research questions that would be important to a more collectivistic culture that have not been discussed in this text.
- How does community sharing differ from equality matching?

*Competition and Aggression: A Uniquely American Way of Life?*

No one can deny the high level of aggression and violence in U.S. society. Tales of murder, rape, muggings, and other violent crimes fill our daily papers. And it is not a misperception that violence is "as American as apple pie," as one observer put it (Berkowitz, 1993). The facts support such a contention. For example, the number of murders of men 15 to 24 years of age is higher in the United States than in any other developed country (see Figure 15-6).

Other indicators of aggression suggest that there are substantial differences in the amount and kind of aggression displayed across various cultures. Before considering such

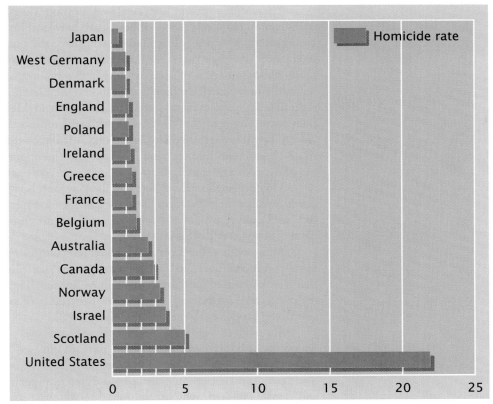

**Figure 15-6   Number of killings annually per 100,000 men between the ages of 15 and 24** (*Source:* Fingerhut & Kleinman, 1990.)

data, however, it is important to keep in mind how difficult it is to study aggression in different cultural contexts, and even more so to then make valid cross-cultural comparisons.

The magnitude of the problem is suggested by recalling the difficulty we had in initially coming up with a precise definition of "aggression" in Western culture. As we discussed in Chapter 8, most researchers consider aggression to occur only when there is intentional injury or harm to another individual. But how do we assess intention in a culture very different from our own? And how do we even adequately assess the concept of "harm." For example, watching children in a schoolyard one may see them shoving and hitting one another. Such behavior may merely represent play, and have little to do with actual aggression.

Despite such difficulties in examining aggression cross-culturally, researchers have carried out several large-scale, comprehensive studies of aggression that have provided clear evidence of cross-cultural differences in aggression. In one of the most meaningful studies, cross-cultural psychologist William Lambert examined aggression in Kenya, India, Mexico, Okinawa, the Philippines, and the United States (Lambert, 1971).

The study began with an inquiry into how mothers (the primary child care-takers in each of the six cultures) reacted to their own children's displays of aggression toward other children. It turned out that Mexican parents were the most strict, while U.S. mothers showed the greatest tolerance for aggressive behavior in their children. On the other hand, there was a difference in how the mothers reacted to aggression against an adult. For this kind of aggression, the children who lived in Kenya, the Philippines, and Mexico received the greatest punishment, while the least punishment occurred for children in India. Children living in the U.S. and Okinawa received a relatively moderate degree of punishment.

These differences in reactions to aggression are associated with differences in the overall amounts of aggression, although the relationships are neither simple nor obvious. For example, it appears that children who have the greatest level of social activity and interaction (the ones that have the most opportunity to behave aggressively) differ from those with lower levels of social activity in the amount of aggression they show. Furthermore, the most active children appear to have best learned the social values of the culture regarding aggression. Hence, the active children in Mexico are less aggressive, because their aggression is reacted to strongly, while the more active children in the United States tend to be more aggressive (the lesson they learn from their parents). On the other hand, relatively inactive children, who have not had the opportunity to acquire the social values of their society as well, show differing patterns of aggression.

This explanation for differences in aggression between various cultures is complex, but it explains the differences fairly adequately. However, the important point to draw is that each culture produces a specific set of socialization pressures that lead to different degrees of aggressive behavior.

Along with differences among various cultures in levels of aggression, there are some commonalities. Perhaps the clearest universal principle of aggressive behavior is that it is committed more by males than by females. There is no known culture in which males are less aggressive than females. Regardless of whether we look at children or adults, the gender difference holds (Segall, 1988).

Although it is clear that men act more aggressively than women, a definitive explanation for the difference in behavior remains elusive. While an explanation based on innate, biological factors seems most obvious, this is not the only possibility. For example, parents and society in general hold different expectations about aggression for male and female children, who are subjected to different socialization pressures. Congruent with such a notion, some research indicates that in a variety of cultures boys are explicitly urged and taught to behave aggressively, whereas a girl's aggression is discouraged (Barry et al., 1976; Eagly & Steffen, 1986a, 1986b).

Another theory meant to explain the higher aggressiveness of males relates to child-rearing practices (Whiting, 1965). Because males in almost all societies are raised by women, aggressive behavior is favored by males as part of an effort to differentiate and distinguish themselves from their female care-takers. In order to establish their masculine identity, then, male children adopt what they see as a dominant behavioral pattern of adult males—acting aggressively.

Ultimately, there is no definitive explanation for the higher levels of male aggression found around the world, nor for the general pervasiveness of aggressive behavior. Given the disparities in displays of aggressive behavior between various cultures, high levels of aggression are not a necessary part of the human condition, despite its preva-

The level of aggression displayed by members of a society is related to the way in which parents react to their children's aggression.

*"What's amazing to me is that this late in the game we still have to settle our differences with rocks."*

Drawing by Ziegler. © 1992 by the New Yorker Magazine, Inc.

lence in certain cultures. In fact, a growing body of work carried out by social psychologists suggests ways of minimizing global aggression and promoting global cooperation and peace.

---

*Promoting World Peace: Toward a Just World*

According to one count, the world has experienced at least 14,500 wars during the course of recorded history (Montagu, 1976). The tally continues to grow today, as cultures and societies come into violent conflict. In some areas, cruel and inhuman methods such as "ethnic cleansing" and organized rape are being used to bring about social change.

Yet the absence of organized conflicts in nonhuman species argues that there is hardly an instinctual basis for warlike behavior. In fact, it may be the very sophistication of humans' cognitive and intellectual abilities that permits them to wage war on such a grand and deadly scale (Groebel & Hinde, 1989).

Consequently, as a United Nations statement suggested after World War II, ". . . since wars begin in the minds of men, it is in the minds of men that defenses of peace must be constructed." The field of social psychology has produced several research approaches to better understand how peace can be preserved and a just world established.

**cross-cutting relations**
the linking and integration of groups in work, education, and recreation.

**INCREASING CROSS-CUTTING RELATIONS.** **Cross-cutting relations** are relations that link and integrate groups in work, education, and recreation. Social psychologist Morton Deutsch (1973) suggests that the development of cross-cutting relations enables people to understand the essential similarities of all humans and to develop ties and feelings of connectedness.

Cross-cutting relations can be produced in several ways. For instance, countries can arrange educational and cultural exchanges and joint scientific and technical projects. Through education about others' customs and habits, people can come to understand the basic similarity of others, even those who appear, on the surface, quite different (Staub, 1988).

Cross-cutting relations, interactions that link and integrate people of different cultures in work, educational, and recreational settings, aid in the quest for world peace.

**REDUCING TENSIONS BETWEEN COUNTRIES.**    Despite the breakup of the Soviet Union, international tension remains a fact of life in today's world. Religious fundamentalist fanaticism, ethnic cleansing, and warlords fighting for power in such places as Bosnia, Somalia, Iraq, and Haiti all represent continuing hot spots that threaten world peace. One method that social psychologists have devised for reducing tension is known as the **graduated and reciprocated initiative in tension reduction**, or **GRIT**.

Notwithstanding its formidable designation, the idea behind GRIT is really quite simple (Osgood, 1962, 1979). According to the plan, one side in an international dispute announces and then makes a unilateral but relatively minor concession. The concession is small enough not to leave the country vulnerable to attack, but large enough to put pressure on the other side to make a concession of its own. GRIT begins to yield results if the sequence is repeated, with each side making reciprocal concessions in response to the other side's concession.

The effectiveness of GRIT is supported by at least one actual example, known as the "Kennedy experiment" (Etzioni, 1969). In a major speech in 1963, U.S. President John Kennedy announced that the United States was unilaterally going to stop testing nuclear weapons in the atmosphere. He said the tests would not be started again unless another country began them first. He also suggested that American attitudes toward the Soviet Union should be reexamined and that Americans should do all that they could to try to get the Soviet Union to coexist in peace with the United States.

The speech marked the start of a series of reciprocal moves on the part of the Soviet Union and the United States. The Soviet Union responded rapidly—and positively—to Kennedy's overture by praising his speech and by agreeing to an American request to allow observers from the United States to intercede in a conflict that was occurring in Yemen.

In turn, the United States responded with a reciprocal easing of its foreign policy by giving full recognition to the Soviet-backed United Nations delegation from Hungary. Ultimately, the give-and-take resulted in the Soviet Union's decision to end production of strategic bombers and in the signing of a limited nuclear test ban treaty.

The "experiment" ended prematurely with the assassination of President Kennedy, and the war in Vietnam clouded and ultimately prevented further reciprocal concessions on the part of both the United States and the Soviet Union. Still, it appears that the

**graduated and reciprocated initiative in tension reduction (GRIT)** a method of reducing tension in which one side makes a unilateral but relatively minor concession, thus pressuring the other side to make a similar concession.

basic strategies of GRIT had brought about a successful reduction in tension and armaments, at least for a limited period of time.

**REDUCING NATIONALISTIC ATTITUDES.**    Some social psychologists have distinguished between patriotic attitudes and nationalistic attitudes. According to social psychologist Seymour Feshbach (1990), patriotic attitudes reflect a positive emotional relationship to one's nation, but nationalistic attitudes reflect a desire for superiority and power over other national groups.

Survey research shows that people strongest in nationalistic attitudes are the most ready to go to war, but the relationship between patriotic tendencies and willingness to go to war is considerably less pronounced. Such findings suggest that schools should teach the distinction between nationalism and patriotism. More specifically, Feshbach argues that our society should emphasize **internationalism**, the focus on the opportunities and problems shared by the peoples of the world (Feshbach, 1990).

**internationalism**
the focus on the opportunities and problems shared by the peoples of the world.

**CREATING A POSITIVE MULTICULTURAL SOCIETY.**    Whether or not the U.S. is prepared, American society is becoming multicultural. The number of people who belong to minority groups is soaring, while the proportion of majority group members continues to decline. For instance, by the year 2000 the percentage of population that is African-American is projected to increase by 13 percent over current numbers, and the percentage of Hispanic individuals will rise by 22 percent (U.S. Department of Education, 1993).

Whether society can reap the benefits of such an increasingly multicultural society remains an open question. Merely placing members of minority and majority groups in proximity does not guarantee any automatic benefits. In fact, as we discussed in Chapter 3, the benefits of multiculturalism come only when people interact in certain kinds of ways. For example, unless society promotes multicultural interaction in equal-status, close, and cooperative settings that allow for equality and the disconfirmation of negative stereotypes, benefits are unlikely to materialize.

On the other hand, if the conditions that promote beneficial contact between majority and minority group members can be attained, society will profit. Furthermore, as people come to learn about and comprehend each other better within their own society, one outgrowth should be a better understanding of people from different cultures.

In sum, increased experience with people from diverse cultural backgrounds may well enhance people's understanding of those living in other cultures. We might expect, and certainly hope, that such understanding will lead to increasing efforts to produce peaceful settlements of world problems and, overall, a more just world.

## ▶ REVIEW & RETHINK

### Review

- Societies have different levels of aggression.
- Differences in aggression between societies are related to child-rearing practices.
- Social psychologists have devised several techniques to promote peace.

### Rethink

- Studying aggression in our own culture is made difficult by not knowing how to define aggression. How is this problem accentuated in cross-cultural studies of aggression?

*Continued on next page*

- Why might socially active children be more aggressive? What implications does this have for the possibility of reducing aggression through intergroup contact?
- When researchers attempt to demonstrate that a human phenomenon is predicated on biological mechanisms, they may try to show that the phenomenon exists in all cultures. Discuss the pros and cons of this approach with respect to the study of male aggressiveness.
- If GRIT has demonstrated its potential utility, why hasn't it played a larger role in U.S. foreign policy? What difficulties interfere with the translation of social psychology to governmental policy?

# LOOKING BACK ◄ ◄ ◄ ◄ ◄ ◄ ◄ ◄ ◄ ◄ ◄ ◄ ◄ ◄ ◄ ◄ ◄ ◄ ◄ ◄ ◄ ◄ ◄ ◄ ◄

## What models explain the basic structure of organizations?

1. Organizations—groups of people working together to attain common goals—operate according to several different models. The bureaucratic model represents the attempt to apply rationality and efficiency to the functioning of organizations. The human relations model emphasizes the social psychological structure of an organization. Contingency models focus on how specific features of an organization's environment affect the way it operates.

2. Because none of the previous approaches has proven fully successful, some organizations have turned to the Japanese model, which includes a lifetime employment guarantee, quality circles, shared responsibility, and adherence to the principle of *kaizen,* the constant search for improvement.

## How do organizations maintain particular cultures and teach them to the organization's newcomers?

3. Organizational culture is the dominant pattern of basic assumptions, perceptions, thoughts, feelings, and attitudes held by members of an organization. The basic features of an organizational culture include regularities in behavior, norms, shared values and philosophy, and organizational climate.

4. Organizational socialization is the process by which a newcomer to an organization comes to behave and hold attitudes similar to those of others in the organization. Socialization moves through a series of stages: investigation, socialization, maintenance, resocialization, and remembrance.

## How is information communicated in organizations?

5. Organizations vary in terms of centralization—the degree to which people occupying a position can communicate with others. People who occupy central positions in highly centralized groups tend to be relatively satisfied and become leaders.

## What is culture, and does it affect basic social psychological processes?

6. Culture comprises the learned behaviors, beliefs, and attitudes that are characteristic of an individual society or population. One basic dimension along which cultures vary relates to individualism versus collectivism. In individualistic societies, personal identity, uniqueness, freedom, and individual worth are central. In contrast, collectivism holds that the group's well-being is more important than that of the individual.

## What impact does a society's level of individualism and collectivism have on social behavior?

7. Individualism and collectivism affect such factors as attributional styles, helpfulness and altruism, and interpersonal relationships. Furthermore, there are four basic models of social

relations across different cultures: community sharing, authority ranking, equality matching, and market pricing.

### To what extent are high levels of competitiveness and aggression uniquely American?

8.  Aggression is not unique to any one culture, but the characteristic level of aggression varies considerably from one culture to another. These differences may be traced in part to child-rearing practices. There are also commonalities between cultures. For example, males universally display higher levels of aggression than females.

### What ways have social psychologists developed to promote world peace?

9.  Social psychologists have devised several methods to promote world peace and move closer to a just world. Among the methods are increasing cross-cutting relations, reducing tensions between countries, reducing nationalistic attitudes, and creating a positive multicultural society.

## KEY TERMS AND CONCEPTS

*organization (p. 474)*

*bureaucratic model (of organizations) (p. 475)*

*human relations model (of organizations) (p. 475)*

*contingency model (of organizations) (p. 476)*

*Japanese model (of organizations) (p. 476)*

*quality circles (p. 476)*

*organizational culture (p. 478)*

*organizational subculture (p. 479)*

*organizational socialization (p. 481)*

*mentor (p. 483)*

*centralization (of communication network) (p. 484)*

*information saturation (p. 484)*

*culture (p. 485)*

*individualism (p. 486)*

*collectivism (p. 486)*

*kinship relationships (p. 488)*

*community sharing (p. 489)*

*authority ranking (p. 489)*

*equality matching (p. 489)*

*market pricing (p. 489)*

*cross-cutting relations (p. 495)*

*graduated and reciprocated initiative in tension reduction (GRIT) (p. 496)*

*internationalism (p. 497)*

## FOR FURTHER RESEARCH AND STUDY

Miner, J. B. (1992). *Industrial-organizational psychology*. New York: McGraw-Hill.

An overview of organizations in the business world, taking an applied perspective on organizations.

Fiske, A. T. (1993). *Structures of social life: The four elementary forms of human relations*. New York: Free Press.

This book provides a fascinating look at human relations across cultures, focusing on the four fundamental components of social interaction.

Segall, M. H., Dasen, P. R., Berry, J. W., & Poortinga, Y. H. (1990). *Human behavior in global perspective: An introduction to cross-cultural psychology*. Boston: Allyn & Bacon.

Moghaddam, F. M., Taylor, D. M., & Wright, S. C. (1993). *Social psychology in cross-cultural perspective*. New York: Freeman.

Lonner, W. J., & Malpass, R. S. (1993). *Psychology and culture*. Boston: Allyn & Bacon.

Three broad, thought-provoking introductions to the cross-cultural factors relating to the social aspects of behavior.

# EPILOGUE

Our journey through the field of social psychology has ended with a consideration of groups and organizations. Beginning in the previous chapter, where we discussed how aggregates of people join together to form groups, we moved to the larger arena of organizations. We considered different models of organizations and the basic processes that underlie their functioning. Finally, we discussed culture and society, reflecting on the contributions social psychologists have made to the quest for peace and world justice.

As we've seen throughout this book, social psychologi-cal theory and research have made significant contributions to our understanding of how the social world operates. At the same time, such work has led to significant applied contributions, producing real improvement in people's lives.

Yet the story of social psychology remains incomplete. The field is advancing on many fronts, continuing to unfold and grow. New theories are being developed, research continues, and applications continue to be derived. To quote poet Robert Browning, "The best is yet to be."

# GLOSSARY

**ABC tripartite model** the notion that attitudes are composed of three components: an affective component, a behavioral component, and a cognitive component. (10)

**abstract modeling** The tendency, as one gets older, to build general rules and principles, and rather than always modeling others' specific behaviors, to draw generalized principles that underlie the behaviors we have observed. (9)

**accessibility** the degree to which an attitude can be brought to mind. (10)

**acquired immune deficiency syndrome (AIDS)** a fatal disease caused by a virus that destroys the body's immune system and that has no known cure. (5)

**action identification theory** the theory that people's interpretation of their own behavior varies in terms of whether the behavior is seen at a high or low level. (4)

**active behavioral coping** a response to disease in which the victim mobilizes to actively fight the illness. (5)

**actor-observer bias** the tendency for people to attribute their own behavior to situational requirements, while people observing that same behavior tend to attribute it to the person's stable dispositions. (4)

**agape** according to Lee, love that is selfless, in which partners put their lover's welfare before their own. (7)

**agentic professions** professions based on accomplishing tasks. (3)

**aggression** intentional injury or harm to another person. (8, 9)

**aggressive cues** learned stimuli that have previously been associated with aggression. (8)

**altruism** helping behavior that is beneficial to others but requires clear self-sacrifice. (8)

**altruistic personality** a trait suggesting that certain individuals have enduring personality characteristics that consistently lead them to help. (8)

Note: Numbers in parentheses refer to the chapter number where the term appears.

**androgynous** a state in which gender roles encompass characteristics thought typical of both sexes. (3)

**anxious–ambivalent attachment** a style of attachment seen in children who show great distress when separated from their caregivers, but who appear angry on their return. (6)

**applied research** research meant to provide practical solutions to immediate problems. (1)

**archival research** research in which an investigator analyzes existing records or documents in an effort to confirm a hypothesis. (1)

**attachment** the positive emotional bond that develops between a child and a particular individual. (6)

**attitudes** learned predispositions to respond in a favorable or unfavorable manner to a particular person, object, or idea. (10)

**attribution approaches** approaches to social cognition that seek to identify how people understand the causes of others' and their own behavior. (2)

**attribution training** a situation in which inaccurate, harmful attributions are replaced with more accurate and beneficial ones. (5)

**attributional approach (to media aggression)** the explanation that suggests that the conditions to which people attribute the aggression they observe have a significant effect upon their subsequent aggression. (9)

**attributional model of helping and emotions** a model suggesting that the nature of an attribution for a request for help determines a person's emotional response and the nature of help provided. (8)

**attributional style** a tendency to make particular kinds of causal attributions across different situations. (5)

**audience pleasing** behavior designed to make an audience feel good. (4)

**authority ranking** the model of social relations in which different status relationships are primary. (15)

**autokinetic effect** the illusion that occurs when a small, stationary light in a darkened room appears to move. (12)

**availability heuristic** a rule for judging the likelihood of an event by considering the ease with which it can be recalled from memory. (2)

**avoidant attachment**    a style of attachment that characterizes relationships in which the child appears relatively indifferent to caregivers and avoids interactions with them. (6)

**avoidant coping**    a response to disease in which the victim refuses to think about the illness and evades or postpones action to deal directly with the disease. (5)

**balance theory**    the theory that people strive for consistency, or balance, in their thoughts, feelings, and attitudes toward others. (6)

**base-rate fallacy**    the tendency to underemphasize base-rate data because of the influence of more prominent, although ultimately less meaningful, information. (2)

**base-rate information**    data regarding the frequency with which some event occurs in the general population. (2)

**beautiful-is-good stereotype**    the belief that physically attractive people have a wide range of positive characteristics. (6)

**behavioral intention**    the probability that people place on the likelihood that they will engage in a behavior that is relevant to a held attitude. (10)

**belief in a just world**    the notion that people tend to deserve what happens to them. (2)

**brainstorming**    a procedure designed to generate ideas, in which group members are asked to produce as many (and as uninhibited) ideas as they possibly can and to withhold criticism in order to optimize creativity. (14)

**bureaucratic model (of organizations)**    the organizational model that attempts to achieve success in the workplace organization by applying rationality and efficiency to the functioning of the organization. (15)

**cataclysmic events**    strong stressors that occur suddenly and affect many people simultaneously. (5)

**catharsis**    the process of discharging aggressive energy that is continually built up within people. (8)

**central route persuasion**    route to persuasion based on the logic, merit, or strength of the arguments. (11)

**central traits**    characteristics that serve to organize an impression of another person and provide a framework for interpreting information that is subsequently received. (2)

**centralization (of communication network)**    the degree to which people occupying a position in an organization can communicate with others in the organization. (15)

**close relationships**    relationships characterized by at least one of three factors: emotional attachment, need fulfillment, and interdependence. (7)

**coercive power**    the power a person holds based on the ability to deliver punishments. (13)

**cognitive algebra approach**    an explanation for impression formation that suggests that perceivers consider each individual trait, evaluate each trait individually in isolation from the others, and then combine the evaluations into an overall judgment. (2)

**cognitive approaches (to interpersonal attraction)**    an approach that focuses on how people perceive the nature of a relationship they hold with others. (6)

**cognitive consistency**    an approach to attitudes that focuses on the ways in which people strive to maintain consistency within and between attitudes and how they manage to reconcile inconsistencies of which they are aware. (10)

**cognitive dissonance**    a state of psychological tension that is aroused when a person simultaneously holds contradictory cognitions. (10)

**cognitive miser model**    model associated with the schema approaches to social cognition that suggests that because of people's limited information-processing capabilities, they expend no more than the minimum effort necessary to solve a social problem or answer a social question. (2)

**cognitive neoassociationistic model**    the argument put forth by Berkowitz that aversive circumstances produce negative affect in the form of anger, hostility, or irritation. (8)

**cohabitation**    the state in which an unmarried couple choose to live together. (7)

**collective behavior**    a situation that occurs in groups of people who are relatively unorganized, yet hold a sense of unity and may work toward similar goals. (9)

**collectivism**    the belief that the group's well-being is more important than that of the individual. (15)

**communal professions**    professions based on relationships. (3)

**communal relationship**    a relationship in which the participants feel mutual responsibility for each other, and provide benefits according to the other's needs or in order to exhibit concern for the other person. (7)

**community sharing**    the model of social relations in which group membership and group identity are central. (15)

**companionate love**    the strong affection we have for those with whom our lives are deeply involved. (7)

**comparison level theories**    the theory that suggests that attraction to others is based on comparison to some hypothetical baseline. (6)

**compliance**    yielding to direct, explicit appeals meant to produce certain behavior or agreement to a particular point of view. (12)

**conditions**    the differing treatments that are given to the different groups in an experiment. (1)

**confederates**    employees or colleagues of the experimenter who pose as subjects in an experiment and who may be used to produce a scene that has impact on subjects, engaging and involving them. (1)

**conformity**    a change in behavior or attitudes brought about by a desire to follow the beliefs or standards of others. (12)

**confounding**    situation in an experiment in which factors other than the independent variable are allowed to vary. (1)

**confusion of responsibility**    a situation in which observers assume that a person who is actually aiding a victim is in some way responsible for the emergency situation. (8)

**consensus information**    data regarding the degree to which other people react similarly in the same situation. (2)

**consistency information** knowledge regarding the degree to which people react in the same way in different situations. (2)

**consumer behavior** buying habits and effects of advertising on buyer behavior. (11)

**contact hypothesis** the theory that under the appropriate conditions, direct contact between hostile groups will reduce prejudice. (3)

**contingency model of leadership** the notion that leader effectiveness is based on three contingencies: the nature of leader–member relations, the task structure, and the leader's power. (13)

**contingency model (of organizations)** the model that focuses on how specific features of an organization's environment affect the operation. (15)

**control** the degree to which an experimenter is able to limit and restrict events within the experiment to those that are intended. (1)

**control group** the no-treatment or alternative-treatment group in an experiment. (1)

**coping** the effort to control, reduce, or learn to tolerate the threats that lead to stress. (5)

**correlational research** research that seeks to identify whether an association or relationship between two factors exists—regardless of whether one factor produces changes in the other. (1)

**correspondence (between attitude and behavior)** the similarity between an individual's attitude and his or her relevant behavior. (10)

**correspondent inferences** observers' notions of how closely an overt behavior or action represents a specific underlying intention, trait, or disposition. (2)

**covert measure of attitude** an approach to the measurement of attitudes in which the measurement technique is disguised. (10)

**creative nonadherence** a response to medical regimens in which the patient adjusts or augments treatment prescribed by a physician, relying instead on his or her own medical judgment and experience. (5)

**cross-cutting relations** the linking and integration of groups in work, education, and recreation. (15)

**culture** the learned behaviors, beliefs, and attitudes that are characteristic of an individual society or population. (15)

**cycle of violence hypothesis** the hypothesis suggesting that abuse and neglect suffered by children lead them to be predisposed as adults to abusing and neglecting their own children. (9)

**daily hassle** (or **background stressor**) a minor irritant that produces minor stress to an individual. (5)

**date rape** the act of rape that occurs on a first date, casual date, or involves a romantic acquaintance. (9)

**deception** research methods that disguise or mislead subjects regarding the actual purpose of a study. (1)

**decision/commitment component (of Sternberg's love model)** the component of love that embodies both the initial cognition that one loves another person and the longer-term determination to maintain that love. (7)

**defense mechanism** an unconscious reaction to threat that reduces anxiety by distorting or denying the actual nature of the situation. (5)

**defensive attributions** attributions that help observers deal with perceived inequities in others' lives in order to maintain the belief that the world is just. (2)

**dehumanization** a justification for illicit activity in which the victim is portrayed as lacking human characteristics and consequently not being worthy of equitable and considerate treatment. (13)

**deindividuation** the reduction of a person's sense of individuality and the corresponding increase in the willingness to engage in deviant behavior. (9)

**demand characteristics** the cues that subjects use in an experiment to provide information regarding what is expected or regarding appropriate behavior. (1)

**dependent variable** the variable that is measured in an experiment and is expected to change as a result of the experimental manipulation. (1)

**descriptive self-disclosure** a situation in which people share facts about their lives. (7)

**desensitization** a reduction in the negative reaction to aggressive stimuli. (9)

**deterrence** the strategy that the threat of large-scale retaliation against an enemy attack is the best method of preventing an initial attack. (9)

**diffusion of responsibility** the tendency for people to feel that responsibility for acting is shared, or diffused, among those present. (8)

**discrimination** the behavioral manifestation of stereotypes and prejudice. (3)

**disinhibition hypothesis** the suggestion that exposure to media violence reduces people's normal inhibitions against behaving aggressively. (9)

**display rules** the implicit rules that define what type of nonverbal behavior is appropriate for a given situation or interpersonal relationship, and what type is not. (4)

**dispositional causes** reasons for behavior that rest on the personality traits and characteristics of the individual. (2)

**distinctiveness information** knowledge regarding the extent to which the same behavior occurs in relation to other people or stimuli. (2)

**distraction-conflict theory** the explanation of social facilitation effects that suggests that the presence of others is a distraction, dividing our attention between the task at hand and the others who are present. (14)

**door-in-the-face technique** a technique of social influence in which a large request, whose refusal is expected, is followed by a smaller one. (12)

**double standard** the view that premarital sex was permissible for men but not for women. (7)

**downward social comparison** a situation in which one compares oneself with others who are inferior or worse off. (4)

**dual-process approach** an approach to social influence that suggests that minority influence differs in degree and in kind from majority influence. (12)

**egoism**   behavior that is motivated by self-benefit. (8)

**elaboration likelihood model**   the notion that central route persuasion occurs when the recipient carefully considers arguments and expends a cognitive effort in elaborating the meaning and implication of a message. (11)

**emergent norm perspective**   the norm suggesting that a group definition of appropriate behavior arises in violent mobs. (9)

**emotion-focused coping**   the conscious regulation of emotion as a way of dealing with stress. (5)

**emotional isolation**   a situation in which a person feels a lack of deep emotional attachment to one specific person. (6)

**empathy**   an emotional response corresponding to the feelings of another person. (8)

**empathy–altruism hypothesis**   the notion that empathy lies at the heart of altruistic behavior. (8)

**entrapment**   a justification for illicit activity in which a person is lured into committing a crime by a law enforcement agent. (13)

**equality matching**   the model of social relations in which all people are seen as equal and the underlying principle is that everyone should get a fair and equal share of resources. (15)

**equity theory**   the theory that suggests that people not only take into account their own outcomes, but also the outcomes that are perceived to be attained by others. (6)

**eros**   Lee's term for intense, emotional, and passionate love. (7)

**evaluation apprehension**   the phenomenon in which the presence of others leads to the inference that the audience is evaluating us, a circumstance that produces physiological arousal. (14)

**evaluation research**   a technique designed to determine the effects of a research program—specifically, whether it is meeting its goals—and to contribute information to help improve the program in the future. (1)

**evaluative self-disclosure**   a situation in which an individual communicates information about personal feelings. (7)

**exchange relationships**   associations based on an economic model of interaction in which people seek to maximize their benefits and minimize their costs. (7)

**excitation transfer model**   a situation in which physiological arousal acts to intensify subsequent emotional experiences, even if they are unrelated to the initial arousal. (8)

**exemplification**   a technique in which people attempt to create an impression of moral superiority and integrity. (4)

**experiment**   procedure to test a hypothesis. (1)

**experimental research**   research designed to discover causal relationships between various factors, in which the researcher deliberately introduces a change in a situation in order to observe the effect that change has upon the situation. (1)

**experimenter expectations**   a situation that may arise in an experiment in which the experimenter unintentionally communicates cues to subjects about the way they are expected to behave in a given experimental condition. (1)

**expert power**   the power a person holds because of his or her superior knowledge and abilities. (13)

**false consensus effect**   the tendency to overestimate the degree of agreement with our own opinions, beliefs, and attributes. (2)

**fear appeals**   messages regarding attitude change that are designed to produce apprehension and anxiety if the message is not followed. (11)

**field study**   a research investigation carried out in a naturally occurring setting. (1)

**foot-in-the-door technique**   a technique of social influence in which the target is first asked to agree to a small request, but later asked to comply with a more important one. (12)

**free-riders**   people who exert minimal effort in group activity but benefit from the group's rewards, leading the other group members to reduce their efforts. (14)

**frustration**   the thwarting or blocking of some ongoing behavior directed toward a desired goal. (8)

**frustration–aggression hypothesis**   the notion that frustration always leads to aggression of some sort, and that aggression is always the result of some form of frustration. (8)

**fundamental attribution error**   the tendency to overattribute others' behavior to dispositional causes, and the failure to recognize the importance of situational causes. (2)

**gender roles**   the set of expectations, defined by society, that indicate what is appropriate behavior for men and women. (3)

**gender schema**   the cognitive framework that organizes information relevant to gender. (3)

**generalization**   the ability to apply the results of a study to other settings and subject populations beyond those immediately employed in the experiment. (1)

**graduated and reciprocated initiative in tension reduction (GRIT)**   a method of reducing tension in which one side makes a unilateral but relatively minor concession, thus pressuring the other side to make a similar concession. (15)

**great person theory of leadership**   the notion that certain people are born to lead others. (13)

**group**   two or more people who interact with one another, perceive themselves as a group, and are interdependent. (14)

**group cohesiveness**   the extent to which the members of a group find the group attractive. (14)

**group polarization**   an exaggeration of a group's initial tendencies following group discussion. (14)

**group structure**   the regular, stable patterns of behavior in groups. (14)

**groupthink**   a type of thinking in which group members share such strong motivation to achieve consensus that they lose the ability to critically evaluate alternative points of view. (14)

**Guttman scale**   a measurment that presents a gradation of attitudes, ranging from least extreme to the most extreme. (10)

**hard sell**   an advertising strategy that focuses on the qualities of the product itself. (11)

**hardiness**   a personality characteristic associated with a lower rate of stress-related illness. (5)

**heuristics** principles or "rules of thumb" that permit people to make decisions on the basis of limited information and with relatively little cognitive effort. (11)

**human relations model (of organizations)** the organizational model that emphasizes the social interactions and the psychological state of members of the organization. (15)

**hypothesis** a prediction stated in a way that permits it to be tested. (1)

**hypothetical constructs** abstract concepts that cannot be directly observed. (10)

**identity** the combination of roles and group categories to which a person belongs, along with the set of personal meanings and experiences related to the roles and categories. (4)

**idiosyncrasy credit** a psychological "currency" that permits deviation from the group. (12)

**illusory correlation** the overestimation by a perceiver of the strength of a relationship between two variables. (3)

**immune system** the body's natural line of defense against disease. (5)

**independent variable** the variable that is manipulated in the experiment by the researchers. (1)

**individualism** the belief in the worth of personal identity, uniqueness, and freedom. (15)

**information saturation** a situation in an organization in which people in central positions experience an overload of communication from other group members. (15)

**informational power** the power a person holds because of the specific content of his or her knowledge. (13)

**informational social influence** pressure to conform that emanates from our assumption that others have knowledge we lack. (12)

**informative advertising** advertising designed to introduce new products, suggest new ways of using an existing product, or correct false impressions about a product in a way that produces demand for a particular class of products. (11)

**informed consent** agreement between the researchers and the subjects in an experiment in which the researchers fully disclose and explain to the subjects the possible risks and benefits of the experiment. (1)

**ingratiation** a deliberate effort to make a favorable impression, often through flattery. (4,6)

**ingroup** a group to which a person feels he or she belongs. (3)

**ingroup–outgroup bias** the tendency to hold less favorable views about groups to which we do not belong, while holding more favorable opinions about groups to which we do belong. (3)

**insufficient justification** a situation in which people perform, for a minimal inducement, a behavior that is discrepant with their true attitude. (10)

**interactional approach to leadership** the notion that different situations call for different kinds of leaders. (13)

**interdependence** the degree of influence two people have over each other and the quantity of activities in which they jointly engage. (7)

**internationalism** the focus on the opportunities and problems shared by the peoples of the world. (15)

**interpersonal attraction** the degree of liking that people have for one another. (6)

**interpersonal repulsion** the desire to escape from another's presence; the opposite of interpersonal attraction. (6)

**intimacy** the process in which a person communicates important feelings and information to another through a process of self-disclosure. (7)

**intimacy component (of Sternberg's love model)** the component of love that encompasses feelings of closeness, affection, and connectedness. (7)

**intimidation** the process of communicating an ability and inclination to provide negative outcomes to others. (4)

**Japanese model (of organizations)** the organizational model that emphasizes decision making by group consensus, shared responsibility, and concerns for employee welfare. (15)

**jigsaw technique** a procedure for increasing intergroup interaction in which people are given a small amount of information and then required to teach the material to a set of partners in a group. (3)

**kinship relationships** relationships involving relatives. (15)

**knowledge function of attitudes** the aspect of attitudes that permits people to organize and make sense of the world. (10)

**labeling theory of passionate love** the theory offered by Hatfield and Berscheid in which people experience romantic love when two events occur together: intense physiological arousal and situational cues that indicate that "love" is the appropriate label for the feelings they are experiencing. (7)

**laboratory study** a research investigation conducted in a controlled setting explicitly designed to hold events constant. (1)

**learned helplessness** the belief that no control can be exerted over one's environment. (5)

**least preferred coworker (LPC)** the person in a group whom the leader identifies as the one individual with whom it is most difficult to work. (13)

**legitimate power** the power a person holds because of the formal position or role that person occupies. (13)

**Likert scale** an approach to the measurement of attitudes in which objects are rated on the basis of a numbered evaluative response scale. (10)

**loneliness** the inability to maintain the level of affiliation one desires. (6)

**low-balling** a technique in which an initial agreement is reached, but then the seller reveals additional costs. (12)

**ludos** Lee's term for playful love, in which the partners view the relationship as a kind of game-playing situation. (7)

**major intersection** the stage of a strong, binding relationship in which the partners increasingly reveal intimate and important attitudes and feelings about themselves. (7)

**mandate phenomenon** a situation in which a person with strong support exceeds the group norms and seeks even more power. (13)

**mania**   according to Lee, love that is possessive and demanding, and in which jealousy is common. (7)

**market pricing**   the model of social relations in which people interact with others in a "psychological marketplace," attempting to maximize the value of their relationships with others, comparing what they might do with various alternatives, and choosing their course of action according to rational criteria that will maximize their psychological gain. (15)

**matching hypothesis**   the hypothesis that people are attracted to others who have a level of physical attractiveness similar to their own. (6)

**mentor**   an informal instructor who acts as a socialization guide for a newcomer. (15)

**mere exposure effect**   the phenomenon that repeated exposure to any stimulus increases the positivity of its evaluation. (6)

**minor intersection**   the early stages of mutuality in which people are hesitant to disclose information about themselves. (7)

**minority group**   a group in which the members have significantly less power, control, and influence over their own lives than do members of a dominant majority. (3)

**mirror-image perceptions**   views that duplicate those held by one's opponent. (9)

**misattribution training**   a situation in which people are led to replace their accurate but harmful attributions with inaccurate but more beneficial attributions. (5)

**models**   people whose behavior can be imitated and who provide a guide to appropriate behavior. (8)

**moderate intersection**   an intermediate stage of relationship development in which the degree of self-disclosure increases. (7)

**modern racism**   a subtle form of prejudice in which people appear, on the surface, not to harbor prejudice, but actually do hold racist attitudes. (3)

**motivated tactician model**   an approach to social cognition that suggests that the way people view the world depends on their goals, motivations, and needs. (2)

**motivational bias**   sources of error that stem from a need to present oneself well, either to impress others or to maintain one's own sense of self-esteem. (2)

**mutuality**   a situation in which the individuals in a relationship share knowledge of each other, experience a sense of responsibility for the other person, and develop a set of personal norms informally regulating their relationship. (7)

**naturalistic observation**   a process in which investigators observe some naturally occurring behavior but do not intervene in the situation. (1)

**need complementarity hypothesis**   the notion that individuals are attracted to others who have significantly different personalities but whose needs complement theirs. (6)

**need for affiliation**   the desire to establish and maintain relationships with other people. (6)

**need for cognition**   a person's habitual level of thoughtfulness and cognitive activity. (11)

**need for power**   a personality characteristic in which an individual has a tendency to seek impact, control, or influence over others, and a need to be seen as a powerful person (13)

**negative affect model of aggression**   Baron's notion that high temperatures, as well as other aversive stimuli in the environment, can lead to higher aggression, but only up to a point. (8)

**negative-state relief (NSR) model**   a model that seeks to explain the relationship between bad mood and helping behavior by considering the consequences of prosocial behavior for the help provider. (8)

**nonparticipant observation**   the type of naturalistic observation in which the researcher records people's behavior in a given setting but does not actually enter into it. (1)

**norm**   general standards or expectations regarding appropriate behavior. (14)

**norm of noninvolvement**   a standard of behavior that causes people to avoid becoming psychologically (and physically) entangled with others. (8)

**norm of reciprocity**   the norm asserting that we should help others because they have helped us in the past or may help us in the future. (8)

**norm of social responsibility**   the norm that suggests people should respond to the reasonable needs of others, and that all people have a societal obligation to aid those in need. (8)

**normative approach (to media aggression)**   the notion that viewing media depictions can lead people to assume that aggression is a socially acceptable behavior. (9)

**normative social influence**   pressure that reflects expectations regarding appropriate behavior held by those belonging to groups. (12)

**nuclear freeze**   a situation in which the world's nuclear powers pledge to build no new nuclear weapons. (9)

**obedience**   a change in behavior that is due to the commands of others in authority. (12)

**operationalization**   the process of translating a hypothesis into specific testable procedures that can be measured and observed. (1)

**organization**   a group of people working together to attain common goals. (15)

**organizational culture**   the dominant pattern of basic assumptions, perceptions, thoughts, feelings, and attitudes held by members of an organization. (15)

**organizational socialization**   the process by which an individual comes to behave like and hold attitudes similar to those of others in an organization. (15)

**organizational subculture**   the shared set of assumptions, perceptions, thoughts, feelings, and attitudes that are held by a relatively small minority of members of an organization and that differ from the dominant organizational culture. (15)

**outgroup**   a group to which a person feels he or she does not belong. (3)

**outgroup homogeneity bias**   the perception that there is greater variability among the members of outgroups than within one's own ingroup. (3)

**overjustification**    a situation in which incentives are used to bring about behavior that would have been done voluntarily, without any incentive. (4)

**participant observation**    the type of naturalistic observation in which the researcher actually engages in the activities of the people being observed. (1)

**passion component (of Sternberg's love model)**    the component of love that is made up of the motivational drives relating to sex, physical closeness, and romance. (7)

**passionate (or romantic) love**    the representation of a state of intense absorption in someone that includes intense physiological arousal, physiological interest, and care for the needs of another. (7)

**perceived behavioral control**    the factor in behavioral intention that takes into account the ease or difficulty of carrying out the behavior, based on prior experience and anticipated barriers in performing it. (10)

**peripheral route persuasion**    route to persuasion based on factors unrelated to the nature or quality of the content of a persuasive message. (11)

**permissiveness with affection standard**    the view that premarital intercourse is permissible for both men and women if it occurs within a long-term, committed, or loving relationship. (7)

**person perception approaches**    approaches to social cognition that consider the way an individual's traits are assessed and combined to form an overall impression. (2)

**person positivity bias**    the tendency to rate others in a generally positive manner, also known as the "Pollyanna effect". (2)

**personal norms**    our own personal sense of obligation to help a specific person in a specific situation. (8)

**personal space**    the area around a person's body which others may not enter. (6)

**personal stressor**    a major event in an individual's life that has immediate negative consequences. (5)

**pluralistic ignorance**    a situation that occurs when bystanders in an emergency use the behavior of others to determine whether help is actually required. (8)

**possible selves**    the aspects of the self that relate to the future. (4)

**POSSLQs**    persons of the opposite sex sharing living quarters—the term given by the U.S. Department of the Census to couples who cohabitate. (7)

**post-decision cognitive dissonance**    a phenomenon following the resolution of cognitive dissonance in which the chosen alternative becomes more positive and the unchosen one becomes more negative. (10)

**posttraumatic stress disorder**    a phenomenon in which victims of major incidents reexperience the original stress-producing event and associated feelings in flashbacks or dreams. (5)

**power semantic**    the power or status level that an individual has in relation to another. (4)

**pragma**    the third of Lee's secondary categories of love, in which practical concerns underlie love. (7)

**prejudice**    the negative (or positive) evaluations or judgments of members of a group that are based primarily on membership

in the group and not necessarily on the particular characteristics of individual members. (3)

**prescriptive norms**    norms that suggest to people the ways they ought to behave. (14)

**primacy effect**    the effect on perception when information received early has a stronger impact than information received later. (2)

**primary appraisal**    the assessment of an event to determine whether its implications are positive, neutral, or negative. (5)

**priming**    the process by which recent exposure to stimuli such as people, ideas, or even mere words influences the interpretation of new information. (2)

**private self-consciousness**    an individual's awareness of inner thoughts. (4)

**problem-focused coping**    the process of attempting to manage a stressful problem or situation. (5)

**process loss**    the aspects of a group's interaction patterns that hinder performance. (14)

**production blocking**    the process loss that reflects the strongly held social norm that only one person in a group can speak at a given time. (14)

**proscriptive norms**    norms that inform people about behaviors they should avoid. (14)

**prosocial behavior**    helping behavior that benefits others. (8)

**prototypes**    schemas that organize a group of traits into meaningful personality types or categories. (2)

**psychographics**    a method for dividing people into lifestyle profiles that are related to purchasing patterns. (11)

**psychosomatic disorders**    medical problems caused by the interaction of psychological, emotional, and physical difficulties. (5)

**public self-consciousness**    an individual's awareness of his or her outward behavior and appearances that are visible to others. (4)

**quality circles**    a method originated in Japan in which small groups within a workplace organization meet regularly to solve problems and ensure excellence. (15)

**racism**    prejudice directed at people because of their race. (3)

**random assignment**    in an experiment, the method of assigning subjects to particular groups on the basis of chance. (1)

**rape**    the act of one person forcing another to submit to sexual activity such as intercourse or oral-genital sex. (9)

**reactance**    a disagreeable emotional and cognitive reaction to the restriction of one's freedom. (5)

**reactivity**    behavior that occurs as a result of subjects' awareness that they are being studied. (1)

**realistic conflict theory**    the notion that prejudice is the outcome of a direct competition over valued, but limited, resources. (3)

**recency effect**    the effect on perception when information received later has a stronger impact than information received earlier. (2)

**reciprocal concessions**    a technique of social influence in which requesters appear to make a compromise (by reducing the size of their initial request), thereby inviting a concession on the part of those who initially refused the request. (12)

**reciprocity of liking**    a situation in which you like those who like you. (6)

**reciprocity of self-disclosure**    a situation in which people who are the recipients of intimate information respond in kind. (7)

**referent power**    the power a person holds based on the ability to act as a model for the behavior of others. (13)

**reinforcement-affect model**    the premise that liking follows the basic principles of learning embodied in classical and operant conditioning. (6)

**Relationship Closeness Inventory**    a system used to objectively measure the strength of relationships. (7)

**relative deprivation**    the sense that one lacks a desired resource in comparison with another group, which is perceived to have more. (3)

**reminder advertising**    advertising designed to keep consumers thinking about a product or to reinforce the message that preferring a brand is appropriate. (11)

**replication**    the process of verifying the original results of an experiment by reproducing the results. (1)

**representativeness heuristic**    a rule in which people are judged by the degree to which they represent a certain category. (2)

**reward power**    the power a person holds based on the ability to provide rewards. (13)

**riot**    a public disorder created by groups of people. (9)

**risky shift**    the situation in which groups often tend to make riskier decisions than individuals solving the same problems on their own. (14)

**role**    the behaviors that are associated with and come to be expected of people in a given position. (14)

**Romeo and Juliet effect**    the phenomenon in which couples who experience strong parental interference in their relationships report greater love for one another than those with little interference. (7)

**schema approaches**    approaches to social cognition that consider how information is organized and stored in memory and how this information is used as a guideline to understand behavior. (2)

**schemas**    organized bodies of information stored in memory. (2)

**script**    the organized knowledge people hold regarding a particular situation and the way events in that situation unfold. (2)

**secondary appraisal**    the assessment of whether one's coping abilities and resources are adequate to overcome the harm, threat, or challenge posed by the potential stressor. (5)

**secure attachment**    a style of attachment that characterizes a positive, healthy relationship between a child and an adult, based primarily on trust in the adult's comfort and love. (6)

**selective demand advertising**    advertising designed to establish or modify attitudes about a particular brand of product or service, compared with other brands of the same kind of product or service. (11)

**selective exposure**    a phenomenon that occurs when people seek out information that supports a choice they have made and avoid information that is inconsistent with the choice. (10)

**self function of attitudes**    the aspect of attitudes that enables people to create and maintain a positive self-image. (10)

**self-affirmation theory**    the notion that people deal with dissonance by seeking to assert their self-adequacy as individuals. (10)

**self-awareness**    a state in which attention is focused on the self. (4)

**self-complexity**    the phenomenon of viewing oneself as having many distinct facets. (5)

**self-concept**    a person's sense of identity, the set of beliefs about what he or she is like as an individual. (4)

**self-construction**    self-presentation meant to corroborate an individual's own view of self. (4)

**self-disclosure**    a situation in which information about the self is exchanged with others. (5)

**self-discrepancy theory**    the argument that the discrepancy between people's self-concept and their self-guides leads to negative emotions and ultimately to lower psychological well-being. (5)

**self-efficacy**    an individual's learned expectations regarding success. (4)

**self-esteem**    the affective component of self, a person's general and specific positive and negative self-evaluations. (4)

**self-evaluation maintenance theory**    a theory that predicts that people will react to the accomplishments of important people in their lives by showing either jealousy or pride. (4)

**self-fulfilling prophecy**    the tendency for people to act in a way that is congruent with their expectation, belief, or cognition about an event or behavior, thereby increasing the likelihood that the event or behavior will occur. (2)

**self-handicapping**    a tactic in which people set up circumstances that allow them to avoid attributing poor performance to low ability and instead allow them to attribute it to less-threatening causes. (4)

**self-monitoring**    a regulating of one's behavior to meet the demands of a situation or the expectations of others. (4)

**self-perception theory**    the notion that people become aware of their own attitudes, dispositions, emotions, and other internal states through observation of their own behavior. (4)

**self-presentation**    the process by which people attempt to create specific, generally positive impressions regarding themselves—also known as impression management. (4)

**self-promotion**    an individual's efforts or techniques designed to make him or her appear more competent. (4)

**self-schema**    the organized body of information that relates to a person's self. (4)

**self-serving bias**    the tendency to attribute personal success to internal factors (such as skill, ability, or effort), while attributing failure to external factors (such as bad luck). (2, 4)

**semantic differential**    an approach to the measurement of attitudes in which objects are rated on the basis of a pair of adjectives that are opposites, such as, good/bad, attractive/unattractive. (10)

**sexism**    prejudice directed at people because of their gender. (3)

**single-process approach**    an approach to social influence that suggests that both majorities and minorities employ similar influence techniques. (12)

**situational approach to leadership**    the notion that people become leaders due to the characteristics of the situation in which they find themselves. (13)

**situational causes**    reasons for behavior that rest on the demands or constraints of a given social setting. (2)

**sleeper effect**    the notion that the persuasiveness of a message increases with the passage of time. (11)

**social cognition**    the study of how people understand and make sense of others and of themselves. (2)

**social combination rules**    the guidelines used by members of groups to decide what needs to be done and how the task should be divided up among group members. (14)

**social comparison**    the need to evaluate one's own behavior, abilities, expertise, and opinions by comparing them to those of other people. (6)

**social decision scheme**    the way in which individual judgments and preferences are combined into a collective decision. (14)

**social facilitation**    the phenomenon in which the presence of others leads to improvements in performance. (14)

**social identity theory**    the notion that people use group membership as a source of pride and self-worth. (3)

**social impact theory**    the notion that the effect of a majority on a minority rests on three basic factors—the majority's strength, immediacy, and number. (12)

**social influence**    real or imagined pressure from others that results in a change in behavior or attitude. (12)

**social isolation**    a situation in which a person suffers from a lack of friends, associates, or relatives. (6)

**social learning theory** (or **observational learning**)    the theory that people learn social behavior through observing and imitating the behavior of others. (8, 10)

**social learning view of prejudice**    the theory that people develop prejudice and stereotypes about members of various groups in the same way they learn other attitudes, beliefs, and values. (3)

**social loafing**    the phenomenon in which individual effort decreases when people engage in shared group activity. (14)

**social power**    the power a person holds based on the ability to control and shape another's behavior. (13)

**social psychology**    the scientific study of how people's thoughts, feelings, and actions are affected by others. (1)

**social reality**    a person's understanding that is derived from how other people act, think, feel, and view the world. (4)

**social support**    assistance and comfort supplied by a network of caring, interested people. (5)

**social supporter**    a person holding a position similar to one's own. (12)

**sociobiology**    a new field of study that considers the biological roots of social behavior. (8)

**soft sell**    an advertising strategy that links a product with a pleasant image related to the product's use. (11)

**solidarity semantic**    the degree of shared social experience between two people. (4)

**statistical significance**    represents an outcome that would be expected to occur by chance less than five times out of 100. (1)

**status**    the evaluation of a role or person by the group. (12, 14)

**stereotypes**    a set of beliefs and expectations about members of a group that are held simply on the basis of their membership in the group. (3)

**stimulus-value-role (SVR) theory**    the theory that relationships proceed in a fixed order through a series of three stages. (7)

**storge**    Lee's term for love in which friendship and companionship prevail. (7)

**stress**    The response to events that threaten or challenge a person. (5)

**stressor**    circumstances that produce threats to an individual's well-being. (5)

**subjective norms**    the factor in behavioral intention that takes into account the perceived social pressure to carry out the behavior. (10)

**subjects**    participants in an experiment. (1)

**superordinate goals**    goals simultaneously shared by members of conflicting groups. (3)

**supplication**    the process of creating the impression that one is needy, weak, and dependent. (4)

**surface contact**    the second level of pair relatedness, in which both people are aware of each other. (7)

**survey research**    research in which an investigator chooses people to represent some larger population and asks them a series of questions about their behavior, thoughts, or attitudes. (1)

**techniques of neutralization**    justifications used to explain behavior that violates society's standards of conduct. (13)

**terrorism**    the use or threat of violence against particular or random targets for the purpose of achieving political aims. (9)

**thanatos**    Freud's view that humans have a primitive instinct he called a death drive. (8)

**that's-not-all technique**    a technique of social influence in which the salesperson offers a deal at an initial, often inflated price, then immediately offers an incentive, discount, or bonus to clinch the deal. (12)

**theoretical research**    research designed specifically to test some explanation of social behavior. (1)

**theories**    broad explanations and predictions of phenomena of interest. (1)

**theory of planned behavior**    the notion that suggests that the likelihood that a person will behave in a way that is congruent with an attitude depends on a measured, rational decision-making process in which a combination of several factors is considered. (10)

**theory of social penetration**    a theory by Altman and Taylor that suggests that relationships gradually progress through increasingly deeper intimacy. (7)

**transformational leaders**    leaders who spur their followers into behavior that surpasses their own personal interests. (13)

**treatment**    the procedure in an experiment provided by an investigator. (1)

**treatment group**    the group that receives the treatment in an experiment. (1)

**two-factor theory of emotion**    the notion that emotions are a joint result of nonspecific physiological arousal and the interpretation of the arousal. (4)

**Type A behavior pattern**    a pattern of behavior characterized by competitiveness, impatience, a tendency toward frustration, and hostility. (5)

**Type B behavior pattern**    a pattern of behavior characterized by noncompetitiveness, patience, and a lack of aggression. (5)

**ultimate attribution error**    the tendency among people holding strong stereotypes to attribute negative behavior on the part of a minority group member to dispositional characteristics, and correspondingly, to attribute positive behavior on the part of a minority group member to situational factors. (3)

**unilateral awareness**    the level in which individuals view others in terms of their outward characteristics. (7)

**uplift**    minor positive events that make people feel good, even if only temporarily. (5)

**values clarification**    a procedure in which students are encouraged to examine their values. (9)

**victimization**    a justification used by perpetrators of violent actions to claim that the act was the fault of the victim. (13)

**violence**    the deliberate attempt to carry out serious physical injury. (9)

**voir dire**    proceedings at the start of a trial in which prospective jurors can be questioned as to their impartiality and background in order to eliminate those who are biased toward or against a particular side. (13)

# REFERENCES

Aaker, D. A., & Biel, A. L. (Eds.). (1993). *Brand equity and advertising: Advertising's role in building strong brands.* Hillsdale, NJ: Erlbaum.

Aaker, D. A., & Myers, J. G. (1987). *Advertising management.* Englewood Cliffs, NJ: Prentice-Hall.

Abelson, R. P. (1981). The psychological status of the script concept. *American Psychologist, 36,* 715-729.

Abramson, L. Y., Metalsky, G. I., & Alloy, L. B. (1989). Hopelessness depression: A theory-based subtype. *Psychological Review, 96,* 358-372.

Adams, G. R., & Crane, P. (1980). An assessment of parents' and teachers' expectations of preschool children's social preference for attractive or unattractive children and adults. *Child Development, 51,* 224-231.

Aderman, D., & Berkowitz, L. (1983). Self-concern and the unwillingness to be helpful. *Social Psychology Quarterly, 46,* 293-301.

Aguirre, B. E., Quarantelli, E. L., & Mendoza, J. L. (1988). The collective behavior of fads: The characteristics, effects, and career of streaking. *American Sociological Review, 53,* 569-584.

Ainsworth, M. D. (1985). Patterns of attachment. *Clinical Psychologist, 38*(2), 27-29.

Ainsworth, M. D. S., Blehar, M. C., Waters, E., & Wall, S. (1978). *Patterns of attachment: A psychological study of the strange situation.* Hillsdale, NJ: Erlbaum.

Ainsworth, M. S. (1979). Infant-mother attachment. *American Psychologist, 34*(10), 932-937.

Ajzen, I. (1985). From intentions to actions: A theory of planned behavior. In J. Kuhland & J. Beckman (Eds.), *Action-control: From cognitions to behavior.* Heidelberg: Springer.

Ajzen, I. (1987). Attitudes, traits, and actions: Dispositional prediction of behavior in personality and social psychology. In L. Berkowitz (Ed.), *Advances in experimental social psychology* (Vol. 20). San Diego: Academic Press.

Ajzen, I. (1988). *Attitudes, personality, and behavior.* Stratford, England: Open University Press.

Ajzen, I., & Fishbein, M. (1977). Attitude-behavior relations: A theoretical analysis and review of empirical research. *Psychological Bulletin, 84,* 888-918.

Ajzen, I., & Fishbein, M. (1980). *Understanding attitudes and predicting social behavior.* Englewood Cliffs, NJ: Prentice-Hall.

Ajzen, I., Timko, C., & White, J. B. (1982). Self-monitoring and the attitude-behavior relation. *Journal of Personality and Social Psychology, 42,* 426-435.

Allen, M., & Stiff, J. B. (1989). Testing three models for the sleeper effect. *Western Journal of Speech Communication, 53,* 411-426.

Allen, V. L. (1965). Situational factors in conformity. In L. Berkowitz (Ed.), *Advances in experimental social psychology* (Vol. 2). New York: Academic Press.

Allen, V. L. (1975). Social support for nonconformity. In L. Berkowitz (Ed.), *Advances in experimental social psychology* (Vol. 8). New York: Academic Press.

Allen, V. L., & Levine, J. M. (1971). Social support and conformity: The role of independent assessment of reality. *Journal of Experimental Social Psychology, 7,* 48-58.

Alley, T. R. (1988). *Social and applied aspects of perceiving faces.* Hillsdale, NJ: Erlbaum.

Alley, T. R., & Cunningham, M. R. (1991). Average faces are attractive, but very attractive faces are not average. *Psychological Science, 2,* 123-125.

Allport, F. H. (1924). *Social psychology.* Boston: Houghton Mifflin.

Allport, G. W., & Postman, L. J. (1945). The basic psychology of rumor. *Transactions of the New York Academy of Sciences, 8* (Series II), 61-81.

Allred, K. D., & Smith, T. W. (1989). The hardy personality: Cognitive and physiological responses to evaluate threat. *Journal of Personality and Social Psychology, 56,* 257-266.

Alpert, J. J. (1964). Broken appointments. *Pediatrics, 34,* 127-132.

Altman, I., & Taylor, D. A. (1973). *Social penetration: The development of interpersonal relationships.* New York: Holt, Rinehart & Winston.

Amabile, T. M. (1983). *The social psychology of creativity.* New York: Springer-Verlag.

Amabile, T. M., Hennessey, B. A., & Grossman, B. S. (1986). Social influences on creativity: The effects of contracted-for reward. *Journal of Personality and Social Psychology, 50,* 14-23.

Ambady, N., & Rosenthal, R. (1992). Thin slices of expressive behavior as predictors of interpersonal consequences: A meta-analysis. *Psychological Bulletin, 111,* 256-274.

Ambady, N., & Rosenthal, R. (1993). Half a minute: Predicting teacher evaluations from thin slices of nonverbal behavior and physical attractiveness. *Journal of Personality and Social Psychology, 64,* 431-441.

American College Health Association. (1989). *Guidelines on acquaintance rape.* Washington, DC: American College Health Association.

American Humane Association. (1991). Annual cases reported. Englewood, CO: American Humane Association.

American Psychological Association. (1990). *Guidelines for ethical conduct in the care and use of animals.* Washington, DC: American Psychological Association.

American Psychological Association. (1993a). APA personnel survey. Washington, DC: *American Psychological Association.*

American Psychological Association. (1993b). Proportion of PhDs in social psychology awarded to women. Washington, DC: *American Psychological Association.*

Andersen, S. M., & Klatzky, R. L. (1987). Traits and social stereotypes: Levels of categorization in person perception. *Journal of Personality and Social Psychology, 53,* 235-246.

Anderson, C. A. (1989). Temperature and aggression: Ubiquitous effects of heat on occurrence of human violence. *Psychological Bulletin, 106,* 74-96.

Anderson, C. A., & Anderson, D. C. (1984). Ambient temperature and violent crime: Tests of the linear and curvilinear hypotheses. *Journal of Personality and Social Psychology, 46,* 91-97.

Anderson, C. A., & DeNeve, K. M. (1992). Temperature, aggression, and the negative affect escape model. *Psychological Bulletin, 111,* 347-351.

Anderson, N. H. (1965). Averaging versus adding as a stimulus-combination rule in impression formation. *Journal of Experimental Psychology, 70,* 394-400.

Anderson, N. H. (1974). Cognitive algebra integration theory applied to social attribution. In L. Berkowitz (Ed.), *Advances in experimental social psychology* (Vol. 7, pp. 1-101). New York: Academic Press.

Anderson, N. H. (1981). *Foundations of information integration theory.* New York: Academic Press.

Anderson, T. A. (1992, March 15). Terry Anderson looks back: Blindfold and chains. *New York Times,* A10.

Andison, F. S. (1977). TV violence and viewer aggression: A cumulation of study results: 1956-1976. *Public Opinion Quarterly, 41,* 314-331.

Andrews, J. C., Durvasula, S., & Akhter, S. H. (1990). A framework for conceptualizing and measuring the involvement construct in advertising research. *Journal of Advertising, 19* (4), 27-40.

Antoni, M. H. (1993). Stress management: Strategies that work. In D. Goleman & J. Gurin (Eds.), *Mind-body medicine.* Yonkers, NY: Consumer Reports Books.

Archer, D., Pettigrew, T. F., & Aronson, E. (1992). Making research apply: High stakes public policy in a regulatory environment. *American Psychologist, 47,* 1233-1236.

Arena, J. M. (1984, April). A look at the opposite sex. *Newsweek on Campus,* p. 21.

Aries, E. J., & Johnson, F. L. (1983). Close friendship in adulthood: Conversational content between same-sex friends. *Sex Roles, 9,* 1183-1197.

Arkin, R. M., & Baumgardner, A. H. (1985). Self-handicapping. In J. H. Harvey & G. Weary (Eds.), *Attribution: Basic issues and applications* (pp. 169-202). New York: Academic Press.

Arms, R. L., Russell, G. W., & Sandiland, M. L. (1979). Effects of viewing aggressive sports on the hostility of spectators. *Social Psychology Quarterly, 42,* 275-279.

Aron, A., Dutton, D. G., Aron, E. N., & Iverson, A. (1989). Experiences of falling in love. *Journal of Social and Personal Relationships, 6,* 243-257.

Aronson, E. (1988). *The social animal* (3rd ed.). San Francisco: W. H. Freeman.

Aronson, E. (1991). How to change behavior. In R. C. Curtis & G. Stricker (Eds.), *How people change: Inside and outside therapy.* New York: Plenum.

Aronson, E., & Bridgeman, D. (1979). Jigsaw groups and the desegregated classroom: In pursuit of common goals. *Journal of Personality and Social Psychology, 35,* 438-446.

Aronson, E., Ellsworth, P. C., Carlsmith, J. M., & Gonzales, M. H. (1990). *Methods of research in social psychology* (2nd ed.). New York: McGraw-Hill.

Aronson, E., & Golden, B. W. (1962). The effect of relevant and irrelevant aspects of communicator credibility on attitude change. *Journal of Personality, 30,* 135-146.

Aronson, E., & Mills, J. (1959). The effect of severity of initiation on liking for a group. *Journal of Abnormal and Social Psychology, 59,* 177-181.

Aronson, E., Stephan, W., Sikes, J., Blaney, N., & Snapp, M. (1978). *Cooperation in the classroom.* Beverly Hills, CA: Sage.

Aronson, E., Willerman, B., & Floyd, J. (1966). The effect of a pratfall on increasing interpersonal attractiveness. *Psychonomic Science, 4,* 227-228.

Asch, S. E. (1946). Forming impressions of personality. *Journal of Abnormal and Social Psychology, 41,* 258-290.

Asch, S. E. (1951). Effects of group pressure upon the modification and distortion of judgments. In H. Guetzkow (Ed.), *Groups, leadership, and men.* Pittsburgh, PA: Carnegie Press.

Asch, S. E. (1952). *Social psychology.* Englewood Cliffs, NJ: Prentice-Hall.

Asch, S. E. (1955). Opinions and social pressure. *Scientific American, 193,* 31-55.

Asch, S. E. (1956). Studies of independence and conformity: A minority of one against a unanimous majority. *Psychological Monographs, 70,* 416.

Asch, S. E., & Zukier, H. (1984). Thinking about persons. *Journal of Personality and Social Psychology, 46,* 1230-1240.

Associated Press. (1985, May 10). Man convicted of killing wife who begged to die.

*Attorney General's Commission on Pornography: Final report.* (1986, July). Washington, DC: U.S. Department of Justice.

Austin, W. (1979). Justice, freedom, and self-interest in intergroup conflict. In W. G. Austin & S. Worchel (Eds.), *The social psychology of intergroup relations.* Monterey, CA: Brooks/Cole.

Axelrod, S., & Apsche, J. (1982). *The effects of punishment on human behavior.* New York: Academic Press.

Bach, G., & Wyden, P. (1968). *The intimate enemy: How to fight fair in love and marriage.* New York: Avon.

Baldwin, W., Cain, V., Evans, J., Hofferth, S., & Kamenske, G. (1987). *Summary of research funded by DBSB.* Bethesda, MD: National Institute of Child Health and Development, Center for Population Research.

Bandura, A. (1973). *Aggression: A social learning analysis.* Englewood Cliffs, NJ: Prentice-Hall.

Bandura, A. (1974). Behavior theory and the models of man. *American Psychologist, 29,* 859-869.

Bandura, A. (1977). *Social learning theory.* Englewood Cliffs, NJ: Prentice-Hall.

Bandura, A. (1978). Social learning theory of aggression. *Journal of Communication. 28,* 12-29.

Bandura, A. (1982). Self-efficacy mechanisms in human agency. *American Psychologist, 37,* 122-147.

Bandura, A. (1983). Psychological mechanisms of aggression. In R. G. Geen & E. I. Donnerstein (Eds.), *Aggression: Theoretical and empirical reviews, Vol. 1: Theoretical and methodological issues.* New York: Academic Press.

Bandura, A. (1986). *Social foundations of thought and action.* Englewood Cliffs, NJ: Prentice-Hall.

Bandura, A. (1988). Perceived self-efficacy: Exercise of control through self-belief. In J. P. Dauwalder, M. Perez, & V. Hobbi (Eds.), *Annual series of European research in behavior therapy* (Vol. 2). Lisse, The Netherlands: Swets & Zietlinger.

Bandura, A. (1993). Perceived self-efficacy in cognitive development and functioning. *Educational Psychologist, 28,* 117-148.

Bandura, A., Grusec, J. E., & Menlove, F. L. (1967). Vicarious extinction of avoidance behavior. *Journal of Personality and Social Psychology, 5,* 16-23.

Bandura, A., Ross, D., & Ross, S. (1963). Vicarious reinforcement and imitative learning. *Journal of Abnormal and Social Psychology, 67,* 601-607.

Bandura, A., & Schunk, D. H. (1981). Cultivating competence, self-efficacy, and intrinsic interest through proximal self-motivation. *Journal of Personality and Social Psychology, 41,* 586-598.

Banuazizi, A., & Movahedi, S. (1975). Interpersonal dynamics in a simulated prison: A methodological analysis. *American Psychologist, 30,* 152-160.

Bar-Hillel, M. (1980). The base-rate fallacy in

probability judgments. *Acta Pscyhologica, 44,* 211-233.

Barber, J. D. (1985). *The presidential character: Predicting performance in the White House* (3rd ed.) Englewood Cliffs, NJ: Prentice-Hall.

Barber, J. D. (1992a, May/June). How to choose a president. *Psychology Today, 25,* 54-91.

Barber, J. D. (1992b). Prediction as a test for hypothesis: Application to the psychology of presidents. *Political Psychology, 13,* 543-552.

Bargh, J. A. (1989a). Conditional automaticity: Varieties of automatic influence in social perception and cognition. In J. S. Uleman & J. A. Bargh (Eds.), *Unintended thought: Causes and consequences for judgment, emotion, and behavior.* New York: Guilford.

Bargh, J. A. (1989b). Auto-Motives: Preconscious determinants of social interaction. In J. S. Uleman & J. A. Bargh (Eds.) *Unintended thought* (pp. 93-130). New York: Guilford Press.

Bargh, J. A., & Pietromonaco, P. (1982). Automatic information processing and social perception: The influence of trait information presented outside of conscious awareness on impression formation. *Journal of Personality and Social Psychology, 43,* 437-449.

Baron, J. N., & Bielby, W. T. (1986). The proliferation of job titles in organizations. *Administrative Science Quarterly, 31,* 561-586.

Baron, R. A. (1983). The control of human aggression: An optimistic perspective. *Journal of Social and Clinical Psychology, 1,* 97-119.

Baron, R. A., & Greenberg, J. (1990). *Behavior in organizations: Understanding and managing the human side of work* (3rd ed.). Boston: Allyn & Bacon.

Baron, R. A., & Kepner, C. R. (1970). Model's behavior and attraction toward the model as determinants of adult aggressive behavior. *Journal of Personality and Social Psychology, 14,* 335-344.

Baron, R. A., & Ransberger, V. M. (1978). Ambient temperature and the occurrence of collective violence: The "long, hot summer" revisited. *Journal of Personality and Social Psychology, 36,* 351-360.

Baron, R. A., Russell, G. W., & Arms, R. L. (1984). Negative ions and behavior. *Journal of Personality and Social Psychology, 48,* 746-754.

Baron, R. S. (1986). Distraction-conflict theory: Progress and problems. In L. Berkowitz (Ed.), *Advances in experimental social psychology* (Vol. 20). New York: Academic Press.

Baron, R. S., Kerr, N. L., & Miller, N. (1992). *Group process, group decision, group action.* Pacific Grove, CA: Brooks/Cole.

Barrett, G. V., & Bass, B. M. (1970). Comparative surveys of managerial attitudes and behavior. In J. Bradburn (Ed.), *Comparative management: Teaching, training and research.* New York: Graduate School of Business Administration, New York University.

Barry, H., III, Josephson, L., Lauer, E., & Marshall, C. (1976). Traits inculcated in childhood: Cross-cultural codes V. *Ethnology, 15,* 83-114.

Bass, B. M. (1985). *Leadership and performance beyond expectations.* New York: Free Press.

Bass, B. M. (1990). *Bass & Stogdill's handbook of leadership: Theory, research, & managerial applications* (3rd ed.). New York: Free Press.

Bass, B. M., & Avolio, B. J. (1990). *Manual: The multifactor leadership questionnaire.* Palo Alto, CA: Consulting Psychologists Press.

Batra, R., Lehmann, D. R., & Singh, D. (1993). The brand personality component of brand goodwill: Some antecedents and consequences. In D. A. Aaker & A. L. Biel (Eds.), *Brand equity and advertising: Advertising's role in building strong brands.* Hillsdale, NJ: Erlbaum.

Batson, C. D. (1990a). Good Samaritans—or priests and Levites? Using William James as a guide in the study of religious prosocial motivation. Special Issue: Centennial celebration of The Principles of Psychology. *Personality and Social Psychology Bulletin, 16,* 758-768.

Batson, C. D. (1990b). How social an animal? The human capacity for caring. *American Psychologist, 45,* 336-346.

Batson, C. D. (1991). *The altruism question: Toward a social-psychological answer.* Hillsdale, NJ: Erlbaum.

Batson, C. D. (1993). Communal and exchange relationships: What is the difference? *Personality and Social Psychology Bulletin, 19,* 677-683

Batson, C. D., Batson, J. G., Slingsy, J. K., Harrell, K. L., Peekna, H. M., & Todd, R. M. (1991). Empathic joy and the empathy-altruism hypothesis. *Journal of Personality and Social Psychology, 61,* 413-426.

Batson, C. D., Cochran, P. J., Biederman, M. F., Bloser, J. L., Ryan, M. J., & Vogt, B. (1978). Failure to help when in a hurry: Callousness or conflict? *Personality and Social Psychology Bulletin, 4,* 97-101.

Batson, C. D., & Oleson, K. C. (1991). Current status of the empathy-altruism hypothesis. *Review of Personality and Social Psychology, 12,* 62-85.

Baumeister, R. F. (1982). A self-presentational view of social phenomena. *Psychological Bulletin, 91,* 3-26.

Baumeister, R. F. (1988). Masochism as escape from self. *Journal of Sex Research, 25,* 28-59.

Baumeister, R. F. (1990). Suicide as escape from self. *Psychological Review, 97,* 90-113.

Baumeister, R. F. (1991). *Escaping the self.* New York: Basic Books.

Baumeister, R. F. (Ed.). (1993). *Self-esteem: The puzzle of low self-regard.* New York: Plenum.

Baumeister, R. F., & Hutton, D. G. (1987). A self-presentational perspective on group processes. In B. Mullen & G. R. Goethals (Eds.), *Theories of group behavior.* New York: Springer-Verlag.

Baumeister, R. F., Hutton, D. G., & Tice, D. M. (1989). Cognitive processes during deliberate self-presentation: How self-presenters alter and misinterpret the behavior of their interaction partners. *Journal of Experimental Social Psychology, 25,* 59-78.

Baumeister, R. F., & Jones, E. E. (1978). When self-presentation is constrained by the target's knowledge: Consistency and compensation. *Journal of Personality and Social Psychology, 36,* 608-618.

Baumgardner, A., Lake, A. E., & Arkin, R. M. (1985). Claiming mood as a self-handicap: The influence of spoiled and unspoiled public identities. *Personality and Social Psychology Bulletin, 11,* 349-357.

Baumgardner, A. H. (1991). Claiming depressive symptoms as a self-handicap: A protective self-presentation strategy. *Basic and Applied Social Psychology, 12,* 97-113.

Baumrind, D. (1964). Some thoughts on the ethics of reading Milgram's "Behavioral study of obedience." *American Psychologist, 19,* 421-423.

Bazerman, M. H., Giuliano, T., & Appelman, A. (1984). Escalation of commitment in individual and group decision making. *Organizational Behavior and Human Performance, 33,* 141-152.

Beaman, A. L., Cole, C. M., Preston, M., Klentz, B., & Steblay, N. M. (1983). Fifteen years of foot-in-the-door research: A meta-analysis. *Personality and Social Psychology Bulletin, 9,* 181-196.

Beck, A. T. (1991). Cognitive therapy: A 30-year perspective. *American Psychologist, 46,* 368-375.

Beck, A. T., Rush, A. J., Shaw, B. F., & Emery, G. (1979). *Cognition therapy of depression.* New York: Guilford Press.

Becker, M. H. (1985). Patient adherence to prescribed therapies. *Medical Care, 23,* 539-555.

Beckman, H. B., & Frankel, R. M. (1984). The effect of physician behavior on the collection of data. *Annals of Internal Medicine, 101,* 692-696.

Beckman, L. (1970). Effects of students' performance on teachers' and observers' attributions of causality. *Journals of Educational Psychology, 61,* 76-82.

Bell, J., & Garthwaite, P. H. (1987). The psychological effects of service in British Antarctica: A study using the General Health

Questionnaire. *British Journal of Psychiatry,* *150,* 213-218.

Bell, P. A. (1978). Affective state, attraction, and affiliation: Misery loves happy company, too. *Personality and Social Psychology Bulletin,* *4,* 616-619.

Bell, P. A. (1992). In defense of the negative affect escape model of heat and aggression. *Psychological Bulletin, 111,* 342-346.

Belmore, S. M. (1987). Determinants of attention during impression formation. *Journal of Experimental Psychology: Learning, Memory, and Cognition, 13,* 480-489.

Belsky, J., Garduque, L., & Hrncir, E. (1984). Assessing performance, competence, and executive capacity in infant play: Relations to home environment and security of attachment. *Developmental Psychology, 20,* 406-417.

Belsky, J., Rovine, M., & Fish, M. (1989). The developing family system. In M. Gunnar (Ed.), *Systems and development: Minnesota symposium on child psychology, Volume 22.* Hillsdale, NJ: Erlbaum.

Bem, D. J. (1967). Self-perception theory. In L. Berkowitz (Ed.), *Advances in experimental social psychology* (Vol. 6, pp. 1-62). New York: Academic Press.

Bem, D. J. (1967). Self-perception: An alternative interpretation of cognitive dissonance phenomena. *Psychological Review, 74,* 183-200.

Bem, D. J., & McConnell, H. K. (1970). Testing the self-perception explanation of dissonance phenomena: On the salience of premanipulation attitudes. *Journal of Personality and Social Psychology, 14,* 23-31.

Bem, D. J. (1972). Self-perception theory: In L. Berkowitz (Ed.), *Advances in experimental and social psychology* (Vol. 6, pp. 1-62). New York: Academic Press.

Bem, S. L. (1974). The measurement of psychological androgyny. *Journal of Consulting and Clinical Psychology, 42,* 155-162.

Bem, S. L. (1982). Gender schema theory and self-schema theory compared: A comment on Markus, Crane, Bernstein, and Siladi's "Self-schemas and gender." *Journal of Personality and Social Psychology, 43,* 1192-1194.

Bem, S. L. (1983). Gender schema theory and its implications for child development: Raising gender-aschematic children in a gender-schematic society. *Signs, 8,* 598-616.

Bem, S. L. (1984). Androgyny and gender schema theory: A conceptual and empirical integration. *Nebraska Symposium on Motivation, 32,* 179-226.

Bem, S. L. (1987). Gender schema theory and its implications for child development: Raising gender-aschematic children in a gender-schematic society. In R. M. Walsh (Ed.), *The psychology of women: Ongoing debates.* New Haven: Yale University Press.

Bem, S. L. (1993). *Lenses of gender.* New Haven, CT: Yale University Press.

Bem, S. L., & Lewis, S. A. (1975). Sex role adaptability: One consequence of psychological androgyny. *Journal of Personality and Social Psychology, 31,* 634-643.

Bem, S. L., Martyna, W., & Watson, C. (1976). Sex typing and androgyny: Further explorations of the expressive domain. *Journal of Personality and Social Psychology, 34,* 1016-1023.

Bennett, M. (1977). Testing management theories cross-culturally. *Journal of Applied Psychology, 62,* 578-581.

Benson, H. (1993). The relaxation response. In D. Goleman & J. Gurin (Eds.), *Mind-body medicine.* Yonkers, NY: Consumer Reports Books.

Bentler, P. M., & Newcomb, M. D. (1978). Longitudinal study of marital success and failure. *Journal of Consulting and Clinical Psychology, 46,* 1053-1070.

Benton, D., Kumari, N., & Brain, P. F. (1982). Mild hypoglycemia and questionnaire measures of aggression. *Biological Psychology, 14,* 129-135.

Berg, J. H., & Archer, R. L. (1982). Responses of self-disclosure and interaction goals. *Journal of Experimental Social Psychology, 18,* 501-512.

Berger, D. (1986, January). Theory into practice: The FCB grid. *European Research,* 35-46.

Berger, J. (1988, March 16). Teachers of the gifted fight accusations of elitism. *The New York Times,* p. 36.

Berglas, S., & Jones, E. E. (1978). Drug choice as a self-handicapping strategy in response to noncontingent success. *Journal of Personality and Social Psychology, 36,* 405-417.

Berkowitz, L. (1972). Social norms, feelings, and other factors affecting helping and altruism. In L. Berkowitz (Ed.), *Advances in experimental social psychology* (Vol. 6). New York: Academic Press.

Berkowitz, L. (1974). Some determinants of impulsive aggression: The role of mediated associations with reinforcements for aggression. *Psychological Review, 81,* 165-176.

Berkowitz, L. (1984). Some effects of thoughts on anti- and prosocial influences of media events: A cognitive-neoassociation analysis. *Psychological Bulletin, 95,* 410-427.

Berkowitz, L. (1989). Frustration-aggression hypothesis: Examination and reformulation. *Psychological Bulletin, 106,* 59-73.

Berkowitz, L. (1990). On the formation and regulation of anger and aggression: A cognitive-neoassociationistic analysis. *American Psychologist, 45,* 494-503.

Berkowitz, L. (1993). *Aggression: Its causes, consequences, and control.* New York: McGraw-Hill.

Berkowitz, L., & Geen, R. G. (1966). Film violence and the cue properties of available targets. *Journal of Personality and Social Psychology, 3,* 525-530.

Berkowitz, L., & LePage, A. (1967). Weapons as aggression-eliciting stimuli. *Journal of Personality and Social Psychology, 7,* 202-207.

Berkowitz, L., & Powers, P. C. (1979). Effects of timing and justification of witnessed aggression on the observers' punitiveness. *Journal of Research in Personality, 13,* 71-80.

Berlyne, D. E. (1970). Novelty, complexity, and hedonic value. *Perception and Psychophysics, 8,* 279-286.

Bernieri, F. J., & Rosenthal, R. (1991). Interpersonal coordination: Behavior matching and interactional synchrony. In R. S. Feldman & B. Rimé (Eds.), *Fundamentals of nonverbal behavior.* Cambridge, England: Cambridge University Press.

Berrenberg, J. L., Rosnik, D., & Kravcisin, N. J. (1991). Blaming the victim: When disease prevention programs misfire. *Current Psychology Research and Reviews, 9,* 415-420.

Berry, D. S. (1990). Taking people at face value: Evidence for the kernel of truth hypothesis. *Social Cognition, 8,* 343-361.

Berry, J. W. (1966). Temne and Eskimo perceptual skills. *International Journal of Psychology, 1,* 207-229.

Berry, J. W. (1967). Independence and conformity in subsistence-level societies. *Journal of Personality and Social Psychology, 7,* 415-418.

Berscheid, E. (1985). Interpersonal attraction. In G. Lindzey and E. Aronson (Eds.), *Handbook of social psychology* (Vol. 2). New York: Random House.

Berscheid, E., Graziano, W., Monson, T., & Dermer, M. (1976). Outcome dependency: Attention, attribution, and attraction. *Journal of Personality and Social Psychology, 34,* 978-989.

Berscheid, E., Snyder, M., & Omoto, A. M. (1989a). The Relationship Closeness Inventory: Assessing the closeness of interpersonal relationships. *Journal of Personality and Social Psychology, 57,* 792-807.

Berscheid, E., Snyder, M., & Omoto, A. M. (1989b). Issues in study close relationships: Conceptualizing and measuring closeness. In C. Hendrick (Ed.), *Review of personality and social psychology: Vol. 10. Close relationships.* Newbury Park, CA: Sage.

Berscheid, E., & Walster, E. (1974). Physical attractiveness. In L. Berkowitz (Ed.), *Advances in experimental social psychology* (Vol. 7, pp. 157-215). New York: Academic Press.

Berscheid, E., & Walster, E. (1978). *Interpersonal attraction* (2nd ed.). Reading, MA: Addison-Wesley.

Berscheid, E., Walster, E., & Campbell, R.

(1974). Grow old with me. Cited in E. Berscheid & E. Walster, Physical attractiveness. In L. Berkowitz (Ed.), *Advances in experimental social psychology* (Vol. 7). New York: Academic Press.

Best, C., Dansky, B. S., & Kilpatrick, D. G. (1992). Medical students' attitudes about female rape victims. *Journal of Interpersonal Violence, 7,* 175-188.

Biaggio, M. K. (1980). Anger arousal and personality characteristics. *Journal of Personality and Social Psychology, 39,* 352-356.

Bianchi, S. M., & Spain, D. (1986). *American women in transition.* New York: Russell Sage Foundation.

Biernat, M., Manis, M., & Nelson, T. E. (1991). Stereotypes and standards of judgment. *Journal of Personality and Social Psychology, 60,* 485-499.

Biernat M., & Wortman, C. B. (1991). Sharing of home responsibilities between professionally employed women and their husbands. *Journal of Personality and Social Psychology, 60,* 844-860.

Birnbaum, M. H., & Mellers, B. A. (1979). Stimulus recognition may mediate exposure effects. *Journal of Personality and Social Psychology, 37,* 391-394.

Birnbaum, M. H., & Sotoodeh, Y. (1991). Measurement of stress: Scaling magnitudes of life changes. *Psychological Science, 2,* 236-243.

Black, L. E., Eastwood, M. M., Sprenkle, D. H., & Smith, E. (1991). An exploratory analysis of the construct of leavers versus left as it relates to Levinger's social exchange theory of attractions, barriers, and alternative attractions. Special Issue: Marital instability and divorce outcomes: Issues for therapists and educators. *Journal of Divorce and Remarriage, 15*(1-2), 127-139.

Blais, M. (1993, June). The Ruehling class. *Lear's, 6,* 50-53.

Blanchard, F. A., Lilly, R., & Vaughn, L. A. (1991). Reducing the expression of racial prejudice. *Psychological Science, 2,* 101-105.

Blanck, P. D. (1991). What empirical research tells us: Studying judges' and juries' behavior. *American University Law Review, 40,* 775-804.

Blanck, P. D. (Ed.). (1993). *Interpersonal expectations: Theory, research and applications.* Cambridge, England: Cambridge University Press.

Blanck, P. D., & Rosenthal, R. (1992). Nonverbal behavior in the courtroom. In R. S. Feldman (Ed.), *Applications of nonverbal behavioral theory and research.* Hillsdale, NJ: Erlbaum.

Blascovich, J. J., & Katkin, E. S. (Eds.). (1993). *Cardiovascular reactivity to psychological stress and disease.* Washington, DC: American Psychological Association.

Blass, T. (1991). Understanding behavior in the Milgram obedience experiment: The role of personality, situations, and their interactions. *Journal of Personality and Social Psychology, 60,* 398-413.

Blass, T., & Krackow, A. (1991, June). *The Milgram obedience experiments: Students' views vs. scholarly perspectives and actual findings.* Paper presented at the annual meeting of the American Psychological Society, Washington, D. C.

Bohner, G., Bless, H., Schwarz, N., & Strack, H. (1988) What triggers causal attributions? The impact of valence and subjective probability. *European Journal of Social Psychology, 18,* 335-348.

Bond, M. (Ed.). (1988). *The cross-cultural challenge to social psychology.* Newbury Park, CA: Sage.

Boone, L. E., & Krutz, D. L. (1986). *Contemporary marketing* (5th ed.). Chicago: Dryden.

Borgida, E. (1982). Legal reform of rape laws: Social psychogical and constituional considerations. In L. Bickman (Ed.), *Applied Social Psychology Annual, 2.*

Bornstein, R. F., & D'Agostino, P. R. (1992). Stimulus recognition and the mere exposure effect. *Journal of Personality and Social Psychology, 63,* 545-552.

Borrello, G. M., & Thompson, B. (1990). An hierarchical analysis of the Hendrick-Hendrick measure of Lee's typology of love. *Journal of Social Behavior and Personality, 5,* 327-342.

Bossard, J. H. S. (1932). Residential proinquity as a factor in mate selection. *American Journal of Sociology, 38,* 219-224.

*Boston Sunday Globe, TV Week.* (1992, May 31). Boston, MA.

Bower, G. H. (1986). Prime time in cognitive psychology. In P. Eelen (Ed.), *Cognitive research behavior therapy: Beyond the conditioning paradigm.* Amsterdam: North Holland Publishers.

Bowlby, J. (1969). *Attachment and loss.* New York: Basic Books.

Boyanowsky, E. O., Allen, V. L., Bragg, B. W., & Lepinski, J. (1981). Generalization of independence created by social support. *Psychological Record, 31,* 475-488.

Boyd, J. R., Covington, T. R., Stanaszek, W. F., & Coussons, R. T. (1974). Drug defaulting, II. Analysis of noncompliance patterns. *American Journal of Hospital Pharmacy, 31,* 485-491.

Boyden, T., Carroll, J. S., & Maier, R. A. (1984). Similarity and attraction in homosexual males: The effects of age and masculinity-femininity. *Sex Roles, 10,* 939-948.

Boyll, J. R. (1991). Psychological, cognitive, personality and interpersonal factors in jury verdicts. *Law and Psychology Review, 15,* 163-184.

Bradbury, T. N., & Fincham, F. D. (1990). Attributions in marriage: Review and critique. *Psychological Bulletin, 107,* 3-33.

Bradbury, T. N., & Fincham, F. D. (1992). Attributions and behavior in marital interaction. *Journal of Personality and Social Psychology, 63,* 613-628

Bray, R. M., Johnson, D., & Chilstrom, J. T., Jr. (1982). Social influence by group members with minority opinions: A comparison of Hollander and Moscovici. *Journal of Personality and Social Psychology, 43,* 78-88.

Bray, R. M., & Noble, A. M. (1978). Authoritarianism and decisions of mock juries: Evidence of jury bias and group polarization. *Journal of Personality and Social Psychology, 36,* 1424-1430.

Breakwell, G. M. (1992). *Social psychology of identity and the self concept.* New York: Academic Press.

Breay, E., & Gentry, M. (1990, April). *Perceptions of a sexual double standard.* Paper presented at the Eastern Psychological Association annual meeting, Philadelphia.

Breckler, S. J. (1984). Empirical validation of affect, behavior, and cognition as distinct components of attitude. *Journal of Personality and Social Psychology, 47,* 1191-1205.

Brehm, J. W. (1956). Post-decision changes in desirability of alternatives. *Journal of Abnormal and Social Psychology 52,* 384-389.

Brehm, J. W., & Mann, M. (1975). Effect of importance of freedom and attraction to group members on influence produced by group pressure. *Journal of Personality and Social Psychology, 31,* 816-824.

Brehm, S. S., & Brehm, J. W. (1981). *Psychological reactance.* New York: Academic Press.

Brehm, S. S. (1988). Passionate love. In R. J. Sternberg and M. L. Barnes (Eds.), *The psychology of love* (pp. 232-263). New Haven, CT: Yale University Press.

Brehm, S. S. (1992). *Intimate relationships* (2nd ed.). New York: McGraw-Hill.

Brennan, J. (1991, August 21). Key words influence stands on minorities. *Los Angeles Times,* A5.

Brewer, M. B. (1988). A dual process model of impression formation. In T. K. Srull & R. S. Wyer, Jr. (Eds.), *Advances in social cognition* (Vol. 1, pp. 1-36). Hillsdale, NJ: Erlbaum.

Brewer, M. B. (1991). The social self: On being the same and different at the same time. *Personality and Social Psychology Bulletin, 17,* 475-482.

Brewer, M. B., & Kramer, R. M. (1985). The psychology of intergroup attitudes and behavior. *Annual Review of Psychology, 36,* 219-243.

Brewer, M. B., & Lui, L. L. (1989). The primacy of age and sex in the structure of person categories. *Social Cognition, 7,* 262-274.

Brickner, M. A., Harkins, S. G., & Ostrom, T. M. (1986). Effects of personal involvement: Thought-provoking implications for social loafing. *Journal of Personality and Social Psychology, 51,* 763-770.

Bridges, J. S. (1988). Sex differences in occupational performance expectations. *Psychology of Women Quarterly, 12,* 75-90.

Brinkerhoff, D. B., & Booth, A. (1984). Gender, dominance, and stress. *Journal of Social and Biological Structures, 7,* 159-177.

Brockner, J., & Swap, W. C. (1983). Resolving the relationships between placebos, misattribution, and insomnia: An individual-differences perspective. *Journal of Personality and Social Psychology, 45,* 32-42.

Brodsky, S. L., & Scogin, F. R. (1988). Inmates in protective custody: First data on emotional effects. *Forensic Reports, 1,* 267-280.

Brody, J. E. (1992, August 11). To predict divorce, ask 125 questions. *New York Times,* C1, C9.

Broeder, D. W. (1959). The University of Chicago jury project. *Nebraska Law Review, 38,* 744-760.

Broverman, I. K., Vogel, S. R., Broverman, D. M., Clarkson, F. E., & Rosenkrantz, P. S. (1972). Sex-role stereotypes: A current appraisal. *Journal of Social Issues, 28,* 59-78.

Brown, J. D. (1991). Staying fit and staying well: Physical fitness as a moderator of life stress. *Journal of Personality and Social Psychology, 60,* 368-375.

Brown, J. D., & McGill, K. L. (1989). The cost of good fortune: When positive life events produce negative health consequences. *Journal of Personality and Social Psychology, 54,* 321-329.

Brown, R. (1986). *Social psychology* (2nd ed.) New York: Free Press.

Brown, R., Condor, S., Matthews, A., & Wade G. (1986). Explaining intergroup differentiation in an industrial organization. *Journal of Occupational Psychology, 59,* 273-286.

Brown, R., & Gilman, A. (1960). The pronouns of power and solidarity. In T. A. Sebok (Ed.), *Style in language* (pp. 253-276). Cambridge, MA: M. I.T. Press.

Brown, R. J., & Williams, J. (1984). Group identification: The same thing to all people? *Human Relations, 37,* 547-564.

Bryan, J. H., & Test, M. A. (1967). Models and helping: Naturalistic studies in aiding behavior. *Journal of Personality and Social Psychology, 6,* 400-407.

Buckalew, L. W., & Sallis, R. E. (1986). Patient compliance and medication perception. *Journal of Clinical Psychology, 42,* 49-53.

Buckhout, R. (1975). Nearly 2000 witnesses can be wrong. *Social Action and the Law, 2,* 7.

Bull, R., & Rumsey, N. (1988). *The social psychology of facial appearance.* New York: Springer-Verlag.

Buller, D. B., & Street, R. L., Jr. (1992). Physician-patient relationships. In R. S. Feldman (Ed.), *Applications of nonverbal behavioral theories and research.* Hillsdale, NJ: Erlbaum.

Bureau of the Census. (1990). *Statistical abstract of the United States.* Washington, DC: U. S. Government Printing Office.

Burger, J. M. (1992). *Desire for control: Personality, social, and clinical perspectives.* New York: Plenum.

Burger, J. M., & Petty, R. E. (1981). The lowball compliance technique: Task or person commitment? *Journal of Personality and Social Psychology, 40,* 492-500.

Burgess, E. W., & Wallin, P. (1953). *Engagement and marriage.* Philadelphia: Lippincott.

Burgess, R. L., & Huston, T. L. (Eds.). (1979). *Social exchanges in developing relationships.* New York: Academic Press.

Burgoon, M., & Miller, M. D. (1990). Overcoming resistance to persuasion via contiguous reinforcement and repetition of message. *Psychological Reports, 66,* 1011-1022.

Burkitt, I. (1992). *Social selves.* Newbury Park, CA: Sage.

Bush, P. J., & Osterweis, M. (1978). Pathways to medicine use. *Journal of Health and Social Behavior, 19,* 179-189.

Bushman, B. J., & Geen, R. G. (1990). Role of cognitive-emotional mediators and individual differences in the effects of media violence on aggression. *Journal of Personality and Social Psychology, 58,* 156-163.

Buss, A. H. (1961). *The psychology of aggression.* New York: Wiley.

Buss, A. H., & Durkee, A. (1957). An inventory for assessing different kinds of hostility. *Journal of Consulting Psychology, 21,* 343-349.

Buss, D. M. (1991). Conflict in married couples: Personality predictors of anger and upset. *Journal of Personality, 59,* 663-688.

Byrne, D. (1971). *The attraction paradigm.* New York: Academic Press.

Byrne, D., & Clore, G. L. (1966). Predicting interpersonal attraction toward strangers presented in three different stimulus modes. *Psychonomic Science, 4.*

Byrne, D., & Clore, G. L. (1970). A reinforcement model of evaluative responses. *Personality: An International Journal, 1,* 103-128.

Byrne, D., Clore, G. L., & Smeaton, G. (1986). The attraction hypothesis: Do similar attitudes affect anything? *Journal of Personality and Social Psychology, 51,* 1167-1170.

Byrne, D., & Murnen, S. K. (1988). Maintaining loving relationships. In R. J. Sternberg & M. L. Barnes (Eds.), *The psychology of love.* New Haven, CT: Yale University Press.

Cacioppo, J. T., Marshall-Goodell, B. S., Tassinary, L. G., & Petty, R. E. (1992). Rudimentary determinants of attitudes: Classical conditioning is more effective when prior knowledge about the attitude stimulus is low than high. *Journal of Experimental Social Psychology, 28,* 207-233.

Cacioppo, J. T., & Petty, R. E. (1979). Effects of message repetition and position on cognitive response, recall, and persuasion. *Journal of Personality and Social Psychology, 37,* 97-109.

Cacioppo, J. T., & Petty, R. E. (1981). Lateral asymmetry in the expression of cognition and emotion. *Journal of Experimental Psychology, Human Perception and Performance, 7,* 333-341.

Cacioppo, J. T., & Petty, R. E. (1982). The need for cognition. *Journal of Personality and Social Psychology, 42,* 116-131.

Cacioppo, J. T., & Petty, R. E. (1984). The need for cognition: Relationship to attitudinal processes. In R. P. McGlynn, J. E. Maddux, C. D. Stoltenberg, & J. H. Harvey (Eds.), *Interfaces in psychology: Social perception in clinical counseling psychology* (pp. 113-139). Lubbock, TX: Texas Tech Press.

Cacioppo, J. T., Petty, R. E., Kao, C. F., & Rodriguez, R. (1986). Central and peripheral routes to persuasion: An individual difference perspective. *Journal of Personality and Social Psychology, 51,* 1032-1043.

Cacioppo, J. T., Petty, R. E., & Losch, M. E. (1986). Attributions of responsibility for helping and doing harm: Evidence for confusion of responsibility. *Journal of Personality and Social Psychology, 50,* 100-105.

Cacioppo, J. T., Petty, R. E., Losch, M. E., & Kim, H. S. (1986). Electromyographic activity over facial muscle regions can differentiate the valence and intensity of affective reactions. *Journal of Personality and Social Psychology, 50,* 260-268.

Cacioppo, J. T., Petty, R. E., & Morris, K. J. (1983). Effects of need for cognition on message evaluation, recall, and persuasion. *Journal of Personality and Social Psychology, 45,* 805-818.

Cacioppo, J. T., & Tassinary, L. G. (Eds.). (1990). *Principals of psychophysiology: Physical, social and inferential elements.* Cambridge, England: Cambridge University Press.

Cadwell, S. (1991). Twice removed: The stigma suffered by gay men with AIDS. Special Issue: Men & men's issues in social work theory and practice. *Smith College Studies in Social Work, 61,* 236-246.

Calder, B. J., Insko, C. A., & Yandell, B. (1974). The relation of cognitive and memorial processes to persuasion on a simulated jury trial. *Journal of Applied Social Psychology, 4,* 62-93.

Calder, B. J., & Sternthal, B. (1980). Television commercial wear-out: An information-processing view. *Journal of Marketing Research, 17,* 173-186.

Caldwell, M. A., & Peplau, L. A. (1984). The balance of power in lesbian relationships. *Sex Roles, 23,* 713-725.

Camerena, P. M., Sarigiani, P. A., & Petersen, A. C. (1990). Gender-specific pathways to intimacy in early adolescence. *Journal of Youth and Adolescence, 19,* 19-32.

Campbell, D. T. (1967). Stereotypes and the perception of group differences. *American Psychologist, 49,* 949-952.

Campbell, J. D., & Fairey, P. J. (1989). Informational and normative routes to conformity: The effect of faction size as a function of norm extremity and attention to the stimulus. *Journal of Personality and Social Psychology, 57,* 457-468.

Candee, D., & Kohlberg, L. (1987). Moral judgment and moral action: A reanalysis of Haan, Smith, and Block's (1986) free-speech data. *Journal of Personality and Social Psychology, 52,* 554-564.

Cantor, N., & Mischel, W. (1979). Prototypes in person perception. In L. Berkowitz (Ed.), *Advances in experimental social psychology* (Vol. 12). New York: Academic Press.

Cantrill, J. G., & Seibold, D. R. (1986). The perceptual contrast explanation of sequential request strategy effectiveness. *Human Communication Research, 13,* 253-267.

Capozza, D., & Nanni, R. (1986). Differentiation processes for social stimuli with different degrees of category representativeness. *European Journal of Social Psychology, 16,* 399-412.

Carducci, B. J., & Deuser, P. S. (1984). The foot-in-the-door technique: Initial request and organ donation. *Basic and Applied Social Psychology, 5,* 75-81.

Carlo, G., Eisenberg, N., Troyer, D., Switzer, G., & Speer, A. L. (1991). The altruistic personality: In what contexts is it apparent? *Journal of Personality and Social Psychology, 61,* 450-458.

Carlson, M., Charlin, V., & Miller, N. (1988). Positive mood and helping behavior: A test of six hypotheses. *Psychological Bulletin, 102,* 91-108.

Carlson, M., Marcus-Newhall, A., & Miller, N. (1989). Evidence for a general construct of aggression. *Personality and Social Psychology Bulletin, 15,* 377-389.

Carlson, M., Marcus-Newhall, A., & Miller, N. (1990). Effects of situational aggression cues: A quantitative review. *Journal of Personality and Social Psychology, 58,* 622-633.

Carlson, M., & Miller, N. (1987). Explanation of the relation between negative mood and helping. *Psychological Bulletin, 102,* 91-108.

Carroll, S. J., Perkowitz, W. T., Lurigio, A. J., & Waver, F. M. (1987). Sentencing goals, causal attributions, ideology, and personality. *Journal of Personality and Social Psychology, 50,* 107-118.

Carver, C. (1990). *Optimism and coping with cancer.* Paper presented at the Conference on "Hostility, Coping and Health," Lake Arrowhead, CA.

Carver C. S., Pozo, C., Harris, S. D., Noriega, V., Scheier, M. F., Robinson, D. S., Ketcham, A. S., Moffat, F. L., Jr., & Clark, K. C. (1993). How coping mediates the effect of optimism on distress: A study of women with early stage breast cancer. *Journal of Personality and Social Psychology, 65,* 375-390.

Carver, C. S., & Scheier, M. F. (1985). Aspect of self and the control of behavior. In B. R. Schlenker (Ed.), *The self and social life* (pp. 146-172). New York: McGraw-Hill.

Cash, T. F., & Derlega, V. J. (1978). The matching hypothesis: Physical attractiveness among same-sexed friends. *Personality and Social Psychology Bulletin, 4,* 240-243.

Castellan, N. J., Jr. (Ed.). (1993). *Individual and group decision making.* Hillsdale, NJ: Erlbaum.

Catania, J. A., Coates, T. J., Stall, R., Turner, H., Peterson, J., Hearst, N., Dolcini, M. M., Hudes, E., Gagnon, J., Wiley, J., & Groves, R. (1992, November 13). Prevalence of AIDS-related risk factors and condom use in the United States. *Science, 258,* 1101-1106.

CDC (Centers for Disease Control). (1991). *Incidence of sexually transmitted diseases.* Atlanta: Centers for Disease Control.

CDC (Centers for Disease Control). (1992, January). *Most students sexually active: Survey of sexual activity.* Atlanta: Centers for Disease Control.

Chaiken, S. (1979). Communicator physical attractiveness and persuasion. *Journal of Personality and Social Psychology, 37,* 1387-1397.

Chaiken, S. (1980). Heuristic versus systematic information processing and the use of source versus message cues in persuasion. *Journal of Personality and Social Psychology, 39,* 752-766.

Chaiken, S. (1987). The heuristic model of persuasion. In M. P. Zanna, J. M. Olson, & C. P. Herman (Eds.), *Social influence: The Ontario Symposium* (Vol. 5). Hillsdale, NJ: Erlbaum.

Chaiken, S., & Stangor, S. (1987). Attitudes and attitude change. *Annual Review of Psychology, 38,* 575-630.

Chamberlain, K., & Zika, S. (1990). The minor events approach to stress: Support for the use of daily hassles. *British Journal of Psychology, 81,* 469-481.

Chandra, S. (1973). The effects of group pressure on perception: A cross-cultural conformity study. *International Journal of Psychology, 8,* 37-39.

Chapkis, W. (1986). *Beauty secrets: Women and the politics of appearance.* Boston: South End Press.

Chemers, M. M., & Ayman, R. (Eds.). (1993). *Leadership in the 1990s: Substance and shadow.* San Diego, CA: Academic Press.

Cheng, P. W., & Novick, L. R. (1990). A probalistic contrast model of causal induction. *Journal of Personality and Social Psychology, 58,* 545-567.

Cherlin, A. J., Furstenberg, F. F., Jr., Chase-Lansdale, P. L., Kiernan, K. E., Robins, P. K., Morrison, D. R., & Teitler, J. O. (1991, June 7). Longitudinal studies of effects of divorce on children in Great Britain and the United States. *Science, 252,* 1386-1389.

Christianson, S. (1992). Emotional stress and eyewitness memory: A critical review. *Psychological Bulletin, 112,* 284-309.

Chwalisz, K., Diener, E., & Gallagher, D. (1988). Autonomic arousal feedback and emotional experience: Evidence from the spinal-cord injured. *Journal of Personality and Social Psychology, 54,* 820-828.

Cialdini, R. (1993). *Influence: Science and practice* (3rd ed.). New York: HarperCollins.

Cialdini, R. B. (1988). *Influence: Science and practice* (2nd ed.). Glenview, IL: Scott, Foresman.

Cialdini, R. B. (1991). Altruism or egoism? That is (still) the question. *Psychological Inquiry, 2,* 124-126.

Cialdini, R. B., & Fultz, J. (1990). Interpreting the negative mood-helping literature via "mega"-analysis: A contrary view. *Psychological Bulletin, 107,* 210-214.

Cialdini, R. B., & Kenrick, D. T. (1976). Altruism as hedonism: A social development perspective on the relationship of negative mood state and helping. *Journal of Personality and Social Psychology, 34,* 907-914.

Cialdini, R. B., Kenrick, D. T., & Baumann, D. J. (1982). Effects of mood on prosocial behavior in children and adults. In N. Eisenberg (Ed.), *The development of prosocial behavior.* Orlando, FL: Academic Press.

Cialdini, R. B., & Petty, R. E. (1981). Anticipatory opinion effects. In R. E. Petty, T. M. Ostrom, & T. C. Brock (Eds.), *Cognitive responses in persuasion.* Hillsdale, NJ: Erlbaum.

Cialdini, R. B., Schaller, M., Houlihan, D., Arps, K., Fultz, J., & Beaman, A. L. (1987). Empathy-based helping: Is it selflessly or selfishly motivated? *Journal of Personality and Social Psychology, 52,* 749-758.

Cialdini, R. B., Vincent, J. E., Lewis, S. K., Catalan, J., Wheeler, D., & Darby, B. L. (1975). Reciprocal concessions procedure for inducing compliance: The door-in-the-face technique. *Journal of Personality and Social Psychology, 31*, 206-215.

CIRE (Cooperative Institutional Research Program of the American Council on Education). (1990). *The American freshman: National norms for fall 1990.* Los Angeles: American Council on Education.

Claes, J. A., & Rosenthal, D. A. (1990). Men who batter women: A study in power. *Journal of Family Violence, 5*, 215-224.

Clark, H. H. (1985). Language use and language users. In G. Lindzey & E. Aronson (Eds.), *Handbook of social psychology* (Vol. 2, 3rd ed.). New York: Random House.

Clark, M., & Mills, J. (1993). The difference between communal and exchange relationships: What it is and is not. *Personality and Social Psychology Bulletin, 19*, 684-691.

Clark, M., Mills, J., & Powell, M. C. (1986). Keeping track of needs in communal and exchange relationships. *Journal of Personality and Social Psychology, 51*, 333-338.

Clark, M. L., & Ayers, M. (1992). Friendship similarity during early adolescence: Gender and racial patterns. *Journal of Psychology, 126*, 393-405.

Clark, M. S. (1984). Record keeping in two types of relationships. *Journal of Personality and Social Psychology, 47*, 549-557.

Clark, M. S., & Mills, J. (1979). Interpersonal attraction in exchange and communal relationships. *Journal of Personality and Social Psychology, 37*, 12-24.

Clark, M. S., Mills, J. R., & Corcoran, D. M. (1989). Keeping track of needs and inputs of friends and strangers. *Personality and Social Psychology Bulletin, 15*, 533-542.

Clark, M. S., & Reis, H. T. (1988). Interpersonal processes in close relationships. *Annual Review of Psychology, 39*, 609-672.

Clark, R. D., & Sechrest, L. B. (1976). The mandate phenomenon. *Journal of Personality and Social Psychology, 34*, 1057-1061.

Clark, R. D., III, & Maass, A. (1988). Social categorization in minority influence. *European Journal of Social Psychology, 18*, 347-364.

Clark, R. D., III, & Maass, A. (1990). The effects of majority size on minority influence. *European Journal of Social Psychology, 20*, 99-117.

Clavier, D. W., & Kalupa, F. B. (1983). Public rebuttals to "trial by television." *Public Relations Review, 9*, 24-36.

Coats, E. J., Feldman, R. S., & Schwartzberg, S. (1994). *Critical thinking: General principles and case studies.* New York: McGraw-Hill.

Cobb, N. (1992, February 9). How they met. *Parade*, 12-15.

Cohen, C. E. (1981). Person categories and social perception: Testing some boundaries of the processing effects of prior knowledge.

*Journal of Personality and Social Psychology, 40*, 441-452.

Cohen, S., Tyrrell, D. A., & Smith, A. P. (1993). Negative life events, perceived stress, negative affect, and susceptibility to the common cold. *Journal of Personality and Social Psychology, 64*, 131-140.

Colvin, C. R., & Funder, D. C. (1991). Predicting personality and behavior: A boundary on the acquaintanceship effect. *Journal of Personality and Social Psychology, 60*, 884-894.

Compton, W. M., Cottler, L. D., Decker, S. H., Meager, D., & Stringfellow, R. (1992). Legal needle buying in St. Louis. *American Journal of Public Health, 82*, 595-596.

Comstock, G., & Strasburger, V. C. (1990). Deceptive appearances: Television violence and aggressive behavior. Conference: Teens and television (1988, Los Angeles, California). *Journal of Adolescent Health Care, 11*, 31-44.

Condon, J. W., & Crano, W. D. (1988). Inferred evaluation and the relation between attitude similarity and interpersonal attraction. *Journal of Personality and Social Psychology, 54*, 789-797.

Condry, J. (1977). Enemies of exploration: Self-initiated versus other-initiated learning. *Journal of Personality and Social Psychology, 35*, 459-477.

Cook, S. W. (1976). Ethical issues in the conduct of research in social relations. In C. Sellitz, L. S. Wrightsman, & S. W. Cook, *Research methods in social relations* (3rd ed., pp. 199-249). New York: Holt, Rinehart and Winston.

Cook, T. D., Gruder, C. L., Hennigan, K. M., & Flay, B. R. (1979). History of the sleeper effect: Some logical pitfalls in accepting the null hypothesis. *Psychological Bulletin, 86*, 662-679.

Cooley, C. H. (1902). *Human nature and the social order.* New York: Scribners.

Cooper, J., & Fazio, R. (1984) A new look at dissonance theory. In L. Berkowitz (Ed.), *Advances in experimental social psychology* (Vol. 17). New York: Academic Press.

Cotton, J. L. (1993). *Employee involvement.* Newbury Park, CA: Sage.

Cottrell, N. B. (1972). Social facilitation. In C. G. McClintock (Ed.), *Experimental social psychology* (pp. 185-236). New York: Holt.

Cowan, N. (1992). Verbal memory span and the timing of spoken recall. *Journal of Memory and Language, 31*, 668-684.

Cowan, P. A., & Cowan, C. P. (1988). Changes in marriage during the transition to parenthood: Must we blame the baby? In G. Y. Michaels & W. A. Goldberg (Eds.), *The transition to parenthood: Current theory and research.* Cambridge, England: Cambridge University Press.

Crandall, R. (1972). Field extension of the frequency-affect findings. *Psychological Reports, 31*, 371-374.

Crocker, J., & Luhtanen, R. (1990). Collective self-esteem and ingroup bias. *Journal of Personality and Social Psychology, 58*, 60-67.

Crohan, S. E. (1992). Marital happiness and spousal consensus on beliefs about marital conflict: A longitudinal investigation. *Journal of Social and Personal Relationships, 9*, 89-102.

Crosby, F. J. (1991). *Juggling: The unexpected advantages of balancing career and home for women, their families, and society.* New York: Free Press.

Cross, H. A., Halcomb, C. G., & Matter, W. W. (1967). Imprinting and exposure learning in rats given early auditory stimulation. *Psychonomic Science, 10*, 223-234.

Croyle, R. T., & Cooper, J. (1983). Dissonance arousal: Physiological evidence. *Journal of Personality and Social Psychology, 45*, 782-791.

Croyle, R. T., & Hunt, J. R. (1991). Coping with health threat: Social influence processes in reactions to medical test results. *Journal of Personality and Social Psychology, 60*, 382-389.

Cruse, D., & Leigh, B. C. (1987). "Adam's Rib" revisited: Legal and non-legal influences on the processing of trial testimony. *Social Behavior, 2*, 221-230.

Cryan, J. R. (1987). The banning of corporal punishment: In child care, school and other educative settings in the United States. *Childhood Education, 63*, 146-153.

Csoka, L. S., & Bons, P. M. (1978). Manipulating the situation to fix the leader's style—Two validation studies of Leader Match. *Journal of Applied Psychology, 63*, 295-300.

Cummings, J. (1987, October 6). An earthquake aftershock: Calls to mental health triple. *New York Times*, p. A-1.

Cunningham, M. R. (1979). Weather, mood and helping behavior: Quasi-experiments with the Sunshine Samaritan. *Journal of Personality and Social Psychology, 37*, 1947-1956.

Cunningham, M. R. (1986). Measuring the physical in physical attractiveness: Quasi-experiments on the sociobiology of female facial beauty. *Journal of Personality and Social Psychology, 50*, 925-935.

Cunningham, M. R., Barbee, A. P., & Pike, C. L. (1990). What do women want? Facial-metric assessment of multiple motives in the perception of male facial physical attractiveness. *Journal of Personality and Social Psychology, 59*, 61-72.

Curtis, R. C., & Miller, K. (1986). Believing another likes or dislikes you: Behavior making the beliefs come true. *Journal of Personality and Social Psychology, 51*, 284-290.

Cutrona, C. (1982). Transition to college: Loneliness and the process of social adjustment. In L. A. Peplau & D. Perlman (Eds.), *Loneliness: A sourcebook of current theory, research, and therapy*. New York: Wiley.

Dabbs, J. M., Jr., Frady, R. L., Carr, T. S., & Besch, N. F. (1987). Saliva testosterone and criminal violence in young adult prison inmates. *Psychosomatic Medicine, 49*, 174-182.

Dabbs, J. M., Jr., & Morris, R. (1990) Testosterone, social class, and antisocial behavior in a sample of 4,462 men. *Psychological Science, 1*, 209-211.

da Gloria, J., Duda, D., Pahlavan, F., & Bonnet, P. (1989). "Weapons effect" revisited: Motor effects of the reception of aversive stimulation and exposure to pictures of firearms. *Aggressive Behavior, 15*, 265-271.

Dailey, D. M. (1979). Adjustment of heterosexual and homosexual couples in pairing relationships: An exploratory study. *Journal of Sex Research, 15*, 143-157.

Dane, F. C., & Wrightsman, L. S. (1982). Effects of defendants' and victims' characteristics on jurors' verdicts. In N. Kerr & R. Bray (Eds.), *The psychology of the courtroom*. New York: Academic Press.

Danziger, S., & Wheeler, D. (1975). Economics of crime: Punishment or income redistribution. *Review of Social Economy, 33*, 113-131.

Darley, J. M., & Batson, C. D. (1973). "From Jerusalem to Jericho": A study of situational and dispositional variables in helping behavior. *Journal of Personality and Social Psychology, 27*, 100-108.

Darley, J. M., Fleming, J. H., Hilton, J. L., & Swan, W. B. (1988). Dispelling negative expectancies: The impact of interaction goals and target characteristics on the expectancy confirmation process. *Journal of Experimental Social Psychology, 24*, 19-36.

Darley, J. M., & Latané, B. (1968), Bystander intervention in emergencies: Diffusion of responsibility. *Journal of Personality and Social Psychology, 8*, 377-383.

Darley, J. M., & Schultz, T. R. (1990). Moral rules: Their content and acquisition. *Annual Review of Psychology, 25*, 525-556.

Dashiell, J. F. (1930). An experimental analysis of some group effects. *Journal of Abnormal and Social Psychology, 25*, 190-199.

Davidson, A. R., & Jaccard, J. J. (1979). Variables that moderate the attitude-behavior relation: Results of a longitudinal survey. *Journal of Personality and Social Psychology, 45*, 997-1009.

Davidson, D., & Hirtle, S. C. (1990). Effects of nondiscrepant and discrepant information on the use of base rates. *American Journal of Pscyhology, 103*, 343-357.

Davis, J. H. (1969). *Group performance*. Reading, MA: Addison-Wesley.

Davis, M. S. (1968). Variations in patients' compliance with doctors' advice: An empirical analysis of patterns of communication. *American Journal of Public Health, 58*, 274-288.

Deal, T. E., & Kennedy, A. A. (1982). *Corporate cultures: The rites and rituals of corporate life*. Reading, MA: Addison-Wesley.

Deaton, A. V. (1985). Adaptive noncompliance in pediatric asthma: The parent as expert. *Journal of Pediatric Psychology, 10*, 1-14.

Deaux, K. (1992). Personalizing identity and socializing self. In G. Breakwell (Ed.), *Social psychology of identity and the self-concept*. London: Academic Press.

Deaux, K. (1993). Reconstructing social identity. *Personality and Social Psychology Bulletin, 19*, 4-12.

Deaux, K., & Lewis, L. L. (1984). The structure of gender stereotypes: Interrelationships among components and gender label. *Journal of Personality and Social Psychology, 46*, 991-1004.

DeBono, K. G., & Packer, M. (1991). The effects of advertising appeal on perceptions of product quality. *Personality and Social Psychology Bulletin, 17*, 194-200.

DeBono, K. G., & Telesca, C. (1990). The influence of source physical attractiveness on advertising effectiveness: A functional perspective. *Journal of Applied Social Psychology, 20*, 1383-1395.

Deci, E. L., & Ryan, R. M. (1985). *Intrinsic motivation and self-determination in human behavior*. New York: Plenum Press.

DeFrank, R. S., Matteson, M. T., Schweiger, D. M., & Ivancevich, J. M. (1985). The impact of culture on the management practices of Japanese and American CEOs. *Organizational Dynamics, 13*, 62-70.

Delgado, J. M. R. (1969). *Physical control of the mind*. New York: Harper & Row.

Demare, D., Briere, J., & Lips, H. M. (1988). Violent pornography and self-reported likelihood of sexual aggression. *Journal of Research in Personality, 22*, 140-153.

DeMott, J. S. (1985, May 6). Fiddling with the real thing (Coca Cola changes formula). *Time, 125*, 54-56.

Dengerink, H. A., & Covey, M. K. (1983). Implications of an escape-avoidance theory of aggressive response to attack. In R. G. Geen & E. I. Donnerstein (Eds.), *Aggression: Theoretical and empirical reviews, Vol. 1: Theoretical and methodological issues*. New York: Academic Press.

Denmark, F. L. (1980). Psyche: From rocking the cradle to rocking the boat. *American Psychologist, 35*, 1057-1065.

DeParle, J. (1993, March 19). Sharp criticism for head start, even by friends. *New York Times*, p. A1.

DePaulo, B. M. (1992). Nonverbal behavior and self-presentation. *Psychological Bulletin, III*, 203-243.

Derlega, V. J. (1988). Self-disclosure: Inside or outside the mainstream of social psychological research? [Special Issue]: The state of social psychology: Issues, themes, and controversies. *Journal of Social Behavior and Personality, 3*, 27-34.

Derlega, V. J., & Berg, J. H. (1987). *Self-disclosure: Theory, research, and therapy*. New York: Plenum.

Derlega, V. J., Metts, S., Petronio, S., & Margulis, S. T. (1993). *Self-disclosure*. Newbury Park, CA: Sage.

Derlega, V. J., Wilson, M., & Chaikin, A. L. (1976). Friendship and disclosure reciprocity. *Journal of Personality and Social Psychology, 34*, 578-587.

Desforges, D. M., Lord, C. G., Ramsey, S. L., Mason, J. A., VanLeeuwen, M. D., West, S. C., & Lepper, M. R. (1991). Effects of structured cooperative contact on changing negative attitudes toward stigmatized social groups. *Journal of Personality and Social Psychology, 60*, 531-544.

Deutsch, M. (1973). *The resolution of conflict: Constructive and destructive processes*. New Haven, CT: Yale University Press.

Deutsch, M., & Gerard, H. B. (1955). A study of normative and informational social influence upon individual judgment. *Journal of Abnormal and Social Psychology, 51*, 629-636.

Devine, P. G. (1989). Stereotypes and prejudice: Their automatic and controlled components. *Journal of Personality and Social Psychology, 56*, 5-18.

Devine, P. G., Monteith, M. J., Zuwerink, J. R., & Elliot, A. J. (1991). Prejudice with and without compunction. *Journal of Personality and Social Psychology, 60*, 817-830.

deWolfe, T. E., & Jackson, L. A. (1984). Birds of a brighter feather: Level of moral reasoning and similarity of attitude as determinants of interpersonal attraction. *Psychological Reports, 54*, 303-308.

Dewsbury, D. A. (1981). Effects of novelty on copulatory behavior: The Coolidge effect and related phenomena. *Psychological Bulletin, 89*, 464-482.

Diamond, S. S. (1993). Instructing on death: Psychologists, juries, and judges. *American Psychologist, 48*, 423-434.

Diehl, M., & Stroebe, W. (1987). Productivity loss in brainstorming groups: Toward the solution of a riddle. *Journal of Personality and Social Psychology, 53*, 497-509.

Diehl, M., & Stroebe, W. (1991). Productivity loss in idea-generating groups: Tracking down the blocking effect. *Journal of Personality and Social Psychology, 61*, 392-403.

Diener, E. (1980). Deindividuation: The absence of self-awareness and self-regulation in group members. In P. B. Paulus (Ed.), *Psychology of group influence* (pp. 209-242). Hillsdale, NJ: Erlbaum.

Dietz, P. E., Harry, B., & Hazelwood, R. R. (1986). Detective magazines: Pornography for the sexual sadist? *Journal of Forensic Sciences, 31,* 197-211.

Dillard, J. P. (1991). The current status of research on sequential-request compliance techniques. [Special Issue]: Meta-analysis in personality and social psychology. *Personality and Social Psychology Bulletin, 17,* 283-288.

Dillard, J. P., Hunter, J. E., & Burgoon, M. (1984). Sequential-request persuasive strategies: Meta-analysis of foot-in-the-door and door-in-the-face. *Human Communication Research, 10,* 461-488.

DiMatteo, M. R., & DiNicola, D. D. (1982). *Achieving patient compliance: The psychology of the medical practitioner's role.* New York: Pergamon.

Dindia, K., & Allen, M. (1992). Sex differences in self-disclosure: A meta-analysis. *Psychological Bulletin, 112,* 106-124.

Dion, K. K. (1972). Physical attractiveness and evaluations of children's transgressions. *Journal of Personality and Social Psychology, 24,* 207-213.

Dion, K. L., & Dion, K. K. (1988). Romantic love: Individual and cultural perspectives. In R. J. Sternberg & M. L. Barnes (Eds.), *The psychology of love.* New Haven, CT: Yale University Press.

Dodge, K. A., Bates, J. E., & Petit, G. S. (1990, December 20). Mechanisms in the cycle of violence. *Science, 250,* 1678-1683.

Dohrenwend, B. S., Dohrenwend, B. P., Dodson, M., & Shrout, P. E. (1984). Symptoms, hassles, social supports, and life events: The problem of confounded measures. *Journal of Abnormal Psychology, 93,* 222-230.

Dolgin, K. G., Meyer, L., & Schwartz, J. (1991). Effects of gender, target's gender, topic, and self-esteem on disclosure to best and middling friends. *Sex Roles, 25,* 311-329.

Doll, J., & Ajzen, I. (1992). Accessibility and stability of predictors in the theory of planned behavior. *Journal of Personality and Social Psychology, 63,* 754-765.

Dollard, J., Doob, L. W., Miller, N. E., Mowrer, O. H., & Sears, R. R. (1939). *Frustration and aggression.* New Haven, CT: Yale University Press.

Dollinger, S. J., & Clancy, S. M. (1993). Identity, self, and personality: II. Glimpses through the autophotographic eye. *Journal of Personality and Social Psychology, 64,* 1064-1071.

Donnerstein, E., & Berkowitz, L. (1981). Victim reactions in aggressive erotic films as a factor in violence against women. *Journal of Personality and Social Psychology, 41,* 710-724.

Donnerstein, E. I., & Linz, D. G. (1986). Mass media sexual violence and male viewers: Current theory and research. *American Behavioral Scientist, 29,* 601-618.

Donnerstein, M., & Donnerstein, E. (1977). Modeling in the control of interracial aggression: The problem of generality. *Journal of Personality, 45,* 100-116.

Donnerstein, M., & Donnerstein, E. (1978). Direct and vicarious censure in the control of interracial aggression. *Journal of Personality, 46,* 162-175.

Doob, A. N., & Beaulieu, L. A. (1992). Variation in the exercise of judicial discretion with young offenders. *Canadian Journal of Criminology, 34,* 35-50.

Dorfman, P. W., & Stephan, W. G. (1984). The effects of group performance on cognitions, satisfaction, and behavior: A process model. *Journal of Management, 10,* 173-192.

Doris, J. (Ed.). (1991). *The suggestibility of children's recollection: Implications for eyewitness testimony.* Hyattsville, MD: American Psychological Association.

Dovidio, J. F., Allen, J. L., & Schroeder, D. A. (1990). Specificity of empathy-induced helping: Evidence for altruistic motivation. *Journal of Personality and Social Psychology, 59,* 249-260.

Dovidio, J. F., Ellyson, S. L., Keating, C. F., Heltman, K., & Brown, C. E. (1988). The relationship of social power to visual displays of dominance between men and women. *Journal of Personality and Social Psychology, 54,* 233-242.

Dovidio, J. F., & Gaertner, S. L. (1986). *Prejudice, discrimination, and racism: Theory and research.* Orlando, FL: Academic Press.

Dovidio, J. F., & Gaertner, S. L. (1991). Changes in the expression of racial prejudice. In H. Knopke, J. Norrell, & R. Rogers (Eds.), *Opening doors: An appraisal of race relations in contemporary America.* Tuscaloosa: University of Alabama Press.

Downs, A. C., & Lyons, P. M. (1991). Natural observations of the links between attractiveness and initial legal judgments. *Personality and Social Psychology Bulletin, 17,* 541-547.

Drabman, R. S., & Thomas, M. H. (1974). Exposure to filmed violence and children's tolerance of real life aggression. *Personality and Social Psychology Bulletin, 1,* 198-199.

Drigotas, S. M. (1993). Similarity revisted: A comparison of similarity-attraction versus dissimilarity-repulsion. *British Journal of Social Psychology, 32,* 365-378.

Driscoll, R., Davis, K. W., & Lipitz, M. E. (1972). Parental interference and romantic love. *Journal of Personality and Social Psychology, 24,* 1-10.

Drogin, B. (1992, January 28). Rapes that are "not as heinous." *Los Angeles Times,* p. 1.

DuBois, D. L., & Hirsch, B. J. (1990). School and neighborhood friendship patterns of Blacks and Whites in early adolescence. *Child Development, 61,* 524-536.

Dubrovsky, V. J., Kiesler, S., & Sethna, B. N. (1991). The equalization phenomenon: Status effects in computer-mediated and face-to-face decision-making groups. *Human Computer Interaction, 6,* 119-146.

Duck, S. (1988). *Relating to others.* Chicago: Dorsey.

Duck, S. W. (Ed.). (1982). Based on: *Personal relationships: Vol. 4. Dissolving personal relationships.* New York: Academic.

Duck, S. W. (1984). *Personal relationships 4: Dissolving personal relationships.* Duluth, MN: Academic Press.

Duckitt, J. (1992). Psychology and prejudice: A historical analysis and integrative framework. *American Psychologist, 47,* 1182-1193.

Dunkel-Schetter, C., Folkman, S., & Lazarus, R. S. (1987). Correlates of social support receipt. *Journal of Personality and Social Psychology, 53,* 71-80.

Dutton, D. G., & Aron, A. P. (1974). Some evidence for heightened sexual attraction under conditions of high anxiety. *Journal of Personality and Social Psychology, 30,* 510-517.

Duval, S., & Wicklund, R. A. (1972). *A theory of objective self-awareness.* New York: Academic Press.

Duval, T. S., & Duval, V. H. (1987). Level of perceived coping ability and attribution for negative events. *Journal of Social and Clinical Psychology, 5,* 452-468.

Duval, T. S., Duval, V. H., & Mulilis, J. P. (1992). Effects of self-focus, discrepancy between self and standard, and outcome expectancy favorability on the tendency to match self to standard or to withdraw. *Journal of Personality and Social Psychology, 62,* 340-348.

Dye, E., & Roth, S. (1990). Psychotherapists' knowledge about and attitudes toward sexual assault victim clients. *Psychology of Women Quarterly, 14,* 191-212.

Dziokonski, W., & Weber, S. J. (1977). Repression-sensitization, perceived vulnerability, and the fear appeal communication. *Journal of Social Psychology, 102,* 105-112.

Eagly, A., & Chaiken, S. (1993). *The psychology of attitudes.* Fort Worth, TX: Harcourt Brace Jovanovich.

Eagly, A., & Crowley, M. (1986). Gender and helping behavior: A meta-analytic review of the social psychological literature. *Psychological Bulletin, 100,* 283-308.

Eagly, A., & Mladinic, A. (1989). Gender stereotypes and attitudes toward women and men. *Personality and Social Psychology Bulletin, 15,* 543-558.

Eagly, A. H. (1987). *Sex differences in social behavior: A social role interpretation.* Hillsdale, NJ: Erlbaum.

Eagly, A. H., & Carli, L. L. (1981). Sex of researchers and sex-typed communications as determinants of sex differences in influence-ability: A meta-analysis of social influence-studies. *Psychological Bulletin, 90,* 1-20.

Eagly, A. H., & Chaiken, S. (1993). *The psychology of attitudes.* Fort Worth: Harcourt Brace Jovanovich.

Eagly, A. H., & Chravala, C. (1986). Sex differences in conformity: Status and gender-role interpretations. *Psychology of Women Quarterly, 10,* 203-220.

Eagly, A. H., & Johnson, B. T. (1990). Gender and leadership style: A meta-analysis. *Psychological Bulletin, 108,* 233-256.

Eagly, A. H., & Steffen, V. J. (1984). Gender stereotypes stem from the distribution of women and men into social roles. *Journal of Personality and Social Psychology, 46,* 735-754.

Eagly, A. H., & Steffen, V. J. (1986a). Gender and aggressive behavior: A meta-analytic review of the social psychological literature. *Psychological Bulletin, 100,* 309-330.

Eagly, A. H., & Steffen, V. J. (1986b). Gender stereotypes, occupational roles, and beliefs about part-time employees. *Psychology of Women Quarterly, 10,* 252-262.

Eagly, A. H., Makhijani, M. G., & Klonsky, B. G. (1992). Gender and evaluation of leaders: A meta-analysis. *Psychological Bulletin, 111,* 3-22.

Eagly, A. H., Wood, W., & Chaiken, S. (1978). Causal inferences about communicators and their effect on opinion change. *Journal of Personality and Social Psychology, 36,* 424-435.

Eagly, A. H., Wood, W., & Fishbaugh, L. (1981). Sex differences in conformity: Surveillance by the group as a determinant of male nonconformity. *Journal of Personality and Social Psychology, 40,* 384-394.

Ebbesen, E. B., Kjos, G. L., & Konecni, V. J. (1976). Spatial ecology: Its effects on the choice of friends and enemies. *Journal of Experimental Social Psychology, 12,* 505-518.

Ebbesen, E. B., & Konecni, V. J. (1982). An analysis of the bail system. In. V. J. Konecni & E. B. Ebbesen (Eds.), *A social-psychological analysis* (pp. 191-229). San Francisco: Freeman.

Eccles, J. S. (1987). Gender roles and women's achievement-related decisions. *Psychology of Women Quarterly, 11,* 135-171.

Eccles, J. S., Jacobs, J. E., & Harold, R. D. (1990). Gender role stereotypes, expectancy effects and parents' socialization of gender differences. *Journal of Social Issues, 46,* 183-201.

Eccles, J. S., Wigfield, A., Flanagan, C. A., Miller, C., Reuman, D. A., & Yee, D. (1989). Self-concepts, domain values, and self-esteem: Relations and changes at early adolescence. *Journal of Personality, 57,* 283-310.

*Economist.* (1992, September 5). The team dream. *324,* 69.

Eden, D. (1990). Pygmalion without interpersonal contrast effects: Whole groups gain from raising manager expectations. *Journal of Applied Psychology, 75,* 394-398.

Egeland, J. A., Gerhard, D. S., Pauls, D. L., Sussex, J. N., Kidd, K. K., Allen, C. R., Hostetter, A. M., & Housman, D. E. (1987). Bipolar effective disorders linked to DNA markers on chromosome 11. *Nature, 325,* 783-787.

Eisenberg, N. (1986). *Altruistic emotion, cognition, and behavior.* Hillsdale, NJ: Erlbaum.

Eisenberg, N. (1991). Meta-analytic contributions to the literature on prosocial behavior. *Personality and Social Psychology Bulletin, 17,* 273-282.

Eisenberg, N., Cialdini, R. B., McCreath, H., & Shell, R. (1989). Consistency-based compliance in children: When and why do consistency procedures have immediate effects? *International Journal of Behavioral Development, 12,* 351-367.

Either, K. A., & Deaux, K. (1990). Hispanics in ivy: Assessing identity and perceived threat. Special Issue: Gender and ethnicity: Perspectives on dual status. *Sex Roles, 22,* 427-440.

Ekman, P., Friesen, W., & O'Sullivan, M. (1988). Smiles when lying. *Journal of Personality and Social Psychology, 54,* 414-420.

Ekman, P. Friesen, W. V., & Ellsworth, P. (1972). *Emotion in the human face.* Elmsford, NY: Pergamon Press.

Ekman, P., & O'Sullivan, M. (1991). Facial expression: Methods, means, and moues. In R. S. Feldman & B. Rimé (Eds.), *Fundamentals of Nonverbal Behavior.* Cambridge, England: Cambridge University Press.

Elkin, R. A., & Leippe, M. R. (1986). Physiological arousal, dissonance, and attitude change: Evidence for a dissonance-arousal link and a "Don't remind me" effect. *Journal of Personality and Social Psychology, 51,* 55-65.

Elliott, S. (1992, July 29). Adoring or abhoring the Camel. *The New York Times, 141,* C16.

Ellison, R. (1952). *Invisible man.* New York: Random House.

Elwork, A., Sales, B. D., & Alfini, J. J. (1982). *Making jury instructions understandable.* Charlottesville, VA: Miche.

Engel, J. F., & Blackwell, R. D. (1982). *Consumer behavior* (4th ed.). Hillsdale, NJ: Erlbaum.

Englis, B. G. (Ed.). (1993). *Global and multinational advertising.* Hillsdale, NJ: Erlbaum.

Erickson, M., Egeland, B., & Sroufe, L. (1985). The relationship between quality of attachment and behavior problems in a high-risk sample. In I. Bretherton & E. Waters (Eds.), Growing point in attachment theory and research. *Monographs of the Society for Research in Child Development, 50*(1-2, Serial No. 209).

Eron, L. D. (1982). Parent-child interaction, television violence, and aggression of children. *American Psychologist, 37,* 197-211.

Eron, L. D., & Huesmann, L. R. (1984). The control of aggressive behavior by changes in attitudes, values, and the conditions of learning. In R. J. Blanchard & D. C. Blanchard (Eds.), *Advances in the study of aggression* (Vol. 1). New York: Academic Press.

Eron, L. D., Huesmann, L. R., Lefkowitz, M. M., & Walder, L. O. (1972). Does television violence cause aggression? *American Psychologist, 27,* 253-263.

Espin, O. M. (1986). Cultural and historical influences on sexuality in Hispanic/Latin women. In J. Cole (Ed.), *All American women: Lines that divide, ties that bind.* New York: Free Press.

Esser, J. K., & Lindoerfer, J. S. (1989). Groupthink and the space shuttle Challenger accident: Toward a quantitative case analysis. *Journal of Behavioral Decision Making, 2,* 167-177.

Evans, D. L. (1993, March 1). The wrong examples. *Newsweek,* 10.

Evans, P. D. (1990). Type A behavior and coronary heart disease: When will the jury return? *British Journal of Psychology, 81,* 147-157.

Evuleocha, S. U., & Ugbah, S. D. (1989). Stereotypes, counter-stereotypes, and Black television images in the 1990s. *Western Journal of Black Studies, 13,* 197-205.

Eyuboglu, N., & Atac, O. A. (1991). Informational power: A means for increased control in channels of distribution. *Psychology and Marketing, 8,* 197-213.

Fazio, R. H. (1989). On the power and functionality of attitudes: The role of attitude accessibility. In A. R. Pratkanis & A. G. Greenwald (Eds.), *Attitude structure and function.* Hillsdale, NJ: Erlbaum.

Fazio, R. H. (1990). Multiple processes by which attitudes guide behavior: The MODE model as an integrative framework. In M. Zanna (Ed.), *Advances in experimental social psychology.* San Diego, CA: Academic Press.

Fazio, R. H., Blascovich, J., & Driscoll, D. M. (1992). On the functional value of attitudes: The influence of accessible attitudes on the ease and quality of decision making. *Personality and Social Psychology Bulletin, 18,* 388-401.

Fazio, R. H., Powell, M. C., & Williams, C. J. (1989). The role of attitude accessibility in the attitude-to-behavior process. *Journal of Consumer Research, 16,* 280-288.

Fazio, R. H., Sanbonmatsu, D. M., Powell, M. C., & Kardes, F. R. (1986). On the automatic activation of attitudes. *Journal of Personality and Social Psychology, 50,* 229-238.

Fazio, R. H., Zanna, M. P., & Cooper, J. (1977). Dissonance and self-perception: An integrative view of each theory's proper domain of application. *Journal of Experimental Social Psychology, 13,* 464-479.

Fehr, B. (1988). Prototype analysis of the concepts of love and commitment. *Journal of Personality and Social Psychology, 55,* 557-579.

Fehr, B., & Russell, J. A. (1991). The concept of love viewed from a prototype perspective. *Journal of Personality and Social Psychology, 60,* 425-438.

Fehr, L. A. (1979). Media violence and catharsis in college females. *Journal of Social Psychology, 109,* 307-308.

Feingold, A. (1988). Matching for attractiveness in romantic partners and same-sex friends: A meta-analysis and theoretical critique. *Psychological Bulletin, 104,* 226-235.

Feingold, A. (1992a). Good-looking people are not what we think. *Psychological Bulletin, 111,* 304-341.

Feingold, A. (1992b). Gender differences in mate selection preferences: A test of the parental investment model. *Psychological Bulletin, 112,* 125-139.

Feldman, R. S. (1976). Nonverbal disclosure of deception and interpersonal affect. *Journal of Educational Psychology, 68,* 807-816.

Feldman, R. S. (Ed.). (1982). *Development of nonverbal behavior in children.* New York: Springer-Verlag.

Feldman, R. S. (Ed.). (1990). *The social psychology of education: Current research and theory.* Cambridge, England: Cambridge University Press.

Feldman, R. S. (Ed.). (1992). *Applications of nonverbal behavioral theories and research.* Hillsdale, NJ: Erlbaum.

Feldman, R. S., Philippot, P., & Custrini, R. J. (1991). Social competence and nonverbal behavior. In R. S. Feldman & B. Rimé (Eds.), *Fundamentals of nonverbal behavior.* Cambridge, England: Cambridge University Press.

Feldman, R. S., & Rimé, B. (Eds.). (1991). *Fundamentals of nonverbal behavior.* Cambridge, England: Cambridge University Press.

Feldman, R. S., & Theiss, A. J. (1982). The teacher and student as Pygmalions: The joint effects of teacher and student expectation. *Journal of Educational Psychology, 74,* 217-223.

Fellner, C. H., & Marshall, J. R. (1981). Kidney donors revisited. In J. P. Rushton & R. M. Sorrentino (Eds.), *Altruism and helping behavior* (pp. 351-365). Hillsdale, NJ: Erlbaum.

Fenigstein, A. (1984). Self-consciousness and the overperception of self as a target. *Journal of Personality and Social Psychology, 47,* 860-870.

Fenigstein, A., Scheier, M. F., & Buss, A. H. (1975). Public and private self-consciousness: Assessment and theory. *Journal of Consulting and Clinical Psychology, 43,* 522-527.

Feshbach, S. (1980). Child abuse and the dynamics of human aggression and violence. In J. Gerbner, C. J. Ross, & E. Zigler (Eds.), *Child abuse: An agenda for action.* New York: Oxford University Press.

Feshbach, S. (1984). The catharsis hypothesis, aggressive drive, and the reduction of aggression. *Aggressive Behavior, 10,* 91-101.

Feshbach, S. (1990). Psychology, human violence, and the search for peace: Issues in science and social values. *Journal of Social Issue, 46,* 183-198.

Feshbach, S., & Weiner, B. (1986). *Personality* (2nd ed.). Lexington, MA: Heath.

Festinger, L. (1954). A theory of social comparison processes. *Human Relations, 7,* 117-140.

Festinger, L. (1957). *A theory of cognitive dissonance.* Stanford, CA: Stanford University Press.

Festinger, L., & Carlsmith, J. M. (1959). Cognitive consequences of forced compliance. *Journal of Abnormal and Social Psychology, 58,* 203-210.

Festinger, L., Riecken, H. W., & Schachter, S. (1956). *When prophecy fails.* Minneapolis: University of Minnesota Press.

Festinger, L., Schachter, S., & Back, K. (1950). *Social pressures in informal groups: A study of a housing community.* New York: Harper.

Fiedler, F. E. (1967). *A theory of leadership effectiveness.* New York: McGraw-Hill.

Fiedler, F. E. (1978). The contingency model and the dynamics of the leadership process. In L. Berkowitz (Ed.), *Advances in experimental social psychology* (Vol. 2). New York: Academic Press.

Fiedler, F. E. (1987). When to lead, when to stand back. *Psychology Today, 21,* 26-27.

Fiedler, F. F., & Garcia, J. E. (1987). *Leadership: Cognitive resources and performance.* New York: Wiley.

Figley, C. R. (1973). Child density and the marital relationship. *Journal of Marriage and the Family, 35,* 272-282.

Fincham, F. D., & Bradbury, T. N. (1992). Assessing attributions in marriage: The relationship attribution measure. *Journal of Personality and Social Psychology 62,* 457-468.

Fincham, F. D., & Bradbury, T. N. (1993). Marital satisfaction, depression, and attributions: A longitudinal analysis. *Journal of Personality and Social Psychology, 64,* 442-452.

Finck, H. T. (1902). *Romantic love and personal beauty: Their development, causal relations, historic and national peculiarities.* London: Macmillan.

Fingerhut, L. A., & Kleinman, J. C. (1990). International and interstate comparisons of homicide among young males. *Journal of the American Medical Association, 263,* 3292-3295.

Fischer, C. S. (1976). *The urban experience.* San Diego, CA: Harcourt Brace Jovanovich.

Fischer, K., Schoeneman, T. J., & Rubanowitz, D. E. (1987). Attributions in the advice columns: II. The dimensionality of actors' and observers' explanations for interpersonal problems. *Personality and Social Psychology Bulletin, 13,* 458-466.

Fischer, W. F. (1963). Sharing in pre-school children as a function of amount and type of reinforcement. *Genetic Psychology Monographs, 68,* 215-245.

Fischman, J. (1987). Type A on trial. *Psychology Today, 21,* 42-50.

Fishbein, M., & Aizen, I. (1975). *Belief, attitude, intention and behavior: An introduction to theory and research.* Reading, MA: Addison-Wesley.

Fisher, I. (1992, March 15). Man shoots attacker, then tries to save him. *The New York Times,* p. A-33.

Fisher, J. D., Bell, P. A., & Baum, A. (1984). *Environmental psychology* (2nd ed.). New York: Holt, Rinehart & Winston.

Fisher, J. D., & Fisher, W. A. (1992). Changing AIDS-risk behavior. *Psychological Bulletin, 111,* 455-474.

Fisher, J. D., Nadler, A., Hart, E., & Whitcher, S. J. (1981). Helping the needy helps the self. *Bulletin of the Psychonomic Society, 17,* 190-192.

Fisher, W. A., & Misovich, S. J. (1990). Evolution of college students' AIDS related behavioral responses, attitudes, knowledge, and fear. *AIDS Education and Prevention, 2,* 322-337.

Fiske, A. P. (1991). *Structures of social life: The four elementary forms of human relations.* New York: Free Press.

Fiske, S. T. (1987). People's reactions to nuclear war: Implications for psychologists. *American Psychologist, 42,* 207-217.

Fiske, S. T. (1992). Thinking is for doing: Portraits of social cognition from Daguerreotype to laserphoto. *Journal of Personality and Social Psychology, 63,* 877-889.

Fiske, S. T., Bersoff, D. N., Borgida, E., Deaux, K., & Heilman, M. E. (1991). Social science research on trial: Use of sex stereotyping research in Price Waterhouse v. Hopkins. *American Psychologist, 46,* 1049-1060.

Fiske, S. T., & Neuberg, S. L. (1990). A continuum of impression formation, from category-based to individuating processes: Influences of information and motivation on attention and interpretation. In M. P. Zanna (Ed.), *Advances in experimental social psychology* (Vol. 23, pp. 1-74). New York: Academic Press.

Fiske, S. T., & Pavelchak, M. A. (1986). Category-based versus piecemeal-based affective responses: Developments in schema-triggered affect. In R. M. Sorrentino & E. T. Higgins (Eds.), *Handbook of motivation and cognition: Foundations of social behavior* (pp. 167-203). New York: Guilford Press.

Fiske, S. T., Pratto, F., & Pavelchak, M. A. (1983). Citizens' images of nuclear war: Content and consequences. *Journal of Social Issues, 39,* 41-65.

Fiske, S. T., & Taylor, S. E. (1991). *Social cognition* (2nd ed.). New York: McGraw-Hill.

Fiske, S. T., & Von Hendy, H. M. (1992). Personality feedback and situational norms can control stereotyping processes. *Journal of Personality and Social Psychology, 62,* 577-596.

Folkman, S., & Lazarus, R. S. (1980). An analysis of coping in a middle-aged community sample. *Journal of Health and Social Behavior, 21,* 219-239.

Folkman, S., & Lazarus, R. S. (1988). Coping as a mediator of emotion. *Journal of Personality and Social Psychology, 54,* 466-475.

Forgas, J. P., & Dobosz, B. (1980). Dimensions of romantic involvement: Towards a taxonomy of heterosexual relationships. *Social Psychology Quarterly, 43,* 290-300.

Forsyth, D. (1990). *Group dynamics.* Pacific Grove, CA: Brooks/Cole.

Forward, J., Canter, R., & Krisch, N. (1976). Role-enactment and deception: Alternative paradigms? *American Psychologist, 31,* 595-604.

Fowler, F. J. (1981). Evaluating a complex crime control experiment. *Applied Social Psychology Annual, 2,* 165-187.

Fowler, F. J., Jr. (1993). *Survey research methods.* Newbury Park, CA: Sage.

Fox, S. (1984). *The mirror makers.* New York: Morrow.

Försterling, F. (1985). Attributional retraining: A review. *Psychological Bulletin, 98,* 495-512.

Försterling, F. (1989). Models of covariation and attribution: How do they relate to the analogy of analysis of variance? *Journal of Personality and Social Psychology, 57,* 615-625.

Frable, D. E., & Bem, S. L. (1985). If you're gender-schematic, all members of the opposite sex look alike. *Journal of Personaltiy and Social Psychology, 49,* 459-468.

Frager, R. (1970). Conformity and anti-conformity in Japan. *Journal of Personaltiy and Social Psychology, 15,* 203-310.

Freedman, J. L. (1984). Effects of television violence on aggressiveness. *Psychological Bulletin, 96,* 227-246.

Freedman, J. L., & Fraser, S. C. (1966). Compliance without pressure: The foot-in-the-door technique. *Journal of Personality and Social Psychology, 8,* 528-548.

Freedman, R. (1986). *Beauty bound.* Lexington, MA: D. C. Heath.

French, J. R. P., Jr., & Raven, B. H. (1959). The bases of social power. In D. Cartwright (Ed.), *Studies in social power.* Ann Arbor: University of Michigan Press.

Freud, S. (1920). *A general introduction to psychoanalysis.* New York: Boni & Liveright.

Frey, D. (1986). Recent research on selective exposure to information. In L. Berkowitz (Ed.), *Advances in experimental social psychology* (Vol. 19). New York: Academic Press.

Frey, D., Fries, A., & Osnabrugge, G. (1983). Reactions to failure after taking a placebo: A study of dissonance reduction. *Personality and Social Psychology Bulletin, 9,* 481-488.

Frey, D., & Wicklund, R. A. (1978). A clarification of selective exposure: The impact of choice. *Journal of Experimental Social Psychology, 14,* 132-139.

Friedland, N., Keinan, G., & Regev, Y. (1992). Controlling the uncontrollable: Effects of stress on illusory perceptions of controllability. *Journal of Personality and Social Psychology, 63,* 923-931.

Friedman, M., Thoresen, C. E., Gill, J. J., Powell, L. H., Ulmer, D., Thompson, L., Price, V. A., Rabin, D. D., Breall, W. S., Dixon, T., Levy, R., & Bourg, E. (1984). Alteration of type A behavior and reduction in cardiac recurrences in postmyocardial infarction patients. *American Heart Journal, 108,* 237-248.

Friendly, D. T. (1985, March 18). This isn't Shakespeare. *Newsweek,* 62

Fuchs, I., Eisenberg, N., Hertz-Lazarowitz, R., & Sharabany, R. (1986). Kibbutz, Israeli city and American children's moral reasoning about prosocial moral conflicts. *Merrill-Palmer Quarterly, 32,* 37-50.

Fulero, S. M., & Penrod, S. D. (1990). Attorney jury selection folklore: What do they think and how can psychologists help? *Forensic Reports, 3,* 233-259.

Funder, D. C. (1987). Errors and mistakes: Evaluating the accuracy of social judgment. *Psychological Bulletin, 101,* 75-90.

Gabrenya, W. K., Latané, B., & Wang, Y. (1983). Social loafing in cross-cultural per-spective: Chinese on Taiwan. *Journal of Cross-Cultural Psychology, 14,* 368-384.

Gabrenya, W. K., Jr., Wang, Y. E., & Latané, B. (1981). *Social loafing among Chinese overseas and U. S. students.* Paper presented at the Asian Conference of the International Association for Cross-Cultural Psychology, Taipei, Taiwan, R.O.C.

Gaertner, S. L., & Dovidio, J. F. (1986). The aversive form of racism. In J. F. Dovidio & S. L. Gaertner (Eds.), *Prejudice, discrimination, and racism: Theory and research* (pp. 61-89). Orlando, FL: Academic Press.

Gaertner, S. L., Mann, J., Murrell, A., & Dovidio, J. F. (1989). Reducing intergroup bias: The benefits of recategorization. *Journal of Personality and Social Psychology, 57,* 239-249.

Gaertner, S. L., Mann, J. A., Dovidio, J. F., Murrell, A. J., & Pomare, M. (1990). How does cooperation reduce intergroup bias? *Journal of Personality and Social Psychology, 59,* 692-704.

Gallup, G. G., Jr. (1977). Self-recognition in primates: A comparative approach to the bidirectional properties of consciousness. *American Psychologist, 32,* 329-337.

Gallup Poll (1969, 1978, 1987). Poll on sexual intercourse before marriage.

Gardner, W. L. (1992). Lessons in organizational dramaturgy: The art of impression management. *Organizational Dynamics, 21,* 33-46.

Gatchel, R. J., & Baum, A. (1983). *An introduction to health psychology.* Reading, MA: Addison-Wesley.

Gecas, V., & Schwalbe, M. L. (1983). Beyond the looking-glass self: Social structure and efficacy-based self-esteem. *Social Psychology Quarterly, 46,* 77-88.

Geen, R. G. (1989). Alternative conceptions of social facilitation. In P. Paulhus (Ed.), *Psychology of group influence* (2nd ed.). Hillsdale, NJ: Erlbaum.

Geen, R. G., & Donnerstein, E. (1983). *Aggression: Theoretical and empirical reviews.* New York: Academic Press.

Geen, R. G., & Quanty, M. B. (1977). The catharsis of aggression: An evaluation of a hypothesis. In L. Berkowitz (Ed.), *Advances in experimental social psychology* (Vol. 10). New York: Academic Press.

Gelles, R. J., & Cornell, C. P. (1990). *Intimate violence in families* (2nd ed.). Newbury Park, CA: Sage.

Gelman, D. (1990, July 23). The mind of the rapist. *Newsweek,* pp. 46-52.

Gentry, W. D., & Kobasa, S. C. O. (1984). Social and psychological resources mediating stress-illness relationships in humans. In W.

D. Gentry (Ed.), *Handbook of behavioral medicine.* New York: Guilford Press.

Gerard, H. B. (1988). Scholl desegregation: The social science role. In P. A. Katz & K. A. Taylor (Eds.), *Eliminating racism: Profiles in controversy.* New York: Plenum.

Gerard, H. B., Whilhelmy, R. A., & Conolley, E. S. (1968). Conformity and group size. *Journal of Personality and Social Psychology, 8,* 79-82.

Gerbner, G., Gross, L., Jackson-Beeck, M., Jeffries-Fox, S., & Signorielli, N. (1978). Cultural indicators: Violence profile No. 9. *Journal of Communications, 28,* 176-207.

Gergen, K. J. (1967). Social psychology as history. *Journal of Personality and Social Psychology, 26,* 309-320.

Gergen, K. J. (1973). Social psychology as history. *Journal of Personality and Social Psychology, 26,* 309-320.

Gergen, K. J. (1982). *Toward transformation in social knowledge.* New York: Springer-Verlag.

Gettys, L. D., & Cann, A. (1981). Children's perception of occupational sex stereotypes *Sex Roles, 7,* 301-308.

Giacalone, R. A., & Rosenfeld, P. (1986). Self-presentation and self-promotion in an organizational setting. *Journal of Social Psychology, 126,* 321-326.

Gibbons, F. X. (1990). Sexual standards and reactions to pornography: Enhancing behavioral consistency through self-focused attention. *Journal of Personality and Social Psychology, 36,* 976-987.

Gibbons, F. X., & Wicklund, R. A. (1982). Self-focused attention and helping behavior. *Journal of Personality and Social Psychology, 43,* 462-474.

Gibbons, F. X., & Wright, R. A. (1983). Self-focused attention and reactions to conflicting standards. *Journal of Research in Personality, 17,* 263-273.

Gibbs, J. P. (1989a). Conceptualization of terrorism. *American Sociological Review, 54,* 329-340.

Gibbs, N. (1989b, January 9). For goodness' sake. *Time,* 20-24.

Gil, D. G. (1970). *Violence against children: Physical abuse in the United States.* Cambridge, MA: Harvard University Press.

Gilbert, D. T. (1989). Thinking lightly about others: Automatic components of the social inference process. In J. S. Uleman & J. A. Bargh (Eds.), *Unintended thought: Causes and consequences for judgment, emotion, and behavior.* New York: Guilford.

Gilbert, D. T., & Hixon, J. G. (1991). The trouble thinking: Activation and application of stereotypic beliefs. *Journal of Personality and Social Psychology, 60,* 509-517.

Gilbert, D. T., McNulty, S. E., Giuliano, T. A., & Benson, J. E. (1992). Blurry words and fuzzy deeds: The attribution of obscure behavior. *Journal of Personaltiy and Social Psychology, 62,* 18-25.

Gilbert, D. T., & Osborne, R. E. (1989). Thinking backward: Some curable and incurable consequences of cognitive busyness. *Journal of Personality and Social Psychology, 54,* 940-949.

Gilbert, D. T., Pelham, B. W., & Krull, D. S. (1988). Of thoughts unspoken: Social inference and the self-regulation of behavior. *Journal of Personality and Social Psychology, 55,* 685-694.

Gillig, P. M., & Greenwald, A. G. (1974). Is it time to lay the sleeper effect to rest? *Journal of Personality and Social Psychology, 29,* 132-139.

Gioia, D. A., & Sims, H. P. (1985). Self-serving bias and actor-observer differences in organizations: An empirical analysis. *Journal of Applied Social Psychology, 15,* 547-563.

Glaser, R., Rice, J., Speicher, C. E., Stout, J. C., & Kiecolt-Glaser, J. K. (1986). Stress depresses interferon production by leukocytes and concomitant with a decrease in natural killer cell activity. *Behavioral Neuroscience, 100,* 675-678.

Glenn, N. D. (1990). Quantitative research on marital quality in the 1980s: A critical review. *Journal of Marriage and the Family, 52,* 818-831.

Glenn, N. D., & Weaver, C. N. (1988). The changing relationship of marital status to reported happiness. *Journal of Marriage and the Family, 50,* 317-324.

Glick, P., Zion, C., & Nelson, C. (1988). What mediates sex discrimination in hiring decisions? *Journal of Personality and Social Psychology, 55,* 178-186.

Goethals, G. R., & Darley, J. (1977). Social comparison theory: An attributional approach. In J. M. Suls & R. L. Miller (Eds.), *Social comparison processes: Theoretical and empirical perspectives* (pp. 259-278). Washington, DC: Hemisphere.

Goethals, G. R., & Zanna, M. P. (1979). The role of social comparison in choice of shifts. *Journal of Personality and Social Psychology, 37,* 1469-1476.

Gold, G. J., & Raven, B. H. (1992). Interpersonal influence strategies in the Churchill-Roosevelt bases-for-destroyers exchange. *Journal of Social Behavior and Personality, 7,* 245-272.

Gold, J. A., Ryckman, R. M., & Mosley, N. R. (1984). Romantic mood induction and attraction to a dissimilar other: Is love blind? *Personality and Social Psychology Bulletin, 10,* 358-368.

Goldman, K. (1993, September 17). Candice Bergen leads the list of top celebrity endorsers. *Wall Street Journal,* B1.

Goleman, D. (1985, February 5). Mourning: New studies affirm its benefits. *New York Times,* pp. C1-C2.

Goleman, D. (1989, February 21). Want a happy marriage? Learn to fight a good fight. *New York Times,* C1, C6.

Goleman, D. (1990, July 17). Aggression in men: Hormone levels are a key. *New York Times,* C1, C6.

Goode, W. J. (1976). Family disorganization. In R. Merton & R. Nisbett (Eds.), *Contemporary social problems* (4th ed.). New York: Harcourt Brace Jovanovich.

Goodwin, S. E., & Mahoney, M. J. (1975). Modification of aggression through modeling: An experimental probe. *Journal of Behavior Therapy and Experimental Psychiatry, 6,* 200-202.

Googans, B., & Burden, D. (1987). Vulnerability of working parents: Balancing work and home roles. *Social Work, 32,* 295-300.

Gordon, R. A., & Vicari, P. J. (1992). Eminence in social psychology: A comparison of textbook citation, Social Sciences Citation Index, and research productivity rankings. *Pesonality and Social Psychology Bulletin, 18,* 26-38.

Gottman, J. M. (1993). *What predicts divorce? The relationship between marital processes and marital outcomes.* Hillsdale, NJ: Erlbaum.

Gottman, J. M., Buehlman, K. T., & Katz, L. F. (1992). *Journal of Family Psychology, 1.*

Gottman, J. M., & Krokoff, L. J. (1989). Marital interaction and satisfaction: A longitudinal view. *Journal of Consulting and Clinical Psychology, 57(1),* 47-52.

Gouldner, A. W. (1960). The notion of reciprocity: A preliminary statement. *American Sociological Review, 25,* 161-178.

Graeff, C. L. (1983). The situational leadership theory: A critical view. *Academy of Management Review, 8,* 285-291.

Graham, S. (1992). "Most of the subjects were white and middle class": Trends in published research on African Americans in selected APA journals, 1970-1989. *American Psychologist, 47,* 629-639.

Grambs, J. D. (1989). *Women over forty: Visions and realities.* New York: Springer.

Granberg, D. (1987). Candidate preference, membership group, and estimates of voting behavior. *Social Cognition, 5,* 323-335.

Granberg, D., & Holmberg, S. (1990). The person positivity and principal actor hypotheses. *Journal of Applied Social Psychology, 20,* 1879-1901.

Grasmick, H. G., Bursik, R. J., & Kimpel, M. (1991). Protestant fundamentalism and attitudes toward corporal punishment of children. *Violence and Victims, 6,* 283-298.

Gray, A., Jackson, D. N., & McKinlay, J. B. (1991). The relation between dominance, anger, and hormones in normally aging men: Results from the Massachusetts male aging study. *Psychosomatic Medicine, 53,* 375-385.

Graziano, A. M., Lindquist, C. M., Kunce, L. J., & Munjal, K. (1992). Physical punishment in childhood and current attitudes: An exploratory comparison of college students in the United States and India. *Journal of Interpersonal Violence, 7,* 147-155.

Green, S. K., Lightfoot, M. A., Bandy, C., & Buchanan, D. R. (1985). A general model of the attribution process. *Basic and Applied Social Psychology, 6,* 159-179.

Greenberg, J., & Folger, R. (1988). *Controversial issues in social research methods.* New York: Springer-Verlag.

Greenwald, A. G. (1975). On the inconclusiveness of crucial cognitive tests of dissonance versus self-perception theories. *Journal of Experimental Social Psychology, 11,* 490-499.

Greenwald, A. G. (1989). Why attitudes are important: Defining attitude and attitude theory 20 years later. In A. R. Pratkanis, S. J. Breckler, & A. G. Greenwald (Eds.), *Attitude structure and function.* Hillsdale, NJ: Erlbaum.

Greenwell, J., & Dengerink, H. A. (1973). The role of perceived versus actual attack in human physical aggression. *Journal of Personality and Social Psychology, 26,* 66-71.

Greydanus, D. E., Pratt, H. H., Greydanus, S. E., & Hoffman, A. D. (1992). Corporal punishment in schools: A position paper of the Society for Adolescent Medicine. *Journal of Adolescent Health, 13,* 240-246.

Griffiths, M. D., & Shuckford, G. L. (1989). Desensitization to television violence: A new model. *New Ideas in Psychology, 7,* 85-89.

Groebel, J., & Hinde, R. (Eds.). (1989). *Aggression and war: Their biological and social bases.* Cambridge, England: Cambridge University Press.

Grusec, J. E. (1982). Socialization processes and the development of altruism. In J. P. Rushton & R. M. Sorrentino (Eds.), *Altruism and helping behavior.* Hillsdale, NJ: Erlbaum.

Grusec, J. E. (1991). The socialization of altruism. In M. S. Clark (Ed.), *Prosocial behavior.* Newbury Park, CA: Sage.

Grusec, J. E., & Dix, T. (1986). The socialization of prosocial behavior: Theory and reality. In C. Zahn-Waxler, E. M. Cummings, & R. Iannotti (Eds.), *Altruism and aggression: Biological and social origins.* New York: Cambridge University Press.

Grusec, J. E., & Skubiski, S. L. (1970). Model nurturance, demand characteristics of the modeling experiment, and altruism. *Journal of Personality and Social Psychology, 14,* 352-359.

Grush, J. E. (1980). Impact of candidate expenditures, regionality, and prior outcomes on the 1976 Democratic presidential primaries. *Journal of Personality and Social Psychology, 38,* 337-347.

Gubernick, L. (1986). The nose knows. *Forbes,* 280-281.

Guetzkow, H. (1968). Differentiation of roles in task-oriented groups. In D. Cartwright & A. Zander (Eds.), *Group dynamics: Research and theory* (3rd ed.). New York: Harper & Row.

Gunter, B. (1983). Do aggressive people prefer violent television? *Bulletin of the British Psychological Society, 36,* 166-168.

Gunter, B. (1988). The importance of studying viewers' perceptions of television violence. [Special Issue]: Violence on television. *Current Psychology Research and Reviews, 7,* 26-42.

Gunter, B., & Furnham, A. (1986). Sex and personality differences in recall of violent and non-violent news from three presentation modalities. *Personality and Individual Differences, 7,* 829-837.

Gupta, U., & Singh, P. (1982). An exploratory study of love and liking and type of marriages. *Indian Journal of Applied Psychology, 19,* 92-97.

Guttman, L. (1944). A basis for scaling qualitative data. *American Sociological Review, 9,* 139-150.

Hackel, L. S., & Ruble, D. N. (1992). Changes in the marital relationship after the first baby is born: Predicting the impact of expectancy disconfirmation. *Journal of Personality and Social Psychology, 62,* 944-957.

Hackman, J. R., & Morris, C. G. (1975). Group tasks, group interaction process, and group performance effectiveness: A review and proposed integration. In L. Berkowitz (Ed.), *Advances in experimental social psychology* (Vol. 8). New York: Academic Press.

Haidt, J., Koller, S. H., & Dias, M. G. (1993). Affect, culture, and morality, or is it wrong to eat your dog? *Journal of Personality and Social Psychology, 65,* 613-628.

Halal, W. E. (1974). Toward a general theory of leadership. *Human Relations, 27,* 401-416.

Halberstadt, A. G. (1991). Toward an ecology of expressiveness: Family socialization in particular and a model in general. In R. S. Feldman & B. Rimé (Eds.), *Fundamentals of nonverbal behavior.* Cambridge, England: Cambridge University Press.

Hall, E. T. (1966). *The hidden dimension.* Garden City, NY: Doubleday.

Hall, J. A., Roter, D. L., & Rand, C. S. (1981). Communication of affect between patient and physician. *Journal of Health and Social Behavior, 22,* 18-30.

Hall, R. G., Varca, P. E., & Fisher, T. D. (1986). The effect of reference groups, opinion polls, and attitude polarization on attitude formation and change. *Political Psychology, 7,* 309-321.

Hallinan, M. T., & Williams, R. A. (1989). Interracial friendship choices in secondary schools. *American Sociological Review, 54,* 67-78.

Hamill, R., Wilson, T. D., & Nisbett, R. E. (1980). Insensitivity to sample bias: Generalizing from atypical cases. *Journal of Personality and Social Psychology, 39,* 578-589.

Hamilton, D. L. (1979). A cognitive-attributional analysis of stereotyping. In L. Berkowitz (Ed.), *Advances in experimental social psychology* (Vol. 12, pp. 53-84). New York: Academic Press.

Hamilton, D. L., & Gifford, R. K. (1976). Illusory correlation in interpersonal perception: A cognitive basis of stereotypic judgments. *Journal of Experimental Social Psychology, 12,* 393-407.

Hamilton, D. L., & Rose, T. L. (1980). Illusory correlation and the maintenance of stereotypic beliefs. *Journal of Personality and Social Psychology, 39,* 832-845.

Hamilton, D. L., Sherman, S. J., & Ruvolo, C. M. (1990). Stereotype-based expectancies: Effects on information processing and social behavior. *Journal of Social Issues, 46,* 35-60.

Hamilton, D. L., & Trolier, T. K. (1986). Stereotypes and stereotyping: An overview of the cognitive approach. In J. F. Dovidio & S. L. Gaertner (Eds.), *Prejudice, discrimination, and racism* (pp. 127-163). Orlando, FL: Academic Press.

Hamilton, M., & Yee, J. (1990). Rape knowledge and propensity to rape. *Journal of Research in Personality, 24,* 111-122.

Hamilton, V. L. (1976). Individual differences in ascriptions of responsibility, guilt, and appropriate judgment. In G. Berman, C. Nemeth, & N. Vidmar (Eds.), *Psychology and the law.* Lexington, MA: Heath.

Hammer, J. (1992a, October 26). Must Blacks be buffoons? *Newsweek,* 70-71.

Hammer, J. (1992b, May 18). Back of the block. *Newsweek, 119,* 40-44.

Hampton, R. L., Gullotta, T. P., Adams, G. R., Potter, E. H., & Weissberg, R. (1993). *Family violence: Prevention and treatment.* Newbury Park, CA: Sage.

Haney, C., Banks, C., & Zimbardo, P. (1973). Interpersonal dynamics in a simulated prison. *International Journal of Criminology and Penology, 1,* 69-97.

Hansen, C. H. (1989). Priming sex-role stereotypic even schemas with rock music videos:

Effects on impression favorability, trait inferences, and recall of subsequent male-female interaction. *Basic and Applied Social Psychology, 10,* 371-391.

Hardy, C., & Latané, B. (1986). Social loafing on a cheering task. *Social Science, 71,* 165-172.

Harkins, S. G. (1987). Social loafing and social facilitation. *Journal of Experimental Social Psychology, 23,* 1-18.

Harkins, S. G., & Petty, R. E. (1982). Effects of task difficulty and task uniqueness on social loafing. *Journal of Personality and Social Psychology, 43,* 1214-1229.

Harkins, S. G., & Petty, R. E. (1987). Information utility and the multiple source effect. *Journal of Personality and Social Psychology, 52,* 260-268.

Harkins, S. G., & Szymanski, K. (1989). Social loafing and group evaluation. *Journal of Personality and Social Psychology, 56,* 934-941.

Harris, M. J. (1990). Effect of interaction goals on expectancy confirmation in a problem-solving context. *Personality and Social Psychology Bulletin, 16,* 521-530.

Harris, M. J. (1991). Controversy and cumulation: Meta-analysis and research on interpersonal expectancy effects. *Personality and Social Psychology Bulletin, 17,* 316-322.

Harris, M. J., Milich, R., Corbitt, E. M., Hoover, D. W., et al. (1992). Self-fulfilling effects of stigmatizing information on children's social interactions. *Journal of Personality and Social Psychology, 63,* 41-50.

Harris, R. N., Snyder, C. R., Higgins, R. L., & Schrag, J. L. (1986). Enhancing the prediction of self-handicapping. *Journal of Personality and Social Psychology, 51,* 1191-1199.

Harrison, A. A. (1977). Mere exposure. In L. Berkowitz (Ed.), *Advances in experimental social psychology* (Vol. 10). New York: Academic Press.

Harrow, J., & Loewenthal, D. E. (1992). Management research supervision: Some users' perspectives on roles, interventions and power. *Management Education and Development, 23,* 54-64.

Harvey, J. H. (1989). People's naive understandings of their close relationships: Attributional and personal construct perspectives. *International Journal of Personal Construct Psychology, 2,* 37-48.

Harvey, J. H., & Weary, G. (Eds.). (1984). *Attribution: Basic issues and applications.* New York: Academic Press.

Hass, R. G. (1981). Effects of source characteristics on the cognitive processing of persuasive messages and attitude change. In R. Petty, T. Ostrom, & T. Brock (Eds.), *Cognitive response in persuasion.* Hillsdale, NJ: Erlbaum.

Hass, R. G., & Eisenstadt, D. (1990). The effects of self-focused attention on perspective-taking and anxiety. *Anxiety Research, 2,* 165-176.

Hass, R. G., & Grady, K. (1975). Temporal delay, type of forewarning, and resistance to influence. *Journal of Experimental Social Psychology, 11,* 459-469.

Hatfield, E. (1988). Passionate and companionate love. In R. J. Sternberg & M. L. Barnes (Eds.), *The psychology of love* (pp. 191-217). New Haven: Yale University Press.

Hatfield, E., & Sprecher, S. (1986). *Mirror, mirror . . . The importance of looks in everyday life.* Albany, NY: SUNY Press.

Hattie, J. (1992). *Self-concept.* Hillsdale, NJ: Erlbaum.

Hayduk, L. A. (1978). Personal space: An evaluative and orienting overview. *Psychological Bulletin, 85,* 117-134.

Haynes, R. B., Wang, E., & da-Mota-Gomes, M. (1987). A critical view of interventions to improve compliance with prescribed medications. *Patient Education and Counseling, 10,* 155-166.

Hays, R. B. (1984). The development and maintenance of friendship. *Journal of Personality and Social Relationships, 1,* 75-98.

Hays, R. B. (1985). A longitudinal study of friendship development. *Journal of Personality and Social Psychology 48,* 909-924.

Hedrick, T. E., Bickman, L., & Rog, D. J. (1993). *Planning applied research design.* Newbury Park, CA: Sage.

Heider, F. (1958). *The psychology of interpersonal relations.* New York: Wiley.

Heller, R. F., Saltzstein, H. D., & Caspe, W. B. (1992). Heuristics in medical and non-medical decision-making. *Quarterly Journal of Experimental Psychology Human Experimental Psychology, 44A,* 211-235.

Hendrick, C., & Hendrick, S. (1986). A theory and method of love. *Journal of Personality and Social Psychology, 50,* 392-402.

Hendrick, C., & Hendrick, S. (1989). Research on love: Does it measure up? *Journal of Personality and Social Psychology, 56,* 784-794.

Hendrick, C., & Seyfried, B. A. (1974). Salience of similarity awareness and attraction: A comparison of balance vs reinforcement predictions. *Memory and Cognition, 2,* 1-4.

Hendrick, S. S., & Hendrick, C. (1992). *Romantic love.* Newbury Park, CA: Sage.

Henley, N. (1977). *Body politcs: Power, sex, and nonverbal communication.* Englewood Cliffs, NJ: Prentice-Hall.

Hensel, N. H. (1991). Social leadership skills in young children. *Roeper Review, 14,* 4-6.

Henson, K. T. (1985). Corporal punishment: Ten popular myths. *High School Journal, 69,* 107-109.

Hepworth, J. T., & West, S. G. (1988). Lynchings and the economy: A time-series reanalysis of Hovland & Sears (1940). *Journal of Personality and Social Psychology, 55,* 239-247.

Herek, G. M., Kimmel, D. C., Amaro, H., & Melton, G. B. (1991). Avoiding heterosexist bias in psychological research. *American Psychologist, 46,* 957-963.

Herr, P. M. (1986). Consequences of priming: Judgment and behavior. *Journal of Personality and Social Psychology, 51,* 1106-1115.

Herringer, L. G., & Garza, R. T. (1987). Perceptual accentuation in minimal groups. *European Journal of Social Psychology, 17,* 347-352.

Hersh, S. (1970). *My Lai 4: A report on the massacre and its aftermath.* New York: Vintage Books.

Heslin, R., & Sommers, P. M. (1987). The sleeper effect: Susceptibility of selective avoiders who hold extreme views. *Psychological Reports, 61,* 982.

Hess, R. D., et al. (1980). Maternal expectations for mastery of developmental tasks in Japan and the United States. *International Journal of Psychology, 15,* 259-271.

Hess, R. D., Azuma, H., Kashiwagi, K., Dickson, W. P., Nagano S., Holloway, S., Miyake, K., Price, G., Hatano, G., & McDevitt, T. (1986). Family influences on school readiness and achievement in Japan and the United States: An overview of a longitudinal study. In H. Stevenson, H. Azuma, & K. Hakuta (Eds.) *Child development and education in Japan.* New York: W. H. Freeman.

Hewston, M., Stroebe, W., Codol, J. P., & Stephenson, G. M. (1988). *Introduction to social psychology: A European perspective.* Oxford, England: Blackwill.

Higgins, E. T. (1989). Self-discrepancy theory: What patterns of self-beliefs cause people to suffer? In L. Berkowitz (Ed.), *Advances in experimental and social psychology* (Vol. 22, pp. 93-136). New York: Academic Press.

Higgins, E. T., Rholes, C. R., & Jones, C. R. (1977). Category accessibility and impression formation. *Journal of Experimental Social Psychology, 13,* 141-154.

Higgins, E. T., & Sorrentino, R. M. (Eds.). (1990). *Handbook of motivation and cognition: Foundations of social behavior* (Vol. 1). New York: Guilford Press.

Higgins, E. T., Strauman, T., & Klein, R. (1986). Standards and the process of self-evaluation: Multiple effects from multiple stages. In R. M. Sorrentino & E. T. Higgins (Eds.), *Handbook of motivation and cognition: Foundations of social behavior* (pp. 23-63). New York: Guilford Press.

Higgins, R. L., & Snyder, C. R. (1989). Excuses gone awry: An analysis of self-defeating excuses. In R. C. Curtis (Ed.), *Self-defeating behaviors: Experimental research, clinical impressions, and practical implications.* New York: Plenum.

Higgins, R. L., Snyder, C. R., & Berglas, S. (1990). *Self-handicapping: The paradox that isn't.* New York: Plenum.

Hildum, D. C., & Brown, R. W. (1956). Verbal reinforcement and interviewer bias. *Journal of Abnormal and Social Psychology, 15,* 150-160.

Hill, C. T., & Stull, D. E. (1981). Sex differences in effects of social and value similarity in same-sex friendship. *Journal of Personality and Social Psychology, 41,* 488-502.

Hill, E. L., & Pfeifer, J. E. (1992). Nullification instructions and juror guilt ratings: An examination of modern racism. Carolinas Psychology Conference (1991, Raleigh, North Carolina). *Contemporary Social Psychology, 16,* 6-10.

Hilton, A., Potvin, L., & Sachdev, I. (1989). Ethnic relations in rental housing: A social psychological approach. *Canadian Journal of Behavioural Science, 21,* 121-131.

Hilton, J. L., & Darley, J. M. (1991). The effects of interaction goals on person perception. In M. P. Zanna (Ed.), *Advances in experimental social psychology* (Vol. 24). San Diego, CA: Academic Press.

Hilton, J. L., Miller, D. T., Fein, S., & Darley, J. M. (1990). When dispositional inferences are suspended: Diagnosing and calibrating traits. *Revue internationale de Psychologie Sociale, 3,* 519-537.

Hinge, J. B. (1991, August 6). "Sad" ad in "sad" program found effective. *Wall Street Journal,* B6.

Hinsz, V. (1990). Cognitive and consensus processes in group recognition memory performance. *Journal of Personality and Social Psychology, 54.*

Hiroto, D. S., & Seligman, M. E. P. (1975). Generality of learned helplessness in man. *Journal of Personality and Social Psychology, 31,* 311-327.

Hirt, E. R., Deppe, R. K., & Gordon, L. J. (1991). Self-reported versus behavioral self-handicapping: Empirical evidence for a theoretical distinction. *Journal of Personality and Social Psychology, 61,* 981-991.

Hoberman, H. M. (1990). Study group report on the impact of television violence on adolescents. Conference: Teens and television (1988, Los Angeles, California). *Journal of Adolescent Health Care, 11,* 45-49.

Hobfoll, S. E., Spielberger, C. D., Breznitz, S., Figley, C., Folkman, S., Lepper-Green, B., Meichenbaum, D., Milgram, N. A., Sandler, I., Sarason, I., & van der Kolk, B. (1991).

War-related stress: Addressing the stress of war and other traumatic events. *American Psychologist, 46,* 848-855.

Hoffman, L. R., & Maier, N. R. F. (1961). Sex differences, sex composition, and group problem solving. *Journal of Abnormal and Social Psychology, 63,* 454-456.

Hoffman, L. W. (1989). Effects of maternal employment in the two-parent family. *American Psychologist, 44,* 283-292.

Hoffman, M. L. (1981). Is altruism part of human nature? *Journal of Personality and Social Psychology, 40,* 121-137.

Hofstede, G. (1980). *Culture's consequences.* Beverly Hills, CA: Sage.

Hogg, M. A., & Hardie, E. A. (1992). Prototypicality, conformity and depersonalized attraction: A self-categorization analysis of group cohesiveness. *British Journal of Social Psychology, 31,* 41-56.

Holahan, C. J., & Moos, R. H. (1987). Personal and contextual determinants of coping strategies. *Journal of Personality and Social Psychology, 52,* 946-955.

Holahan, C. J., & Moos, R. H. (1990). Life stressors, resistance factors, and improved psychological functioning: An extension of the stress resistance paradigm. *Journal of Personality and Social Psychology, 58,* 909-917.

Holland, J. C., & Lewis, S. (1993). Emotions and cancer: What do we really know? In D. Goleman & J. Gurin (Eds.), *Mind-body medicine.* Yonkers, NY: Consumer Reports Books.

Hollander, E. P. (1958). Conformity, status, and idiosyncrasy credit. *Psychological Review, 65,* 117-127.

Hollander, E. P. (1980). Leadership and social exchange processes. In K. J. Gergen, M. Greenberg, & R. Willis (Eds.), *Social exchange: Advances in theory and research.* New York: Plenum.

Hollander, E. P. (1985). Leadership and power. In G. Lindzey & E. Aronson (Eds.), *Handbook of social psychology* (3rd ed., Vol. 2, pp. 485-537). New York: Random House.

Hollander, E. P., Julian, J. W., & Haaland, G. (1965). Conformity process and prior group support. *Journal of Personality and Social Psychology, 2,* 852-850.

Holloway, S. D. (1988). Concepts of ability and effort in Japan and the United States. *A Review of Educational Research,* 58, 327-345.

Holloway, S. D., Kashiwagi, K., Hess, R. D., & Azuma, H. (1986). Causal attributions by Japanese and American mothers and children about performance in mathematics. *International Journal of Psychology, 21,* 269-286.

Holmes, J. G., & Boon, S. D. (1990). Developments in the field of close relationships:

Creating foundations for intervention strategies. *Personality and Social Psychology Bulletin, 16,* 23-41.

Holmes, T. H., & Rahe, R. H. (1967). The social readjustment scale. *Journal of Psychosomatic Research, 11.*

Holtgraves, T., Srull, T. K., & Socall, D. (1989). Conversation memory: The effects or speaker status on memory for the assertiveness of conversation remarks. *Journal of Personality and Social Psychology, 56,* 149-160.

Homer, P. M., & Kahle, L. R. (1990). Source expertise, time of source identification, and involvement in persuasion: An elaborative processing perspective. *Journal of Advertising, 19, 1,* 30-39.

Hopkins v. Price Waterhouse, 618 F. Supp. 1109 (D. D. C. 1985).

Hopkins v. Price Waterhouse, No. 84-3040, slip op. (D. D. C. May 14, 1990) (on remand).

Hornstein, G. A., & Truesdell, S. E. (1988). Development of intimate conversation in close relationships. *Journal of Social and Clinical Psychology, 7,* 49-64.

Hornstein, H. A., Heilman, M. E., Mone, E., & Tartell, R. (1987). Responding to contingent leadership behavior. *Organizational Dynamics, 15,* 56-65.

Horowitz, I. A. (1980). Juror selection: A comparison of two methods in several criminal cases. *Journal of Applied Social. Psychology, 10,* 86-99.

Hosch, H. M., & Platz, S. J. (1984). Self-monitoring and eyewitness accuracy. *Personality and Social Psychology Bulletin, 10,* 289-292.

Houston, B. K. (1983). Psychophysiological responsibilities and the Type A behavior patter. *Journal of Research in Personality, 17,* 22-39.

Hovland, C. I., & Janis, I. L. (Eds.). (1959). *Personality and persuadability.* New Haven, CT: Yale University Press.

Hovland, C. I., Lumsdaine, A. A., & Sheffield, F. D. (1949). *Experiments in mass communication.* Princeton, NJ: Princeton University Press.

Hovland, C. I., & Sears, R. R. (1940). Minor studies in aggression: VI. Correlation of lynchings with economic indices. *Journal of Psychology, 9,* 301-310.

Hovland, C. I., & Weiss, W. (1951). The influence of source credibility on communication effectiveness. *Public Opinion Quarterly, 15,* 635-650.

Hsu, F. L. K. (1983). *Rugged individualism reconsidered.* Knoxville: University of Tennessee Press.

Huesmann, L. R. (1986). Psychological processes promoting the relation between exposure to media violence and aggressive behavior by the viewer. *Journal of Social Issues, 42,* 125-139.

Huesmann, L. R., & Eron, L. D. (Eds.). (1986). *Television and the aggressive child: A cross-national comparison.* Hillsdale, NJ: Erlbaum.

Huesmann, L. R., Eron, L. D., Klein, R., Brice, P., & Fischer, P. (1983). Mitigating the imitation of aggressive behaviors by changing children's attitudes about media violence. *Journal of Personality and Social Psychology, 45,* 899-910.

Huesmann, L. R., Lagerspetz, K., & Eron, L. D. (1984). Intervening variables in the TV violence-aggression relation: Evidence from two countries. *Developmental Psychology, 20,* 746-775.

Hughes, J. O., & Sandler, B. R. (1987). *"Friends" raping friends: Could it happen to you?* Washington, DC: Association of American Colleges.

Hui, C. H. (1986). Fifteen years of pornography research: Does exposure to pornography have any effects? Hong Kong Psychological Society: Psychosocial aspects of pornography (1986, Hong Kong). *Bulletin of the Hong Kong Psychological Society,* Nos. 16-17, 41-62.

Hui, C. H. (1988). Measurement of individualism-collectivism. *Journal of Research in Personality, 22,* 17-36.

Hull, J. G., Van Treuren, R. R., & Virnelli, S. (1987). Hardiness and health: A critique and alternative approach. *Journal of Personality and Social Psychology, 53,* 518-530.

Hunter, C. E., & Ross, M. W. (1991). Determinants of health-care workers' attitudes toward people with AIDS. *Journal of Applied Social Psychology, 21,* 947-956.

Hunter, J. A., Stringer, M., & Watson, R. P. (1991). Intergroup violence and intergroup attributions. *British Journal of Social Psychology, 30,* 261-266.

Huston, T., & Levinger, G. (1978). Interpersonal attraction and relationships. *Annual Review of Psychology, 29,* 115-156.

Huston, T. L., & Vangelisti, A. L. (1991). Socioemotional behavior and satisfaction in marital relationships: A longitudinal study. *Journal of Personality and Social Psychology, 61,* 721-733.

Hutton, D. G., & Baumeister, R. F. (1992). Self-awareness and attitude change: Seeing oneself on the central route to persuasion. *Personality and Social Psychology Bulletin, 18,* 68-75.

Hyde, J. S. (1990). *Understanding human sexuality.* New York: McGraw-Hill.

Hyler, S. E., Gabbard, G. O., & Schneider, I. (1991). Homicidal maniacs and narcissistic parasites: Stigmatization of mentally ill persons in the movies. Annual Meeting of the American Psychiatric Association (1989, San Francisco, California). *Hospital and Community Psychiatry, 42,* 1044-1048.

Iacobucci, D., & McGill, A. L. (1990). Analysis of attribution data: Theory testing and effects estimation. *Journal of Personality and Social Psychology, 59,* 426-441.

Insko, C. A. (1965). Verbal reinforcement of attitude. *Journal of Personality and Social Psychology, 2,* 621-623.

Insko, C. A., Sedlak, A. J., & Lipsitz, A. (1982). A two-valued logic or two-valued balance resolution of the challenge of agreement and attraction effects in p-o-x triads, and a theoretical perspective on conformity and hedonism. *European Journal of Social Psychology, 12,* 143-167.

Inui, T. S., & Carter, W. B. (1985). Problems and prospects for health services research on provider-patient communication. *Medical Care, 23,* 521-538.

Ironson, G. (1993, April). National Institutes of Health symposium on gender and stress. Bethesda, Maryland.

Isen, A. M., Clark, M., & Schwartz, M. F. (1976). Duration of the effect of good mood on helping: "Footprints on the sands of time." *Journal of Personality and Social Psychology, 34,* 385-393.

Isen, A. M., & Levin, P. F. (1972). Effect of feeling good on helping: Cookies and kindness. *Journal of Personality and Social Psychology, 21,* 384-388.

Isenberg, D. J. (1986). Group polarization: A critical review and meta-analysis. *Journal of Personality and Social Psychology, 58,* 487-498.

Jaccard, J., Helbig, D. W., Wan, C. K., Gutman, M. A., & Kritz-Silverstein, D. C. (1990). Individual differences in attitude-behavior consistency: The prediction of contraceptive behavior. *Journal of Applied Social Psychology, 20,* 576-617.

Jackson, J. M. (1986). In defense of social impact theory: Comment on Mullen. *Journal of Personality and Social Psychology, 50,* 511-513.

Jackson, J. M., & Harkins, S. G. (1985). Equity in effort: An explanation of the social loafing effect. *Journal of Personality and Social Psychology, 49,* 1199-1206.

Jacobson, M. B., Antonelli, J., Winning, P. U., & Opeil, D. (1977). Women as authority figures: The use and nonuse of authority. *Sex Roles, 4,* 43-50.

Jaffe, Y., & Yinon, Y. (1979). Retaliatory aggression in individuals and groups. *European Journal of Social Psychology, 9,* 177-186.

Jahoda, G. (1986). Nature, culture and social psychology. *European Journal of Social Psychology, 16,* 17-30.

James, W. (1890). *Principles of psychology.* New York: Holt.

Jamieson, D. W., Lydon, J. E., Stewart, G., & Zanna, M. P. (1987). Pygmalion revisited:

New evidence for student expectancy effects in the classroom. *Journal of Educational Psychology, 79,* 461-466.

Janda, L. H., & Klenke-Hamel, K. E. (1980). *Human sexuality.* New York: Van Nostrand.

Janis, I. L. (1967). Effects of fear arousal on attitude change: Recent developments in theory and experimental research. In L. Berkowitz (Ed.), *Advances in experimental social psychology* (Vol. 3). New York: Academic Press.

Janis, I. L. (1972). *Victims of groupthink: A psychological study of foreign-policy decisions and fiascoes.* Boston: Houghton Mifflin.

Janis, I. L. (1982). Counteracting the adverse effects of concurrence-seeking in policy-planning groups: Theory and research perspectives. In H. Brandstatter, J. H. Davis, & G. Stocker-Kreichgauer (Eds.), *Group decision making.* New York: Academic Press.

Janis, I. L. (1989). *Crucial decisions: Leadership in policy-making management.* New York: Free Press.

Janoff-Bulman, R. (1992). *Shattered assumptions: Towards a new psychology of trauma.* New York: Free Press.

Jemmott, J. B., III, Pettigrew, T. F., & Johnson, J. T. (1983, August). *The effects of in-group versus out-group membership in social perception.* Paper presented at the 91st Annual Convention of the American Psychological Association, Anaheim, CA.

Jenner, H. (1990). The Pygmalion Effect: The importance of expectancies. *Alcoholism Treatment Quarterly, 7,* 127-133.

Jervis, R., Lebow, R. N., & Stein, J. G., with Morgan, P. M., & Snyder, J. L. (1985). *Psychology and deterrence.* Baltimore: Johns Hopkins University Press.

Joffe, J. (1992). Bosnia: The return of history. *Commentary, 94,* 24-29.

Johar, J. S., & Sirgy, M. J. (1991). Value-expressive versus utilitarian advertising appeals: When and why to use which appeal. *Journal of Advertising, 20* (3), 23-33.

Johnson, M. P., Huston, T. L., Gaines, S. O., & Levinger, G. (1992). Patterns of married life among young couples. [Special Issue]: Social networks. *Journal of Social and Personal Relationships, 9,* 343-364.

Johnson-George, C., & Swap, W. (1982). Measurement of specific interpersonal trust: Construction and validation of a scale to assess trust in a specific other. *Journal of Personality and Social Psychology, 43,* 1306-1317.

Jones, D. C. (1991). Friendship satisfaction and gender: An examination of sex differences in contributors to friendship satisfaction. *Journal of Social and Personal Relationships, 8,* 167-185.

Jones, E. (1961). *The life and work of Sigmund Freud.* New York: Basic Books.

Jones, E. E. (1964). *Ingratiation: A social psychological analysis.* New York: Appleton-Century-Crofts.

Jones, E. E. (1990). *Interpersonal perception.* New York: Freeman.

Jones, E. E., & Berglas, S. (1978). Control of attributions about the self through self-handicapping strategies: The appeal of alcohol and the role of under-achievement. *Personality and Social Psychology Bulletin, 4,* 200-206.

Jones, E. E., & Davis, K. E. (1965). A theory of correspondent inferences: From acts to dispositions. In L. Berkowitz (Ed.), *Advances in experimental social psychology* (Vol. 2). New York: Academic Press.

Jones, E. E., Gergen, K. J., & Davis, K. E. (1961). Role playing variations and their informational value on person perception. *Journal of Abnormal and Social Psychology, 63,* 302-310.

Jones, E. E., & Goethals, G. R. (1972). *Order effects in impression formation: Attribution context and the nature of the entity.* Morristown, NJ: General Learning Press.

Jones, E. E., & Harris, V. A. (1967). The attribution of attitudes. *Journal of Experimental and Social Psychology, 3,* 1-24.

Jones, E. E., & Nisbett, R. E. (1972). The actor and the observer: Divergent perceptions of the causes of behavior. In E. E. Jones, D. E. Kanouse, H. H. Kelley, R. E. Nisbett, S. Valins, & B. Weiner (Eds.), *Attribution: Perceiving the causes of behavior* (pp. 79-94). Morristown, NJ: General Learning Press.

Jones, E. E., & Pittman, T. S. (1982). Toward a general theory of strategic self-presentation. In J. Suls (Ed.), *Psychological perspectives on the self.* Hillsdale, NJ: Erlbaum.

Jones, R. A. (1985). *Research methods in the social and behavioral sciences.* Sunderland, MA: Sinauer.

Jones, R. W., & Bates, J. E. (1978). Satisfaction in male homosexual couples. *Journal of Homosexuality, 3,* 217-224.

Joule, R. V. (1987). La dissonance cognitive: Un état de motivation? / Arousal properties of dissonance. *Année Psychologique, 87,* 273-290.

Jourard, S. M. (1971). *The transparent self.* New York: Van Nostrand Reinhold.

Judd, C. M., Drake, R. A., Downing, J. W., & Krosnick, J. A. (1991). Some dynamic properties of attitude structures: Context-induced response facilitation and polarization. *Journal of Personality and Social Psychology, 60,* 193-202.

Judd, C. M., & Park, B. (1988). Out-group homogeneity: Judgments of variability at the individual and group levels. *Journal of Personality and Social Psychology, 54,* 778-788.

Judd, C. M., Ryan, C. S., & Park, B. (1991). Accuracy in the judgment of in-group and out-group variability. *Journal of Personality and Social Psychology, 61,* 366-379.

Julian, J. W., Bishop, D. W., & Fiedler, F. E. (1966). Quasitherapeutic effects of inter-group competition. *Journal of Personality and Social Psychology, 5,* 321-327.

Julius, Mara. (1990, Nov. 18). Gender differences in mortality as a result of anger-coping styles and blood pressure. Paper presented at the Gerontological Society of America, Boston, MA.

Jurma, W. E., & Wright, B. C. (1990). Follower reactions to male and female leaders who maintain or lose reward power. *Small Group Research, 21,* 97-112.

Jussim, L., Milburn, M., & Nelson, W. (1991). Emotional openness: Sex-role stereotypes and self-perceptions. *Representative Research in Social Psychology, 19,* 35-52.

Kagehiro, D. K. (1990). Defining the standards of proof in jury instructions. *Psychological Science, 1,* 194-200.

Kagitcibasi, C. (1984). Socialization in traditional society: A challenge to psychology. *International Journal of Psychology, 19,* 145-157.

Kahneman, D., & Tversky, A. (1973). On the psychology of prediction. *Psychological Review, 80,* 237-251.

Kalb, M. (1983). The conception of the alternative and the decision to divorce. *American Journal of Psychotherapy, 37,* 346-356.

Kallgren, C. A., & Wood, W. (1986). Access to attitude-relevant information in memory as a determinant of attitude-behavior consistency. *Journal of Experimental Social Psychology, 22,* 328-338.

Kamins, M. A., Marks, L. J., & Skinner, D. (1991). Television commercial evaluation in the context of program induced mood: Congruency versus consistency effects. *Journal of Advertising, 20,* 1-14.

Kanner, A. D., Coyne, J. C., Schaefer, C. & Lazarus, R. (1981). Comparison of two modes of stress measurement: Daily hassles and uplifts versus major life events. *Journal of Behavioral Medicine, 4,* 14.

Kanouse, D. E., & Hanson, L. R., Jr. (1972). Negativity in evaluations. In E. E. Jones, D. E. Kanouse, H. H. Kelley, R. E. Nisbett, S. Valins, & B. Weiner (Eds.). *Attribution: Perceiving causes of behavior.* Morristown, NJ: General Learning Press.

Kantrowitz, B. (1992, August 3). Teenagers and AIDS. *Newsweek,* 45-50.

Kaplan, M. F. (1975). Information integration in social judgment: Interaction of judge and informational components. *Human judgment and decision processes.* New York: Academic Press.

Kaplan, M. F., & Anderson, N. H. (1973). Information integration theory and reinforcement theory as approaches to interpersonal attraction. *Journal of Personality and Social Psychology, 28,* 301-312.

Kaplan, M. F., & Miller, C. E. (1987). Group decision making and normative versus informational influence: Effects of type of issue and assigned decision rule. *Journal of Personality and Social Psychology, 53,* 306-313.

Kaplan, R. M., Sallis, J. F., Jr., & Patterson, T. L. (1993). *Health and human behavior.* New York: McGraw-Hill.

Karasawa, M. (1988). Effects of cohesiveness and inferiority upon ingroup favoritism. *Japanese Psychological Research, 30,* 49-59.

Karau, S. J., & Williams, K. D. (1993). Social loafing: A meta-analytic review and theoretical integration. *Journal of Personality and Social Psychology, 65,* 681-706.

Karlen, N. (1993, July 11). Lollapalooza lover story. *New York Times,* Sec. 9, pp. 1, 9.

Karlins, M., Coffman, T. L., & Walters, G. (1969). On the fading of social stereotypes: Studies in three generations of college students. *Journal of Personality and Social Psychology, 13,* 1-16.

Kassin, S. M. (1983). Deposition testimony and the surrogate witness: Evidence for a "messenger effect" in persuasion. *Personality and Social Psychology Bulletin, 9,* 281-288.

Kassin, S. M., Ellsworth, P. C., & Smith, V. L. (1989). The "general acceptance" of psychological research on eyewitness testimony: A survey of the experts. *American Psychologist, 44,* 1089-1098.

Kassin, S. M., Reddy, M. E., & Tulloch, W. F. (1990). Juror interpretations of ambiguous evidence: The need for cognition, presentation, order, persuasion. *Law and Human Behavior, 14,* 43-55.

Katz, D., & Braly, K. (1933). Racial stereotypes of one hundred college students. *Journal of Abnormal and Social Psychology, 28,* 280-290.

Katz, I., & Hass, R. G. (1988). Racial ambivalence and American Value Conflict: Correlational and priming studies of dual cognitive structures. *Journal of Personaltiy and Social Psychology, 55,* 893-905.

Katz, P. A. (Ed.). (1976). *Towards the elimination of racism.* New York: Pergamon.

Kaufman, J., & Zigler, E. (1987). Do abused children become abusive parents? *American Journal of Orthopsychiatry, 57,* 186-192.

Keating, C. F. (1985). Human dominance signals: The primate in us. In S. L. Ellyson & J. F. Dovidio (Eds.), *Power, dominance, and nonverbal behavior.* New York: Springer-Verlag.

Kelley, H. H. (1950). The warm-cold variable in first impressions of persons. *Journal of Personality, 18*, 431-439.

Kelley, H. H. (1967). Attribution theory in social psychology. *Nebraska Symposium on Motivation, 15*, 192-238.

Kelley, H. H. (1972). Attribution in social interaction. In E. E. Jones et al. (Eds.), *Attribution: Perceiving the causes of behavior*. Morristown, NJ: General Learning Press.

Kelley, H. H. (1991). Research on interpersonal relationships. *Japanese Journal of Experimental Social Psychology, 30*, 259-267.

Kelley, H. H., Berscheid, E., Christensen, A., Harvey, J. H., Huston, T. L., Levinger, G., McClintock, E., Peplau, L. A., & Peterson, D. R. (1983). *Close relationships*. New York: Freeman.

Kelley, H. H., & Michela, J. L. (1980). Attribution theory and research. *Annual Review of Psychology, 31*, 457-501.

Kello, A., & Ruisel, I. (1979). Effect of personality traits on group status in sportsmen. *Studia Psychologica, 21*, 155-159.

Kelly, E. L., & Conley, J. J. (1987). Personality and compatibility: A prospective analysis of marital stability and marital satisfaction. *Journal of Personality and Social Psychology, 52*, 27-40.

Kelman, H. C. (1967). Human use of human subjects: The problem of deception in social psychological experiments. *Psychological Bulletin, 67*, 1-11.

Kelman, H. C. (1968). *A time to speak: On human values and social research*. San Francisco: Jossey-Bass.

Kelman, H. C., & Hamilton, V. L. (1989). *Crimes of obedience*. New Haven, CT: Yale University Press.

Kelman, H. C., & Lawrence, L. (1972). Assignment of responsibility in the case of Lt. Calley: Preliminary report on a national survey. *Journal of Social Issues, 28*, 177-212.

Kerckhoff, A. C., & Davis, K. E. (1962). Value consensus and need complementarity in mate selection. *American Sociological Review, 27*, 295-303.

Kernis, M. H., Cornell, D. P., Sun, C., Berry, A., & Harlow, T. (1993). There's more to self-esteem than whether it is high or low: The importance of stability of self-esteem *Journal of Personality and Social Psychology, 65*, 1190-1204.

Kerr, N. L. (1983). Motivation losses in small groups: A social dilemma analysis. *Journal of Personality and Social Psychology, 45*, 819-828.

Kerr, N. L., & Bruun, S. (1981). Ringelmann revisited: Alternative explanations for the social loafing effect. *Journal of Personality and Social Psychology, 37*, 224-231.

Kerr, N. L., & Bruun, S. E. (1983). Dispensibility of member effort and group motivation losses: Free-rider effects. *Journal of Personality and Social Psychology, 12*, 78-94.

Kerwin, J., & Shaffer, D. R. (1991). The effects of jury dogmatism on reactions to jury nullification instructions. *Personality and Social Psychology Bulletin, 17*, 140-146.

Kessen, W. (1979). The American child and other cultural inventions. *American Psychologist, 34*, 815-820.

Kiecolt-Glaser, J. K., & Glaser, R. (1991). Psychosocial factors, stress, disease, and immunity. In R. Ader, D. L. Felten, & N. Cohen (Eds.), *Psychoneuroimmunology*. San Diego, CA: Academic Press.

Kiecolt-Glaser, J. K., Glaser, R., Dyer, C., Shuttleworth, E., Orgrocki, P., & Speicher, C. E. (1987). Chronic stress and immunity in family caregivers of Alzheimer's disease victims. *Psychosomatic Medicine, 49*, 523-535.

Kiecolt-Glaser, R., & Kiecolt-Glaser, J. K. (1993). Mind and immunity. In D. Goleman & J. Gurin (Eds.), *Mind-body medicine*. Yonkers, New York: Consumer Reports Books.

Killian, L. M. (1980). Theory of collective behavior: The mainstream revisited. In H. M. Blalock Jr. (Ed.), *Sociological theory and Research*. New York: Free Press.

Kim, Y., & Stevens, J. H. (1987). The socialization of prosocial behavior in children. *Childhood Education, 63*, 200-206.

Kinder, D. R., Abelson, R. P., & Fiske, S. T. (1979). *Developmental Research on candidate instrumentation: Results and recommendations*. Report available from Center for Political Studies, ISR, University of Michigan.

Kinder, D. R., & Sears, D. O. (1985). Public opinion and political action. In G. Lindzey & E. Aronson (Eds.), *Handbook of social psychology* (3rd ed.). New York: Random House.

Kipnis, D. (1976). *The powerholders*. Chicago: University of Chicago Press.

Kipnis, D., Castell, J., Gergen, M., & Mauch, D. (1976). Metamorphic effects of power. *Journal of Applied Psychology, 61*, 127-135.

Kipnis, D. M. (1974). Inner direction, other direction and achievement motivation. *Human Development, 17*, 321-343.

Klein, J. G. (1991). Negativity effects in impression formation: A test in the political arena. *Personality and Social Psychology Bulletin, 17*, 412-418.

Kleinke, C. L. (1986). *Meeting and understanding people*. New York: Freeman.

Klentz, B., & Beaman, A. L. (1981). The effects of type of information and method of dissemination on the reporting of a shoplifter. *Journal of Applied Social Psychology, 11*, 64-82.

Klineberg, O. (1990). A personal perspective on the development of social psychology. *Annals of the New York Academy of Sciences, 602*, 35-50.

Knight, G. P., Johnson, L. G., Carlo, G., & Eisenberg, N. (1994). A multiplicative model of the dispositional antecedents of a prosocial behavior: Predicting more of the people more of the time. *Journal of Personality and Social Psychology, 66*, 178-183.

Kobasa, S. C. (1979). Stressful life events, personality and health: An inquiry into hardiness. *Journal of Personality and Social Psychology, 37*, 1-11.

Kohn, A. (1988, October). Beyond selfishness. *Psychology Today*, 34-38.

Kolbert, E. (1993, March 20). Perot to hold his own vote, but this time on television. *New York Times*, 6.

Kolditz, T. A., & Arkin, R. M. (1982). An impression management interpretation of the self-handicapping strategy. *Journal of Personaltiy and Social Psychology, 43*, 492-502.

Koss, M. P., Dinero, T. E., Siebel, C. A., & Cox, S. L. (1988). Stranger and acquaintance rape: Are there differences in the victim's experience? *Psychology of Women Quarterly, 12*, 1-24.

Kotler, P. (1986). *Principles of marketing* (3rd ed.). Englewood Cliffs, NJ: Prentice-Hall.

Kotre, J., & Hall, E. (1990). *Seasons of life*. Boston: Little, Brown.

Krackhardt, D., & Porter, L. W. (1986). The snowball effect: Turnover embedded in communication networks. *Journal of Applied Psychology, 71*, 50-55.

Krahe, B. (1992). *Personality and social psychology: Towards a synthesis*. Newbury Park, CA: Sage.

Kravitz, D. A., & Martin, B. (1986). Ringelmann rediscovered: The original article. *Journal of Personaltiy and Social Psychology, 50*, 936-941.

Kreuz, L. E., & Rose, R. M. (1972). Assessment of aggressive behavior and plasma testosterone in a young criminal population. *Psychosomatic Medicine, 34*, 321-332.

Kristiansen, C. M., & Giulietti, R. (1990). Perceptions of wife abuse: Effects of gender attitudes toward women, and just-world beliefs among college students. *Psychology of Women Quarterly, 14*, 177-189.

Kruglanski, A., & Mackie, D. M. (1989). Majority and minority influence: A judgmental process analysis. In W. Stroebe & M. Hewstone (Eds.), *Advances in European social psychology*. London: Wiley.

Kruglanski, A. E., & Mayseless, O. (1987). Motivational effects in the social comparison of opinions. *Journal of Personality and Social Psychology, 53*, 834-842.

Kruglanski, A. W., & Freund, T. (1983). The freezing and unfreezing of lay-inferences: Effects of impressional primacy, ethnic stereotyping, and numerical anchoring. *Journal of Experimental Social Psychology, 19,* 448-468.

Kruglanski, A. W., & Webster, D. M. (1991). Group members' reactions to opinion deviates and conformists at varying degrees of proximity to decision deadline and of environmental noise. *Journal of Personality and Social Psychology, 61,* 212-225.

Kryzanowski, E., & Stewin, L. (1985). Developmental implications in youth counseling: Gender socialization. *International Journal for the Advancement of Counseling, 8,* 265-278.

Kunda, Z. (1990). The case of motivated reasoning. *Psychological Bulletin, 108,* 480-498.

Kurdek, L. A. (1991). Correlates of relationship satisfaction in cohabiting gay and lesbian couples: Integration of contextual, investment, and problem-solving models. *Journal of Personality and Social Psychology,, 61,* 910-922.

Kushler, M. G. (1989). Use of evaluation to improve energy conservation programs: A review and case study. *Journal of Social Issues, 45,* 153-168.

Lakey, B., & Heller, K. (1985). Response biases and the relation between negative life events and psychological symptoms. *Journal of Personality and Social Psychology, 49,* 1662-1668.

Lamb, M. E. (1982). The bonding phenomenon: Misinterpretations and their implications. *Journal of Pediatrics, 101,* 555-557.

Lambert, W. W. (1971). Cross-cultural backgrounds to personality development and the socialization of aggression: Findings from the Six Culture study. In W. W. Lambert & R. Weisbrod (Eds.), *Comparative perspectives on social psychology.* Boston: Little, Brown.

Lamm, H. (1988). A review of our research on group polarization: Eleven experiments on the effects of group discussion on risk acceptance, probability estimation, and negotiation positions. ONR Conference: The psychology of the social group (1987, London, England). *Psychological Reports, 62,* 807-813.

Lamm, H., & Myers, D. G. (1978). Group-induced polarization of attitudes and behavior. In L. Berkowitz (Ed.), *Advances in experimental social psychology* (Vol. 2, pp. 145-195). New York: Academic Press.

Landy, D., & Aronson, E. (1969). The influence of the character of the criminal and his victim on the decisions of simulated jurors. *Journal of Experimental Social Psychology, 5,* 141-152.

Langer, E. J. (1989a). *Mindfulness.* Reading, MA: Addison-Wesley.

Langer, E. J. (1989b). Minding matters. In L. Berkowitz (Ed.), *Advances in experimental social psychology* (Vol. 22). New York: Academic Press.

Langlois, J. H., Roggman, L. A., Casey, R. J., Ritter, J. M., Rieser-Danner, L. A., & Jenkins, V. Y. (1987). Infant preferences for attractive faces: Rudiments of a stereotype? *Developmental Psychology, 23,* 363-369.

Langlois, J. H., Roggman, L. A., & Rieser-Danner, L. A. (1990). Infants' differential social responses to attractive and unattractive faces. *Developmental Psychology, 26,* 153-159.

LaPiere, R. T. (1934). Attitudes vs. action. *Social Forces, 13,* 230-237.

Larsen, K. S., Triplett, J. S., Brant, W. D., & Langenberg, D. (1979). Collaborator status, subject characteristics, and conformity in the Asch paradigm. *Journal of Social Psychology, 108,* 259-263.

Lassiter, G. D., Stone, J. I., & Weigold, M. F. (1988). Effect of leading questions on the self-monitoring correlation. *Personality and Social Psychology Bulletin, 13,* 537-545.

Laszlo, J. (1986). Scripts for interpersonal situations. *Studia Psychologica, 28,* 125-135.

Latané, B. (1981). The psychology of social impact. *American Psychologist, 36,* 343-356.

Latané, B., & Darley, J. M. (1968). Group inhibition of bystander intervention. *Journal of Personality and Social Psychology, 10,* 215-221.

Latané, B., & Darley, J. M. (1970). *The unresponsive bystander: Why doesn't he help?* New York: Appleton-Century-Crofts.

Latané, B., & Nida, S. (1981). Ten years of research on group size and helping. *Psychological Bulletin, 89,* 308-324.

Latané, B., & Wolf, S. (1981). The social impact of majorities and minorities. *Psychological Review, 88,* 438-453.

Laughlin, P. R. (1980). Social combination process of cooperative, problem-solving groups at verbal intellective tasks. In M. Fishbein (Ed.), *Progress in social psychology* (Vol. 1). Hillsdale, NJ: Erlbaum.

Lazarus, R. (1991). *Emotion and adaptation.* Oxford, England: Oxford University Press.

Lazarus, R., DeLongis, A., Folkman, S., & Gruen, R. (1985). Stress and adaptation outcomes: The problem of confounded measures. *American Psychologist, 40,* 770-779.

Lazarus, R. S. (1968). Emotions and adaptation: Conceptual and empirical relations. In W. Arnold (Ed.), *Nebraska symposium on motivation.* Lincoln: University of Nebraska Press.

Lazarus, R. S., & Cohen, J. B. (1977). Environmental stress. In I. Altman & J. F. Wohlwill (Eds.), *Human behavior and the environment: Current theory and research* (Vol. 2). New York: Plenum.

Lazarus, R. S., & Folkman, S. (1984). Stress, appraisal, and coping. New York: Springer.

Leana, C. R. (1985). A partial test of Janis' groupthink model: Effects of group cohesiveness and leader behavior on defective decision making. *Journal of Management, 11,* 5-17.

Leary, M. R. (1979). Levels of disconfirmability and social psychology theory: A response to Greenwald. *Personality and Social Psychology Bulletin, 5,* 149-153.

Leary, M. R., & Shepperd, J. A. (1986). Behavioral self-handicaps versus self-reported handicaps: A conceptual note. *Journal of Personality and Social Psychology, 51,* 1265-1268.

Leavitt, H. J. (1951). Some effects of certain communication patterns on group performance. *Journal of Abnormal and Social Psychology, 46,* 38-50.

Lebow, R. N., & Stein, J. G. (1987). Beyond deterrence. *Journal of Social Issues, 43,* 5-71.

Lee, A. M. (1983). *Terrorism in North Ireland.* Bayside, NY: General Hall.

Lee, J. A. (1974). The styles of loving. *Psychology Today, 8,* 43-50.

Lee, J. A. (1977). A typology of styles of loving. *Personality and Social Psychology Bulletin, 3,* 173-182.

Lee, J. A. (1988). Love styles. In R. J. Sternberg & M. J. Barnes (Eds.), *The psychology of love.* New Haven, CT: Yale University Press.

Lee, M. E., Matsumoto, D., Kobayashi, M., Krupp, D., Maniatis, E. F., & Roberts, W. (1992). Cultural influences on nonverbal behavior in applied settings. In R. S. Feldman (Ed.), *Applications of nonverbal behavioral theories and research.* Hillsdale, NJ: Erlbaum.

Lehman, D. R., & Taylor, S. E. (1988). Date with an earthquake: Coping with a probable, unpredictable disaster. *Personality and Social Psychology Bulletin, 13,* 546-555.

Leigh, H., & Reiser, M. F. (1980). *The patient.* New York: Plenum.

Leland, J. (1992, November 2). The selling of sex. *Newsweek,* 95-103.

Lemoine, J., & Mougne, C. (1983). Why has death stalked the refugees? *Natural History, 92,* 6-19.

Lepore, S. J., Evans, G. W., & Schneider, M. L. (1991). Dynamic role of social support in the link between chronic stress and psychological distress. *Journal of Personality and Social Psychology, 61,* 889-909.

Lepper, M. (1983b). Social control processes, attributions of motivation, and the internalization of social values. In E. T. Higgins,

D. N. Rubble, & W. W. Hartup (Eds.), *Social cognition and social development: A sociocultural perspective.* New York: Cambridge University Press.

Lepper, M. R. (1983a). Extrinsic reward and intrinsic motivation: Implications for the classroom. In J. M. Levine & M. C. Wung (Eds.), *Teacher and student perceptions: Implications for learning* (pp. 281-317). Hillsdale, NJ: Erlbaum.

Lepper, M. R., & Greene, D. (1978). *The hidden costs of reward.* Hillsdale, NJ: Erlbaum.

Lepper, M. R., Greene, D., & Nisbett, R. E. (1973). Undermining children's intrinsic interest with extrinsic rewards: A test of the "overjustification" hypothesis. *Journal of Personality and Social Psychology, 28,* 129-137.

Lerner, M. J. (1980). *The belief in a just world: A fundamental delusion.* New York: Plenum.

Lerner, M. J., & Meindl, J. R. (1981). Justice and altruism. In J. P. Rushton & R. M. Sorrentino (Eds.), *Altruism and helping behavior: Social, personality, and developmental perspectives.* Hillsdale, NJ: Erlbaum.

Leung, K., & Bond, M. H. (1984). The impact of cultural collectivism on reward allocation. *Journal of Personality and Social Psychology, 47,* 793-804.

Leventhal, H. (1970). Findings and theory in the study of fear communications. In L. Berkowitz (Ed.), *Advances in experimental social psychology* (Vol. 5, pp. 119-186). New York: Academic Press.

Leventhal, H., Nerenz, D., & Leventhal, E. (1985). Feelings of threat and private views of illness: Factors in dehumanization in the medical care system. In A. Baum and J. E. Singer (Eds.), *Advances in environmental psychology* (Vol. 4). Hillsdale, NJ: Erlbaum.

Levin, J., & McDevitt, J. (1993). *Hate crimes: The rising tide of bigotry and bloodshed.* New York: Plenum.

Levine, J. M. (1989). Reaction to opinion deviance in small groups. In P. B. Paulhus (Ed.), *Psychology of group influence* (2nd ed.). Hillsdale, NJ: Erlbaum.

LeVine, R. A., & Campbell, D. T. (1972). *Ethnocentrism: Theories of conflict, ethnic attitudes and group behavior.* New York: Wiley.

Levine, R. V. (1993, February). Is love a luxury? *American Demographics,* 27-29.

Levinger, G. A. (1974). A three-level approach to attraction: Toward an understanding of pair relatedness. In T. L. Huston (Ed.), *Foundations of interpersonal attraction.* New York: Academic.

Levinger, G. A. (1983). Development and change. In H. H. Kelley et al. *Close relationships.* San Francisco: Freeman.

Levinger, G. A., Senn, D. J., & Jorgensen, B. W. (1970). Progress toward permanence in courtship: A test of the Kerckhoff-Davis hypothesis. *Sociometry, 33,* 427-443.

Levinson, S. C. (1980). Speech act theory: The state of the art. *Language and Linguistics Teaching: Abstracts, 1,* 5-24.

Levy, S. M., Lee, J., Bagley, C., & Lippman, M. (1988). Survival hazard analysis in first recurrent breast cancer patients. Seven-year follow-up. *Psychosomatic Medicine, 50,* 520-528.

Levy, S. M., & Roberts, D. C. (1992). Clinical significance of psychoneuroimmunology: Prediction of cancer outcomes. In N. Schneiderman, P. McCabe, & A. Baum (Eds.), *Stress and disease processes.* Hillsdale, NJ: Erlbaum.

Lewin, K. (1931). *Die psychologische Situation bein Lohn und Strafe.* Leipzig: S. Hirzel.

Lewin, K. (1935). *A dynamic theory of personality.* New York: McGraw-Hill.

Lewin, K. (1936). *Principles of topological psychology.* New York: McGraw-Hill.

Lewin, K. (1943). Forces behind food habits and methods of change. *Bulletin of the National Research Council, 108,* 35-65.

Lewin, K. (1951). *Field theory in social science.* New York: Harper.

Lewin, K., Lippitt, R., & White, R. K. (1939). Patterns of aggressive behavior in experimentally created "social climates." *Journal of Social Psychology, 10,* 271-299.

Lewis, C. S. (1958). *The allegory of love: A study in medieval traditions.* New York: Oxford University Press.

Lewis, M., & Brooks-Gunn, J. (1979). *Social cognition and the acquisition of self.* New York: Plenum.

Lewittes, H. J. (1988). Just being friendly means a lot: Women, friendship, and aging. *Women and Health, 14,* 139-159.

Ley, P. (1982). Giving information to patients. In J. R. Eiser (Ed.), *Social psychology and behavioral medicine.* New York: Wiley.

Ley, P., Bradshaw, P. W., Kincey, J. A., & Atherton, S. T. (1977). Increasing patients' satisfaction with communications. *British Journal of Social and Clinical Psychology, 15,* 403-413.

Ley, R. (1977). Encoding specificity and unidirectional associates in cued recall. *Memory and Cognition, 5,* 523-528.

Liebert, R. M. (1975). Modeling and the media. *School Psychology Digest, 4,* 22-29.

Liebert, R. M., & Sprafkin, J. (1988). *The early window: Effects of television on children and youth* (3rd ed.). New York: Pergamon.

Likert, R. (1932). A technique for the measurement of attitudes [Special issue]. *Archives of Psychology, 140.*

Linneweber, V., Mummendey, A., Bornewasser, M., & Loschper, G. (1984). Classification of situations specific to field and behaviour: The context of aggressive interactions in schools. *European Journal of Social Psychology, 14,* 281-295.

Linville, P. W. (1982). The complexity-extremity effect and age-based stereotyping. *Journal of Personality and Social Psychology, 42,* 193-211.

Linville, P. W. (1987). Self-complexity as a cognitive buffer against stress-related illness and depression. *Journal of Personality and Social Psychology, 52,* 663-676.

Linville, P. W., Fischer, G. W., & Salovey, P. (1989). Perceived distributions of the characteristics of in-group and out-group members: Empirical evidence and a computer simulation. *Journal of Personality and Social Psychology, 57,* 165-188.

Linville, P. W., & Jones, E. E. (1980). Polarized appraisals of outgroup members. *Journal of Personality and Social Psychology, 38,* 689-703.

Linz, D., Donnerstein, E., & Penrod, S. (1987). The findings and recommendations of the attorney general's commission on pornography. *American Psychologist, 42,* 946-953.

Linz, D. G., Donnerstein, E., & Adams, S. M. (1989). Physiological desensitization and judgments about female victims of violence. *Human Communication Research,* p. 5.

Lipka, R. P., & Brinthaupt, T. M. (Eds.). (1992). *Self-perspectives across the life span.* Albany: State University of New York Press.

Lipman, J. (1991, September 4). Celebrity pitchmen are popular again. *Wall Street Journal,* B1.

Lipman, J. (1992, March 10). Surgeon general says it's high time Joe Camel quit. *Wall Street Journal,* B1, B7.

Lippa, R. (1976). Expressive control and the leakage of dispositional introversion-extroversion during role-playing teaching. *Journal of Personality, 44,* 541-559.

Lippa, R., & Donaldson, S. I. (1990). Self-monitoring and idiographic measures of behavioral variability across interpersonal relationships. *Journal of Personality, 58,* 465-479.

Lisak, D., & Roth, S. (1988). Motivational factors in nonincarcerated sexually aggressive men. *Journal of Personality and Social Psychology, 55,* 795-802.

Liskin, L. (1985, November-December). Youth in the 1980s: Social and health concerns 4. *Population Reports, 8.*

Loftus, E. F. (1993). Psychologists in the eyewitness world. *American Psychologist, 48,* 550-552.

Loftus, E. F., & Ketcham, K. (1991). *Witness for the defense: The accused, the eyewitness who puts memory on trial.* New York: St. Martin's Press.

Loftus, E. F., & Palmer, J. C. (1974). Reconstruction of automobile destruction: An example of the interface between language and memory. *Journal of Verbal Learning and Verbal Behavior, 13,* 585-589.

Logan, G. D., & Cowan, W. B. (1984). On the ability to inhibit thought and action: A theory of an act of control. *Psychological Review, 91,* 295-327.

Lord, C. G., Lepper, M. R., & Mackie, D. (1984). Attitude prototypes as determinants of attitude-behavior consistency. *Journal of Personality and Social Psychology, 46,* 1254-1266.

Lorenz, K. (1966). *On aggression.* New York: Harcourt Brace Jovanovich.

Lorenz, K. (1974). *Civilized man's eight deadly sins.* New York: Harcourt Brace Jovanovich.

Lortie-Lussier, M. (1987). Minority influence and idiosyncrasy credit: A new comparison of the Moscovici and Hollander theories of innovation. *European Journal of Social Psychology, 17,* 431-446.

Lott, A. J., & Lott, B. E. (1974). The role of reward in the formation of positive interpersonal attitudes. In T. L. Huston (Ed.), *Foundations of interpersonal attraction* (pp. 171-189). New York: Academic Press.

Lott, B. (1987). Sexist discrimination as distancing behavior: I. A laboratory demonstration. *Psychology of Women Quarterly, 11,* 47-58.

Love, K. D., & Aiello, J. R. (1980). Using projective techniques to measure interaction distance: A methodological note. *Personality and Social Psychology Bulletin, 6,* 102-104.

Luckey, E. B., & Bain, J. K. (1970). Children: A factor in marital satisfaction. *Journal of Marriage and the Family, 32,* 43-44.

Luginbuhl, J. (1992). Comprehension of judges' instructions in the penalty phase of a capital trial: Focus on mitigating circumstances. *Law and Human Behavior, 16,* 203-218.

Luginbuhl, J., & Palmer, R. (1991). Impression management aspects of self-handicapping: Positive and negative effects. *Personality and Social Psychology Bulletin, 17,* 655-662.

Luks, A. (1988, October). Helper's high. *Psychology Today,* 39-42.

Luthans, F. (1989). *Organizational behavior* (5th ed.). New York: McGraw-Hill.

Lysak, H., Rule, B. G., & Dobbs, A. R. (1989). Conceptions of aggression: Prototype or defining features? *Personality and Social Psychology Bulletin, 15,* 233-243.

Lytton, H., & Romney, D. M. (1991). Parents' differential socialization of boys and girls: A meta-analysis. *Psychological Bulletin, 109,* 267-296.

Maas, A., & Clark, R. D. (1983). Internalization versus compliance: Differential processes underlying minority influence and conformity. *European Journal of Social Psychology, 13,* 197-215.

Maas, A., & Clark, R. D., III. (1984). Hidden impact of minorities: Fifteen years of minoirty influence research. *Psychological Bulletin, 95,* 428-450.

Maccoby, E. E., & Jacklin, C. N. (1974). *The psychology of sex differences.* Stanford, CA: Stanford University Press.

MacDermid, S. M., Huston, T. L., & McHale, S. M. (1990). Changes in marriage associated with the transition to parenthood: Individual differences as a function of sex-role attitudes and changes in division of labor. *Journal of Marriage and the Family, 52,* 475-486.

Macher, K. (1986). The politics of organizations. *Personnel Journal, 65,* 80-84.

Mackie, D. M. (1987) Systematic and nonsystematic processing of majority and minority persuasive communications. *Journal of Personality and Social Psychology, 53,* 41-52,

Mackie, D. M., & Worth, L. T. (1991). Feeling good, but not thinking straight: The impact of positive mood on persuasion. In J. Forgas (Ed.), *Emotion and social judgments.* Oxford, England: Pergamon Press.

Mackie, D. M., Worth, L. T., & Allison, S. T. (1990). Outcome-based inferences and the perception of change in groups. *Social Cognition, 8,* 325-342.

MacNeil, M. K., & Clark, R. D., III. (1984). Hidden impact of minorities: Fifteen years of minority influence research. *Psychological Bulletin, 95,* 428-450.

MacNeil, M. K., & Sherif, M. (1976). Norm change over subject generations as a function of arbitrariness of prescribed norms. *Journal of Personality and Social Psychology, 34,* 762-773.

Macrae, C. N., Milne, A. B., & Bodenhausen, G. V. (1994). Stereotypes as energy-saving devices: A peek inside the cognitive toolbox. *Journal of Personality and Social Psychology, 66,* 37-47.

Madden, T. J., Ellen, P. S., & Ajzen, I. (1992). A comparison of the theory of planned behavior and the theory of reasoned action. *Personality and Social Psychology Bulletin, 18,* 3-9.

Maddie, S. R., Barone, P. T., & Puccetti, M. C. (1987). Stressful events are indeed a factor in physical illness: Reply to Schroeder and Costa (1984). *Journal of Personality and Social Psychology, 52,* 833-843.

Maddux, C. D., Stoltenberg, C. O., & Harvey, J. H. (Eds.). (1989). *Interfaces in psychology: Social perception in clinical and counseling psychology.* Lubbock, TX: Texas Tech Press.

Maddux, J. E., & Rogers, R. W. (1983). Protection motivation and self-efficacy: A revised theory of fear appeals and attitude change. *Journal of Experimental Social Psychology, 19,* 469-479.

Maddux, J. E., & Rogers, R. W. (1980). Effects of source expertness, physical attractiveness, and supporting arguments on persuasion: A case of brains over beauty. *Journal of Personality and Social Psychology, 39,* 833-843.

Magalhaes, R. (1984). Organisation development in Latin countries: Fact or fiction? *Leadership and Organization Development Journal, 5,* 17-21.

Mahler, M. S., Pine, F., & Bergman, A. (1975). *The psychological birth of the human infant.* New York: Basic Books.

Mahoney, E. R. (1983). *Human sexuality.* New York: McGraw-Hill.

Maier, N. R. F., & Solem, A. R. (1952). The contribution of a discussion leader to the quality of group thinking: The effective use of minority opinions. *Human Relations, 5,* 277-288.

Major, B., & Konar, E. (1984). An investigation of sex differences in pay expectations and their possible causes. *Academy of Management Journal, 27,* 777-792.

Malamuth, N. M., & Check, J. V. P. (1985). The effects of aggressive pornography on beliefs in rape myths: Individual differences. *Journal of Research in Personality, 15,* 436-446.

Malatesta, C. Z., & Lamb, C. (1987, August). *Emotion socialization during the second year.* Paper presented at the Annual Meeting of the American Psychological Association, New York City.

Malloy, T. E., & Albright, L. (1990). Interpersonal perception in a social context. *Journal of Personality and Social Psychology, 58,* 419-428.

Mann, L. (1980). Cross-cultural studies in small groups. In H. C. Triandis & R. W. Brislin (Eds.), *Handbook of cross-cultural psychology* (Vol. 5). Boston: Allyn & Bacon.

Mann, L., Newton, J. W., & Innes, J. M. (1982). A test between deindividuation and emergent norm theories of crowd aggression. *Journal of Personality and Social Psychology, 42,* 260-272.

Manucia, G. K., Baumann, D. J., & Cialdini, R. B. (1984). Mood influences on helping: Direct effects or side effects? *Journal of Personality and Social Psychology, 46,* 357-364.

Marco, C. A., & Suls, J. (1993). Daily stress and the trajectory of mood: Spillover, response assimilation, contrast, and chronic negative affectivity. *Journal of Personality and Social Psychology, 64,* 1053-1063.

Margolin, L. (1989). Gender and the prerogatives of dating and marriage: An experimental assessment of a sample of college students. *Sex Roles, 20,* 91-102.

Marino, R. V., Rosenfeld, W., Narula, P., & Karakurum, M. (1991). Impact of pediatricians' attire on children and parents. *Journal of Developmental and Behavioral Pediatrics, 12,* 98-101.

Markman, H. J. (1981). Prediction of marital distress: A 5-year follow-up. *Journal of Consulting and Clinical Psychology, 49*, 760-762.

Markman, H. J. (1991). Constructive marital conflict is *not* an oxymoron. [Special Issue]: Negative communication in marital interaction: A misnomer? *Behavioral Assessment, 13*, 83-96.

Marks, G., & Miller, N. (1987). Ten years of research on the false-consensus effect: An empirical and theoretical review. *Psychological Bulletin, 102*, 72-90.

Markus, G. B. (1982). Political attitudes during an election year: A report of the 1980 NES Panel Study. *American Political Science Review, 76*, 538-560.

Markus, H. (1977). Self-schemata and processing information about the self. *Journal of Personality and Social Psychology, 35*, 63-78.

Markus, H., & Nurius, P. (1986). Possible selves. *American Psychologist, 41*, 954-969.

Markus, H., & Sentis, K. P. (1982). The self in social information processing. In J. Suls (Ed.), *Psychological perspectives on the self* (Vol. 1, pp. 41-70). Hillsdale, NJ: Erlbaum.

Markus, H. R., & Kitayama, S. (1991). Culture and the self: Implications for cognition, emotion, and motivation. *Psychological Review, 98*, 224-253.

Markus, H. R., Smith, J., & Moreland, R. L. (1985). Role of the self-concept in the perception of others. *Journal of Personality and Social Psychology, 49*, 1494-1512.

Mars, D. (1981). Creativity and urban policy leadership. *Journal of Creative Behavior, 15*, 199-204.

Marsh, H. W. (1986). Global self-esteem: Its relation to specific facets of self-concept and their importance. *Journal of Personality and Social Psychology, 51*, 1224-1236.

Marshall, G. D., & Zimbardo, P. G. (1979). Affective consequences of inadequately explained physiological arousal. *Journal of Personality and Social Psychology, 37*, 970-988.

Martin, A. J. (1975). *One man, hurt.* New York: Macmillan.

Martin, B. A. (1989). Gender differences in salary expectations. *Psychology of Women Quarterly, 13*, 87-96.

Marton, J. P., & Acker, L. E. (1982). Television provoked aggression: Effects of gentle, affection-like training prior to exposure. *Child Study Journal, 12*, 27-43.

Marx, M. B., Garrity, T. F., & Bowers, F. R. (1975). The influence of recent life experience on the health of college freshmen. *Journal of Psychosomatic Research, 19*, 87-98.

Maslow, A. H. (1987). *Motivation and personality* (3rd ed.). New York: Harper & Row.

Mason, J. W. (1975). A historical view of the stress field. *Journal of Human Stress, 1*, 6-12, 22-37.

Mathis, J. O., & Lampe, R. E. (1991). Corporal punishment: A TACD issue. *TACD Journal, 19*, 27-32.

Matlon, R. J., Davis, J. W., Catchings, B. W., & Derr, W. R. (1986). Factors affecting jury decision-making. *Social Action and the Law, 12*, 41-48.

Matsuda, N. (1985). Strong, quasi-, and weak conformity among Japanese in the modified Asch procedure. *Journal of Cross-Cultural Psychology, 16*, 83-97.

Matsui, T., Kakuyama, T., & yOnglatco, M. U. (1987). Effects of goals and feedback on performance in groups. *Journal of Applied Psychology, 72*, 407-415.

Matsui, Y. (1981). A structural analysis of helping. *Japanese Journal of Psychology, 52*, 226-232.

Matsumoto, D. (1990). Cultural similarities and differences in display rules. *Motivation and Emotion, 14*, 195-214.

Matsumoto, D., & Ekman, P. (1989). American-Japanese cultural differences in intensity ratings of facial expressions of emotion. *Motivation and Emotion, 13*, 1989.

Matthews, K. A. (1982). Psychological perspectives on the type A behavior pattern. *Psychological Bulletin, 91*, 293-323.

McAllister, A., Perry, C. Killen, J., Slinkard, L. A., & Maccoby, N. (1980). Pilot study of smoking, alcohol and drug abuse prevention. *American Journal of Public Health, 70*, 719-721.

McArthur, L. A. (1972). The how and what of why: Some determinants and consequences of causal attribution. *Journal of Personality and Social Psychology, 22*, 171-193.

McArthur, L. Z., & Berry, D. S. (1987). Cross-cultural agreement in perceptions of baby-faced adults. *Journal of Cross-Cultural Psychology, 18*, 165-192.

McCann, C. D., Ostrom, T. M., Tyner, L. K., & Mitchell, M. L. (1985). Person perception in heterogeneous groups. *Journal of Personality and Social Psychology, 49*, 1449-1459.

McCarthy, M. J. (1991, March 18). Marketers zero in on their customers. *The Wall Street Journal.*, p. B1.

McCaul, K. D., Veltum, L. G., Boyechko, V., & Crawford, J. J. (1990). Understanding attributions of victim blame for rape: Sex, violence, and foreseeability. *Journal of Applied Social Psychology, 20*, 1-26.

McCauley, C. R., & Segal, M. E. (1987). Social psychology of terrorist groups. In C. Hendrick (Ed.), *Group processes and intergroup relations: Review of personality and social psychology* (Vol. 9). Newbury Park, CA: Sage.

McCauley, C. R., & Segal, M. E. (1989). Terrorist individuals and terrorist groups: The normal psychology of extreme behavior. In J.

Groebel, & J. H. Goldstein (Eds.), *Terrorism: Psychological perspectives.* Seville, Spain: Publicaciones de la Universidad de Sevilla.

McConahay, J. B. (1986). Modern racism, ambivalence and the modern racism scale. In J. F. Dovidio & S. L. Gaertner (Eds.), *Prejudice, discrimination, and racism: Theory and research* (pp. 91-125). Orlando, FL: Academic Press.

McConahay, J. B., Hardee, B. B., & Batts, V. (1981). Has racism declined in America? It depends on who is asking and what is asked. *Journal of Conflict Resolution, 25*, 563-579.

McGarry, J., & Hendrick, C. (1974). Communicator credibility and persuasion. *Memory and Cognition, 2*, 82-86.

McGarty, C., Turner, J. C., Hogg, M. A., & David, B., et al. (1992). Group polarization as conformity to the prototypical group member. *British Journal of Social Psychology, 31*, 1-19.

McGrath, J. E. (1988). (Ed.). *The social psychology of time: New perspectives.* Newbury Park, CA: Sage.

McGuire, W. J. (1964). Inducing resistance to persuasion. In L. Berkowitz (Ed.), *Advances in experimental and social psychology* (Vol. 1). New York: Academic Press.

McGuire, W. J. (1985). Attitudes and attitude change. In G. Lindzey & E. Aronson (Eds.), *Handbook of social psychology* (3rd ed., Vol. 2). New York: Random House.

McHugo, G. J., Lanzetta, J. R., & Bush, L. K. (1991). The effect of attitudes on emotional reactions to expressive displays of political leaders. *Journal of Nonverbal Behavior, 15*, 19-41.

McKelvie, S. J. (1990). The Asch primacy effect: Robust but not infallible. *Journal of Social Behavior and Personality, 5*, 135-150.

McKenna, J. J. (1983). Primate aggression and evolution: An overview of sociobiological and anthropological perspectives. *Bulletin of the American Academy of Psychiatry and the Law, 11*, 105-130.

McKillip, J., & Riedel, S. L. (1983). External validity of matching on physical attractiveness for same and opposite sex couples. *Journal of Applied Social Psychology, 13*, 328-337.

McKinlay, J. B. (1975). Who is really ignorant—physician or patient? *Journal of Health and Social Behavior, 16*, 3-11.

McPhail, P. (1991). *The myth of the madding crowd.* New York: de Gruyter.

McQueen, M. (1991, May 17). Voters' responses to poll disclose huge chasm between social attitudes of blacks and whites. *Wall Street Journal*, A16.

Medway, F. J., & Smircic, J. M. (1992). Willingness to use corporal punishment among school administrators in South Carolina. *Psychological Reports, 7*, 65-66.

Meehan, A. M., & Janik, L. M. (1990). Illusory correlation and the maintenance of sex role stereotypes in children. *Sex Roles, 22*, 83-95.

Mehrabian, A. (1968a). Inference of attitude from the posture orientation and distance of a communicator. *Journal of Consulting and Clinical Psychology, 32*, 296-308.

Mehrabian, A. (1968b). Relationship of attitude to seated posture, orientation, and distance. *Journal of Personality and Social Psychology, 10*, 26-30.

Meindl, J. R., & Lerner, M. J. (1985). Exacerbation of extreme responses to an out-group. *Journal of Personality and Social Psychology, 47*, 71-84.

Mentzer, S. J., & Snyder, M. L. (1982). The doctor and the patient: A psychological perspective. In G. S. Sanders, & J. Suls (Eds.), *Social psychology of health and illness* (pp.161-181). Hillsdale, NJ: Erlbaum.

Metee, D. R., & Aronson, E. (1974). Affective reactions to appraisal from others. In T. L. Huston (Ed.), *Foundations of interpersonal attraction* (pp. 235-283). New York: Academic Press.

Metts, S., Cupach, W. R., & Bejlovec, R. A. (1989). "I love you too much to ever start liking you": Redefining romantic relationships. *Journal of Personality and Social Psychology, 37*, 602-607.

Mewborn, C. R., & Rogers, R. W. (1979). Effects of threatening and reassuring components of fear appeals on physiological and verbal measures of emotion and attitudes. *Journal of Experimental Social Psychology, 15*, 242-253.

Meyer, J. P., & Mulherin, A. (1980). From attribution to helping: An analysis of the mediating effects of affect and expectancy. *Journal of Personality and Social Psychology, 39*, 201-210.

Meyer, J. P., & Pepper, S. (1977). Need compatibility and marital adjustment in young married couples. *Journal of Personality and Social Psychology, 35*, 331-342.

Meyer, T. P. (1972). The effects of sexually arousing violent films on aggressive behavior. *Journal of Sex Research, 8*, 324-331.

Michaels, M. (1988, December 26). Hands across the workplace. *Time*, 13-17.

Midlarsky, E., Bryan, J. H., & Brickman, P. (1973). Aversive approval: Interactive effects of modeling and reinforcement on altruistic behavior. *Child Development, 44*, 321-328.

Miell, D. E., & Duck, S. W. (1986). Strategies in developing friendship. In V. J. Derlega & B. A. Winstead (Eds.), *Friendship and social interaction*. New York: Springer-Verlag.

Milavsky, J. R., Kessler, R. C., Stipp, H. H., & Rubens, W. S. (1982). *Television and aggression: A panel study*. New York: Academic Press.

Milgram, S. (1965). Some conditions of obedience and disobedience to authority. *Human Relations, 18*, 57-75.

Milgram, S. (1974). *Obedience to authority*. New York: Harper & Row.

Milgram, S. (1977a, October). Subject reaction: The neglected factor in the ethics of experimentation. *Hastings Center Report*. 19-23.

Milgram, S. (1977b). *The individual in a social world: Essays and experiments*. Reading, MA: Addison-Wesley.

Milgram, S. (1992). *The individual in a social world* (2nd ed.). New York: McGraw-Hill.

Miller, C. E., Jackson, P., Mueller, J., & Schersching, C. (1987). Some social psychological effects of group decision rules. *Journal of Personaltiy and Social Psychology, 52*, 325-332.

Miller, C. E. (1985). Group decision making under majority and unanimity decision rules. *Social Psychology Quarterly, 48*, 354-363.

Miller, C. E. (1989). The social psychological effects of group decision rules. In P. B. Paulhus (Ed.), *Psychology of group influence*. 2nd Ed. Hillsdale, NJ: Erlbaum.

Miller, C. T., & Felicio, D. M. (1990). Person positivity bias: Are individuals liked better than groups? *Journal of Experimental Social Psychology, 26*, 408-420.

Miller, D. T., & McFarland, C. (1987). Pluralistic ignorance: When similarity is interpreted as dissimilarity. *Journal of Personality and Social Psychology, 53*, 298-305.

Miller, D. T., & McFarland, C. (1991). When social comparison goes awry: The case of pluralistic ignorance. In J. Suls & T. Wills (Eds.), *Social comparison: Contemporary theory and research*. Hillsdale, NJ: Erlbaum.

Miller, G. R., & Stiff, J. B. (1992). Applied issues in studying deceptive communication. In R. S. Feldman (Ed.), *Applications of nonverbal behavioral theories and research*. Hillsdale, NJ: Erlbaum.

Miller, J. G. (1984). Culture and the development of everyday social explanation. *Journal of Personality and Social Psychology, 46*, 961-978.

Miller, J. G., & Bersoff, D. M. (1992). Culture and moral judgment: How are conflicts between justice and interpersonal responsibilities resolved? *Journal of Personality and Social Psychology, 62*, 541-554.

Miller, J. G., Bersoff, D. M., & Harwood, R. L. (1990). Perceptions of social responsibility in India and in the United States: Moral imperatives or personal decisions? *Journal of Personality and Social Psychology, 58*, 33-47.

Miller, L. C. (1990). Intimacy and liking: Mutual influence and the role of unique relationships. *Journal of Personality and Social Psychology, 59*, 50-60.

Miller, L. C., & Kenny, D. A. (1986). Reciprocity of self-disclosure at the individual and dyadic levels: A social relationship analysis. *Journal of Personality and Social Psychology, 50*, 713-719.

Miller, N., & Brewer, M. B. (1984). *Groups in contact: The psychology of desegregation*. New York: Academic Press.

Miller, S. J. (1986). Conceptualizing interpersonal relationships. *Generations, 10*, 6-9.

Mills, J., & Aronson, E. (1965). Opinion change as a function of communicator's attractiveness and desire to influence. *Journal of Personality and Social Psychology, 1*, 173-177.

Mills, J., & Clark, M. S. (1986). Communications that should lead to perceived exploitation in communal and exchange relationships. *Journal of Social and Clinical Psychology, 4*, 225-234.

Mineka, S., & Henderson, R. W. (1985). Controllability and predictability in acquired motivation. *Annual Review of Psychology, 36*, 495-529.

Miner, J. B. (1992). *Industrial-organizational psychology*. New York: McGraw-Hill.

Mitchell, A. (1983). *The nine American lifestyles: Who we are & where we're going*. New York: Macmillan.

Mitchell, J., & Dodder, R. A. (1983). Types of neutralization and types of delinquency. *Journal of Youth and Adolescence, 12*, 307-318.

Mitchell, T. R. (1982). *People in organizations: An introduction to organizational behavior* (2nd ed.). New York: McGraw-Hill.

Moffat, M. (1989). *Coming of age in New Jersey*. New Brunswick, NJ: Rutgers University Press.

Moghaddam, F. M., Taylor, D. M., & Wright, S. C. (1993). *Social psychology in cross-cultural perspective*. New York: Freeman.

Mohr, L. B. (1992). *Impact analysis for program evaluation*. Newbury Park, CA: Sage.

Molm, L. D. (1988). The structure and use of power: A comparison of reward and punishment power. *Social Psychology Quarterly, 51*, 108-122.

Monahan, J., & Loftus, E. F. (1982). The psychology of law. *Annual Reviews, 33*, 441-475.

Mongeau, P. A., & Garlick, R. (1988). Social comparison and persuasive arguments as determinants of group polarization. *Communication Research Reports, 5*, 120-125.

Montagu, A. (1976). *The nature of human aggression*. New York: Oxford University Press.

Monteith, M. F. (1993). Self-regulation of prejudiced responses: Implications for progress in prejudice-reduction efforts. *Journal of Personality and Social Psychology, 65*, 469-485.

Moore, D. S., & Erickson, P. O. (1985). Age, gender, and ethnic differences in sexual and contraceptive knowledge, attitude, and behavior. *Family and Community Health, 8,* 38-51.

Moore-Ede, M. (1993). *The twenty-four hour society.* Boston: Addison-Wesley.

Moorhead, G., Ference, R., & Neck, C. P. (1991). Group decision fiascoes continue: Space shuttle Challenger and a revised groupthink framework. *Human Relations, 44,* 539-550.

Moran, G., & Comfort, J. C. (1986). Neither "tentative" nor "fragmentary": Verdict preference of impaneled felony jurors as a function of attitude toward capital punishment. *Journal of Applied Psychology, 71,* 146-155.

Moreland, R. L., & Levine, J. M. (1982). Socialization in small groups: Temporal changes in individual-group relations. In L. Berkowitz (Ed.), *Advances in experimental social psychology* (Vol. 15). New York: Academic Press.

Moreland, R. L., & Levine, J. M. (1988). Group dynamics over time: Development and socialization in small groups. In J. E. McGrath (Ed.), *The social psychology of time: New perspectives.* Newbury Park, CA: Sage.

Moreland, R. L., & Levine, J. M. (1989). Newcomers and oldtimers in small groups. In Paulhus, P. B. (Ed.), *Psychology of group influence* (2nd ed.). Hillsdale, NJ: Erlbaum.

Moretti, M. M., & Higgins, E. T. (1990). Relating self-discrepancy to self-esteem: The contribution of discrepancy beyond actual-self ratings. *Journal of Experimental and Social Psychology, 26,* 108-123.

Morgan, M. (1983). Symbolic victimization and real world fear. *Human Communication Research, 9,* 146-157.

Morgan, P. M. (1977). *Deterrence: A conceptual analysis.* Beverly Hills, CA: Sage.

Morris, D., Collett, P., Marsh, P., & O'Shaughnessy, M. (1979). *Gestures: Their origins and distribution.* Briarcliff Manor, NY: Stein & Day.

Morris, W. N., Worchel, J. L., Bois, J. L., Pearson, J. A., Rountree, C. A., Samaha, G. M., Wachtler, J., & Wright, S. L. (1976). Collective coping with stress: Group reactions to fear, anxiety, and ambiguity. *Journal of Personality and Social Psychology, 33,* 674-679.

Morton, T. L. (1978). Intimacy and reciprocity of exchange: A comparison of spouses and strangers. *Journal of Personality and Social Psychology, 36,* 72-81.

Moscovici, S., & Faucheaux, C. (1972). Social influence, conformity bias, and the study of active minorities. In L. Berkowitz (Ed.), *Advances in experimental social psychology* (Vol. 6). New York: Academic Press.

Moscovici, S., Lage, E., & Naffrechoux, M. (1969). Influence of a consistent minority on the responses of a majority in a color perception task. *Sociometry, 32,* 365-380.

Moscovici, S., & Mugny, G. (1983). Minority influence II: Minority influence. In C. Nemeth (Ed.), *Social psychology: Classic and contemporary integrations.* Chicago: Rand McNally.

Moses, J. M. (1992, August 10.) Bias against minorities. *Wall Street Journal,* p. B2.

Mosher, D. L., & Anderson, R. D. (1986). Macho personality, sexual aggression, and reactions to guided imagery of realistic rape. *Journal of Research in Personality, 20,* 77-94.

Moss, M. K., & Page, R. A. (1972). Reinforcement and helping behavior. *Journal of Applied Social Psychology, 2,* 360-371.

Muehlenhard, C. L., & Hollabaugh, L. C. (1988). Do women sometimes say no when they mean yes? The prevalence and correlates of women's token resistance to sex. *Journal of Personality and Social Psychology, 54,* 872-879.

Mugny, G., & Perez, J. A. (1991). *The social psychology of minority influence.* Hillsdale, NJ: Erlbaum.

Mullen, B. (1986). Strength and immediacy of sources: A meta-analytic evaluation of the forgotten elements of social impact theory. *Journal of Personality and Social Psychology, 48,* 1458-1466.

Mullen, B., & Hu, L. (1989). Perception of ingroup and outgroup variability. A meta-analytic integration. *Basic and Applied Social Psychology, 29,* 11-28.

Mullen, B., & Johnson, C. (1990). Distinctiveness-based illusory correlations and stereotyping: A meta-analytic integration. *British Journal of Social Psychology, 29,* 11-28.

Mullen, B., Johnson, C., & Salas, E. (1991). Productivity loss in brainstorming groups: A meta-analytic integration. *Basic and Applied Social Psychology, 12,* 3-23.

Murstein, B. I. (1976). *Who will marry whom? Theories and research in marital choice.* New York: Springer.

Murstein, B. I. (1986). *Paths to marriage.* Beverly Hills, CA: Sage.

Murstein, B. I. (1987). A clarification and extension of the SVR theory of dyadic pairing. *Journal of Marriage and the Family, 49,* 929-933.

Myers, D. G. (1982). Polarizing effects of social interaction. In H. Brandstatter, J. H. Davis, & G. Stocker-Kreichgauer (Eds.), *Group decision making.* New York: Academic Press.

Myers, D. G., & Lamm, H. (1976). The group polarization phenomenon. *Psychological Bulletin, 83,* 602-627.

Nagao, D. H., & McClain, L. (1983, May). *The effects of judge's instructions concerning reasonable doubt on mock juror's verdicts.* Paper presented at the annual meeting of the Midwestern Psychological Association, Chicago, IL.

Nagata, Y. (1980). Status as a determinant of conformity to and deviation from the group norm. *Japanese Journal of Psychology, 51,* 152-159.

Nail, P. R. (1986). Toward an integration of some models and theories of social response. *Psychological Bulletin, 100,* 190-206.

Naroll, R., Bullough, V. L., & Naroll, F. (1974). *Military deterrence in history: A pilot cross-historical survey.* Albany: State University of New York Press.

Nass, G. D. (1978). *Marriage and the family.* Reading, MA: Addison-Wesley.

Natarajan, V. (1979). Defensive avoidance hypothesis in fear arousal research. *Indian Journal of Clinical Psychology, 6,* 21-26.

National Child Abuse and Neglect Data Systems. (1991). Working Paper 2. Summary Data Component. U.S. Department of Health and Human Services, National Child Abuse and Neglect.

Neimeyer, R. A., & Mitchell, K. A. (1988). Similarity and attraction: A longitudinal study. *Journal of Social and Personal Relationships, 5,* 131-148.

Nelson, S. D. (1974). Nature/nurture revisited I: A review of the biological bases of conflict. *Journal of Conflict Resolution, 18,* 285-335.

Nemeth, C. (1986). Differential contributions of majority and minority influence. *Psychological Review, 93,* 1-10.

Nemeth, C., & Kwan, J. L. (1985). Originality of word associations as a function of majority vs. minority influence. *Social Psychology Quarterly, 48,* 277-282.

Nemeth, C., Mayseless, O., Sherman, J., & Brown, Y. (1990). Exposure to dissent and recall of information. *Journal of Personality and Social Psychology, 58,* 429-437.

Neuberg, S. L. (1989). The goal of forming accurate impressions during social interactions: Attenuating the impact of negative expectancies. *Journal of Personality and Social Psychology 56,* 374-386.

*New Yorker* (1986, August 25). Cartoon, p. 75.

*New York Times.* (1982, December 21). Subway altruism.

*New York Times.* (1984, May 20). The new addicts. p. 50.

Newcomb, T. M. (1961). *The acquaintance process.* New York: Holt, Rinehart & Winston.

Nicholson, W. D., & Long, B. C. (1990). Self-esteem, social support, internalized homophobia, and coping strategies of HIV+ gay men. *Journal of Consulting and Clinical Psychology, 58*, 873-876.

Niedenthal, P. M., & Cantor, N. (1986). Affective responses as guides to category-based inferences. *Motivation and Emotion, 10*, 217-232.

NIH (National Institute of Health). (1993). Application for Intramural Support. Bethesda, MD: National Institute of Health.

Nisbett, R. E., & Ross, L. (1980). *Human inference: Strategies and shortcomings of social judgment.* Englewood Cliffs, NJ: Prentice-Hall.

Nixon, H. L. (1976). Team orientations, interpersonal relations, and team success. *Research Quarterly, 47*, 429-435.

Noller, P. (1992). Nonverbal communication in marriage. In R. S. Feldman (Ed.), *Applications of nonverbal behavioral theories and research.* Hillsdale, NJ: Erlbaum.

Northrop, C. E. (1990, February). How good Samaritan laws do and don't protect you. *Nursing, 20* (2), 50-51.

*Obedience.* (1965). Distributed by the New York University Film Library and Pennsylvania State University, PCR. Copyright 1965 by Stanley Milgram.

Office of Technology Assessment. (1990). *Unconventional cancer treatments.* Washington, DC: Government Printing Office.

Ohman, R. (1993, March 8). Cartoon. *Newsweek,* p. 17.

Oliner, S. P., & Oliner, P. M. (1988). *The altruistic personality: Rescuers of Jews in Nazi Europe.* New York: Free Press.

Olson, J. M., Herman, C. P., & Zanna, M. P. (Eds.). (1986). *Relative deprivation and social comparison: The Ontario Symposium* (Vol. 4). Hillsdale, NJ: Erlbaum.

Olson, J. M., & Ross, M. (1988). False feedback about placebo effectiveness: Consequences for the misattribution of speech anxiety. *Journal of Experimental Social Psychology, 24*, 275-281.

Olweus, D. (1986). Aggression and hormones: Behavioral relationships with testosterone and adrenaline. In D. Olweus, J. Block, & M. Radke-Yarrow (Eds.), *Development of antisocial and prosocial behaviors: Research, theories, and issues.* Orlando, FL: Academic Press.

Orne, M. T., & Holland, C. C. (1968). On the ecological validity of laboratory deceptions. *International Journal of Psychiatry, 6*, 282-293.

Ornstein, R. F. (1989). Exposure and affect: Overview and meta-analysis of research, 1968-1987. *Psychological Bulletin, 106*, 265-289.

Orvis, B. R., Cunningham, J. D., & Kelley, H. H. (1975). A closer examination of causal inference: The role of consensus, distinctiveness and consistency information. *Journal of Personality and Social Psychology, 32*, 605-616.

Osberg, T. M., & Shrauger, J. S. (1986). Retrospective versus prospective causal judgments of self and others' behavior. *Journal of Social Psychology, 126*, 169-178.

Osborn, A. F. (1957). *Applied imagination.* New York: Scribners.

Osgood, C. E. (1962). *An alternative to war or surrender.* Urbana: University of Illinois Press.

Osgood, C. E. (1979). GRIT for MBFR: A proposal for unfreezing force-level postures in Europe. *Peace Research Reviews, 8*, 77-92.

Osgood, C. E., Suci, G. J., & Tannenbaum, P. H. (1957). *The measurement of meaning.* Urbana, IL: University of Illinois Press.

Oskamp, S. (1977) *Attitudes and opinions.* Englewood Cliffs, NJ: Prentice-Hall.

Ostrom, T. M. (1969). The relationship between the affective, behavioral and cognitive components of attitudes. *Journal of Experimental Social Psychology, 5*, 12-30.

Ostrom, T. M. (1977). Between-theory and within-theory conflict in explaining context effects in impression formation. *Journal of Experimental Social Psychology, 13*, 492-503.

Ouchi, W. G. (1981). *Theory Z: How American business can meet the Japanese challenge.* Reading, MA: Addison-Wesley.

Oyserman, D. (1993). The lens of personhood: Viewing the self and others in a multicultural society. *Journal of Personality and Social Psychology, 65*, 993-1009.

Pace, T. M. (1988). Schema theory: A framework for research and practice in psychotherapy. *Journal of Cognitive Psychotherapy, 2*, 147-163.

Parlee, M. B. (1979, October). The friendship bond. *Psychology Today, 13*, 43-45.

Patterson, A. H. (1986). Scientific jury selection: The need for a case specific approach. *Social Action and the Law, 11*, 105-109.

Pavlov, I. (1927). *Conditioned reflexes.* Oxford: Oxford University Press.

Peck, C. L., & King, N. J. (1982). Increasing patient compliance with prescriptions. *Journal of the American Medical Association, 248*, 2874-2877.

Pelham, B. W., & Swann, W. B., Jr. (1989). From self-conceptions to self-worth: The sources and structure of self-esteem. *Journal of Personality and Social Psychology, 57*, 672-680.

Pendleton, M. G., & Batson, C. D. (1979). Self-presentation and the door-in-the-face technique for inducing compliance. *Personality and Social Psychology Bulletin, 5*, 77-81.

Pennebaker, J. W. (1990). *Opening up: The healing power of confiding in others.* New York: Morrow.

Pennebaker, J. W., & Beall, S. (1986). Confronting a traumatic event: Toward an understanding of inhibition and disease. *Journal of Abnormal Psychology, 95*, 274-281.

Pennington, N., & Hastie, R. (1990). Practical implications of psychological research on juror and jury decision making. *Personality and Social Psychology Bulletin, 16*, 90-105.

Pennington, N., & Hastie, R. (1992). Explaining the evidence: Tests of the story model for juror decision making. *Journal of Personality and Social Psychology, 62*, 189-206.

Penrod, S., & Cutler, B. L. (1987). Assessing the competence of juries. In I. B. Weiner & A. K. Hess (Eds.), *Handbook of forensic psychology.* New York: Wiley.

Pepitone, A. (1987). The role of culture in theories of social psychology. In C. Kagitcibasi (Ed.), *Growth and progress in cross-cultural psychology.* Lisse, The Netherlands: Swets & Zeitlinger.

Peplau, L. A., & Cochran, S. D. (1990). A relationship perspective on homosexuality. In D. P. McWhirter, S. A. Sanders, & J. M. Reinisch (Eds.), *Homosexuality/heterosexuality: The Kinsey scale and current research.* New York: Oxford University Press.

Peplau, L. A., Micelli, M., & Morasch, B. (1982). Loneliness and self-evaluation. In L. A. Peplau & D. Perlman (Eds.), *Loneliness: A sourcebook of current theory, research, and therapy.* New York: Wiley.

Peplau, L. A., Padesky, C., & Hamilton, M. (1982). Satisfaction in lesbian relationships. *Journal of Homosexuality, 8*, 23-25.

Peplau, L. A., & Perlman, D. (Eds.). (1982). *Loneliness: A sourcebook of current theory, research and therapy.* New York: Wiley.

Perdue, C. W., Dovidio, J. F., Gurtman, M. B., & Tyler, R. B. (1990). Us and them: Social categorization and the process of intergroup bias. *Journal of Personality and Social Psychology, 59*, 475-486.

Perloff, R. M. (1993). *The dynamics of persuasion.* Hillsdale, NJ: Erlbaum.

Peter, J. P., & Olson, J. C. (1987). *Consumer behavior: Marketing strategy perspectives.* Homewood, IL: Irwin.

Peters, L. H., Hartke, D. D., & Pohlmann, J. T. (1985). Fiedler's contingency theory of leadership: An application of the meta-analysis procedures of Schmidt and Hunter. *Psychological Bulletin, 97*, 274-285.

Peterson, C., & Barrett, L. C. (1987). Explanatory style and academic performance among university freshmen. *Journal of Personality and Social Psychology, 53*, 603-607.

Peterson, K. C., Prout, M. F., & Schwartz, R. A. (1991). *Post-traumatic stress disorder: A clinician's guide.* New York: Plenum.

Pettigrew, T. F. (1979). The ultimate attribution error: Extending Allport's cognitive analysis of prejudice. *Personality and Social Psychology Bulletin, 5,* 461-476.

Pettigrew, T. F. (1989). The nature of modern racism in the United States. *Revue Internationale de Psychologie Sociale, 2,* 291-303.

Pettingale, K. W., Morris, T., Greer, S., & Haybittle, J. L. (1985). Mental attitudes to cancer: An additional prognostic factor. *Lancet,* p. 750.

Petty, R., Harkins, S., & Williams, K. (1980). The effects of diffusion of cognitive effort on attitudes: An information processing view. *Journal of Personality and Social Psychology, 38,* 81-92.

Petty, R. E., & Cacioppo, J. T. (1984). The effects of involvement on response to argument quantity and quality: Central and peripheral routes to persuasion. *Journal of Personality and Social Psychology, 46,* 69-81.

Petty, R. E., & Cacioppo, J. T. (1986a). The elaboration likelihood model of persuasion. In L. Berkowitz (Ed.), *Advances in experimental social psychology* (Vol. 19). Orlando: Academic Press.

Petty, R. E., & Cacioppo, J. T. (1986b). *Communication and persuasion: Central and peripheral routes to attitude change.* New York: Springer-Verlag.

Petty, R. E., Cacioppo, J. T., & Schumann, D. (1983). Central and peripheral routes to advertising effectiveness: The moderating role of involvement. *Journal of Consumer Research, 10,* 134-148.

Petty, R. E., & Krosnick, J. A. (Eds.). (in press). *Attitude strength: Antecedents and consequences.* Hillsdale, NJ: Erlbaum.

Petty, R. E., Schumann, D. W., Richman, S. A., & Strathman, A. J. (1993). Positive mood and persuasion: Different roles for affect under high- and low-elaboration conditions. *Journal of Personality and Social Psychology, 64,* 5-20.

Philippot, P., Schwarz, N., Carrera, P., DeVries, N., & VanYperen, N. W. (1991). Differential effects of priming at the encoding and judgment stage. *European Journal of Social Psychology, 21,* 293-302.

Phillips, D. P. (1982). The impact of fictional television stories on U.S. adult fatalities: New evidence on the effect of the mass media on violence. *American Journal of Sociology, 87,* 1340-1359.

Phillips, D. P. (1986). Natural experiments on the effects of mass media violence on fatal aggression: Strengths and weaknesses of a new approach. In L. Berkowitz (Ed.), *Advances in experimental social psychology* (Vol. 19). Orlando, FL: Academic Press.

Pierce, C. M. (1984). Television and violence: Social psychiatric perspectives. 136th Annual Meeting of the American Psychiatric Associa-

tion (1983, New York, New York). *American Journal of Social Psychiatry, 4,* 41-44.

Pietromonaco, P. R., & Markus, H (1985). The nature of negative thoughts in depression. *Journal of Personality and Social Psychology, 48,* 799-807.

Piirto, R. (1991). *Beyond mind games: The marketing power of psychographics.* Ithaca, NY: American Demographics.

Piliavin, J. A., & Callero, P. L. (1991). *Giving blood: The development of an altruistic identity.* Baltimore: Johns Hopkins University Press.

Piliavin, J. A., Evans, D. E., & Callero, P. (1984). Learning to "give unnamed strangers": The process of commitment to regular blood donation. In E. Staub, D. Bar-Tal, J. Karylowski, & J. Reykowski (Eds.), *The development and maintenance of prosocial behavior: International perspectives.* New York: Plenum.

Piliavin, J. A., & Piliavin, I. M. (1972). Effect of blood on reactions to a victim. *Journal of Personality and Social Psychology, 23,* 353-361.

Platz, S. J., & Hosch, H. M. (1988). Cross-racial/ethnic eyewitness identification: A field study. *Journal of Applied Social Psychology, 18,* 972-984.

Plous, S. (1988). Disarmament, arms control, and peace in the nuclear age. Political objectives and relevant research. *Journal of Social Issues, 44,* 133-154.

Pollack, D. A., Rhodes, P., Boyle, C. A., Decoufle, P., & McGee, D. L. (1990). Estimating the number of suicides among Vietnam veterans. *American Journal of Psychiatry, 147,* 772-776.

Popenoe, D. (1987). Beyond the nuclear family: A statistical portrait of the changing family in Sweden. *Journal of Marriage and the Family, 49,* 173-183.

Pratkanis, A., & Aronson, E. (1991). *The age of propaganda: The everyday use and abuse of persuasion.* New York: Freeman.

Pratkanis, A. R., & Greenwald, A. G. (1989). A sociocognitive model of attitude structure and function. In L. Berkowitz (Ed.), *Advances in experimental social psychology* (Vol. 22). New York: Academic Press.

Pratkanis, A. R., Greenwald, A. G., Leippe, M. R., & Baumgardner, M. H. (1988). In search of reliable persuasion effects: III. The sleeper effect is dead: Long live the sleeper effect. *Journal of Personality and Social Psychology, 54,* 203-218.

Prentice-Dunn, S. (1990). Perspectives on research classics: Two routes to collective violence. *Contemporary Social Psychology, 14,* 217-218.

Prentice-Dunn, S., & Rogers, R. W. (1982). Effects of public and private self-awareness on deindividuation and aggression. *Journal of Personality and Social Psychology, 43,* 503-513.

Prentice-Dunn, S., & Rogers, R. W. (1983). Deindividuation in aggression. In R. G. Geen & E. I. Donnerstein (Eds.), *Aggression: Theoretical and empirical reviews* (Vol. 2). New York: Academic Press.

Price, D. W., & Goodman, G. S. (1990). Visiting the wizard: Children's memory for a recurring event. *Child Development, 61,* 664-680.

Price, K. H. (1987). Decision responsibility, task responsibility, identifiability, and social loafing. *Organizational Behavior and Human Decision Processes, 40,* 330-345.

Price, L., Rust, R., & Kumar, V. (1986). In J. Olson & K. Sentis (Eds.), *Advertising and consumer psychology* (Vol. 3). New York: Praeger.

Price Waterhouse v. Hopkins, 109 S. Ct. 1775 (1989).

Prislin, R., Akrap, L., & Sprah, B. (1987). Self-monitoring and attitude-behaviour relationship. *Revija za Psihologiju, 17,* 37-45.

Provorse, D., & Sarata, B. (1989). The social psychology of juvenile court judges in rural communities. *Journal of Rural Community Psychology, 10,* 3-15.

Proxmire, W. (1975). Press release, U.S. Senate Office. Washington, DC.

Pryor, J. B., & Reeder, G. D. (Eds.). (1993). *The social psychology of HIV infection.* Hillsdale, NJ: Erlbaum.

PsychINFO. (1991, January). The PsychINFO Basic Workshop. Washington, DC: American Psychological Association. *Psychological Bulletin, 107,* 210-214.

Pyszczynski, T., & Greenberg, J. (1987). Self-regulatory perseveration and the depressive self-focusing style: A self-awareness theory of depression. *Psychological Bulletin, 102,* 122-138.

Quanty, M. B. (1976). Aggression catharsis: Experimental investigations and implications. In R. G. Geen & E. C. O'Neal (Eds.), *Perspectives on aggression.* New York: Academic Press.

Quattrone, G. A. (1982). Overattribution and unit formation. When behavior engulfs the person. *Journal of Personality and Social Psychology, 42,* 593-607.

Quattrone, G. A. (1986). On the perception of a group's variability. In S. Worchel & W. G. Austin (Eds.), *Psychology of intergroup relations* (2nd ed.). Chicago: Nelson Hall.

Quinn, M. (1990, January 29). Don't aim that pack at us. *Time,* p. 60.

Ragland, D. R., & Brand, R. J. (1988). Type A behavior and mortality from coronary heart disease. *New England Journal of Medicine, 313,* 65-69.

Rahe, R. H., & Arthur, R. J. (1978). Life change and illness studies: Past history and future directions. *Human Stress, 4,* 3-15.

Rajecki, D. W. (1989). *Attitudes* (2nd ed.). Sunderland, MA: Sinauer.

Rapoff, M. A., & Christophersen, E. R. (1982). Improving compliance in pediatric practice. *Pediatric Clinics of North America, 29*, 339-357.

Rastogi, P. N. (1987). Essence of leadership. *Vikalpa, 12*, 37-41.

Raven, B. H. (1988, August). *French and Raven 30 years later: Power, interaction and personal influence.* Paper presented at the International Congress of Psychology, Sydney, Australia.

Raven, B. H. (1992). A power/interaction model of interpersonal influence: French and Raven thirty years later. *Journal of Social Behavior and Personality, 7*, 217-244.

Raven, B. H. (1993). The bases of power: Origins and recent developments. *Journal of Social Issues, 49*, 227-251.

Reader, N., & English, H. B. (1947). Personality factors in adolescent female friendships. *Journal of Consulting Psychology, 11*, 212-220.

Rebellow, K. (1992, February 24). Microsoft: Bill Gates's baby is on top of the world. Can it stay there? *Business Week*, 60-64.

Reeves, R. A., Baker, G. A., Boyd, J. G., & Cialdini, R. B. (1991). The door-in-the-face technique: Reciprocal concessions vs. self-presentational explanations. *Journal of Social Behavior and Personality, 6*, 545-558.

Rehder, R. R., & Smith, Marta, M. (1986). KAIZEN and the art of labor relations. *Personnel Journal, 65*, 82-93.

Reich, W. (Ed.). (1990). *Origins of terrorism: Psychologies, ideologies, theologies, states of mind.* Hillsdale, NJ: Erlbaum.

Reifman, A., Klein, J. G., & Murphy, S. T. (1989). Self-monitoring and age. *Psychology and Aging, 4*, 245-246.

Reifman, A. S., Larrick, R. P., & Fein, S. (1991). Temper and temperature on the diamond: The heat-aggression relationship in major league baseball. *Personality and Social Psychology Bulletin, 17*, 580-585.

Reimer, J., Paolitto, D. P., & Hersch, R. H. (1983). *Promoting moral growth: From Piaget to Kohlberg* (2nd ed.). New York: Longman.

Reinisch, J. M. (1981). Prenatal exposure to synthetic progestins increases potential for aggression in humans. *Science, 211*, 1171-1173.

Reis, H. T. (1990). The role of intimacy in interpersonal relations. [Special Issue]: Social support in social and clinical psychology. *Journal of Social and Clinical Psychology, 9*, 15-30.

Reis, H. T., & Shaver, P. (1988). Intimacy as an interpersonal process. In S. Duck (Ed.), *Handbook of personal relationships: Theory, relationships and interventions.* Chichester, England: Wiley.

Reis, H. T., Wilson, I. M., Monestere, C., Bernstein, S., Clark, K., Seidl, E., Franco, M., Gioioso, E., Freeman, L., & Radoane, K. (1990). What is smiling is beautiful and good. *European Journal of Social Psychology, 20*, 259-267.

Reisenzein, R. (1983). The Schachter theory of emotion: Two decades later. *Psychological Bulletin, 94*, 239-264.

Reiss, I. L. (1960). *Premarital sexual standards in America.* New York: Free Press.

Reiss, M. J. (1984). Human sociobiology. *Zygon Journal of Religion and Science, 19*, 117-140.

Reskin, B. F., & Visher, C. A. (1986). The impacts of evidence and extralegal factors in jurors' decisions. *Law and Society Review, 20*, 423-438.

Reynolds, K. D., & West, S. G. (1989). Attributional constructs: Their role in the organization of social information memory. *Basic and Applied Social Psychology, 10*, 119-130.

Ricci Bitti, P. E., & Poggi, I. (1991) Symbolic nonverbal behavior: Talking through gestures. In R. S. Feldman & B. Rimé (Eds.), *Fundamentals of nonverbal behavior.* Cambridge, England: Cambridge University Press.

Rice, B. (1988). The selling of life-styles. *Psychology Today, 22*, 46-50.

Rimé, B., & Schiaratura, L. (1991). Gesture and speech In R. S. Feldman & B. Rimé (Eds.), *Fundamentals of nonverbal behavior.* Cambridge, England: Cambridge University Press.

Ringelmann, M. (1913). Research on animate sources of power: The work of man. *Annales de l'Institut National Agronomique, 2e série, tome XII*, 1-40.

Riordan, C. A., & Tedeschi, J. T. (1983). Attraction in aversive environments: Some evidence for classical conditioning and negative reinforcement. *Journal of Personality and Social Psychology, 44*, 683-692.

Roark, A. E., & Sharah, H. S. (1989). Factors related to group cohesiveness. *Small Group Behavior, 20*, 62-69.

Robbins, M. W. (1990, December 10). Sparing the child: How to intervene when you suspect abuse. *New York Magazine*, 42-53.

Robins, C. J. (1988). Attributions and depression: Why is the literature so inconsistent? *Journal of Personality and Social Psychology, 54*, 236-247.

Robinson, R. J., Keltner, D., & Ross, L. (1991). Misconstruing the views of the "other side": Real and perceived differences in three ideological conflicts. Working Paper No. 18, Stanford Center on Conflict and Negotiation, Stanford University.

Robinson, T. T., & Carron, A. V. (1982). Personal and situational factors associated with dropping out versus maintaining participation in competitive sport. *Journal of Sport Psychology, 4*, 364-378.

Robinson-Staveley, K., & Cooper, J. (1990). Mere presence, gender, and reactions to computers: Studying human-computer interaction in the social context. *Journal of Experimental Social Psychology, 26*, 168-183.

Roethlisberger, F. J., & Dickson, W. V. (1939). *Management and the worker.* Cambridge, MA: Harvard University Press.

Rofé, Y. (1984). Stress and affiliation: A utility theory. *Psychological Bulletin, 91*, 235-250.

Rogers, M., Miller, N., Mayer, F. S., & Duval, S. (1982). Personal responsibility and salience of the request for help: Determinants of the relation between negative affect and helping behavior. *Journal of Personality and Social Psychology, 43*, 956-970.

Rogers, R. W. (1983). Cognitive and physiological processes in fear appeals and attitude change: A revised theory of protection motivation. In J. T. Cacioppo & R. E. Petty (Eds.), *Social psychophysiology.* New York: Guilford.

Rohlen, T. P. (1973). "Spiritual education" in a Japanese bank. *American Anthropologist, 75*, 1542-1562.

Rojas, L., & Gil, R. M. (1989). The diagnosis of public mental health care bureaucracies. Second World Basque Congress: Diagnosis in psychiatry (1987, Bilbao, Spain). *British Journal of Psychiatry, 154(Suppl.)*, 96-100.

Rokeach, M. (1971). Long-range experimental modification of values, attitudes, and behavior. *American Psychologist, 26*, 453-459.

Romano, S. T., & Bordieri, J. E. (1989). Physical attractiveness stereotypes and students' perceptions of college professors. *Psychological Reports, 64*, 1099-1102.

Ronis, D. L., & Greenwald, A. G. (1979). Dissonance theory revised again: Comment on the paper by Fazio, Zanna, and Cooper. *Journal of Experimental Social Psychology, 15*, 62-69.

Ronis, D. L., Yates, J. F., & Kirscht, J. P. (1989). Attitudes, decisions, and habits as determinants of repeated behavior. In A. R. Pratkanis, S. J. Breckler, & A. G. Greenwald (Eds.), *Attitude structure and function.* Hillsdale, NJ: Erlbaum.

Rosenbaum, M. E. (1986). The repulsion hypothesis: On the nondevelopment of relationships. *Journal of Personality and Social Psychology, 51*, 1156-1166.

Rosenberg, D. (1992, October). Good Samaritan engineers. *Technology Review, 95 (7)*, 18.

Rosenberg, L. A. (1961). Group size, prior experience, and conformity. *Journal of Abnormal and Social Psychology, 63*, 436-437.

Rosenblatt, P. C., & Anderson, R. M. (1981). Human sexuality in cross-cultural perspective. In M. Cook (Ed.), *The bases of human sexual attraction*. London and New York: Academic Press.

Rosenhan, D. L. (1970). The natural socialization of altruistic autonomy. In J. R. Macaulay & L. Berkowitz (Eds.), *Altruism and helping behavior*. New York: Academic Press.

Rosenman, R. H. (1990). Type A behavior pattern: A personal overview. *Journal of Social Behavior and Personality, 5*, 1-24.

Rosenman, R. H., Brand, R. J., Sholtz, R. I., & Friedman, M. (1976). Multivariate prediction of coronary heart disease during 8.5 year follow-up in the western collaborative group study. *American Journal of Cardiology, 37*, 903-910.

Rosenthal, R. (1976). *Experimenter effects in behavioral research*. New York: Irvington.

Rosenthal, R. (1991). Teacher expectancy effects: A brief update 25 years after the Pygmalions experiment. *Journal of Research in Education, 1*, 3-12.

Rosenthal, R., & Jacobson, L. (1968). *Pygmalion in the classroom: Teacher: Teacher expectation and pupils' intellectual development*. New York: Holt, Rinehart and Winston.

Roskos-Ewoldsen, D. R., & Fazio, R. H. (1992). The accessibility of source likability as a determinant of persuasion. *Personality and Social Psychology Bulletin, 18*, 19-25.

Ross, D., Greene, D., & House, P. (1977). The false consensus phenomenon: An attributional bias in self-perception and social-perception processes. *Journal of Experimental Social Psychology, 13*, 279-301.

Ross, L. (1977). The intuitive psychologist and his shortcomings. Distortions in the attribution process. In L. Berkowitz (Ed.), *Advances in experimental social psychology* (Vol. 10, pp. 174-221). New York: Academic Press.

Ross, L., & Nisbett, R. E. (1991). *The person and the situation*. New York: McGraw-Hill

Rossi, P. H., & Berk, R. A. (1985). Varieties of normative consensus. *American Sociological Review, 50*, 333-347.

Rothbart, M., & John, O. P. (1985). Social Categorization and behavioral episodes: A cognitive analysis of the effects of intergroup contact. *Journal of Social Issues, 41*, 81-104.

Rotton, J., & Frey, J. (1985). Air pollution, weather, and violent crimes: Concomitant time-series analysis of archival data. *Journal of Personality and Social Psychology, 49*, 1207-1220.

Rubenstein, C. (1982, July). Psychology's fruit flies. *Psychology Today*, 83-84.

Rubin, J. Z., & Friedland, N. (1986). Theater of terror. *Psychology Today, 20*, 18-19, 22, 24, 26-28.

Rubin, L. B. (1985). *Just friends: The role of friendship in our lives*. New York: Harper & Row.

Rubin, Z. (1973). *Liking and loving*. New York: Holt.

Rubin, Z. (1988). Preface. In R. J. Sternberg and M. L. Barnes (Eds.), *The psychology of love*. New Haven: Yale University Press.

Rubin, Z., Hill, C. T., Peplau, L. A., & Dunkel-Schetter, C. (1980). Self-disclosure in dating couples: Sex roles and the ethic of openness. *Journal of Marriage and the Family, 42*, 305-317.

Rule, B. G., & Ferguson, T. J. (1986). The effects of media violence on attitudes, emotions, and cognitions. *Journal of Social Issues, 42*, 29-50.

Rumelhart, D. E. (1984). Schemata and the cognitive system. In R. S. Wyer, Jr., & T. K. Siull (Eds.), *Handbook of social cognition*. Hillsdale, NJ: Erlbaum.

Rushton, J. P. (1975). Generosity in children: Immediate and long-term effects of modeling, preaching, and moral judgment. *Journal of Personality and Social Psychology, 31*, 459-466.

Russell, D., Cutrona, C. E., Rose, J., & Yurko, K. (1984). Social and emotional loneliness: An examination of Weiss's typology of loneliness. *Journal of Personality and Social Psychology, 46*, 1313-1321.

Russell, D. E. H., & Howell, N. (1983). The prevalence of rape in the United States revisited. *Signs, 8*, 688-695.

Russell, G. W. (1983). Psychological issues in sports aggression. In H. H. Goldstein (Ed.), *Sports violence*. New York: Springer-Verlag.

Russell, G. W. (1985). Spectator moods at an aggressive sports event. *Journal of Sport Psychology, 3*, 217-227.

Rutkowski, G. K., Gruder, C. L., & Romer, D. (1983). Group cohesiveness, social norms, and bystander intervention. *Journal of Personality and Social Psychology, 44*, 545-552.

Ruvolo, A., & Markus, H. (1992). Possible selves and performance power: The power of self-relevant imagery. *Social Cognition, 9*, 95-124.

Ryff, C. D. (1991). Possible selves in adulthood and old age: A tale of shifting horizons. *Psychology and Aging, 6*, 286-295.

Sacks, M. H. (1993). Exercise for stress control. In D. Goleman & J. Gurin (Eds.), *Mind-body medicine*. Yonkers, NY: Consumer Reports Books.

Sagatun, I. J., & Knudsen, J. H. (1982). Attributional self presentation for actors and observers in success and failure situations. *Scandinavian Journal of Psychology, 23*, 243-252.

Saks, M. J. (1977). *Jury verdicts: The role of group size and social decision rule*. Lexington, MA: Lexington.

Salovey, P., Mayer, J. D., & Rosenhan, D. L. (1991). Mood and helping: Mood as a motivator of helping and helping as a regulator of mood. *Review of Personality and Social Psychology, 12*, 215-237.

Salovey, P., & Rodin, J. (1985). Cognitions about the self: Connecting feeling states and social behavior. In P. Shaver (Ed.), *Self, situations, and social behavior: Review of Personality and Social Psychology* (Vol. 6). Beverly Hills, CA: Sage.

Salovey, P., & Rosenhan, D. L. (1989). Mood states and prosocial behavior. In H. L. Wagner & A. S. R. Manstead (Eds.), *Handbook of psychophysiology: Emotion and social behavior*. Chichester, England: John Wiley.

Samora, J., Saunders, L., & Larson, R. F. (1961). Medical vocabulary knowledge among hospital patients. *Journal of Health and Social Behavior, 2*, 83-89.

Sande, G. N., Goethals, G. R., & Radloff, C. E. (1988). Perceiving one's own traits and others': The multifaceted self. *Journal of Personality and Social Psychology, 54*, 13-20.

Sanders, G. S. (1983). An attentional process model of social facilitation. In A. Hare, H. Bumberg, V. Kent, & M. Davies (Eds.), *Small groups*. London: Wiley.

Sanitioso, R., & Kunda, Z. (1991). Ducking the collection of costly evidence: Motivated use of statistical heuristics. *Journal of Behavioral Decision Making, 4*, 161-178.

Sanna, L. J. (1992). Self-efficacy theory: Implications for social facilitation and social loafing. *Journal of Personality and Social Psychology, 62*, 774-786.

Sanoff, A. P., & Minerbrook, S. (1993, April 19). Race on campus. *U.S. News and World Report*, 52-64.

Sarasan, S., Johnson, J. H., & Siegel, J. M. (1978). Assessing the impact of life changes: Development of the Life Experiences Survey. *Journal of Consulting and Clinical Psychology, 46*, 932-946.

Sarason, I. G., Sarason, B. R., & Pierce, G. R. (1990). Anxiety, cognitive interference, and performance. *Journal of Social Behavioral and Personality, 5*, 1-18.

Saunders, D. G., & Size, P. B. (1986). Attitudes about woman abuse among police officers, victims, and victim advocates. *Journal of Interpersonal Violence, 1*, 25-42.

Schachter, S. (1959) *The psychology of affiliation*. Stanford, CA: Stanford University Press.

Schachter, S., & Singer, J. (1962). Cognitive, social, and physiological determinants of the emotional state. *Psychological Review, 69*, 379-399.

Schaefer, R. T., & Lamm, R. P. (1992). *Sociology* (4th ed.). New York: McGraw-Hill.

Schaller, M., & Cialdini, R. B. (1990). Happiness, sadness, and helping: A motivational integration. In R. M. Sorrentino & E. T.

Higgins (Eds.), *Handbook of motivation and cognition: Foundations of social behavior* (Vol. 2). New York: Guilford.

Schatz, R. T., & Fiske, S. T. (1992). International reactions to the threat of nuclear war: The rise and fall of concern in the eighties. *Political Psychology, 13,* 1-29.

Scheier, M. F., & Carver, C. S. (1992). Effects of optimism on psychological and physical well-being: Theoretical overview and empirical update. *Cognitive Therapy and Research, 16,* 201-228.

Scheier, M. F., & Carver, C. S. (1993). On the power of positive thinking: The benefits of being optimistic. *Current Directions in Psychological Science, 2,* 26-30.

Schein, E. H. (1990). Organizational culture. *American Psychologist, 45,* 109-119.

Schellhardt, T. D. (1991, October 18). Attractiveness aids men more than women. *The Wall Street Journal.,* p. B1.

Schiffenbauer, A., & Schiavo, R. S. (1976). Physical distance and attraction: An intensification effect. *Journal of Experimental Social Psychology, 12,* 274-282.

Schindenhette, S. (1990, February 5). After the verdict, solace for none. *People Weekly, 33,* 76-80.

Schlenker, B. (1980). *Impression management: The self-concept, social identity, and interpersonal relations.* Monterey, CA: Brooks/Cole.

Schlenker, B. R. (1982). Translating actions into attitudes: An identity-analytic approach to the explanation of social conduct. In L. Berkowitz (Ed.), *Advances in experimental social psychology* (Vol. 15, pp. 193-247). New York: Academic Press.

Schlenker, B. R., & Weigold, M. F. (1992). Interpersonal processes involving impression regulation and management. *Annual Review of Psychology, 43,* 133-168.

Schlenker, B. R., Weigold, M. F., & Hallam, J. R. (1990). Self-serving attributions in social context: Effects of self-esteem and social pressure. *Journal of Personality and Social Psychology, 58,* 855-863.

Schlesinger, B. (1982)., Lasting marriages in the 1980's. *Conciliation Courts Review, 20,* 43-49.

Schneier, C. E. (1978). The contingency model of leadership: An extension to emergent leadership and leader's sex. *Organizational Behavior and Human Performance, 21,* 220-239.

Schoeneman, T. J., & Rubanowitz, D. E. (1985). Attributions in the advice columns: Actors observers, causes and reasons. *Personality and Social Psychology Bulletin, 11,* 315-325.

Schouten, P. G. W., & Handelsman, M. M. (1987). Social basis of self-handicapping: The case of depression. *Personality and Social Psychology Bulletin, 13,* 103-110.

Schultz, N. R., Jr., & Moore, D. (1984). Loneliness: Correlates, attributions, and coping among older adults. *Personality and Social Psychology Bulletin, 10,* 67-77.

Schumann, D. W., Petty, R. E., & Clemons, D. S. (1990). Predicting the effectiveness of different strategies of advertising variation: A test of the repetition-variation hypotheses. *Journal of Consumer Research, 17,* 192-202.

Schunk, D. H. (1991). Self-efficacy and academic motivation. Special Issue: Current issues and new directions in motivational theory and research. *Educational Psychologist, 26,* 207-231.

Schuster, E., & Eldeston, E. M. (1907). *The inheritance of ability.* London: Dulave & Co.

Schwartz, J. (1993). Marketing the verdict. *American Demographics,* 52-55.

Schwarz, N., Bless, H., & Bohner, G. (1991). Mood and persuasion: Affective states influence the processing of persuasive communications. In M. P. Zanna (Ed.), *Advances in experimental social psychology* (Vol. 24). San Diego, CA: Academic Press.

Schwarz, N., Bless, H., Strack, F., Klumpp, G., Rittenauer-Schatka, H., & Simons, A. (1991). Ease of retrieval as information: Another look at the availability heuristic. *Journal of Personality and Social Psychology, 61,* 195-202.

Scott, C. R. (1990, November 7). As baby boomers age, fewer couples untie the knot. *The Wall Street Journal,* B1, B8.

Sears, D. O. (1982). The person-positivity bias. *Journal of Personality and Social Psychology, 44,* 233-250.

Sears, D. O. (1986). College sophomores in the laboratory: Influences of a narrow data base on social psychology's view of human nature. *Journal of Personality and Social Psychology, 51,* 515-530.

Sears, D. O., & Funk, C. L. (1991). The role of self-interest in social and political attitudes. In M. P. Zanna (Ed.), *Advances in experimental social psychology* (Vol. 24.). San Diego: Academic Press.

Sears, D. O., & Kinder, D. R. (1985). Whites' opposition to busing: On conceptualizing and operationalizing group conflict. *Journal of Personality and Social Psychology, 48,* 1141-1147.

Sears, D. O., & McConahay, J. B. (1981). *The politics of violence: The new urban Blacks and the Watts riot.* Lanham, MD: University Press of America.

Seashore, S. E. (1954). *Group cohesiveness in the industrial work group.* Ann Arbor, MI: Institute for Social Research.

Segal, M. W. (1974). Alphabet and attraction: An unobtrusive measure of the effect of propinquity in a field setting. *Journal of Personality and Social Psychology, 30,* 654-657.

Segall, M. H. (1988). Cultural roots of aggressive behavior. In M. Bond (Ed.), *The cross-cultural challenge to social psychology.* Newbury Park, CA: Sage.

Seguin, D. G., & Horowitz, I. A. (1984). The effects of "death qualification" on juror and jury decisioning: An analysis from three perspectives. *Law and Psychology Review, 8,* 49-81.

Seligman, M. E. P. (1975). *Helplessness: On depression, development, and death.* San Francisco: Freeman.

Selye, H. (1976). *The stress of life.* New York: McGraw-Hill.

Seta, J. J., & Seta, C. E. (1987). Payment and value: The generation of an evaluation standard and its effect on value. *Journal of Experimental Social Psychology, 23,* 285-301.

Shaffer, D. R., Pegalis, L. J., & Cornell, D. P. (1991). Interactive effects of social context and sex role identity on female self-disclosure during the acquaintance process. *Sex Roles, 24,* 1-19.

Shaffer, D. R., Pegalis, L. J., & Cornell, D. P. (1992). Gender and self-disclosure revisited: Personal and contextual variations in self-disclosure to same-sex acquaintances. *Journal of Social Psychology, 132,* 307-315.

Shaffer, D. R., Plummer, D., & Hammock, G. (1986). Hath he suffered enough? Effects of jury dogmatism, defendant similarity, and defendant's pretrial suffering on juridic decisions. *Journal of Personality and Social Psychology, 50,* 1059-1067.

Shaffer, D. R., Smith, J. E., & Tomarelli, M. (1982). Self-monitoring as a determinant of self-disclosure reciprocity during the acquaintance process. *Journal of Personality and Social Psychology, 43,* 163-175.

Shanab, M. E., & O'Neill, P. (1979). The effects of contrast upon compliance with socially undesirable requests in the door-in-the-face paradigm. *Canadian Journal of Behavioural Science, 11,* 236-244.

Shapiro, D. E., Boggs, S. R., Melamed, B. G., & Graham-Pole, J. (1992). The effect of varied physician affect on recall, anxiety, and perceptions in women at risk for breast cancer: An analogue study. *Health Psychology, 11,* 61-66.

Sharpe, D., Adair, G. J., & Roese, N. J. (1992). Twenty years of deception research: A decline in subjects' trust? *Personality and Social Psychology Bulletin, 18,* 585-590.

Shaver, P., Hazan, C., & Bradshaw, D. (1988). Love as attachment: The integration of three behavioral systems. In R. J. Sternberg & M. L. Barnes (Eds.), *The psychology of love.* New Haven, CT: Yale University Press.

Shaver, P., & Klinnert, M. (1982). Schachter's theory of affiliation and emotion: Implications of developmental research. In L. Wheeler (Ed.), *Review of personality and social psychology* (Vol. 3). Beverly Hills, CA: Sage.

Shaver, P. R., & Hazan, C. (1987). Being lonely, falling in love: Perspectives from attachment theory. [Special Issue]: Loneliness: Theory, research, and applications. *Journal of Social Behavior and Personality, 2,* 105-124.

Shaver, P. R., & Hazan, C. (1988). A biased overview of the study of love. *Journal of Social and Personal Relationships, 5,* 473-501.

Shavitt, S. (1989). Operationalizing functional theories of attitude. In A. R. Pratkanis, S. J. Breckler, & A. G. Greenwald (Eds.), *Attitude structure and function.* Hillsdale, NJ: Erlbaum.

Shaw, M. E. (1981). *Group dynamics: The psychology of small group behavior.* New York: McGraw-Hill.

Shaw, M. E., & Harkey, B. (1976). Some effects of congruency of member characterisitics and group structure upon group behavior. *Journal of Personality and Social Psychology, 34,* 412-418.

Sheatsley, P. B., & Feldman, J. J. (1964). The assassination of President Kennedy: A preliminary report on public attitude and behavior. *Public Opinion Quarterly, 28,* 189-215.

Sheppard, B. H., Hartwick, J., & Warshaw, P. R. (1988). The theory of reasoned action: A meta-analysis of past research with recommendations for modifications and future research. *Journal of Consumer Research, 15,* 325-343.

Shepperd, J. A., & Arkin, R. M. (1989a). Self-handicapping: The moderating roles of public self-consciousness and task importance. *Personality and Social Psychology Bulletin, 15,* 252-265.

Shepperd, J. A., & Arkin, R. M. (1989b). Determinants of self-handicapping: Task importance and the effects of preexisting handicaps on self-generated handicaps. *Personality and Social Psychology Bulletin, 15,* 101-112.

Sherif, M. (1935). A study of some social factors in perception. *Archives of Psychology,* No. 187.

Sherif, M. (1936). *The psychology of social norms.* New York: Harper.

Sherif, M. (1966). *In common predicament: Social psychology of intergroup conflict and cooperation.* Boston: Houghton Mifflin.

Sherif, M., & Sherif, C. W. (1969). *Social psychology* (rev. ed.). New York: Harper & Row.

Sherman, B. L., & Dominick, J. R. (1986). Violence and sex in music videos: TV and rock 'n' roll. *Journal of Communication, 36,* 79-93.

Shiffrin, R. M., & Dumais, S. T. (1981). The development of automatism. In J. R. Anderson (Ed.), *Cognitive skills and their acquisition.* Hillsdale, NJ: Erlbaum

Shiffrin, R. M., & Schneider, W. (1977). Controlled and automatic human information processing: II. Perceptual learning, automatic attending, and a general theory. *Psychological Review, 84,* 127-190.

Shotland, R. L. (1985, June). When bystanders just stand by. *Psychology Today, 19,* 50-55.

Shrauger, J. S. (1975). Responses to evaluation as a function of initial self-perceptions. *Psychological Bulletin, 82,* 581-596.

Sigall, H., & Ostrove, N. (1975). Beautiful but dangerous: Effects of offender attractiveness and nature of the crime on juridic judgment. *Journal of Personality and Social Psychology, 31,* 410-444.

Signorella, M. L., & Frieze, I. H. (1989). Gender schemas in college students. *Psychology, a Journal of Human Behavior, 26,* 16-23.

Silver, R. L., & Wortman, C. B. (1980). Coping with undesirable life events. In J. Barber, & M. E. P. Seligman (Eds.), *Human helplessness: Theory and application.* New York: Academic Press.

Silverstein, B., Perdue, L., Peterson, B., & Kelly, E. (1986). The role of the mass media in promoting a thin standard of bodily attractiveness for women. *Sex Roles, 14,* 519-532.

Simon, S. B., Howe, L. V., & Kirschenbaum, H. (1972). *Values clarification: A handbook of practical strategies for teachers and students.* New York: Hart.

Simpson, G. E., & Yinger, J. M. (1985). *Racial and cultural minorities: An analysis of prejudice and discrimination* (5th ed.). New York: Harper & Row.

Simpson, J. A. (1987). The dissolution of romantic relationships: Factors involved in relationship stability and emotional distress. *Journal of Personality and Social Psychology, 53,* 683-692.

Singer, R. D. (1961). Verbal conditioning and generalization of prodemocratic responses. *Journal of Abnormal and Social Psychology, 63,* 43-46.

Singh, D. (1993). Adaptive significance of female physical attractiveness: Role of waist-to-hip ratio. *Journal of Personality and Social Psychology, 65,* 293-307.

Sinha, J. B. P. (1990). Role of psychology in national development. In G. Misra (Ed.), *Applied social psychology in India.* New Delhi: Sage.

Sistrunk, F., & McDavid, J. W. (1971). Sex variable in conformity behavior. *Journal of Personality and Social Psychology, 17,* 200-207.

Skinner, B. F. (1957). *Verbal behavior.* New York: Macmillan.

Skinner, B. F. (1983). *A matter of consequences.* New York: Knopf.

Skowronski, J. J., & Carlston, D. E. (1989). Negativity and extremity biases in impression formation: A review of explanations. *Psychological Bulletin, 105,* 131-142.

Slovic, P., Fischhoff, B., & Lichenstein, S. (1976). Cognitive processes and societal risk taking. In J. S. Carroll & J. W. Payne (Eds.), *Cognition and social behavior* (pp. 165-184). Hillsdale, NJ: Erlbaum.

Slowiaczek, L. M., Klayman, J., Sherman, S. J., & Skov, B. (1989). Information selection and use in hypothesis testing: What is a good question? What is a good answer? Unpublished manuscript.

Smadi, A. A. (1991). Dynamics of marriage as interpreted through control theory. *Journal of Reality Therapy, 10,* 44-50.

Smeaton, G., Byrne, D., & Murnen, S. K. (1989). The repulsion hypothesis revisited: Similarity irrelevance or dissimilarity bias? *Journal of Personality and Social Psychology, 56,* 54-59.

Smith, C. A., & Ellsworth, P. C. (1987). Patterns of appraisal and emotion related to taking an exam. *Journal of Personality and Social Psychology, 52,* 475-488.

Smith, E. (1988, May). Fighting cancerous feelings. *Psychology Today,* pp. 22-23.

Smith, K. D., Keating, J. P., & Stotland, E. (1989). Altruism reconsidered: The effect of denying feedback on a victim's status to empathic witnesses. *Journal of Personality and Social Psychology, 57,* 641-650.

Smith, M. B. (1990). Psychology in the public interest: What have we done? What can we do? *American Psychologist, 45,* 530-536.

Smith, P. B., Peterson, M. F., Bond, M., & Misumi, J. (1990). Leader style and leader behaviour in individualistic and collectivistic cultures. In S. Iwawaki, Y. Kashima, & K. Leung (Eds.), *Innovations in cross-cultural psychology.* Amsterdam, The Netherlands: Swets & Zeitlinger.

Smith, T. W. (1992). Hostility and health: Current status of a psychosomatic hypothesis. *Health Psychology, 11,* 139-150.

Smith, V. L. (1991a). Impact of pretrial instructions on jurors' information processing and decision making. *Journal of Applied Psychology, 76,* 220-228.

Smith, V. L. (1991b). Prototypes in the courtroom: Lay representations of legal concepts. *Journal of Personality and Social Psychology, 61,* 857-872

Snyder, C. R., & Higgins, R. L. (1988). Excuses: Their effective role in the negotiation of reality. *Psychological Bulletin, 104,* 23-35.

Snyder, D. R., Higgins, R. L., & Stucky, R. J. (1983). *Excuses: Masquerades in search of grace.* New York: Wiley-Interscience.

Snyder, M. (1974a). When belief creates reality. In L. Berkowitz (Ed.), *Advances in experimental social psychology* (Vol. 18). New York: Academic Press.

Snyder, M. (1974b). The self-monitoring of expressive behavior. *Journal of Personality and Social Psychology, 30,* 526-537.

Snyder, M. (1977). Impression management. In L. S. Wrightsman (Ed.), *Social psychology in the seventies* (pp. 115-145). New York: Wiley.

Snyder, M. (1979). Self-monitoring processes. In L. Berkowitz (Ed.), *Advances in experimental social psychology* (Vol. 12). New York: Academic Press.

Snyder, M. (1987). *Public appearances/private realities: The psychology of self-monitoring.* New York: W. H. Freeman.

Snyder, M. (1992). Motivational foundations of behavioral confirmation. In L. Berkowitz (Ed.), *Advances in experimental social psychology* (Vol. 25). San Diego, CA: Academic Press.

Snyder, M. (1993). Basic research and practical problems: The promise of a "functional" personality and social psychology. *Personality and Social Psychology Bulletin, 19,* 251-264.

Snyder, M., Campbell, B. H., & Preston, E. (1982). Testing hypotheses about human nature: Assessing the accuracy of social stereotypes. *Social Cognition, 1,* 256-272.

Snyder M., & DeBono, K. G. (1985). Appeals to images and claims about quality: Understanding the psychology of advertising. *Journal of Personality and Social Psychology, 49,* 586-597.

Snyder M., & DeBono, K. G. (1989). Dopamine and schizophrenia. In A. R. Pratkanis, S. J. Breckler, & A. G. Greenwald (Eds.), *Attitude structure and function.* Hillsdale, NJ: Erlbaum.

Snyder, M., & Gangestad, S. (1986). On the nature of self-monitoring: Matters of assessment, matters of validity. *Journal of Personality and Social Psychology, 51,* 125-139.

Snyder, M., Gangestad, S., & Simpson, J. A. (1983). Choosing friends as activity partners: The role of self-monitoring. *Journal of Personality and Social Psychology, 45,* 1061-1072.

Snyder, M., & Simpson, J. A. (1984). Self-monitoring and dating relationships. *Journal of Personality and Social Psychology, 47,* 1281-1291.

Snyder, S. H. (1987, April 30). Parkinson's disease: A cure using brain transplants? *Nature, 326,* 824-825.

Solomon, Z. (1993). *Combat stress reaction: The enduring toll of war.* New York: Plenum.

Sorenson, S. B., & Siegel, J. M. (1992). Gender, ethnicity, and sexual assault: Findings from the Los Angeles Epidemiological catchment area study. *Journal of Social Issues, 48,* 93-104.

Spanier, G. B. (1983). Married and unmarried cohabitation in the United States: 1980. *Journal of Marriage and the Family, 45,* 277-288.

Spence, J. T., Helmreich, R., & Stapp, J. (1973). A short version of the Attitude toward Women Scale (AWS). *Bulletin of the Psychonomic Society, 2,* 219-220.

Spiegel, D. (1993). Social support: How friends, family, and groups can help. In D. Goleman & J. Gurin (Eds.), *Mind-body medicine.* Yonkers, NY: Consumer Reports Books.

Spiegel, D., Bloom, J. R., Kraemer, H. C., & Gottheil, E. (1989, October 14). Effect of psychosocial treatment on survival of patients with metastic breast cancer. *Lancet, 2,* 888-891.

Spivey, C. B., & Prentice-Dunn, S. (1990). Assessing the directionality of deindividuated behavior: Effects of deindividuation, modeling, and private self-consciousness on aggressive and prosocial responses. *Basic and Applied Social Psychology, 11,* 387-403.

Staats, A. W., & Staats, C. K. (1958). Attitudes established by classical conditioning. *Journal of Abnormal and Social Psychology, 57,* 37-40.

Stang, D. J. (1973). Six theories of repeated exposure and affect. *Catalog of Selected Documents in Psychology, 126.*

Stang, D. J. (1976). Group size effects on conformity. *Journal of Social Psychology, 98,* 175-181.

Stangor, C., Lynch, L., Changming, D., & Glass, B. (1992). Categorization of individuals on the basis of multiple social features. *Journal of Personality and Social Psychology, 62,* 207-218.

Stangor, C., Sullivan, L. A., & Ford, T. E. (1991). Affective and cognitive determinants of prejudice. *Social Cognition, 9,* 359-380.

Stasser, G., Kerr, N. L., & Davis, J. H. (1989). Influence processes and consensus models in decision-making groups. In P. B. Paulhus (Ed.), *Psychology of group influence* (2nd ed.). Hillsdale, NJ: Erlbaum.

Stasson, M. F., & Davis, J. H. (1989). The relative effects of the number of arguments, number of argument sources and number of opinion positions in group-mediated opinion change. *British Journal of Social Psychology, 28,* 251-262.

Staub, E. (1971). A child in distress: The influence of nurturance and modeling on children's attempts to help. *Developmental Psychology, 5,* 124-133.

Staub, E. (Ed.). (1978). *Positive social behavior and morality: Vol. 1. Social and personal influences.* New York: Academic Press.

Staub, E. (1988). The evolution of caring and nonaggressive persons and societies. *Journal of Social Issues, 44,* 81-100.

Staub, E. (1989). *The roots of evil: The origins of genocide and other group violence.* Cambridge, England: Cambridge University Press.

Steblay, N. M. (1987). Helping behavior in rural and urban environments: A meta-analysis. *Psychological Bulletin, 102,* 346-356.

Steele, C. M. (1988). The psychology of self-affirmation: Sustaining the integrity of the self. In L. Berkowitz (Ed.), *Social psychological studies of the self: Perspectives and programs* (pp. 261-302). San Diego, CA: Academic Press.

Steele, C. M., & Liu, T. J. (1981). Making the dissonant act unreflective of self: Dissonance avoidance and the expectancy of a value-affirming response. *Personality and Social Psychology Bulletin, 7,* 393-397.

Steele, C. M., & Liu, T. J. (1983). Dissonance processes as self-affirmation. *Journal of Personality and Social Psychology, 45,* 5-19.

Steinberg, L., Belsky, J., & Meyer, R. B. (1991). *Infancy, childhood, & adolescence.* New York: McGraw-Hill.

Steinberg, L., & Silverberg, S. B. (1987). Influences on marital satisfaction during the middle stages of the family life cycle. *Journal of Marriage and the Family, 49,* 751-760.

Steiner, I. (1972). *Group process and productivity.* New York: Academic.

Steiner, I. (1976). Task-performing groups. In J. W. Thibaut, J. T. Spence, & R. C. Carson (Eds.), *Contemporary topics in social psychology.* Morristown, NJ: General Learning Press.

Stephan, W. G. (1985). Intergroup relations. In G. Lindzey & E. Aronson (Eds.), *Handbook of social psychology* (Vol. 2, pp. 599-658). New York: Random House.

Stephan, W. G. (1986). The effects of school desegregation: An evaluation 30 years after *Brown.* In M. J. Saks & L. Saxe (Eds.), *Advances in applied social psychology* (Vol. 3, pp. 181-206). Hillsdale, NJ: Erlbaum.

Sternberg, R. J. (1985). Implicit theories of intelligence, creativity, and wisdom. *Journal of Personality and Social Psychology, 49,* 607-627.

Sternberg, R. J. (1986). A triangular theory of love. *Psychological Review, 93,* 119-135.

Sternberg, R. J. (1987). Liking versus loving: A comparative evaluation of theories. *Psychological Bulletin, 102,* 331-345.

Sternberg, R. J. (1988). Triangulating love. In R. J. Sternberg & M. J. Barnes (Eds.), *The psychology of love.* New Haven, CT: Yale University Press.

Stevenson, H. W. (1992, December). Learning from Asian schools. *Scientific American*, 70-75.

Stevenson, H. W., & Lee, Shin-Ying. (1990). Contexts of achievement: A study of American, Chinese, and Japanese children. *Monographs of the Society for Research in Child Development, No. 221, 55*, Nos. 1-2.

Stevenson, H. W., & Stigler, J. W. (1992). *The learning gap: Why our schools are failing and what we can learn from Japanese and Chinese education*. New York: Summit.

Stewart, D. W., & Kamins, M. A. (1993). *Secondary research: Information sources and methods*. Newbury Park, CA: Sage.

Stewart, J. E., II. (1980). Defendant's attractiveness as a factor in the outcome of criminal trials: An observational study. *Journal of Applied Social Psychology, 10*, 348-361.

Stewart, R. H. (1965). Effect of continuous responding on the order effect in personality impression formation. *Journal of Personality and Social Psychology, 1*, 161-165.

Stogdill, R. M. (1974). *Handbook of leadership: A survey of theory and research*. New York: The Free Press.

Stokes, J. P. (1983). Components of group cohesion: Intermember attraction, instrumental value, and risk taking. *Small Group Behavior, 14*, 163-173.

Stone, G. C. (1979). Patient compliance and the role of the expert. *Journal of Social Issues, 35*, 34-59.

Storms, M. D. (1973). Videotape and the attribution process: Reversing actors' and observers' points of view. *Journal of Personality and Social Psychology, 27*, 165-175.

Storms, M. D., & McCaul, K. (1976). Attribution processes and emotional exacerbation of dysfunctional behavior. In J. H. Harvey, W. J. Ickes, & R. F. Kidd (Eds.), *New directions in attribution research* (Vol. 1). Hillsdale, NJ: Erlbaum.

Storms, M. D., & Nisbett, R. E. (1970). Insomnia and the attribution process. *Journal of Personality and Social Psychology, 16*, 219-328.

Strack, F., Martin, L., & Stepper, S. (1988). Inhibiting and facilitating conditions of the human smile: A nonobtrusive test of the facial feedback hypothesis. *Journal of Personality and Social Psychology, 54*, 768-777.

Straus, M., Gelles, R., & Steinmetz, S. K. (1980). *Behind closed doors: Violence in the American family*. Garden City, NY: Anchor Press.

Straus, M. A., & Gelles, R. J. (Eds.). (1990). *Physical violence in American families*. New Brunswick, NJ: Transaction.

Strawn, D. V., & Buchanan, R. W. (1976). Jury confusion: A threat to justice. *Judicature, 59*, 478-483.

Striacker, L. J., Messick, S., & Jackson, D. N. (1969). Dimensionality of social influence. *Proceedings of the 76th annual convention of the American Psychological Association, 1968, 3*, 189-190.

Stroebe, W., Diehl, M., & Abakoumkin, G. (1992). The illusion of group effectivity. *Personality and Social Psychology Bulletin, 18*, 643-650.

Strube, M. (Ed.). (1990). Type A behavior [Special Issue]. *Journal of Social Behavior and Personality, 5*.

Strube, M. J., Miles, M. E., & Finch, W. H. (1981). The social facilitation of a simple task: Field tests of alternative explanations. *Personality and Social Psychology Bulletin, 7*, 701-707.

Suarez, E. C., & Williams, R. B., Jr. (1992). Interactive models of reactivity: The relationship between hostility and potentially pathogenic physiological responses to social stressors. In N. Schneiderman, P. McCabe, & A. Baum (Eds.), *Stress and disease processes*. Hillsdale, NJ: Erlbaum.

Suchner, R. W., & Jackson, D. (1976). Responsibility and status: A causal or only a spurious relationship? *Sociometry, 39*, 243-256.

Sudefeld, P., & Borrie, R. A. (1978). Sensory deprivation, attitude change, and defense against persuasion. *Canadian Journal of Behavioural Science, 10*, 16-27.

Sue, S., Smith, S. E., & Caldwell, C. (1973). Effects of inadmissible evidence on the decisions of simulated jurors: A moral dilemma. *Journal of Applied Social Psychology, 3*, 345-353.

Suls, J., & Rosnow, J. (1988). Concerns about artifacts in behavioral research. In M. Morawski (Ed.), *The rise of experimentation in American psychology* (pp. 163-187). New Haven, CT: Yale University Press.

Suls, J., & Wills, T. A. (Eds.). (1991). *Social comparison: Contemporary theory and research*. Hillsdale, NJ: Erlbaum.

Sulzer-Azaroff, B., & Mayer, G. R. (1991). *Behavior analysis for lasting change*. Fort Worth, TX: Holt.

Sutherland, E. H., & Cressey, D. R. (1974). *Principles of criminology* (9th ed.). New York: Lippincott.

Sutker, P. B., Uddo, M., Brailey, K., & Allain, A. N., Jr. (1993). War-zone trauma and stress-related symptoms in Operation Desert Shield/Storm (ODS) returnees. *Journal of Social Issues, 49*, 33-49.

Sweeney, P. D., Anderson, K., & Bailey, S. (1986). Attributional style in depression: A meta-analytic review. *Journal of Personality and Social Psychology, 50*, 974-991.

Sweeney, P. D., & Gruber, K. L. (1984). Selective exposure: Voter information preferences and the Watergate affair. *Journal of Personality and Social Psychology, 46*, 1208-1221.

Sweet, E. (1985, October). Date rape: The story of an epidemic and those who deny it. *Ms/Campus Times*, pp. 56-59.

Sykes, G., & Matza, D. (1957). Techniques of neutralization: A theory of delinquency. *American Sociological Review, 22*, 664-670.

Symonds, M. (1975). Victims of violence: Psychological effects and after effects. *The American Journal of Psychoanalysis, 35*, 19-26.

Szymanski, K., & Harkins, S. (1987). Social loafing and self-evaluation with a social standard. *Journal of Personality and Social Psychology, 53*, 891-897.

Tachibana, Y., Ohgishi, M., & Monden, K. (1984). Experimental study of aggression and catharsis in Japanese. *Perceptual and Motor Skills, 58*, 207-212.

Tajfel, H. (1974). Social identity and intergroup behaviour. *Social Science Information, 13*, 65-93.

Tajfel, H. (1979). Individuals and groups in social psychology. *British Journal of Social and Clinical Psychology, 18*, 183-190.

Tajfel, H. (1982). *Social identity and intergroup relations*. London: Cambridge University Press.

Tajfel, H., & Turner, J. C. (1986). The social identity theory of intergroup behavior. In S. Worchel & W. G. Austin (Eds.), *Psychology of intergroup relations*. Chicago: Nelson Hall.

Takolditz, J., & Palmer, R. (1991). Impression management aspects of self-handicapping: Positive and negative effects. *Personality and Social Psychology Bulletin, 17*, 655-662.

Tanford, S., & Penrod, S. (1984). Social interference processes in juror judgments of multiple-offense trials. *Journal of Personality and Social Psychology, 47*, 749-765.

Tannen, D. (1991). *You just don't understand*. New York: Ballantine.

Tannenbaum, A. S. (1980). Organizational psychology. In H. C. Triandis & R. W. Brislin (Eds.), *Handbook of cross-cultural psychology: Social psychology* (Vol. 5). Boston: Allyn & Bacon.

Tavris, C., & Sadd, S. (1977). *The Redbook report on female sexuality*. New York: Delacorte.

Tayeb, M. (1987). Contingency theory and culture: A study of matched English and the Indian manufacturing firms. *Organization Studies, 8*, 241-261.

Taylor, D. G. (1982). Pluralistic ignorance and the spiral of silence: A formal analysis. *Public Opinion Quarterly, 46*, 311-335.

Taylor, D. M., Doria, J., & Tyler, J. K. (1983). Group performance and cohesiveness: An attribution analysis. *Journal of Social Psychology, 119*, 187-198.

Taylor, D. M., & Jaggi, V. (1974). Ethnocentrism and causal attribution in a south Indian context. *Journal of Cross Cultural Psychology, 5*, 162-171.

Taylor, G. (1990, July 9). Good Samaritans kick. *The National Law Journal, 12 (44)*, 2.

Taylor, M. S., Locke, E. A., Lee, C., & Gist, M. E. (1984). Type A behavior and faculty research productivity: What are the mechanisms? *Organizational Behavior and Human Performance, 34*, 402-418.

Taylor, R. G. (1984). The potential impact of humanistic psychology on modern administrative style: II. Administrative models and psychological variants. *Psychology: A Quarterly Journal of Human Behavior, 21*, 1-9.

Taylor, S. E. (1981). The interface of cognitive and social psychology. In J. Harvey (Ed.), *Cognition, social behavior, and the environment* (pp. 189-211). Hillsdale, NJ: Erlbaum.

Taylor, S. E. (1991a). Asymmetrical effects of positive and negative events: The mobilization-minimization hypothesis. *Psychological Bulletin, 110*, 67-85.

Taylor, S. E. (1991b). *Health psychology*. New York: McGraw-Hill.

Taylor, S. E., & Brown, J. D. (1988). Illusion and well-being: A social psychological perspective on mental health. *Psychological Bulletin, 103*, 193-210.

Taylor, S. E., Buunk, B. P., & Aspinwall, L. G. (1990). Social comparison, stress, and coping. *Personality and Social Psychology Bulletin, 16*, 74-89.

Taylor, S. E., & Fiske, S. T. (1978). Salience, attention, and attribution: Top of the head phenomena. In L. Berkowitz (Ed.), *Advances in experimental social psychology* (Vol. 11, pp. 249-288). New York: Academic Press.

Taylor, S. E., Helgeson, V. S., Reed, G. M., & Skokan, L. A. (1991). Self-generated feelings of control and adjustment to physical illness. *Journal of Social Issues, 47*, 91-109.

Taylor, S. E., & Thompson, S. C. (1982). Stalking the elusive "vividness" effect. *Psychological Review, 89*, 155-181.

Taylor, S. P., & Pisano, R. (1971). Physical aggression as a function of frustration and physical attack. *Journal of Social Psychology, 84*, 261-267.

Tennen, H., Suls, J., & Affleck, G. (1991). Personality and daily experience: The promise and the challenge. *Journal of Personality, 59*, 313-338.

Teske, R. H., & Hazlett, M. H. (1985). A scale for measurement of attitudes toward handgun control. *Journal of Criminal Justice, 13*, 373-379.

Tesser, A., & Brodie, M. (1971). A note on the evaluation of a computer date. *Psychonomic Science, 23*, 300.

Tesser, A., & Shaffer, D. R. (1990). Attitudes and attitude change. *Annual Review of Psychology, 41*, 479-523.

Tessor, A. (1988). Toward a self-evaluation maintenance model of social behavior. In L. Berkowitz (Ed.), *Advances in experimental and social psychology* (Vol. 21, pp. 181-227). New York: Academic Press.

Tetlock, P. E., Peterson, R. S., McGuire, C., Chang, S., & Feld, P. (1992). Assessing political group dynamics: A test of the groupthink model. *Journal of Personality and Social Psychology, 63*, 403-425.

t'Hart, P. (1991). Irving L. Janis' victims of groupthink. *Political Psychology, 12*, 247-278.

Thibaut, J. W., & Kelley, H. H. (1959). *The social psychology of groups*. New York: Wiley.

Thomas, M. H., & Drabman, R. S. (1978). Effects of television violence on expectations of other's aggression. *Personality and Social Psychology Bulletin, 4*, 73-76.

Thomas, M. H., Horton, R. W., Lippincott, E. C., & Drabman, R. S. (1977). Desensitization to portrayals of real-life aggression as a function of television violence. *Journal of Personality and Social Psychology, 35*, 450-458.

Thompson, M. G., & Heller, K. (1990). Facets of support related to well-being: Quantitative social isolation and perceived family support in a sample of elderly women. *Psychology and Aging, 5*, 535-544.

Thompson, S. C. (1988, August). *An intervention to increase physician-patient communication*. A paper presented at the annual meeting of the American Psychological Association, Atlanta.

Thompson, S. C., Nanni, C., & Schwankovsky, L. (1990). Patient-oriented interventions to improve communication in a medical office visit. *Health Psychology, 9*, 390-404.

Thoresen, C. E., & Low, K. G. (1990). Women and the Type A behavior pattern: Review and commentary. *Journal of Social Behavior and Personality, 5*, 117-133.

Thornton, B. (1992). Repression and its mediating influence on the defensive attribution of responsibility. *Journal of Research in Personaltiy, 26*, 44-57.

Thornton, B., Hogate, L., Moirs, K., Pinette, M., & Presby, W. (1986). Physiological evidence for an arousal-based motivational bias in the defensive attribution of responsibility. *Journal of Experimental Social Psychology, 22*, 148-162.

Timaeus, E. (1968). Untersuchungen zum sogenannten konformen Verhatten. *Zeitschrift für experimentelle und angewandte Psychologie, 15*, 176-194.

Titus, T. G. (1991). Effects of rehearsal instructions on the primacy effect in free recall. *Psychological Reports, 68*, 1371-1377.

Tjosvold, D., & Deemer, D. K. (1980). Effects of controversy within a cooperative or competitive context on organizational decision making. *Journal of Applied Psychology, 65*, 590-595.

Tolstedt, B. E., & Stokes, J. P. (1984). Self-disclosure, intimacy, and the depenetration process. *Journal of Personality and Social Psychology, 46*, 84-90.

Tomita, S. K. (1990). The denial of elder mistreatment by victims and abusers: The application of neutralization theory. *Violence and Victims, 5*, 171-184.

Torrence, E. P. (1954). Some consequences of power differences on decision making in permanent and temporary three-man groups. *Research Studies, State College of Washington, 22*, 130-140.

Tosi, H. L. (1991). The organization as a context for leadership theory: A multilevel approach. *Leadership Quarterly, 2*, 205-228.

Tosi, H. L., & Slocum, J. W. (1984). Contingency theory: Some suggested directions. *Journal of Management, 10*, 9-26.

Traugott, M. W., & Price, V. E. (1991, November). *Exit polls in the 1989 Virginia gubernatorial race: Where did they go wrong?* Paper presented at the annual meeting of the Midwest Association for Public Opinion Research, Chicago.

Triandis, H. (1988). Collectivism vs. individualism: A reconceptualization of a basic concept in cross-cultural psychology. In C. Bagley & G. K. Verma (Eds.), *Personality, cognition and values: Cross-cultural perspectives in childhood and adolescence*. London: Macmillan.

Triandis, H. C. (1989). The self and social behavior in differing cultural contexts. *Psychological Review, 96*, 506-520.

Triplett, N. (1897). The dynamogenic factors in pacemaking and competition. *American Journal of Psychology, 9*, 507-533.

Trope, Y., & Higgins, E. T. (1993). The what, when, and how of dispositional inference: New answers and new questions. *Personality and Social Psychology Bulletin, 19*, 493-500.

Tulving, E., & Schacter, D. L. (1990, January 19). Priming and human memory systems. *Science, 247*, 301-306.

Turk, D. C., & Meichenbaum, D. (1991). Adherence to self-care regimens: The patient's perspective. In R. H. Rozensky, J. J. Sweet, & S. M. Tovian (Eds.), *Handbook of clinical psychology in medical settings*. New York: Plenum.

Turner, J. C. (1987). *Rediscovering the social group: A self-categorization theory*. New York: Basil Blackwell.

Turner, M. E., Pratkanis, A. R., Probasco, P., & Leve, C. (1992). Threat, cohesion, and group effectiveness: Testing a social identity maintenance perspective on groupthink. *Journal of Personality and Social Psychology, 63*, 781-796.

Tuthill, D. M., & Forsyth, D. R. (1982). Sex differences in opinion conformity and dissent. *Journal of Social Psychology, 116*, 205-210.

Tyler, T. R., & McGraw, K. M. (1983). The threat of nuclear war: Risk interpretation and behavioral response. *Journal of Social Issues, 39*, 25-40.

U.S. Bureau of Census. (1993a). Current projections of the population makeup of the United States. Washington, DC.

U.S. Bureau of Census. (1993b). Cohabitation in the United States. Washington, DC.

U.S. Bureau of Census. (1993c). Figures on cohabitation.

U.S. Bureau of Labor Statistics. (1993) Average wages earned by women compared to men. Washington, DC.

U.S. Commission on Civil Rights. (1990). *Intimidation and violence: Racial and religious bigotry in the United States.* Washington, DC: U. S. Commission on Civil Rights.

U.S. Department of Education. (1993). Minority population projections. Washington, DC.

U.S. Department of Justice. (1990). *Sourcebook of criminal justice statistics.* Washington, DC: U.S. Department of Justice.

*U.S. News & World Report.* (1991, May 6). P. 91.

Unger, R. K., & Crawford, M. E. (1992). *Women and gender: A feminist psychology.* Philadelphia, PA: Temple University Press.

United States: A laboratory comparison using 3-month-old infants. *Developmental Psychology, 24*, 398-406.

United We Stand America. (1993, March 20). The first national referendum on government reform sponsored by United We Stand American. *TV Guide*, 41.

Ussher, J. (1989). *The psychology of the female body.* London: Routledge.

Ussher, J. (1990). Choosing psychology or not throwing the baby out with the bathwater. In E. Burman (Ed.), *Feminists and psychological practice.* London: Sage.

Valins, S. (1966). Cognitive effects of false heartrate feedback. *Journal of Personality and Social Psychology, 4*, 400-408.

Vallacher, R. R., Robin, R., & Wegner, D. M. (1987). What do people think they're doing? Action identification and human behavior. *Pscyhological Review, 94*, 3-15.

Vallacher, R. R., & Wegner, D. M. (1985). *A theory of action identification.* Hillsdale, NJ: Erlbaum.

Vallacher, R. R., & Wegner, D. M. (1989). Levels of personal agency: Individual variation in action identification. *Journal of Personality and Social Psychology, 57*, 660-671.

Vallerand, R. J., Deshaies, P., Cuerrier, J., Pelletier, L. G., & Mongeua, C. (1992). Ajzen and Fishbein's theory of reasoned action as applied to moral behavior: A confirmatory analysis. *Journal of Personality and Social Psychology, 62*, 98-109.

Van Hook, E., & Higgins, E. T. (1988). Self-related problems beyond the self-concept: Motivational consequences of discrepant self-guides. *Journal of Personality and Social Psychology, 55*, 625-633.

Van Knippenberg, A., & Wilke, H. (1988). Social categorization and attitude change. *European Journal of Social Psychology, 18*, 395-406.

Van Manen, S., & Pietromonaco, P. (1994). Acquaintance and consistency influence memory from interpersonal information. Unpublished manuscript. University of Massachusetts at Amherst.

Varela, J. A. (1971). *Psychological solutions to social problems.* New York: Academic Press.

Verplanck, W. S. (1955). People processing: Strategies of organizational socialization. *Organizational Dynamics* (summer).

Vollrath, D. A., Sheppard, B. H., Hinsz, V. B., & Davis, J. H. (1989) Memory performance by decision-making groups and individuals. *Organizational Behavior and Human Decision Processes, 43*, 289-300.

Vonk, R. (1993). The negativity effect in trait ratings and in open-ended descriptions of persons. *Personality and Social Psychology Bulletin, 19*, 269-278.

Von Lang, J., & Sibyll, C. (Eds.). (1983). *Eichmann interrogated.* Translated from the German by Ralph Manheim. New York: Farrar, Straus & Giroux.

Wagley, C., & Harns, M. (1958). *Minorities in the new world.* New York: Columbia.

Waitzkin, H. (1985). Information giving in medical care. *Journal of Health and Social Behavior, 26*, 81-101.

Waitzkin, H., & Stoeckle, J. D. (1976). Information control and the micropolitics of health care. *Journal of Social Issues, 10*, 263-276.

Wall, P. M. (1965). *Eyewitness identification in criminal cases.* Springfield, IL: Charles C. Thomas.

Wallach, L., & Wallach, M. A. (1991). Why altruism, even though it exists, cannot be demonstrated by social psychological experiments. *Psychological Inquiry, 2*, 153-155.

Walsh, N. A., Meister, L. A., & Kleinke, C. L. (1977). Interpersonal attraction and visual behavior as a function of perceived arousal and evaluation by an opposite sex person. *Journal of Social Psychology, 103*, 65-74.

Walster, E., Walster, G. W., & Traupmann, J. (1978). Equity and premarital sex. *Journal of Personality and Social Psychology, 36*, 82-92.

Walster, (Hatfield) E., Aronson, V., Abrahams, D., & Rottman, L. (1966). Importance of physical attractiveness in dating behavior. *Journal of Personality and Social Psychology, 4*, 508-516.

Walster, (Hatfield) E., Walster, G. W., & Berscheid, E. (1978). *Equity: Theory and research.* Boston: Allyn and Bacon.

Walster, (Hatfield) E., & Walster, G. W. (1978). *Love.* Reading, MA: Addison-Wesley.

Warren, P. E., & Walker, I. (1991). Empathy, effectiveness and donations to charity: Social psychology's contribution. *British Journal of Social Psychology, 30*, 325-337.

Warren, R., & Kurlychek, R. T. (1981). Treatment of maladaptive anger and aggression: Catharsis vs behavior therapy. *Corrective and Social Psychiatry and Journal of Behavior Technology, Methods and Therapy, 27*, 135-139.

Warshaw, R. (1988). *I never called it rape: The "Ms." report on recognizing, fighting, and surviving date rape and acquaintance rape.* New York: Harper & Row.

Waters, H. F. (1993, July 12). Networks under the gun. *Newsweek*, 64-66.

Watkins, M. J., & Peynircioglu, Z. F. (1984). Determining perceived meaning during impression formation: Another look at the meaning change hypothesis. *Journal of Personality and Social Psychology, 46*, 1005-1016.

Webb, E. J., Campbell, D. T., Schwartz, D., & Sechrest, L. (1966). *Unobstrusive measures: Nonreactive research in the social sciences.* Chicago: Rand McNally.

Weber, M. (1952). The essentials of bureaucratic organization: An ideal-type construction. In R. K. Merton et al. (Eds.), *A reader in bureaucracy.* Glencoe, IL: Free Press.

Wegner, D. M. (1989). *White bears and other unwanted thoughts: Suppression, obsession, and the psychology of mental control.* New York: Viking.

Wegner, D. M., Schneider, D. J., Knutson, B., & McMahon, S. R. (1991). Polluting the stream of consciousness: The effect of thought suppression on the mind's environment. *Cognitive Therapy and Research, 15*, 141-152.

Wegner, D. M., Shortt, J. W., Blake, A. W., & Page, M. S. (1990). The suppression of exciting thoughts. *Journal of Personality and Social Psychology, 58*, 409-418.

Wegner, D. M., Vallacher, R. R., & Dizadji, D. (1989). Do alcoholics know what they're doing? Identifications of the act of drinking. *Basic and Applied Social Psychology, 10*, 197-210.

Weinberger, M., Hiner, S. L., & Tierney, W. M. (1987). In support of hassles as a measure of stress in predicting health outcomes. *Journal of Behavioral Medicine, 10*, 19-32.

Weiner, B. (1980). A cognitive (attribution) emotion-action model of motivated behavior: An analysis of judgments of helpgiving. *Journal of Personality and Social Psychology, 39*, 186-200.

Weiner, M., & Mehrabian, A. (1968). *Language within language: Immediacy, a channel in verbal communication*. New York: Appleton-Century-Crofts.

Weiner, N., Pandy, J., & Latané, B. (1981). *Individual and group productivity in the United States and India*. Paper presented at the American Psychological Association, Los Angeles.

Weinstein, S., Weinstein, C., & Drozdenko, R. (1984). Brain wave analysis. *Psychology and Marketing, 1*, 17-42.

Weintraub, M. (1976). Intelligent noncompliance and capricious compliance. In L. Lasagna (Ed.), *Patient compliance*. Mt. Kisco, NY: Futura.

Weiss, R. L. (1980). Strategic behavioral marital therapy: Toward a model for assessment and intervention. In J. P. Vincent (Ed.), *Advances in family intervention, assessment and theory*. Greenwich, CT: JAI Press.

Weiss, R. S. (1973). *Loneliness: The experience of emotional and social isolation*. Cambridge, MA: M. I.T. Press.

Weldon, E., & Weingart, L. R. (1993). Group goals and group performance. *British Journal of Social Psychology, 32*, 307-334.

Wells, G. L. (1993). What do we know about eyewitness identification? *American Psychologist, 48*, 553-571.

Werner, P. D., & LaRussa, G. W. (1985). Persistence and change in sex-role stereotypes. *Sex Roles, 12*, 1089-1100.

Wetzel, C. G., & Walton, M. D. (1985). Developing biased social judgments: The false-consensus effect. *Journal of Personality and Social Psychology, 49*, 1352-1359.

Wheeler, L. (1974). Social comparison and selective affiliation. In T. L. Huston (Ed.), *Foundations of interpersonal attraction* (pp. 309-328). New York: Academic Press.

Wheeler, L., Reis, H. T., & Bond, M. H. (1989). Collectivism-individualism in everyday social life: The middle kingdom and the melting pot. *Journal of Personality and Social Psychology, 57*, 79-86.

Wheeless, L. R., Wheeless, V. E., & Dickson-Markman, F. (1982). A research note: The relations among social and task perceptions in small groups. *Small Group Behavior, 13*, 373-384.

White, G. (1989). Media and violence: The case of professional football championship games. *Aggressive Behavior, 15*, 423-433.

White, J. W., & Humphrey, J. A. (1991). Young people's attitudes toward rape. In A. Parrot & L. Bechhofer (Eds.), *Acquaintance rape: The hidden crime*. New York: Wiley.

White, J. W., & Koss, M. P. (1991). Adolescent sexual aggression within heterosexual relationships: Prevalence, characteristics, and causes. In H. E. Barbaree, W. L. Marshall, & D. R. Laws (Eds.), *The juvenile sexual offender*. New York: Guilford Press.

White, P. A. (1992). The anthropomorphic machine: Causal order in nature and the world view of common sense. *British Journal of Psychology, 83*, 61-96.

White, R. (1984). *Fearful warriors: A psychological profile of U. S.-Soviet relations*. New York: Free Press.

White, R. K. (1977). Misperception in the Arab-Israeli conflict. *Journal of Social Issues, 33*, 190-221.

Whiting, B. B. (1965). Sex identity conflict and physical violence: A comparative study. *American Anthropologist, 67*, 123-140.

Whiting, B. B., & Edwards, C. P. (1988). *Children of different worlds: The foundation of social behavior*. Cambridge: Harvard University Press.

Whiting, B. M., & Whiting, J. W. (1975). *Children of six countries: A psychological analysis*. Cambridge, MA: Harvard University Press.

Whittaker, J. O., & Meade, R. D. (1967). Social pressure in the modification and distortion of judgment: A cross-cultural study. *International Journal of Psychology, 2*, 109-113.

Whyte, W. F. (1981). *Street corner society: The social structure of an Italian slum* (3rd ed.). Chicago: University of Chicago Press.

Wicker, A. W. (1969). Attitudes versus actions: The relationship of verbal and overt behavioral responses to attitude objects. *Journal of Social Issues, 25*, 41-78.

Wicklund, R. A. (1975). Objective self awareness. In L. Berkowitz (Ed.), *Advances in experimental social psychology* (Vol. 8). New York: Academic Press.

Wicklund, R. A., & Frey, D. (1980). Self awareness theory: When the self makes a difference. In D. M. Wegner & R. R. Vallacher (Eds.), *The self in social psychology* (pp. 31-54). New York: Oxford University Press.

Widdicombe, S. (1988). Dimensions of adolescent identity. *European Journal of Social Psychology, 18*, 471-483.

Widmeyer, W. N., & Loy, J. W. (1988). When you're hot, you're hot! Warm-cold effects in first impressions of persons and teaching effectiveness. *Journal of Educational Psychology, 60*, 89-99.

Widom, C. S. (1989). Does violence beget violence? A critical examination of the literature. *Psychological Bulletin, 106*, 3-28.

Wiebe, D. J. (1991). Hardiness and stress moderation: A test of proposed mechanisms. *Journal of Personality and Social Psychology, 60*, 89-99.

Wilder, D. A. (1977). Perception of groups, size of opposition, and social influence. *Journal of Experimental Social Psychology, 19*, 173-177.

Wilder, D. A. (1981). Perceiving persons as a group: Categorization and intergroup relations. In D. L. Hamilton (Ed.), *Cognitive processes in stereotyping and intergroup behavior* (pp. 213-258). Hillsdale, NJ: Erlbaum.

Wilder, D. A. (1984). Intergroup contact: The typical member and the exception to the rule. *Journal of Experimental Social Psychology, 20*, 177-194.

Wilder, D. A. (1986). Social categorization: Implications for creation and reduction of intergroup bias. In L. Berkowitz (Ed.), *Advances in experimental social psychology* (Vol. 19). San Diego, CA: Academic.

Wilder, D. A. (1990). Some determinants of the persuasive power of in-groups and the out-groups: Organization of information and attribution of independence. *Journal of Personality and Social Psychology, 59*, 1202-1213.

Wilder, D. A., & Allen, V. L. (1977). Veridical social support, extreme social support, and conformity. *Representative Research in Social Psychology, 8*, 33-41.

Wiley, M. G., & Eskilson, A. (1982). Coping in the corporation: Sex role constraints. *Journal of Applied Social Psychology, 12*, 1-11.

Williams, J. E., & Best, D. L. (1990). *Measuring sex stereotypes: A multination study*. Newbury Park, CA: Sage.

Williams, J. M. (1984). Assertiveness as a mediating variable in conformity to confederates of high and low status. *Psychological Reports, 55*, 415-418.

Williams, K. D., Harkins, S., & Latané, B. (1981). Identifiability as a deterrent to social loafing: Two cheering experiments. *Journal of Personality and Social Psychology, 40*, 303-311.

Williams, K. D., Jackson, J. M., & Karau, S. J. (1992). Collective hedonism: A social loafing analysis of social dilemmas. In D. A. Schroeder (Ed.), *Social dilemmas: Social psychological perspectives*. New York: Praeger.

Williams, K. D., & Karau, S. J. (1991). Social loafing and social compensation: The effects of expectations of co-worker performance. *Journal of Personality and Social Psychology, 61*, 570-581.

Williams, K. D., & Williams, K. B. (1984). *Social loafing in Japan: A cross-cultural development study*. Paper presented at the Midwestern Psychological Association, Chicago.

Williams, R. B., Jr. (1993). Hostility and the heart. In D. Goleman, & J. Gurin (Eds.), *Mind-body medicine*. Yonkers, NY: Consumer Reports Books.

Williams, R. B., Jr., Barefoot, J. C., Haney, T. L., Harrell, F. E., Jr., Blumenthal, J. A., Pryor, D. B., & Peterson, B. (1988). Type A behavior and angiographically documented coronary atherosclerosis in a sample of 2,289 patients. *Psychosomatic Medicine, 50,* 139-152.

Wills, T. A. (1981). Downward comparison principles in social psychology. *Psychological Bulletin, 90,* 245-271.

Wilson, E. (1975). *Sociobiology: The new synthesis.* Cambridge, MA: Harvard University Press.

Wilson, E. (1978). *On human nature.* Cambridge, MA: Harvard University Press.

Wilson, J. P., & Petruska, R. (1984). Motivation, model attributes, and prosocial behavior. *Journal of Personality and Social Psychology, 46,* 458-468.

Wilson, J. P., & Raphael, B. (Eds.). (1993). *International handbook of traumatic stress syndromes.* New York: Plenum.

Wilson, M., & Lynxwiler, J. (1988). Abortion clinic violence as terrorism. *Terrorism, 11,* 263-273.

Wilson, T., & Linville, P. (1982). Improving academic performance of college freshmen: Attribution therapy revisited. *Journal of Personality and Social Psychology, 42,* 367-376.

Wilson, T., & Linville, P. (1985). Improving the performance of college freshmen with attributional techniques. *Journal of Personality and Social Psychology, 49,* 287-293.

Winch, R. F. (1958). *Mate selection: A study of complementary needs.* New York: Harper & Row.

Winkel, F. W. (1991). Police communication programs aimed at burglary victims: A review of studies and an experimental evaluation. *Journal of Community and Applied Social Psychology, 1,* 275-289.

Winter, D. G. (1973). *The power motive.* New York: Free Press.

Winter, D. G. (1987). Leader appeal, leader performance, and the motive profile of leaders and followers: A study of American presidents and elections. *Journal of Personality and Social Psychology 52,* 196-202.

Winter, D. G. (1988). The power motive in women—and men. *Journal of Personality and Social Psychology, 54,* 196-202.

Wissler, R. L., & Saks, M. J. (1985). On the inefficacy of limiting instructions: When jurors use prior conviction evidence to decide on guilt. *Law and Human Behavior, 9,* 37-48.

Wober, J. M. (1978). Televised violence and paranoid perception: The view from Great Britain. *Public Opinion Quarterly, 42,* 315-321.

Wolf, S. (1985). Manifest and latent influence of majorities and minorities. *Journal of Personality and Social Psychology, 48,* 899-908.

Wolf, S., & Latané, B. (1983). Majority and minority influence on restaurant preferences.

*Journal of Personality and Social Psychology, 45,* 282-292.

Wolf, S., & Montgomery, D. A. (1977). Effects of inadmissible evidence and level of judicial admonishment to disregard on the judgments of mock jurors. *Journal of Applied Social Psychology, 7,* 205-219.

Won-Doornick, M. J. (1979). On getting to know you: The association between the stage of a relationship and reciprocity of self-disclosure. *Journal of Experimental Social Psychology, 15,* 229-241.

Wood, J. (1989). Theory and research concerning social comparisons of personal attributes. *Psychological Bulletin, 106,* 231-248.

Wood, J. V., Saltzberg, J. A., & Goldsamt, L. A. (1990). Does affect induce self-focused attention? *Journal of Personality and Social Psychology, 5,* 899-908.

Wood, S. (1990). Tacit skills, the Japanese management model and new technology. Special Issue: Skills, qualifications, employment. *Applied Psychology: An International Review, 39,* 169-190.

Wood, W. (1987) A meta-analytic review of sex differences in group performance. *Psychological Bulletin, 102,* 53-71.

Wood, W., & Karten, S. J. (1986). Sex differences in interaction style as a product of perceived sex differences in competence. *Journal of Personality and Social Psychology, 50,* 341-347.

Wood, W., Polek, D., & Aiken, C. (1985). Sex differences in group task performance. *Journal of Personality and Social Psychology, 48,* 63-71.

Wood, W., Wong, F. Y., & Chachere, J. G. (1991). Effects of media violence on viewers' aggression in unconstrained social interaction. *Psychological Bulletin, 109,* 371-383.

Workman, J. E., & Johnson, K. K. (1991). The role of cosmetics in impression formation. *Clothing and Textiles Research Journal, 10,* 63-67.

World Health Organization. (1993). *The HIV/AIDS Pandemic: 1993 Overview* (Document WHO/GPA/EVA/93.1, Global Program on AIDS). Geneva, Switzerland: World Health Organization.

Worth, L. T., & Mackie, D. M. (1987). Cognitive mediation of positive affect in persuasion. *Social Cognition, 5,* 76-94.

Wright, L. (1988). The Type A behavior pattern on coronary artery disease. *American Psychologist, 43,* 2-14.

Wrightsman, L. S. (1991). *Psychology and the legal system* (2nd ed.). Belmont, CA: Brooks/Cole.

Wuensch, K. L., Castellow, W. A., & Moore, C. H. (1991). Effects of defendant attractiveness and type of crime on juridic judgment. *Journal of Social Behavior and Personality, 6,* 713-724.

Wyatt, G. E. (1992). Sociocultural context of African American and white American women's rape. *Journal of Social Issues, 48,* 77-91.

Wyer, R. S., Jr. (1988). Social memory and social judgment. In P. R. Solomon, G. R. Goethals, C. M. Kelley, & B. R. Stephens (Eds.), *Perspectives in memory research.* New York: Springer-Verlag.

Wyer, R. S., Jr., & Srull, T. K. (Eds.), (1993). *Perspectives on anger and emotion.* Hillsdale, NJ: Erlbaum.

Xiaohe, X., & Whyte, M. K. (1990). Love matches and arranged marriages: A Chinese replication. *Journal of Marriage and the Family, 52,* 709-722.

Yang, K. S., & Ho, D. Y. F. (1988). The role of yuan in Chinese social life: A conceptual and empirical analysis. In A. C. Paranjpe, D. Y. F. Ho, & R. W. Rieber (Eds.), *Asian contributions to psychology.* New York: Praeger.

Yang, N., & Linz, D. (1990). Movie ratings and the content of adult videos: The sex-violence ratio. *Journal of Communication, 40,* 28-42.

Younger, J. C., Walker, L., & Arrowood, A. J. (1977). Postdecision dissonance at the fair. *Personality and Social Psychology Bulletin, 3,* 284-287.

Yukl, G., & Falbe, C. M. (1990). Influence tactics and objectives in upward, downward, and lateral influence attempts. *Journal of Applied Psychology, 75,* 132-140.

Yukl, G., & Falbe, C. M. (1991). Importance of different power sources in downward and lateral relations. *Journal of Applied Psychology, 76,* 416-423.

Zaccaro, S. J. (1984). Social loafing: The role of task attractiveness. *Personality and Social Psychology Bulletin, 10,* 99-106.

Zajonc, R. B. (1965). Social facilitation. *Science, 149,* 269-274.

Zajonc, R. B. (1968). The attitudinal effects of mere exposure. *Journal of Personality and Social Psychology, 9,* 1-27.

Zajonc, R. B., Adelmann, P. K., Murphy, S. T., & Niedenthal, P. M. (1987). Convergence in the physical appearance of spouses. *Motivation and Emotion, 11,* 335-346.

Zajonc, R. B., Heingartner, A., & Herman, E. M. (1969). Social enhancement and impairment of performance in the cockroach. *Journal of Personaltiy and Social Psychology, 13,* 83-92.

Zanna, M. P., & Cooper, J. (1974). Dissonance and the pill: An attribution approach to studying the arousal properties of dissonance. *Journal of Personality and Social Psychology, 29,* 703-709.

Zebrowitz, L., & Montepare, J. M. (1990). Impressions of babyfaced and mater-faced individuals across the lifespan. Manuscript in preparation, cited in Zebrowitz, 1990.

Zebrowitz, L. A. (1990). *Social perception*. Pacific Grove, CA: Brooks/Cole.

Zebrowitz, L. A., Olson, K., & Hoffman, K. (1993). Stability of babyfaceness and attractiveness across the life span. *Journal of Personaltiy and Social Psychology, 64*, 453-466.

Zebrowitz-McArthur, L. (1988). Person perception in cross-cultural perspective. In M. H. Bond (Ed.), *The cross-cultural challenge to social psychology*. Newbury Park, CA: Sage.

Zelen, S. L. (Ed.). (1991). *New models, new extensions of attribution theory*. New York: Springer-Verlag.

Zevon, M., & Corn, B. (1990). Paper presented at the annual meeting of the American Psychological Association, Boston.

Zillman, D. (1983). Transfer of excitation in emotional behavior. In J. T. Cacioppo & R. E. Petty (Eds.), *Social psychophysiology*. New York: Academic Press.

Zillman, D. (1984). *Connections between sex and aggression*. Hillsdale, NJ: Erlbaum.

Zillman, D. (1988). Cognition-excitation interdependencies in aggressive behavior. *Aggressive Behavior, 14*, 51-64.

Zillman, D. (1993). Mental control of angry aggression. In D. M. Wegner & J. W. Pennebaker (Eds.), *Handbook of mental control*. Englewood Cliffs, NJ: Prentice Hall.

Zillman, D., Bryant, J., Comisky, P. W., & Medoff, N. J. (1981). Excitation and hedonic valence in the effect of erotica on motivated intermale aggression. *European Journal of Social Psychology, 11*, 233-252.

Zillman, D., Hoyt, J. L., & Day, K. D. (1974). Strength and duration of the effect of aggressive, violent, and erotic communications on subsequent aggressive behavior. *Communication Research, 1*, 286-306.

Zillman, D., Katcher, A., & Milavsky, B. (1972). Excitation transfer from physical exercise to subsequent aggressive behavior. *Journal of Experimental Social Psychology, 8*, 247-259.

Zimbardo, P. (1975). Transforming experimental research into advocacy for social change. In M. Deutsch & H. Hornstein (Eds.), *Applying social psychology: Implications for research, practice, and training*. Hillsdale, NJ: Erlbaum.

Zimbardo, P. G. (1970). The human choice: Individuation, reason, and order versus deindividuation, impulse, and chaos. In W. J. Arnold & D. Levine (Eds.), *Nebraska Symposium on Motivation: 1969* (Vol. 17, pp. 237-307). Lincoln: University of Nebraska Press.

Zimbardo, P. G. (1973). On the ethics of intervention in human psychological research: With special reference to the Stanford prison experiment. *Cognition, 2*, 243-256.

Zinberg, N. E. (1976). Normal psychology of the aging process, revisited (I): Social learning and self-image in aging. *Journal of Geriatric Psychiatry, 9*, 131-150.

Zuckerman, M. (1971). Physiological measures of sexual response in the human. *Psychological Bulletin, 75*, 297-239.

Zullow, H. M., & Seligman, M. E. P. (1990a). "Pessimistic rumination predicts defeat of presidential candidates, 1900 to 1984": Response. *Psychological Inquiry, 1*, 80-85.

Zullow, H. M., & Seligman, M. E. P. (1990b). Pessimistic rumination predicts defeat of presidential candidates: 1900-1984. *Psychological Inquiry, 1*, 52-61.

# PHOTO ACKNOWLEDGMENTS

**PART I**

*Opener:* Page 2, Joe McDonnell, "Breaking Away" Bronze

**CHAPTER 1**

*Opener:* Page 4, August Mosca, "Straphangers." Courtesy of Grand Central Art Galleries, Inc.

Page 5, Reuters/*Bettmann* (left), *AP/Wide World Photos* (right); p. 8 (clockwise from top left), Roger Dollarhide/*Monkmeyer Press*, Rhoda Sidney/*Monkmeyer Press*, Rhoda Sidney/*Stock Boston, Inc.*; p. 13, Bob Daemmrich/*The Image Works* (left), *Stock Boston, Inc.* (right); p. 29, Bob Daemmrich/*Stock Boston, Inc.* (top), Rhoda Sidney/*Photoedit* (bottom); p. 35, Dion Ogust/ *The Image Works*

**PART II**

*Opener:* Page 40, Harry Marinsky, sculptor, "Vernissage," 1978. Bronze, 39″ high × 43″ long. Courtesy of Hammer Galleries

**CHAPTER 2**

*Opener:* Page 42, Frida Kahlo, "El camión, 1929," Oleo sobre tela/26 × 55 cm. Collection of Dolores Olmeda, Mexico, D.F.

Page 43, *AP/Wide World Photos* (left), *AP/Wide World Photos* (right); p. 45, Robert Brenner/*Photoedit*; p. 46, Bob Daemmrich/*The Image Works*; p. 48 (all seven photos), *Matsumoto & Ekman*; p. 50, Steven Marks/Stock Photos, Inc./*The Image Bank*; p. 52, Bob Daemmrich/*The Image Works*; p. 53, Spencer Grant/*Monkmeyer Press* (left), Bob Daemmrich/*The Image Works* (right); p. 54, Elena Rooraid/*Photoedit*; p. 62, *Focus on Sports*; p. 63, Bob Daemmrich/*Stock Boston, Inc.*; p. 65, Charles Gupton/*Stock Boston, Inc.*; p. 70, McCarten/*Photoedit*; p. 72; David Young-Wolff/*Photoedit*

**CHAPTER 3**

*Opener:* Page 78, David Hammons, artist, "Free Nelson Mandela," 1987. Stencil, printed in color, cut from outdoor postered site, 29 × 28″. © Artists Rights Society, 1995. Reproduccion autorizada por el Instituto Nacional de Bellas Artes & Literatura

Page 79, *Miami Herald*; p. 82, L.L. Chryslin/*The Image Bank*; p. 83, Bob Daemmrich/*The Image Works*; p. 85, UPI/*Bettmann*; p. 86, Mark Antman/*The Image Works*; p. 90, Alan Carey/*The Image Works*; p. 94, Elena Rooraid/*Photoedit*; p. 99, J. Kramer/*The Image Works* (left), Bob Daemmrich/*Stock Boston, Inc.* (right); p. 101, Cynthia Johnson/© *Time Magazine*

**PART III**

*Opener:* Page 108, George Segal, sculptor, "Woman Painting Her Fingernails," 1962. Plaster, wood, glass, mirror, cloth, nail polish, 55 × 35 × 25″. Collection of Mrs. Farn Schniewind, Neviges, Germany. Courtesy of the Sidney Janis Gallery, NY

**CHAPTER 4**

*Opener:* Page 110, Rimma Gerlovina & Valeriy Gerlovin, "Manyness, 1990." Ektacolor print, 48 × 48″. Courtesy of Steinbaum Krauss Gallery, NYC

Page 111, *AP/Wide World Photos* (left), Reuters/*Bettmann* (right); p. 113, Richard Hutchings/*Photoedit* (left), Lawrence Migdale/*Stock Boston, Inc.* (right); p. 114, Tony Freeman/*Photoedit*; p. 117, Bob Daemmrich/*Stock Boston, Inc.*; p. 121, Charles Gupton/*Stock Boston, Inc.*; p. 124, Reuters/*Bettmann*; p. 125, Joseph Nettis/*Stock Boston, Inc.*; p. 127, Robert Brenner/*Photoedit*; p. 134, UPI/*Bettmann*; p. 135, Bob Daemmrich/*The Image Works*; p. 137, Reuters/*Bettmann*; p. 138 (all three photos), Paul Ekman/*Department of Psychiatry, University of California, San Francisco*

**CHAPTER 5**

*Opener:* Page 142, Keith Haring, "Untitled" (*Three Dancing Figures*), 1989. Polyurethane enamel on aluminum, 45 × 66 × 50″. Photo courtesy of the Tony Shafrazi Gallery, New York. © 1995 The Estate of Keith Haring

Page 143, *Rich Frishman*; p. 144, Michael Siluk/*The Image Works*; p. 147, Bill Aron/*Photoedit*; p. 153, Edrington/*The Image Works* (left), John Eastcott/*The Image Works* (right); p. 154, N. Rowan/*The Image Works*; p. 158, Bob Daemmrich/*The Image Works* (left), Tony Clark/*The Image Works* (right); p. 159, Bob Daemmrich/*The Image Works*; p. 161, Robert Brenner/*Photoedit*; p. 167, J. Griffin/*The Image Works*

**PART IV**

*Opener:* Page 176, Eve Renée Nele, "The Couple," 1961. Bronze, 21½ × 133⅛″. Courtesy of Bayerische Staatsgemaldesammlungen, Munich

**CHAPTER 6**

*Opener:* Page 178, Diego Rivera, "Dance in Tehuantepec" (version of "La Zandunga" Fresco in the Secretaria de Educación Publica), 1928. Oil on canvas, 78⅜ × 63¾″. Collection of IBM Corporation, Armonk, New York

Page 179, Reuters/*Bettmann* (left), *University of Massachusetts at Amherst* (right); p. 180, Explorer/*Photo Researchers, Inc.*; p. 182, Michael Weisbrot/*Stock Boston, Inc.*; p. 183, Robert Brenner/*Photoedit*; p. 185, Richard Pasley/*Stock Boston, Inc.*; p. 188, Derek Berwin/*The Image Bank*; p. 189, Vanessa Vick/*Photo Researchers, Inc.*; p. 191, Jim Harrison/*Stock Boston, Inc.*; p. 197, Mike Okoniewski/*The Image Works* (top), Mark Antman/*The Image Works* (bottom); p. 202 (left), Merlino/*The Image Works*; p. 202 (right), Peter Paul Rubens, detail of "Debarquement de Marie de Medicis au Port de Marseille, le 3 Novembre 1600," courtesy of the Louvre, Paris

### CHAPTER 7

*Opener:* Page 208, Romare Bearden, "Family Dinner," 1968. Collage on board, 30 × 40″. Toledo Museum of Art, Estate of Romare Bearden

Page 209, *Ebet Roberts*; p. 213 (clockwise from top left), Richard Pasley/*Stock Boston, Inc.*, W. Hill/*The Image Works*, Deborah Davis/*Photoedit*, Bob Daemmrich/*Stock Boston, Inc.*; p. 222, Reuters/*Bettmann*; p. 226 (clockwise from left), S. Villeger/*Explorer*/*Photo Researchers, Inc.*, Robin Tooker/*National Institute on Aging*, Martha Bates/*Stock Boston, Inc.*; p. 230, Arlene Collins/*Monkmeyer Press*; p. 232, Michael Siluk/*The Image Works*; p. 233: Reuters/*Bettmann*

### PART V

*Opener:* Page 242, The Momument at the Majdanek death camp in the Poland Jewish Museum. Photo: © Ira Nowinski, 1944

### CHAPTER 8

*Opener:* Page 244, Darren Waterston, artist, Poster for Amnesty International. Courtesy of Darren Waterston/Amnesty International

Page 245, *Freda Leinwand*; p. 247, *AP/Wide World Photos*; p. 251, UPI/*Bettmann*; p. 257, *AP/Wide World Photos*; p. 258, Trevor, Inc./*Monkmeyer Press*; p. 260, Nola Tully/*Sygma*; p. 261, Reuters/*Bettmann* (top), Charles Gupton/*Stock Boston, Inc.* (bottom); p. 263, Topham/*The Image Works* (left), George H. Harrison/*Grant Heilman Photography*; p. 271, Reuters/*Bettmann*

### CHAPTER 9

*Opener:* Page 276, Suzanne Pines, artist, "Barn Raising," 1993. Oil on linen, 52 × 78″. Commerce Bancshares Collection, Kansas City, Missouri. Courtesy of the Fishbach Gallery, New York

Page 277, Reuters/*Bettmann*; p. 280, Mary Kate Denny/*Photoedit*; p. 285, Robert Brenner/*Photoedit*; p. 288, Frank Siteman/*Monkmeyer Press*; p. 289, Tony Freeman/*Photoedit*; p. 293, Bob Daemmrich/*Stock Boston, Inc.*; p. 296, Reuters/*Bettmann*; p. 298, Keystone/*The Image Works*; p. 299, *Library of Congress*; p. 302, Lawrence Migdale/*Stock Boston, Inc.*; p. 303, David Young-Wolff/*Photoedit*

### PART VI

*Opener:* Page 310, Bill Barrett, "Baille Merengue" Bronze, 1989. 12 × 7 × 6′. Courtesy of Bill Barrett

### CHAPTER 10

*Opener:* Page 312, Ed McGowin, "Grown Men Playing with the Planet Earth," 1991. Oil on canvas with carved and painted wood frame, 52 × 52″. Courtesy of Ed McGowin

Page 313, Courtesy of Coca-Cola; p. 314, Reuters/*Bettmann*; p. 317, Reuters/*Bettmann* (left), AP/Wide World Photos (right); p. 318, *American Dairy Association*; p. 319, AP/Wide World Photos; p. 323, Bob Daemmrich/*The Image Works*; p. 327, Renate Hiller/*Monkmeyer Press*; p. 328, David R. Frazier/*Photo Researchers, Inc.*; p. 334, UPI/*Bettmann*; p. 337, Tony Savino/*The Image Works*

### CHAPTER 11

*Opener:* Page 344, Frank Romero, "The Closing of Whittier Boulevard," 1984. Oil on canvas, 6 × 10′. Courtesy of the Douglas M. Parker Studio

Page 345, Michael Newman/*Photoedit*; p. 347, *AP/Wide World Photos*; p. 348, *Healthmax*; p. 352, courtesy of Reebok; p. 357, *American Cancer Society*; p. 358, courtesy of Greater Miami & The Beaches; p. 363, *Reader's Digest*; p. 364, *Fidelity Investments*; p. 367, *Joop*; p. 368, *Rogaine* (top), Dougal Thornton/*The Moorings, Ltd.* (bottom); p. 372, *Kellogg Co.*

### PART VII

*Opener:* Page 378, George Segal, "Walk, Don't Walk," 1976. Plaster, cement, metal, painted wood and electric light, 264.2 × 182.9 × 182.9 cm. Purchase, with funds from the Louis and Bessie Adler Foundation, Inc.; Seymour M. Klein, President, the Gilman Foundation, Inc.; the Howard and Jean Lipman Foundation, Inc.; and the National Endowment for the Arts. Photography by Jerry L. Thompson, NY

### CHAPTER 12

*Opener:* Page 380, George Tooker, "Government Bureau," 1956. Egg tempera on gesso panel, 19⅝ × 29⅝″. The Metropolitan Museum of Art, New York. George A. Hearn Fund, 1956

Page 381, Reuters/*Bettmann*; p. 383, L. Kolvoord/*The Image Works*; p. 385, Bob Daemmrich/*Stock Boston, Inc.*; p. 390, "Portrait of Darwin" (left), "Portrait of Susan B. Anthony/*Bettmann* (right); p. 395, Robert Brenner/*Photoedit*; p. 397, Spencer Grant/*Photo Researchers, Inc.*; p. 402, AP/Wide World Photos; p. 403 (left and right), copyright 1965 by Stanley Milgram, from the film *Obedience,* distributed by the New York University Film Library; p. 406, M. Greenlar/*The Image Works*

### CHAPTER 13

*Opener:* Page 410, Zhang Hongtu, "Chairman Mao," #11, 1989. Acrylic on laser printer collage, 11 × 8″

Page 411, AP/Wide World Photos; p. 414, David R. Frazier/*Photo Researchers, Inc.*; p. 420 (left and right), *Michael Justice*; p. 423, Ida Wyman/*Monkmeyer Press*; p. 424, Michael Newman/*Photoedit*; p. 429 (clockwise from top left), AP/Wide World Photos, Bettmann, AP/Wide World Photos; p. 433, Mark Richards/*Photoedit*

### PART VIII

*Opener:* Page 442, Marisol, "Poor Family," 1986. Wood, charcoal, stone, plastic doll, 6′ 6″ × 13′ × 7′. Courtesy of the Sidney Janis Gallery. © Marisol/VAGA, New York, 1995

### CHAPTER 14

*Opener:* Page 444, David Hockney, "The Printers at Gemini, Los Angeles, April 1982." Composite Poloroid, 38 × 55⁷⁄₁₆″. © David Hockney

Page 445, *NASA*; p. 447 (clockwise from top left), Mike Okoniewski/*The Image Works*, Bob Daemmrich/*The Image Works*, Paul Conklin/*Monkmeyer Press*; p. 449, Reuters/*Bettmann*; p. 452, UPI/*Bettmann*; p. 455 (left and right), Bob Daemmrich/*Stock Boston, Inc.*; p. 457, AP/Wide World Photos; p. 463 (clockwise from top left), Spencer Grant/*Monkmeyer Press*, Bob Daemmrich/*Stock Boston, Inc.*, Bob Daemmrich/*Stock Boston, Inc.*, Janet Century/*Photoedit*

### CHAPTER 15

*Opener:* Page 472, Paul Gaugin, "The Siesta," 1893. Oil on canvas. © from the Private Collection of the Hon. & Mrs. Walter H. Annenberg. Philadelphia Museum of Art

Page 473, *Photo Researchers, Inc.*; p. 475, *Bettmann* (left), Rhoda Sidney/*Picture Person Plus* (right); p. 476, Bob Daemmrich/*The Image Works*; p. 479, Jim Pickerell/*The Image Works* (left), David Young-Wolff/*Photoedit* (right); p. 481, Alan Oddie/*Photoedit*; p. 494, John Eastcott/YVA Momatiuk/*The Image Works*; p. 496, Jeff Greenberg/*The Image Works*

# NAME INDEX

# SUBJECT INDEX